Introduction to Mediation, Moderation, and Conditional Process Analysis

Methodology in the Social Sciences

David A. Kenny, Founding Editor

Todd D. Little, Series Editor

www.guilford.com/MSS

This series provides applied researchers and students with analysis and research design books that emphasize the use of methods to answer research questions. Rather than emphasizing statistical theory, each volume in the series illustrates when a technique should (and should not) be used and how the output from available software programs should (and should not) be interpreted. Common pitfalls as well as areas of further development are clearly articulated.

RECENT VOLUMES

DOING STATISTICAL MEDIATION AND MODERATION
  Paul E. Jose

LONGITUDINAL STRUCTURAL EQUATION MODELING
  Todd D. Little

BAYESIAN STATISTICS FOR THE SOCIAL SCIENCES
  David Kaplan

CONFIRMATORY FACTOR ANALYSIS FOR APPLIED RESEARCH, SECOND EDITION
  Timothy A. Brown

PRINCIPLES AND PRACTICE OF STRUCTURAL EQUATION MODELING, FOURTH EDITION
  Rex B. Kline

HYPOTHESIS TESTING AND MODEL SELECTION IN THE SOCIAL SCIENCES
  David L. Weakliem

REGRESSION ANALYSIS AND LINEAR MODELS: CONCEPTS, APPLICATIONS, AND IMPLEMENTATION
  Richard B. Darlington and Andrew F. Hayes

GROWTH MODELING: STRUCTURAL EQUATION AND MULTILEVEL MODELING APPROACHES
  Kevin J. Grimm, Nilam Ram, and Ryne Estabrook

PSYCHOMETRIC METHODS: THEORY INTO PRACTICE
  Larry R. Price

INTRODUCTION TO MEDIATION, MODERATION, AND CONDITIONAL PROCESS ANALYSIS, SECOND EDITION: A REGRESSION-BASED APPROACH
  Andrew F. Hayes

MEASUREMENT THEORY AND APPLICATIONS FOR THE SOCIAL SCIENCES
  Deborah L. Bandalos

Introduction to
Mediation, Moderation, and Conditional Process Analysis

A Regression-Based Approach

SECOND EDITION

Andrew F. Hayes

Series Editor's Note by Todd D. Little

THE GUILFORD PRESS
New York   London

Copyright © 2018 The Guilford Press
A Division of Guilford Publications, Inc.
370 Seventh Avenue Suite 1200, New York, NY 10001-1020
www.guilford.com

Printed in the United States of America

This book is printed on acid-free paper.

Last digit is print number: 9   8   7   6   5   4   3   2   1

Library of Congress Cataloging-in-Publication Data

Names: Hayes, Andrew F., author.
Title: Introduction to mediation, moderation, and conditional process
  analysis : a regression-based approach / Andrew F. Hayes.
Description: Second edition. | New York : Guilford Press, [2018] | Series:
  Methodology in the social sciences | Includes bibliographical references
  and index.
Identifiers: LCCN 2017039263 | ISBN 9781462534654 (hardcover)
Subjects: LCSH: Social sciences—Statistical methods. | Mediation
  (Statistics) | Regression analysis.
Classification: LCC HA31.3 .H39 2018 | DDC 001.4/22—dc23
LC record available at *https://lccn.loc.gov/2017039263*

Series Editor's Note

As I mentioned in the first edition of this book, it's a good thing that research questions have become more nuanced. We are no longer satisfied with demonstrating simple associations or unqualified multivariate associations. Our research questions are delving into the realm of process, mechanism, and the conditional features that impact how a process or mechanism might unfold: "How?," "In what way?," "By which pathway?," and "Under which circumstances?" exemplify the burning questions that we now want to answer. These kinds of questions now sit squarely on accurate applications of mediation and moderation analysis principles. Enter Andrew Hayes. Andy has devoted much of his academic acumen to understanding the causal foundations of mediation and moderation and to effectively applying the statistical tools that will implicate the causal elements of human behavior. He has even gone so far as to develop PROCESS (now in version 3), his free, user-friendly tool for SPSS and SAS that simplifies many of the tasks in testing for mediation and moderation.

The first edition was an indisputable classic. This second edition is even better! Andy has added many critical new features to this edition while maintaining all of the great features of the first edition. New features include clearly distinguished example code in SAS, SPSS, and R as well as thoroughly annotated output from version 3 of PROCESS, including the 13 new preprogrammed models that he has added, and a new Appendix B that describes how to create models in PROCESS or customize preprogrammed models. The additional material on multicategorical variables and how to combine parallel and serial mediation only enhances the already rich material of the first edition. Moreover, the practical tips and advice that Andy imparts throughout (and especially in the final chapter) as well as the broadened data examples from published studies are invaluable.

Andy's treatment of conditional process modeling provides you with a definitive statement of where both theory and practice with these topics has evolved and where we are headed. Andy's presentation of the cutting edge on these topics is easy to follow and grasp. Beginning with a review of ordinary least squares regression, the book covers the estimation and computation of direct and indirect effects in mediation analysis, modern methods of inference about indirect effects, models with multiple mediators, estimating and probing of interactions in moderation analysis, conditional direct and indirect effects, testing moderated mediation, and other topics pertaining to exploring, quantifying, and answering questions about the mechanisms and contingencies of process-related effects. Andy details each step of analysis using real data examples along with tips on writing up and reporting mediation analyses, moderation analyses, and conditional process models. Applied researchers will enjoy this work as a go-to resource for how to test and report on their tests of mediation and moderation. Andy gifts us with an easy-to-follow guide to the techniques that allow each of us to navigate the tangled web of today's refined research questions.

Andy is a great communicator. He's taught scores of workshops and short courses on mediation and moderation. The popularity of his workshops is a testament to the well-honed didactic devices that he has perfected and which you will find presented throughout his book. As you will discover, no topic or issue that is essential to accurately applying a mediation or moderation analysis is given slight treatment. Andy presents it all and covers it thoroughly, clearly, and satisfyingly. The dessert to this intellectual meal comes in the form of the sweet elements Andy provides throughout his book. His wit and wisdom permeate this resource. It's a work that is both essential and easy to enjoy.

As you read and begin to fully appreciate the nuance in using these procedures, you will also list Andrew Hayes as an MVM (most valuable methodologist). As an MVM, Andy has crafted a resource that will be a staple in the personal library of every serious researcher. It will be your personal guide to asking and answering the new wave of complex research questions. With better answers to better questions, we all will be better off.

Todd D. Little
Again at The Short Branch Saloon
Lakeside, Montana

Preface

When research in an area is in its earliest phases, attention is typically focused on establishing evidence of a relationship between two variables, X and Y, and ascertaining whether the association is causal or merely an artifact of design, measurement, or otherwise unaccounted-for influences. But as a research area develops and matures, focus eventually shifts away from demonstrating the existence of an effect toward understanding the mechanism or mechanisms by which the effect operates, as well as establishing its boundary conditions or contingencies. Answering such questions of *how* and *when* results in a deeper understanding of the phenomenon or process under investigation, and gives insights into how that understanding can be applied.

Analytically, questions of *how* are typically approached using *process* or *mediation analysis*, whereas questions of *when* are most often answered through *moderation analysis*. The goal of mediation analysis is to establish the extent to which some putative causal variable, X, influences some outcome, Y, through one or more *mediator* variables. For example, there is evidence that violent video game play can enhance the likelihood of aggression outside of the gaming context. Perhaps violent video game players come to believe through their interaction with violent game content that others are likely to aggress, that doing so is normative, or that it is an effective solution to problems, or perhaps it desensitizes them to the pain others feel, thereby leading them to choose aggression as a course of action when the opportunity presents itself. In contrast, an investigator conducting a moderation analysis seeks to determine whether the size or sign of the effect of X on Y depends in one way or another on (i.e., "interacts with") a moderator variable or variables. In the realm of video game effects, one might ask whether the effect of violent video game play on later aggression depends on the player's sex, age, or ethnicity, or personality factors such as trait aggressiveness, or whether the game is played competitively or cooperatively.

Both substantive researchers and methodologists have recently come to appreciate that an analysis focused on answering only *how* or *when* questions is going to be incomplete. A more fine-grained understanding of a phenomenon comes from uncovering and describing the contingencies of mechanisms—"the when of the how." The analytical integration of moderation and mediation analysis was highlighted in some of the earliest work on mediation analysis, but it is only in the last 10 years or so that methodologists have begun to talk more extensively about how to do so. Described using easily confused terms such as *moderated mediation* and *mediated moderation*, the goal is to empirically quantify and test hypotheses about the contingent nature of the mechanisms by which X exerts its influence on Y. For example, such an analysis could be used to establish the extent to which the influence of violent video game play on aggressive behavior through the mechanism of expectations about the aggressive behavior of others depends on age, sex, the kind of game (e.g., first-person shooter games relative to other forms of violent games), or the player's ability to manage anger. This can be accomplished by piecing together parameter estimates from a mediation analysis with parameter estimates from a moderation analysis and combining these estimates in ways that quantify the conditionality of various paths of influence from X to Y.

Mediation and moderation analysis are two of the more widely used statistical methods in the social, behavioral, and health sciences, as well as business, medicine, and other areas. Some of the most highly cited papers in social science methodology this century are about mediation or moderation analysis. Indeed, it is nearly imperative these days that readers and producers of research understand the distinction between these concepts and know how to implement moderation and mediation analysis in their own work. The book you are now holding is one of the few book-length treatments covering the statistical analysis of both mechanisms and contingencies. The contents of this book, classroom-tested in university courses and workshops I have conducted throughout the world over the last few years, cover the fundamentals of mediation and moderation analysis as well as their integration in the form of *conditional process analysis*, a term I introduced in the first edition. Once you turn the final page, you will be well prepared to conduct analyses of the sort you see here and describe those analyses in your own research.

This is an introductory book, in that I cover only basic principles here, primarily using data from simple experimental or cross-sectional studies of the sort covered in most elementary statistics and research design courses. I do not provide much coverage of longitudinal research, multilevel analysis, latent variables, repeated measures, or the analysis of categorical outcomes, for instance, though I touch on these topics in the final chapter. I presume no special background in statistics or knowledge of matrix algebra or advanced statistical methods such as structural equation modeling. All the methods described are based entirely on principles of ordinary least squares regression (Chapter 2 introduces and reviews these principles). Most students in the social and behavioral sciences who have taken a first course in statistical methods and research design will be able to understand and apply the methods described here, as will students of public health, business, and various other disciplines.

The examples I use throughout these pages are based on data from published studies that are publicly available on the book's web page at *www.afhayes.com*, so you can replicate and extend the analyses reported. To facilitate the implementation of the methods introduced and discussed, I introduce a computational aid in the form of a freely available macro for SPSS and SAS (named PROCESS) beginning in Chapter 3. PROCESS combines many of the functions of computational tools about which I have written and published over the years (tools that go by such names as INDIRECT, SOBEL, MODPROBE, and MODMED) into a single integrated command. PROCESS takes the computational burden off the shoulders of the researcher by estimating the models, calculating various effects of interest, and implementing modern and computer-intensive methods of inference, such as bootstrap confidence intervals for indirect effects and the Johnson–Neyman technique in moderation analysis. Example PROCESS commands are provided throughout the book, and SPSS users not interested in using the syntax version of PROCESS can install a dialog box into SPSS that makes the use of PROCESS literally as simple as pointing and clicking. This can greatly facilitate the teaching of the methods described here to students who are just getting started in the use of computers for data analysis.

This book is suitable as either a primary text for a specialized course on moderation or mediation analysis or a supplementary text for courses in regression analysis. It can be used by educators, researchers, and graduate students in any discipline that uses social science methodologies, including psychology, sociology, political science, business, and public health. It will benefit the reader as a handy reference to modern approaches to mediation and moderation analysis, and Appendix A is critical to users of PROCESS, as it is the only official source of documentation for this powerful add-on for SPSS and SAS. This book will be useful to anyone interested in identifying the contingencies of effects and associations, understanding and testing hypotheses about the mechanisms behind causal effects, and describing and exploring the conditional nature of the mechanisms by which causal effects operate.

You will find 14 chapters between the front and back covers defining five broad parts of the book. The first part, containing Chapters 1 and 2, introduces the concepts in moderation and mediation analysis and provides an example of their integration in the form of a conditional process model. I also cover a bit about my philosophy on the link between statistics and causality and describe how we should not let the limitations of our data dictate the mathematical tools we bring to the task of trying to understand what our data may be telling us. In Chapter 2, I overview ordinary least squares regression analysis. I assume that most readers of this book have been exposed to least squares regression analysis in some form already, but for those who have not or for whom much time has passed since their last regression analysis, this review will be useful, while also introducing the reader to my way of thinking and talking about linear modeling.

The second part focuses exclusively on mediation analysis. In Chapter 3, I describe how linear regression can be used to conduct a simple path analysis of a three-variable $X \rightarrow M \rightarrow Y$ causal system. The estimation and interpretation of direct and indirect effects is the first focus of this chapter, first with a dichotomous causal agent X and then with a continuous X. After an introduction to PROCESS, I cover inference about direct and indirect effects, with an emphasis on newer statistical methods such as bootstrap confidence intervals that have become the standard in the 21st century for testing hypotheses about mechanisms in a mediation analysis. Chapter 4 covers dealing with confounds, estimation and interpretation of models with multiple X or Y variables, and quantifying effect size. In this chapter I also provide the rationale for why the historically significant *causal steps* procedure is no longer recommended by people who think about mediation analysis for a living. Chapter 5 then builds on the fundamentals of mediation analysis by discussing models with multiple mediators, including the parallel and serial multiple mediator model. Chapter 6, new to this second edition of the book, is dedicated exclusively to mediation analysis when X is a multicategorical variable, such as in an experiment with three or more groups constructed through a random assignment procedure.

Part III temporarily puts aside mediation analysis and shifts the discussion to moderation analysis. In Chapter 7, I show how a multiple regression model can be made more flexible by allowing one variable's effect to depend linearly on another variable in the model. The resulting *moderated multiple regression model* allows an investigator to ascertain the extent to which X's influence on outcome variable Y is contingent on or *interacts with* a *moderator* variable W. Interpretation of a moderated multiple regression model is facilitated by visualizing and probing the moderation, and techniques for doing so are introduced, along with how PROCESS can be used to make the task a lot easier than it has been in the past. Whereas Chapter 7 focuses exclusively on the case where X is a dichotomous variable and W is a continuum, Chapter 8 continues this line of analysis to models where X is quantitative rather than dichotomous. It also discusses the equivalence between the 2×2 factorial analysis of variance and moderated multiple regression, as well as why it is not necessary to enter variables into a model hierarchically to test a moderation hypothesis. Chapter 9 covers myths and truths about the need to mean-center or standardize variables in a moderation analysis, models with more than one moderator, and comparing conditional effects in complex multiple moderator models. Chapter 10, the last chapter in Part III of the book, new to this edition, is dedicated to testing a moderation hypothesis using regression analysis when X or W is a multicategorical variable.

The fourth part of the book, Chapters 11 through 13, integrates the concepts and lessons described in the prior two by introducing *conditional process analysis*. A model that includes both a mediation and a moderation component is a conditional process model—a model in which the direct and/or indirect effect of X on Y through M is moderated by or conditioned on one or more variables. Chapter 11 offers an overview of the history of this form of modeling—sometimes referred to as *moderated mediation analysis*—and provides examples in the literature of such conditional processes hypothesized or tested. An introduction to the concepts of conditional direct and indirect effects is provided, along with their mathematical bases, and an example conditional process analysis is provided, including estimation and inference using regression analysis or, more conveniently, using PROCESS. Chapter 12 provides a further example of a conditional process model with moderation of both the direct and indirect effects simultaneously, and shows the equivalence between this one specific model form and something known as *mediated moderation*. But I take a stand in this chapter and argue that unlike moderated mediation, mediated moderation is not a particularly interesting concept or phenomenon and probably not worth hypothesizing or testing. Chapter 13 is new to this edition and addresses an example of conditional process analysis when X is a multicategorical variable.

The last part of the book contains only one chapter. Chapter 14 addresses various questions that I am frequently asked by readers of the prior edition of this book, people who have taken workshops from me, or others who have contacted me by email over the years. The largest section in Chapter 14 is dedicated to writing about mediation, moderation, and conditional process analysis. The rest of the chapter touches on various miscellaneous issues and questions and a (typically) brief response to each, from my perspective at least.

The appendices are very important, as they are the best source of information about how to use PROCESS. Appendix A is essentially a user's manual for PROCESS that discusses how to set up the macro and construct a PROCESS command, and it discusses various options available in PROCESS that vary depending on the analysis being conducted. Appendix B is entirely new to this edition of the book and focuses on an important new feature in the latest release of PROCESS that allows you to set up or customize construct your own model rather than having to rely on one of the many preprogrammed models built into PROCESS.

I have taken care to maintain a light and conversational tone throughout the book while discussing the concepts and analyses without getting heavily into the mathematics behind them. I believe that maintaining a reader's interest is one of the more important facets of scientific writing, for if one's audience becomes bored and attention begins to wander, the power and influence of the message is reduced. Indeed, it is this philosophy about writing that guides the advice I give in Chapter 14, where I talk about how to report a mediation, moderation, or conditional process analysis. Most important, the advice I offer in this part of the book is intended to empower you as the one best positioned to determine how you tell the story your data are telling you.

New to This Edition

You are holding the second edition of *Introduction to Mediation, Moderation, and Conditional Process Analysis*. This new edition is longer by roughly 200 pages than the first edition released in 2013. The additional pages include several new chapters, another appendix, and a variety of new sections dispersed throughout the book. In addition, some sections of chapters from the first edition were reorganized or relocated to different chapters. Perhaps most significantly, examples of analyses using PROCESS have been modified to reflect changes to the syntax and features with the release of PROCESS version 3 with this book. Below is a nonexhaustive list of changes in this edition:

- A condensed regression analysis review in Chapter 2 (shortened from two chapters).

- Annotated PROCESS outputs throughout the book to make it easier to find relevant sections of output corresponding to discussion in the book.

- A substantially rewritten Appendix A to reflect changes to the syntax, options, and defaults in PROCESS version 3 compared to version 2.

- Modified conceptual diagrams in the templates section of Appendix A, along with the addition of 13 new preprogrammed models to PROCESS that combine serial and parallel mediation and that estimate moderated serial mediation models.

- A new Appendix B describing how to create models in PROCESS from scratch as well as how to edit preprogrammed, numbered models.

- A new real-data example from an experimental study published by Chapman and Lickel (2016) and used in Chapters 7, 8, and 12.

- R code in several chapters for visualizing interactions, Johnson–Neyman plots, and plots of the relationship between indirect effects and moderators.

- A new section on models that combine parallel and serial mediation (section 5.5).

- A change in the discussion of effect size measures in mediation analysis corresponding to those now available in PROCESS output (section 4.3).

- A new chapter on mediation analysis with a multicategorical antecedent variable (Chapter 6).

- A new section on the difference between testing for interaction and probing an interaction (section 7.5).

- A new section on the dangers of manually centering and standardizing variables (section 9.3).

- A new section on testing the difference between conditional effects in models with more than one moderator (section 9.5).

- A new chapter on moderation analysis with multicategorical antecedent or moderator variables (Chapter 10).

- A new focus in the chapters on conditional process analysis on a formal test of moderation of an indirect effect using the *index of moderated mediation* (Hayes, 2015).

- A new chapter on conditional process analysis with a multicategorical antecedent variable (Chapter 13).

- An expanded final chapter on miscellaneous issues and frequently asked questions, including some guidance on the analysis of repeated measures data and references to consult when modeling variables that are discrete and better analyzed with something other than ordinary least squares regression.

Acknowledgments

I began writing this book well before the first word of it was typed. Several years ago, I started receiving invitations from former strangers, many of whom are now colleagues and friends, to come speak on the topic of papers I have published or to conduct workshops on material related to this book. These invitations allowed me to interact with people I otherwise would not likely have ever had the opportunity to get to know. Speaking to audiences diverse in background and interests has provided a means to fine-tune and hone my message as my own ideas and philosophy about the contents of this book evolved. Without those invitations, the hospitality of my hosts, and the time sacrifices they made orchestrating and coordinating my visits, this book would not be anything like what it is, nor would it have evolved from the first to the second edition in the way that it has. So I offer my thanks to Paul Allison, H. Onur Bodur, Leslie Booren, Adrian Brügger, Jonathan Cohen, Roberta Crouch, Grete Dyb, Truls Erikson, Joseph Fletcher, Shira Dvir Gvirsman, Tilo Hartmann, Kristina Klein, Hans-Joachim Knopf, Catherine Lamberton, Todd D. Little, Kelley Main, Jörg Matthes, Osvaldo Morera, Peter Neijens, Harmen Oppewal, Deirdre O'Shea, Jochen Peter, Torsten Pieper, Carolin Plewa, Nicolas Pontes, Michelle Salyers, Jennifer Skeem, Graham Stead, Toon Taris, Annika Tovote, Gülden Ülkümen, Jens Vogelgesang, Claes de Vreese, Etty Wielenga-Meijer, Anna Woodcock, and everyone else who has spent time with me during my travels talking about their research interests and their lives.

As much as I enjoy speaking and teaching abroad, I do most of my teaching a mere 3 miles from my house. I have had the pleasure of teaching graduate students, both beginning and advanced, working on degrees in my home department of Psychology, my second home in the School of Communication, and elsewhere at Ohio State University. Their questions over the years have helped me sharpen my language when it comes to describing abstract concepts in terms that are concrete without being too imprecise or oversimplified. I appreciate their tolerance for numerous typos on PowerPoint slides, patience with my occasional need to repeat myself when I botch an explanation, and now and again waiting attentively as I retype SPSS or SAS code that generates a string of errors when using macros and other tools I invented but can't always remember how to use.

Heartfelt thanks also go to numerous people who have been generously willing to donate their data for use in my classes, workshops, and journal articles, and this book. These include Daniel Ames, George Bonanno, Nyla Branscombe, Heike Bruch, Jonathan Cohen, Michael S. Cole, Carsten K. W. De Dreu, Ryan Duffy, Naomi Ellemers, Chip Eveland, Francis Flynn, Donna Garcia, Friedrike X. R. Gerstenberg, Al Gunther, Sri Kalyanaraman, Brian Lickel, Anthony Mancini, Jörg Matthes, Erik Nisbet, Kirsi Peltonen,

Jeffrey Pollack, Raija-Leena Punamäki, Michael Schmitt, Michael Slater, S. Shyam Sundar, Nurit Tal-Or, Yariv Tsfati, Eric Van Epps, and Frank Walter. Writing and reading about methodology is much more interesting when examples are based on real data from existing and published studies rather than hypothetical studies made up for the purpose of illustration. For the record, I should point out that all analyses conducted in this book and claims I make based on others' data are my own and are not necessarily endorsed by those who collected the data in the first place.

C. Deborah Laughton and Seymour Weingarten at The Guilford Press have been very supportive and enthusiastic about this project and others I have worked on for them, and I appreciate their contributions before the writing began, during the production process, and as the first edition evolved into the second. No doubt they will continue to influence its course well into the future. Matthew Fritz offered a review of the manuscript of the first edition prior to production, and I appreciate his insights and recommendations.

The support of my wife, Carole, and kids, Conor and Julia, has been critical. As anyone who has been a part of a research team knows, a study is much more than just the journal article that describes it. There is much that happens behind the scenes of a study that is invisible to outsiders but without which the study just doesn't get done. My family is similar to members of a research lab in that sense. Fortunately, they understand the time commitment that a project like this entails. This is the third time in 15 years they have had to put up with the divided attention that comes with writing a book, especially as the due date approaches, and I appreciate their tolerance.

Finally, I would also like to tell the world in writing about the gratitude I feel toward my father for buying me my first computer in high school, and my mother for allowing me to lock myself away in my room as I taught myself BASIC. I imagine my father didn't think long or deeply about his decision to spend $300 on a Commodore VIC-20 back in the early 1980s, but it is the machine I learned to program on, and it turned out this decision had a big influence on where I ended up in my professional life. Without this early introduction to computer science, I probably wouldn't have chosen this career, I probably wouldn't have written PROCESS, and, as a consequence, this book simply would not exist.

Contents

Data files for the examples used in the book and files
containing the SPSS and SAS versions of PROCESS are
available on the companion web page at *www.afhayes.com.*

Part I

FUNDAMENTALS

1

Introduction

Research that establishes the mechanism or mechanisms by which effects operate or the conditions that facilitate and inhibit such effects deepens our understanding of the phenomena scientists study. Mediation analysis and moderation analysis are used to establish evidence or test hypotheses about such mechanisms and boundary conditions. Conditional process analysis is used when one's research goal is to describe the boundary conditions of the mechanism or mechanisms by which a variable transmits its effect on another. Using a regression-based path-analytic framework, this book introduces the principles of mediation analysis, moderation analysis, and their unification as conditional process analysis. In this initial chapter, I provide a conceptual overview of moderation and mediation and describe an example of a conditional process analysis that combines elements of both mediation and moderation analysis. After articulating my perspective on the use of statistical methods when testing causal processes, followed by a discussion of conceptual and statistical diagrams, I end with a synopsis of each of the chapters in this book.

1.1   A Scientist in Training

As an undergraduate student studying psychology at San Jose State University back in the late 1980s, one of the first empirical research projects I undertook was a study on the relationship between students' attitudes about college and their selection of seat in the classroom. I developed an instrument that purportedly (although in hindsight, not really) measured whether a person felt getting a college education was generally a good and important thing to do or not. After the participants in the study completed the instrument, I presented each of them with a diagram of a generic college classroom, with seats arranged in a 6 (row) by 5 (column) matrix, and I asked them to mark which seat they would choose to sit in if they could choose any seat in the classroom. Based on which row he or she selected,

I scored how close to the front of the room that participant preferred (6 = front row, 5 = second row, 4 = third row, and so forth).

With these two measurements collected from over 200 students at San Jose State, I could test my prediction that students with a more positive attitude about college (i.e., who scored higher on my attitude scale) would prefer sitting closer to the front of the classroom. Indeed, when I calculated Pearson's coefficient of correlation between the two measurements, I found the relationship was positive as expected, $r = 0.27$. Furthermore, a hypothesis test revealed that the probability of obtaining a correlation this extreme or more extreme from zero (positive or negative, as I tested the hypothesis two-tailed even though my prediction was directional) was too small ($p < .001$) to consider it just a fluke or "chance." Naturally, I was excited, not realizing as I do now that *any* result is exciting whether consistent with a prediction or not. Unfortunately, three anonymous reviewers did not share my enthusiasm, and the then-editor of the *Journal of Nonverbal Behavior* let me know in no uncertain terms that this finding was neither of sufficient interest nor derived with sufficient rigor to warrant publication. Rather than rewriting the paper and resubmitting elsewhere, I filed the paper away and moved to upstate New York to pursue a PhD in social psychology.

After more than 20 years, I still have this paper, and now and then I take it out of my file drawer when reflecting on where I have been in my professional life and where I am going. Looking at it now, it is clear to me that the reviewers were correct and the editor's decision sound and justified. Even if the study had been conducted with the kind of rigor I now ask of myself and my own students, in the paper I offered nothing but speculation as to why this association existed. Furthermore, I could not establish the direction of cause, if any. Although I argued that variations in attitudes caused variation in seat choice, it is just as plausible that where one sits influences one's attitude about college. For example, perhaps students who sit closer to the front receive more attention and feedback from the instructor, can hear and see better and therefore learn more, and this in turn leads them to feel better about the college experience in general. Even if I was able to ascertain why the association exists or the direction of cause, I was in no position to be able to describe its boundary conditions, such as the type of people in whom this relationship would be expected to be larger or smaller. For instance, no doubt there are many bright students who love the college experience but for one reason or another choose to sit in the back, just as there are students who sit in the front even though they would much rather be somewhere else—anywhere else—than in that classroom.

I have learned many lessons about research over the years—lessons that began with that first early and unsuccessful attempt at academic publishing. I have learned that research is tough, that it takes patience, and that our egos often get too involved when we interpret feedback from others. Although this particular study never was published, I have learned that resilence to rejection combined with persistence following failure often does lead to success. But I think one of the more important lessons I've learned being both a producer and a consumer of research is how much more impressive a study is when it can speak to more than just whether an effect exists, whether a relationship is different from zero, or whether two groups differ from each other. Instead, some of the best research I have done and the best research I have read goes further by answering not only "whether" or "if," but also "how" and "when." Approaches to analyzing one's data with the goal of answering these latter two questions is the topic of this book.

1.2 Questions of Whether, If, How, and When

Questions of "whether" or "if" focus primarily on whether two variables are related, causally or otherwise, or if something is more or less likely to happen in one set of circumstances or conditions than another. Such questions are often the first ones a scientist-in-training asks, sometimes merely by observing the world around him or her and wondering about it. For example, when I ask undergraduate students in a research methods class to conceive and design a research project, one of the popular topics is the effects of exposure to the thin-is-ideal standard on self-esteem and body dissatisfaction. Term after term, students want to design a study to see if women who are exposed to images of women depicted in beauty magazines, the Internet, popular television, and music videos—as thin and beautiful—suffer in some way from this exposure. I believe this is such a popular topic because it is nearly impossible to avoid the daily bombardment by the media of depictions of what the ideal woman should look like and, by extension, what society seems to value. Naturally, many wonder whether this is bad for women and society—if women's sense of worth, image of their bodies, and likelihood of disordered eating are affected by this exposure.

Questions of the whether or if variety also serve as a starting point in our quest to understand the effects of something that has happened in society, when a new technology is developed, when a new problem confronts the people of a community or nation, and so forth. After the twin towers of the World Trade Center in New York City were brought down by terrorists on September 11, 2001, researchers started asking whether and what kind of physical and psychological health effects it had on those who experienced it (e.g., Cukor et al., 2011; DiGrande et al., 2008), those who only observed it from a distance (e.g., Mijanovich & Weitzman, 2010), or how people's behavior changed after the event (e.g., Richman, Shannon, Rospenda, Flaherty, & Fendrich, 2009). And a genre of television known as *political entertainment* has spawned much research about its viewers and whether programs like *The Daily Show* serve to politically educate, mobilize, or demotivate those who view them (e.g., Baumgartner & Morris, 2006; Xenos & Becker, 2009).

The empirical literature in most every scientific discipline is replete with research that provides answers to questions of whether or if, and for good reason. Many theoretical and applied questions in the sciences focus on whether there is evidence of association between some presumed causal antecedent X and some putative consequent or outcome Y. Is a particular therapeutic method effective at reducing depression (e.g., Hofmann & Smits, 2008)? Does combining drugs with psychotherapy work better than therapy alone (e.g., Cuijpers, van Straten, Warmeredam, & Andersson, 2009)? Does playing violent video games or watching violent television make people aggressive (e.g., Anderson & Bushman, 2001; Anderson et al., 2010)? Does exposure to negative political advertisements turn people off from participating in the political process (e.g., Lau, Silegman, Heldman, & Babbit, 1999)? Are the children of divorced parents more prone to behavioral or psychological problems than children of married parents (e.g., Amato, 2001; Amato & Keith, 1991; Weaver & Schofield, 2015)? Does rewarding performance at work increase employee satisfaction and reduce turnover (e.g., Judge, Piccolo, Podsakoff, Shaw, & Rich, 2010)? What sets science apart from armchair speculation is that we can answer such questions by collecting data. Being able to establish that two variables are associated—that an effect or relationship of some kind exists—is in part what science is about, and research that does so is worth undertaking. Indeed, the drive to answer questions of this sort is one of the things that motivates scientists to get up in the morning.

But establishing association does not translate into deep understanding even when a causal association can be established. We know that we better understand some phenomenon when we can answer not only whether X affects Y, but also *how* X exerts its effect on Y, and *when* X affects Y and when it does not. The "how" question relates to the underlying psychological, cognitive, or biological process that causally links X to Y, whereas the "when" question pertains to the boundary conditions of the causal association—under what circumstances, or for which types of people, does

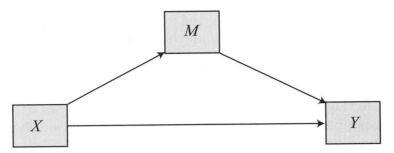

FIGURE 1.1. A simple mediation model with a single mediator variable *M* causally located between *X* and *Y*.

X exert an effect on *Y* and under what circumstances, or for which type of people, does *X* not exert an effect?

Mediation

A researcher whose goal is to establish or test how *X* exerts its effect on *Y* frequently postulates a model in which one or more intervening variables *M* is located causally between *X* and *Y*. One of the simplest forms of such a model is depicted in Figure 1.1. These intervening variables, often called *mediators*, are conceptualized as the mechanism through which *X* influences *Y*. That is, variation in *X* causes variation in one or more mediators *M*, which in turn causes variation in *Y*. For example, there is evidence that exposure to the thin ideal through the mass media is a risk factor if not an actual cause of body dissatisfaction in women (e.g., Grabe, Ward, & Hyde, 2008; Levine & Murnen, 2009). But how does this occur? Research suggests that internalization of the norm functions as a mediator of this relationship (Lopez-Guimera, Levine, Sanchez-Cerracedo, & Fauquet, 2010). Women who report greater exposure (or who are given greater exposure experimentally) to the thin-as-ideal image of women are more likely to internalize this image and seek thinness as a personal goal than those with less exposure. Such internalization, in turn, leads to greater body dissatisfaction (Cafri, Yamamiya, Brannick, & Thompson, 2005). So internalization of the standard portrayed by the media is one mechanism that links such exposure to body dissatisfaction. Of course, other mechanisms may be at work too, and Lopez-Guimera et al. (2010) discuss some of the other potential mediators of the effect of such exposure on women's beliefs, attitudes, and behavior.

Investigators interested in examining questions about mechanism resort to *process modeling* to empirically estimate and test hypotheses about the two pathways of influence through which *X* carries its effect on *Y* depicted in Figure 1.1, one *direct* from X to Y and the other *indirect* through M. More popularly known as *mediation analysis*, this type of analysis is extremely common in virtually all disciplines. Some of the most highly cited journal articles in methodology both historically (e.g., Baron & Kenny, 1986) and more recently (e.g., MacKinnon, Lockwood, Hoffman, & West, 2002; Preacher & Hayes, 2004, 2008a) discuss mediation analysis and various statistical approaches to quantifying and testing hypotheses about direct and indirect effects of X on Y. I describe the fundamentals of mediation analysis in Chapters 3 through 6.

Moderation

When the goal is to uncover the boundary conditions of an association between two variables, moderation analysis is used. An association between two variables X and Y is said to be moderated when its size or sign depends on a third variable or set of variables W. Conceptually, moderation is depicted as in Figure 1.2, which represents moderator variable W influencing the magnitude of the causal effect of X on Y. Moderation is also known as *interaction*. For example, experimental studies of exposure to the thin-as-ideal standard reveal that such exposure tends to have a larger effect on body dissatisfaction and affect among women who have already internalized the thin-as-ideal standard (see, e.g., Groetz, Levine, & Murnen, 2002). In other words, relative to women who strive for thinness as a personal goal, women who buy in less to the social norm that thinner is better are less likely to show evidence of body dissatisfaction after exposure to thin models through media images. So internalization of the norm (W) functions as moderator of the effect of exposure to images reflecting the thin-as-ideal norm (X) on body dissatisfaction (Y).

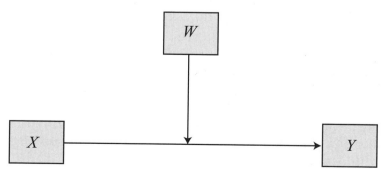

FIGURE 1.2. A simple moderation model with a single moderator variable W influencing the size of X's effect on Y.

Statistically, moderation analysis is typically conducted by testing for *linear interaction* between X and W in a model of Y. With evidence that X's effect on Y is moderated by W, the investigator typically will then quantify and describe the contingent nature of the association or effect by estimating X's effect on Y at various values of the moderator, an exercise known as *probing an interaction*. The principles of moderation analysis are introduced in Chapters 7 to 10.

This example illustrates that the answers to how and when questions can be intertwined. A variable could function as either a mediator or a moderator, depending on how the phenomenon under investigation is being conceptualized and tested. And in principle, the same variable could serve both roles simultaneously for certain processes that evolve and operate over long periods of time. For instance, early exposure to media images that portray the thin-as-ideal norm can persuade adolescents that thin is indeed better, which results in body dissatisfaction given that few women can live up to this unrealistic and even unhealthy standard. Of course, not all young women will buy into this message. Among those who do, once this norm has been internalized and adopted as a personal goal, it is more likely to influence how such women perceive themselves following later exposure to this norm relative to those who don't believe thinner is better.

1.3 Conditional Process Analysis

It is not difficult to find examples of mediation and moderation analysis in the empirical literature, and there have been numerous papers and book chapters emphasizing the value of moderation and mediation analysis to further understanding processes of interest to researchers in specific disciplines, many of which also provide methodological tutorials (e.g., Baron & Kenny, 1986; Breitborde, Srihari, Pollard, Addington, & Woods, 2010; Bryan, Schmiege, & Broaddus, 2007; Dawson, 2014; Dearing & Hamilton, 2006; Eveland, 1997; Fairchild & McQuillin, 2010; Frazier, Tix, & Barron, 2004; Gogineni, Alsup, & Gillespie, 1995; Harty, Sella, & Kadosh, 2017; Hayes & Rockwood, 2017; Holbert & Stephenson, 2003; James & Brett, 1984; Kraemer, Wilson, Fairburn, & Agras, 2002; Krause, Serlin, Ward, & Rony, 2010; Lockhart, MacKinnon, & Ohlrich, 2011; MacKinnon, Fairchild, & Fritz, 2007; Magill, 2011; Maric, Wiers, & Prins, 2012; Mascha, Dalton, Kurz, & Saager, 2013; Namazi & Namazi, 2016; Preacher & Hayes, 2008b; Ro, 2012; Schmidt & Scimmelmann, 2014; VanderWeele, 2016; Whisman & McClelland, 2005; Windgassen, Goldsmith, Moss-Morris, & Chalder, 2016). However, many of these articles don't discuss the combination of mediation and moderation in the same model. This lesser attention to the integration of moderation and mediation analysis may be due in part to the fact that analytical procedures that combine moderation and mediation were introduced to the research community in anything resembling a systematic fashion only in the last 15 years or so. For instance, Muller, Judd, and Yzerbyt (2005) write about the mediation of a moderated effect and the moderation of a mediated effect, Edwards and Lambert (2007) provide a framework for testing hypotheses that combine moderation and mediation using path analysis, and Preacher, Rucker, and Hayes (2007) introduce the concept of the "conditional indirect effect" as a quantification of the contingent nature of a process or mechanism and provide techniques for estimation and inference (additional articles include Morgan-Lopez & MacKinnon, 2006; Fairchild & MacKinnon, 2009).

In part as a result of these articles, researchers are now frequently throwing around terms such as "mediated moderation," "moderated mediation," and "conditional indirect effects," but often are only somewhat awkwardly implementing the corresponding analytical methods because of a lack of clear guidance from methodologists for how to properly do so and write about it. To be sure, the few methodology articles that do exist attempt to speak to the user, and some provide statistical software code or tools to ease the implementation of the methods discussed, but only so much can be accomplished in a single journal article. Furthermore, the advice that does exist is fragmented and spread across multiple articles in different journals. Part IV of this book is dedicated to the analytical integration of mediation and moderation using a data-analytical strategy I termed *conditional process modeling* or *conditional process analysis* in the first edition of this book in 2013 as well as in a book chapter published around the same time (Hayes & Preacher, 2013). Since then, the term has gained some traction and is now appearing not only in the text of scientific articles but even in the titles of the articles themselves (e.g., Barz et al., 2016; Beullens & Vandenbosch, 2016; Desorsiers, Vine, Curtiss, & Klemanski, 2014; Livingston, Christianson, & Cochran, 2016; Palmer, Koenig-Lewis, & Assad, 2016; Quratulain & Khan, 2015).

Conditional process analysis is used when one's research goal is to describe the conditional nature of the mechanism or mechanisms by which a variable transmits its effect on another and testing hypotheses about such contingent effects. As discussed earlier, mediation analysis is used to quantify and examine the direct and indirect pathways through which an antecedent variable X transmits its effect on a consequent variable Y through one or more intermediary or mediator variables.[1] Moderation analysis is used to examine how the effect of antecedent variable X on a consequent Y

---

[1]*Antecedent* and *consequent* variables will be formally defined in section 1.5.

depends on a third variable or set of variables. Conditional process analysis is both of these in combination and focuses on the estimation and interpretation of the conditional nature (the moderation component) of the indirect and/or direct effects (the mediation component) of X on Y in a causal system. Although not always described using this term, the methodology articles mentioned earlier have prompted an increasingly widespread adoption of this analytical method. It is not difficult to find examples of conditional process analysis in the empirical literature of many disciplines, including social psychology (Kung, Eibach, & Grossmann, 2016; Osborne, Huo, & Smith, 2015; Wu, Balliet, & Van Lange, 2015), health psychology (Webb, Fiery, & Jafari, 2016), developmental psychology (Canfield & Saudino, 2016; Thomas & Bowker, 2015), clinical psychology and psychiatry (Goodin et al., 2009; Lee, Ahn, Jeong, Chae, & Choi, 2014; Rees & Freeman, 2009; Torres & Taknint, 2015), cognitive psychology (Rodriguez & Berry, 2016), public health (Blashill & Wal, 2010), sociology (Augustine, 2014; Li, Patel, Balliet, Tov, & Scollon, 2011), women's studies (Gaunt & Scott, 2014; Sibley & Perry, 2010), public administration (Smith, 2016), biological psychology and neuroscience (Little et al., 2015; Oei, Tollenaar, Elzinga, & Spinhoven, 2010; Thai, Taber-Thomas, & Pérez-Edgar, 2016), business, marketing, and management (Felipe, Rodan, & Leal-Rodriguez, 2016; Karnal, Machiels, Orth, & Mai, 2016; Smith, Martinez, & Sabat, 2016), and communication (Goodboy, Martin, & Brown, 2016; Gvirsman, 2014; Johnson, Slater, Silver, & Ewoldsen, 2016), among others.

A concrete example will help to clarify just what conditional process analysis is all about. In 2011, the U.S. Congress held the American and world economies hostage over largely politically motivated disagreements and fighting over the conditions under which the amount of money the government is allowed to borrow can be raised—the so-called *debt ceiling*. In part as a result of this political bickering and a failure of Congress to adequately address spending and revenue problems, Standard & Poor's lowered the credit rating of the U.S. government for the first time in history, from AAA to AA+. In this time frame, U.S. unemployment was at a recent high at over 9%, housing prices were falling, and so too was the value of people's retirement portfolios. In roughly this same time frame, the Greek economy was bailed out by the International Monetary Fund, the European Union was facing economic instability, and an earthquake followed by a tsunami and near-nuclear meltdown at a power plant in Japan roiled the Japanese people and its economy. Not to downplay the significance of a bad economy for the public at large, but imagine owning a business in this kind of environment, where your economic livelihood and your ability to pay your workforce and your creditors depends on a public that is reluctant to let go of its money.

It is in this context that Pollack, VanEpps, and Hayes (2012) conducted a study examining the affective and cognitive effects of economic stress on entrepreneurs. Of primary interest was whether economic stress prompts business owners to contemplate pursuing other careers, giving up their entrepreneurial roles, and just doing something else instead. But Pollack et al. (2012) went further than asking only whether economic stress is related to such "withdrawal intentions." They proposed that such economic stress leads to depressed affect, which in turn enhances a business owner's intention to leave entrepreneurship and pursue another vocation. This is a question about not whether but *how*. On top of this, they proposed that entrepreneurs who are more socially connected to others in their field would be less susceptible to the deleterious effects of economic stress. Having the support of other entrepreneurs in your business community could help to buffer the effects of that stress on depression and, in turn, the desire to leave the business. This proposed explanation addresses a question of *when*. Under what circumstances, or for which type of people, is the effect of stress on depression and business withdrawal intentions large versus small or even zero?

To conduct this study, Pollack et al. (2012) sent a survey to members of Business Networking International, a social networking group for small business owners. The 262 respondents were asked a series of questions used to score the economic stress they felt related to their business (higher score = more stress), whether and how much they thought about withdrawing from entrepreneurship (higher score = greater intentions to leave), the extent to which they felt various emotions (e.g., discouraged, hopeless, inadequate) related to their business over the last year (higher score = more depressed affect), and how many people they spoke to, e-mailed, or met with face-to-face about their business on a daily basis from this networking group (higher score = more social ties).

Somewhat surprisingly perhaps, there was no evidence of an association between economic stress and withdrawal intentions. Entrepreneurs who reported feeling more economic stress were no more or less likely to report greater intentions to withdraw from their business than those who felt less stress ($r = 0.06, p > .05$). But that is not the whole story, for this finding belies what is a more interesting, nuanced, and, ultimately, conditional process. A moderation analysis revealed that those who reported relatively higher stress did report relatively higher withdrawal intentions compared to those with lower stress (i.e., the relationship was positive), but this was true only among those with relatively few social ties with network members. Among

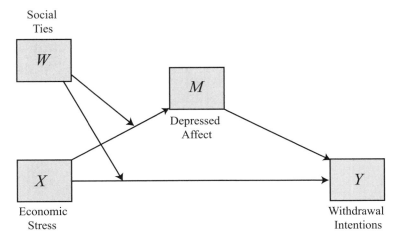

FIGURE 1.3. A conceptual diagram of a conditional process model corresponding to the Pollack et al. (2012) study.

those who reported relatively more social ties, there was little or even a *negative* association between economic stress and withdrawal intentions. So social ties seemed to buffer the effects of stress on desire to withdraw from their business enterprise. This is *moderation*; social ties moderates the effect of economic stress on withdrawal intentions.

Pollack et al. (2012) proposed that the effect of economic stress on entrepreneurial withdrawal intentions operated through business-related negative affect. That is, economic uncertainty and the resulting stress it produces bums business owners out, makes them feel inadequate and helpless, and leads them to choose to pursue other careers. This is *mediation*. In fact, participants who reported more economic stress did report more depressed affect ($r = 0.34, p < .01$), and those who reported more depressed affect reported greater intentions to withdraw ($r = 0.42, p < .01$). But this process, according to Pollack et al. (2012), can be "interrupted" by strong social ties. Having people you can lean on, talk to, or bounce ideas off to manage the business-related stress can reduce the effects of such stress on how you feel and therefore how you think about your future as a business owner. The evidence was consistent with the interpretation that economic stress affects how business owners feel, depending on their social ties. Entrepreneurs under relatively more economic stress who also had relatively few social ties reported relatively more business-related depressed affect. But among those with relatively more social ties, economic stress was unrelated or even negatively related to negative affect. So social ties moderated the effect of stress on negative affect as well as on withdrawal intentions.

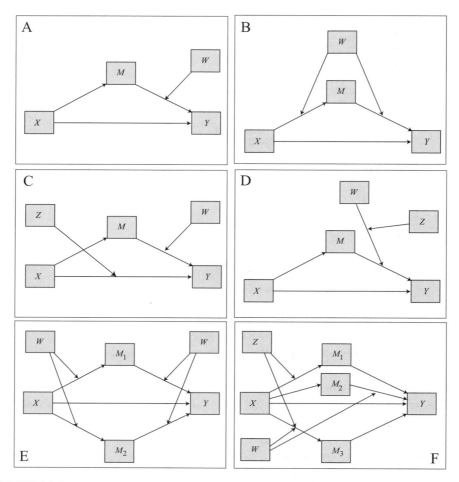

FIGURE 1.4. Some variants of a conditional process model, from quite simple (A) to fairly complex (F).

A conceptual diagram of a conditional process model corresponding to this example can be found in Figure 1.3. This diagram depicts what some have called *moderated mediation* and others have called *mediated moderation*. In fact, it depicts both. It has been given other labels as well, such as a *direct effect and first stage moderation model* (Edwards & Lambert, 2007). Regardless, observe that this diagram depicts two moderated relationships, one from economic stress to depressed affect ($X \rightarrow M$), and the other from economic stress to withdrawal intentions ($X \rightarrow Y$), both of which are diagrammed as moderated by social ties (W). In addition, there is an indirect effect of economic stress on withdrawal intentions through depressed affect depicted ($X \rightarrow M \rightarrow Y$), but because this indirect effect includes a component that is proposed as moderated (the $X \rightarrow M$ association), the indirect effect is also moderated or *conditional*. The direct effect of economic stress on with-drawal intentions ($X \to Y$) is also depicted as moderated. According to this diagram, it too is conditional, for it depends on social ties. Thus, the process linking economic stress to withdrawal intentions through depressed affect is moderated or conditional, hence the term *conditional process model.* Throughout this book I describe how to piece the components of this model together and estimate and interpret direct and indirect effects, moderated as well as unmoderated.[2]

The example depicted in Figure 1.3 is only one of the forms that a conditional process model can take. A few additional possibilities can be found in Figure 1.4, but these still represent only some of the many, many ways that moderation and mediation can be combined into a single integrated model. Panel A depicts a model in which the $M \to Y$ effect is moderated by W, called a *second stage moderation model* in terms introduced by Edwards and Lambert (2007). For examples of this model in published research, see Boren and Veksler (2015), Canfield and Saudino (2016), and Kuwabara, Yu, Lee, and Galinsky (2016). The model in panel B adds moderation of the $X \to M$ effect to the model in panel A, yielding a *first and second stage moderation model* (Edwards & Lambert, 2007). Papadaki and Giovalolias (2015) and Thai et al. (2016) provide examples of this model. Panel C is like the model in panel A but adds moderation of the direct effect of X ($X \to Y$) by Z. Panel D depicts moderation of the $M \to Y$ effect by W, which itself is moderated by Z. See Fries, Brown, Carroll, and Arkin (2015) and Krieger and Sarge (2013) for examples. Panels E and F show models with more than one mediator. The model in panel E is similar to panel B but includes moderation by W of all effects to and from M_1 and M_2 (see, e.g., Jones et al., 2013; Takeuchi, Yun, & Wong, 2011). Panel F depicts a complex model (see Andreeva et al., 2010) with three mediators and two moderators. In this model, the $X \to M_3$ effect is moderated by both W and Z, the $X \to M_1$ effect is moderated by Z, and the $M_2 \to Y$ effect is moderated by W.

1.4 Correlation, Causality, and Statistical Modeling

The study of economic stress in entrepreneurs just described illustrates what conditional process analysis is all about, but it also illustrates what some construe as a weakness of mediation analysis in general, as well as

---

[2]It turns out in this case that there was no evidence that the direct effect of economic stress on withdrawal intentions was moderated by social ties, even though the so-called *total effect* was moderated. The moderation of the total effect of economic stress on withdrawal intentions is not depicted in Figure 1.3. The distinction between a total effect and a direct effect will be introduced in Chapter 3.

how liberally people often attribute causality as the mechanism producing the associations observed in any kind of study. These findings come from a cross-sectional survey. This study is what is often called called *observational* rather than experimental. All measurements of these entrepreneurs were taken at the same time, there is no experimental manipulation or other forms of experimental control, and there is no way of establishing the causal ordering of the relationships observed. For example, people who are feeling down about their business might be more likely to contemplate withdrawing, and as a result they work less, network less often with other business leaders, and feel more stress from the economic pressures that build up as a result. The nature of the data collection makes it impossible to establish what is causing what. In terms of the three criteria often described as necessary conditions for establishing causation (covariation, temporal ordering, and the elimination of competing explanations), this study establishes, at best, only covariation between variables in the causal system.

Experimentation and, to a lesser extent, longitudinal research offer some advantages over cross-sectional research when establishing causal association. For example, suppose economic stress was experimentally manipulated in some way, but otherwise the same results were found. In that case, we would be in a much better position to argue direction of cause, at least in part. Random assignment to levels of economic stress would ensure that neither social ties, depressed affect, nor withdrawal intentions could be affecting the stress the study participants felt. It also guarantees that economic stress and depressed affect are not spuriously associated, meaning they share a common cause. But random assignment would not help establish the correct temporal ordering of depressed affect and withdrawal intentions. Although it could be that economic stress influences depressed affect which, in turn, influences withdrawal intentions ($X \rightarrow M \rightarrow Y$), it remains possible that economic stress influences withdrawal intentions, which then influences depressed affect ($X \rightarrow Y \rightarrow M$).

To deal with this limitation of one-shot experimental studies, a sequence of experimental studies can help to some extent (see Stone-Romero & Raposa, 2010). First, one attempts to establish that X causes M and Y in one experimental study. Success at doing so can then be followed with a second experimental study to establish that M causes Y rather than Y causing M. The estimates from such analyses (perhaps including a moderation component as well) could then be pieced together to establish the nature (conditional or not) of the indirect effects of X on Y through M. But as Spencer, Zanna, and Fong (2005) note, it is not always easy or even possible to establish convincingly that the M measured in the first study is the same as the M that is manipulated in the second study. Absent such equivalence, the ability of a sequence of experiments to establish a causal chain of events is compromised.

Collecting data on the same variables over time is an alternative approach to studying causal processes, and doing so offers some advantages. For instance, rather than measuring entrepreneurs only once, it would be informative to measure their experience of economic stress on multiple occasions, as well as their depressed affect and intentions to withdraw from entrepreneurial activity. If economic stress influences withdrawal intentions through its effect on depressed affect, then you'd expect that people who are under more stress *than they were before* would express stronger intentions to withdraw *than they expressed earlier* as a result of feeling more depressed affect *than they were feeling earlier*. But covariation over time does not imply cause, just as covariation at a single time fails to establish a causal association. There are statistical procedures that attempt to disentangle contemporaneous from time-lagged association (e.g., Finkel, 1995), and there is a growing literature on moderation and mediation analysis, as well as their combination, in longitudinal studies (e.g., Bauer, Preacher, & Gil, 2006; Cole & Maxwell, 2003; Cheong, MacKinnon, & Khoo, 2003; Selig & Preacher, 2009). With the exception of a brief treatment in section 14.7, I do not address this literature or corresponding methods in this book.

Some advance the argument that scientists really should not attempt to model purportedly causal processes with data that do not afford causal interpretation, such as when the data are purely correlational in nature. For instance, Maxwell, Cole, and Mitchell (2011) take the position that trying to get at causal processes using mediation analysis with correlational data is "almost certainly futile" (p. 836). And Trafimow (2015) edited an entire issue of *Basic and Applied Social Psychology* dedicated to the position that mediation analysis as widely practiced and interpreted is fundamentally flawed, and published with "no effort to be locally fair" as a goal but, rather, to "reduce the dependence of social psychologists on this questionable paradigm."[3]

My perspective is much more relaxed than these extreme positions. We don't use statistical methods to make causal inferences. Establishing cause and effect is more a problem in research design and logical analysis than one in data analysis. Statistical methods are just mathematical tools that allow us to discern order in apparent chaos, or signals of processes that may be at work amid random background noise or other processes we haven't incorporated into our models. The inferences that we make about cause are

[3]These quotes are from the call for papers sent to the listserv of Division 5 of the American Psychological Association on January 8, 2015.

not products of the mathematics underneath the modeling process. Rather, the inferences we make are products of our minds—how we interpret the associations we have observed, the signal we believe we have extracted from the noise. To be sure, we can and should hold ourselves to a high standard. We should strive to design rigorous studies that allow us to make causal inferences with clarity when possible. But we won't always be able to do so given constraints on resources, time, the availability of data, the generosity of research participants, and research ethics. We should not let the limitations of our data collection efforts constrain the tools we bring to the task of trying to understand what our data might be telling us about the processes we are studying. But we absolutely should recognize the limitations of our data and couch our interpretations with the appropriate caveats and cautions.

Causality is the cinnamon bun of social science. It is a sticky concept, and establishing that a sequence of events is a causal one can be a messy undertaking. As you pick the concept apart, it unravels in what seems like an endless philosophical spiral of reductionism. Even if we can meet the criteria of causality when testing a simple $X \rightarrow M \rightarrow Y$ model, what is the mechanism that links X and M, and M to Y? Certainly, those causal processes must themselves come into being through some kind of mechanism. What are the mediators of the individual components of the causal chain? And what mediates the components of those components? And if those mediators can be established as such, what mediates those effects?

In other words, we have never really explained an association entirely, no matter how many intervening variables we propose and account for linking X and Y. This does not mean that it is not worth thinking deeply about what cause means or discussing and debating what kinds of standards we must hold ourselves to as scientists in order to accept causal interpretations. But that isn't going to happen in this book. There are other books and journal articles on the topic of causality if you want to explore the concept on your own (e.g., Davis, 1985; Holland, 1986; Morgan & Winship, 2007; Pearl, 2009), and there is a growing chorus of quantitative social scientists who reject the regression-based orientation I outline here on the grounds that linear modeling and statistical adjustment simply don't do the job many people claim it does. That said, this book is about statistically modeling relationships—relationships that may but may not be causal in the end—and I think you will find the techniques and tools described here useful in your quest to understand your data and test some of your theoretical propositions and hypotheses. Just how large an inferential chasm between data and claim you attempt to leap is your decision to make, as is how you go about justifying your inference to potential critics. I will not, nor should I or anyone else, forbid you to use the methods described here just because your data are *only* correlational in nature.

1.5   Statistical and Conceptual Diagrams, and Antecedent and Consequent Variables

When discussing our ideas about the relationships between variables with colleagues or when giving a lecture or trying to describe our ideas in research articles, we often do so using what I am calling a *conceptual diagram* in this book. I have already used conceptual diagrams three times in this introductory chapter, once for mediation in Figure 1.1, one for moderation in Figure 1.2, and again for the conditional process model depicted in Figure 1.3. A conceptual diagram represents a set of relationships between variables, with the direction of the arrow representing what we are treating as either the direction of causal flow, or merely denoting which variable is considered predictor (with an arrow pointing away from it) and which is considered outcome (with an arrow pointing at it) in the process one is describing or theorizing. Conceptual diagrams are not the same as what are known as *path diagrams* in the structural equation modeling literature. A conceptual diagram does not represent a set of mathematical equations the way that a path diagram does. A conceptual diagram is used merely to convey ideas about relationships, whether causal, noncausal, or moderated, between variables.

A *statistical diagram*, by contrast, is like a path diagram, in that it represents a set of equations, in visual form, corresponding to a conceptual diagram. The statistical diagram visually depicts how the effects represented in a conceptual diagram would actually be estimated by a mathematical model, such as a linear regression model. An example of a statistical diagram for a simple moderation model as depicted in conceptual form in Figure 1.5, panel A, can be found in Figure 1.5, panel B. In a statistical diagram, boxes represent explicitly measured or *observed* variables (i.e., variables that actually exist in one's dataset), and the solid unidirectional arrows represent *predictor of* or *predicted from*, depending on whether the arrow points to or from the variable. It may be that two variables connected by an arrow are in fact causally related, with the direction of causal flow represented by the direction of the arrow. But resist the temptation to interpret solid unidirectional arrows in a statistical diagram as necessarily implying something about causality. That may not be what they are intended to convey, although they may, depending on context. No distinction is made in a statistical diagram between "cause of" and "predictor of."

Throughout this book, any variable in a statistical diagram that has an arrow pointing at it I will call a *consequent variable*, and any variable that has an arrow pointing away from it I will call an *antecedent variable*. I will also use these terms when referring to variables in a model expressed in equation form. *Antecedent* is synonymous with *predictor* or *independent* variable, and *consequent* is synonymous with *dependent* or *outcome* variable. If a variable in a statistical diagram has an arrow pointing at it, it is a consequent variable by definition, and it is being predicted by all antecedents that send an arrow to it. The number of consequent variables in a statistical diagram corresponds to the number of equations the diagram represents.

A consequent variable may or may not be an antecedent variable, depending on whether it sends an arrow to another variable. A variable can be both antecedent and consequent in some models discussed later in the book, meaning that the same variable can be an outcome or dependent variable in one equation but a predictor or independent variable in another equation. Antecedent and consequent variables are similar to but not the same as *exogeneous* and *endogeneous* variables in the language of structural equation modeling. An endogeneous variable in structural equation modeling is a consequent variable by definition, but an endogeneous variable can't also be an exogeneous variable in structural equation modeling terms, whereas a consequent variable can also be an antecedent variable if it sends an arrow to another variable.

Looking at Figure 1.5, it is apparent that there are four observed variables in this model, three of which are antecedent and one of which is consequent. Because there is only one consequent variable in this diagram, it represents a single equation of the form

$$Y = i_Y + b_1 X_1 + b_2 W_2 + b_3 XW + e_Y \tag{1.1}$$

as will be discussed in detail in Chapter 7. In this model, the consequent variable Y is being predicted by three antecedent variables, X, W, and XW (the latter being the product of X and W) because Y receives an arrow from each of these antecedents. That is, these three antecedents are predictors of the consequent Y because they point an arrow at Y.

Any variable functioning as a consequent in a statistical model is assumed to be predicted from its antecedent variables with some degree of error. The error in estimation of a consequent variable is represented in a statistical diagram with the letter e and a dashed line pointing at its corresponding consequent variable. The subscript for an error will be the same as the label given to the consequent variable it is attached to. I use a dashed line rather than a solid line because we don't usually think of the error in estimation as a predictor of the consequent (which would be denoted by a solid arrow), although it could be construed in that way.

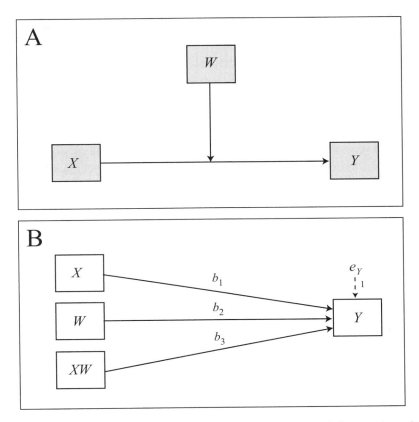

FIGURE 1.5. A simple moderation model depicted as a conceptual diagram (panel A) and a statistical diagram (panel B).

Observe in Figure 1.5 that each arrow in the statistical diagram has a label attached to it. Labels attached to arrows between variables represent the regression coefficients for each antecedent variable in the statistical model of the consequent. Depending on whether the diagram depicts a model prior to estimation of the coefficients or conveys the results after model estimation, these labels will either be numbers or some other symbol, such as a letter of the alphabet. For instance, without information about the values of b_1, b_2, and b_3, it makes sense to label them symbolically and generically in this way, because their values are not known. However if a diagram is being used to depict the results *after* estimation of the model, one might instead use the actual regression coefficients calculated using the data available. In this case, b_1, b_2, b_3 could be replaced with numbers like 0.235, −0.127, and 0.221, respectively. Alternatively, one might use the labels in the diagram but place their estimated values in a table corresponding to the diagram. The label attached to an arrow leading from a consequent's error in estimation will typically be 1, as errors in estimation are almost always given a weight of 1 in a linear model.[4]

In regression analysis, we generally assume that the antecedents of a common consequent either are or might be correlated with each other. Such assumed covariation between antecedent variables is often depicted in path diagrams using curved bidirectional arrows. However, I will not depict such covariation in a statistical diagram, because doing so can very quickly make a compact visual representation of a set of equations very complex and cluttered, and its meaning harder to discern. As a general rule, all antecedent variables not connected with a unidirectional arrow are assumed to be correlated. There may be occasions when it is necessary to include certain covariances in a statistical diagram in order to convey important estimation information, such as in models that combine moderation and mediation. I will do so when needed.

Linear regression models such as those represented by equation 1.1 typically contain a *regression constant* or *intercept*, denoted here as i_Y because equation 1.1 is a model of consequent Y. It may be that this constant is fixed to zero as a result of certain transformations of the data, such as mean centering or standardization, but that doesn't mean it doesn't exist when it isn't formally specified in the equation. I will not visually depict the constant in a statistical diagram corresponding to that model because, like covariation between antecedents, doing so adds unnecessary visual clutter while providing no information that is particularly relevant to interpretation. But its absence from the diagram should not be interpreted as its absence from the model.

To reduce the potential for confusing a conceptual diagram and a statistical diagram, I make clear in the figure captions whether a diagram corresponds to a model in statistical or conceptual form. In addition, because a conceptual diagram is not intended to be a representation of an equation or set of equations, a conceptual model will not depict the errors in estimation, whereas a statistical model will. Finally, all variables in a conceptual model will be denoted by gray boxes, as opposed to the white boxes used in a statistical diagram.

1.6 Statistical Software

I believe that the widespread adoption of modern methods of analysis is greatly facilitated when these methods are described using software with which people are already familiar. Most likely, you already have access

---

[4]Equation 1.1 could be written as $Y = i_Y + b_1X_1 + b_2X_2 + b_3XW + 1e$. The weight of 1 given to e in equation 1.1 is implied by its absence.

to the statistical software I will emphasize in this book, primarily SAS and IBM SPSS Statistics (the latter of which I refer to henceforth simply as SPSS). Although other software could be used (such as Mplus, LISREL, AMOS, or other structural equation modeling programs), most of these don't implement at least some of the procedures I emphasize in this book. And by eliminating the need to learn a new software language, I believe you more quickly develop an understanding and appreciation of the methods described herein.

Throughout the pages that follow I will emphasize estimation of model parameters using ordinary least squares (OLS) regression. Although any program that can conduct OLS regression analysis can estimate the parameters of most of the models I describe, such programs can only get you so far when taken off the shelf. For instance, no program I am aware of implements the Johnson–Neyman technique for probing interactions, and neither SPSS nor SAS can generate bootstrap confidence intervals for products of parameters, a method I advocate for inference in mediation analysis and conditional process analysis. Over the last several years, I have been publishing on moderation and mediation analysis and providing various tools for SPSS and SAS in the form of "macros" that simplify the analyses I describe in this book. You may have used one of these tools yourself, such as INDIRECT (Preacher & Hayes, 2008a), MODMED (Preacher et al., 2007), SOBEL (Preacher & Hayes, 2004), or MODPROBE (Hayes & Matthes, 2009).

But each of these tools was designed for a specific task and not others, and keeping track of which tool should be used for which analysis can be difficult. So rather than confuse you by describing the ins-and-outs of each of these tools, I designed a new macro, released with the first edition of this book, called PROCESS that integrates most of the functions of my earlier macros into one handy command or dialog box, and with additional features not available in my other macros. PROCESS has become very popular, and my prediction is that you will come to love PROCESS and will find yourself turning to it again and again in your professional life. If you have used PROCESS before, you will find the latest version is dramatically improved relative to earlier releases described in the first edition of this book. PROCESS is freely available and can be downloaded from *www.processmacro.org*, and its features are documented with various examples throughout this book and also in Appendix A. I recommend familiarizing yourself with the documentation before attempting to use PROCESS. You should also check back now and then with *www.processmacro.org* to see if any updates have been released since you last downloaded it.

The advent of the graphic user interface (GUI) in the 1980s made data analysis a point-and-click enterprise for some and turned what is a distasteful task for many into something that is actually quite fun. Yet I still believe there is value to understanding how to instruct your preferred software package to perform using syntax or "code." In addition to providing a set of instructions that you can easily save for use later or give to collaborators and colleagues, syntax is easier to describe in books of this sort than is a set of instructions about what to click, drag, point, click, and so forth, and in what sequence. Users of SAS have no choice but to write in code, and although SPSS is highly popular in part because of its easy-to-navigate user interface, and I do provide a GUI-based version of PROCESS, I nevertheless will describe all SPSS instructions using syntax. In this book, all code for whatever program I am using or describing at that moment will be denoted with **courier** typeface in a box. For SPSS commands, the code will be set in a black box with white text, as below.

```
process y=intent/x=exposure/m=attitude/w=social/model=8/boot=10000.
```

But for SAS code, I will use a white box with black text. So the SAS version of the command above will look like

```
%process (data=example,y=intent,x=exposure,m=attitude,w=social,model=8,
    boot=10000);
```

Some commands will not fit in a single line in this book and must be carried below to the next line. When this occurs, it will be denoted by indentation of the continuing text, as in the SAS example above. A command has ended when you see a *command terminator*. In SPSS, the command terminator is a period ("."), whereas in SAS it is the semicolon (";"). A failure to include a command terminator at the end of your command is likely to confuse your software, and a string of errors is likely.

New to this edition of the book, in several chapters I provide R code for visualizing interactions and moderated direct and indirect effects. R code will stand out from the SPSS and SAS code through the use of a gray box and black letters, as in

```
plot(y=attitude,x=skeptic,pch=15)
```

1.7   Overview of This Book

This book is divided into five thematic parts as well as a few appendices. The first part, which you are reading now, consists of the introductory material in this chapter as well as an overview of the fundamentals of linear regression analysis in Chapter 2. These chapters should be considered important prerequisite reading. If you are not familiar with linear regression analysis, almost nothing in this book will make any sense to you. So although the temptation to skip the material in this first part may be strong, do so at your own risk.

Chapters 3 through 6 define the second part, which is devoted to mediation analysis. Chapter 3 illustrates the principles of elementary path analysis, with a focus on the partitioning of the total effect of antecedent variable X on consequent variable Y into direct and indirect effects, as well as means of making statistical inference about direct and indirect effects. Chapter 4 discusses the disadvantages of older approaches to mediation analysis, some controversies such as confounding and causal order, and it addresses models with multiple causal antecedent or consequent variables. Chapter 5 extends the principles and methods introduced in Chapter 3 into the realm of multiple mediator models—models of causal influence that are transmitted by two or more intervening variables operating in parallel or in sequence. This second part of the book ends with Chapter 6, new to this edition, that focuses on mediation analysis when the causal antecedent variable X is multicategorical.

The third part is Chapters 7 through 10, and the topic is moderation analysis. In Chapter 7, I define the concept of a conditional effect and show how to set up a linear model that allows the effect of one variable on another to depend linearly on a third variable. I illustrate how a hypothesis of moderation is tested and how to interpret the regression coefficients of the corresponding model. I also introduce a few methods of dissecting the conditional nature of association and show how to construct a visual representation of moderation. Chapter 8 illustrates the generality of the procedure introduced in Chapter 7, including interaction between quantitative variables or between dichotomous moderators and focal antecedents. Chapter 9 addresses various miscellaneous issues in the estimation of models that allow one variable's effect to depend on another, such as models with multiple interactions, and a debunking of myths and misunderstandings about centering and standardization in moderation analysis. Chapter 10, new to this edition, concludes the moderation analysis section of the book by extending the principles described in the prior chapters to models with a multicategorical focal antecedent or moderator.

Chapters 11 through 13 define the fourth part of the book. The topic is conditional process analysis. Chapter 11 provides numerous examples of conditional process models proposed and estimated in the literature, introduces the important concepts of conditional and unconditional direct and indirect effects, describes how they are defined mathematically, and shows how they are estimated. Chapter 12 provides a slightly more complex analytical example of conditional process analysis while also illustrating the distinction between moderated mediation and mediated moderation. Chapter 13 integrates principles from Chapters 6, 10, 11, and 12, applying them to a conditional process analysis with a multicategorical antecedent variable.

The fifth section of the book contains only one chapter that closes the body of the book. Chapter 14 addresses various miscellaneous issues and frequently asked questions about the analysis of the mechanisms and their contingencies. Some of the topics include how to approach a complex analysis, scientific writing, a brief treatment of repeated measures designs, and whether a variable can be both moderator and mediator in the same model.

Most statistical methods books include appendices, and this one is no exception. Appendix A is the documentation for PROCESS, a macro freely available for SPSS and SAS that greatly simplifies the analyses I describe in this book. PROCESS has evolved considerably since the release of the first edition of this book, and a new Appendix B describes one of its greatest new features: a new syntax structure allowing you to build a model from scratch rather than having to rely on the preprogrammed models. PROCESS has become quite popular in the last few years, but not everyone trying to use it understands clearly just what it does or exactly how it works. I recommend reading the documentation before using PROCESS in any research you are going to attempt to publish.

This is an introductory book, and so there are many important, interesting, and some could say critical points and controversies that I gloss over or completely ignore. For example, all of the analyses I illustrate are done using OLS regression-based path analysis, which assumes fixed effects, continuous outcomes, and the absence of random measurement error. Of course, we generally don't measure without error, and it is well known that a failure to account for random measurement error in the variables in a linear model can produce bias and possibly misleading results. And often our outcomes of interest are not continuous. Rather, they may take one of two values or perhaps are measured on a course ordinal scale. In such cases OLS regression is not appropriate. I also neglect repeated measures and multilevel designs, with the exception of a brief discussion in section 14.7. These are all interesting and important topics, to be sure, and there is a developing literature in the application of mediation and moderation analysis, as well as their combination, to such problems. But assuming you don't plan on abandoning OLS regression any time soon as a result of some of its weaknesses and limitations, I believe you will be no worse for the wear and, I predict, even a bit better off once you turn the last page and have developed an understanding of how to use OLS regression to model complicated, contingent processes.

1.8 Chapter Summary

The outcome of an empirical study is more impressive, more influential, and more helpful to our understanding of an area of scientific inquiry if it establishes not only *whether* or *if* X affects Y but also *how* and *when* that relationship holds or is strong versus weak. If all effects exist through some kind of mechanism, and all effects have some kind of boundary conditions, then the most complete analysis answers both the how and when question simultaneously. In this chapter I have introduced the concepts of mediation (how X influences Y) and moderation (when X influences Y) and their combination in the form of a conditional process model. Although data analysis cannot be used to demonstrate or prove causal claims, it can be used to determine whether the data are consistent with a proposed causal process. Thus, the methods described in this book are useful for testing causal processes even absent data that lend themselves to unequivocal causal interpretation. My emphasis throughout this book is on the use of regression-based path analysis as a means of estimating various effects of interest (direct and indirect, conditional and unconditional). In order to grasp the material throughout this book, the basic principles of linear modeling using regression analysis must be well understood. Thus, the next chapter provides on overview of the fundamentals of linear regression analysis.

2
Fundamentals of Linear Regression Analysis

Ordinary least squares (OLS) regression analysis serves as the foundation for much of what is discussed in this book. In this chapter, I provide an overview of the principles of OLS regression, including the estimation process, measuring the fit of a model, interpretation of information a linear regression yields, and the fundamentals of statistical inference.

During the U.S. Presidential election of 2000 between Texas governor George W. Bush and Vice President Al Gore, the Bush campaign released a television advertisement in which he described the world as one of "terror, madmen, and missiles." He argued the need for a "sharpened sword" in a dangerous world and promised that if elected, he would rebuild a military suffering from aging equipment and low morale, help to protect the United States and its allies from blackmail by other countries by constructing a missile defense system, and that his foreign policy would be one "with a touch of iron" motivated by U.S. interests. Similarly, in the 2016 campaign between Hillary Clinton and Donald J. Trump, Trump warned voters of the dangers of policies of the Democrats that could allow terrorists from the Middle East and "rapists and drug dealers" from Mexico easy access to American soil and a safe place to perpetrate their crimes. The not-so-subtle message used by these politicians is that this is a scary world full of people who want to harm the United States, and by electing Bush or Trump as President, we will all be safer.

Politicians are not the only ones to use emotions in their attempt to influence the public. Consider a public service announcement produced by the Environmental Defense Fund in which a man appearing to be in his 40s stands on a railroad track as a locomotive, whistle blaring, screams toward him. As the screen transitions back and forth between his face and various shots of the train from different angles, he states matter of factly, "Global warming. Some say irreversible consequences are 30 years away."

Another shot of the train is shown, and the camera then focuses on his face as he states in a smug tone, "30 years? That won't affect me," at which point he steps aside to reveal a young girl standing behind him on the tracks. The camera zooms in on her worried face just before the train hits her.

Such advertisements attempt to appeal to the base nature of humanity by tugging at our hearts rather than engaging our heads. The assumption is that people's actions are guided by how they feel. If you want to stimulate people to act (e.g., vote for a particular politician, donate to a cause, or otherwise mobilize to affect change) appeal to their emotions while giving them a course of action to deal with the emotion that results from the message. Emotional appeals have been used as a persuasive device for as long as people have been able to communicate, and no doubt they will be around as long as we are.

In this chapter, I introduce some principles of linear regression analysis using data from a study examining the extent to which people's beliefs about whether and how government should enact new laws to reduce the impact of an environmental crisis is related to their emotional responses to that potential crisis. Linear regression is the foundation of most of the methods I describe in this book, so a solid understanding of the fundamentals of linear regression is essential. I assume that most readers have been exposed to linear regression in some form before discovering this book, and so some of the material will be review. Even so, I encourage everyone to read this chapter. Not only will it help to refresh your understanding of linear regression, but you will also find it easier to understand the material in chapters that follow with familiarity of my way of talking about linear regression. Furthermore, I introduce some notation in these two chapters that will be used throughout the book.

2.1 Correlation and Prediction

To what extent are people's beliefs about the role government should play in mitigating the potential effects of a global crisis related to their emotional reactions to such a crisis? To answer this question, I rely on data from 815 residents of the United States (417 female, 398 male) who expressed a willingness to participate in online surveys in exchange for various incentives. The sampling procedure was designed such that the respondents roughly represent the U.S. population. The dataset (named GLBWARM) can be downloaded from the web page for this book located on at *www.afhayes.com*.

The dataset contains a variable constructed from how each participant responded to five questions about the extent to which he or she supports various policies or actions by the U.S. government to mitigate the threat of global climate change. Examples include "How much do you support or oppose increasing government investment for developing alternative energy like biofuels, wind, or solar by 25%?" and "How much do you support or oppose creating a 'Cap and Trade' policy that limits greenhouse gases said to cause global warming?" Response options were scaled from "Strongly opposed" (coded 1) or "Strongly support" (7), with intermediate labels to denote intermediate levels of support. An index of support for government action to reduce climate change was constructed for each person by averaging responses to the five questions (GOVACT in the data file).

The dataset also contains a variable quantifying participants' negative emotional responses to the prospect of climate change. This variable was constructed using participants' responses to a question that asked them to indicate how frequently they feel each of three emotions when thinking about global warming: "worried," "alarmed," and "concerned." Response options included "not at all," "slightly," "a little bit," "some," "a fair amount," and "a great deal." These responses were numerically coded 1 to 6, respectively, and each participant's responses were averaged across all three emotions to produce a measure of *negative emotions about climate change* (NEGEMOT in the data file). This variable is scaled such that higher scores reflect feeling stronger negative emotions.

Do people who feel stronger negative emotions about the prospect of climate change report greater support for government action than those who feel such negative emotions to a lesser extent? The scatterplot in Figure 2.1 depicts the association between support for government action and negative emotions about climate change. This scatterplot was generated SPSS using the command

```
graph/scatterplot=negemot with govact.
```

and then edited using the binning function and various other features in SPSS. A comparable command in SAS is

```
proc sgscatter data=glbwarm;plot govact*negemot;run;
```

Looking at the scatterplot, it appears that there is a tendency for those who report relatively stronger negative emotions about climate change to also be relatively more supportive of government action to help mitigate climate change. To be sure, the association isn't perfect by any means, but the trend is fairly clear.

Our eyes can deceive us, so it is always a good idea to quantify association rather than relying only on a visual depiction such as a scatterplot. *Pearson's product moment correlation*, symbolically known as Pearson's *r*, is a

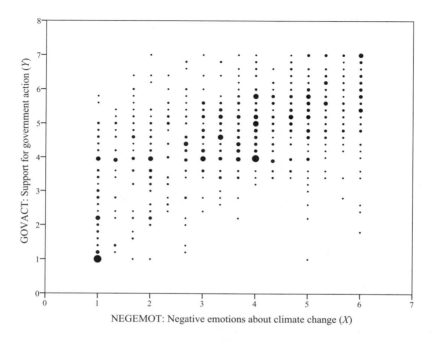

FIGURE 2.1. A scatterplot of the association between negative emotions about climate change and support for government action to mitigate climate change. (Note: The size of the dot reflects the number of cases at that point on the plot.)

handy measure of association that is the foundation of most of the methods discussed in this book. It can be used to quantify linear association between two quantitative variables, a quantitative and a dichotomous variable, as well as between two dichotomous variables. Mathematically,

$$r \approx \frac{\sum_{j=1}^{n} Z_{X_j} Z_{Y_j}}{n}$$

where Z_{X_j} and Z_{Y_j} are X and Y for case j in *standardized* form, meaning expressed as deviation from their sample means in standard deviation units:

$$Z_{X_j} = \frac{X_j - \overline{X}}{SD_X} \qquad Z_{Y_j} = \frac{Y_j - \overline{Y}}{SD_Y}$$

where SD_X and SD_Y are the standard deviations of X and Y, respectively, $\overline{X}$ and $\overline{Y}$ are their sample means, and the summation is over all n cases in the data. Pearson's r can range between -1 and 1, although values of 1 and -1 would rarely be observed in real data. The closer r is to 1, ignoring sign, the stronger the *linear* association. The sign of r corresponds to the

Correlations

		NEGEMOT: Negative emotions about climate change	GOVACT: Support for government action
NEGEMOT: Negative emotions about climate change	Pearson Correlation	1	.578
	Sig. (2-tailed)		.000
	N	815	815
GOVACT: Support for government action	Pearson Correlation	.578	1
	Sig. (2-tailed)	.000	
	N	815	815

FIGURE 2.2. SPSS output showing Pearson's correlation between negative emotional responses to climate change (NEGEMOT) and support for government action (GOVACT).

direction of the linear association between X and Y. Pearson's r is positive if relatively high values of X tend to be paired with relatively high values of Y, and relatively low values of X tend to be paired with relatively low values of Y. Pearson's r is negative if relatively high values on X tend to be paired with relatively low values on Y, and relatively low values on X tend to be paired with relatively high values of Y. Pearson's r will be close to zero when there is no apparent order to the pairing of values of X and Y, or when the association is better characterized as nonlinear (as Pearson's r is a measure of linear association, not just any kind of association).

There are many procedures in SPSS and SAS that can be used to generate Pearson's r. In SPSS, the command

```
correlations variables = negemot govact.
```

calculates Pearson's r as well as the means and standard deviations for both variables. In SAS, try

```
proc corr data=glbwarm;var negemot govact;run;
```

The SPSS output generated by this command can be found in Figure 2.2. As can be seen, Pearson's $r = 0.578$. The positive sign for r confirms what is seen in the scatterplot in Figure 2.1. Participants in this study who reported relatively stronger negative emotions about climate change were also relatively more supportive of government action.

If two variables X and Y are correlated, this implies that if you were to use knowledge of case j's measurement on X to estimate case j's measurement on Y, doing this for all j cases should produce estimates that are more accurate than if one were to merely estimate $Y_j = \overline{Y}$ for every case in the data. Indeed, one interpretation of Pearson's correlation between two variables X and Y is that it provides an estimate as to how many standard deviations from the sample mean on Y a case is given how many standard deviations from the sample mean the case is on X. More formally,

$$\hat{Z}_{Y_j} = r_{XY}Z_{X_j}$$

where $\hat{Z}_{Y_j}$ is the estimated value of Z_{Y_j}. For instance, a person who is one-half of a standard deviation above the mean ($Z_X = 0.5$) in negative emotions is estimated to be $\hat{Z}_Y = 0.578(0.5) = 0.289$ standard deviations from the mean in his or her support for government action. The sign of $\hat{Z}_Y$ is positive, meaning that this person is estimated to be above the sample mean (i.e., more supportive than average). Similarly, someone who is two standard deviations below the mean ($Z_X = -2$) in negative emotions is estimated to be $\hat{Z}_Y = 0.578(-2) = -1.156$ standard deviations from the mean in support for government action. In this case, $\hat{Z}_Y$ is negative, meaning that such a person is estimated to be below the sample mean in support for government action (i.e., less supportive than average).

Of course, these are just estimates of Y from X. Rarely would they be exactly correct for any particular case in a data file. Rather, they are *expectations* extracted from what is known about the association between X and Y. In statistics, as in life, rarely are our expectations perfectly met. But we hope those expectations come close to reality. Unlike in life, in statistics, we have a numerical means of gauging how close our expectations derived from the association between X and Y are to reality. That gauge is the size of Pearson's r. The closer it is to one (ignoring sign), the more consistent those expectations are with the reality of our data.

So correlation and prediction are closely connected concepts. If two variables are correlated with each other, then you should be able to use information about values on one variable in the X,Y pairs to estimate with at least some degree of accuracy the values on the other variable in the pair.

2.2   The Simple Linear Regression Model

A linear regression model is an equation that links one or more input variables to an output variable by exploiting information contained in the association between inputs and output. The input variables are often called *predictor*, *independent*, or *explanatory variables*, but in Chapter 1 I introduced the term *antecedent variable*, so I will use that term. The output variable is called the *criterion*, *outcome*, or *dependent variable*, synonyms for *consequent variable*, a term also introduced in Chapter 1. Many of the statistical procedures that scientists use can be represented in the form of a regression model, such as the independent groups t-test and analysis of variance.

The goal when conducting a linear regression analysis is to estimate various *parameters* of the regression model such that the resulting equation yields estimates of the consequent variable from one or more antecedent variables that are as good as can be, given how one defines "good" and various assumptions one makes about the association between the variables, such as linearity. The information that comes from a regression model can be used to test hypotheses about the processes that link antecedents and consequent, which antecedents should be used and which ignored when attempting to explain variation in the consequent, and various other things that scientists are interested in.

A *simple* linear regression model is one of the more rudimentary forms a regression model takes, in that it contains only a single antecedent variable. The simple linear regression model is

$$Y_j = i_Y + bX_j + e_j \tag{2.1}$$

where Y_j and X_j refer to case j's measurement on a consequent and antecedent variable, respectively, b is the *regression coefficient* or *regression weight* for antecedent variable X, i_Y is the *regression constant*, and e_j is the error in estimation of case j's value of Y from case j's value of X, also known as a *residual*. The process of estimating a regression model is referred to as *regressing Y on X*. When analyzing data using a linear regression model, we know X_j and Y_j, as these are the data. Our goal is to find what we don't know, i_Y and b, and then interpret information the regression model yields once those are derived.

Suppose we did know i_Y and b. In that case, we could generate an estimate of Y from X with a variant of this model:

$$\hat{Y}_j = i_Y + bX_j \tag{2.2}$$

where $\hat{Y}_j$ is case j's *estimated*, *fitted*, or *predicted* value of Y given case j's X value. Substituting equation 2.2 into equation 2.1 yields

$$Y_j = \hat{Y}_j + e_j$$

and isolating e_j yields

$$e_j = Y_j - \hat{Y}_j$$

Thus, the residual e_j in equation 2.1 is the difference between case j's estimated value for Y from equation 2.2 and case j's actual value of Y.

Putting all this together, if we knew i_Y and b, we could generate an estimate of case j's Y value from case j's X value. This estimate likely will not be exactly equal to Y_j, however. The difference between Y_j and $\hat{Y}_j$ is case j's residual, which represents the difference between case j's actual value on Y and what Y is estimated to be given j's value of X.

There is an infinitely large number of pairs of values of i_Y and b that could be used to generate estimates of Y from X from equation 2.2. But when you estimate a linear regression model using the *ordinary least squares criterion*, you will get only one of the many possible pairs. The pair of values for the regression constant and coefficient that an ordinary least squares (OLS) regression procedure yields is special in that it minimizes the *residual sum of squares* ($SS_{residual}$), defined as

$$SS_{residual} = \sum_{j=1}^{n} \left(Y_j - \hat{Y}_j\right)^2 = \sum_{j=1}^{n} e_j^2 \qquad (2.3)$$

Observe from equation 2.3 that $SS_{residual}$ cannot be negative (as the sum of a bunch of squared values must be positive) and that if $\hat{Y}_j = Y_j$ for all n cases in the data, then $SS_{residual} = 0$. As the discrepancy between the estimated and actual values of Y increases, so too does $SS_{residual}$. In any dataset, the largest that $SS_{residual}$ could possibly be is the *total sum of squares*, defined as

$$SS_{total} = \sum_{j=1}^{n} \left(Y_j - \bar{Y}\right)^2$$

So OLS regression (i.e., regression analysis using the least squares criterion) derives the values of i_Y and b in equations 2.1 and 2.2 that produce the best fitting model of the data as defined by the least squares criterion—meaning that they make $SS_{residual}$ as small as it can possibly be, and certainly somewhere between 0 and SS_{total}.

Most popular statistical packages include a routine for estimating an OLS regression model. For instance, in SPSS and SAS, a simple regression model estimating support for government action to mitigate the effects of climate change (Y) from negative emotions regarding climate change (X) would be generated using the commands

```
regression/statistics defaults ci/dep=govact/method=enter negemot.
```

```
proc reg data=glbwarm;model govact=negemot/stb clb;run;
```

The resulting SPSS output can be found in Figure 2.3. The regression constant and regression coefficient can be found under the heading "Unstandardized Coefficients: B" in the model coefficients table. As can be seen, $i_Y = 2.757$ and $b = 0.514$; thus, the best fitting OLS regression model is

$$\hat{Y}_j = 2.757 + 0.514X_j \qquad (2.4)$$

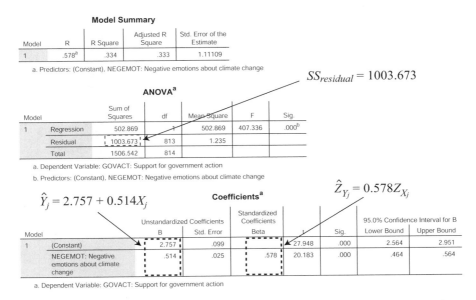

Model Summary

Model	R	R Square	Adjusted R Square	Std. Error of the Estimate
1	.578[a]	.334	.333	1.11109

a. Predictors: (Constant), NEGEMOT: Negative emotions about climate change

$SS_{residual} = 1003.673$

ANOVA[a]

Model		Sum of Squares	df	Mean Square	F	Sig.
1	Regression	502.869	1	502.869	407.336	.000[b]
	Residual	1003.673	813	1.235		
	Total	1506.542	814			

a. Dependent Variable: GOVACT: Support for government action
b. Predictors: (Constant), NEGEMOT: Negative emotions about climate change

$\hat{Y}_j = 2.757 + 0.514X_j$

$\hat{Z}_{Y_j} = 0.578Z_{X_j}$

Coefficients[a]

Model		Unstandardized Coefficients		Standardized Coefficients		Sig.	95.0% Confidence Interval for B	
		B	Std. Error	Beta	t		Lower Bound	Upper Bound
1	(Constant)	2.757	.099		27.948	.000	2.564	2.951
	NEGEMOT: Negative emotions about climate change	.514	.025	.578	20.183	.000	.464	.564

a. Dependent Variable: GOVACT: Support for government action

FIGURE 2.3. SPSS output from a simple regression analysis estimating support for government action to mitigate climate change from negative emotions about climate change.

These two values of i_Y and b are the pair of values that make $SS_{residual}$ as small as it can possibly be in a model of the form $\hat{Y}_j = i_Y + bX_j$. Observe in Figure 2.3 that $SS_{residual} = 1003.673$. No model of the form in equation 2.1 would produce a smaller $SS_{residual}$.

Using equation 2.4, an estimate for each person's support for government action ($\hat{Y}$) can be generated given information about that person's negative emotions about climate change (X). For instance, for someone with a negative emotions score of $X = 4$, the model generates $\hat{Y} = 2.757 + 0.514(4) = 4.813$. Suppose this person's actual support for government action, Y, is 3.6. If so, then this person's residual would be $e = 3.6 - 4.813 = -1.213$. The model *overestimates* this person's support for government action by 1.213 units.

The simple regression equation can be represented visually in the form of a line on a two-dimensional plane. In Figure 2.4, the regression line has been superimposed on a scatterplot of the data. Using this visual representation, an approximation of $\hat{Y}$ can be obtained by choosing a value on the horizontal axis, projecting up vertically until you intersect the line, and then projecting horizontally to the vertical axis. The point at which the horizontal projection touches the vertical axis is $\hat{Y}$ from the regression model. For example, as can be seen in Figure 2.4, when $X = 3$, the model

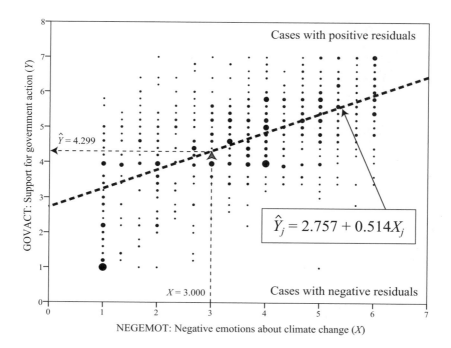

FIGURE 2.4. A visual representation of the least squares regression equation (the dotted line) estimating support for government action (*Y*) from negative emotions about climate change (*X*).

yields $\hat{Y}$ somewhere between 4 and 4.5. From the model in its precise mathematical form (equation 2.4), the estimate for $X = 3$ is $\hat{Y} = 4.299$.

Interpretation of the Constant and Regression Coefficient

The simple linear regression model links *X* to *Y* mathematically by expressing the association between *X* and *Y* in the form of an equation for a line. Thinking back to secondary school, recall that the equation for a line has two components: the *slope*, and the *Y-intercept*. In the linear regression equation, the regression coefficient corresponds to the slope of the line, and for this reason, the regression coefficient is sometimes called the *regression slope*. It quantifies how much two cases that differ by one unit on *X* are estimated to differ on *Y*. More formally, for any value $X = x$,

$$b = [\hat{Y}|(X = x)] - [\hat{Y}|(X = x - 1)] \tag{2.5}$$

where the vertical line "|" means "conditioned on," "given," or "when." Thus, equation 2.5 can be read "*b* equals the estimated value of *Y* when $X = x$ minus the estimated value of *Y* when $X = x$ minus 1." So applied to the climate change example, two cases that differ by one unit in their negative emotions about climate change are estimated to differ by $b = 0.514$ units in their support for government action.

The sign of b conveys information about the relative difference in Y. If b is positive, the case one unit higher on X is estimated to be b units higher on Y, whereas if b is negative, the case one unit higher on X is estimated to be b units lower on Y. Here, b is positive, so a person one unit higher in negative emotions is estimated to be 0.514 units *more* supportive of government action to mitigate global climate change.

The regression constant is conceptually equivalent to the Y-intercept in the equation for a line. It quantifies the estimated value of Y when $X = 0$. In Figure 2.4, the regression constant corresponds to the point at which the regression line crosses the vertical axis. However, this will not always be true, for where the line crosses the vertical axis will depend on how such a figure is constructed. If the vertical axis is drawn vertically up from the point $X = 0$, then the constant is indeed the Y-intercept, but if the vertical axis begins at some other point on the X scale, the regression line will cross the vertical axis at a location different from the regression constant.

In the climate change model, $i_Y = 2.757$. This is the estimated support for government action for someone who measures zero on the negative emotions scale. Although this has clear mathematical meaning, substantively it makes no sense because the negative emotions scale is bounded between 1 and 6. Often the regression constant has no substantive interpretation, but sometimes it does. It depends on how X is scaled and whether $X = 0$ has any substantive meaning.

It is possible to make i_Y substantively meaningful by *mean-centering* X prior to estimating the regression model. To mean-center a variable, the sample mean is subtracted from all measurements of that variable in the data:

$$X'_j = X_j - \overline{X} \tag{2.6}$$

where X'_j is mean-centered X_j. Estimating Y from X' produces a model with exactly the same fit as defined by $SS_{residual}$ and other measures discussed below. Furthermore, b will be the same as when X is used as the antecedent variable. However, the regression constant will change to reflect the rescaling of X. The constant is still interpreted as the estimated value of Y when $X' = 0$, but note from equation 2.6 that $X' = 0$ when $X = \overline{X}$. So i_Y is the estimated value of Y_j when $X_j = \overline{X}$.

Applied to the climate change example, when negative emotions about climate change is mean-centered prior to estimation of equation 2.1, the resulting regression model is $\hat{Y}_j = 4.587 + 0.514X'_j$. As promised, b is unaffected by mean-centering of X. The constant tells us that the estimated support for government action is $i_Y = \overline{Y} = 4.587$, for someone who is average in his or her negative emotional reactions to climate change.

The Standardized Regression Model

Thus far, the interpretation of the regression coefficients in a regression model has been couched in *unstandardized* or *raw metric* form. Many regression routines will also produce a version of the model in *standardized* form. The standardized regression model is what results when all variables are first standardized prior to estimation of the model by expressing each measurement in units of standard deviations from the sample mean. When this is done, the resulting model takes the form

$$\hat{Z}_{Y_j} = \tilde{b} Z_{X_j} \qquad (2.7)$$

where Z_Y and Z_X are standardized versions of Y and X, and $\tilde{b}$ is the *standardized regression coefficient* for X. Notice that the standardized regression model appears not to contain a constant. In fact, it does, although the constant in a standardized regression model is always zero, so there is no need to include it in equation 2.7.

Although one could formally standardize X and Y prior to estimating the regression model, this typically isn't necessary. Most statistical packages that conduct OLS regression will provide the standardized regression model in a section of output. In the SPSS output in Figure 2.3, for instance, the standardized regression coefficient can be found under a column labeled "Standardized coefficients." Thus, in the climate change model, the standardized regression equation is $\hat{Z}_{Y_j} = 0.578 Z_{X_j}$, where Z_Y and Z_X are standardized support for government action and standardized negative emotions, respectively.

The standardized regression coefficient is interpreted as the expected difference in Y, *in standard deviations*, between two cases that differ by *one standard deviation* on X. Thus, two people who differ by one standard deviation in their negative emotions about climate change are estimated to differ by $\tilde{b} = 0.578$ standard deviations in their support for government action. The positive coefficient means that the person with more negative emotions is estimated to have stronger support for government action to mitigate climate change. Notice that the standardized regression coefficient is exactly equal to Pearson's correlation between X and Y. This will be true in any regression model with only one antecedent, but does not generalize to models with more than one antecedent.

Simple Regression with a Dichotomous Antecedent Variable

In linear regression equation, an antecedent variable can be either a quantitative dimension (e.g., as in the example thus far) or a dichotomous variable. An example of a dichotomous variable would be whether a person is male or female, or which of two conditions a participant was assigned to in an experiment or clinical trial, such as whether a person in a drug study received the experimental drug or a placebo. No modifications are necessary to the mathematics when using a dichotomous variable an an antecedent.

To illustrate, I will use a linear regression analysis to estimate differences between men and women (X) in their support for government action to mitigate climate change (Y). The GLBWARM data file contains a variable (SEX) coding whether the participant is male (coded 1, 51.2% of the participants) or female (coded 0, 48.8%). Calculating the mean support for government action in each sex reveals men are slightly less supportive of government action on average ($\overline{Y}_{male} = 4.450, SD = 1.528$) than are women ($\overline{Y}_{female} = 4.718, SD = 1.165$). Regressing Y on X

```
regression/statistics defaults ci/dep=govact/method=enter sex.
```

```
proc reg data=glbwarm;model govact=sex/stb clb;run;
```

yields

$$\hat{Y}_j = 4.718 - 0.268X_j$$

as can be seen in the SAS output in Figure 2.5. The regression constant i_Y is still the estimated value of Y when $X = 0$. In this case, females are coded $X = 0$, so $\hat{Y} = 4.718$. This is the estimated support for government action among females, and it corresponds to the sample mean for females: $i_Y = \overline{Y}_{female} = 4.718$. The regression coefficient retains its mathematical interpretation as the estimated difference in Y between two cases that differ by one unit on X, with the negative sign telling us that the case higher on X is estimated to be lower on Y. This is consistent with the means reported earlier. Males, who are coded one unit higher on X relative to females, are lower on average in the support for government action. Furthermore, observe that the difference between the means is exactly 0.268 units on the scale (i.e., $\overline{Y}_{male} - \overline{Y}_{female} = 4.450 - 4.718 = -0.268$). So the regression coefficient quantifies the difference between the group means.

In simple regression with a dichotomous antecedent variable, the model will generate estimates for Y that correspond to the means of the two groups. It was demonstrated earlier that for females, $X = 0$ and so the model generates $\hat{Y} = 4.718 - 0.268(0) = 4.718 = \overline{Y}_{female}$. For males, $X = 1$ and the model generates $\hat{Y} = 4.718 - 0.268(1) = 4.450 = \overline{Y}_{male}$.

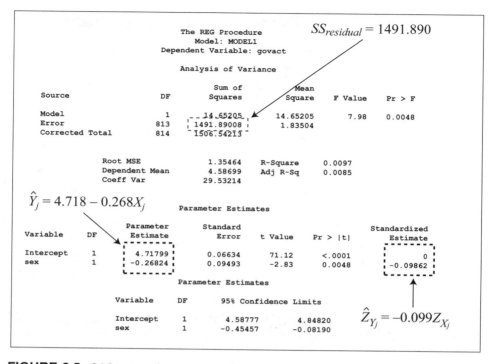

FIGURE 2.5. SAS output from a simple regression analysis estimating support for government action to mitigate global climate change (*Y*) from participant sex (*X*).

Although the model will always generate the group means, the regression coefficient and regression constant will depend on how the two groups are coded. For instance, suppose females were coded $X = -1$ and males were coded $X = 1$. In that case, the regression model would be $\hat{Y} = 4.584 - 0.134X$. Now $b = -0.134$ is one-half of the difference between those means and i_Y is the unweighted mean of the means: $(\overline{Y}_{\text{male}} + \overline{Y}_{\text{female}})/2$. But the model still reproduces the group means. For females, $\hat{Y} = 4.584 - 0.134(-1) = 4.718$, and for males, $\hat{Y} = 4.584 - 0.134(1) = 4.450$.

When *X* is a dichotomous variable, the regression coefficient will always be some function of the difference between the values of the codes used to code groups. Specifically, if the larger numerical code is X_L and the smaller numerical code is X_S,

$$b = \frac{\overline{Y}_{X_L} - \overline{Y}_{X_S}}{X_L - X_S}$$

where $\overline{Y}_{X_L}$ and $\overline{Y}_{X_S}$ are the group means for the two groups coded $X = X_L$ and $X = X_S$, respectively. For instance, if the two groups differ by two units on *X*, then *b* is one-half of the difference between the group means. If they differ by three units on *X*, then *b* is one-third of the mean difference, and so forth. I recommend getting in the habit of always coding a dichotomous variable such that the two groups differ by only one unit, so that b can be interpreted as the difference between the group means. I will usually use 0 and 1 in this book.

A Caution about the Standardized Regression Coefficient. The standardized regression model estimating support for government action from sex is

$$\hat{Z}_{Y_j} = -0.099 Z_{X_j}$$

Thus, $i_Y = 0$ and $\tilde{b} = -0.099$. Although $\tilde{b}$ can be interpreted in mathematical terms as the estimated difference in Y, in standard deviations, between two cases that differ by one standard deviation on X, this is not meaningful substantively. The number of standard deviations by which two groups differ on a dichotomous variable coding groups will depend on the distribution of the cases across the two groups. In these data, 48.8% of the sample is female ($X = 0$) and 51.2% is male ($X = 1$). The standard deviation of X is 0.499. So females and males differ by just over two standard deviations on X. That means that $\tilde{b}$ is just about one-half of the mean difference between males and females in standard deviation units of Y.

If this were always the case, it would be easy enough to remember that we should just multiply $\tilde{b}$ by about two in order to interpret it as a mean difference in standard deviations of Y. However, the number of standard deviations the groups differ on X is a function of the distribution of the cases across the two groups. If the groups were split, say, 40:60, they would differ by about 2.04 standard deviations on X, and $\tilde{b}$ would be less than half of the mean difference in standardized Y. If they were split 30:70, they would differ by about 2.17 standard deviations, and $\tilde{b}$ would be even smaller. At a 20:80 split, the groups differ by 2.5 standard deviations on X, and $\tilde{b}$ is smaller still. The more X favors one group, the more standard deviations the groups will differ on X, and the smaller $\tilde{b}$ will be.

My point is that when an antecedent variable is dichotomous, our substantive interest naturally focuses on differences between the groups on Y. If groups are coded such that they differ by one unit on X, then b is always the mean difference between the groups on Y. Not so for $\tilde{b}$. The standardized regression coefficient is a function of both the mean difference and the distribution of the cases across the groups. This is an undesirable property of $\tilde{b}$ when X is dichotomous. *I recommend that the standardized regression coefficient for a dichotomous antecedent variable not be interpreted or reported*.

If you desire an index of a mean difference in standard deviation units, I recommend standardizing Y but not the dichotomous X and then interpreting the *unstandardized* regression coefficient in a model estimating Z_Y from

X. In such a model, b is a *partially* standardized regression coefficient. In the simple regression example with negative emotions as the sole antecedent variable, doing so yields

$$\hat{Z}_{Y_j} = 0.096 - 0.197X_j$$

The constant i_Y is the mean standardized Y for females, and b is the mean difference between males and females in standard deviations of Y. So men are estimated to differ from women by 0.197 standard deviations in their support for government action. The negative sign for b means males are lower than females, on average, in their support. The partially standardized regression coefficient will not depend on the distribution of the cases into the two groups defined by X.

A Note on Symbolic Representations

A brief digression is in order at this point. It is important when reporting the results of an analysis to define the symbols you use unless there is a strong convention, for a failure to do so can invite confusion. Different uses of b and β in regression analysis are an important case in point. There is much inconsistency in the substantive and methodology literature as to how regression coefficients are symbolized in unstandardized versus standardized form. Some use b or B to refer to the unstandardized regression coefficient and β to refer to the standardized regression coefficient. Others, rather than using β, spell it out by referencing "beta weights" or just talk about the "betas." Some use β to refer to a population regression coefficient, to distinguish it from a sample estimate, others use β as the unstandardized regression weight, and there are still others who use $\hat{\beta}$ to refer to a sample unstandardized regression coefficient and leave the hat off for its corresponding population or "true" value. In this book, I use $\tilde{b}$ for the standardized regression weight.

Ultimately, the symbols we use are for the most part arbitrary. We can use any symbols we want. My point is that you should not assume others will know what symbols you use mean, for your familiar symbols to represent certain concepts may not be understood as representing those concepts by all. The same applies to terms such as "beta coefficient" or other verbalizations of symbols. Best to define your symbols in advance, or otherwise let your reader know what your symbols mean when used in text and tables. This will help others better understand and interpret your work.

2.3   Alternative Explanations for Association

That "correlation does not imply causation" is etched into the brains of all scientists. If variables X and Y are correlated, that doesn't mean that X causes Y or that Y causes X. The ability to infer cause–effect is not even a statistical matter in the end. Rather, it is the design of one's study, the data collection procedures one employs, and theoretical plausibility that most directly influence whether a cause–effect claim can be made and with what degree of confidence, not the size or sign of a statistical index of association. Absent certain design features, numerous processes both systematic and haphazard can induce association between two variables. These processes function as alternative explanations for an association, and they interfere with a researcher's ability to make causal claims. The greater the number of such alternative explanations, the less comfortable we must be making cause–effect claims from nothing other than association between variables.

Recall from section 2.2 that negative emotions about climate change and support for government action to mitigate climate change are positively related. Does this mean that if we could just make people more anxious and scared about climate change, they would be more supportive of government action? Perhaps, but of course mere association between these two variables is not sufficient to warrant such a causal inference. Alternative explanations abound.

In this section I entertain some alternative explanations, but only after first describing a few more of the variables available in the GLBWARM data file. Recall that negative emotions about climate change was operationalized from participants' responses as to how frequently they reported feeling concerned, worried, and alarmed when thinking about climate change. At the same time, participants were asked how frequently they felt "hopeful," "encouraged," and "optimistic" about global climate change using the same 1- to 6-point scale. A measure of *positive emotions about climate change* was constructed as the average response a participant provided to these three items (POSEMOT in the data). Like negative emotions, positive emotions is scaled such that higher scores reflect feeling more positive emotion about the prospect of climate change.

Participants were also asked to rate their political ideology (IDEOLOGY in the data file) on a 1 (very liberal) to 7 (very conservative) scale in response to the question "How would you describe your views on most political matters?" Respondents, as a collective, represented the entire spectrum of political ideology, with 39% responding moderate or middle of the road (a rating of 4) and the remaining participants distributing themselves in about equal number on both sides of this middle point.

Consider some plausible alternative explanations for the association observed between negative emotions and support for government action. Perhaps this association reflects only a difference between men and women in how emotional they are about just about *anything* and in their beliefs about the ability of government to effectively solve social problems. That is, perhaps something about how men and women are socialized leads them to differ on both of these dimensions. Indeed, males report less strong negative emotions ($r = -0.117$) as well as less support for government action than females ($r = -0.099$). So it may be that emotional responses to climate change and support for government action are related not through some cause–effect mechanism but, rather, are *spuriously associated*. Two variables are spuriously associated if their association is induced as a result of a shared cause—in this case, biological sex.

Alternatively, we know that in the United States, people who identify as politically conservative tend to believe that government should play a limited role in the lives of its citizens. Conservatives tend to favor low taxes, minimal regulation of business by government, and are less supportive of government-provided social services and benefits. By contrast, people who identify as politically liberal favor a greater role of government and tend to favor social safety net programs, such as economic assistance for the disadvantaged and unemployed, strict regulation of business, and higher taxes so that government can provide services for its people. That is, individual differences between people in their support for government policies are attributable in part to differences between them in their political ideology. Not surprisingly, the evidence from this study is consistent with this proposition, as those who self-reported as relatively more politically conservative reported relatively less support for government action to mitigate climate change ($r = -0.418$).

Importantly, there is research suggesting that conservatives and liberals have different emotional lives and experiences (see, e.g., Leone & Chirumbolo, 2008; Napier & Jost, 2008; Vigil, 2010). If so, then the association between emotional reactions to climate change and support for government action may merely be an *epiphenomenon* of the effect of political ideology on support for government action. An association between X and Y is epiphenomenal if X is correlated with a cause of Y but does not itself causally influence Y. Many things correlated with the cause of Y will also tend to be correlated with Y. But that doesn't make all those things causes of Y as well. Indeed, in these data, political ideology is correlated with negative emotional responses to climate change ($r = -0.349$), with conservatives reporting less negative emotion than liberals. So it is possible the association observed between negative emotional responses to climate change and support for government action is epiphenomenal. We don't need to assume that ideology causally influences emotions felt in order to invoke epiphenomenality as an alternative explanation for this association.

Or perhaps it is not negative emotions specifically, but general emotionality that leads to greater support for government action. In these data, there is a positive association between positive and negative emotions felt about climate change ($r = 0.128$). Given that people who report relatively more anxiety and concern about climate change also report feeling relatively more optimistic and excited, for example, the unique role of negative relative to positive emotions in this process is obscured. Is it that anxiety and worry lead people to feel that action must be taken by government, or is just the tendency to get worked up and be emotional about things that prompts such people to seek out solutions to problems from a variety of different sources, including the government?

Such is the problem facing the interpretation of association between two variables. Typically there are many processes that can explain association, some causal, others not. Some alternative explanations can be ruled out logically or theoretically. Others can be dealt with prior to data collection by using a design that rules them out a priori, such as experimentation. If negative emotions were experimentally manipulated in some fashion and people were randomly assigned to feel negative emotions or not about climate change, then differences between these experimentally constructed groups in their support for government action following the manipulation has a clearer causal interpretation. Random assignment tends to equate groups, on average, at the start of the study on all variables other than the manipulated variable. If nothing other than the variable the researcher intends to vary differentiates the groups at the beginning of the study, differences observed on a consequent variable of interest can be interpreted as resulting causally from differences between them on the manipulated variable.

When experimental manipulation is not possible, not desired, or simply didn't happen during data collection, *multiple linear regression* can be used as a fallback option for dealing with at least some alternative explanations for an association. What makes the association between two variables X and Y ambiguous is that people who differ on X and Y also likely differ on many other things, and it may be those things that are responsible for the association. Multiple regression gives a researcher a means of engaging in a kind of mathematically aided counterfactual reasoning by estimating what the association between X and Y would be if people did not differ on the other antecedent variables in the regression model. It does this by "mathematically equating" people (or whatever the unit of analysis is) on those variables. This equating process is also called *partialing out* those other variables from the association between X and Y, or *statistically controlling* for those variables. These other variables are sometimes called *covariates* in the lingo of linear models, but in practice they are just antecedent variables in the regression model of Y, just as X is.

2.4 Multiple Linear Regression

The simple linear regression model is easily extended to the estimation of a consequent variable using more than one antecedent variable. Including more than one antecedent in a regression model allows you to simultaneously investigate the role of multiple influences on a consequent variable. An additional and important benefit of the multiple regression model is that it provides various measures of *partial association* that quantify the component of the association between an antecedent and a consequent that is unique to that antecedent relative to other antecedent variables in the model. In so doing, multiple regression allows you to examine the plausibility of various explanations for an association between two variables, such as spuriousness or epiphenomenality discussed in section 2.3. This is useful because such alternative explanations reduce the confidence you can muster as to whether an association can plausibly be interpreted as causal—something you often wish to claim. Although ruling out certain alternative explanations for an association statistically through multiple regression analysis does not itself justify causal claims, it can help as you build an argument that the association may be causal.

In its most general form, a multiple linear regression model with k antecedent variables takes the form

$$Y_j = i_Y + b_1 X_{1j} + b_2 X_{2j} + \ldots + b_k X_{kj} + e_j \tag{2.8}$$

where X_{ij} is case j's measurement on antecedent variable i, b_i is the regression coefficient for antecedent variable X_i, and all other terms are defined as before. The model can also be expressed in terms of fitted values of Y by eliminating the residual, as such

$$\hat{Y}_j = i_Y + b_1 X_{1j} + b_2 X_{2j} + \ldots + b_k X_{kj} \tag{2.9}$$

Simple regression is a special case of equations 2.8 and 2.9 with $k = 1$. Using the ordinary least squares criterion, an OLS regression routine will derive a multiple regression model containing a constant i_Y and k regression coefficients, one for each of the k antecedent variables, that minimizes $SS_{residual}$. However, there are some important differences between simple and multiple regression in terms of both interpretation of the regression weights and questions the model can be used to answer.

Some of the terms in equations 2.8, and 2.9 involve two subscripts i and j denoting antecedent number and case, respectively. To simply notation, henceforth I will remove the j subscript denoting case, since any regression analysis will involve regressing the consequent on one or more antecedent variables each measured a set of n cases in a data file. When the j subscript is removed entirely, equations 2.8 and 2.9 become

$$Y = i_Y + b_1X_1 + b_2X_2 + \ldots + b_kX_k + e$$

and

$$\hat{Y}_j = i_Y + b_1X_{1j} + b_2X_{2j} + \ldots + b_kX_{kj}$$

To illustrate the estimation and interpretation of a multiple regression model, I simultaneously regress support for government action on negative emotions about climate change, positive emotions about climate change, political ideology, sex, and age in years. With these five antecedent variables denoted X_1, X_2, X_3, X_4, and X_5, respectively, the model is

$$\hat{Y} = i_Y + b_1X_1 + b_2X_2 + b_3X_3 + b_4X_4 + b_5X_5 \tag{2.10}$$

In SPSS and SAS, this is accomplished using the command

```
regression/statistics defaults ci/dep=govact/method=enter negemot
   posemot ideology sex age.
```

```
proc reg data=glbwarm;model govact=negemot posemot ideology sex age
   /stb clb;run;
```

Output generated by the SPSS command can be found in Figure 2.6. The regression constant (in the row labeled "Constant") is 4.064, and the five regression coefficients for negative emotions, positive emotions, ideology, sex, and age are, respectively, $b_1 = 0.441$, $b_2 = -0.027$, $b_3 = -0.218$, $b_4 = -0.010$, and $b_5 = -0.001$. In the form of an equation and expressing the model in terms of the estimated value of Y, the model is

$$\hat{Y} = 4.064 + 0.441X_1 - 0.027X_2 - 0.218X_3 - 0.010X_4 - 0.001X_5 \tag{2.11}$$

Model Summary

Model	R	R Square	Adjusted R Square	Std. Error of the Estimate
1	.623[a]	.388	.385	1.06728

← R, R^2, and the standard error of estimate

a. Predictors: (Constant), AGE: Respondent age at last birthday, POSEMOT: Positive emotions about climate change, NEGEMOT: Negative emotions about climate change, SEX: female(0) or male(1), IDEOLOGY: Political ideology (conservatism)

ANOVA[a]

Model		Sum of Squares	df	Mean Square	F	Sig.
1	Regression	585.019	5	117.004	102.717	.000[b]
	Residual	921.523	809	1.139		
	Total	1506.542	814			

← $MS_{residual} = 1.139$

a. Dependent Variable: GOVACT: Support for government action

b. Predictors: (Constant), AGE: Respondent age at last birthday, POSEMOT: Positive emotions about climate change, NEGEMOT: Negative emotions about climate change, SEX: female(0) or male(1), IDEOLOGY: Political ideology (conservatism)

Coefficients[a]

Model		Unstandardized Coefficients B	Std. Error	Standardized Coefficients Beta	t	Sig.	95.0% Confidence Interval for B Lower Bound	Upper Bound
1	(Constant)	4.064	.205		19.791	.000	3.661	4.467
	NEGEMOT: Negative emotions about climate change	.441	.026	.495	16.676	.000	.389	.493
	POSEMOT: Positive emotions about climate change	-.027	.028	-.027	-.951	.342	-.082	.028
	IDEOLOGY: Political ideology (conservatism)	-.218	.027	-.243	-8.071	.000	-.271	-.165
	SEX: female(0) or male(1)	-.010	.077	-.004	-.131	.896	-.161	.141
	AGE: Respondent age at last birthday	-.001	.002	-.016	-.552	.581	-.006	.003

a. Dependent Variable: GOVACT: Support for government action

$$\hat{Y}_j = 4.064 + 0.441X_1 - 0.027X_2 - 0.218X_3 - 0.010X_4 - 0.001X_5$$
$$\hat{Z}_{Y_j} = 0.495Z_{X_1} - 0.027Z_{X_2} - 0.243Z_{X_3} - 0.004Z_{X_4} - 0.016Z_{X_5}$$

FIGURE 2.6. SPSS output from a multiple regression analysis estimating support for government action to mitigate global climate change (Y) from negative (X_1) and positive (X_2) emotions about climate change, political ideology (X_3), sex (X_4), and age (X_5).

Interpretation of the Constant and Partial Regression Coefficients

The regression constant in a multiple regression model is $\hat{Y}$ for a case with measurements of 0 on all antecedent variables in the model. In this example, $i_Y = 4.064$, but this estimate of Y is rather nonsensical substantively given that 0 is outside the bounds of the scale of measurement of emotions (both positive and negative emotions have a lower bound of 1) as well as ideology (which is a 1 to 7 scale) and age.

Interpretative focus in multiple regression is typically directed toward the regression coefficients rather than the constant. To understand their interpretation, consider what the regression model estimates for someone with measurements of three on negative emotions ($X_1 = 3$), four on positive emotions ($X_2 = 4$), two on ideology ($X_3 = 2$), and who is male ($X_4 = 1$) and 30 years old ($X_5 = 30$). According to equation 2.11,

$$\hat{Y} = 4.064 + 0.441(3) - 0.027(4) - 0.218(2) - 0.010(1) - 0.001(30) = 4.803$$

Now consider another male who has the same positive emotions, ideology, and age, yet measures one point higher on the negative emotions scale ($X_1 = 4$). For that person, the model estimates

$$\hat{Y} = 4.064 + 0.441(4) - 0.027(4) - 0.218(2) - 0.010(1) - 0.001(30) = 5.244$$

So these two people who differ by one unit on X_1 but are the same on X_2, X_3, X_4, and X_5 are estimated to differ by $5.244 - 4.803 = 0.441$ units on support for government action. But this is b_1. It makes no difference what values X_2, X_3, X_4, and X_5 are set to. If they are held fixed, two cases that differ by one unit on X_1 are estimated to differ by b_1 units on Y. This interpretation applies to all partial regression coefficients in a multiple regression model such as this. Most generally, if we let $\mathbf{X}$ refer to a set of values on all variables except variable X_i, then

$$b_i = [\hat{Y} \mid (X_{is} = x; \mathbf{X})] - [\hat{Y} \mid (X_{it} = x - 1; \mathbf{X})]$$

That is, b_i is the estimated difference in Y between two cases s and t that are the same on all antecedent variables except X_i but that differ by one unit on X_i. As in simple regression, the sign of the regression coefficient tells whether the case one unit higher on X_i is estimated to be higher on Y (when b_i is positive) or lower on Y (when b_i is negative).

When negative emotions about climate change was the only antecedent variable in the model, we saw in section 2.2 that two people who differ by one unit in negative emotions are estimated to differ by 0.514 units in the support for government policies to mitigate its effects. But we said in section 2.3 that there are some explanations for this association that disrupt our ability to infer that this is a cause–effect relationship. From the multiple regression analysis, we have found that two people of the same sex, age, ideology, and positive emotions about climate change but who differ by one unit in their negative emotions are estimated to differ by 0.441 units in their support for government action. This is a slightly smaller difference in support than when sex, age, ideology, and positive emotions were not held constant or *statistically controlled*, but the partial regression coefficient between negative emotions and support for government action is not zero. This suggests that the association observed cannot be attributed to spuriousness or epiphenomenality with respect to these four variables. Of course, it could be that there are some other differences between people in their negative emotions that produce this association that we haven't accounted for yet.

So to statistically control for one or more covariates when quantifying the association between some antecedent X_i and a consequent Y, simply include the covariates in the model along with X_i. Unfortunately, one can never know whether an association observed between an antecedent or consequent is causal or can be attributed to some other variable or variables that haven't been statistically controlled for in the model. But knowing that a relationship of interest persists when holding other things constant at least eliminates some alternative explanations. Ultimately, the best one can do absent data that afford more unequivocal causal interpretation is attempt to control for covariates that critics might argue are responsible for the association you are claiming is causal, in the hope that those critics will be satisfied if the association of interest stands up to the statistical control process.

The Standardized Regression Model

In a multiple regression model, b_i is interpreted as the estimated difference in Y between two cases that differ by one unit on X_i but that are equal on all other variables in the model. This interpretation applies to the standardized regression coefficients in a multiple regression model, but the meaning of "one unit" is different following standardization. If X_i and Y are both standardized (regardless of whether or not the other antecedent variables are standardized), $\tilde{b}_i$ is the estimated difference in standard deviations of Y between two cases that differ by one standard deviation on X_i but are equal on all other antecedent variables in the model. However, unlike in simple regression, the standardized regression coefficient b_i in a multiple regression model is usually not equivalent to the Pearson correlation between X_i and Y.

In this example, the standardized regression model is

$$\hat{Z}_Y = 0.495 Z_{X_1} - 0.027 Z_{X_2} - 0.243 Z_{X_3} - 0.004 Z_{X_4} - 0.016 Z_{X_5}$$

Here, $\tilde{b}_1 = 0.495$, so we can say that two people who differ by one standard deviation in negative emotions (X_1) but who express the same positive emotions and are of the same ideology, sex, and age are estimated to differ by 0.495 standard deviations in their support for government action, with the person higher in negative emotions expressing greater support. And because $\tilde{b}_3 = -0.243$, we can say that two people who differ by one standard deviation on the ideology scale but who express the same positive and negative emotions and are of the same age and sex are estimated to differ by 0.243 standard deviations in support for government action, with the person who is more conservative expressing less support. However, as discussed in section 2.2, it would not be accurate to say that men and women who are of the same ideology, age, and emotions are estimated to differ by 0.004 standard deviations in support for government action. You should not interpret or report the standardized regression coefficient for a dichotomous antecedent variable in a regression model.

The standardized regression coefficients generated automatically by an OLS regression program will be based on a model in which all X_i and Y variables are standardized. However, in a multiple regression model, one can standardize only some of the antecedent variables rather than all of them if one chooses. This would have to be done before estimating the model. Once this is done and the model generated, the *unstandardized regression coefficients* rather than the standardized regression coefficients are interpreted. The unstandardized coefficients will be in standardized form for those antecedent variables that were first standardized manually. That is, for standardized X_i, $b_i = \tilde{b}_i$. The coefficients for antecedent variables that were not standardized will be in *partially standardized* form because Y but not those antecedents are in a standardized metric. For such variables, $b_i \neq \tilde{b}_i$. If Y is standardized but X_i is not, b_i is interpreted as the number of standard deviations by which two cases that differ by one unit on X_i are estimated to differ on Y.

Applying this reasoning, we could manually standardize support for government action and all the antecedent variables except sex, but keep sex (X_4) in its original form. This will give us a sensible measure of the partial relationship between sex and support for government action in the metric of standardized units of the consequent.[1] Doing so results in

$$\hat{Z}_Y = 0.004 + 0.495Z_{X_1} - 0.027Z_{X_2} - 0.243Z_{X_3} - 0.007X_4 - 0.016Z_{X_5}$$

Notice that the regression coefficients for all but X_4 are unchanged relative to the completely standardized regression model. But $b_4 = -0.007$ now has a sensible interpretation. We can say that men and women differ by 0.007 standard deviations in their support for government action when all other variables in the model are held constant. The negative sign means that men are less supportive of government action than women.

---

[1]If you are only interested in the partially standardized regression coefficient for the unstandardized antecedent, it isn't necessary to standardize the other antecedents, as whether or not they are standardized will not affect the partially unstandardized regression coefficient for the unstandardized antecedent variable of interest.

It is possible to calculate standardized regression coefficients using the unstandardized coefficients and the standard deviations of the antecedent and consequent variables. The formula is

$$\tilde{b}_i = b_i \left(\frac{SD_{X_i}}{SD_Y} \right) \tag{2.12}$$

If you want a partially standardized regression coefficient, with X_i kept in its original metric, divide $\tilde{b}_i$ by SD_{X_i}. This would be equivalent to removing SD_{X_i} from the numerator in equation 2.12.

When you decide to standardize some variables but not others prior to estimating a regression model, make sure you consider the effects of missing data in the eventual analysis. Many regression programs use listwise deletion, deleting any case in the analysis that is missing data on any of the variables in the regression model. Suppose you standardize variable X_1, but some of the cases with data on X_1 are missing data on X_2 or Y (or both). When you put X_1 and X_2 into the regression model of Y, your regression program might delete those cases that are missing data on X_2 and Y prior to estimating the model. But now Z_{X_1} is no longer a legitimate standardized form of X_1 because the original standardization was based on the mean and standard deviation of a different subset of cases than are actually being used in the analysis.

2.5 Measures of Model Fit

The regression equation minimizes $SS_{residual}$ and is therefore the best fitting linear model by the least squares criterion. The size of $SS_{residual}$ can be thought of as a measure of *lack* of fit, for larger values are associated with a greater discrepancy betweeen Y and $\hat{Y}$. However, its absolute size has no meaning, for it is determined by sample size as well as the scale of measurement of Y. All else being equal, as n increases, so too does $SS_{residual}$. And $SS_{residual}$ is not comparable across models of different consequent variables even if the antecedent variables are the same.

There are other measures of fit derived from $SS_{residual}$ that deal with one or both of these problems with $SS_{residual}$ to at least some degree. The first is the *mean squared residual* ($MS_{residual}$), sometimes called the *mean squared error* (*MSE*), defined most generally for any linear regression model as

$$MS_{residual} = \frac{SS_{residual}}{n - k - 1} \tag{2.13}$$

where k is the number of antecedent variables in the regression model. The quantity $n - k - 1$ in the denominator of equation 2.13 is also called the *residual degrees of freedom* or $df_{residual}$. The mean squared residual can be thought of as a sample-size corrected residual sum of squares. It is approximately the average squared residual. A value closer to zero represents better fit. As can be seen in Figure 2.6, in the climate change example, $MS_{residual} = 1.139$. Because the least squared criterion results in a minimization of $SS_{residual}$, it follows that it also minimizes $MS_{residual}$.

Like $SS_{residual}$, $MS_{residual}$ is a scale-bound measure of fit, in that it depends on the metric of measurement of Y. Furthermore, it lacks interpretability, primarily because it is based on a squared metric (i.e., the squared residuals). An alternative measure of fit is the square root of the mean squared residual, known as the *standard error of estimate*, defined as

$$\text{Standard error of estimate} = \sqrt{MS_{residual}} = \sqrt{\frac{SS_{residual}}{n-k-1}}$$

The standard error of estimate does not have the noninterpretability problem that $MS_{residual}$ has. It can be interpreted as approximately the average amount by which Y differs from $\hat{Y}$ ignoring sign. It is also approximately equal to the standard deviation of the residuals. In the climate change example, the standard error of estimate is 1.067 (see Figure 2.6). This is approximately how much, on average, $\hat{Y}$ differs from Y when you ignore the sign of the error. Because the standard error of estimate is just a transformation of $SS_{residual}$, it too is minimized by the least squares criterion.

All three of these measures of fit are scale-bound measures. Different metrics of Y will produce different values of $SS_{residual}$, $MS_{residual}$, and the standard error of estimate. A measure of fit which eliminates this problem is the multiple correlation coefficient R and its square, R^2. Recall from section 2.2 that $SS_{residual}$ is bound between 0 and SS_{total}, where SS_{total} is the sum of the squared differences between Y and $\overline{Y}$. SS_{total} can be thought of as the fit of a model in which Y is estimated to be $\overline{Y}$ for every case in the data, as if one entirely ignored the information contained in the antecedents that could be used to estimate Y with greater precision than the use of this naive strategy of predicting $\overline{Y}$ for every case. Whenever there is some linear association between antecedents and consequent, however small that association is, $SS_{residual}$ will be smaller than SS_{total}. It has to be, but it won't be smaller than zero.

Considering the naive model as a reference model, R^2 quantifies the distance the best fitting linear regression model has traveled between this naive reference model and a perfectly fitting model. Mathematically,

$$R^2 = 1 - \frac{SS_{residual}}{SS_{total}} \tag{2.14}$$

Because $SS_{residual}$ is minimized by the least squared criterion, it follows that this criterion maximizes R^2 and also R. R and R^2 are bound between 0 and 1.

R^2 is commonly interpreted as the proportion of the variance in Y explained by the model. A perfectly fitting model explains all the variation in Y, so $R = R^2 = 1$, whereas the naive model that predicts $\hat{Y} = \overline{Y}$ for all cases, $R = R^2 = 0$. In the climate change model, $R^2 = 0.388$. So negative and positive emotions, age, sex, and ideology together explain $0.388 \times 100 = 38.8\%$ of the variance in people's support for government action.

R can also be interpreted as the Pearson correlation between Y and $\hat{Y}$. This interpretation makes it most clear how R and R^2 can be construed as a measure of model fit. In a good-fitting model, the correlation between what the model estimates for Y and the actual values of Y across the n cases in the data should be large. If this correlation is small, it would be hard to argue that this model does a particularly good job in accounting for or explaining individual differences in Y.

The multiple correlation coefficient R, as well its square, are scale-free metrics, meaning the fit of two models can be compared using the relative sizes of their R or R^2 values even when they are models of different consequent variables. In addition, this measure of fit is mostly independent of sample size. All other things being equal, R and R^2 will tend to be somewhat larger in smaller samples, but the association between sample size and the multiple correlation rapidly levels off as sample size increases. For all practical purposes, R and R^2 for two models based on different sample sizes can be directly compared so long as one sample size is not very small. However, you can't fairly compare R or R^2 between models that differ in the number of antecedents, because the multiple correlation will tend to be larger in models that contain more antecedent variables. This is because R can never go down and almost always goes up when an antecedent variable is added to a model. In section 2.6, I discuss an inferential test for differences in fit that is based on values of R^2 computed in two models that differ in the number of antecedents.

2.6   Statistical Inference

Consider the following thought experiment. Imagine that the 815 people in the GLBWARM data file represent a census of the population of planet Earth. There are no other people on the planet. So the GLBWARM data set is a data set of the entire population. If we were to estimate support for government action to mitigate the effects of climate change from negative emotions, positive emotions, ideology, sex, and age, then we could generate the *population regression model* that minimizes the residual sum of squares. This population regression model would take the form

$$\hat{Y} = _Ti_Y + _Tb_1X_1 + _Tb_2X_2 + _Tb_3X_3 + _Tb_4X_4 + _Tb_5X_5 \qquad (2.15)$$

where the T prescript $_T$ represents the "true" or population value of the regression coefficient. So in this example, with X_1 being negative emotions about climate change, $_Tb_1 = 0.441$. This is the regression coefficient for negative emotions in the model of support for government action in the analysis reported in section 2.4.

Now suppose that rather than a census of this planet of 815 people you had only 50 people from the 815 inhabitants of Earth in your study, and you obtained these 50 by randomly sampling from the population of 815 inhabitants. In this sample of 50, you regress support for government action on these same five antecedents. This sampling process wouldn't change $_Tb_1$, of course, because it is a fixed property of the population. But in this model, the regression coefficient for negative emotions, b_1, which is your *estimate* of $_Tb_1$, would almost certainly not be equal to the true value $_Tb_1 = 0.441$. It would be something different because of *sampling variance*.

To illustrate sampling variance, try running the code below in SPSS with the GLBWARM data file open.

```
compute u=rv.uniform(0,1).
sort cases by u.
temporary.
select if ($casenum < 51).
regression/dep=govact/method=enter negemot posemot ideology sex age.
```

If you prefer SAS, try

```
data glbwarm;set glbwarm;u=uniform(0);run;
proc sort data=glbwarm;by u;run;
proc reg data = glbwarm (OBS = 50);model govact = negemot posemot
ideology sex age;run;
```

This code randomly selects 50 people from the 815 in the GLBWARM data and then estimates the partial regression coefficient for negative emotions in a model of support for government action, holding positive emotions, sex, age, and ideology constant using OLS regression. When I did this in SPSS, I got $b_1 = 0.467$. When I did it again, I got $b_1 = 0.392$. And yet again, the result was $b_1 = 0.419$. Figure 2.7 depicts a histogram of values of b_1 from 10,000 repetitions of this procedure. Notice that the 10,000 estimates of $_Tb_1$ vary considerably, from a low of about 0.02 to a high of 0.85, with

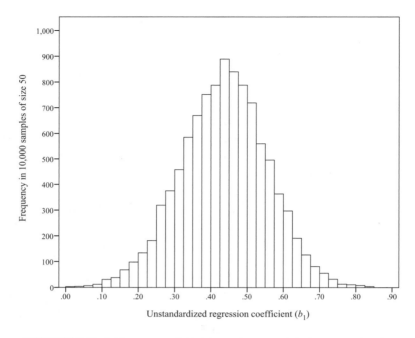

FIGURE 2.7. A histogram of 10,000 estimates of $_Tb_1$ in a sample of 50.

most of the estimates somewhere between 0.30 and 0.60. This is sampling variance.

The original data collection effort that resulted in the 815 cases in the GLBWARM data file can be thought of as the result of a single trial from a similar sampling process but undertaken on a larger scale. The 815 people who participated in this study represent a single subset of people—a *sample*—from a much larger collection of people who could have been in the study but, in part by the luck of the draw, simply were not. That is, these 815 are analogous to the 50 selected from the 815 in the thought experiment described earlier. This "larger collection" is typically referred to as the *population*. In the previous example, the 815 sole inhabitants of Earth were the population. But in the actual study, the population is much, much larger, presumably. That population might be all people living in the United States, all people willing to participate in online surveys, or something of the sort. Regardless, if this entire population provided data in this study (whatever that population is), then $_Tb_1$ could be known exactly. No estimation would be needed. But given that data analysis is generally undertaken only on a subset of the population, all that can be done is to estimate $_Tb_1$ using the data available. We hope that the estimate, b_1, is close to the true value, but we can never know for certain how close it is because we have observed only a single sample-specific estimate of the true value based on the data available. A different random sample of 815 would have produced a different estimate of $_Tb_1$, because b_1 is subject to sampling variance whenever the sample size is smaller than the population size.

There are several inferential problems we often face when conducting a regression analysis. One inference focuses on testing a hypothesis about the regression coefficient for antecedent i, $_Tb_i$, or, alternatively, generating an interval estimate that demarcates the lower and upper boundaries between which $_Tb_i$ is likely to reside with a certain degree of confidence—a *confidence interval*. We have an arsenal of statistical theory and method that can be brought into service to help with the inference. A second inferential problem revolves around whether adding a set of antecedents to an existing model of a consequent improves the fit of the model. I address each of these next.

Testing a Null Hypothesis

When testing a hypothesis about a regression coefficient, an assumption is made about $_Tb_i$ and then a decision is made about the plausibility of that assumption given the data available. The assumption is the *null hypothesis* and it is statistically pitted against the *alternative hypothesis*, which is the logical complement of the null hypothesis. In regression, the null hypothesis most typically tested is that X_i and Y are linearly uncorrelated in the population. In a simple regression model (i.e., only one antecedent), this is a null hypothesis about simple association, but in multiple regression, the null hypothesis is about partial association: is there a linear relationship between X_i and Y when all other antecedents are held fixed. If X_i is unrelated to Y, then X_i should be given no weight in the derivation of the estimate of Y. This corresponds to a null hypothesis that $_Tb_i = 0$ and an alternative hypothesis that $_Tb_i \neq 0$. Symbolically,

$$H_0 : \quad _Tb_i = 0$$
$$H_a : \quad _Tb_i \neq 0$$

To decide between the null hypothesis and the alternative hypothesis, it is necessary to derive the probability of the obtained association between X_i and Y or something more extreme from the null hypothesis in either direction (for a *two-tailed* or *nondirectional* test) assuming the null hypothesis is true. This probability is the *p-value* for the obtained result. If the *p*-value is no larger than the level of significance for the test (typically, the level of significance or α-*level* used is 0.05), then the null hypothesis is rejected in favor of the alternative hypothesis. Rejection of the null hypothesis implies that there is some association between X_i and Y in the population (holding the covariates constant, if any), with the direction of the association in the population implied by the direction of the obtained estimate of the association in the sample.

The p-value is derived by converting the obtained regression coefficient b_i to deviation from the null hypothesis in standard error units and then calculating the probability of such a departure from the null hypothesis using the $t(df_{residual})$ distribution, where $df_{residual}$ is the residual degrees of freedom for the regression model. The standard error of b_i, calculated by any OLS regression program, quantifies how much b_i tends to deviate from $_Tb_i$. Along with the standard error, most all regression programs also calculate the ratio of the estimate to its standard error and a p-value for testing the null hypothesis.

The SPSS output in Figure 2.6 provides a test of the null hypothesis that $_Tb_1 = 0$, where X_1 is negative emotions about climate change. In this sample of 815 participants, $b = 0.441$, with an estimated standard error (se_{b_1}) of 0.026 (provided under the column heading "Std Error" in the SPSS output). Dividing b_1 by its standard error yields

$$t(809) = \frac{b_1}{se_{b_1}} = \frac{0.441}{0.026} = 16.962$$

where 809 is the $df_{residual}$ for the model. The t statistic is reported more precisely by SPSS as $t = 16.676$. This result has a p-value that is so tiny it appears to be zero in the output (under the heading "Sig").[2] Of course, the p-value is not zero, and it should not be interpreted or reported as such. With three decimals of resolution in the output, we know $p < .0005$, which is less than $\alpha = 0.05$ (or any other α-level one could imagine actually using). The null hypothesis can be rejected in favor of the alternative, meaning we can conclude that $_Tb_1 \neq 0$. The obtained result of $b_1 = 0.441$ is too discrepant from zero to attribute it to the vagaries of random sampling error or "chance." Having ruled out zero and with b_1 in the positive direction, we can conclude $_Tb_1 > 0$. In substantive terms, there is evidence that in the population, there is a positive association between negative emotions about climate change and support for government action when all the other antecedent variables in the model are held fixed. People who feel negative emotions to a greater extent are relatively more supportive of such actions.

---

[2]Throughout this book, there will be small discrepancies between the computations done in the text by hand, which are completed to only the third decimal place, with output found in various computer outputs or tables based on computer outputs. Computer-generated outputs are based on computations done to much greater precision—at least the eighth decimal place and typically more.

It is possible to test a null hypothesis that the association between X_i and Y is some value other than zero, but this is rarely done in practice. Typically our theories and beliefs about the phenomena under investigation are not so sophisticated that they give rise to sensible predictions about the absolute size of an association. Instead, they usually are only precise enough to be able to predict the direction of the association. Thus, ruling out zero is important, using a null hypothesis test or some other procedure, because doing so allows an investigator to make a claim about the direction of the association (see, e.g., Cortina & Dunlap, 1997; O'Keefe, 2011).

Interval Estimation

An alternative approach to inference is *interval estimation*, also known as the construction of a *confidence interval* for $_Tb_i$. There is much debate in the literature as to the relative merits and disadvantages of null hypothesis testing and confidence intervals. I will not take a stand on this debate in this book and instead refer you to Cortina and Dunlap (1997) for a good discussion.

In any single sample, b_i is our best guess of the value of $_Tb_i$. It is a *point estimate* of $_Tb_i$. If the sample is large enough and the sampling process mimics something akin to random sampling from the population, we can be pretty confident that b_i will be near $_Tb_i$. The standard error for b_i gives us information as to just how much a point estimate is likely to deviate from $_Tb_i$ on average given the sample size used. Yet b_i almost certainly is not exactly equal to $_Tb_i$. A confidence interval acknowledges this uncertainty as a range in which $_Tb_i$ is likely to reside with a specified degree of confidence.

A good OLS program will provide a confidence interval for b_i if requested, so hand computation is rarely required. Typically, a 95% confidence interval is used, and this is usually the default in most statistics programs. The formula for a $c\%$ confidence interval is

$$b_1 - t_{c\%}se_{b_1} \leq {}_Tb_1 \leq b_1 + t_{c\%}se_{b_1} \qquad (2.16)$$

where $t_{c\%}$ is the value of t that cuts off the upper $(100-c)/2\%$ of the $t(df_{residual})$ distribution from the rest of the distribution, where c is the confidence level desired. For instance, for a 95% confidence interval, we need the value of t that cuts off the upper 2.5% of the $t(df_{residual})$ distribution from the rest. These "critical values of t" are available in most all introductory statistics books as well as more advanced ones. In the climate change example, $t_{c\%}$ for $df_{residual} = 809$ is 1.962, and so

$$0.441 - 1.962(0.026) \leq {}_Tb_1 \leq 0.441 + 1.962(0.026)$$

That is, we can be 95% confident that $_Tb_1$ is somewhere between 0.390 and 0.492. The output in Figure 2.6 provides the confidence interval with slightly higher accuracy than these hand computations: $0.389 \leq {_T}b_1 \leq 0.493$. So we can be pretty sure that $_Tb_1$ is positive and somewhere between 0.389 and 0.493 when all other variables in the model are held constant.

Testing a Hypothesis about a Set of Antecedent Variables

Multiple regression can also be used to test a hypothesis about a set of antecedent variables in the model. For instance, considering *emotions* as a set (i.e., both positive and negative emotions), are emotional reactions to climate change related to support for government action while holding constant ideology, sex, and age? With negative and positive emotions being X_1 and X_2 in our regression model, this question can be framed in terms of the following null and alternative hypotheses:

$$H_0: \quad {_T}b_1 \text{ and } {_T}b_2 = 0$$
$$H_a: \quad {_T}b_1 \text{ or } {_T}b_2 \text{ or both} \neq 0$$

Conducting this test requires the estimation of R^2 for two regression models. Model 1 has only sex, age, and political ideology as antecedents. This model yields $R_1^2 = 0.177$. Model 2 contains all the antecedent variables in Model 1 as well as the two emotion variables. This model yields $R_2^2 = 0.388$. A p-value is then constructed by converting the difference between the squared multiple correlations to an F-ratio and finding the p-value corresponding to this F.

Most generally, to test a null hypothesis that all partial regression coefficients for a set of m antecedents in a regression model are equal to zero, the F-ratio is calculated as

$$F\left(m, df_{residual_2}\right) = \frac{df_{residual_2}\left(R_2^2 - R_1^2\right)}{m\left(1 - R_2^2\right)} \tag{2.17}$$

where R_1^2 and R_2^2 are the squared multiple correlations for Models 1 and 2, respectively, Model 2 includes the m antecedent variables as well as all the antecedent variables in Model 1, and $df_{residual_2}$ is the residual degrees of freedom for Model 2. The p-value for F is derived from the $F(m, df_{residual_2})$ distribution. Applied to this example, $R_1^2 = 0.177$, $R_2^2 = 0.388$, $m = 2$, and $df_{residual_2} = 809$, and so

$$F(2, 809) = \frac{809\,(0.388 - 0.177)}{2\,(1 - 0.388)} = 139.632, p < .001$$

The null hypothesis can be rejected. Emotional reactions to climate change are related to support for government action holding political ideology, sex, and age constant. This test can also be interpreted as a test whether the model with the m additional variables in Model 2 fits better than the one that excludes them (Model 1). In this example, we can conclude that the model that includes positive and negative emotions fits better (i.e., estimates Y with greater accuracy) than the one that does not include these two variables.

These computations are laborious if done by hand, but most good OLS regression routines have a means of implementing this test. In SPSS, the command is

```
regression/statistics defaults change/dep=govact/method=enter ideology
    sex age/method=enter negemot posemot.
```

and in SAS, the command is

```
proc reg data=glbwarm;model govact=negemot posemot ideology sex age;
    test negemot=0,posemot=0;run;
```

There are two special cases of this test worthy of mention. First, when Model 1 and Model 2 differ by only one antecedent variable, meaning $m = 1$, the F-ratio generated by equation 2.17 is the square of the t statistic for that antecedent variable in a model that includes all the antecedent variables, and their p-values will be the same. Thus, the t-test for a regression coefficient can be interpreted as a test of whether a model that includes that antecedent variable fits better than one that excludes it.

The second special case is when $m = k$, where k is the number of antecedent variables in your regression model. In that case, Model 1 is a model that includes only a regression constant, and Model 2 includes all k of the antecedent variables. The change in R^2 is the squared multiple correlation for the model including all k antecedents. The null hypothesis tested is that *all* $b_i = 0$ and the alternative hypothesis is that *at least one* $b_i \neq 0$. The null and alternative hypotheses can also be framed in terms of the "true" multiple correlation $_TR^2$. The null hypothesis is $_TR^2 = 0$ and the alternative is $_TR^2 > 0$. Most statistics programs generate this test automatically when you conduct a regression analysis. In Figure 2.6, the test is found in the section labelled "ANOVA." As can be seen, $F(5, 809) = 102.717, p < .0005$. So we can reject the null hypothesis. But in the types of analyses we focus on in this book, rarely is the outcome of this test interesting because rejection of this null hypothesis results in only the vague claim that there is some association between one of the antecedents and the consequent. We usually are interested in the regression coefficients themselves, not the overall fit of the model.

Process Inference

The previous discussion couches the inferential goal of data analysis in terms of populations. That is, sampling variation adds a discrepancy between the association between two variables observed in a sample and the true association in the population. This "true" association is conceptualized as the association that would have been observed if all members of the population to which an inference is desired provided data to the study. Equivalently, it is conceptualized as the association that would have been observed if the sample was infinite in size, or at least as large as the population itself. Regardless, sample-to-sample variation that results when using sample sizes smaller than the size of the population is conceptualized as being due to the random sampling process.

Given that the vast majority of researchers do not randomly sample from specified populations when recruiting research participants, some have questioned the value of the population model of inference and advocated alternative conceptualizations and statistical techniques. This is not the place to go into this large and interesting literature (see, e.g., Bear, 1995; Berger, 2000; Edgington, 1964, 1978, 1995; Frick, 1998; Kennedy, 1995; Ludbrook & Dudley, 1998; Lunneborg, 2000; May, Masson, & Hunter, 1989; May & Hunter, 1993; Mook, 1987; Oja, 1987; Still & White, 1981; ter Braak, 1992). Suffice it to say that in my experience, most researchers appreciate that rarely is population inference the goal, although it is sometimes. Rather, more often, researchers are interested in making inferences about the *processes at work generating the pattern of association observed* rather than what the association would be if all members of some population participated in the study.

These processes at work can be expressed in terms of true values or parameters, such as $_Tb_i$, but these symbols mean something different under a process model of inference. The true regression coefficient in process inference terms can be thought of as a representation of the mathematical weight given to the input X_i in the process that generates the output Y. In the same way that a quality control expert observes only some of the product coming off a production line, a researcher is privy to only a subset of the outputs the process generates; outputs from the process at work among those participants who were included in the study and measured on the input and output variables. Importantly, b_i departs from $_Tb_i$ because only a small subset of possible outputs from the process has been observed. We try to infer $_Tb_i$ from what is available to us as researchers. We don't need to assume what is available represents a random sample from some population of outputs. Indeed, if you think of the process as a production line, there is no defined population to make an inference about, as the process will generate outputs as long as there are inputs given to it. Instead, the inference is about the process at work linking inputs to outputs—the gears of a *data generating machine*.

Consider the null hypothesis that $_Tb_1 = 0$ in the climate change example. Such a hypothesis, if true, is akin to saying that the psychological, biological, or cognitive process that gives rise to individual beliefs about what government should do about climate change (output Y) does not use negative emotional responses to the crisis (X_i) as an input when all other inputs are held fixed. Alternatively, the null stipulates that these emotional reactions receive no weight (hence, $_Tb_1 = 0$) in the mental calculus generating responses to questions about beliefs about government action. If this were true, then we'd expect to see an association between X_1 and Y in the sample, using b_1 as the measure of partial association, that is no larger than what a *random* process would tend to generate, such as randomly assigning values of Y to patterns of values of the antecedent variables. But if the obtained value of b_1 is larger than what a random process would tend to produce, this leads to the conclusion that there is some systematic process linking X_1 to Y (i.e., negative emotions or something confounded with such emotions is being used as an input to the mental calculus). In other words, $_Tb_1 \neq 0$.

Absent random sampling from a specified population, process inferences do not allow the kind of population generalizations that random sampling affords. Rather, such inferences are specific to the process generating the observed data and thus are sample-specific. But this is perfectly acceptable to most scientists, for population inference is not often the objective. Being able to establish that a random process is not at work producing an association opens the door to other more interesting explanations that probably motivated the study in the first place. In this specific example, however, if one is willing to accept that the sampling method used to recruit participants to fill out the online survey yielded a fairly representative sample of the target population (residents of the United States), generalization can be made about both process and population.

2.7 Multicategorical Antecedent Variables

Every antecedent variable in the examples thus far has been either dichotomous (meaning containing only two values, such as codes for two groups) or quantitative in nature, where the numbers in the data represent a quantity of something. But you will often find yourself wanting to include an antecedent variable in a regression model that is multicategorical, with the data coding which of more than two groups a case belongs in. For example, you might have two experimental groups and a control group in a variable, with the numbers 0, 1, and 2 coding the three groups. When such a variable is of kind rather than quantity, you can't just include such a variable in a model as is, because a regression program will interpret the numbers as quantities. Special procedures are needed to represent membership in one of more than two groups.

To include a multicategorical antecedent variable representing g groups in a regression model, it must be represented with $g - 1$ variables using one of a variety of different group coding systems. One popular system for coding groups is *indicator coding*, also known as *dummy coding*. With indicator coding, $g - 1$ *indicator variables* containing either a zero or one represent which of the g groups a case belongs in, and these indicator variables are used as antecedents in a regression model. To construct indicator codes, create $g - 1$ variables D_i for each case set to 1 if the case is in group i, otherwise set D_i to zero. This procedure is represented in Table 2.1. Because only $g - 1$ variables are created, one of the groups does not receive its own indicator variable. Instead, as can be seen, the group that doesn't get its own indicator receives a zero on all $g - 1$ D_i indicator variables. This group is called the *reference* or *baseline* group.

For instance, if your multicategorical antecedent represents three groups, estimate

$$\hat{Y} = b_0 + b_1 D_1 + b_2 D_2$$

where D_1 and D_2 are indicator codes as just described. In this model, b_1 is the difference in $\hat{Y}$ between the reference group and the group set to 1 on D_1. Similarly, b_2 is the difference in $\hat{Y}$ between the reference group and the group set to 1 on D_2. The regression constant, b_0 is $\hat{Y}$ for the reference group. These turn out to be group means or differences between means, as discussed below.

I illustrate this method using the global warming data. In the GLB-WARM data, there is a variable named PARTYID that codes whether a person identified as a Democrat (1), an Independent (2), or a Republican (3). The mean support for government action to mitigate the effects of climate change are 5.064, 4.605, and 3.925 for these three groups, respectively. The code below constructs two indicators, one for Democrats and one for Republicans, with Independents as the reference category, and then estimates the model:

```
compute d1=(partyid=1).
compute d2=(partyid=3).
regression/dep=govact/method=enter d1 d2.
```

TABLE 2.1. Indicator Coding of g Categories

Group	D_1	D_2	$\cdots$	D_i	$\cdots$	D_{g-1}
1	1	0	$\cdots$	0	$\cdots$	0
2	0	1	$\cdots$	0	$\cdots$	0
$\vdots$						
i	0	0	$\cdots$	1	$\cdots$	0
$\vdots$						
$g-1$	0	0	$\cdots$	0	$\cdots$	1
g	0	0	$\cdots$	0	$\cdots$	0

```
data glbwarm;set glbwarm;
d1=(partyid=1);d2=(partyid=3);run;
proc reg data=glbwarm;model govact=d1 d2;run;
```

The resulting regression equation is[3]

$$\hat{Y} = 4.605 + 0.459D_1 - 0.680D_2$$

In this equation $b_0 = 4.605$ corresponds to $\overline{Y}$ for the reference group, which in this example is the Independents. The regression coefficient for D_1 is $b_1 = 0.459$, which is the mean difference in support for government action between Democrats and Independents ($5.064 - 4.605 = 0.459$). And the regression coefficient for D_2, $b_2 = -0.680$, is the mean difference in support for government action between Republicans and Independents ($3.925 - 4.605 = -0.680$). For this model, $R^2 = 0.131$, and a test of the fit of the model (see section 2.6) yields $F(2, 812) = 61.243, p < .0005$. This is equivalent to the F-ratio from a single factor analysis of variance comparing the three means. We can reject the null hypothesis and conclude that Democrats, Independents, and Republicans differ on average in their support for government action to mitigate the effects of global climate change. Both of the regression coefficients for D_1 and D_2 are statistically significant, leading to the conclusion that the corresponding pairs of means (Democrats versus Independents for b_1, Republicans versus Independents for b_2) are statistically different from each other.

[3]There are no missing data in the GLBWARM data file, so this SAS code is appropriate. If any cases were missing on PARTYID, this SAS code would result in anyone missing on PARTYID as an Independent. To properly code missing data as such, the missing data need to be explicitly coded with two more lines in the data step: **if (partyid=.) then d1=.;if (partyid=.) then d2=.**

The indicator codes representing membership in the categories of a multicategorical antecedent variable can be included in a model with additional antecedents. If the multicategorical variable is thought of as a covariate, then all the other effects estimated by the model will be estimated holding the multicategorical covariate fixed. Or one could ask whether the groups differ on average on the consequent variable when all other antecedent variables in the model are held constant. This question could be answered using the method described in section 2.6, first estimating R^2 for a model that includes all antecedents except the multicategorical one and then seeing how much R^2 increases when the indicator codes are added to the model. For instance, in a model estimating support for government action from negative emotions, positive emotions, ideology, sex, and age, $R^2 = 0.388$. When the two indicator variables coding party identification are added, $R^2 = 0.392$. This increase of 0.004 is not quite statistically significant, $F(2, 807) = 2.586, p = .076$, so we can't conclude that Democrats, Independents, and Republicans who are the same on the other five antecedent variables differ on average in their support for government action. This is equivalent to a single factor analysis of covariance comparing the three means, with the other antecedent variables functioning as covariates.

Indicator coding is only one of many ways of representing a multicategorical antecedent variable in a regression model. Other methods are discussed in later sections of this book. For a more detailed presentation of this topic, see Darlington and Hayes (2017) or Davis (2010).

2.8 Assumptions for Interpretation and Statistical Inference

Regression is a handy tool to have in your statistical toolbox. Its utility as a "general data analytic system" (Cohen, 1968) will be apparent throughout this book. But it is a human invention that isn't perfect, it can lead you astray if used indiscriminately, and it is founded on some assumptions that aren't always realistic or likely to be met in the circumstances in which the method is applied. These assumptions are worth understanding, but they are abstract and can be confusing at first, and they are hard to do justice to in just a few paragraphs. A more thorough discussion of the assumptions of OLS regression than I provide here can be found in a short monograph by Berry (1993).

Before introducing these assumptions, I will make my perspective clear. Because assumption violations can have some adverse effects on inference sometimes, we should be mindful of the assumptions OLS regression makes. At the same time, I do not believe you should lose too much sleep over the potential that you have violated one or more of those assumptions. Most likely you have, even if statistical tests of the assumptions you might employ say otherwise. Statistical models are tools we use to help us understand our data, and they can give us insights that are only approximations of reality. The question is not whether we have violated an assumption, but how much doing so is likely to lead us astray when we interpret our results and the inferences we make from them. OLS regression is widely used by researchers because it is fairly easy to understand and describe, widely implemented in software that is readily available, and tends to do a good job approximating reality much of the time when used thoughtfully. Those advantages of OLS regression far outweigh some of the costs of abandoning it for other perhaps better but much more complicated and less well-understood methods. To be sure, be respectful of the complexities and properties of your data and do your best to analyze them with methods best suited, but don't obsess over every minor assumption violation. *Throughout this book, I assume you have contemplated the appropriateness of OLS regression for your problem and have decided you are comfortable and want to forge ahead.*

Linearity

When using OLS regression to model some consequent variable of interest Y, you must be willing to assume that the relationship between the variables in the model are linear in nature, or at least approximately linear. The regression coefficient for X_i generated by optimizing the fit of the model using the least squares criterion quantifies how much two cases that differ by one unit on X_i but are equal on all other antecedents in the model are estimated to differ on Y. This interpretation is not conditioned on a specific value of X_i. In other words, regardless of which value of X_i you choose, a case with $X_i = x_i + 1$ is estimated to differ by b_i units on Y relative to a case with $X_i = x_i$. This assumption would be violated if, *in reality*, the difference in Y between two cases that differ by one unit on X_i depends on X_i.

The linearity assumption is important because if it is violated, this jeopardizes the meaningfulness of the interpretation of the regression coefficient (e.g., Darlington & Hayes, 2017). If in reality, the difference in Y between cases differing by one unit on X_i depends on X_i, then b_i isn't an inadequate description across the range of X_i of how differences in X_i map onto differences in Y. Of course, we do not know reality. If we did, we wouldn't need to build a model and make inferences using such a model. All we can do is use our data to try to model what that reality looks like. Fortunately, we can also use our data to test whether the assumption of linearity is plausible given the data available. In addition, it is possible to model nonlinear relationships using OLS regression. For details on testing and modeling nonlinear relationships with OLS regression, see Darlington and Hayes (2017), or Fox (1991).

Normality

The assumption of *normality* states that the errors in estimation of consequent variable Y, conditioned on $\hat{Y}$, are normally distributed.[4] This assumption is one of the least important in linear regression analysis. Simulation research suggests that only the most severe violations of the normality assumption substantially affect the validity of statistical inferences from a regression analysis unless the sample size is quite small (e.g., Duncan & Layard, 1973; Edgell & Noon, 1984; Havlicek & Peterson, 1977; Hayes, 1996). However, non-normality can influence sampling variance in some circumstances in such a way that power of hypothesis tests is reduced. The power of a hypothesis test is the probability of it correctly rejecting a false null hypothesis.

This assumption is rarely met in practice primarily because of the measurement procedures researchers typically use. Often, measurement scales are bounded by zero, such as when a variable is a count of things (e.g., how many good friends a person has, how many phone calls a person made today, etc.). Measurement scales also sometimes produce discrete data, meaning only a few unique values are observed on the measurement scale. An example would be the use of a 7-point scale asking someone to evaluate how much he or she likes a television program, or how shy he or she is. Technically speaking, the normal distribution is a continuous distribution, so no model of such a variable using OLS regression would generate normally distributed errors in estimation. Finally, many if not most things that researchers study and measure are not normally distributed, in spite of claims made in many statistics books about the ubiquity of the normal distribution (cf., Micceri, 1989). When modeling non-normal consequent variables using OLS regression, the errors in estimation also tend not to be normal.

Violation of the normality assumption is certain when using OLS regression to analyze consequent variables that are discrete or bounded on the lower or upper end of the measurement scale. For example, OLS regression is not ideal for modeling dichotomous consequent variables. Logistic or probit regression is more appropriate. For coarse ordinal scales with only a few measurement categories, some kind of ordinal regression model (e.g.,

---

[4]Contrary to the beliefs of some, the assumption of normality does not pertain to the distribution of Y itself or to the predictors of Y in the regression model. Regression analysis makes no assumption about the shape of these distributions.

probit or ordinal logit regression) would be preferred to OLS regression, although there is some debate in the literature over just how much damage is done when modeling coarsely measured consequent variables with OLS. Count consequent variables are better analyzed with Poisson or negative binomial regression, but again, use of OLS is not uncommon or entirely inappropriate if certain precautions are taken. Long (1997) provides a nice introduction to all of these methods.

Homoscedasticity

The assumption of *homoscedasticity* is a complex one. Roughly (although incompletely), it states that the errors in estimation of Y are equally variable conditioned on $\hat{Y}$. When this condition is not met, the errors in estimation are said to be *heteroscedastic*. Heteroscedasticity can affect both the validity of inference and reduce statistical power of hypothesis tests and influence the accuracy of confidence intervals for regression coefficients, depending on the form of the heteroscedasticity. Simulation research suggests that mild violations of the homoscedasticity assumption are not too much of a concern (e.g., Hayes, 1996), but the assumption is still worth taking seriously. There are some informal tests of homoscedasticity, such as eyeballing a scatterplot of the residuals as a function of $\hat{Y}$, as well as some formal tests of the null hypothesis that the errors in estimation are homoscedastic. See Breusch and Pagan (1979), Berry (1993), Cohen, Cohen, West, and Aiken (2003), Cook and Weisberg (1983), Darlington and Hayes (2017), Downs and Rocke (1979), Goldfeld and Quandt (1965), and White (1980) for a discussion of some of the conditions that can produce heteroscedasticity and various tests of this assumption.

Homoscedasticity is not required for derivation of the regression coefficients. Rather heteroscedasticity exerts its effect on inference through its effect on the standard error of regression coefficients. The standard error estimator programmed into most OLS regression routines is based on this assumption. If you have reason to believe the homoscedasticity assumption has been violated, increasing the sample size will not help like it does when the normality assumption is violated (Hayes, 1996; Long & Ervin, 2000). The PROCESS procedure for SPSS and SAS described throughout this book provides an option for the use of inferential methods in regression analysis that don't assume homoscedasticity, such as heteroscedasticity-consistent covariance estimators. For a concise introduction to and discussion of these estimators, see Hayes and Cai (2007) or Long and Ervin (2000).

Independence

OLS regression also assumes the errors in estimation are statistically independent. In the most basic terms, two things are independent if information about one gives no information about the other. If the errors in estimation are independent, this means that for all (i, j) pairs of observations, there is no information contained in the error in estimation of Y for case i that could be used to estimate the error in estimation of Y for case j.

Many processes can result in a violation of independence. For example, subsets of cases may share something that is related to Y, and a failure to account for that thing in the model can result in estimation errors that are nonindependent. An example would be studies that are based on some kind of cluster sampling procedure. In studies of school-age children, for instance, children are often selected for inclusion in a study based on a random sampling of classrooms in a school or in a district. Ten of the children in the study may be students of Mr. Jones at Tremont Elementary, 10 may be from Mrs. Peterson's class at Barrington Elementary, another 20 may come from Mrs. Stewart's room at Hastings Elementary, and so forth. Suppose the goal is to estimate performance on a statewide achievement test from how many days of school a child has missed. The problem is that achievement of students in a particular class is certainly determined in part by how good the teacher is at his or her job, or how kids are assigned to teachers. If Mr. Jones is an exceptionally gifted teacher relative to other teachers, or teaches the exceptionally gifted children in the school, the model will probably tend to underestimate the performance of relatively more of his students. In other words, the errors in estimation would tend to be positive for students in Mr. Jones's class in greater relative frequency than they would for students from other classes. This would be a violation of the independence assumption.

Another example would be ignoring familial relationships when using participants from the same family. Suppose, for instance, you wanted to examine the relationship between income and marital satisfaction by asking 50 husband–wife dyads to each report how satisfied they are in their marriage and how much money they each make. If you regressed the 100 satisfaction measurements on the 100 income measurements to test the hypothesis that income and satisfaction are positively related, the result would almost certainly be contaminated by violation of the independence assumption. The satisfaction of one person in a marriage is almost certainly predictable from how satisfied his or her partner is. As a result, the signs of the errors in estimation for husband and wife pairs are more likely to be the same than different.

Like does heteroscedasticity, nonindependence affects the accuracy of the estimation of the standard error of regression coefficients, as the OLS standard error estimator assumes independence of errors in estimation. Whether the standard error is over- or underestimated will depend on the form of nonindependence, but typically the result is underestimation. If the standard error is underestimated, this means that hypothesis tests will be invalid, and confidence intervals too narrow relative to what they should be when the independence assumption is met. Additional discussion of some of the causes and consequences of nonindependence, as well as how to properly handle it analytically when it is not ignorable, can be found in such places as Grawitch and Munz (2004), Griffin and Gonzales (1995), Hayes (1996), Kenny and Judd (1986), Kenny, Mannetti, Pierro, Livi, and Kashy (2002), Luke (2004), O'Connor (2004), and Raudenbush and Bryk (2002).

2.9 Chapter Summary

Ordinary least squares regression analysis is one of the more useful analytical tools a researcher has available, and it is the foundation of many of the statistical methods that researchers use. Understanding how to estimate and interpret a regression model is important, for regression analysis is the method I will emphasize in my discussion of mediation, moderation, and conditional process analysis in this book.

A simple regression model is a mathematical representation of the association between a consequent variable Y and an antecedent variable X. Using the least squares criterion, a linear regression routine derives the regression constant and regression coefficient(s) defining the best equation linking the antecedent variable(s) to the consquent variable. The regression equation generates estimates of Y for each case in the data from those cases' values on X while minimizing the discrepancy between the actual values of Y and what the equation estimates for Y.

Two variables X and Y may be correlated as a result of a number of different processes. Investigators often want to interpret association in causal terms, but when there are alternative explanations, causal language must be worded carefully with the appropriate caveats and cautions. Differences between people on both X and Y may be due to some kind of causal effect of X on Y, but it could be because people who differ on X and Y also differ on other variables that influence both X and Y, thereby inducing spurious association between X and Y. Or X may be correlated with a cause of Y and therefore also be correlated with Y even though it itself is not a cause of Y, a phenomenon known as epiphenomenal association. Multiple regression can be used to rule out some alternative explanations for an association between X and Y by including variables representing those alternative explanations as covariates in a linear regression model estimating Y from X. When this is done, a multiple regression model generates partial regression coefficients that quantify the association between X and Y when holding all other antecedent variables in the model constant. Understanding this statistical control process, as well as how to interpret a regression model with more than one antecedent variable, is important because most of the models estimated in the rest of this book, starting with Chapter 3 on mediation analysis, will include more than one antecedent variable.

Part II

MEDIATION ANALYSIS

3

The Simple Mediation Model

In this chapter, I introduce the elements of mediation analysis, with a focus on the most basic mediation model possible consisting of a causal antecedent variable linked to a single consequent variable through a single intermediary variable or *mediator*. This very popular and widely estimated *simple mediation model* is used to introduce the mechanics of path analysis and to demonstrate how a variable's effect on an outcome can be partitioned into direct and indirect effects that can be quantified using OLS regression. Inferential tests for direct and indirect effects are presented, with an emphasis on approaches that do not make unnecessary assumptions.

There is a body of research in the persuasion and attitude change literature on the differential effects of gain versus loss framing in influencing behavior (e.g., O'Keefe & Jensen, 1997). A gain frame message is one that emphasizes all the things you will acquire or gain if you engage in the behavior advocated by the message. For example, if you wanted to persuade your friend to stop smoking, you could make the argument to him that if he stops smoking, he will feel physically better each day, he will live to an older age, and more people will like him. By contrast, a message framed in terms of losses emphasizes all the things he will lose if he fails to engage in the behavior advocated. For example, you could tell your friend how his health will deteriorate, he will die younger, and his friends will eventually abandon him if he doesn't stop smoking.

The literature suggests that in some circumstances, gain frame messages are more effective at influencing people, whereas in other circumstances, loss frames work better. In other words, the effect of message framing is *moderated* because it depends on the circumstance. As discussed in Chapter 1, establishing the boundary conditions of an effect and identifying those factors that influence the size of an effect are important scientific goals.

But just as important to scientific understanding and the application of that understanding is figuring out *how* effects occur in the first place. For instance, if a study shows that a gain frame message works better than a loss frame message at influencing smokers to quit, what is it about gain framing that results in greater behavior change? What is the *mechanism* at work that leads to a greater likelihood of smoking cessation after being told about all the potential gains that can occur if one quits smoking rather than all the losses one will experience by continuing to smoke? Is it that messages framed in terms of gains empower people more than loss framed messages, which in turn enhances the likelihood of taking action? Or perhaps loss frame messages are more likely to prompt lots of counterarguing, which reduces the persuasiveness of the message relative to gain frame messages.

Whereas answering questions about *when* or *for whom* is the domain of moderation analysis, questions that ask about *how* pertain to *mediation*, the focus of this and the next three chapters. In this chapter, I introduce the *simple mediation model* and illustrate using OLS regression-based path analysis how the effect of an antecedent variable X on some final consequent Y can be partitioned into two paths of influence, *direct* and *indirect*. I show that the procedure one follows to derive these paths of influence does not depend on whether X is dichotomous or continuous. I also discuss various approaches to making inferences about direct and indirect effects in this most simple of mediation models.

3.1   The Simple Mediation Model

Mediation analysis is a statistical method used to evaluate evidence from studies designed to test hypotheses about how some causal antecedent variable X transmits its effect on a consequent variable Y. What is the mechanism, be it emotional, cognitive, biological, or otherwise, by which X influences Y? Does framing an anti-smoking message in gain as opposed to loss terms (X) influence the likelihood of smoking cessation (Y) because the type of frame influences how much people counterargue, which in turn influences behavior? Or maybe loss framing leads to certain negative emotional reactions, such as anxiety, which disrupt systematic message processing and elaboration, which in turn reduces the effectiveness of the message.

The most basic of mediation models—the simple mediation model—is represented in conceptual diagram form in Figure 3.1. As can be seen, this model contains two consequent variables (M) and (Y) and two antecedent variables (X) and (M), with X causally influencing Y and M, and M causally influencing Y. A simple mediation model is any causal system in which at least one causal antecedent X variable is proposed as influencing an outcome Y through a single intervening variable M. In such a model,

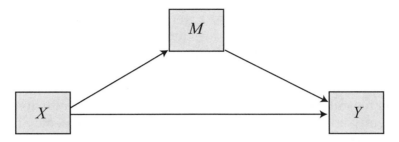

FIGURE 3.1. A conceptual diagram of a simple mediation model.

there are two pathways by which X can influence Y. These pathways are found by tracing the ways one can get from X to Y while never tracing in a direction opposite to the direction an arrow points. One pathway leads from X to Y without passing through M and is called the *direct effect* of X on Y. The second pathway from X to Y is the *indirect effect* of X on Y through M. It first passes from antecedent X to consequent M and then from antecedent M to consequent Y. The indirect effect represents how Y is influenced by X through a causal sequence in which X influences M, which in turn influences Y.

In a mediation model, M is typically called a *mediator variable*, though the terms *intermediary variable*, *surrogate variable*, and *intermediate endpoint* are used in some fields. In the example thus far, counterarguing and anxiety are conceptualized as potential mediators of the effect of framing on likelihood of smoking cessation. They represent a possible or proposed mechanism—the contents of the "black box"—by which message framing influences behavior. Once X exerts its effect on M, then M's causal influence on Y produces variation in Y.

Historically, questions of "how" have been thought of as sensible to ask only after one first has established evidence of association between X and Y. As a result, mediation analysis would be undertaken only when one has successfully demonstrated that X and Y are associated. This rationale is based on one of the three criteria popularly described as necessary to establish cause–effect: correlation between X and Y (the other two criteria being establishing that X precedes Y, and ruling out competing explanations). Thus, suppose one finds no average difference in the likelihood of smoking cessation (Y) between two groups of smokers in an experiment exposed to differently framed anti-smoking messages (X) designed to change behavior. What point would there be in trying to explain how message framing affects behavior when one has no evidence of a difference in behavior following exposure to differently framed messages? If one has no actual evidence that X is related to Y, then, so the argument goes, X does not affect Y, so there is no "how" question to answer.

This conceptualization of mediation analysis as a statistical means of "accounting for an effect" may in part be due to the popularization of a particular approach to mediation analysis I describe in section 4.1 but which is no longer recommended. This approach has dominated mediation analysis until recently, still remains widely used, and has become deeply ingrained in how scientists think. On the surface, it seems that the existence of an association between X and Y would be a reasonable precondition of trying to explain the underlying effect of X on Y. But there is a growing awareness of and appreciation that such thinking is misguided and outdated. As Bollen (1989) stated some years ago in a couple of sentences tucked away on page 52 of his popular book *Structural Equations with Latent Variables*, "lack of correlation does not disprove causation" and "correlation is neither a necessary nor a sufficient condition of causality." This seems contrary to conventional wisdom and what is taught in graduate school or printed in research methods books. Yet it is true, and most scholars of mediation analysis have now adopted the perspective Bollen articulated (see, e.g., Cerin & MacKinnon, 2009; Hayes, 2009; Hayes & Rockwood, 2017; MacKinnon, 2008; Rucker, Preacher, Tormala, & Petty, 2011; Shrout & Bolger, 2002; Zhao, Lynch, & Chen, 2010). Mediation analysis as practiced now no longer imposes evidence of simple association between X and Y as a precondition.

The simple mediation model is the most rudimentary mediation model one can estimate, and no doubt it greatly oversimplifies the complex dynamics through which X influences Y in real processes that scientists study. In later chapters, I describe more complex mediation models that are more realistic, such as models in which X transmits its effect on Y through multiple mechanisms represented with different mediators. Nevertheless, a thorough understanding of this model is important. Simple mediation models are routinely estimated and their components interpreted in the empirical social psychological (e.g., Newheiser & Barreto, 2014; Petrocelli, Rubin, & Stevens, 2016), cognitive (e.g., Banks, Tartar, & Welhaf, 2014; Lavenure et al., 2016), clinical (e.g., Dubois-Comtois, Moss, Cyr, & Pascuzzo, 2014; Nelson, Shankman, & Proudfit, 2014), environmental (e.g., An, Colarelli, O'Brien, & Boyajian, 2016), health (e.g., Doue & Roussiau, 2016; Walker, Harrison, Brown, Thorpe, & Szanton, 2016), political (e.g., de Moore, 2015; Wohl & Branscombe, 2009), medical (e.g., Cao-Lei et al., 2016; Meade, Conn, Skalski, & Safren, 2011), educational (e.g., Coetzee, 2014; Paige, Rasinski, Magpuri-Lavell, & Smith, 2014), communication (e.g., Goodboy et al., 2016; Joseph, Afifi, & Denes, 2016; Knobloch-Westerwick, 2014; Nathanson

& Fries, 2014), occupational safety (e.g., Morgan, Jones, & Harris, 2013), family studies (e.g., Bergman, Cummings, & Davies, 2014; Waldinger & Schultz, 2016), women's studies (e.g., Mittal, Senn, & Carey, 2013), and organizational behavior, management, and marketing (e.g., Boren, 2014; Gao, Huang, & Simonson, 2014; Schaerer, Swaab, & Galinsky, 2015) literature, among many other disciplines. Indeed, it would be tough to read the literature in many fields without encountering models of this sort being advanced and tested empirically.

A second reason for understanding this rather rudimentary three-variable causal model is that the principles described in this chapter will be applied later in this book to more complex models that also are very popular in many empirical disciplines. So an understanding of the concepts discussed in this chapter is necessary to progress further in this book and to understand the research published in your chosen area.

When thinking about whether a phenomenon or theory you are studying could be conceptualized as a mediation process, it is important to keep in mind that mediation is ultimately a causal explanation. It is assumed that the relationships in the system are causal, and, importantly, that M is causally located *between* X and Y. It must be assumed, if not also empirically substantiated, that X causes M, which in turn causes Y. M cannot possibly carry X's effect on Y if M is not located causally between X and Y.

Some argue that absent data that allow one to confidently infer cause–effect, a mediation model cannot and should not be estimated or interpreted. I have already articulated my perspective on the relationship between statistics, research design, and cause in Chapter 1, but my position is worth repeating here. I believe that one can conduct a mediation analysis even if one cannot unequivocally establish causality given the limitations of one's data collection and research design. It is often, even typically, the case that the data available for analysis do not lend themselves to unequivocally causal claims, perhaps because the data are purely correlational, collected at a single time point, and with no experimental manipulation or random assignment. Sometimes theory or solid argument is the only foundation upon which a causal claim can be built given limitations of our data. But I see no problem in conducting the kind of analysis I describe here and subsequent chapters even when causal claims rest on shaky empirical ground. It is our brains that interpret and place meaning on the mathematical procedures used, not the procedures themselves. So long as we couch our causal claims with the required cautions and caveats given the nature of the data available, we can apply any mathematical method we want to understand and model relationships between variables.

3.2   Estimation of the Direct, Indirect, and Total Effects of *X*

When empirically testing a causal process that involves a mediation component, of primary interest is the estimation and interpretation of the direct and indirect effects along with inferential tests thereof. To derive these effects, one must also estimate the constituent components of the indirect effect, meaning the effect of X on M as well as the effect of M on Y, although the constituent components of the indirect effect are not of primary interest in modern mediation analysis. Many researchers often estimate the total effect of X on Y as well, although doing so is not required for the purpose of interpretation. I define the total effect later.

The simple mediation model represented in the form of a statistical diagram can be found in Figure 3.2. Notice that in comparing Figures 3.1 and 3.2, there is little difference between the conceptual and statistical diagrams representing a simple mediation model. As there are two consequent variables in this diagram, two linear models are required, one for each consequent. This statistical diagram represents two equations:

$$M = i_M + aX + e_M \tag{3.1}$$
$$Y = i_Y + c'X + bM + e_Y \tag{3.2}$$

where i_M and i_Y are regression constants, e_M and e_Y are errors in the estimation of M and Y, respectively, and a, b, and c' are the regression coefficients given to the antecedent variables in the model in the estimation of the consequents. The coefficients of the model are treated as estimates of the putative causal influences of each variable in the system on others, and the analytical goal is to estimate these coefficients, piece them together, and interpret. These coefficients can be estimated by conducting two OLS regression analyses using the procedures that come with SPSS, SAS, R, and other statistical packages, using a structural equation modeling program such as LISREL, AMOS, Mplus, or EQS, or through the use of PROCESS, mentioned first in Chapter 1 and illustrated in the next section. In a simple mediation model, it generally makes no difference, although without additional computational aids, OLS regression procedures that come with most statistical packages will not get you all the information you need to conduct some of the more preferred inferential tests described later in this chapter. For now, we can talk about the coefficients and effects in the model without concerning ourselves with the specifics of the method used to estimate them.

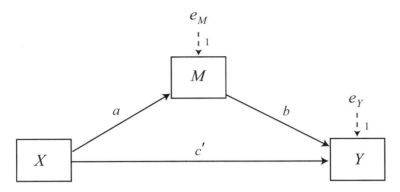

FIGURE 3.2. A statistical diagram of the simple mediation model.

The Direct Effect of *X* on *Y*

In equation 3.2, c' estimates the direct effect of X on Y. A generic interpretation of the direct effect is that two cases that differ by one unit on X but are equal on M are estimated to differ by c' units on Y. More formally,

$$c' = [\hat{Y} \mid (X = x, M = m)] - [\hat{Y} \mid (X = x - 1, M = m)] \qquad (3.3)$$

where m is any value of M, | means *conditioned on* or *given*, and the hat over Y means *estimated* or *expected* from the model. In other words, for two cases with $M = m$ but that differ by one unit on X, c' is the estimated value of Y for the case with $X = x$ minus the estimated value of Y for the case with $X = x - 1$. As can be determined looking at equation 3.3, the sign of c' tells whether the case one unit higher on X is estimated to be higher ($c' = +$) or lower ($c' = -$) on Y. So a positive direct effect means that the case higher on X is estimated to be higher on Y, whereas a negative direct effect means that the case higher on X is estimated to be lower on Y. In the special case where X is dichotomous, with the two values of X differing by a single unit (e.g., $X = 1$ and $X = 0$), $\hat{Y}$ can be interpreted as a group mean, so $c' = [\overline{Y} \mid (X = x, M = m)] - [\overline{Y} \mid (X = x - 1, M = m)]$, meaning c' estimates the difference between the two group means holding M constant. This is equivalent to what in analysis of covariance terms is called an *adjusted mean difference*.

The Indirect Effect of *X* on *Y*

Before defining the indirect effect, it is first necessary to discuss what a and b in equations 3.1 and 3.2 estimate. In this model, a quantifies how much two cases that differ by one unit on X are estimated to differ on M, with the sign determining whether the case higher on X is estimated to be higher (+) or lower (−) on M. That is,

$$a = [\hat{M} \mid (X = x)] - [\hat{M} \mid (X = x - 1)]$$

When X is a dichotomous variable and the two groups are coded such that they differ by one unit on X (e.g., 0 and 1), a in equation 3.1 represents the difference between the two group means on M: $a = [\overline{M} \mid (X = x)] - [\overline{M} \mid (X = x - 1)]$.

The b coefficient from equation 3.2 has an interpretation analogous to c', except with M as the antecedent. Two cases that differ by one unit on M but that are equal on X are estimated to differ by b units on Y. As with a and c', the sign of b determines whether the case higher on M is estimated as higher (+) or lower (−) on Y:

$$b = [\hat{Y} \mid (M = m, X = x)] - [\hat{Y} \mid (M = m - 1, X = x)]$$

The indirect effect of X on Y through M is the product of a and b. For instance, if $a = 0.5$ and $b = 1.3$, then the indirect effect of X on Y through M is $ab = 0.65$. The indirect effect tells us that two cases that differ by one unit on X are estimated to differ by ab units on Y as a result of the effect of X on M which, in turn, affects Y. The indirect effect will be positive (meaning the case higher on X is estimated to be higher on Y) if a and b are both positive or both negative, whereas it will be negative (meaning the case higher on X is estimated to be lower on Y) if either a or b, but not both, is negative.

Although one can interpret the indirect effect without considering the signs of a and b, doing so can be dangerous, because the sign of ab is determined by two different configurations of the signs of a and b. A certain theory you are testing might predict ab to be positive because, according to the process the theory explains, a and b should both be positive. But what if a and b turned out to be negative in your analysis? This would yield a positive indirect effect as predicted, yet this pattern of results for a and b is exactly opposite to what the theory predicts, and this should cast some doubt on whether the theory is adequately describing the process generating your data.

The Total Effect of X on Y

The direct and indirect effects perfectly partition how differences in X map on to differences in Y, the *total effect* of X and denoted here as c. The total effect c quantifies how much two cases that differ by one unit on X are estimated to differ on Y. That is,

$$c = [\hat{Y} \mid (X = x)] - [\hat{Y} \mid (X = x - 1)]$$

In a simple mediation model, c can be derived by estimating Y from X alone:

$$Y = i_{Y*} + cX + e_{Y*} \tag{3.4}$$

When X is a dichotomous variable coded by a single unit difference, c is the difference between the group means on Y: $c = [\overline{Y} \mid (X = x)] - [\overline{Y} \mid (X = x-1)]$. Regardless of whether X is dichotomous, the total effect of X on Y is equal to the sum of the direct and indirect effects of X:

$$c = c' + ab$$

This relationship can be rewritten as $ab = c - c'$, which provides another definition of the indirect effect. The indirect effect is the difference between the total effect of X on Y and the effect of X on Y controlling for M, the direct effect.

   The equivalence between the total effect of X and the sum of the direct and indirect effects can be illustrated by substituting equation 3.1 into equation 3.2, thereby expressing Y as a function of only X:

$$Y = i_Y + c'X + b(i_M + aX + e_M) + e_Y$$

which can be equivalently written as

$$Y = (i_Y + bi_M) + (ab + c')X + (e_Y + be_M) \tag{3.5}$$

Equation 3.5 is a simple linear function of X, just as is equation 3.4. In fact, equations 3.4 and 3.5 are identical if you make the following substitutions: $c = ab + c'$, $i_{Y*} = i_Y + bi_M$, and $e_{Y*} = (e_Y + be_M)$. So $ab + c'$ has the same interpretation as c. The sum of the direct and indirect effects quantifies how much two cases that differ by one unit on X are estimated to differ on Y.

   It is important to recognize that this mathematics, whereby $c = c' + ab$, applies when Y and M are estimated using OLS regression, meaning analyzed as continuous variables using the OLS criterion for maximizing fit of the model. It also works when using a maximum-likelihood-based model of continuous outcomes, such as when using a structural equation modeling program. It does not apply when using other modeling methods that deviate from what is known in the generalized linear modeling literature as an *identity link* in the model. For example, suppose your outcome variable is dichotomous or a three- or four-category ordinal variable and you use logistic or probit regression rather than OLS regression to estimate b, c, and c' in equations 3.2 and 3.4. In that case, c usually will not be equal to $c' + ab$. The inequality has given rise to a large literature in mediation analysis about how to partition an effect into direct and indirect components for such analytical problems. I do not address corresponding methods in this book, as this is a more advanced topic, but I elaborate on this point in the last chapter and provide some references.

3.3   Example with Dichotomous X: The Influence of Presumed Media Influence

To illustrate the estimation of direct and indirect effects in a simple mediation model, I use data from a study conducted in Israel by Tal-Or, Cohen, Tsfati, and Gunther (2010). The data file is named PMI and can be downloaded from *www.afhayes.com*. The participants in this study (43 male and 80 female students studying political science or communication at a university in Israel) read one of two newspaper articles describing an economic crisis that may affect the price and supply of sugar in Israel. Approximately half of the participants ($n = 58$) were given an article they were told would be appearing on the front page of a major Israeli newspaper (henceforth referred to as the *front page* condition). The remaining participants ($n = 65$) were given the same article but were told it would appear in the middle of an economic supplement of this newspaper (referred to here as the *interior page* condition). Which of the two articles any participant read was determined by random assignment. In all other respects, the participants in the study were treated equivalently, the instructions they were given were the same, and all measurement procedures were identical in both experimental conditions.

After the participants read the article, they were asked a number of questions about their reactions to the story. Some questions asked participants how soon they planned on buying sugar and how much they intended to buy. Their responses were aggregated to form an *intention to buy sugar* measure (REACTION in the data file), such that higher scores reflected greater intention to buy sugar (sooner and in larger quantities). They were also asked questions used to quantify how much they believed that others in the community would be prompted to buy sugar as a result of exposure to the article, a measure of *presumed media influence* (PMI in the data file).

Tal-Or et al. (2010) reasoned that relative to an article buried in the interior of a newspaper, an article published on the front page would prompt a belief that others are likely to be influenced by the possibility of a shortage and so would go out and buy sugar. This belief that others were going to respond in this way would, in turn, prompt the participant to believe he or she should also go out and buy sugar. That is, people would use their beliefs about how others would respond to the article anticipating a price

TABLE 3.1. Descriptive Statistics for Presumed Media Influence Study

		Y REACTION	M PMI	Y adjusted
Front page ($X = 1$)	Mean	3.746	5.853	3.616
	SD	1.452	1.267	
Interior page ($X = 0$)	Mean	3.250	5.377	3.362
	SD	1.608	1.338	
	Mean	3.484	5.602	
	SD	1.550	1.321	

increase and supply shortage as a guide to determining their own behavior (i.e.,"Others are going to buy up all the sugar, so I should act while I still can, before prices skyrocket and supplies disappear").

The statistical model is diagrammed in Figure 3.3, and the descriptive statistics for each variable in the two conditions can be found in Table 3.1. To estimate the effects of the manipulation (X in Figure 3.3, with the front page condition coded 1 and the interior page condition coded 0) on likelihood of buying sugar (Y in Figure 3.3), directly as well as indirectly through presumed media influence (M in Figure 3.3), the coefficients of two linear models defined by equations 3.1 and 3.2 can be generated using any OLS regression program. There are many statistical programs available that can estimate the coefficients of a model such as this with ease. For example, using the PMI data file, in SPSS the commands below estimate a, b, and c':

```
regression/dep=pmi/method=enter cond.
regression/dep=reaction/method=enter cond pmi.
```

The total effect (c) can be calculated as the sum of the direct and indirect effects from the resulting models, or with a third regression analysis:

```
regression/dep=reaction/method=enter cond.
```

In SAS, PROC REG implements ordinary least squares regression, and the commands below estimate the regression coefficients:

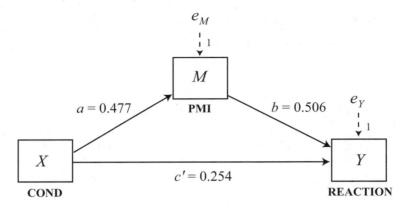

FIGURE 3.3. Simple mediation model for presumed media influence study in the form of a statistical diagram.

```
proc reg data=pmi;
    model pmi=cond;model reaction=cond pmi;model reaction=cond;
run;
```

The regression analysis is summarized in Table 3.2, and the regression coefficients are superimposed on the statistical diagram of the model in Figure 3.3. As can be seen, $a = 0.477$, $b = 0.506$, $c' = 0.254$. In terms of equations 3.1 and 3.2 but eliminating the error term and expressing in terms of estimated M and Y,

$$\hat{M} = 5.377 + 0.477X$$
$$\hat{Y} = 0.527 + 0.254X + 0.506M$$

The a coefficient tells us that two cases that differ by one unit on X are estimated to differ by $a = 0.477$ units on M. So those assigned to the front page condition ($X = 1$) are, on average, 0.477 units higher (because a is positive) in their presumed media influence than those assigned to the interior page condition ($X = 0$). As discussed earlier, because the groups are coded on X using a single unit difference, a is the difference between the group means on M: $a = [\overline{M} \mid (X = 1)] - [\overline{M} \mid (X = 0)]$. That is, $a = \overline{M}_{front} - \overline{M}_{interior} = 5.853 - 5.377 \approx 0.477$ (the difference between 0.477 and 0.476 is simply the result of rounding error producing by doing these computations by hand to only the third decimal place).

The regression coefficient for presumed media influence, $b = 0.506$, means that two people assigned to the same experimental condition (i.e., equal on X) but that differ by one unit in their presumed media influence (M) are estimated to differ by 0.506 units in intention to buy sugar (Y). That

TABLE 3.2. Model Coefficients for the Presumed Media Influence Study

Antecedent		Consequent						
		M (PMI)				Y (REACTION)		
		Coeff.	SE	p		Coeff.	SE	p
X (COND)	a	0.477	0.236	.045	c'	0.254	0.256	.322
M (PMI)		—	—	—	b	0.506	0.097	$<.001$
Constant	i_M	5.377	0.162	$<.001$	i_Y	0.527	0.550	.340
		$R^2 = 0.033$				$R^2 = 0.206$		
		$F(1, 121) = 4.088, p = .045$				$F(2, 120) = 15.557, p < .001$		

is, $b = [\hat{Y} \mid (M = m, X = x)] - [\hat{Y} \mid (M = m - 1, X = x)]$. The sign of b is positive, meaning that those relatively higher in presumed media influence are estimated to be relatively higher in their intentions to buy sugar.

The indirect effect is quantified as the product of the effect of the manipulation of article location on presumed media influence (a) and the effect of presumed media influence on intentions to buy sugar when article location is held fixed (b). Doing the math by multiplying these two coefficients yields the indirect effect of the manipulation of article location on intentions to buy sugar through presumed media influence: $ab = 0.477(0.506) = 0.241$. So relative to those assigned to the interior page condition, those who read an article they were told was to be published in the front page of the newspaper were, on average, 0.241 units higher in their likelihood of buying sugar as a result of the effect of the location of the article on presumed media influence which, in turn, putatively affected people's intentions to buy sugar.

The estimated direct effect of the location of the article on likelihood of buying sugar is $c' = 0.254$. That is, two cases that differ by one unit on X but are equal on M are estimated to differ by 0.254 units on Y. Because the two groups were coded such that they differ by one unit on X, substantively, we can say that independent of the effect of presumed media influence on likelihood of buying sugar (because M is being held constant in the derivation of c'), participants assigned to the front page condition ($X = 1$) are estimated to be 0.254 units higher on average in their likelihood of buying sugar than those assigned to the interior page condition ($X = 0$). That is, $[\overline{Y} \mid (X = 1, M = m)] - [\overline{Y} \mid (X = 0, M = m)] = 0.254$.

We could put specific values on these two means by selecting a value of M at which to condition Y and then estimate Y from X and M using equation 3.2. A sensible choice is to condition on being average on the mediator, which produces the *adjusted means* for Y (see Table 3.1), denoted here as $\overline{Y}^*$:

$$\overline{Y}^* = i_Y + b\overline{M} + c'X \qquad (3.6)$$

For instance, those assigned to the front page condition ($X = 1$) but who are average ($\overline{M} = 5.602$) in their presumed media influence are estimated to have a score of

$$\overline{Y}^* = 0.527 + 0.506(5.602) + 0.254(1) = 3.616$$

on average, on the intentions measure. In contrast, those assigned to the interior page condition ($X = 0$) who are average in presumed media influence are estimated to have a score of

$$\overline{Y}^* = 0.527 + 0.506(5.602) + 0.254(0) = 3.362$$

on average in their intentions. This difference between these two adjusted means is, of course, 0.254 and is independent of the choice of M at which the estimations of Y are derived.

The total effect of the manipulation on intentions to buy sugar can be derived by summing the direct and indirect effects. In this case, the total effect is $c' + ab = 0.254 + 0.241 = 0.495$, meaning those who read the article they were told was to be published on the front page were, on average, 0.495 units higher in their intention to buy sugar than those told it would be published in the interior of the newspaper. In a simple mediation model such as this, the total effect of X can be estimated merely by regressing Y on X alone, without M in the model. The coefficient for X is the total effect, and it corresponds to the difference between the means of the two groups (i.e., $\overline{Y}_{\text{front}} - \overline{Y}_{\text{interior}} = 3.746 - 3.250 = 0.496$), which is c (within expected rounding error produced by hand computation).

When X is a dichotomous variable coded by a one-unit difference, and assuming in the equation below that X is coded 0 and 1 for the two groups, the relationship between the total, direct, and indirect effects can be expressed in terms of differences between the means of the two groups along with the effect of M on Y controlling for X:

$$\underbrace{(\overline{Y}_{X=1} - \overline{Y}_{X=0})}_{\text{Total effect } (c)} = \underbrace{(\overline{Y}^*_{X=1} - \overline{Y}^*_{X=0})}_{\text{Direct effect } (c')} + \underbrace{(\overline{M}_{X=1} - \overline{M}_{X=0})\, b}_{\text{Indirect effect } (ab)}$$

Substituting statistics from the previous analysis,

$$\underbrace{(3.746 - 3.250)}_{\text{Total effect } (c)} = \underbrace{(3.616 - 3.362)}_{\text{Direct effect } (c')} + \underbrace{(5.853 - 5.377)\,0.506}_{\text{Indirect effect } (ab)}$$

Estimation of the Model in PROCESS for SPSS and SAS

Throughout this book I will rely on a handy tool I created for SPSS and SAS called PROCESS, instructions on the use of which can be found in Appendices A and B and in various places in this book when appropriate. One of the features of PROCESS is that it can estimate the regression coefficients in a simple mediation model such as this, as well as in more complex models involving two or more mediators, while providing an estimate of the indirect effect, various inferential tests, and additional information to be discussed later. Furthermore, it can be used for moderation analysis and modeling that combines moderation and mediation. The SPSS version of the PROCESS command for the analysis just conducted is

```
process y=reaction/x=cond/m=pmi/total=1/normal=1/model=4/seed=31216.
```

In SAS, the equivalent command is

```
%process (data=pmi,y=reaction,x=cond,m=pmi,total=1,normal=1,model=4,
    seed=31216);
```

Output from the SPSS version of PROCESS can be found in Figure 3.4. Using OLS regression, PROCESS model 4 estimates equations 3.1 and 3.2 and thereby provides a, b, and c' along with standard regression statistics such as R^2 for each of the equations. It also creates a section of output containing the direct and indirect effects of X. The **total=1** option generates output for c, the total effect of X on Y. Additional options in this command and other features of PROCESS will be revealed as necessary throughout this book and are also described in the documentation in Appendices A and B.

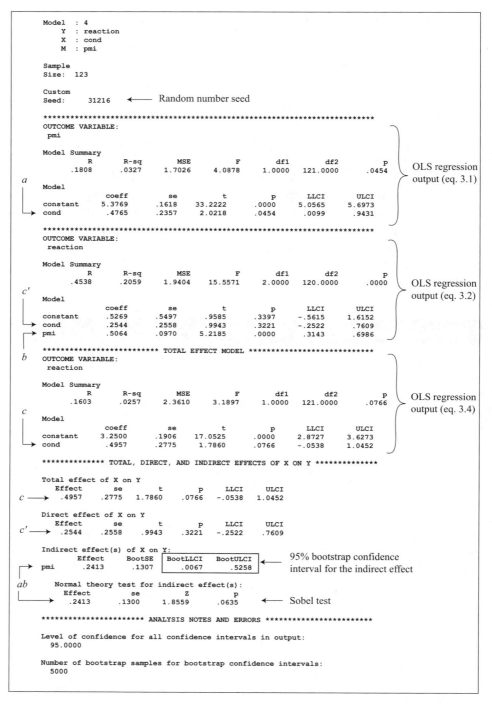

FIGURE 3.4. Output from the PROCESS procedure for SPSS for the presumed media influence simple mediation analysis.

3.4 Statistical Inference

The previous section was dedicated to describing how the effect of X on Y in a simple mediation model can be partitioned into direct and indirect components. When these effects are estimated using OLS regression, it will always be true in any data set that $c = c' + ab$. But these effects as represented by c, c', and ab are sample-specific instantiations of their true values $_Tc$, $_Tc'$, and $_Ta_Tb$. They describe the association between variables in the data available, but they say nothing about generalizability. Typically, investigators are interested in generalizability, either by seeing whether "chance" can be discounted as a plausible explanation for the obtained effect by conducting a hypothesis test, or by acknowledging the sampling variance inherent in any estimate through the construction of an interval estimate for these effects. Inference about the direct, indirect, and total effects of X is the topic of this section.

Inference about the Total Effect of X on Y

In a simple mediation model, the total effect of X on Y is the sum of the direct effect of X on Y and indirect effect of X on Y through M. Whereas there are many choices available for inferences about the indirect effect, inference for the total effect is simple and straightforward. Although the total effect is the sum of two pathways of influence, it can be estimated by regressing Y on just X, without M in the model. The regression coefficient for X in that model, c in equation 3.4, is the total effect of X. Inference can be framed in terms of a null hypothesis test ($H_0 : {}_Tc = 0$ versus the alternative $H_a : {}_Tc \neq 0$) or whether an interval estimate for $_Tc$ includes zero.

The mechanics of both procedures are described in section 2.6. Any OLS regression program provides the output necessary to implement both approaches, as does the PROCESS procedure with the use of the **total** option. The **total** option in PROCESS is one of many "toggle" options, meaning that PROCESS will either do it (when the argument is set to 1) or not (when the argument is set to 0). So adding **total=1** to the PROCESS command line tells SPSS to show the model that generates the total effect of X on Y in a section of the output. The default argument is zero, meaning that if you just leave out the **total** option entirely, PROCESS will not show this model generating the total effect of X.

Because we asked for it, you can find the total effect in the PROCESS output in Figure 3.4 under the section labeled "Total effect of X on Y" or in the model information under "Total Effect Model." As can be seen, the total effect is $c = 0.496$ but it just misses statistical significance using an

$\alpha = 0.05$ decision criterion, $t(121) = 1.786, p = 0.077$. With 95% confidence, $_Tc$ resides somewhere between -0.054 and 1.045.

Inference about the Direct Effect of X on Y

The direct effect quantifies the estimated difference in Y between two cases that are equal on M but differ by one unit on X. Inference for the direct effect of X on Y in a mediation analysis is typically undertaken using the standard method used for inference for any regression coefficient in a regression model. This involves testing a null hypothesis about $_Tc'$ against an alternative hypothesis or the construction of a confidence interval for $_Tc'$. Except in unusual circumstances, researchers focus on ascertaining whether a claim that $_Tc'$ is different from zero is justified based on the data available. If so, this supports the argument that X is related to Y independent of the mechanism represented by M. If not, one can claim that there is no evidence of association between X and Y when the mechanism through M is accounted for. In other words, X does not affect Y independent of M's effect on Y.

In terms of a null hypothesis, this means testing $H_0 : _Tc' = 0$ against the alternative $H_a : _Tc' \neq 0$. Framed in terms of a confidence interval, this involves determining whether an interval estimate for $_Tc'$ includes zero. The mechanics of both procedures are described in section 2.6. Any OLS regression program provides the output necessary to implement both approaches, as does the PROCESS procedure.

In the presumed media influence study, is there evidence of a direct effect of the placement of the sugar shortage article on intentions to buy sugar? The answer to this question can be found in two locations in the PROCESS output in Figure 3.4. In the section labeled "Total, Direct, and Indirect Effects of X on Y" is the direct effect along with its standard error, t-value, p-value, and 95% confidence interval. This information is also found in the section labeled "Outcome Variable: reaction" in the row labeled "cond," which is the variable name for the experimental manipulation. As can be seen, the direct effect is not statistically different from zero, $c' = 0.254, t(120) = 0.994, p = .322$. The null hypothesis that $_Tc' = 0$ cannot be rejected. The interval estimate for $_Tc'$ is -0.252 to 0.761 with 95% confidence. This confidence interval does include zero, so zero cannot be confidently ruled out as a plausible value for the direct effect. Of course, the hypothesis test and confidence interval lead to the same inference, as they are just different ways of packaging the same information.

Inference about the Indirect Effect of *X* on *Y* through *M*

The indirect effect quantifies how much two cases that differ by a unit on *X* are estimated to differ on *Y* as a result of *X*'s influence on *M*, which in turn influences *Y*. The indirect effect is relevant as to whether *X*'s effect on *Y* can be said to be transmitted through the mechanism represented by the $X \to M \to Y$ causal chain of events. As with the direct effect, investigators typically want to know whether the data allow for the claim that this estimated difference in *Y* attributable to this mechanism can be said to be different from zero. If so, one can claim *M* serves as a mediator of the effect of *X* on *Y*. As with inference about the direct effect, this inference can be formulated in terms of a null hypothesis test about $_T a_T b$ or by constructing an interval estimate.

In this section I describe only a few of the approaches to statistical inference for the indirect effect that have been proposed. There are many more available, and new ones are always being introduced in the methodology literature. The ones on which I focus here have been used widely in the past or have become popular recently, and so they are worth emphasizing. For a discussion of some of the approaches I neglect here, see Biesanz, Falk, and Savalei (2010), Falk and Biesanz (2016), MacKinnon et al. (2002), MacKinnon (2008), Preacher and Hayes (2008b), Preacher and Selig (2012), and Yuan and MacKinnon (2009).

The Normal Theory Approach. Also called the *product of coefficients* approach to inference, the *Sobel test*, and the *delta method*, the normal theory approach is based on the same theory of inference used for inference about the total and direct effect and many other inferential tests described in elementary statistics books. With an estimate of the standard error of *ab* and assuming the sampling distribution of *ab* is normal, a *p*-value for *ab* can be derived given a specific null hypothesized value of $_T a_T b$, or an interval estimate can be generated.

Before the normal theory approach can be implemented, an estimate of the standard error of *ab* is needed. There are a few such estimators circulating in the literature that have been used in mediation analysis (see, e.g., Aroian, 1947; Baron & Kenny, 1986; Goodman, 1960; MacKinnon, Warsi, & Dwyer, 1995; Sobel, 1982), and they are all a function of *a* and *b* and their standard errors. One known as the *second order* standard error is

$$se_{ab} = \sqrt{a^2 se_b^2 + b^2 se_a^2 + se_a^2 se_b^2} \qquad (3.7)$$

where se_a^2 and se_b^2 are the squared standard errors of *a* and *b*, respectively. All the information needed to calculate se_{ab} is available in whatever program you might use to estimate *a* and *b*. No special software is otherwise needed.

For instance, from the presumed media influence results in Table 3.2, $a = 0.477$, $b = 0.506$, $se_a = 0.236$, and $se_b = 0.097$. Plugging this information into equation 3.7 yields the second-order estimate of the standard error of the indirect effect

$$se_{ab} = \sqrt{0.477^2 0.097^2 + 0.506^2 0.236^2 + 0.236^2 0.097^2} = 0.130$$

With an estimate of the standard error of the indirect effect, the null hypothesis that $_Ta_Tb = 0$ can be tested against the alternative that $_Ta_Tb \neq 0$ by taking the ratio of ab to its standard error,

$$Z = \frac{ab}{se_{ab}},$$

and deriving the proportion of the standard normal distribution more extreme than $\pm Z$. For the indirect effect in the presumed media influence study, $Z = 0.241/0.130 = 1.854$. A table of two-tailed normal probabilities for $Z = 1.854$ yields $p = .064$. This test results in a failure to reject the null hypothesis of no indirect effect using an $\alpha = 0.05$ decision criterion, although some might be comfortable talking about this as "marginally significant" evidence of a positive indirect effect.

If you prefer confidence intervals over null hypothesis testing, the standard error of ab can be used to generate an interval estimate for $_Ta_Tb$ by assuming normality of the sampling distribution of ab and applying equation 3.8:

$$ab - Z_{ci\%}se_{ab} \leq {}_Ta_Tb \leq ab + Z_{ci\%}se_{ab} \tag{3.8}$$

where ci is the confidence desired (e.g., 95) and $Z_{ci\%}$ is the value of the standard normal distribution above which $(100 - ci)/2\%$ percent of the distribution resides. For a 95% confidence interval, $Z = 1.96$. Thus,

$$0.241 - 1.96(0.130) \leq {}_Ta_Tb \leq 0.241 + 1.96(0.130)$$

$$-0.014 \leq {}_Ta_Tb \leq 0.496$$

So we can be 95% confident that $_Ta_Tb$ is somewhere between -0.014 and 0.496. As with the null hypothesis test, zero cannot be ruled out as a plausible value for $_Ta_Tb$, meaning we cannot say definitively that the indirect effect of the location of the article on intentions to buy sugar through presumed media influence is different from zero. In other words, we cannot claim that presumed media influence is functioning as a mediator of the effect of X on Y according to the normal theory approach to inference about the indirect effect.

The normal theory approach can be conducted by hand fairly easily, and most good structural equation modeling (SEM) programs conduct this test in some form automatically when estimating a simple mediation model. Outside of an SEM program, most statistical software packages require special add-ons or macros to conduct this test. PROCESS will conduct this test with the use of the **normal** option. The relevant section of output from PROCESS can be found in Figure 3.4 under the section labeled "Normal theory test for indirect effect(s)."

The normal theory approach suffers from two flaws that make it difficult to recommend. First, this method assumes that the sampling distribution of ab is normal. But it has been shown analytically and through simulation that the distribution is irregular in sample sizes that characterize most empirical studies (Bollen & Stine, 1990; Craig, 1936; Stone & Sobel, 1990). Because it is never possible to know for certain whether the sampling distribution is close enough to normal given the characteristics of one's problem to safely apply a method that assumes normality, it is desirable to use a test that does not require this assumption.

Second, simulation research that has compared this approach to various competing inferential methods has shown that it is one of the lowest in power and generates confidence intervals that tend to be less accurate than some methods described next (Hayes & Scharkow, 2013; MacKinnon, Lockwood, & Williams, 2004). If X does influence Y indirectly through M, the normal theory approach is less likely to detect it than competing alternatives. For these two reasons, I recommend you avoid this approach. For the simple mediation model, and in fact all models discussed in this book, it is always possible to employ a better alternative. I describe a few of those alternatives next.

Bootstrap Confidence Interval. As a member of a class of procedures known as *resampling methods*, bootstrapping has been around for decades. It was made possible by the advent of high-speed computing, and as computer power has increased while the expense of that power has declined, bootstrapping is being implemented in modern statistical software with increasing frequency. Bootstrapping is a versatile method that can be applied to many inferential problems a researcher might confront. It is especially useful when the behavior of a statistic over repeated sampling is either not known, too complicated to derive, or highly context dependent. I will not go into all the subtle details about bootstrapping, as there are good articles and entire books devoted to this topic and variations. For very readable overviews, see Good (2001), Lunneborg (2000), Mooney and Duval (1993), Rodgers (1999) and Wood (2005).

Regardless of the inferential problem, the essence of bootstrapping remains constant across applications. The original sample of size n is treated as a miniature representation of the population originally sampled. Observations in this sample are then "resampled" *with replacement*, and some statistic of interest is calculated in the new sample of size n constructed through this resampling process. Repeated over and over—thousands of times ideally—a representation of the sampling distribution of the statistic is constructed empirically, and this empirical representation is used for the inferential task at hand.

In mediation analysis, bootstrapping is used to generate an empirically derived representation of the sampling distribution of the indirect effect, and this empirical representation is used for the construction of a confidence interval for $_Ta_Tb$. Unlike the normal theory approach, no assumption is made about the shape of the sampling distribution of ab. Bootstrap confidence intervals better respect the irregularity of the sampling distribution of ab and, as a result, yield inferences that are more likely to be accurate than when the normal theory approach is used. When used to test a hypothesis, the result is a test with higher power than the normal theory approach.

There are six steps involved in the construction of a bootstrap confidence interval for $_Ta_Tb$:

1. Take a random sample of n cases from the original sample, sampling those cases *with replacement*, where n is the size of the original sample. This is called a *bootstrap sample*.

2. Estimate the indirect effect ab^* in the bootstrap sample, where ab^* is the product of a and b from equations 3.1 and 3.2.

3. Repeat (1) and (2) above a total of k times, where k is some large number, saving the value of ab^* each time. Generally, k of at least a few thousand is preferred. More than 10,000 typically is not necessary, but in principle, the more the better. I use 5,000 in all examples in this book.

4. Sort the k indirect effects ab^* estimated from steps (1), (2), and (3) from low to high.

5. For a $ci\%$ confidence interval, find the value of ab^* in this distribution of k estimates that defines the $0.5(100 - ci)$th percentile of the distribution. This is the lower bound of a $ci\%$ confidence interval. It will be the value of ab^* in ordinal position $0.005k(100 - ci)$ of the sorted distribution.

6. Find the value of ab^* in this distribution of k estimates that defines the $[100 - 0.5(100 - ci)]$th percentile of the distribution. This is the upper bound of a $ci\%$ confidence interval. It will be the value of ab^* in ordinal position $k[1 - 0.005(100 - ci)] + 1$ of the sorted distribution.

To illustrate steps (1), (2), and (3) of this bootstrap sampling and estimation process, Table 3.3 provides a small-scale example. Suppose you have a sample of $n = 10$ cases in a study measured on variables X, M, and Y,

TABLE 3.3. Bootstrap Estimates of a, b, and the Indirect Effect ab When Taking Two Bootstrap Samples from an Original Sample of Size $n = 10$

Original sample				Bootstrap sample 1				Bootstrap sample 2			
Case	X	M	Y	Case	X	M	Y	Case	X	M	Y
1	0	1.500	3.000	4	0	2.500	4.500	10	1	5.000	5.000
2	0	2.000	2.750	8	1	3.000	3.750	3	0	1.000	3.500
3	0	1.000	3.500	2	0	2.000	2.750	7	1	2.500	2.250
4	0	2.500	4.500	3	0	1.000	3.500	5	0	4.500	4.750
5	0	4.000	4.750	1	0	1.500	3.000	6	1	4.500	4.500
6	1	4.500	4.500	2	0	2.000	2.750	8	1	3.000	3.750
7	1	2.500	2.250	6	1	4.500	4.500	8	1	3.000	3.750
8	1	3.000	3.750	8	1	3.000	3.750	4	0	2.500	4.500
9	1	1.500	2.500	5	0	4.000	4.750	10	1	5.000	5.000
10	1	5.000	5.000	9	1	1.500	2.500	2	0	2.000	2.750
a		1.100		a		0.833		a		1.458	
b		0.700		b		0.631		b		0.713	
ab		0.770		ab^*		0.526		ab^*		1.039	

and you want to generate a bootstrap sampling distribution of the indirect effect of X on Y through M. Using the original data in the leftmost columns of the table, the obtained indirect effect is $ab = 0.770$. This is a point estimate of $_Ta_Tb$. A bootstrap confidence interval for $_Ta_Tb$ is constructed by repeatedly taking a random sample of size n from the original sample, with replacement, and estimating the indirect effect in each resample. The middle columns of Table 3.3 contain one such bootstrap sample, which yields an indirect effect of $ab^* = 0.526$. The rightmost columns contain a second bootstrap sample with an indirect effect of $ab^* = 1.039$. As this process is repeated over and over, a distribution of ab^* is built which functions as an empirical proxy for the unknown sampling distribution of ab when taking a random sample of size n from the original population.

This table also illustrates the meaning of random resampling with replacement. Notice in bootstrap sample 1 that cases 2 and 8 from the original sample both appear twice, but by the luck of the draw, cases 7 and 10 do not appear at all. Similarly, bootstrap sample 2 has cases 8 and 10 from the original sample appearing twice, but cases 1 and 9 never appear. That is the nature of random resampling with replacement. This process allows a case to appear multiple times in a bootstrap sample and is necessary in order to mimic the original sampling process, which is the goal of bootstrap sampling. Suppose case 1 in the original sample is "Joe." Joe happened to be contacted for participation in the study and provided data to the effort. In the resampling process, Joe functions as a stand-in for himself and *anyone else like him* in the pool of potential research participants, as defined by Joe's measurements on the variables in the model. The original sampling could have sampled several Joes or none, depending in part on the luck of the draw. The random resampling process is thus akin to repeating the study over and over again but using the data from those who originally provided data to the study in those replications rather than collecting data on a new set of people. Although it may seem like it on the surface, this is not cheating or creating fake data or falsely inflating one's sample size. It is merely a clever means of ascertaining how *ab* varies from sample to sample without having to actually sample repeatedly from the original population but, instead, replicating the sampling process by treating the original sample as a representation of the population.

Steps (5) and (6) are generic ways of describing how the endpoints of a confidence interval are constructed given k bootstrap estimates of the indirect effect. A specific example will help. If a $ci = 95\%$ confidence interval is desired, the lower and upper bounds of the interval are defined as the bootstrap values of ab^* that define the 2.5th and 97.5th percentiles in the distribution of k values of ab^*. Suppose $k = 10,000$. In that case, after sorting the 10,000 values of ab^* obtained from repeated bootstrap sampling from low to high, the 2.5th and 97.5th percentiles of the distribution will be in ordinal positions $0.005(10,000)(100 - 95) = 250$ and $(10,000)[1 - 0.005(100 - 95)] + 1 = 9,751$ in the sorted list, respectively. These are the lower and upper bounds of the 95% confidence interval for $_Ta_Tb$.

Obviously, this is a computationally intensive process that requires a computer. Fortunately, it is not difficult to do, as bootstrapping is either hardwired into some data analysis programs (e.g., Mplus) or special code can be written to implement this approach in many popularly used programs, SPSS and SAS among them. The PROCESS macro will automatically construct a bootstrap confidence interval for any indirect effect it generates in any model it can estimate. Furthermore, using the **save** function and writing a little extra code, you can visualize the bootstrap distribution of the indirect effects.

As can be seen in the PROCESS output in Figure 3.4, a 95% bootstrap confidence interval for the indirect effect of article location on reactions through presumed media influence, using 5,000 bootstrap samples, is 0.007 to 0.526 (under the headings "BootLLCI" and "BootULCI"). So 2.5% of the 5,000 bootstrap estimate were smaller than 0.007, 2.5% were larger than

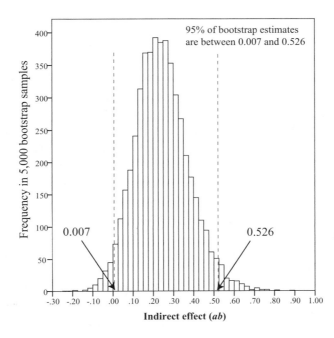

FIGURE 3.5. A histogram of 5,000 bootstrap estimates of the indirect effect in the pre-sumed media influence study.

0.526. As this confidence interval is entirely above zero, this supports the conclusion that the indirect effect is positive. Although it is not technically correct to say that one can reject the null hypothesis that $_Ta_Tb = 0$ with a p-value of no greater than .05, in practice the interpretation of the confidence interval leads to essentially the same substantive claim. There is clear evidence that the indirect effect is positive to a "statistically significant" degree.[1] PROCESS also provides a bootstrap estimate of the standard error of the indirect effect under the heading "Boot SE." This is the standard deviation of the 5,000 bootstrap estimates of the indirect effect.

A visual depiction of the 5,000 bootstrap estimates of ab can be found in Figure 3.5. Although it may not be apparent at first glance, the distri-bution is not normal. It has a slight skew and also is more peaked than a normal distribution. Indeed, a hypothesis test leads to a rejection of the null hypothesis of normality, with evidence of positive skew and kurtosis.

By default, PROCESS generates bootstrap confidence intervals for in-direct effects using 5,000 bootstrap samples. But this can be changed using

[1]A p-value from a null hypothesis test is calculated conditioned on the assumption that the null hypothesis is true. Because a bootstrap confidence interval is not derived based on any assumption about the size of $_Ta_Tb$, it is not correct to say that $p < .05$ if a 95% confidence interval does not include zero.

the **boot** option, specifying the number of bootstrap samples following an equals sign. For example, for 10,000 bootstrap samples, add **boot=10000** to the PROCESS command. And if you prefer a 90% or a 99% confidence interval instead of a 95% confidence interval (the default), PROCESS allows you to change the confidence level for *all* confidence intervals in the output through the **conf** option. For example, for 90% confidence intervals, add **conf=90** to the PROCESS command. Note that bootstrapping is used only for the production of confidence intervals for indirect effects, unless you tell PROCESS to do otherwise. All other confidence intervals in the PRO-CESS output are just ordinary confidence intervals generated as described in section 2.6.[2]

A bootstrap confidence interval calculated using the approach just described is called a *percentile* bootstrap confidence interval, because it is based entirely on values of ab^* that demarcate the upper and lower $(100-ci)/2\%$ of the distribution of k bootstrap estimates of the indirect effect. Alternative approaches to the construction of bootstrap confidence intervals include *bias-correction* and *bias-correction and acceleration*. Bias-corrected bootstrap confidence intervals are like percentile confidence intervals but the endpoints are adjusted as a function of the proportion of k values of ab^* that are less than ab, the point estimate of the indirect effect calculated in the original data. The endpoints will be adjusted upward or downward to varying degrees depending on that proportion. For the acceleration component, an additional adjustment is made based on the skew of the distribution of k bootstrap estimates. The mechanics of the construction of bias-corrected and bias-corrected and accelerated bootstrap confidence intervals can be found in Efron (1987), Efron and Tibshirani (1993), Lunneborg (2000), and Preacher and Selig (2012).

Although the percentile bootstrap confidence interval is the inferential approach I emphasize in this book, it is not without its pitfalls and criticisms, and these are worth acknowledging. First, in order to have much confidence in bootstrap-based inference, it is clearly important that one is able to muster some faith in the quality of one's sample as a reasonable representation of the population distribution of the measured variables. Bootstrapping is founded on the notion that resampling with replacement from one's sample mimics the original sampling process. But if the sample does not adequately represent the population from which the sample was derived, then bootstrapping will produce results that are hard to trust. It is not required that the original sample be obtained randomly from the population, but merely that the distribution of the measured variables roughly

---

[2]The **modelbt** option in PROCESS produces bootstrap confidence intervals for all the regression coefficients. See Appendix A for details.

mirrors the population distributions. Random sampling facilitates this representativeness, of course, but it isn't required.

Second, bootstrapping is particularly useful relative to the normal theory approach in smaller samples, because it is in smaller samples that the non-normality of the sampling distribution of ab is likely to be most severe, the large sample asymptotics of the normal theory approach are harder to trust, and the power advantages of bootstrapping are more pronounced. But if the original sample is *very* small, in principle at least, it is possible that one or two cases that are unusual in some way could distort a bootstrap analysis even more than they do a more traditional inferential procedure. Alternatively, it is possible that bootstrapping may be *better* than other methods in small samples with outliers. Indeed, some of my as of yet unpublished simulation research suggests that bootstrap confidence intervals may be preferred even in small samples with outliers. But more research on this is needed.

Third, because bootstrap confidence intervals are based on random resampling of the data, the endpoints of the confidence interval are not fixed quantities. Rather, each time a bootstrap confidence interval is produced from the same data, a slightly different confidence interval will result. This is bothersome to some people, for ideally two people analyzing the same data using the same method should get exactly the same results. It also could lead to wrongdoing by unscrupulous investigators who simply repeat a bootstrap analysis until a desired result is obtained.

This latter criticism, while legitimate, can be rebutted on the grounds that the sampling variation from analysis to analysis can be made arbitrarily small simply by setting the number of bootstrap samples to a very large number. This raises the question as to how many bootstrap samples is enough. It can be shown that the variation in the estimation of the limits of a confidence interval shrinks remarkably quickly as the number of bootstrap samples increases. Generally speaking, 5,000 to 10,000 bootstrap samples is sufficient in most applications. There is relatively little added value to increasing it above 10,000, as the gain in precision is fairly marginal beyond that. That said, given the speed of today's desktop computing technology, it is not difficult to use a much larger number to keep the variation due to the random resampling process to an absolute minimum. Do 100,000 bootstrap samples, or even 1,000,000 if you want. Let your computer work on the problem while you get a cup of coffee or take a nap.

An alternative way around this problem of the confidence interval as a moving target is called *seeding the random number generator*. Bootstrapping randomly samples the rows of the data file based on information fed to the bootstrapping algorithm by a random number generator. But no random number generator actually generates entirely random numbers. For this reason, random number generators are typically called *pseudo* random number generators. They generate a long sequence of numbers by a systematic algorithm that will eventually repeat itself. When you seed a random number generator, you are telling the generator where to start in the sequence. If you use the same seed twice, each time pulling, say, 5,000 draws from the generator, then the generator will produce the same sequence of 5,000 "random" numbers both times.

PROCESS allows you to seed the random number generator for bootstrapping using the **seed** option. Use any number for the seed you want. In the command on page 91, I used 31216, which happens to be the date I conducted this analysis in day, month, year format (the 3rd of December, 2016). As a result, each time I run this PROCESS command, so long as the order of the rows in the data remains fixed and I don't change the number of bootstrap samples, PROCESS will always generate the same bootstrap confidence interval for the indirect effect. PROCESS will display the seed used at the top of the output, in case you forget what seed you used. If you choose not to use a seed, PROCESS will use a randomly chosen seed, and there is no way of determining what that seed is and so the seed is not displayed in the PROCESS output.

You may find that if you use 31216 as the seed and do the same analysis I report using your version of SPSS or SAS using the PMI data file, you will also get the same bootstrap confidence interval in Figure 3.4. Remarkably, I have found that the seed generalizes across versions of SPSS, and even between SAS and SPSS. So if you give your data to a colleague and provide the seed used for the random number generator, he or she should be able to replicate your results exactly. This may not always be true, as software sometimes changes from version to version, and if the companies decide to change the random number generator used, or if the different programs use different random number generators, then the results using a common seed may not generalize across platforms, versions, or time.

I think it is a good idea to get in the habit of seeding the random number generator when using bootstrapping for inference. This gets around the problem with the confidence interval changing each time you conduct the same analysis, something some people find disturbing. And often we do multiple analyses of the same data, with bootstrapping used in each analysis. If you use the same seed in each analysis, you know that the bootstrap results in each analysis are based on the same set of bootstrap samples.

Alternative "Asymmetric" Confidence Interval Approaches. Observe that the upper and lower bounds of the 95% bootstrap confidence interval calculated earlier are not equidistant from the point estimate of 0.241. The lower bound is $0.241 - 0.007 = 0.234$ units away from the point estimate, and the upper bound is $0.526 - 0.241 = 0.285$ units away. This is not due to the random resampling process but instead reflects the actual asymmetry of the sampling distribution of ab. Confidence intervals (and p-values) based on the normal theory approach to inference, by contrast, impose a symmetry constraint on this distance. The endpoints of a 95% confidence interval using equation 3.8 are necessarily 1.96 standard errors from the point estimate. The endpoints are symmetrical around the point estimate. Thus, percentile bootstrap confidence intervals are called "asymmetric," whereas normal theory confidence intervals are "symmetric." Asymmetric approaches to interval estimation are preferred when the sampling distribution of the estimator is asymmetric, as is usually the case for the sampling distribution of ab.

Bootstrapping is not the only approach to the construction of asymmetric confidence intervals. *Monte Carlo confidence intervals*, like bootstrapping, are simulation-based. This approach relies on the fact that though the distribution of ab is not normal, the sampling distributions of a and b tend to be nearly so. Furthermore, in simple mediation analysis using OLS regression, a and b are independent across repeated sampling (i.e., their covariance is zero). Thus, an empirical approximation of the sampling distribution of ab can be generated by randomly sampling values of a and b from normally distributed populations with $\mu = a$, $\sigma = se_a$ and $\mu = b$, $\sigma = se_b$, respectively, where a, b, se_a, and se_b are the OLS regression coefficients and standard errors from the mediation analysis. The sampled values of a and b are then multiplied together to produce ab^*, and this process is repeated k times. Over the k replications, the upper and lower bounds of the confidence interval for ab can be generated using the procedure described in steps (4) through (6) on page 98. A generic discussion of the Monte Carlo approach to interval estimation can be found in Buckland (1984). MacKinnon et al. (2004) and Preacher and Selig (2012) further describe the application of this approach to mediation analysis. PROCESS implements the Monte Carlo approach through the **mc** option, as described in Appendix A. Appendix C describes another tool in the form of a macro for SPSS and SAS that could be used to generate a Monte Carlo confidence interval even when you don't have the original data, as PROCESS requires.

The *distribution of the product* approach relies on a mathematical approximation of the sampling distribution of the product. This complex method defies nonmathematical description. Suffice it to say that it requires a transformation of ab to a standardized metric, finding the values of the standardized metric that define the upper and lower bounds of the

TABLE 3.4. 95% Confidence Intervals for the Indirect Effect in the Presumed Media Influence Study

Method	Lower Limit	Upper Limit
Normal theory	−0.014	0.496
Percentile bootstrap	0.007	0.526
Monte Carlo	0.008	0.514
Distribution of the product	0.011	0.514

confidence interval for the indirect effect in the standardized metric, and then converting these endpoints back into the original metric of *ab*. Like the Monte Carlo method, all that it needed to implement this approach is *a*, *b*, se_a, and se_b from the mediation analysis. The original data are not needed. For a discussion of this method, see MacKinnon, Fritz, Williams, and Lockwood (2007). Tofighi and MacKinnon (2011) provide R code that implements this approach, as well as Monte Carlo confidence intervals.

Simulation research shows the distribution of product and Monte Carlo confidence interval approaches work pretty well by the standards of relative validity and power, but they are largely exchangeable in that they rarely produce different inferences (Hayes & Scharkow, 2013). Neither approach requires the original data like bootstrapping does. But the product of coefficients approach yields endpoints that are fixed rather than varying randomly as a result of the bootstrapping or the Monte Carlo simulation process.

Does Method Really Matter? In this section I have described four inferential tests for indirect effects. If you were to apply all of these methods to the same data, you will typically find that it makes no difference which method you use, as they tend to produce the same substantive inference about the indirect effect. But sometimes they will disagree, as demonstrated in Table 3.4. This raises the question as to whether there is one better test among them or one that you should trust more than others, especially when they disagree. There is much research comparing the relative performance of these tests (e.g., Biesanz et al., 2010; Fritz & MacKinnon, 2007; Fritz, Taylor, & MacKinnon, 2012; Hayes & Scharkow, 2013; MacKinnon et al., 2004; Preacher & Selig, 2012; Williams & MacKinnon, 2008), and that research says that the answer to this question depends on your relative concern about Type I (claiming an indirect effect exists when it does not) and Type II (failing to detect an indirect effect that is real) errors.

Although the Sobel test (i.e., the normal theory approach) is conservative relative to other methods, if you are very concerned about Type I errors, it can be a good choice. But the power cost of this conservativeness is likely to be too high for most to tolerate. You are more likely to miss an indirect effect that is real using the Sobel test. So as noted earlier, I recommend avoiding it. The bootstrap confidence interval tends to have higher power than the Sobel test. In principle, bias-corrected and bias-corrected and accelerated bootstrap confidence intervals should be better than those generated with the simpler percentile method. However, there is evidence that the bias correction (with or without the acceleration component) can slightly inflate the likelihood of a Type I error when either $_Ta$ or $_Tb$ is zero (see, e.g., Fritz et al., 2012; Hayes & Scharkow, 2013). Unfortunately, you can never know whether $_Ta$ or $_Tb$ is zero, so it is difficult to use these findings to guide your decision about whether to employ a bias correction method. Regardless, if this elevated risk of Type I error rate concerns you, use a percentile bootstrap confidence interval or a Monte Carlo confidence interval instead. The distribution of the product approach also works quite well, but it almost never disagrees with a Monte Carlo confidence interval.

The percentile bootstrap confidence interval has become the more widely recommended method for inference about the indirect effect in mediation analysis. The simulation research summarized above shows it to be among the better methods for making inferences about an indirect effect balancing validity and power considerations, but this could change as new data come in and new tests are invented. Its popularity has also been enhanced by the existence of freely available tools that make it easy to implement using software scientists are already using. For this reason, I emphasize it throughout this book, and it is the default method used by PROCESS when your model contains an indirect effect.

3.5 An Example with Continuous *X*: Economic Stress among Small-Business Owners

In the prior example, I illustrated mediation analysis in a study with a dichotomous *X*. In experiments, *X* frequently takes only one of two values, such as whether a person is randomly assigned to a treatment or a control condition. *X* could be dichotomous in a mediation model even if not experimentally manipulated, such as whether a child is diagnosed with attention-deficit hyperactivity disorder (ADHD) or not (Huang-Pollock, Mikami, Pfiffner, & McBurnette, 2009), maltreated by a parent or not (Shenk, Noll, & Cassarly, 2010), or whether or not a soldier killed someone during combat (Maguen et al., 2011), or simply whether a person is male rather than female (Kimki, Eshel, Zysberg, & Hantman, 2009; Webster & Saucier, 2011) or Caucasian rather than Asian (Woo, Brotto, & Gorzalka, 2011). Even in nonexperimental studies such as these, the total, direct, and indirect effects of X can be expressed in terms of differences in $\overline{Y}$ between the two groups, so long as a coding of X is used that affords such an interpretation.

Of course, not all putative causal agents in a mediation model take the form of a dichotomy. For instance, Gong, Shenkar, Luo, and Nyaw (2007) examined the effect of the number of partners in a joint business venture on venture performance both directly and indirectly through partner co-operation. Landreville, Holbert, and LaMarre (2010) studied the effect of individual differences in frequency of viewing of late-night comedy on fre-quency of political talk during a political campaign. They asked whether more frequent viewing increases political talk in part by increasing interest in viewing political debates, which in turn prompts greater talk. And in an investigation of men with prostate cancer, Orom et al. (2009) reported that men who are relatively more optimistic in their personality find it easier to make decisions about their treatment, because such optimism translates into greater confidence about their decision-making ability, which makes it easier to decide. In these studies, the number of joint venture partners, a person's optimism, and how frequently a person reported watching late-night comedy were measured quantitatively—as matters of degree—rather than in binary terms.

When X is a continuum rather than a dichotomy, the total, direct, and indirect effects cannot be expressed literally in terms of mean differences between discrete groups in the study. Indeed, often there are no two people in the study with exactly the same measurement on X. Nevertheless, no modifications are necessary to the mathematics or procedures described in sections 3.2 through 3.4 to estimate these effects, and the interpretation of these effects otherwise remains unchanged. The total effect of a continuous X on some outcome Y still partitions cleanly into the direct effect and the indirect effect through a mediator M, and these effects can be estimated using the same analytical procedure described thus far.

To illustrate, I use data from the study of economic stress in en-trepreneurs by Pollack et al. (2012) introduced in Chapter 1. The data file corresponding to this study is ESTRESS and can be downloaded from *www.afhayes.com*. Participants in this study were 262 entrepreneurs who were members of Business Networking International, a networking group for small-business owners, who responded to an online survey about re-cent performance of their business as well as their emotional and cognitive reactions to the economic climate. As diagrammed in Figure 3.6, Pollack et al. (2012) proposed that economic stress (X) leads to a desire to disen-

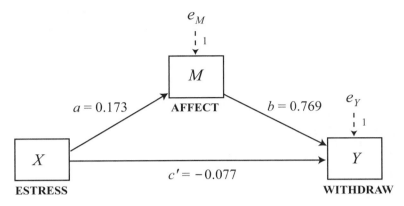

FIGURE 3.6. Simple mediation model for economic stress study in the form of a statistical diagram.

gage from entrepreneurial activities (Y) as a result of the depressed affect (M) such stress produces, which in turns leads to a desire to disengage from entrepreneurship. More specifically, the experience of stress results in feelings of despondency and hopelessness, and the more such feelings of depressed affect result, the greater the desire to withdraw from one's role as a small-business owner to pursue other vocational activities. So depressed affect was hypothesized as a mediator of the effect of economic stress on withdrawal intentions.

The participants in this study (162 male, 100 female) were asked a series of questions about how they felt their business was doing. Their responses were used to construct an index of economic stress (ESTRESS in the data file, with high scores reflecting greater economic stress). They were also asked the extent to which they had various feelings related to their business, such as "discouraged," "hopeless," "worthless," and the like, an aggregation of which was used to quantify business-related depressed affect (AFFECT in the data, with higher scores reflecting more depressed affect). They were also asked a set of questions to quantify their intentions to withdraw from entrepreneurship in the next year (WITHDRAW in the data, with higher scores indicative of greater withdrawal intentions).

The direct and indirect effects of economic stress on withdrawal intentions are estimated just as in the prior example with a dichotomous X. The proposed mediator, depressed affect, is regressed on economic stress (X) to produce a, and withdrawal intentions is regressed on both depressed affect and economic stress, which yields b and c', respectively. In PROCESS, the command to estimate the model is

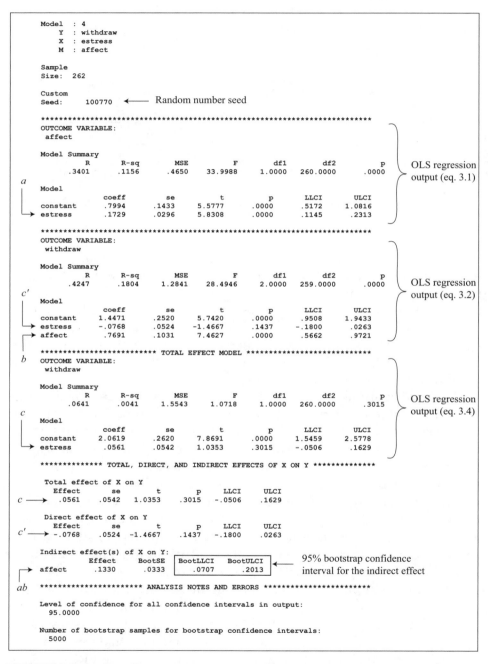

FIGURE 3.7. Output from the PROCESS macro for SPSS for the economic stress simple mediation analysis.

TABLE 3.5. Model Coefficients for the Economic Stress Study

			Consequent					
		M (AFFECT)				Y (WITHDRAW)		
Antecedent		Coeff.	SE	p		Coeff.	SE	p
X (ESTRESS)	a	0.173	0.030	< .001	c′	−0.077	0.052	.146
M (AFFECT)		—	—	—	b	0.769	0.103	< .001
constant	i_M	0.799	0.143	< .001	i_Y	1.447	0.252	< .001
		$R^2 = 0.116$				$R^2 = 0.180$		
		$F(1, 260) = 33.999, p < .001$				$F(2, 259) = 28.495, p < .001$		

```
process y=withdraw/x=estress/m=affect/total=1/model=4/seed=100770.
```

```
%process (data=estress,y=withdraw,x=estress,m=affect,total=1,model=4,
    seed=100770);
```

PROCESS output can be found in Figure 3.7 and is summarized in Table 3.5. As can be seen, $a = 0.173$, $b = 0.769$, and $c′ = -0.077$. In the form of two OLS regression models,

$$\hat{M} = 0.799 + 0.173X$$
$$\hat{Y} = 1.447 - 0.077X + 0.769M$$

Multiplying a and b yields the indirect effect, $ab = 0.173(0.769) = 0.133$. So two entrepreneurs who differ by one unit in their economic stress are estimated to differ by 0.133 units in their reported intentions to withdraw from their business as a result of the tendency for those under relatively more economic stress to feel more depressed affect (because a is positive), which in turn translates into greater withdrawal intentions (because b is positive). This indirect effect is statistically different from zero, as revealed by a 95% bootstrap confidence interval that is entirely above zero (0.071 to 0.201 in the PROCESS output under the headings "BootLLCI" and "BootULCI," respectively).

The direct effect of economic stress, $c′ = -0.077$, is the estimated difference in withdrawal intentions between two business owners experiencing the same level of depressed affect but who differ by one unit in their reported economic stress. The coefficient is negative, meaning that the person feeling more stress but who is equally depressed is estimated to be 0.077 units lower in his or her reported intentions to withdraw from entrepreneurial endeavors. However, as can be seen in the PROCESS output, this direct effect is not statistically different from zero, $t(259) = -1.467, p = .144$, with a 95% confidence interval from -0.180 to 0.026.

The total effect of economic stress on withdrawal intentions is derived by summing the direct and indirect effects, or by regressing withdrawal intentions on economic stress by itself: $c = c' + ab = -0.077 + 0.133 = 0.056$. Two people who differ by one unit in economic stress are estimated to differ by 0.056 units in their reported withdrawal intentions. The positive sign means the person under greater stress reports higher intentions to withdraw from entrepreneurship. However, this effect is not statistically different from zero, $t(260) = 1.035, p = .302$, or between -0.051 and 0.163 with 95% confidence.

3.6   Chapter Summary

Mediator variables function as the conduits through which causal effects operate. When some causal variable X transmits an effect on Y through a mediator M, it is said that X affects Y *indirectly* through M. Indirect effects can be quantified easily using OLS regression and some simple rules of path analysis. X can also affect Y *directly*, meaning independent of its effect on M. These two pathways of influence sum to yield the total effect of X on Y. Innovations in computer-intensive methods have made it possible to conduct inferential tests of an indirect effect without making unnecessary assumptions about the shape of its sampling distribution. These principles and methods were highlighted here in the context of the simple mediation model—a causal model with only a single mediator variable. A solid understanding of these principles and methods is important because they serve as the foundation for the discussion in the next three chapters, which focus on such topics as causal order, causal association versus confounding, effect size, models with more than one mediator, and multicategorical causal antecedents.

4

Causal Steps, Confounding, and Causal Order

In this chapter, I contrast the method of mediation analysis introduced in Chapter 3 with the historically popular *causal steps* approach. I then tackle various threats to the validity of the conclusions one might reach using mediation analysis, including confounding, epiphenomenality, and alternative causal orderings of *X*, *M*, and *Y*. After discussion of various measures of effect size in mediation analysis, I address the estimation of direct and indirect effects in models with multiple causal antecedents and outcome variables.

The fundamentals of statistical mediation analysis was the focus of Chapter 3. This is prerequisite material to understanding more complex models involving more than one mediator and the integration of mediation and moderation analysis discussed in later chapters. Comfort with these principles allows you to conduct mediation analysis and use it to shed light on your research questions and hypotheses about causal processes. In this chapter, I take up a variety of complications, including testing and ruling out various alternative explanations for associations observed in a mediation analysis, effect size, and models with multiple causal agents and outcomes. But first I talk about the historically popular *causal steps* method to mediation analysis and why I don't recommend its use.

4.1 What about Baron and Kenny?

Anyone reading this book who has familiarity with mediation analysis as predominantly practiced until the last decade or so will wonder why I have given no attention to the *causal steps approach*. Although this method can be traced in some form back to the 1950s, it was made popular in the 1980s by a very influential article by Baron and Kenny (1986) published in the

Journal of Personality and Social Psychology. For this reason, the causal steps approach is known to many as the *Baron and Kenny method*. Historically, the vast majority of published mediation analyses are based on the logic of the causal steps approach, and it is still used by some today. However, its popularity is fading. I do not recommend this method for reasons I document below, but only after first describing how a mediation analysis is conducted and interpreted using the causal steps approach.

The causal steps strategy has been used to answer the question as to whether or not a certain variable M functions as a mediator of the relationship between X and Y. In terms of the modeling process, the causal steps approach is pretty much the same as the method already discussed at length. But it differs in one important way by focusing entirely on the outcome of a set of tests of significance for each path in the causal system.

Using the causal steps approach, in order for M to be considered a mediator of the effect of X on Y, you should first establish that there is an effect to be mediated, meaning that X and Y are associated. The litmus test as to whether there is an effect of X on Y is the rejection of the null hypothesis that the total effect $_Tc$, estimated in equation 3.4, is zero. If so, then this criterion is met, and you proceed to the second step. If it is not, all testing stops.

Assuming this first criterion is met, in this second step, the effect of X on M is then estimated using equation 3.1. If a is statistically significant, this meets the second criterion of the causal steps strategy, which requires that X affects M. A failure to reject the null hypothesis that $_Ta = 0$ stops this process in its tracks, and the claim is that M is not a mediator of the effect of X on Y.

If this second criterion is met, then a test of the third criterion is undertaken: that M affects Y controlling for X. To establish this criterion, Y is regressed on both X and M using equation 3.2, and the null hypothesis that $_Tb = 0$ is tested. If this null hypothesis cannot be rejected, the procedure stops with the claim that M is not functioning as a mediator of X's effect on Y.

But if this third criterion is also met, then the direct effect of X (c' in equation 3.2) is compared to the total effect c (from equation 3.4). If c' is closer to zero than c and c' is not statistically significant, then M is said to *completely* mediate X's effect on Y. That is, M entirely accounts for the effect of X on Y. But if c' is closer to zero than c but c' is statistically different from zero, then M *partially* mediates X's effect on Y. Only part of the effect of X on Y is carried through M.

The popularity of this approach is no doubt due to the fact that it is quite simple to understand, it is easy to describe and teach, it is still being taught and recommended by researchers who don't follow the methodology literature, it can be summarized in a few sentences in a scientific report, it does not require specialized software, and it doesn't take a strong background in statistics or data analysis to implement. But recognition has been growing that this approach is not ideal both statistically and philosophically, and these days it is difficult to get away with the use of the causal steps strategy. Gone are the days where one has to meet these "conditions of mediation," as they are often called. It is fair to say that soon you won't be able to publish your research if you rely on the causal steps method. That day may already be here.

To describe some of the problems with the causal steps approach, it is worth first considering what I see as three common-sense principles of inference using statistics. The first is that claims scientists make about some phenomenon should be based on a quantification of the phenomenon that is most directly relevant to the claim. The second is that scientists should base a claim on as few inferential statistical tests as required in order to support that claim. And third, scientists should convey some information to consumers of their research about the uncertainty attached to that claim. Point estimates of effects are fine, but they should supplemented by information about sampling variance or other sources of uncertainty when possible.

With these principles in mind, notice that the causal steps procedure neither formally quantifies the indirect effect nor requires any kind of inferential test about it. Rather, according to the causal steps approach, the existence of an indirect effect is inferred logically from the outcome of a set of null hypothesis tests about a quantification of something other than the indirect effect. This violates the first common-sense principle and is contrary to the way that scientists usually collect evidence and make an argument. When we want to know whether one therapy is more effective than another, we quantify differences between those who do and do not experience that therapy on the outcomes of interest and determine whether there is evidence of a difference with some kind of hypothesis test or a confidence interval. When we want to know whether people who play violent video games frequently are more aggressive than those who play less, we estimate the correlation between violent video game play and aggression, and then conduct some kind of an inferential test about that correlation. Why should inference about indirect effects be any different? Our inferences about indirect effects should be based on an estimate of the indirect effect and whether an inferential procedure justifies the claim that $_Ta_Tb$ is not zero, not on the outcome of a set of hypothesis tests about $_Ta$ and $_Tb$.

A rebuttal to this criticism of the causal steps approach goes something like this:

> "If $_Ta \neq 0$ and $_Tb \neq 0$, then it follows that $_Ta_Tb \neq 0$. And if $_Ta = 0$ or $_Tb = 0$, then $_Ta_Tb = 0$. So why do we need to conduct an inferential test about the indirect effect? We know what we need to know using the causal steps procedure."

Although this sounds sensible, the problem is that it is wrong. Although somewhat rare, one can find that a formal inferential test of $_Ta_Tb$ leads to the conclusion that there is no indirect effect even when both a and b are statistically different from zero. But even more important, it is possible to conclude $_Ta_Tb \neq 0$ even if either a or b (or both) are not statistically significant. Because ab is the proper estimate of the indirect effect, inference should be based on ab, not on individual hypothesis tests of $_Ta$ and $_Tb$. The indirect effect is not estimated as a and b. It is estimated as the *product* of a and b. Statistical significance of a and b are not requirements of mediation by current thinking.

Second, the ability to claim M is a mediator is contingent on the successful rejection of three null hypotheses (about $_Tc$, $_Ta$, and $_Tb$). But hypotheses tests are human inventions that are fallible. They are based on assumptions that may not be met and which can affect their performance. Even when those assumptions are met, we know the possibility remains that a hypothesis test will fail to reject a false null hypothesis, or it will incorrectly reject a true one. The more hypothesis tests one conducts in order to make or support a claim, the more likely one is to make a mistake. It is better to minimize the number of inferential procedures one must employ in order to support a claim. A single inferential test of the indirect effect is all that is needed. So the causal steps approach violates the second common-sense principle.

Third, those who use the causal steps strategy are usually thinking dichotomously about mediation. Is X's effect on Y mediated by M or not? This is a qualitative claim, and one that carries no information about the uncertainty attached to it. This violates the third common-sense principle. We have seen that indirect effects can be quantified, and a confidence interval can be constructed for the indirect effect. Confidence intervals are generally more informative than are qualitative claims about whether an effect exists or not.

Fourth, investigators routinely begin the causal steps procedure by first testing whether X affects Y by conducting a hypothesis test for $_Tc$, the total effect of X. A failure to reject the null hypothesis that $_Tc = 0$ means that the remaining criteria to establish M as a mediator are irrelevant, so the causal steps procedure stops in its tracks. This logic is predicated on the belief that an effect that doesn't exist can't be mediated, so there is no point in trying to explain the mechanism generating such a noneffect.

But this logic is flawed. It is possible for X to exert an effect on Y indirectly through M even if one cannot establish through a hypothesis test that the total effect is different from zero. Although this seems counterintuitive, that doesn't make it not true. The size of the total effect does not constrain or determine the size of the indirect effect. An indirect effect can be different from zero even when the total effect is not. This happens much more than people probably realize. Indeed, we have already seen two examples of such a phenomenon in Chapter 3. Recall that there was evidence consistent with an indirect effect of article location on intentions to purchase sugar through presumed media influence even though the total effect of article location on intentions was not statistically significant. And there was no statistically significant evidence of a total effect of economic stress on withdrawal intentions, even though the indirect effect of economic stress through depressed affect was statistically different from zero using a bootstrap confidence interval. Situations like this, obviously, can happen and probably do more often than people realize or appreciate. For some examples in the literature, see Cole, Walter, and Bruch (2008), Fillo et al. (2016), Hammond, Müller, Carpendale, Bibok, and Liebermann-Finestone (2012), Maguen et al. (2011), Panno, Lauriola, and Pierro (2016), Petrocelli et al. (2016), and Seehuus, Clifton, and Rellini (2015). There is now a general consensus among methodologists (e.g., Bollen, 1989; Cerin & MacKinnon, 2009; Hayes, 2009; LeBreton, Wu, & Bing, 2009; MacKinnon, 2008; Rucker et al., 2011; Shrout & Bolger, 2002; Zhao et al., 2010) that a total effect of X on Y should not be a prerequisite to searching for evidence of indirect effects.

The discomfort this might induce in some who can't fathom the logic of an indirect effect absent evidence of a total effect can be resolved quite easily by acknowledging that the total effect simply is not a good way of thinking about X's effect on Y. Recall that the total effect is equal to the direct effect plus the indirect effect. If these two effects are different in sign, they may add to something close to zero, or even zero itself.[1] Or the indirect effect might be different from zero and estimated with considerable certainty (i.e., a narrow confidence interval) but when added to a direct effect that is small and estimated with lots of uncertainty (i.e., a large confidence interval), the total effect may contain enough sampling error to make it hard to detect as

---

[1]It usually is not difficult to find a sensible substantive interpretation for direct and indirect effects that are opposite in sign. Some label such a phenomenon *suppression* or *inconsistent mediation*, but these are merely labels, not an explanation.

different from zero. Supporting this point, Kenny and Judd (2014) show that an indirect effect of a given size is sometimes easier to detect than a comparably sized total effect. That is, tests of indirect effects are generally higher in power than tests on total effects of the same size. So why would you want to condition a test of an indirect effect on a test of the total effect when the total effect is likely to be tested with less power?

Another situation that can produce a total effect near zero is the existence of subpopulations in which X exerts opposite effects on Y. For instance, perhaps X positively affects Y among males but negatively among females, and something must account for this differential effect. If the effects are similar in magnitude and the sample is evenly split between the sexes, a regression of Y on X that does not account for the differential effect of X on Y between men and women may lead you to the mistaken conclusion that X is unrelated to and therefore does not affect Y. Alternatively, it could be that X is unrelated to Y among some people but positively related to Y among others. If there are enough people in the sample in the first group, the association between X and Y will be diluted to the point that it is difficult to detect without a large sample.

The point is that it is a mistake to condition the hunt for indirect effects on evidence of a total effect of X, and there is general consensus among those who think about mediation analysis on this point. Researchers who use the causal steps strategy and insist on a statistically significant total effect of X before estimating and testing indirect effects will end up underanalyzing their data. They will fail to detect indirect effects when they are there and the result will be false statements about the process generating the data. Fewer mistakes of inference will be made in the long run if this strategy is abandoned.

Mediation without (or even with) evidence of a total effect is evaluated by some researchers using the *test of joint significance*. This test requires that a and b be statistically significant in order to support a claim of mediation, without a corresponding requirement for c. This method requires two tests (rather than just one) and does not yield an interval estimate of the indirect or some other measure of uncertainty. Thus, the test of joint significance violates the second and third common-sense principles. A variation on this approach also used by some is to conduct a test of the indirect effect (such as using a bootstrap confidence interval) only *after* using the causal steps procedure to establish the statistical significance of the individual paths, including the total effect (see, e.g., Robinson & Sutin, 2017). That is, meeting the causal steps criteria is used as a gatekeeper to conducting a more relevant test of the indirect effect. This is simply redundant data analysis, and it will result in reduced statistical power to detect mediation.

The "criteria to establish mediation" are no longer such. It is the test of the indirect effect that matters, not the test on the individual paths in the model.

Finally, because the causal steps strategy is not based on a quantification of the indirect effect, it encourages investigators to think about indirect effects and mediation in purely qualitative terms. If you think in these terms, it becomes difficult to entertain and test more refined questions about processes, such as whether the indirect effect through one mediator is different in size than the indirect effect through another (as discussed in section 5.3). Such qualitative thinking also makes it impossible to conceptualize processes as moderated, which is the focus of the latter few chapters of this book. In order to apply many of the methods covered later, it is necessary to get in the habit of thinking about mediation in quantitative rather than purely qualitative terms.

A Critique of Complete and Partial Mediation

Those who use the causal steps strategy often attempt to articulate their findings in terms of "degree of mediation." Is M a mediator of X's effect on Y at all and, if so, does M completely or partially mediate that effect? Partial mediation implies that the mechanism through M does not entirely account for the association observed between X and Y, whereas complete mediation means that the association between X and Y is entirely accounted for by the indirect mechanism. Although these terms are used in abundance in the scientific literature and frequently are the subject of hypotheses being tested, I argue below that they are empty concepts and should be abandoned.

First, notice that complete and partial mediation are defined only when an investigator has determined that the total effect is different from zero. But we've seen that one can find evidence of an indirect effect absent evidence of a total effect. Thus, in at least some circumstances that do occur in real research, these concepts simply don't apply. This itself is not a criticism of the concepts, but it is important because it means that it is fruitless to try to label a pattern of findings in terms of complete and partial mediation if the pattern of findings is not consistent with the concepts as defined.

Second, there is a sense in which complete mediation seems like a better, more desirable claim, and I think scientists celebrate complete mediation with a bit more excitement and champagne than they do claims of partial mediation. If you propose that M mediates the effect of X on Y and can go away at the end of the study with the claim that M functions as a complete mediator of the effect, this somehow seems like a happier conclusion than the claim that M only partially mediates X's effect. The implication is that if M completely accounts for X's effect, we now knows all we need to know about the process being studied. No one needs to propose other mechanisms that might be at work because the one you've identified entirely accounts for the effect of X. You deserve a prize because you've found the answer. Being able to claim only partial mediation means you haven't finished the job. It is almost a disappointment. Scientists should keep working on the problem, because there is more to understand about the mechanism by which X's effect operates.

As Rucker et al. (2011) nicely illustrated, the problem with this reasoning is that establishing that some variable M completely mediates the effect of X on Y says nothing whatsoever about the existence or absence of other possible mediators of X's effect. Even if you can say you have completely accounted for the effect of X on Y with your favored mediator, this does not preclude another investigator from being able to make the same claim as you, but using a different mediator. If there are multiple mediators that completely mediate X's effect when considered in isolation, then what value is there to claiming that your favored mediator does? It is an empty claim, with no real value or meaning and nothing especially worthy of celebration.

Third, a claim of partial mediation is, in effect, a celebration of a misspecified model. On a philosophical level, all effects are mediated by something. When you claim that M partially mediates X's effect, you are acknowledging that part of X's effect on Y has not been accounted for by M. So what is accounting for X's remaining effect as evidenced by a statistically significant direct effect? Something must be, but whatever it is, it isn't in your model. To be sure, all models are wrong at some level. All our models are misspecified to some degree. I think most researchers recognize this even if they are inclined to believe it is less true for their own models relative to someone else's. But why hypothesize it, and why celebrate when you support a hypothesis of partial mediation? You are hypothesizing and celebrating a misspecified model.

Fourth, consider two investigators who are studying exactly the same process using exactly the same method and exactly the same measurement procedures. Furthermore, imagine that descriptively their results are the same, but that investigator A's study is based on a smaller sample than investigator B's study. If in reality, M only partially accounts for the effect of X on Y, investigator B is more likely than investigator A to claim that M partially mediates X's effect, because investigator B's test of the direct effect (c') will be conducted with more power. So investigator A's findings seem more impressive because the effect of X on Y has been completely accounted for by the indirect mechanism, even though he or she has less data than investigator B. But if complete mediation is a better, more desirable claim than partial mediation, this means that it would be better to limit your sample size such that you have just enough power to be able to claim that M is a mediator, but not enough to detect the direct effect. In other words, if your goal is to establish complete mediation, it is best to use a smaller sample size. Obviously, this is crazy, and it runs absolutely counter to what we generally believe about data collection—that more is better.

Complete and partial mediation are concepts that are deeply ingrained in the thinking of social and behavioral scientists. But I just don't see what they offer our understanding of a phenomenon. They are too sample-size-dependent and the distinction between them has no substantive or theoretical meaning or value of any consequence. I recommend avoiding expressing hypotheses about mediation or results of a mediation analysis using these terms.

4.2   Confounding and Causal Order

One of the beautiful features of experiments is the causal interpretations they afford about differences between groups. Good experimentation is tough and requires lots of careful planning and strict control over experimental procedures, construction of stimuli, treatment of participants, and so forth. But when done well, no research design gives a researcher more confidence in the claim that differences between groups defined by X on some variable of interest is due to X rather than something else. Given that a mediation model is a causal model, the ability to make unequivocal causal claims about the effect of X on M and the direct and total effects of X on Y gives experiments tremendous appeal.

However, mediation models are about more than establishing that X affects M and Y. One must also be comfortable claiming M causes Y. Unfortunately, random assignment to values of X does not establish that M causes Y. Alternative possibilities exist. For example, M may be correlated with some other variable that X is actually affecting, and if that other variable causes Y rather than M, one will go away with the mistaken conclusion that X affects Y indirectly through M when in fact the other variable is the mechanism variable through which X exerts its effect indirectly. This is the phenomenon referred to in section 2.3 as *epiphenomenal association*. That is, the association between M and Y may be an epiphenomenon of the fact that X affects some other variable not in the model, and that other variable affects Y, but because M is correlated with that other variable, it appears that M is the variable through with X's effect on Y is carried. Epiphenomenal association is a serious threat to the validity of the causal inference one makes from a mediation analysis.

Confounding or spurious association also presents a serious validity threat. A causal claim about association is threatened by confounding if the association between the variables can be attributed to a third variable that causally affects both. For example, the fact that children who watch relatively more television are more likely to be overweight (e.g., Brown, Nicholson, Broom, & Bittman, 2011; Jordan, 2010) does not imply with certainty that excessive television viewing causes weight problems. Perhaps parents who don't encourage a healthy lifestyle are more likely to purchase and feed their children less healthy food that is high in fat and calories and are also less likely to encourage their children to play sports, exercise, or engage in other behaviors that are better for their bodies than just watching television. So it isn't necessarily the excessive television viewing causing the weight problems. Perhaps it is the behavior of the parents that causes both excessive television viewing and weight gain in their kids. So differences between the kids' parents in terms of how much they encourage a healthy lifestyle is a potential confound, making it difficult to claim convincingly that watching more TV causes weight gain.

When X is not experimentally manipulated, then things get even worse. Absent random assignment to values of X, *all* of the associations in a mediation model are susceptible to confounding and epiphenomenal association, not just the association between M and Y. Whether one's design includes manipulation and random assignment of X or not, it behooves the researcher to seriously ponder these potential threats to causal inference and, if possible, do something to reduce their plausibility as alternative explanations for associations observed.

Accounting for Confounding and Epiphenomenal Association

Fortunately, epiphenomenal association and confounding as threats to the validity of a causal claim can be managed at least in part through statistical control. If two variables M and Y are epiphemenonally associated or confounded due to their association with some variable C, then the association between M and Y should not exist among people who are equal on C. So, for instance, suppose we studied a bunch of kids with parents who are equivalent to each other in how much they encourage a healthy lifestyle in their children. If we found that among such kids, those who watch relatively more television (M) also are more likely to be overweight (Y), it couldn't possibly be variations between kids in how much their parents encourage healthy lifestyles (C) that accounts for the association because we've held that potential confounding variable constant.

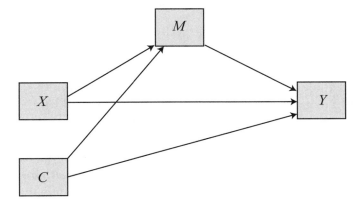

FIGURE 4.1. A conceptual diagram of a simple mediation model with statistical controls.

Often we can't literally hold C constant through research design in this fashion. However, if we have measured C, we can remove C's influence on the quantification of the putative causal associations in a mediation model mathematically, as described in section 2.3. In a mediation analysis, confounding and epiphenomenal association due to C can be ruled out by including C as a predictor in the models of M and Y, represented conceptually in Figure 4.1. Conveniently, adding C to the models of M and Y will also remove C as an epiphenomenal or confounding threat to a causal claim about the association between X and M and X and Y as well as between M and Y.

Of course, controlling for C does not eliminate other potential sources of confounding or epiphenomenal association. Maybe some variable other than C is confounding the associations in the mediation model, or perhaps both C and some other variable are. The possibility of multiple confounds is not a problem, so long as those other variables are measured. They can just be added as additional predictors to the models of M and Y in the mediation analysis.

In practice, researchers frequently have more than one potential confounding variable in mind that they want to statistically partial out of the association between the variables in a simple mediation model. Denoting C as the set of q variables ($q \geq 1$, frequently called *covariates* in this context) that may threaten a claim of causality due to confounding or epiphenomenal association, their effects on the paths in a mediation model (i.e., a, b, and c') can be statistically removed by estimating the coefficients in the following models of M and Y:

$$M = i_M + aX + \sum_{i=1}^{q} f_i C_i + e_M$$

$$Y = i_Y + c'X + bM + \sum_{i=1}^{q} g_i C_i + e_Y$$

As can be seen, the only change relative to equations 3.1 and 3.2 from Chapter 3 is the addition of the q covariates to the models of M and Y. The resulting estimates for a, b, and c' now can be said to be "purified" of the influence of the covariates on their value absent the inclusion of C in the model. The covariates are being held constant mathematically or statistically controlled in the estimation of the other effects in the model.

In this model, c' is still the direct effect of X on Y, ab remains the indirect effect of X on Y through M, and the total effect of X on Y is the sum of the direct and indirect effects, $c' + ab$. The total effect will be equal to c in a model of Y without M but including the q covariates:

$$Y = i_{Y*} + cX + \sum_{i=1}^{q} h_i C_i + e_{Y*} \tag{4.1}$$

The interpretation of the direct, indirect, and total effects remains the same, but with the inclusion of "equal on C," "holding C constant," or "statistically controlling for C" (terms that have the same meaning and can be used interchangeably). So c' quantifies how much two cases that differ by a unit on X are estimated to differ on Y holding M and C constant. The indirect effect, ab, quantifies how much two cases that differ by one unit on X but equal on covariates C are estimated to differ on Y as a result of the effect of X on M, which in turn affects Y. And the total effect of X, c, estimates how much two cases that differ by a unit on X are estimated to differ on Y, statistically controlling for C.

To illustrate, we shall revisit the economic stress study described in section 3.5. Recall that Pollack et al. (2012) assessed the economic stress and business-related depressed affect that 262 entrepreneurs reported experiencing during an economic downturn, as well as their intentions to withdraw from entrepreneurship. The simple mediation analysis was consistent with the claim that economic stress can prompt a desire to withdraw from the business world indirectly through its effect on depressed affect. That is, those who reported experiencing more economic stress felt stronger business-related depressed affect ($a = 0.173$), and those who were experiencing more depressed affect reported a greater intention to withdraw from entrepreneurship even after accounting for economic stress ($b = 0.769$). The indirect effect was statistically different from zero ($ab = 0.133$, with a 95% bootstrap confidence interval from 0.071 to 0.201). There was no evidence of a direct effect of economic stress on withdrawal intentions ($c' = -0.077, p = .144$).

The indirect effect may reflect a bona fide causal sequence of events in which elevated stress leads to depressed affect, which leads to a desire to withdraw from entrepreneurship. But remember that these data come from a one-shot observational study. Nothing was manipulated, nothing was measured over time, and potential confounds abound. For example, the indirect effect may be a manifestation of nothing other than individual differences such as perceptions of one's own confidence and skill in managing a business. People who feel relatively more confident in their abilities may tend to feel relatively less stress in general, perhaps are less prone to feeling negative and down about their business under any circumstances, and enjoy their jobs relatively more than people who are less confident. If so, then statistically controlling for such an individual difference when assessing the indirect effect of economic stress should weaken or eliminate it. That is, among people equal in their confidence, there should be no evidence of an indirect effect of economic stress on withdrawal intentions through depressed affect, because this variable has been taken out of the process that, by this reasoning, induces spurious association between X and M and between M and Y. But if the indirect effect persists even when holding confidence constant, a causal claim remains viable.

This alternative explanation can be put to the test only if something akin to confidence has been measured. Fortunately, Pollack et al. (2012) included a measure of "entrepreneurial self-efficacy" (Chen, Green, & Crick, 1998). This measure indexes a person's confidence in his or her ability to successfully engage in various entrepreneurship-related tasks such as setting and meeting goals, creating new products, managing risk, and making decisions (ESE in the ESTRESS data file). Indeed, compared to participants relatively low in entrepreneurial self-efficacy, those relatively high in entrepreneurial self-efficacy did report feeling relatively less economic stress ($r = -0.158, p = .010$), relatively less business-related depressed affect ($r = -0.246, p < .001$), and reported relatively weaker intentions to withdraw from entrepreneurship ($r = -0.243, p < .001$). So spurious or epiphenomenal association are plausible alternative explanations for at least some of the relationship observed between economic stress, depressed affect, and withdrawal intentions.

To account for the shared association between entrepreneurial self-efficacy and the key variables in the causal model being estimated, entrepreneurial self-efficacy (C_1) is included in the equations for both depressed affect (M) and intentions to withdraw (Y). To illustrate that more than a single variable can be used as a statistical control, I also include sex of the participant (C_2; SEX in the data, 0 = female, 1 = male) and length of time in the business, in years (C_3; TENURE in the data) as predictors.

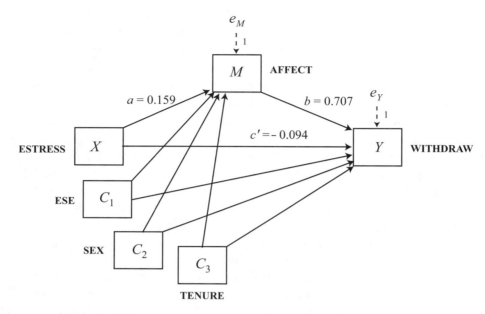

FIGURE 4.2. A statistical diagram of a simple mediation model for the economic stress study with three covariates.

Thus, the equations estimated to quantify the direct and indirect effects of economic stress are

$$M = i_M + aX + f_1C_1 + f_2C_2 + f_3C_3 + e_M \tag{4.2}$$

$$Y = i_Y + c'X + bM + g_1C_1 + g_2C_2 + g_3C_3 + e_Y \tag{4.3}$$

Figure 4.2 depicts the complete model corresponding to these equations in the form of a statistical diagram. As always, the coefficients in equations 4.2 and 4.3 could be estimated using any OLS regression routine, but PROCESS makes it easier while providing the inferential tests for the indirect effect that a set of separate regression analyses will not provide. In SPSS, the PROCESS command is

```
process y=withdraw/x=estress/m=affect/cov=ese sex tenure/total=1/
    model=4/seed=100770.
```

In SAS, use

```
%process (data=estress,y=withdraw,x=estress,m=affect,cov=ese sex
    tenure,total=1,model=4,seed=100770);
```

The only difference between the PROCESS command for this model and the model in Chapter 3 is the addition of the three covariates listed after **cov=**.

TABLE 4.1. Model Coefficients for the Economic Stress Simple Mediation Analysis with Three Covariates

Antecedent		Consequent						
		M (AFFECT)				Y (WITHDRAW)		
		Coeff.	SE	p		Coeff.	SE	p
X (ESTRESS)	a	0.159	0.030	< .001	c'	−0.094	0.053	.077
M (AFFECT)		—	—	—	b	0.707	0.105	< .001
C_1 (ESE)	f_1	−0.155	0.044	.001	g_1	−0.212	0.076	.006
C_2 (SEX)	f_2	0.015	0.086	.863	g_2	0.127	0.144	.378
C_3 (TENURE)	f_3	−0.011	0.006	.086	g_3	−0.002	0.011	.846
Constant	i_M	1.786	0.308	< .001	i_Y	2.746	0.550	< .001
		$R^2 = 0.163$				$R^2 = 0.206$		
		$F(4, 257) = 12.523, p < .001$				$F(5, 256) = 13.282, p < .001$		

By default, any variable in the covariate list will be included as additional antecedent variables in the model of each of the consequents. PROCESS does offer the option of including the covariates in the model of only the mediators, only Y, or distributing the covariates in various ways across the consequents. See the documentation in Appendix A, but when this option is used, it will no longer be true that $c = c' + ab$. I don't recommend overriding the default without a strong principled argument. If you don't include the covariates in all of the consequent models, you will not be controlling for them entirely. But there are some circumstances in which it could be appropriate to do so.

The resulting PROCESS output can be found in Figure 4.3, and the model coefficients are summarized in Table 4.1 and superimposed on the statistical diagram in Figure 4.2. Comparing the PROCESS output for the model controlling for sex, tenure, and entrepreneurial self-efficacy to the output excluding these controls (see Figure 3.7), it can be seen that substantively, nothing has really changed. Even after adjusting for the possibility of spurious or epiphenomenal association resulting from these three covariates, the indirect effect of economic stress on withdrawal intentions through depressed affect is positive and statistically different from zero (point estimate = 0.113, with a 95% bootstrap confidence interval of 0.058 to 0.173). The direct effect is slightly stronger than it was prior to these

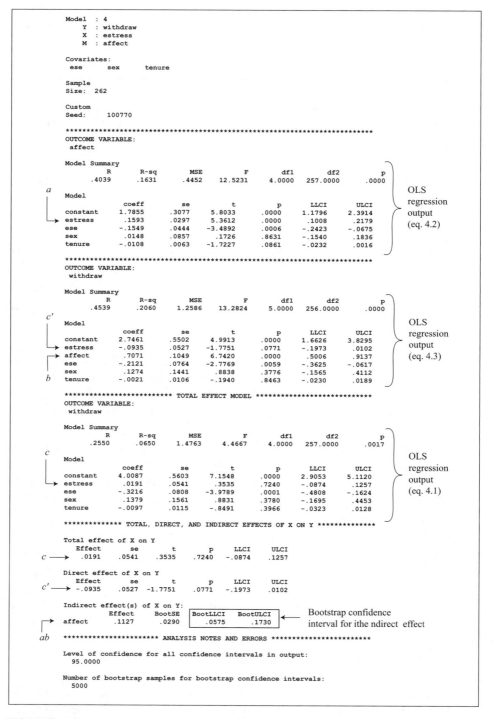

FIGURE 4.3. Output from the PROCESS procedure for SPSS for the economic stress simple mediation analysis with three covariates.

controls in the negative direction, but still not statistically significant by commonly used standards, $c' = -0.094, p = .077$.

Use of the **total=1** option in PROCESS generates the total effect of X on Y while controlling for entrepreneurial self-efficacy, sex, and tenure. Observe that the total effect is $c = 0.019$. As promised, the total effect is equal to the sum of the direct and indirect effects of X: $c = c' + ab = 0.019 = 0.113 + (-0.094)$. This relationship between the total, direct, and indirect effect of X applies to models with covariates so long as the covariates are included in the equations for both Y and M.

This kind of analysis may be done in order to see how sensitive or susceptible the results from a comparable analysis without such controls is to alternative explanations involving those variables being controlled, or it may be done because it is known a priori or based on preliminary analyses that certain variables may be producing spurious association between key variables in the causal system. Ruling out epiphenomenality or spurious association as alternative explanations is an important part of any causal argument that includes associations that are only correlational in nature. This is not to say, however, that we can now interpret these effects unequivocally as causal. Of course, there could be other confounding variables that are producing the associations observed between X, M, and Y that haven't been accounted for in this analysis. This is one of the problems of this approach. One can only account for potential confounds that have been measured, and one can never know whether the correct potential confounds, if they exist, have been statistically controlled. The best one can do when such alternative interpretations may exist for an association is to anticipate those confounding threats, measure them during the study, and hope that no critic is able to conceive a plausible alternative confounding variable that you can't mathematically account for in your analysis.

Causal Order

Even if it were possible to anticipate every possible confound and eliminate its influence on the associations in a mediation model, this does nothing to establish direction of causal order. Mediation is a causal process, and among the criteria for claiming that an association is cause–effect is establishing that the cause precedes the effect in time. Experimental manipulation and random assignment to X all but guarantees that X precedes M and Y in a mediation model. This is because random assignment largely ensures that the groups that define X are equal on M and Y on average at the beginning of the study. Any differences observed between M and Y following random assignment must have occurred after the assignment of cases to groups (assuming no failure of random assignment to equate groups). But random assignment does not ensure that M precedes Y in time. Who is to say that the direction of causal flow runs from X to M to Y? Perhaps the true causal sequence is X to Y to M. For example, in the presumed media influence study, it could be argued that if people believe they should take action in response to the article about a possible sugar shortage in the country, they then project that decision onto the public at large as a form of rationalization for their own beliefs and chosen course of action. That is, beliefs about how one's self is influenced by the media may function as a mediator of the effect of article location on beliefs about how others are likely to be influenced by the media.

If X is not determined through manipulation and random assignment, then any sequence of causal ordering of X, M, and Y must be entertained as a potential candidate for the direction of causal flow. Even in a simple three-variable mediation model absent random assignment to values of X, six possible directions of causal flow are in the running ($X \rightarrow M \rightarrow Y$; $X \rightarrow Y \rightarrow M$; $M \rightarrow X \rightarrow Y$; $M \rightarrow Y \rightarrow X$; $Y \rightarrow X \rightarrow M$; $Y \rightarrow M \rightarrow X$). Hopefully, strong theory or logical impossibility precludes some of these, but it is likely that someone could piece together a sensible argument supporting at least one direction of causal flow other than your preferred interpretation. Consider an alternative proposal to the process modeled in the economic stress study, where depressed affect was construed as a mediator of the effect of economic stress on withdrawal intentions. It may be just as plausible that people who begin to ponder giving up on a business start putting less time into the enterprise, which in time hurts the profit margin, economic stresses mount, and the owner begins to start getting depressed about having to abandon his or her business, laying off employees, and so forth.

Fortunately, sometimes certain alternative directions of causal flow are so implausible that they can be discounted without difficulty. For instance, suppose X is the highest level of education attained by a person prior to age 25, and M is the grade point average of that person's child at the time of graduation from high school. It is impossible that M could cause X in this case. How could the academic performance of a person's child at graduation from high school influence how much education that person receives prior to age 25? If X and M are causally associated, the direction of causal flow must be X to M rather than the reverse.

Good theory may also help to discount some of the possible causal directions. It may be that a certain theory linking X causally to M has already been tested and accepted by the bulk of researchers and theorists in a particular area, and so few would argue that M is likely to affect X. Or perhaps in principle M *could* cause X, but the theory that gives rise to such a possibility is much weaker and less parsimonious than theory that predicts X causes M. In either of these cases, one might be fairly comfortable with the likelihood that X causes M rather than the reverse and feel no need to have to justify that likelihood empirically.

In an attempt to entertain alternative direction of causal flow, one procedure some investigators employ is to estimate a mediation model corresponding to the alternative explanation to see whether the direct and indirect effects are consistent with what that alternative order predicts. For example, Shrum, Lee, Burroughs, and Rindfleisch (2011) proposed that people who engage in heavy television viewing tend to be less satisfied with life than less frequent viewers because excessive consumption of television prompts material values, and such materialism tends to reduce satisfaction with life as one is not able to obtain the goods one desires. The results of a simple mediation analysis based on data from a survey of over 300 residents of the United States were consistent with this process. They found a negative indirect effect of television viewing frequency on life satisfaction just as predicted, but no direct effect. That is, people who reported watching relatively more television tended to be more materialistic, and this materialism was associated with reduced satisfaction with life. Using the same data, they also entertained an alternative model in which materialism influenced life satisfaction indirectly through television viewing frequency. They found no evidence of an indirect effect when the model was respecified with this alternative direction of causal flow.

When this procedure was applied to the presumed media influence study by treating presumed media influence as the final outcome and intentions to buy sugar as the mediator, the results were not consistent with this alternative direction of causal flow. Though the indirect effect of article location on presumed media influence through intentions to buy sugar was indeed positive ($ab = 0.181$), a 95% bootstrap confidence interval (based on 5,000 bootstrap samples) straddled zero (-0.014 to 0.417), unlike when presumed media influence was specified as the mediator. Similarly, when economic stress was specified as the mediator of the effect of withdrawal intentions on depressed affect, there was no evidence of such a process at work, as a bootstrap confidence interval for the indirect effect ($ab = 0.012$) contained zero (-0.013 to 0.044). For additional examples of this strategy in use, see Bizer, Hart, and Jekogian (2012), Chugani, Irwin, and Redden (2015), Coyle, Pillow, Snyder, and Kochunov (2011), Dickert, Kleber, Västfjäll, and Slovic (2016), Druckman and Albin (2011), Giner-Sorolla and Chapman (2017), Greitemeyer and McLatchie (2011), Guendelman, Cheryan, and Monin (2011), Gunn and Finn (2013), Huang, Peck, Mallya, Lupien, and Fiocco (2016), Huang, Sedlovskaya, Ackerman, and Bargh

(2011), Oishi, Seol, Koo, and Miao (2011), Usborne and Taylor (2010), and de Zavala and Cichocka (2011).

The results from the analyses just described by no means establish with certainty that the direction of causal flow is as proposed by Pollack et al. (2012), Shrum et al. (2011), or Tal-Or et al. (2010). Reversing causal pathways in a mediation model will not get you closer to "truth" about direction of cause and effect, as such models are equivalent in the sense that they imply the same relationships between the variables in the model. Indeed, sometimes reversing paths in this matter can even result in conclusions that are the opposite of reality (Lemmer & Gollwitzer, 2017). In the end, only proper design that affords a clear causal interpretation for direction of effects can solve this (see Thoemmes, 2015). However, I am somewhat less skeptical than others about the utility of this practice for piecing together an argument against at least some competing causal orders predicted by alternative theoretical accounts of the process at work. This is an important part of scientific discovery. But sometimes estimation after a reordering of the causal sequence in this fashion does yield evidence consistent with the alternative causal order (see, e.g., Davydov, Shapiro, & Goldstein, 2010; Luksyte & Avery, 2010; Morano, Colella, Robazza, Bortoli, & Capranica, 2011). When this happens, which no doubt does quite frequently, the data are simply uninformative about competing accounts of causal order, and additional study is required using a design that better establishes causal direction.

4.3   Effect Size

In the examples in Chapter 3, interpretations of the direct and indirect effect were couched in quantitative terms in the metrics of X and Y. Two cases that differ by one unit on X are estimated to differ by c' and ab units through the direct and indirect processes, respectively. As these effects are scaled in terms of the metrics of X and Y, they are scale bound and so will be determined by decisions about measurement. So the absolute size of the direct and indirect effects say nothing about whether the effects are large or small in a practical or theoretical sense. They can be made arbitrarily large or small by, for instance, multiplying or dividing X or Y by a constant.

This is not to say that c' and ab are necessarily substantively unmeaningful. On the contrary, they may be quite meaningful. Suppose Y is the number of pounds a person loses in a 2-month period, X is a dichotomous variable coding whether a person attended a half-day weight loss seminar two months prior (1) or only made the waiting list to attend some day in the future (0), and M is a measure of confidence in the ability to lose weight at the close of the seminar. Imagine a simple mediation analysis modeling weight loss reveals a direct effect of attendance at the seminar of $c' = 2$ and an indirect effect of $ab = 5$ through confidence. So those who attended the weight loss seminar lost 7 pounds more on average than those who did not, with 5 of those pounds coming off through the effect of the seminar on confidence which in turn influenced weight loss, and the remaining 2 pounds due to some other process or mechanism not included in the model. A 7-pound weight loss resulting from attending a brief seminar seems like a meaningful effect. One could also say that the indirect effect is (descriptively at least) bigger than the direct effect because they are both measured on the same metric—the metrics of X and Y. As discussed in section 5.3, the metric of the mediator is not a part of the metric of the indirect or direct effects.

Meaningful effect sizes resulting from meaningful metrics such as this are probably not the norm, however, as measurement decisions often result in quantifications of constructs that are on arbitrary scales. In that case, there isn't much that can be done about the ambiguity in interpretation of the size of direct and indirect effects. In addition, "practical" or "theoretical" significance are subjective terms that defy precise quantification. Finally, what might be considered a small effect in one context or by one investigator might be considered relatively large in a different context or by a different investigator. Although there are many rules of thumbs circulating in the literature for labeling an effect as "small," "medium," or "large," these ultimately are just rough guidelines and cannot be applied indiscriminately to any study regardless of content area and regardless of how variables are measured.

The quantification of effect size in mediation analysis is an evolving area of thought and research. Below I describe two measures of effect size that apply to the direct, indirect, and total effects in a mediation model. I also discuss a few measures that have been offered for indirect effects, but each of these has significant problems that limit their value. The measures I discuss here are by no means the only measures available. For an excellent discussion of measures of effect size in mediation analysis, see Preacher and Kelley (2011). I use their notation below.

The Partially Standardized Effect

Consider the mediation analysis examining the effect of economic stress on intentions to withdraw from entrepreneurial activities. Recall from that analysis (described in section 3.5) that two entrepreneurs who differ by one unit in their economic stress were estimated to differ by $ab = 0.133$ units in their withdrawal intentions indirectly through depressed affect, and $c' = -0.077$ units directly, independent of depressed affect. But are these large effects or small ones? Given the arbitrary nature of the measurement scales used (responses to rating scales aggregated over multiple questions), it is hard to say, because the measurement metric is not inherently meaningful. This can be resolved in part by indexing these effects relative to variability between entrepreneurs in their intentions to withdraw from business-related activity. These effects could be considered quite large if there is very little variation in withdrawal intentions, but they could be quite small if there is lots of variation.

The partially standardized effect size (see, e.g., MacKinnon, 2008) is a transformation of an effect that expresses it relative to the standard deviation of Y rather than in the original metric of Y, thereby giving it context relative to variability in the outcome. The formulas for the partially standardized direct and indirect effects are simple:

$$c'_{ps} = \frac{c'}{SD_Y}$$

$$ab_{ps} = \frac{ab}{SD_Y}$$

In the economic stress analysis, $SD_Y = 1.248$, so the direct and indirect effects expressed in partially standardized form are $c'_{ps} = -0.077/1.248 = -0.062$ and $ab_{ps} = 0.133/1.248 = 0.107$. This means that two entrepreneurs who differ by one unit in their economic stress differ by about one-tenth of a standard deviation in their intentions to withdraw from entrepreneurship as a result of the effect of stress on depressed affect, which in turn affects withdrawal intentions. Independent of this indirect mechanism, the entrepreneur one unit higher in economic stress is estimated to be 0.062 standard deviations lower in withdrawal intentions (lower because c'_{ps} is negative). These seem like fairly small effects when conceptualized in terms of variation in withdrawal intentions. But who is to say really, as someone's small effect might be someone else's large effect.

As already discussed many times, the direct and indirect effects sum to yield the total effect of X. So too do the partially standardized direct and indirect effects add to yield the partially standardized total effect. That is,

$$c_{ps} = \frac{c}{SD_Y} = c'_{ps} + ab_{ps}$$

So given two entrepreneurs who differ by one unit in their economic stress, the entrepreneur experiencing more stress is estimated to be $-0.062 + 0.107 = 0.045$ standard deviations higher in intentions to withdraw from entepreneurship as a result of the combined direct and indirect pathways by which stress influences withdrawal intentions.

When X is a dichotomous variable and the two groups are coded such that they differ by one unit on the coding scheme (0 and 1, −0.5 and 0.5, etc.), then c'_{ps} and ab_{ps} can be interpreted as the number of standard deviations in Y that the groups differ on average as a result of the direct and indirect mechanisms. In the presumed media influence simple mediation analysis in section 3.3, $c' = 0.254$, $ab = 0.241$, $SD_Y = 1.550$, and so $c'_{ps} = 0.254/1.550 = 0.164$ and $ab_{ps} = 0.241/1.550 = 0.156$. Those told the story was to be published on the front page of the newspaper were, on average, 0.156 standard deviations higher in their intention to buy sugar as a result of the indirect effect through presumed media influence than were those told the story was to be buried inside the paper. Independent of this mechanism, those told the story was to be on the front page were 0.164 standard deviations higher, on average, in their intentions. These direct and indirect influences sum to give the total estimated mean difference in intention to buy sugar between the two conditions: $0.164 + 0.156 = 0.320$ standard deviations (or, more precisely from Figure 3.4, 0.319 standard deviations).

The Completely Standardized Effect

The partially standardized effect rescales c' and ab to the standard deviation of Y but keeps X in its original metric. Therefore, partially standardized effects are in a scale-bound metric, for their size will depend on the scaling of X. Oftentimes, a difference of one unit on X has little substantive meaning. Removing the scaling of X from the partially standardized effect expresses the direct and indirect effects in terms of the difference in standard deviations in Y between two cases that differ by *one standard deviation* in X. This yields the *completely standardized effect*:

$$c'_{cs} = \frac{SD_X(c')}{SD_Y} = SD_X(c'_{ps})$$

$$ab_{cs} = \frac{SD_X(ab)}{SD_Y} = SD_X(ab_{ps})$$

These two measures are identical to the direct and indirect effects when those effects are calculated using standardized regression coefficients (or standardized X, M, and Y are used in the model rather than X, M, and Y in their original metric). That is, $c'_{cs} = \tilde{c}'$ and $ab_{cs} = \tilde{a}\tilde{b}$ (see, e.g., Cheung, 2009; Preacher & Hayes, 2008b).

In the economic stress study, $SD_X = 1.424$, $SD_Y = 1.248$, $c' = -0.077$, $ab = 0.133$, and so $c'_{cs} = 1.424(-0.077)/1.248 = -0.088$ and $ab_{cs} = $

1.424(0.133)/1.248 = 0.152. These are larger than the partially standardized effects because they reference differences in standard deviations of Y between two people that differ by 1.424 units on X (i.e., one standard deviation) rather than only one unit. So if entrepreneur i is one standard deviation higher in economic stress than entrepreneur j, entrepreneur i is estimated to be 0.152 standard deviations higher in withdrawal intentions as a result of the effect of stress on affect which in turn influences withdrawal intentions. But the direct effect pulls that difference back toward zero, as independent of depressed affect, the more stressed entrepreneur is estimated to be 0.088 standard deviations lower in withdrawal intentions.

As was true with the partially standardized effect, the completely standardized direct and indirect effects add to yield the completely standardized total effect:

$$c_{cs} = \frac{SD_X(c)}{SD_Y} = c'_{cs} + ab_{cs}$$

So the opposing direct and indirect effects translate into an estimated difference of 0.152 + (−0.088) = 0.064 standard deviations in withdrawal intentions between two entrepreneurs that differ by one standard deviation in economic stress. The completely standardized total effect is also equivalent to $\tilde{c}$, the standardized regression coefficient for X in a simple regression model estimating Y from X alone.

The completely standardized effect is generally not meaningful if X is a dichotomous variable. The problem with its use with a dichotomous X is that SD_X is affected by the distribution of the cases into the two groups coded in X (see section 2.4). For example, if the n cases in the sample are equally distributed between the two groups, and assuming the groups are coded with a one-unit difference on X, then $SD_X = 0.50$ (in large samples), and so c'_{cs} and ab_{cs} will be half the size of their corresponding partially standardized values. But if the n cases are distributed unevenly between the two groups, SD_X will be smaller than 0.50, and therefore so too will be c'_{cs} and ab_{cs}, and they will be even more discrepant from c'_{ps} and ab_{ps}.

The discrepancy between the completely and partially standardized effects is itself not a problem. What is a problem is that exactly the same mean difference in Y in standard deviation units resulting from the direct and indirect mechanism (which is what c'_{ps} and ab_{ps} measure) depends on how the cases are distributed into the two groups when the completely standardized effect size measure is used. A measure of effect size for a dichotomous X should not be influenced in this way by something not directly associated with the size of the mean difference. Thus, I cannot recommend the use of the completely standardized effect size when X is a dichotomous variable.

Some (Problematic) Measures Only for Indirect Effects

The partially and completely standardized effects discussed above are certainly not the only approaches to quantifying the size of an indirect effect. Many others have been proposed, and I discuss four of them here. My discussion does not imply endorsement of these measures. Indeed, I offer some arguments for avoiding each and everyone one of these. But you should be aware of them because you will find others reporting them or advocating that you do so.

Ratio of the Indirect Effect to the Total Effect. Historically, mediation analysis has been undertaken when the goal is to establish the process by which an effect operates. Given evidence of an effect of X on Y (the total effect c), mediation analysis can be used to break that effect into its constituent components direct and indirect. A natural question to ask given evidence of an effect of X on Y is how much of the effect of X on Y operates indirectly through M. Alwin and Hauser (1975) and MacKinnon et al. (1995) discuss an effect size measure often interpreted as the proportion of the total effect that is mediated:

$$P_M = \frac{ab}{c} = \frac{ab}{c' + ab}$$

The closer P_M is to one, the more of the effect of X on Y can be said to operate through M, and the closer P_M is to zero, the less of the effect of X on Y is due to the indirect process through M. For instance, in the presumed media influence mediation analysis, $ab = 0.241$ and $c = 0.496$, so $P_M = 0.241/0.496 = 0.486$. So 48.6% of the effect of article location on intentions to buy sugar occurs indirectly through presumed media influence.

Although simple enough to understand, P_M has serious problems that lead me to recommend avoiding this measure. First, a proportion is by definition between 0 and 1, yet P_M is not so constrained. If either ab or c is negative but not both, then $P_M < 0$, and if c is closer to zero than ab, then $|P_M| > 1$. For instance, in the economic stress simple mediation analysis, $ab = 0.133$ and $c = 0.056$, so $P_M = 2.375$. Is it sensible to say that 237.5% of the effect of economic stress on withdrawal intentions is accounted for by the indirect effect through depressed affect? Clearly, it is not. Indeed, as c approaches zero, P_M explodes toward positive or negative infinity, depending on the signs of ab and c.

In addition, P_M is highly unstable from sample to sample (see MacKinnon et al., 1995). It has large sampling variance, and it is not uncommon for a confidence interval for P_M to include zero even when most other measures of effect size for the indirect effect clearly show evidence that the effect is different from zero. Ignoring the problems described earlier, one must have a fairly large sample (at least 500, according to MacKinnon et al., 1995) before one can have much faith in P_M as a description of the magnitude of an indirect effect.

Ratio of the Indirect Effect to the Direct Effect. A variation on the ratio of the indirect to total effect is the ratio of the indirect to the direct effect, which references the size of the indirect effect relative to the direct effect rather than the total effect:

$$R_M = \frac{ab}{c'}$$

R_M is simply a transformation of P_M. A little algebra shows that R_M can be expressed in terms of P_M as

$$R_M = \frac{P_M}{1 - P_M}$$

(see Preacher & Kelley, 2011). If $|R_M| > 1$, then the indirect effect is larger than the direct effect, whereas if $|R_M| < 1$, the indirect effect is smaller than the direct effect. In the special case where the indirect and direct effects are of the same sign, then $R_M > 1$ means that more of the total effect of X on Y is carried indirectly through M, whereas $R_M < 1$ implies that more of the total effect is determined by the direct rather than the indirect effect.

I can't recommend this measure of the size of the indirect effect. Notice that as c' approaches zero, even tiny indirect effects will explode in size relative to the direct effect, as R_M quickly becomes massive with shrinking c'. And as Preacher and Kelley (2011) note, minor sample-to-sample fluctuations in estimates of c' can really sway R_M in one direction or another. Simulation research has verified that like P_M, R_M is unstable as an estimator except in large samples. It simply can't be trusted as a description of the size of the indirect effect unless the sample size is at least 2,000 or so (MacKinnon et al., 1995).

Proportion of Variance in Y Explained by the Indirect Effect. Fairchild, MacKinnon, Toborga, and Taylor (2009) derived a measure of effect size for the indirect effect in simple mediation analysis that is an attempt at quantifying the proportion of the variance in Y attributable to the indirect effect of X on Y through M. Their measure, which they label R^2_{med}, is calculated as

$$R^2_{med} = r^2_{MY} - (R^2_{Y.MX} - r^2_{XY})$$

where r^2_{MY} and r^2_{XY} are the squared correlations between M and Y and X and Y, respectively, and $R^2_{Y.MX}$ is the squared multiple correlation estimating Y from both X and M. The meaningfulness of R^2_{med} is predicated on the assumption that there is an association between X and Y, meaning that

X explains some of the variation in Y. When this occurs, presumably some fraction of that explained variation is attributable to the indirect mechanism. But as we have seen, it is possible for an indirect effect to exist absent evidence of detectable association between X and Y. Rephrased, it is possible for ab to be larger in absolute value than c. In such situations, R^2_{med} can be negative, as in the economic stress example, and this violates its interpretation as a proportion which must by definition be between 0 and 1. So R^2_{med} does not truly have a proportion of variance explained interpretation.

Kappa-Squared. Zero is frequently used as a meaningful reference point against which to discuss the size of an effect. An effect of zero has a clear interpretation. Thus, an effect size that is close to zero is generally seen as small, and the further the index gets from zero, the larger the effect is perceived to be. However, the size of an effect can always be interpreted relative to some other reference, and depending on the choice of reference, any effect can be perceived as large or small. For instance, although a partially standardized indirect effect of 0.50 is certainly larger than zero, it is only a quarter as large as two. So is 0.50 large or small? It depends on what you compare it to.

The newest entrant to the growing list of effect size measures in simple mediation analysis, introduced by Preacher and Kelley (2011), acknowledges that the variances and correlations between the variables observed in the data constrain just how large the indirect effect can be. Given this, it is sensible to gauge the size of an indirect effect relative to how large it could possibly be given these constraints. They call their index "kappa-squared" (κ^2) and define it as the ratio of the indirect effect relative to its maximum possible value in the data:

$$\kappa^2 = \frac{ab}{MAX(ab)}$$

where MAX(ab) is the largest that ab could be given the observed variability of X, Y, and M and their intercorrelations in the data. κ^2 is bound between 0 and 1, which makes it a true proportion, unlike ab/c and R^2_{med}.

I mention κ^2 because the idea of indexing an indirect effect relative to its maximum possible value is very appealing. This idea already has some support in regression analysis, where a correlation (partial or simple) can be interpreted as how large an association is relative to some maximum value that it could be (see Darlington & Hayes, 2017). And you will see some people using κ^2 in their scientific reports. Unfortunately, Wen and Fan (2015) showed that the derivation of the maximum possible value of ab in the denominator of κ^2 contained a computational error, so implementations

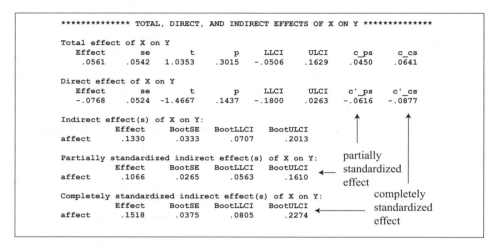

FIGURE 4.4. Effect sizes with bootstrap confidence intervals generated by PROCESS for the economic stress simple mediation analysis.

of κ^2 in existing software are, at least as of the date of the publication of this book, also in error. But this index of effect size otherwise shows promise.

Effect Sizes Available in PROCESS

PROCESS can produce partially and completely standardized measures of total, direct, and indirect effects in mediation models when X is a numerical continuum. For a dichotomous X, PROCESS will not generate the completely standardized effect, as it is not meaningful when X is dichotomous. To obtain these measures in the output, add **effsize=1** to the PROCESS command line. PROCESS also generates confidence intervals for the partially and completely standardized indirect effects using bootstrapping or the Monte Carlo method. An excerpt from the output generated by this option for the economic stress analysis from section 3.5 can be found in Figure 4.4.

4.4   Statistical Power

The power of a test refers to the probability that the test will reject a false null hypothesis. If you propose that X's effect on Y is carried through a mediator M, you would prefer to know that if this is true, you will be able to detect the indirect effect in the study you are planning to conduct. Or after the fact, you might wonder whether your study had sufficient power to detect a nonzero indirect effect. If it did not, you could be criticized for not giving your hypothesis sufficient likelihood of being supported. If your work is funded by someone other than you, it could be perceived as a waste of the funder's money if your study did not have sufficient power to detect an indirect effect.

Personally, I find power analysis little more than a semi-informed game that we play, given that in order to conduct a power analysis (at least an *a priori* power analysis), you need more information than you are likely to have or be in a position to know before the data collection. In mediation analysis, your problem is made more complicated by the fact that an indirect effect is formed as a product of two effects with no agreed upon way of quantifying the magnitude of those effects or their product (something you need to do to assess the power to detect an effect of a given size). Nevertheless, there is small literature on power and sample size selection in mediation analysis, so if power is something you think about, you might want to familiarize yourself with approaches to estimating the power of various methods to detect indirect effects. The simplest read is Fritz and MacKinnon (2007), who provide a table of sample sizes needed to detect an indirect effect of certain sizes using several of the methods I described in Chapter 3. If these tables aren't useful for your purpose, Ma and Zeng (2014) and Zhang (2014) describe how to estimate power in mediation analysis using simulation methods.

4.5   Multiple *X*s or *Y*s: Analyze Separately or Simultaneously?

Researchers sometimes propose that several causal agents (*X* variables) simultaneously transmit their effects on the same outcome through the same mediator(s). For instance, Von Hippel, Issa, Ma, and Stokes (2011) examined the direct and indirect effects of social comparisons with the opportunities of men and of women in their place of work on their perceived likelihood of career advancement through a sense of "stereotype threat." And Simpson et al. (2011) examined how posttherapeutic severity of obsessive-compulsive disorder symptoms is affected by pretreatment severity, pretreatment hoarding, and perceptions of a "working alliance" with the therapist, both directly and indirectly through a patient's adherence to the procedures and strategies taught during cognitive-behavioral therapy.

Multiple *X* Variables

The computation of the direct and indirect effects in models with multiple *X* variables requires no modification to the procedure discussed thus far.

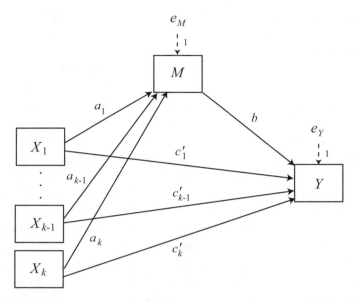

FIGURE 4.5. A simple mediation model with k antecedent X variables.

Each consequent is regressed on the variables in the model that putatively cause it, and the resulting coefficients are pieced together or directly interpreted. But the estimation and interpretation of the effects in such models have some special considerations worth discussing. Primarily, the considerations revolve around the question as to whether the inclusion of multiple Xs in a single model will have any effect on the results one would obtain if one instead estimates several models, each one focusing on a single X variable at a time.

Figure 4.5 represents a simple mediation model with k X variables passing their effects directly to a single Y and indirectly through a single M. In such a model, there are k direct and indirect effects, one of each for each X. There are two consequent variables in this model, so two linear models are required to estimate the effects. These two models are

$$M = i_M + a_1 X_1 + a_2 X_2 + \ldots + a_k X_k + e_M$$

$$Y = i_Y + c'_1 X_1 + c'_2 X_2 + \ldots + c'_k X_k + bM + e_Y$$

and they can be estimated as a set of separate OLS regressions. The indirect effect of X_i on Y through M is $a_i b$, and the direct effect is c'_i. The total effect of X_i is the sum of its direct and indirect effects: $c_i = c'_i + a_i b$. The total effect of X_i on Y could also be estimated by predicting Y from all k Xs but not M:

$$Y = i_{Y*} + c_1 X_1 + c_2 X_2 + \ldots + c_k X_k + e_{Y*}$$

When all k Xs are in the model simultaneously, the direct and indirect effects of X_i are interpreted as the estimated difference in Y between two cases differing by a unit on X_i but that are equal on the other $k - 1$ X_i variables (or, rephrased, holding the remaining $k - 1$ X variables constant, or controlling for those variables). In other words, these represent the direct and indirect effects of X_i on Y that are unique to X_i. As such, these effects are interpreted just as they are when the remaining $k - 1$ X variables are conceptualized as statistical controls rather than variables whose effects are substantively interesting.

In a model with k X variables, the total, direct, and indirect effects of X_i may or may not be the same as the corresponding effects in a simple mediation model that excludes all the other $k - 1$ X variables (as in Figure 3.2). Any differences will depend on the size of the correlations between X_i and the other $k - 1$ Xs, as well as the correlation between other Xs and M and Y.

It is sensible to ask which approach is "better" or "more correct," in terms of the estimates they yield and their substantive meaning. With k causal Xs, should one include all X's in a single model (as did, e.g., Andela & Truchot, 2016; Von Hippel et al., 2011; Weikamp & Göritz, 2016) or estimate k models each with a single X (as did, e.g., Gibbs, Ellison, & Lai, 2011; Han & Shaffer, 2014). The answer is that either approach can be legitimate, and sometimes one can learn from doing it both ways, but it is important to recognize that the direct and indirect effects estimate different things and so interpretation of the results must be undertaken with due care. The former approach, including all Xs in a model, yields an estimate of the part of one X's effect on Y (directly and indirectly through M) that is unique to that X relative to the other Xs in the model. The latter approach, estimating several models each with a single X, yields an estimate of X's direct and indirect effects on Y and, potentially, the effect of other Xs excluded from the model.

The danger in including multiple Xs in a mediation model, as when including statistical controls, is the possibility that highly correlated Xs will cancel out each others' effects. This is a standard concern in linear models involving correlated predictors. Two X variables (or an X variable and a control variable) highly correlated with each other may also both be correlated with M or Y, so when they are both included as predictors of M or Y in a mediation model, they compete against each other in their attempt to explain variation in M and Y. Their regression coefficients quantify their unique association with the model's mediator and outcome variable(s). At the extreme, the two variables end up performing like two boxers in the ring simultaneously throwing a winning blow at the other at precisely the same time. Both get knocked out and neither goes away appearing worthy of a prize. The stronger the associations between the variables in the model, the greater the potential of such a problem. As a result, one could find that when included as the sole X, each variable exerts a direct and/or indirect effect on Y through M, but when considered together, none of them appears to have any effect at all.

Estimation of a Model with Multiple X Variables in PROCESS

One of the limitations of PROCESS is that only a single X variable can be listed in the **x=** part of the command line. However, compare Figure 4.5 to Figure 4.2. Mathematically, these are the same model. The only difference is in the construal of the additional variables sending arrows to M and Y— as either covariates and not of substantive interest or as additional causal influences whose effects are very much of interest. As discussed in section 4.2, PROCESS can estimate a mediation model with covariates as in Figure 4.2, so it follows that it can also estimate a mediation model with multiple X variables. However, in order to estimate the direct and indirect effects of all k X variables in Figure 4.5, PROCESS must be executed k times, each time putting one X_i in the model as X and the remaining $k-1$ X variables as covariates. Each time PROCESS is run, the direct and indirect effects of the variable listed as X will be generated. Repeating $k-1$ times generates the indirect effects for all k X variables. Mathematically, all resulting regression coefficients, direct, and indirect effects will be the same as if they had been estimated simultaneously using a structural equation modeling program.

For instance, consider a mediator model with one mediator (MED), one outcome (DV), and three X variables (IV1, IV2, and IV3). The set of SPSS PROCESS commands below would estimate the effects of IV1, IV2, and IV3 on DV directly and indirectly through MED:

```
process y=dv/x=iv1/m=med/cov=iv2 iv3/model=4/seed=5235.
process y=dv/x=iv2/m=med/cov=iv1 iv3/model=4/seed=5235.
process y=dv/x=iv3/m=med/cov=iv1 iv2/model=4/seed=5235.
```

In SAS, the corresponding set of commands is

```
%process (data=datafile,y=dv,x=iv1,m=med,cov=iv2 iv3,model=4,
    seed=5235);
%process (data=datafile,y=dv,x=iv2,m=med,cov=iv1 iv3,model=4,
    seed=5235);
%process (data=datafile,y=dv,x=iv3,m=med,cov=iv1 iv2,model=4,
    seed=5235);
```

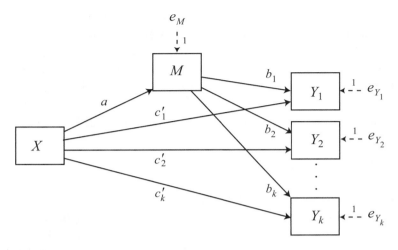

FIGURE 4.6. A simple mediation model with k consequent Y variables.

In this code, the random number generator is seeded with a common (and arbitrary) seed so that at each run, the bootstrap confidence intervals will be based on the same set of bootstrap samples from the data. This trick is easily extended to more complex mediation models described in Chapters 5 and 6 as well as models with statistical controls merely by including the additional mediators and covariates in the PROCESS command.

Multiple Y Variables

Sometimes investigators are interested in the direct and indirect effects of some putative causal antecedent on several different outcome variables. For example, Broeren, Muris, Bouwmeester, van der Heijden, and Abee (2011) estimated the direct and indirect effects of neuroticism (X) on anxiety symptoms (Y_1), depression symptoms (Y_2), and sleep difficulties (Y_3) in 158 Dutch children, with worry (M_1) and rumination (M_2) specified as mediators of neuroticism's effect. And Webster and Saucier (2011) found evidence that following a mortality salience manipulation, gender (X) differences between men and women in homonegativity (Y_1), acceptance of restrictions on the employment opportunities for gay men (Y_2), and affective prejudice toward gay men (Y_3) were mediated by acceptance of traditional gender roles (M_1) but not by empathy (M_2).

A mediation model with k Y variables is displayed in the form of a statistical diagram in Figure 4.6. A close examination of this model shows that it is really just k simple mediation models with a common X and M. Because Y_i is determined only by X and M, the direct and indirect effects of X on Y_i will be the same regardless of whether they are estimated simultaneously with the other $k - 1$ Y variables in the model analytically (which would require a structural equation modeling program) or using k separate analyses, one for each Y variable. PROCESS can be used to estimate the paths in a model such as in Figure 4.6 by running k PROCESS commands, substituting one Y variable for another at each run and seeding the random number generator with a common seed for bootstrapping.

4.6   Chapter Summary

Statistical mediation analysis has changed since the publication of Baron and Kenny (1986). The heyday of the causal steps "criteria to establish mediation" approach is over. Also disappearing in the 21st century is a concern about whether a process can be labeled as complete or partial mediation. Modern mediation analysis emphasizes an explicit estimation of the indirect effect, inferential tests of the indirect effect that don't make unnecessary assumptions, and an acknowledgment that evidence of a statistically significant association between X and Y is not necessary to talk about and model intervening variable processes (in which case the concepts of complete and partial mediation simply don't make sense).

What has not changed over the years are limitations to the causal claims one can make when one's data do not lend themselves to unequivocal causal inference. Confounding and epiphenomenal association can induce noncausal associations between variables in a mediation model, and it behooves researchers to consider such possibilities and at least account for them mathematically in the model with the judicious inclusion of various statistical controls when available. Even if one is comfortable that such alternative explanations are unlikely to account for one's findings, statistical mediation analysis by itself does not substantiate a proposed causal ordering of variables in the causal system. There has been some progress made in the development of various measures of effect size in mediation analysis, but there is no "silver bullet" effect size index that can be unconditionally recommended.

In the next two chapters, I add some additional complexities to the modeling process, first by considering models with more than one mediator. In these next chapters, you will appreciate the importance of understanding the fundamentals of mediation analysis we just covered, as well as the strengths and weaknesses of this statistical approach to understanding mechanisms behind causal effects, for these fundamentals and controversies continue to play an important role in analysis and interpretation of these more complex models.

5

More Than One Mediator

In this chapter, I extend the principles of mediation analysis introduced
in Chapter 3 to models with more than one mediator. Such models allow
a variable's effect to be transmitted to another through multiple mechanisms simultaneously. Two forms of multiple mediator models are introduced here that differ from each other by whether mediators operate in
parallel, without affecting one another, or in serial, with mediators linked
together in a causal chain. By including more than one mediator in a
model simultaneously, it is possible to pit theories against each other by
statistically comparing indirect effects that represent different theoretical
mechanisms.

In Chapter 3 I introduced the fundamentals of statistical mediation
analysis. In the context of a model with a single mediator, I illustrated how
the total effect of a causal antecedent X on consequent Y can be partitioned
into direct and indirect components, and I described various means of
statistically testing hypotheses about total, direct, and indirect effects. As
noted at the beginning of that chapter, the simple mediation model is
frequently used by researchers, but it often oversimplifies the kinds of
phenomena that researchers study. Specifically, because it is based on
only a single mediator variable, it doesn't allow the investigator to model
multiple mechanisms simultaneously in a single integrated model.

This limitation of the simple mediation model is important for at least
four reasons (see, e.g., Preacher & Hayes, 2008a; MacKinnon, 2000, 2008).
First, most effects and phenomena that scientists study probably operate
through multiple mechanisms at once. Of course, all models are wrong to
some extent, and no model will completely and accurately account for all
influences on some variable of interest (cf. MacCallum, 2003). But some
models are more wrong than others. If you have reason to believe that an
antecedent variable's effect on a consequent may or does operate through
multiple mechanisms, a better approach is to estimate a model that allows
for multiple processes at work simultaneously.

Related to this first limitation, it is frequently possible to propose, if not also theoretically likely, that a specific causal influence in a simple mediation model is itself mediated. For instance, the direct effect in a simple mediation model estimates the effect of X on Y independent of M. But there may be identifiable mechanisms responsible for the transmission of this effect. In other words, a direct effect could be interpreted as an estimate of the influence of one or more mechanisms that link X to Y other than the mediator already included in the model. Similarly, in a simple mediation model, the a path estimates the *total* effect of X on M and the b path estimates the *total* effect of M on Y controlling for X. Each of these total effects could, in principle, be partitioned into direct and indirect components through one or more mediators, just as can the total effect of X on Y. Doing so requires the addition of at least one mediator to the simple mediation model.

Third, a proposed mediator could be related to an outcome not because it causes the outcome but because it is correlated with another variable that is causally influencing the outcome. This is the noncausal alternative explanation for an association I referred to in Chapter 2 as *epiphenomenality*. For example, recall the simple mediation analysis of the economic stress study presented in Chapter 3. This model proposed that economic stress influences withdrawal intentions through business-related depressed affect, with depressed affect increased through the experience of economic stress, which in turn enhances desire to withdraw from entrepreneurship. But suppose that in fact it is not depressed business-related affect that is the mediator but role conflict. Perhaps economic stress leads entrepreneurs to have to spend more time at work, away from family and friends, in order to keep their business afloat. This conflict between roles (e.g., role as business leader, provider for the family, spouse, or father or mother) may enhance the desire to change occupations as a means of bringing the demands of competing roles into better balance. If business-related depressed affect were correlated with feelings of role conflict, then a failure to include role conflict in the model as a mediator could result in the mistaken claim that depressed affect is the mediator transmitting the effect of stress on withdrawal intentions.

Finally, the inclusion of multiple mediators between an antecedent and a consequent allows one to pit competing theories of mechanisms against each other. For instance, theory A may postulate that the effect of X on Y is transmitted primarily through mediator A, whereas theory B stipulates that a different mediator B is the conduit through which X affects Y. Inclusion of mediators A and B in an integrated model allows for a formal comparison of the size of the indirect effects of X through them, giving you a means of determining which indirect effect is the stronger of the two (or three, or four, depending on the complexity of the model).

In this chapter, I extend the principles of path analysis and inference described in Chapter 3 to models with more than one mediator. I focus on two forms of the multiple mediator model defined by whether the mediators are linked together in a causal chain (the *serial* multiple mediator model) or are merely allowed to correlate but not causally influence another mediator in the model (the *parallel* multiple mediator model). I also discuss models that blend parallel and serial processes.

5.1   The Parallel Multiple Mediator Model

In a parallel multiple mediator model, antecedent variable X is modeled as influencing consequent Y directly as well as indirectly through two or more mediators, with the condition that no mediator causally influences another. For example, Teixeira et al. (2010) simultaneously examined three potential mediators of the effectiveness of a 30-session, 1-year experimental weight loss intervention among middle-aged women. These mediators included emotional eating (e.g., eating to placate a negative mood), restrained eating (e.g., not eating after feeling full), and perceived barriers to exercise. Figure 5.1 depicts this model in conceptual form. They found that relative to women randomly assigned to a control weight-loss program, those who experienced the experimental method did lose more weight over the year. The mediation analysis suggested that the intervention reduced frequency of emotional eating and increased restraint while eating, which in turn resulted in greater weight loss. But independent of these two mechanisms, there was no evidence that the intervention influenced weight loss by changing perceived barriers to exercise.

A statistical diagram of a parallel multiple mediator model with k mediators is depicted in Figure 5.2. There are other forms that a multiple mediator model can take. A defining feature of the parallel multiple mediator model that distinguishes it from an alternative multiple mediator model, the serial multiple mediator model described in section 5.4, is the constraint that no mediator is modeled as influencing another mediator in the model. This constraint is apparent in Figure 5.2 by the absence of any unidirectional arrows linking any mediator to any other mediator. This is not to say that the mediators are assumed to be independent. In fact, in most circumstances, the mediators are likely to be correlated. Even if they are not, there still may be some advantage to estimating a parallel multiple mediator model with k mediators rather than k simple mediation models. Doing so could result in a power boost for tests of indirect effects if the

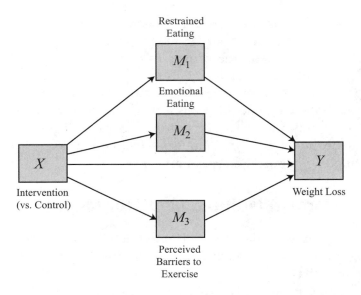

FIGURE 5.1. A conceptual diagram of a parallel multiple mediator model.

mediators are highly correlated with Y but weakly correlated with each other, and doing so affords the ability to compare the sizes of the indirect effects through different mediators.

In principle, the number of mediators one can include in a parallel multiple mediator model is limited only by the number of cases in one's data file and the number of variables one has the foresight to measure as possible mediators. In practice, models with two mediators are most commonly estimated (e.g., Gurmen & Rohner, 2014; Grund & Fries, 2014; Kurti & Dallery, 2014; Pitts & Safer, 2016; Spinhoven, Penninx, Krempeniou, van Hemert, & Elzinga, 2015; Scogin, Morthland, DiNapoli, LaRocca, & Chaplin, 2015). But parallel multiple mediator models can be found with three (e.g., Jones, Willness, & Madey, 2014; Kley, Tuschen-Caffier, & Heinrichs, 2012; Merino, Senra, & Ferreiro, 2016; Vraga, Johnson, Carr, Bode, & Bard, 2014), four (e.g., Alvarez & Juang, 2010; Goldman, Goodboy, & Weber, 2016; Kirby, Jones, & Copello, 2014; Lecheler, de Vreese, & Slouthuus, 2011; Peréz, Abrams, López-Martínez, & Asmundson, 2012), five (e.g., Brandt & Reyna, 2010; Osberg, Billingsley, Eggert, & Insana, 2012; Zadeh, Farnia, & Ungerleider, 2010), six (e.g., Barnhofer & Chittka, 2010; Goldman & Goodboy, 2016; Gonzales, Reynolds, & Skewes, 2011; Veilleux, Skinner, Reese, & Shaver, 2014; Weiss, 2015), and even as many as seven mediators in a model simultaneously (e.g., Anagnostopoulos, Slater, & Fitzsimmons, 2010; Hsu et al., 2012; Lecheler, Bos, & Vliegenthart, 2015) .

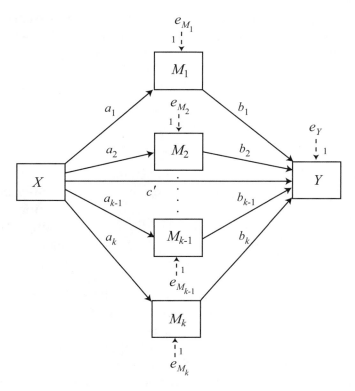

FIGURE 5.2. A statistical diagram representing a parallel multiple mediator model with *k* mediators.

As can be seen in Figure 5.2, a parallel multiple mediator model with *k* mediators has $k + 1$ consequent variables (one for each of the *k* mediators *M* and one for *Y*) and so requires $k + 1$ equations to estimate all the effects of *X* on *Y*. These equations are

$$M_i \;=\; i_{M_i} + a_i X + e_{M_i} \quad \text{for all } i = 1 \text{ to } k \tag{5.1}$$

$$Y \;=\; i_Y + c'X + \sum_{i=1}^{k} b_i M_i + e_Y \tag{5.2}$$

In this set of equations, a_i estimates the effect of *X* on M_i, b_i estimates the effect of M_i on *Y* controlling for *X* and the other $k - 1$ *M* variables, and c' estimates the effect of *X* on *Y* holding all *k* *M* variables constant.

Consider a parallel multiple mediator with three mediators, like the weight loss example introduced earlier. With $k = 3$ mediators, four equations are needed:

$$M_1 = i_{M_1} + a_1 X + e_{M_1} \tag{5.3}$$
$$M_2 = i_{M_2} + a_2 X + e_{M_2} \tag{5.4}$$
$$M_3 = i_{M_3} + a_3 X + e_{M_3} \tag{5.5}$$
$$Y = i_Y + c'X + b_1 M_1 + b_2 M_2 + b_3 M_3 + e_Y \tag{5.6}$$

In equations 5.3, 5.4, and 5.5, a_1, a_2, and a_3 quantify the amount by which two cases that differ by one unit on X are estimated to differ on M_1, M_2, and M_3, respectively. In equation 5.6, b_1 estimates the amount by which two cases that differ by one unit on M_1 differ on Y holding M_2, M_3, and X constant. Similarly, b_2 estimates the amount by which two cases that differ by one unit on M_2 differ on Y holding M_1, M_3, and X constant, and b_3 estimates the amount by which two cases that differ by one unit on M_3 differ on Y holding M_1, M_2, and X constant. Finally, c' estimates the amount by which two cases that differ by one unit on X differ on Y holding M_1, M_2, and M_3 constant.

The interpretations of a_i and c' are not dependent on the scale of measurement of X. Whether X is a dichotomous variable or a continuum, the interpretation is the same. However, when X is a dichotomous variable with the two groups coded by a one unit difference, these can be interpreted as estimated mean differences. For instance, suppose the two groups are coded with $X = 0$ or $X = 1$. In that case, $a_i = [\overline{M}_i \mid (X = 1)] - [\overline{M}_i \mid (X = 0)]$, and $c' = [\overline{Y}^* \mid (X = 1)] - [\overline{Y}^* \mid (X = 0)]$, where $\overline{Y}^*$ is an adjusted mean as defined on page 90, with all mediators set to their sample means: $\overline{Y}^* = i_Y + c'X + \sum_{i=1}^{k} b_i \overline{M}_i$.

Direct and Indirect Effects in a Parallel Multiple Mediator Model

In a parallel multiple mediator as in Figure 5.2, X is modeled to exert its effect on Y through $k + 1$ pathways. One pathway is direct, from X to Y without passing through any of the proposed mediators, and the other k pathways are indirect, each through a single mediator. In a multiple mediator model, the indirect effects are referred to as *specific indirect effects*. Thus, a model with k mediators has k specific indirect effects, one through M_1 $(X \rightarrow M_1 \rightarrow Y)$, one through M_2 $(X \rightarrow M_2 \rightarrow Y)$, and so forth, up through M_k $(X \rightarrow M_k \rightarrow Y)$.

As in a simple mediation model, the indirect effect of X on Y through a given mediator M_i is quantified as the product of paths linking X to Y through M_i. In a parallel multiple mediator model, only two paths link X

to Y through M_i. The first of these paths is the effect of X to M_i, and the second is the path from M_i to Y. The regression coefficients corresponding to these paths, when multiplied together, yield the specific indirect effect of X on Y through M_i. So consider the three-mediator parallel multiple mediator model estimated with equations 5.3 through 5.6. In this model, the specific indirect of X on Y through M_1 is a_1b_1, the specific indirect effect through M_2 is a_2b_2, and the specific indirect effect of X through M_3 is a_3b_3. Most generally, regardless of the number of mediators, the specific indirect effect of X on Y through M_i is estimated as a_ib_i from equations 5.1 and 5.2.

A specific indirect effect is interpreted just as in the simple mediation model, except with the addition of "controlling for all other mediators in the model." Thus, the specific indirect effect of X on Y through M_i is the estimated amount by which two cases that differ by one unit on X are estimated to differ on Y as a result of the effect of X on M_i, which in turn affects Y, holding all other mediators constant.

When added together, the specific indirect effects yield the *total indirect effect* of X on Y through all mediators in the model. In a model with k mediators:

$$\text{Total indirect effect of } X \text{ on } Y = \sum_{i=1}^{k} a_ib_i$$

For example, in a parallel multiple mediator model with three mediators represented by equations 5.3 through 5.6, the total indirect effect of X on Y is $a_1b_1 + a_2b_2 + a_3b_3$.

The direct effect of X quantifies how much two cases that differ by one unit on X are estimated to differ on Y independent of all mediators. As discussed earlier, this is c' in the model of Y from X and all mediators (e.g., equation 5.6 for the three-mediator model, or equation 5.2 more generally).

As in the simple mediation model, the sum of the direct and indirect effects is the total effect of X. In a model with k mediators, from the coefficients in equations 5.1 and 5.2,

$$c = c' + \sum_{i=1}^{k} a_ib_i \tag{5.7}$$

where c is the total effect of X. The total effect can also be estimated by regressing Y on X alone (as in equation 3.4). For instance, in the three-mediator model, $c = c' + a_1b_1 + a_2b_2 + a_3b_3$. Isolation of the total indirect effect in equation 5.7 shows that the total indirect effect is equal to the difference between the total and the direct effects of X:

$$\sum_{i=1}^{k} a_ib_i = c - c'$$

5.2   Example Using the Presumed Media Influence Study

In Chapter 3, I illustrated a simple mediation analysis using the data from a study conducted in Israel in which participants' reactions to a newspaper article about a likely sugar shortage were assessed (Tal-Or et al., 2010). Recall that half of the participants read an article they were told would be published on the front page of Israel's largest daily newspaper, whereas the other half were told it would appear in an internal economic supplement. After reading the article, their beliefs about how others would be influenced were measured (i.e., the extent to which the general public would be prompted to go buy sugar as a result of the article). The model in that chapter placed these beliefs, presumed media influence (PMI in the data file), as the mechanism or mediator intervening between the experimental manipulation of article location (COND in the data file: 1 for those assigned to the front page condition, 0 to the interior page condition) and intentions to buy sugar (REACTION in the data file). That is, people who thought the article was about to be published on the front page would be more inclined to believe that the public would be influenced relative to those told the article would appear in an economic supplement, so they themselves should go out and buy more sugar before it was all gone.

As described at the beginning of this chapter, establishing an indirect effect of X on Y through M through a simple mediation analysis does not imply that M is the only mechanism at work linking X to Y (cf., Rucker et al., 2011). Furthermore, the indirect effect could be due to an epiphenomenal association between the M in a simple mediation model and the "true" mediator or mediators causally between X and Y. Any variable correlated with presumed media influence and also affected by the experimental manipulation of article location could be the actual mediator transmitting the effect of location on intentions to buy sugar.

Fortunately, Tal-Or et al. (2010) recognized this and so had the foresight to measure a variable related to another possible mechanism—perceived issue importance. Perhaps people infer, from where an article is published in the newspaper, the extent to which the issue is something worthy of attention, of local or national significance, and thereby potentially something one should think about and perhaps act upon. So they measured people's beliefs about how important the potential sugar shortage was using two questions that were aggregated to form a perceived importance measure (IMPORT in the data file). Significant to the point made earlier, issue importance is correlated with presumed media influence ($r = 0.282, p < .01$). Those relatively more likely to believe others would be influenced to buy

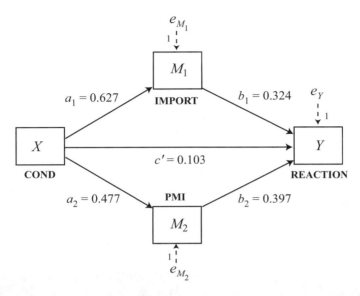

FIGURE 5.3. A statistical diagram of the parallel multiple mediator model for the presumed media influence study.

sugar as a result of reading the article also perceived the sugar shortage as relatively more important. Thus, it is conceivable that presumed media influence only appears to be functioning as a mediator of the effect of article location on peoples' reactions and it is perceptions of importance that is the real mediator.

Estimation of indirect effects in a parallel multiple mediator model with both presumed media influence and perceived importance as mediators would allow for a simultaneous test of each mechanism while accounting for the association between them. Figure 5.3 provides a statistical diagram of the model. As can be seen, it contains three consequent variables, so it requires three equations to estimate all the effects, one for each of the mediators (M_1 and M_2), and one for the outcome Y. The equations for the mediators contain article location (X) as the only predictor, whereas the equation for intentions to buy sugar (Y) includes both article location and the two mediators.

In SPSS, the coefficients of this model are estimated with three regression commands:

```
regression/dep=import/method=enter cond.
regression/dep=pmi/method=enter cond.
regression/dep=reaction/method=enter import cond pmi.
```

The corresponding commands in SAS are

```
proc reg data=pmi;
model import=cond;
model pmi=cond;
model reaction=cond import pmi;
run;
```

The regression coefficients, standard errors, and other statistics pertinent to the model are summarized in Table 5.1, and the path coefficients are superimposed on the statistical diagram in Figure 5.3.

PROCESS greatly simplifies the estimation process by conducting all these regressions in one command, while also generating various additional statistics and inferential tests discussed in section 5.3 but not available in the OLS regression routines built into SPSS and SAS. The PROCESS command below estimates the model and provides output pertinent to statistical inference:

```
process y=reaction/x=cond/m=import pmi/total=1/contrast=1/model=4/
    seed=31216.
```

```
%process (data=pmi,y=reaction,x=cond,m=import pmi,total=1,contrast=1,
    model=4,seed=31216);
```

This PROCESS command looks identical to the command for the simple mediation model in Chapter 3, with a few exceptions. First, because the model contains more than one mediator, more than one variable is provided following **m=**. Notice that the inclusion of an additional mediator does not require a different model number; **model=4** is used for both simple mediation models and parallel multiple mediator models. PROCESS automatically detects the number of variables listed in the **m=** list and estimates a parallel multiple mediator model if it sees more than one variable in the list. The order of the variables in this list is not consequential in model 4 for estimation purposes, although it does influence the order in which information about the models and effects is displayed in the output. The second difference is the addition of the **contrast=1** command, which requests PROCESS to conduct a test of differences between specific indirect effects. This test is described in section 5.3.

From Table 5.1 or Figure 5.4, the three best fitting OLS regression models that define this parallel multiple mediator model are

$$\hat{M}_1 = 3.908 + 0.627X \tag{5.8}$$

$$\hat{M}_2 = 5.377 + 0.477X \tag{5.9}$$

$$\hat{Y} = -0.150 + 0.103X + 0.324M_1 + 0.397M_2 \tag{5.10}$$

TABLE 5.1. Regression Coefficients, Standard Errors, and Model Summary Information for the Presumed Media Influence Parallel Multiple Mediator Model Depicted in Figure 5.3

		Consequent												
		M_1 (IMPORT)					M_2 (PMI)					Y (REACTION)		
Antecedent			Coeff.	SE	p		Coeff.	SE	p		Coeff.	SE	p
X (COND)	a_1		0.627	0.310	.045	a_2	0.477	0.236	.045	c'	0.103	0.239	.666
M_1 (IMPORT)			—	—	—		—	—	—	b_1	0.324	0.071	<.001
M_2 (PMI)			—	—	—		—	—	—	b_2	0.397	0.093	<.001
Constant	i_{M_1}		3.908	0.213	<.001	i_{M_2}	5.377	0.162	<.001	i_Y	−0.150	0.530	.778
			$R^2 = 0.033$				$R^2 = 0.033$				$R^2 = 0.325$		
			$F(1, 121) = 4.094, p = .045$				$F(1, 121) = 4.088, p = .045$				$F(3, 119) = 19.112, p < .001$		

Thus, $a_1 = 0.627$, $a_2 = 0.477$, $b_1 = 0.324$, $b_2 = 0.397$, $c' = 0.103$. The use of the **total** option in PROCESS also generates the total effect, $c = 0.496$, from estimating Y from X alone. Very little of the variance in perceived media influence or issue importance is explained by the manipulation of article location (both $R^2 = 0.033$), but about a third of the variance in intentions to buy sugar is accounted for by both proposed mediators and article location, $R^2 = 0.325$.

The most relevant information pertinent to the process being modeled is the direct and indirect effects of article location on participants' reactions to the article. Starting first with the indirect effect through issue importance, this indirect effect is estimated as $a_1b_1 = 0.627(0.324) = 0.203$. PROCESS does the multiplication automatically and displays the indirect effect in the section of output on page 160 labeled "Indirect effect of X on Y" in the row labeled "import." Two cases that differ by one unit on X (i.e., COND, the front versus the interior page condition in this data set) are estimated to differ by 0.203 units in their intention to buy sugar through perceived importance, with those assigned to the front page condition having higher intentions (because the indirect effect is positive). This positive indirect effect results from two positive constituent effects. Those assigned to the front page condition have stronger intentions to buy sugar as a result of the tendency for those told the article was to be published on the front page to perceive the sugar shortage as more important than those told it would be published in an interior supplement (because a_1 is positive), which in turn was positively related to their own intentions to purchase sugar (because b_1 is positive). Because the two experimental groups are coded by a one-unit difference on X, this indirect effect is equal to the mean difference in perceived importance times the partial effect of perceived importance on reactions: $a_1b_1 = ([\overline{M}_1 \mid (X = 1)] - [\overline{M}_1 \mid (X = 0)])b_1 = (4.535 - 3.908)0.324 = 0.203$.

A second indirect effect of article location on intention to buy sugar is modeled through presumed media influence, estimated as $a_2b_2 = 0.477(0.397) = 0.189$ and provided in the PROCESS output. Those assigned to the front page condition have stronger intentions to buy sugar (by 0.189 units) as a result of the tendency for those told the article was to be published on the front page to perceive others would be influenced by the story more so than those told it would be published in an interior supplement (because a_2 is positive), which in turn was positively related to their own intentions to purchase sugar (because b_2 is positive). This is equivalent to the mean difference in perceived media influence multiplied by the partial effect of presumed media influence on reactions: $a_2b_2 = ([\overline{M}_2 \mid (X = 1)] - [\overline{M}_2 \mid (X = 0)])b_2 = (5.853 - 5.377)0.397 = 0.189$.

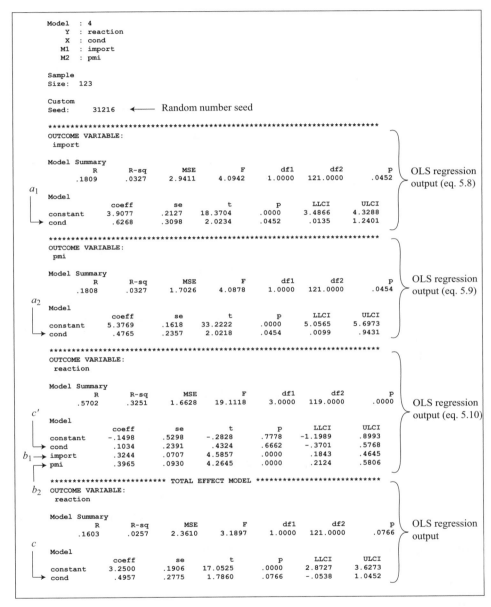

FIGURE 5.4. Output from the PROCESS procedure for SPSS for a parallel multiple mediator model of the presumed media influence data.

(continued)

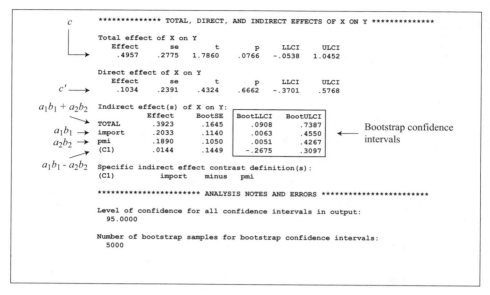

FIGURE 5.4 continued.

In a parallel multiple mediator model, it is possible to talk about the indirect effect of X on Y summed across all mediators. This is the total indirect effect, defined here as $a_1b_1 + a_2b_2 = 0.627(0.324) + 0.477(0.397) = 0.392$. The total indirect effect is positive, meaning that those assigned to the front page condition were, on average, 0.392 units higher in their intention to buy sugar than those assigned to the interior page condition as a result of the effect of article location on the mediators, which in turn influence intentions. The total indirect effect often is not of much interest in a multiple mediator model, and sometimes it will be small even when the specific indirect effects are large, which seems paradoxical. More on this in section 5.6.

The direct effect, $c' = 0.103$, quantifies the effect of the manipulation of article location on intentions to buy sugar independent of the effect of the proposed mediators on those intentions. Irrespective of differences between the groups in their perceived media influence and issue importance and how those mediators relate to intentions to buy sugar, those told the article was to be published on the front page expressed stronger intentions to buy sugar (because c' is positive) than those told it would be published in the interior supplement. Due to the coding of groups by a difference of one unit, c' is equivalent to the difference between adjusted means, as defined and described on page 90. In this case, $c' = [\overline{Y}^* \mid (X = 1)] - [\overline{Y}^* \mid (X = 0)] = 3.538 - 3.435 = 0.103$, where $\overline{Y}^* = -0.150 + 0.103X + 0.324(4.203) + 0.397(5.603)$ from the model of Y.

The total effect of article location on intentions to buy sugar is not determined at all by the mediators proposed as intervening between X and Y. As it was in the simple mediation model, $c = 0.496$. As promised, this total effect partitions cleanly into the direct effect plus the sum of the specific indirect effects:

$$c = c' + a_1b_1 + a_2b_2 = 0.103 + 0.203 + 0.189 = 0.496$$

meaning that the total indirect effect of X (i.e., the sum of the specific indirect effects) is the difference between the total and direct effects of X:

$$c - c' = a_1b_1 + a_2b_2 = 0.496 - 0.103 = 0.203 + 0.189 = 0.392$$

5.3 Statistical Inference

In the prior section, I illustrated the estimation of the equations defining a multiple mediator model using the OLS regression procedures built into SPSS or SAS as well as using the PROCESS procedure. The discussion thus far has been purely descriptive in nature. Statistical inference allows for generalization to the process generating the data or the population from which the sample was derived. The inferential procedures available for effects in the parallel multiple mediator model are similar to those in the simple mediation model. The inclusion of multiple mediators also allows for a formal test of the difference between specific indirect effects. I describe such a test in this section.

Inference about the Direct and Total Effects

As in the simple mediation model, inference about the total and direct effects of X on Y is straightforward. A test of the null hypothesis that $_Tc' = 0$ is available in the output from any statistical package that can estimate equation 5.2 using OLS regression. This test is available in two locations on the PROCESS output in Figure 5.4. As can be seen, $c' = 0.103, t(119) = 0.432, p = .666$. The null hypothesis cannot be rejected. Alternatively, a confidence interval can be constructed using equation 2.16, implemented automatically by PROCESS. From the PROCESS output, $-0.370 \leq {}_Tc' \leq 0.577$. Regardless of which method is used, we cannot claim that participants' reactions to the article differ as a function of article location when presumed media influence and perceived importance are statistically controlled.

The total effect of article location on reactions is the sum of the direct and indirect effects. In this parallel multiple mediator model, the total effect c can be estimated by regressing Y on X alone using any OLS regression program. The coefficient for X is the total effect of X in this regression. The **total** option in PROCESS generates the relevant output. As can be seen in Figure 5.4, $c = 0.496, p = .077$, with a 95% confidence interval between -0.054 and 1.045. This is identical to the total effect of X in the simple mediation example in section 3.3 because the total effect won't be influenced by the number of mediators you place between X and Y.

Inference about Specific Indirect Effects

The normal theory approach for the indirect effect in a simple mediation model described in section 3.4 can be used for statistical inference about specific indirect effects in a parallel multiple mediator model, though for reasons outlined in Chapter 3, I don't recommend this approach. For the specific indirect effect of X on Y through M_i, the second-order standard error estimator is

$$se_{a_i b_i} = \sqrt{a_i^2 se_{b_i}^2 + b_i^2 se_{a_i}^2 + se_{a_i}^2 se_{b_i}^2}$$

where $se_{a_i}^2$ and $se_{b_i}^2$ are the squared standard errors of a_i and b_i. A test of the null hypothesis that $_T a_{iT} b_i = 0$ is constructed by dividing $a_i b_i$ by the estimated standard error and deriving a p-value from the standard normal distribution. Alternatively, a $ci\%$ confidence interval can be constructed as

$$a_i b_i - Z_{ci\%} se_{a_i b_i} \leq {}_T a_{iT} b_i \leq a_i b_i + Z_{ci\%} se_{a_i b_i}$$

where ci is the confidence desired (e.g., 95) and $Z_{ci\%}$ is the value in the standard normal distribution that cuts off the upper $(100 - ci)/2\%$ of the distribution from the rest.

Rounding errors and other inaccuracies are nearly inevitable if these computations are done by hand. PROCESS provides normal theory hypothesis tests for specific indirect effects in a parallel multiple mediator model through the use of the **normal** option.

Bootstrap confidence intervals are the better approach to inference when the original data are available for analysis. No assumptions about the shape of the sampling distribution of $a_i b_i$ are made, and bootstrap confidence intervals tend to be more powerful than competing methods such as the normal theory approach (see Williams & MacKinnon, 2008, for simulation results specific to the multiple mediator model). Using the same procedure described on page 98, a bootstrap confidence interval for a specific indirect effect is constructed by taking a random sample with replacement of size n

from the sample, estimating each specific indirect effect $a_i b_i^*$ in the resulting data, and repeating this resampling and estimation many times. With several thousand bootstrap estimates of each specific indirect effect, endpoints of the confidence interval are calculated. If zero is outside of a $ci\%$ confidence interval, then $_T a_{iT} b_i$ is declared different from zero with $ci\%$ confidence, whereas if the confidence interval straddles zero, the conclusion is that there is insufficient evidence that X affects Y through M_i.

Bootstrap confidence intervals for the specific indirect effects generated by PROCESS using the percentile method can be found in Figure 5.4 under the section of the output that reads "Indirect effect(s) of X on Y." By default, $5,000$ bootstrap samples are generated. Notice that contrary to the conclusion reached using the normal theory approach, the bootstrap confidence intervals support the claim, with 95% confidence, that article location influences reactions indirectly through both perceived importance (0.006 to 0.455) and presumed media influence (0.005 to 0.427), as both confidence intervals are entirely above zero.

Bootstrapping requires the original data. Although this is not usually a problem, there are occasions when the data may not be available. Monte Carlo confidence intervals are a good substitute for bootstrapping in such a circumstance. The estimation of a Monte Carlo confidence interval for a specific indirect effect proceeds similarly to the estimation procedure in the simple mediation model. The major difference in the procedure relates to the fact that there are multiple a and b distributions to simulate in a multiple mediator model. For a multiple mediator model with k mediators, one could simply use the Monte Carlo method described in section 3.4 k times, once for each specific indirect effect, plugging the values of a_i, b_i, se_{a_i}, and se_{b_i} into the Monte Carlo sampling procedure (or the code in Appendix C). An alternative and better approach would acknowledge that the paths from each M to Y in a multiple mediator model are not necessarily independent, and so the Monte Carlo sampling procedure should accommodate this. Preacher and Selig (2012) describe the construction of Monte Carlo confidence intervals in a multiple mediator model and provide R code that does the computation.

Pairwise Comparisons between Specific Indirect Effects

In a multiple mediator model, it is sometimes of interest to test whether one indirect effect is statistically different from another. For instance, is the specific indirect effect of article location on reactions through perceived importance different from the specific indirect effect through presumed media influence? If the indirect effect of X through mediator i (i.e., $a_i b_i$) is pertinent to the mechanism postulated by one theory and the indirect effect of X through mediator j (i.e., $a_j b_j$) quantifies the mechanism relevant to a second theory, an inference about whether $_T a_{iT} b_i = _T a_{jT} b_j$ affords a claim as to whether one mechanism accounts for more of the effect of X on Y than the other mechanism, with an important caveat described below. For examples of such questions in the literature about difference between indirect effects, answered using the approach described here, see Goldman et al. (2016), Hart (2011), Merino et al. (2016), Peréz et al. (2012), and Scogin et al. (2015).

Although it might seem that such a comparison between specific indirect effects would be impossible if the mediators are measured on different metrics, it turns out this is not a problem. A specific indirect effect is interpreted as the amount by which two cases differing by one unit on X are estimated to differ on Y through the intervening variable independent of the other intervening variables. This interpretation does not include the metric of the intervening variable. Specific indirect effects are scaled entirely in terms of the metrics of X and Y (see MacKinnon, 2000, 2008; Preacher & Hayes, 2008a), so two specific indirect effects of the same antecedent on the same consequent can be meaningfully compared even if the mediator variables are measured on different scales. Thus, standardization or other forms of arithmetic gymnastics applied to the measurement scales is not necessary to conduct an inferential test of the equality of specific indirect effects from X to Y in a multiple mediator model.

Two inferential approaches have been most widely discussed and disseminated in the literature. A normal theory approach is described by Preacher and Hayes (2008a) and MacKinnon (2000) based on dividing $a_i b_i - a_j b_j$ by an estimate of its standard error. One estimator of the standard error of the difference is

$$se_{a_i b_i - a_j b_j} = \sqrt{\begin{array}{c} b_i^2 se_{a_i}^2 - 2b_i b_j COV_{a_i a_j} + b_j^2 se_{a_j}^2 + \\ a_j^2 se_{b_j}^2 - 2a_i a_j COV_{b_i b_j} + a_i^2 se_{b_i}^2 \end{array}}$$

where $COV_{a_i a_j}$ is the covariance between a_i and a_j, and $COV_{b_i b_j}$ is the covariance between b_i and b_j. MacKinnon (2000) offers a different standard error estimator that does not require the covariance between a_i and a_j by assuming it is zero, which is equivalent to constraining the correlation between the residuals in the models of M_i and M_j to be zero:

$$se_{a_i b_i - a_j b_j} = \sqrt{b_i^2 se_{a_i}^2 + b_j^2 se_{a_j}^2 + a_j^2 se_{b_j}^2 - 2a_i a_j COV_{b_i b_j} + a_i^2 se_{b_i}^2}$$

The ratio of the difference to its standard error is then calculated and a p-value for a test of the null hypothesis that $_T a_{iT} b_i = _T a_{jT} b_j$ can be derived using the standard normal distribution. Alternatively, a 95% confidence interval for the difference can be computed as

$$(a_ib_i - a_jb_j) \pm 1.96se_{a_ib_i-a_jb_j} \tag{5.11}$$

In this expression, 1.96 can be replaced with an appropriate critical Z from a table of normal probabilities for different confidence levels (e.g., 1.645 for 90% or 2.57 for 99% confidence).

Like all normal theory approaches discussed thus far, this method requires the assumption that the sampling distribution of the difference between specific indirect effects is normal. It turns out that this is a fairly reasonable assumption, but since an assumption can never be proven true, bootstrapping offers an alternative without requiring this assumption. A bootstrap confidence interval is derived by estimating the difference between specific indirect effects over repeated bootstrap sampling and model estimation. Using the resulting empirical approximation of the sampling distribution of the difference between specific indirect effects, a bootstrap confidence interval for the difference can be constructed with the same procedure described thus far.

PROCESS offers bootstrap confidence intervals for pairwise comparisons between specific indirect effects with the addition of **contrast=1** to the PROCESS command. In a model with k mediators, PROCESS will conduct $k(k - 1)/2$ pairwise comparisons, one for each possible difference between specific indirect effects. A confidence interval that does not contain zero provides evidence that the two indirect effects are statistically different from each other, whereas a confidence interval that straddles zero supports the claim of no difference between the specific indirect effects.

The output this option generates for the parallel multiple mediator model of the presumed media influence study can be found in Figure 5.4 in the indirect effects section in the row labeled "(C1)." There is only one comparison listed because in a parallel multiple mediator model with two mediators, there are only two specific indirect effects and so only one pairwise comparison is possible. The PROCESS output provides a key for the meaning of (C1) at the bottom of Figure 5.4, which in this case is the specific indirect effect through importance minus the specific indirect effect through presumed media influence (i.e., $a_1b_1 - a_2b_2$). The point estimate of the difference between specific indirect effects is $0.203 - 0.189 = 0.014$, but a 95% confidence interval straddles zero (-0.268 to 0.310). So we can't say definitively these specific indirect effects are different from each other.

It is tempting to treat this as a test of the difference in *strength* of the mechanisms at work linking X to Y, or that one indirect effect is larger than another in an absolute sense. However, such an interpretation is justified only if the point estimates for the two specific indirect effects being compared are of the same sign. Consider, for instance, the case where $a_i b_i = -0.30$ and $a_j b_j = 0.30$. A test of the difference between these specific indirect effects may lead to the claim that their difference is not zero, but this does not imply the mechanisms are of different strength or that one indirect effect is bigger. The point estimates suggest one mechanism results in a positive difference in Y, whereas the other yields a negative difference of equal magnitude. In an absolute sense, they are equal in size by the point estimates, yet statistically different by an inferential test which considers their sign. But one indirect effect is not *stronger* than the other. Nor can we say that X exerts a larger effect on Y through one of the mediators relative to the other.

But what if you find yourself in a situation where you want to compare the strength of two indirect effects that are different in sign? The literature is largely silent on this, but here is a proposal. Rather than defining the contrast as $a_i b_i - a_j b_j$ and then bootstrapping this difference, instead define the contrast as

$$|a_i b_i| - |a_j b_j| \tag{5.12}$$

and bootstrap this difference, which ignores whether a specific indirect effect is positive or negative. A confidence interval for this difference that does not include zero suggests that the indirect effects are different when you ignore sign, meaning that they differ in strength. But if the confidence interval contains zero, then one cannot definitely claim that the indirect effects are different in strength.

PROCESS will generate bootstrap confidence intervals for all possible pairwise contrasts between indirect effects as defined in equation 5.12. To get the output, use 2 rather than 1 in the argument of the **contrast** command (i.e., **contrast=2**).

Inference about the Total Indirect Effect

A multiple mediator model also contains a *total indirect effect*, defined as the sum of all specific indirect effects. It is possible to conduct an inferential test of the total indirect effect using either the normal theory approach, a bootstrap confidence interval, or a Monte Carlo confidence interval. The normal theory approach requires an estimate of the standard error of the total indirect effect, but the formula for constructing it is quite complicated even in multiple mediator models with only two mediators. Given such complicated expressions and the fact that I do not recommend the normal theory approach to inference about indirect effects, I don't present the details here. They can be found in Preacher and Hayes (2008a) or MacKinnon

(2008). Good SEM programs can conduct a normal theory test of the total indirect effect. PROCESS does not provide this test.

The Monte Carlo approach is available for the total indirect effect in a multiple mediator model using code provided by Preacher and Selig (2012), and PROCESS provides a bootstrap confidence interval. As I discuss in section 5.6, the total indirect effect is often not of much interest, and I generally deemphasize it when interpreting a multiple mediator model. As can be seen in the PROCESS output in Figure 5.4, we can be 95% confident that the total indirect effect of article location through both mediators simultaneously is somewhere between 0.091 and 0.739. This supports the claim that perceived importance and presumed media influence collectively mediate the effect of article location on intentions to buy sugar.

5.4 The Serial Multiple Mediator Model

Examples of the parallel multiple mediator model like that described in the prior section are in abundance in the literature. A distinguishing feature of this model is the assumption that no mediator causally influences another. In practice, mediators will be correlated, but this model specifies that they are not causally so. In the *serial* multiple mediator model, the assumption of no causal association between two or more mediators is not only relaxed, it is rejected outright a priori. The goal when an investigator estimates a serial multiple mediator model is to investigate the direct and indirect effects of X on Y while modeling a process in which X causes M_1, which in turn causes M_2, and so forth, concluding with Y as the final consequent.

Though less common than the parallel multiple mediator model, it is not hard to find exemplars of such models in the literature. For instance, Casciano and Massey (2012) compared the anxiety of residents living in a low-income housing development located in a middle-class neighborhood to a matched group who applied to live in the housing development but remained on the waiting list. They argued that life in a middle-class housing development would reduce exposure to neighborhood disorder (e.g., crime, homeless people, drugs and drug use, violence) relative to those living elsewhere, which would in turn reduce the number of stressful life experiences, which in turn would translate into fewer anxiety symptoms. Their analysis supported the environment → disorder exposure → stressful experiences → anxiety symptoms causal sequence. Other examples in the literature in which a causal process is modeled as operating with mediators linked in serial include Aragón, Clark, Dyer, and Bargh (2015); Bizer et al. (2012); Brown-Iannuzzi, Dotsch, Cooley, and Payne (2017); Chugani et al. (2015);

Feldman (2011); Kan, Lichtenstein, Grant, and Janiszwski (2014); Knobloch-Westerwick and Hoplamazian (2012); Krieger and Sarge (2013); Lachman and Agrigoroaei (2012); Li, Shaffer, and Bagger (2016); Oishi and Diener (2014); Schrift and Moty (2015); Traut-Mattausch, Wagner, Pollatos, and Jones (2015); Tsang, Carpenter, Robers, Frisch, and Carlisle (2014); Valentine, Li, Penki, and Perrett (2014); and Van Jaarsveld, Walker, and Skarlicki (2010).

Serial multiple mediator models can grow in complexity quite rapidly as the number of mediators increases, as increasing the number of mediators increases the number of paths that one can draw between causes and effects. In this section, I restrict discussion to a form of serial mediation in which variables presumed as causally prior are modeled as affecting all variables later in the causal sequence. In a sense, this is the most complex serial mediator model possible because it maximizes the number of paths that need to be estimated. Variations on this model are described in section 5.5 that impose constraints on what variables earlier in the causal sequence affect what variables later.

Two serial multiple mediator models can be found in Figure 5.5 in the form of statistical diagrams. The diagram in panel A depicts a two-mediator model in which X is modeled as affecting Y through four pathways. One pathway is indirect and runs from X to Y through M_1 only, a second indirect path runs through M_2 only, and a third indirect influence passes through both M_1 and M_2 in serial, with M_1 affecting M_2. The remaining effect of X is direct from X to Y without passing through either M_1 or M_2.

This statistical model translates into three equations, because the model contains three consequent variables:

$$M_1 = i_{M_1} + a_1 X + e_{M_1} \tag{5.13}$$
$$M_2 = i_{M_2} + a_2 X + d_{21} M_1 + e_{M_2} \tag{5.14}$$
$$Y = i_Y + c' X + b_1 M_1 + b_2 M_2 + e_Y \tag{5.15}$$

Notice in this set of equations that each consequent has all variables assumed to be causally prior as antecedents. So M_1 is estimated from X alone, M_2 is estimated from X and M_1, and Y is estimated from X, M_1, and M_2.

Figure 5.5, panel B, is a serial multiple mediator model with three mediators representing eight distinct effects of X on Y, seven indirect and one direct. The seven indirect paths are found by tracing every possible way of getting from X to Y through at least one M. The possibilities include three passing through only a single mediator ($X \to M_1 \to Y; X \to M_2 \to Y; X \to M_3 \to Y$), three passing through two mediators in serial

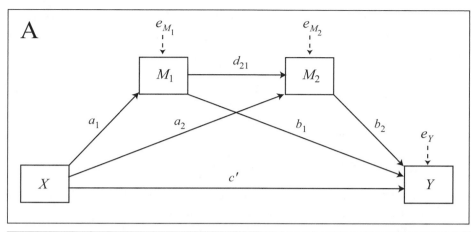

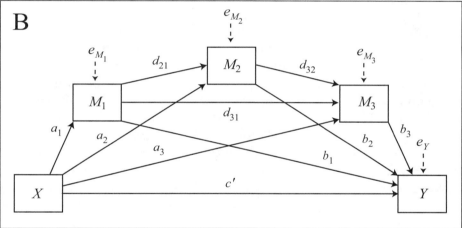

FIGURE 5.5. Two serial multiple mediator models in statistical diagram form with two (panel A) and three (panel B) mediators.

$(X \rightarrow M_1 \rightarrow M_2 \rightarrow Y; X \rightarrow M_1 \rightarrow M_3 \rightarrow Y; X \rightarrow M_2 \rightarrow M_3 \rightarrow Y)$, and one through all three mediators in serial $(X \rightarrow M_1 \rightarrow M_2 \rightarrow M_3 \rightarrow Y)$. As always, the direct effect does not pass through any mediators. The four equations (one for each of the four consequent variables) representing the three-mediator serial multiple mediator model are

$$
\begin{aligned}
M_1 &= i_{M_1} + a_1 X + e_{M_1} \\
M_2 &= i_{M_2} + a_2 X + d_{21} M_1 + e_{M_2} \\
M_3 &= i_{M_3} + a_3 X + d_{31} M_1 + d_{32} M_2 + e_{M_3} \\
Y &= i_Y + c' X + b_1 M_1 + b_2 M_2 + b_3 M_3 + e_Y
\end{aligned}
$$

Most generally, a serial multiple mediator model with k mediators requires $k+1$ equations to estimate because there are $k+1$ consequent variables (one for each of the k mediators, plus one for Y):

$$M_1 = i_{M_1} + a_1 X + e_{M_1}$$
$$M_i = i_{M_i} + a_i X + \sum_{j=1}^{i-1} d_{ij} M_j + e_{M_i} \quad \text{for all } i = 2 \text{ to } k$$
$$Y = i_Y + c' X + \sum_{i=1}^{k} b_i M_i + e_Y$$

Direct and Indirect Effects in a Serial Multiple Mediator Model

In a serial multiple mediator model, the total effect of X on Y partitions into direct and indirect components, just as it does in the simple and parallel multiple mediator models. Regardless of the number of mediators in the model, the direct effect is c' and interpreted as always—the estimated difference in Y between two cases that differ by one unit on X but that are equal on all mediators in the model. The indirect effects, of which there may be many depending on the number of mediators in the model, are all constructed by multiplying the regression weights corresponding to each step in an indirect pathway. And they are all interpreted as the estimated difference in Y between two cases that differ by one unit on X through the causal sequence from X to mediator(s) to Y. Regardless of the number of mediators, the sum of all the specific indirect effects is the total indirect effect of X, and the direct and indirect effects sum to the total effect of X. I illustrate below for two serial multiple mediator models with either two or three mediators, but the procedure generalizes to serial mediator models with any number of mediators.

Two Mediators in Serial. Consider the serial multiple mediator model with two mediators. This model has three specific indirect effects and one direct effect. The three specific indirect effects are each estimated as the product of the regression weights linking X to Y through at least one M. From Figure 5.5 panel A, the specific indirect effect of X on Y through only M_1 is $a_1 b_1$, the specific indirect effect through M_2 only is $a_2 b_2$, and the specific indirect effect through both M_1 and M_2 in serial is $a_1 d_{21} b_2$. Combined, these three indirect effects sum to the total indirect effect of X: $a_1 b_1 + a_2 b_2 + a_1 d_{21} b_2$. When the total indirect effect of X is added to the direct effect of X, the result is c, the total effect of X, which can be estimated from a regression estimating Y from X only, as in equation 3.4. That is,

$$c = c' + a_1 b_1 + a_2 b_2 + a_1 d_{21} b_2$$

As in the simple and parallel multiple mediator models, the total indirect effect of X on Y in the serial multiple mediator model is the difference between the total effect of X on Y and direct effect of X on Y:

$$c - c' = a_1 b_1 + a_2 b_2 + a_1 d_{21} b_2$$

Three Mediators in Serial. These same definitions, rules, and relationships apply to the serial multiple mediator model with three mediators. Considering the three-mediator model in Figure 5.5, there are seven indirect effects estimated as products of regression coefficients. For example, the specific indirect effect of X on Y through M_2 only is $a_2 b_2$. Through M_1 and M_3 in serial, the specific indirect effect is $a_1 d_{31} b_3$. And the specific indirect effect through M_1, M_2, and M_3 in serial is $a_1 d_{21} d_{32} b_3$. Using this same procedure, following all pathways and multiplying coefficients as you go, all seven specific indirect effects can be derived. These sum to the total indirect effect of X on Y through all three mediators: $a_1 b_1 + a_2 b_2 + a_3 b_3 + a_1 d_{21} b_2 + a_1 d_{31} b_3 + a_2 d_{32} b_3 + a_1 d_{21} d_{32} b_3$. When the total indirect effect is added to the direct effect, the result is c, the total effect of X on Y

$$c = c' + a_1 b_1 + a_2 b_2 + a_3 b_3 + a_1 d_{21} b_2 + a_1 d_{31} b_3 + a_2 d_{32} b_3 + a_1 d_{21} d_{32} b_3$$

which means the total indirect effect of X on Y is the difference between the total effect of X on Y and the direct effect of X on Y:

$$c - c' = a_1 b_1 + a_2 b_2 + a_3 b_3 + a_1 d_{21} b_2 + a_1 d_{31} b_3 + a_2 d_{32} b_3 + a_1 d_{21} d_{32} b_3$$

Statistical Inference

Inferential tests of direct and indirect effects are analogous to methods described already for the simple and parallel multiple mediator model. A test of the null hypothesis that the direct effect $_T c'$ is equal to zero is available in the output of any OLS regression routine, and an interval estimate is constructed as described in section 5.3.

A comparable normal theory approach for inference about the indirect effects in a serial multiple mediator model proceeds as usual by dividing the indirect effect by an estimate of the standard error and then deriving the p-value using the standard normal distribution in order to test the null hypothesis that the indirect effect is zero in the population. The same formulas for the standard errors for indirect effects through a single mediator provided in section 5.3 can be used in the serial multiple mediator model for the $a_i b_i$ indirect effects. With two mediators linked in serial, Taylor, MacKinnon, and Tein (2008) provide the standard error of the indirect effect of $a_1 d_{21} b_2$ as

$$se_{a_1 d_{21} b_2} = \sqrt{a_1^2 d_{21}^2 se_{b_2}^2 + a_1^2 b_2^2 se_{d_{21}}^2 + d_{21}^2 b_2^2 se_{a_1}^2}$$

where $se^2_{a_1}$, $se^2_{d_{21}}$, and $se^2_{b_2}$ are the squared standard errors of a_1, d_{21}, and b_2, respectively. The formula for the standard error of the indirect effect involving three or more mediators in serial is complicated and described in Sobel (1982).

Computation of these standard errors by hand is certain to produce inaccuracies, so let a computer do the work for you if you are going to use this approach.[1] But whether computed by hand or by computer, I don't recommend the normal theory approach for the same reasons I don't recommend it in simple or parallel multiple mediation models. It assumes normality of the sampling distribution of the indirect effect—an unrealistic assumption and not necessary to make these days, because simulation research (Taylor et al., 2008) shows that bootstrap confidence intervals generally perform better without making this assumption.

No modifications to the logic or method of bootstrapping is required to apply this method to the indirect effects in a serial multiple mediator model. Bootstrap confidence intervals for indirect effects (specific, total, or pairwise comparisons between) are calculated by repeatedly resampling from the data with replacement, estimating the model in each bootstrap sample, calculating the indirect effects, and deriving the endpoints of a confidence interval for each as described already. An indirect effect (or a difference between two indirect effects) can be deemed different from zero with $ci\%$ confidence if zero is outside of a $ci\%$ confidence interval. If the confidence interval straddles 0, this supports the claim that the indirect effect (or difference between) is not statistically different from zero.

In principle, Monte Carlo confidence intervals can be constructed for all indirect effects in a serial multiple mediator model. As noted earlier, Preacher and Selig (2012) describe Monte Carlo confidence interval construction for specific indirect effects through a single mediator in a parallel multiple mediator model as well as for the total indirect effect. The method and code they illustrate could be adapted without too much difficulty to indirect effects through multiple mediators chained in serial as well.

Example from the Presumed Media Influence Study

The parallel multiple mediator model of the presumed media influence study estimated and interpreted in sections 5.2 and 5.3 assumes no causal association between the mediators. Although plausible, it is perhaps more plausible that people's beliefs about how others are going to be influenced by the media are determined at least in part by perceived issue importance.

---

[1]Some structural equation modeling programs can generate standard errors for complex indirect effects.

That is, perhaps those who perceive a particular article pertains to an issue of local, national, or international importance are more likely to believe that others will be affected by what they read about that important topic, then go out and act based on this information. The psychological logic would go something like this: "This article will be published on the front page, so it must be important, and people will take notice of such an important matter and act by buying sugar to stock up. Therefore, I should go out and buy sugar before supplies are all gone."

This process predicts that even after accounting for the effect of article location on both perceived media influence and perceived importance, there should be some association remaining between these mediators. In a parallel multiple mediator model, the partial correlation between M_1 and M_2 controlling for X is an index of association between mediators remaining after accounting for the effect of X on both. In these data, this partial correlation is .258, $p < .01$. That is, after statistically adjusting for the effect of the experimental manipulation of article location on both perceived importance and presumed media influence, those who perceive the sugar shortage as relatively more important also presume relatively more media influence. Of course, this correlation remaining after accounting for X could be due to other causes outside of the system being modeled, but it may reflect a misspecification resulting from assuming no causal association between M_1 and M_2.

A statistical diagram of a serial multiple mediator model consistent with this proposed process can be found in Figure 5.6. This model contains one direct and three indirect effects of article location on intentions to buy sugar, pieced together by estimating the regression coefficients in equations 5.13, 5.14, and 5.15. In SPSS, the commands are

```
regression/dep=import/method=enter cond.
regression/dep=pmi/method=enter cond import.
regression/dep=reaction/method=enter cond import pmi.
```

In SAS, use

```
proc reg data=pmi;
model import=cond;model pmi=cond import;model reaction=cond import pmi;
run;
```

However, the OLS routine built into SPSS and SAS will not calculate any of the indirect effects for you, nor will it provide any inferential tests of the indirect effects such as bootstrap confidence intervals. Better to use PROCESS, which estimates the coefficients and provides additional information needed for inference all in one fell swoop. In SPSS, try the command below.

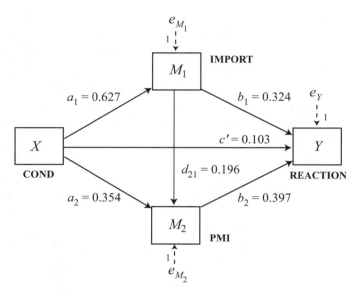

FIGURE 5.6. A statistical diagram of the serial multiple mediator model for the presumed media influence data.

```
process y=reaction/x=cond/m=import pmi/total=1/contrast=1/model=6/
    seed=031216.
```

The equivalent PROCESS command in SAS is

```
%process (data=pmi,y=reaction,x=cond,m=import pmi,total=1,contrast=1,
    model=6,seed=031216);
```

Notice that this PROCESS command looks very similar to the PROCESS command for the parallel multiple mediator model. The major difference is the specification of **model=6**, which tells PROCESS this is a serial multiple mediator model (see Appendix A). When model 6 is specified, the order of the variables listed in the **m=** list matters, unlike in model 4 where order is ignored. The order of the variables in the list of mediators is taken literally as the causal sequence, with the first mediator variable in the list causally prior to the second in the list, and so forth. This PROCESS command will also generate bootstrap confidence intervals for all indirect effects as well as all possible pairwise comparisons between indirect effects using 5,000 bootstrap samples. PROCESS does not provide normal theory tests for indirect effects in a serial multiple mediator model.

PROCESS output can be found in Figure 5.7, and the various model coefficients and other assorted statistics are summarized in Table 5.2. The model coefficients have also been superimposed on the statistical diagram

TABLE 5.2. Regression Coefficients, Standard Errors, and Model Summary Information for the Presumed Media Influence Serial Multiple Mediator Model Depicted in Figure 5.6

			Consequent											
		M_1 (IMPORT)					M_2 (PMI)					Y (REACTION)		
Antecedent		Coeff.	SE	p		Coeff.	SE	p			Coeff.	SE	p
X (COND)	a_1	0.627	0.310	.045	a_2	0.354	0.233	.131		c'	0.103	0.239	.666
M_1 (IMPORT)		—	—	—	d_{21}	0.196	0.067	.004		b_1	0.324	0.071	<.001
M_2 (PMI)		—	—	—		—	—	—		b_2	0.397	0.093	<.001
Constant	i_{M_1}	3.908	0.213	<.001	i_{M_2}	4.610	0.306	<.001		i_Y	−0.150	0.530	.778
		$R^2 = 0.033$				$R^2 = 0.097$					$R^2 = 0.325$		
		$F(1, 121) = 4.094, p = .045$				$F(2, 120) = 6.443, p = .002$					$F(3, 119) = 19.112, p < .001$		

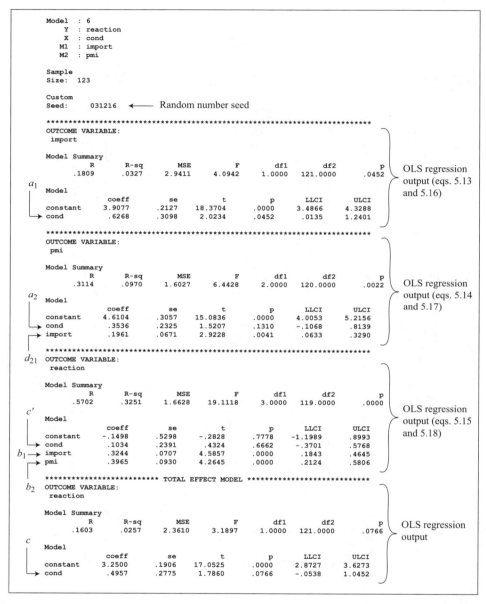

FIGURE 5.7. Output from the PROCESS procedure for a serial multiple mediator analysis of the presumed media influence data.

(continued)

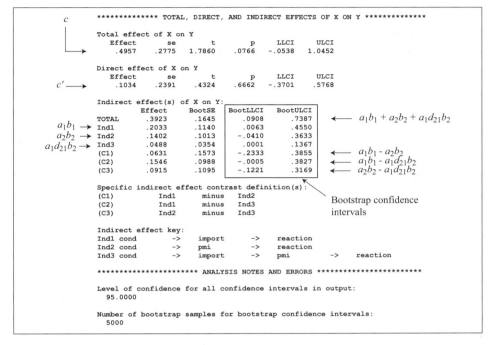

FIGURE 5.7 continued.

for this model in Figure 5.6. Whether extracted from the summary table, the PROCESS output, or the statistical diagram, the model expressed in equation form is

$$\hat{M}_1 = 3.908 + 0.627X \tag{5.16}$$

$$\hat{M}_2 = 4.610 + 0.354X + 0.196M_1 \tag{5.17}$$

$$\hat{Y} = -0.150 + 0.103X + 0.324M_1 + 0.397M_2 \tag{5.18}$$

The direct effect of the manipulation in this serial multiple mediator model is exactly the same as in the parallel multiple mediator model because whether the mediators are modeled as causally influencing each other or not does not change the model of Y. That is, the equation for Y is the same in both models, as they each contain only X, M_1, and M_2 as antecedents. This direct effect is positive but not statistically significant, $c' = 0.103, t(119) = 0.432, p = .666$. As we learned from the parallel multiple mediator model, location of the article in the newspaper is unrelated to intentions to buy sugar independent of the effect of perceived importance and presumed media influence.

This serial multiple mediator model contains four indirect effects estimated as products of regression coefficients linking X to Y. These indirect effects can be found in the PROCESS output along with 95% bootstrap confidence intervals based on 5,000 bootstrap samples. Because an indirect effect in a serial mediation model may pass through several mediators, a complete label can be quite lengthy, so PROCESS uses a shorthand notation to label them along with a key with a lengthier and more descriptive label.

The first indirect effect is the specific indirect effect of article location on reactions through perceived importance of the sugar shortage ($X \rightarrow M_1 \rightarrow Y$), estimated as $a_1 b_1 = 0.627(0.324) = 0.203$ and found in the output in the row labeled "Ind1." This indirect effect can be interpreted as significantly positive because the bootstrap confidence interval is entirely above zero (0.006 to 0.455). Those told the article would appear on the front page of the newspaper perceived the sugar shortage as more important (because a_1 is positive), and this increased importance was associated with an increased intention to buy sugar (because b_1 is positive) independent of presumed media influence.

The second specific indirect effect, labeled "Ind2," is the indirect effect of article location on reactions through only presumed media influence ($X \rightarrow M_2 \rightarrow Y$). Estimated as the product of the effect of article location on presumed media influence (a_2) and the effect of presumed media influence on reactions (b_2), this indirect effect is $0.354(0.397) = 0.140$. However, this path of influence cannot be claimed as definitively different from zero because the bootstrap confidence interval straddles zero (-0.041 to 0.363).

The third indirect effect is found in the output labeled "Ind3." This is the specific indirect effect of article location on reactions through perceived importance and presumed media influence in serial, with importance modeled as affecting presumed media influence, which in turn influences intentions to buy sugar (i.e., $X \rightarrow M_1 \rightarrow M_2 \rightarrow Y$). Estimated as $a_1 d_{21} b_2 = 0.627(0.196)0.397 = 0.049$, this specific indirect effect is significantly positive because the bootstrap confidence interval is above zero (0.0001 to 0.137). Relative to those assigned to the interior page condition, those told the article would appear in the front page perceived the sugar shortage as more important (as a_1 is positive), which in turn was associated with a greater perception that others would be influenced by the article (because d_{21} is positive) and this greater perception of influence on others translated into a greater intention to buy sugar (because b_2 is positive).

A serial multiple mediator model also contains a total indirect effect, estimated as the sum of all the specific indirect effects. As can be seen in the PROCESS output in the row labeled "Total," the total indirect effect is 0.392 and different from zero as determined by a bootstrap confidence interval that does not contain zero (0.091 to 0.739).

The contrast option of PROCESS, specified by adding **contrast=1** to the command line, calculates all possible pairwise comparisons between specific indirect effects. These comparisons are found in the PROCESS output in the rows labeled "(C1)," "(C2)," and so forth, along with a corresponding key toward the bottom. From the PROCESS output, the three differences are

$$C1 = a_1b_1 - a_2b_2 = 0.203 - 0.140 = 0.063$$
$$C2 = a_1b_1 - a_1d_{21}b_2 = 0.203 - 0.049 = 0.155$$
$$C3 = a_2b_2 - a_1d_{21}b_2 = 0.140 - 0.049 = 0.091$$

When used in conjunction with the bootstrapping option in PROCESS, confidence intervals for the comparison are also provided for inference about the difference between specific indirect effects. Notice in the PROCESS output that all of the confidence intervals contain zero. The interpretation is that no specific indirect effect is statistically different than any other specific indirect effect.

If you have been following along very closely, you might have noticed what seems like a conflict in results here. Earlier, we saw that the specific indirect effect of article location on reactions through presumed media influence *alone* is not definitively different from zero, because the bootstrap confidence interval for this specific indirect effect includes zero. The other two specific indirect effects we could claim are different from zero, as their bootstrap confidence intervals are entirely above zero. If you think of these results in terms of the logic of hypothesis testing, you would say that there is no indirect effect through presumed media influence only, but a positive indirect effect through perceived importance only, as well as through perceived importance and then presumed media influence in serial. And yet the bootstrap confidence intervals for differences between any two specific indirect effects all include zero. In hypothesis testing terms, you would conclude from these comparisons that none of the indirect effects differ from each other. Yet how can that be true if some of the indirect effects are different from zero while others are not?

The apparent conflict results from three things you should always keep in mind when interpreting a set of inferential tests in mediation analysis (and, indeed, in any analytical context). First, a test as to whether an effect is different from zero is not the same as a test of whether one effect differs from another effect. They test different hypotheses, and there is no mathematical law that says the result of one test must be consistent with the results of another test of a different hypothesis. Second, difference in significance does not mean statistically different (Gelman & Stern, 2006), just as similarity in significance does not imply statistical equivalence. If an inferential test leads to the conclusion that one thing is different from zero but another is not, that does not mean that those things are necessarily different from each other. This *would* be a conflict if inferential tests were always accurate. But we know that inferential procedures can lead us astray. A failure to reject a null hypothesis doesn't mean the null hypothesis is necessarily true, and rejecting a null hypothesis doesn't mean the null hypothesis is certainly false. Third, there is always uncertainty in our estimates of unknown quantities. Just because a confidence interval includes zero, that doesn't mean that thing we are estimating is zero. The confidence intervals for the difference between the specific indirect effect through presumed media influence alone and either of the other two specific indirect effects includes nonzero values. This means that these specific indirect effects *could be* different. We just can't say definitively that they are because the confidence interval includes zero as a possibility.

5.5   Models with Parallel and Serial Mediation Properties

In a model with two mediators, the only difference between a serial and a parallel multiple mediator model is the inclusion of a causal path from M_1 to M_2. The serial model estimates this effect, whereas the parallel model assumes it is zero, which is equivalent to leaving it out of the model entirely. With more than three mediators, a model can be a blend of parallel and serial mediation processes, depending on which paths between mediators are estimated and which are fixed to zero through their exclusion from the model.

Consider the mediation model in statistical form in Figure 5.8, panel A. This model has three mediators, but but only M_1 has a pathway of influence to the two other mediators M_2 and M_3. More complex versions of such a model would include additional mediators stacked in the parallel process operating between M_1 and Y. Some examples in the literature of a mediation model taking this form include Bombay, Matheson, and Anisman (2012), Gratz, Bardeen, Levy, Dixon-Gordon, and Tull (2015), and Liao, Ho, and Yang (2016).

Using regression analysis, the direct and indirect effects of X on Y in this model can be estimated using four equations, one for each of the three mediators and one for the final consequent Y:

$$M_1 = i_{M_1} + a_1 X + e_{M_1}$$
$$M_2 = i_{M_2} + a_2 X + d_{21} M_1 + e_{M_2}$$

$$M_3 = i_{M_3} + a_3X + d_{31}M_1 + e_{M_3}$$
$$Y = i_Y + c'X + b_1M_1 + b_2M_2 + b_3M_3 + e_Y$$

This model has five specific indirect effects of X on Y, discovered by finding all the ways one can trace from X to Y passing through at least one mediator. Each of these specific indirect effects is quantified as the product of the pathways that link X to Y. Three of these specific indirect effects pass through only one mediator (a_1b_1, a_2b_2, and a_3b_3) and two pass through two mediators ($a_1d_{21}b_2$ and $a_1d_{31}b_3$. The sum of the specific indirect effects is the total indirect effect. The direct effect of X is c'. The specific indirect effects and the direct effect of X sum to produce the total effect of X, which can also be estimated by regressing Y on X alone.

If X feeds immediately into a parallel mediation process, with the parallel process then sending pathways to a common additional mediator, the result is a model such as depicted in Figure 5.8, panel B. This model includes three mediators stacked in parallel, but variations on this model exist in the literature with as few as two mediators in the parallel process to as many as six (see, e.g., Krieger, Katz, Kam, & Roberto, 2012; Moyer-Guse, Chung, & Jain, 2011; Richard & Purnell, 2017; Valdesolo & Graham, 2014).

The direct and indirect effects of X for the model in Figure 5.8, panel B, can be estimated using five equations, one for each of the four mediators and one for the final consequent:

$$M_1 = i_{M_1} + a_1X + e_{M_1}$$
$$M_2 = i_{M_2} + a_2X + e_{M_2}$$
$$M_3 = i_{M_3} + a_3X + e_{M_3}$$
$$M_4 = i_{M_4} + a_4X + d_{41}M_1 + d_{42}M_2 + d_{43}M_3 + e_{M_4}$$
$$Y = i_Y + c'X + b_1M_1 + b_2M_2 + b_3M_3 + b_4M_4 + e_Y$$

This model has seven specific indirect effects, four passing through only one mediator (a_1b_1, a_2b_2, a_3b_3, and a_4b_4), and three passing through two mediators ($a_1d_{41}b_4, a_2d_{42}b_4$, and $a_3d_{43}b_4$). These sum to produce the total indirect effect. The direct effect of X is c' and the direct and indirect effects sum to produce the total effect of X on Y. In this model, as in the others discussed in this chapter, the total effect can also be estimated by regressing Y on X without any of the mediators in the model.

Inference about the total and direct effects come from the regression output for the models of Y (one with all the mediators in the model for the direct effect, and one without the mediators for the total effect) just as in other mediation analyses described thus far. And any of the methods for inference about an indirect effect in sections 5.1 and 5.4 can be used in models such as these. PROCESS simplifies the analysis considerably, as it

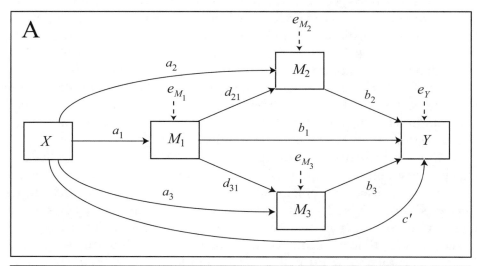

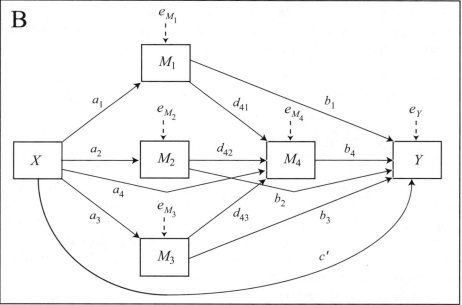

FIGURE 5.8. Some models that combine properties of parallel and serial mediation.

has each of these two forms of a "parallel-serial" model preprogrammed (in Appendix A, models 80 and 81; also see model 82 for an interesting model blending parallel and serial processes). The output will include all regression coefficients with standard errors, t- and p-values, and confidence intervals, as well as bootstrap confidence intervals for all the indirect effects. And the **contrast** option can be used to conduct all possible pairwise comparisons between specific indirect effects.

5.6 Complementarity and Competition among Mediators

This chapter has been dedicated to mediation models containing more than one mediator. At this point, the benefits of estimating multiple mechanisms of influence in a single model are no doubt apparent. But the inclusion of more than one mediator in a model does entail certain risks as well, and at times the results of multiple mediator model may appear to contradict the results obtained when estimating a simpler model with a single mediator. Some of the risks, paradoxes, and contradictions that sometimes can occur are worth some acknowledgement and discussion.

First, a specific indirect effect quantifies the influence of X on Y through a particular mediator while holding constant other mediators. This means that it is possible that a simple mediation analysis reveals evidence of an indirect effect of X on Y through M_1 when M_1 is the sole mediator in the model, but no such indirect effect when M_1 is included in a model along with M_2, M_3, and so forth. This will occur more so or with greater likelihood when the mediators are somewhat correlated, which is precisely the circumstance in which a multiple mediator model is most useful. But when the intercorrelation between mediators becomes too large, the usual problems with collinearity in regression models begin to take hold and muddle the results, as the paths from each mediator to the outcome are estimated controlling for all other mediators. Collinearity between predictors increases sampling variance in estimates of their partial relationships with an outcome (Cohen et al., 2003; Darlington & Hayes, 2017; Fox, 1991), and such sampling variance will propagate throughout the estimates of indirect effects and increase the width of confidence intervals for both asymmetric and symmetric confidence intervals or increase p-values from normal theory tests for specific indirect effects.

With evidence of an indirect effect when a mediator is considered in isolation but not when considered in a model with multiple mediators, it is reasonable to ask which result is correct. But there is no good answer to this question. In fact, they could both be correct because the specific indirect effect in a multiple mediator model estimates something different than the indirect effect in a simple mediation model. The indirect effect in a model with a single mediator confounds influence through that sole mediator and other mediators it may be correlated with but that are excluded from the model. Including correlated mediators in the model allows you to disentangle spurious and epiphenomenal association from potential causal association, but this comes at the cost of greater sampling variance and reduced power for tests of indirect effects.

Second, remember that the total indirect effect of X quantifies how differences in X relate to differences in Y through all mediators at once. Evidence that the total indirect effect is different from zero supports the claim that, taken together, X influences Y indirectly in some fashion through one or more of these mechanisms these mediators represent. However, because the indirect effect is a sum over all specific indirect effects, some seemingly paradoxical results are possible.

One possibility is when the total indirect effect is not different from zero according to the outcome of an inferential test, even though one or more of the specific indirect effects is. Two scenarios can produce such an apparent paradox. Because the total indirect effect is a sum of all specific indirect effects, if those indirect effects differ in sign but are of similar magnitude, their sum very well may be zero or nearly so (see, e.g., MacKinnon, 2008; Hayes, 2009). For instance, people who attend more highly or frequently to political campaign advertisements may be more likely to vote because such exposure leads people to believe that the outcome of the election is consequential to the future, which in turn facilitates turnout. On the other hand, such advertisements often are highly negative in tone, which may reduce trust in government and politicians, which could suppress the likelihood of showing up at the ballot box. Such push-and-pull processes could be at work simultaneously, but because the specific indirect effects are opposite in sign (i.e., a positive effect through perceptions of consequence, but a negative effect through trust in government), they may sum to zero. See Pitts and Safer (2016) for a published example of such opposing indirect effects.

Such a paradox can also result in models with several specific indirect effects that differ in size, even if those specific indirect effects are the same sign. For instance, an investigator might fit a parallel multiple mediator model with four mediators, only one of which is actually transmitting X's effect on Y. The inclusion of a bunch of potential mediators in the model that actually do nothing to carry X's effect on Y can increase the sampling variance of the estimate of the total indirect effect, rendering it not statistically different from zero when subjected to an inferential test.

The opposite is also possible—evidence of a total indirect effect in spite of absence of compelling evidence from inferential tests that any of the specific indirect effects are different from zero. Consider a variation on the example just presented in which *all* of the specific indirect effects are small in size but are of the same sign. If the sample size is relatively small or the mediators highly correlated, sampling variance will rule the day, making it hard to detect a weak signal (i.e., a small specific indirect effect) amid all the sampling noise. But a few weak signals, when added up (i.e., the total indirect effect), may be strong enough to detect with an inferential test because all other things being equal, power is higher when the effect size is larger.

Such apparently paradoxical inconsistencies between inferential tests for total and specific indirect effects result not so much from the statistics but, rather, from our minds by thinking of these effects in binary terms, as either zero or not zero. One escape, which is admittedly difficult given how deeply ingrained the logic of hypothesis testing is in the consciousness of scientists, is to acknowledge the uncertainty inherent in our estimates as communicated through confidence intervals. The fact that a confidence interval for an effect contains zero does not mean the effect is zero. It merely means that zero is in the realm of possibility, or that one cannot say with certainty what the direction of the effect is.

A second escape is to discount the relevance of the total indirect effect when interpreting the results. Although this may not be possible, in some situations, the total indirect effect will have little substantive or theoretical value. The total indirect effect and the outcome of an inferential test thereof are similar to the squared multiple correlation in a regression model or an omnibus test of the equality of several means in analysis of variance. Rejection of the null hypothesis that a regression model fits no better than chance or that all group means are equal in analysis of variance says nothing about the size or statistical significance of the individual predictors in the model or the outcome of various pairwise comparisons between means. One could have a statistically significant R^2 or F-ratio with no significant predictors or pairwise mean comparisons. Conversely, one could find one or more statistically significant predictor variables in a regression model, or two or more statistically significant pairwise comparisons between means even if one is not able to reject the null hypothesis that a model fits no better than chance or that a set of group means are the same using an omnibus test. The total indirect effect is a sum of all specific indirect effects some of which may be large, others small, some positive, some negative. We often estimate multiple mediator models because we are interested in specific mechanisms at work, not the aggregate of all mechanisms. With a few exceptions, such as small specific indirect effects that are too small to detect with the data available but sum to a large total indirect effect, or in a serial multiple mediator model with data collected over time on the same mediator (see, e.g., Cole & Maxwell, 2003, pp. 571–572), inference and interpretation of a multiple mediator model would usually focus more on the direct and specific indirect effects, not the total indirect effect.

5.7   Chapter Summary

In this chapter, I extended the principles of simple mediation analysis introduced in Chapter 3 to models with more than one mediator. Acknowledging and explicitly modeling the multiple mechanisms or pathways of influence between X and Y opens the door to more interesting analytical opportunities and tests. Specific indirect effects estimated in models with mediators operating either in parallel or serial estimate causal influences independent of other processes in the model. Tests that compare specific indirect effects provide a means of pitting competing mechanisms or theories against each other in a single integrated process model.

6

Mediation Analysis with a Multicategorical Antecedent

This chapter further extends the principles of mediation analysis introduced in earlier chapters to mediation questions involving a multicategorical causal antecedent. A multicategorical antecedent variable is one that is categorical but with three or more categories. I show how to estimate and interpret the *relative* total, *relative* direct, and *relative* indirect effects of a multicategorical antecedent variable X on a consequent Y through one or more mediators. Bootstrap inference for the indirect effect described in Chapters 3 and 5 is applied to inference about relative indirect effects. I illustrate the analysis using two systems for representing a multicategorical variable in the model.

In Chapters 3 through 5, I introduced the fundamentals of statistical mediation analysis. In all the examples in those chapters, the causal antecedent X was dichotomous or some kind of quantitative measurement that located the cases in the data on a continuum. I illustrated that a simple path analysis algebra applies regardless of whether X represents two groups or a quantitative, continuous variable. The total effect of X partitions into direct and indirect components, and inference about the indirect effect(s) serves as a statistical test of mediation.

But researchers are often interested in questions about mediation of the effect of an antecedent variable X that is neither dichotomous nor continuous. An example would be when using an experimental design and participants are randomly assigned into one of three or more experimental conditions. For instance, Emery, Romer, Sheerin, Jamieson, and Peters (2014) conducted a study on the effect of cigarette health warning labels on various smoking-related beliefs and behaviors among a sample of smokers. Participants in this study were exposed to one of three warning labels, with the label a participant viewed determined by random assignment. A simple-text-only label merely mentioned the risks of smoking. A simple-text-plus-image label was identical to the simple-text-only label but included an image consistent with the text. A third label included the simple text warning, an image, and some additional text elaborating on the nature of the risks of smoking. They found that the type of label indirectly influenced such outcomes as desire to smoke and feelings about quitting through both emotional (worry) and cognitive (believability) responses to the labels. Some other examples of investigators testing a mediation hypothesis when X is multicategorical include Bohns, Newark, and Xu (2016), Brach, Walsh, and Shaw (2017), Chew, Haase, and Carpenter (2017), Golubickis, Tan, Falben, and Macrae (2016), Hahl (2016), and Windscheid et al. (2016).

In the review of regression analysis principles in Chapter 2, we saw that one cannot include a multicategorical variable as an antecedent variable in a regression analysis unless that variable is first represented in the form of $g - 1$ variables, where g is the number of categories or groups (see section 2.7). In the discussion in that section, indicator coding was used to represent the three groups (political party identification), and differences between the groups on a consequent variable were quantified with $g - 1$ regression coefficients. But when X is represented with more than one variable in a regression model, how can one estimate the total, direct, and indirect effects of X, given that X's effect on M and Y cannot be expressed with a single regression coefficient?

Historically, investigators interested in doing a mediation analysis with a multicategorical antecedent X have resorted to some less optimal strategies than the one I discuss in this chapter. One of these strategies is to throw out all the cases in the data in one or more of the groups such that only two groups remain in the data, and then a mediation analysis is conducted as if X were dichotomous. This is then repeated, returning some of the groups to the data and discarding others, and the analysis undertaken again, until all of the comparisons of interest have been conducted. Using the warning labels study described above as an example, one analysis might be conducted comparing those exposed to the simple-text-only label to those exposed to the simple-test-plus-image label, temporarily discarding those assigned to the elaborated-text-and-image condition as if they were never in the study in the first place. The analysis is then repeated, perhaps returning those in the elaborated-text-and-image condition but discarding those in the simple-text-plus-image condition, thereby allowing for a comparison of the two conditions with an image, again temporarily pretending like the simple-text-only condition didn't exist in the study. One of several of the flaws of this is approach is that it lowers statistical power and increases uncertainty in the estimation of the effects, given that each analysis is done with less data than if the entire sample was analyzed in one analysis.

A second strategy I have seen used is to combine subsets of the groups into one group. For example, those assigned to either of the two warning label conditions that included an image might be treated as a single "text plus image" condition, and a mediation analysis conducted comparing this group to those who received a warning label containing only text. This strategy treats those given an image as if they were in the same condition, even though the information on the labels differed. This procedure is often justified by investigators who perform initial tests comparing the two groups on the mediator and outcome to make sure that they don't differ significantly, with the logic that a failure to find differences justifies combining them into one condition. However, this strategy still carries risks associated with the violation of various assumptions of linear regression analysis, such as homoscedasticity. Furthermore, it disrespects the design, given that the information participants in the two image conditions were given was not actually the same.

A third strategy relies on the causal steps approach to mediation analysis described in Chapter 4. When X is a multicategorical variable, this involves conducting a set of hypothesis tests comparing group means using analysis of variance and covariance, and then piecing together a claim of mediation from the resulting set of hypothesis tests. All of the shortcomings of the causal steps approach that I describe in Chapter 4 apply to mediation analysis with a multicategorical X.

The procedure for mediation analysis that I focus on in this chapter I originally described in Hayes and Preacher (2014). Here I illustrate its logic and use with data from a study on sexual discrimination in the workplace. This procedure does not require discarding any data; the entire sample is analyzed simultaneously. Furthermore, the multicategorical nature of X is respected and retained. No groups are formally combined into one for the sake of analysis. Finally, the regression equations that are used to estimate the direct, indirect, and total effects of X also produce estimates of the mediator(s) and consequent Y that correspond to the means of the groups. As a consequence, the direct and indirect effects of X quantify separation between the group means resulting from the mechanism(s) and the part of the effect of X not attributable to the mechanism(s).

6.1 Relative Total, Direct, and Indirect Effects

In the review of regression analysis in Chapter 2, we saw that a multicategorical antecedent variable with g categories can be used as an antecedent variable in a regression model if it is represented by $g - 1$ variables using some kind of group coding system (see section 2.7). I described indicator

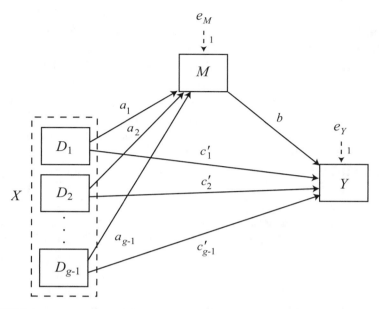

FIGURE 6.1. A statistical diagram of the simple mediation model with a multicategorical antecedent X with g categories.

or dummy coding as one such system, where groups are represented with $g-1$ variables set to either zero or one (see Table 2.1). With indicator coding, one of the g groups is chosen as the *reference group*. Cases in the reference group receive a zero on all $g-1$ variables coding X. Each of the remaining $g-1$ groups gets its own indicator variable that is set to 1 for cases in that group, with all other cases set to zero. Using such a system, which of the g groups a case is in is represented by its pattern of zeros and ones on the $g-1$ indicator variables. These $g-1$ indicator variables are then used as antecedent variables in a regression model as a stand-in for X.

Using such a system to represent a multicategorical X, to conduct a mediation analysis when X is a multicategorical variable, the same procedure can be used that was discussed in Chapter 3, except that the $g-1$ variables representing the g groups are used wherever X originally appeared in the regression equations. A mediation model with a multicategorical X and a single mediator M is represented in the form of a statistical diagram in Figure 6.1. In equation form, the model is

$$M = i_M + a_1D_1 + a_2D_2 + \cdots + a_{g-1}D_{g-1} + e_M \tag{6.1}$$

$$Y = i_Y + c_1'D_1 + c_2'D_2 + \cdots + c_{g-1}'D_{g-1} + bM + e_Y \tag{6.2}$$

where D_j is one of the $g - 1$ variables used to represent the g groups. The regression coefficients in each of these equations can be estimated using ordinary least squares regression. As discussed below, the $g-1$ c' regression coefficients represent *relative* direct effects of X, the $g - 1$ products of the a_j and b coefficients represent *relative* indirect effects of X, and when relative direct and indirect effects are added up, they yield *relative* total effects.

Relative Indirect Effects

Observe that unlike when X is dichotomous or continuous, in Figure 6.1 there are now $g - 1$ paths from X to M, one for each of the $g - 1$ variables representing X. These are the $g - 1$ a coefficients in equation 6.1. Each of these represents a part of the effect of X on M. Their values and their interpretation will depend on the system used for representing the g groups. For instance, if X coded three groups and indicator coding was used with group 3 as the reference, a_1 would be the mean difference in M between those in group 1 and those in group 3. That is, $a_1 = \overline{M}_1 - \overline{M}_3$. Likewise, a_2 is the mean difference in M between those in group 2 and group 3: $a_2 = \overline{M}_2 - \overline{M}_3$. When the pattern of values on the $g - 1$ D variables for each group is substituted into equation 6.1, the result is $\overline{M}$ for that group. So equation 6.1, once estimated using the data available, will generate the g group means on M.

Although there are $g - 1$ regression coefficients in the model of M, there is only one regression coefficient for M in the model of Y. This is b in equation 6.2, and it is interpreted just as it would be if X were continuous or dichotomous. It quantifies how much two cases that differ by one unit on M but that are equal on X are estimated to differ on Y. In this interpretation, being "equal on X" means being in the same group. So b is an estimate of the effect of M on Y when controlling for X. It will not be influenced by the coding system reflected in the $g - 1$ variables representing groups.

Looking at Figure 6.1, you can see that there are $g - 1$ ways to get from X to Y through M, each starting at one of the D_j variables representing groups, then progressing to M, and then to Y. Collecting the paths and multiplying them together as you trace from X to M to Y yields $g - 1$ *relative indirect effects*, defined as $a_j b$. They each quantify a part of the difference in Y between groups resulting from the effect of X on Y through X's effect on M. So unlike in mediation analysis with a dichotomous or continuous X, there is no single indirect effect but, rather, $g - 1$ relative indirect effects. Like the a paths, their interpretation will depend on how the groups are coded. Sticking with indicator coding as earlier, still assuming $g = 3$, and with group 3 as the reference, $a_1 b$ would quantify the difference in Y between group 1 and group 3 resulting from the causal effect of being in group 1 rather than group 3 on M, which in turn affects Y. And a_2b would quantify the difference in Y between group 2 and group 3 resulting from the effect of being in group 2 rather than group 3 on M which in turn carries its effect to Y. Collectively, they quantify the mediation of X's effect on Y through M.

Given that there is no single indirect effect in a model such as this, how can we determine whether M is mediating the effect of X on Y? When X was dichotomous or continuous, this question was answered with an inference about the indirect effect, and a variety of methods discussed in Chapter 3 could be used. But now that there is more than one indirect effect, the inferential problem is a bit more complicated and controversial. The criterion I recommend is that X's effect on Y can be said to be mediated by M if at least one of the $g - 1$ relative indirect effects is different from zero. I recommend a bootstrap confidence interval for inference about the relative indirect effects, for reasons discussed in Chapter 3. However, as will be made clear through the examples and discussion in later sections, this criterion is imperfect because its use can result in different claims about mediation, depending on the system you use for coding the g groups.

Relative Direct Effects

In a mediation model, X can affect Y directly and indirectly through M. That doesn't change when X is a multicategorical variable. The direct effect of X on Y is quantified in equation 6.2 with the $g - 1$ regression coefficients for the $g - 1$ variables representing X. Each c' is a *relative direct effect* and quantifies part of the effect of X on Y that operates directly on Y, without passing through M. For instance, when $g = 3$ and group 3 is the reference group in an indicator coding system, c'_1 is the relative direct effect of being in group 1 rather than group 3 on Y, and c'_2 is the relative direct effect of being in group 2 rather than group 3 on Y. These quantify the component of the difference between the group means on Y not attributable to the mechanism through M. Inference about each relative direct effect comes from ordinary regression output, in the form of a confidence interval or a p-value for testing the null hypothesis that the relative direct effect is equal to zero.

Equation 6.2 can be used to produce what are known in the analysis of covariance literature as *adjusted means*. The adjusted means on Y are estimates of Y for each group when the covariates are set to their sample mean. In a mediation model, the mediator mathematically functions like a covariate, with X's effect on Y estimated after controlling for M. The adjusted means for each group are constructed by plugging the values of the $g - 1$ variables coding that group into equation 6.2, with $\overline{M}$ substituted for

M. The relative direct effects represent differences between these adjusted means, as will be seen by way of example in section 6.2.

Relative Total Effects

In a mediation analysis, the direct and indirect effects of X sum to produce the total effect of X. When X is a multicategorical antecedent, there are $g-1$ relative direct and indirect effects. When the relative direct and indirect effects corresponding to one of the $g-1$ variables coding groups are added together, the result is a *relative total effect*. So the relative total effect for D_j is $c_j = c'_j + a_j b$. Like the relative direct and indirect effects, the interpretation of the relative total effects depends on how the g groups are represented with the $g-1$ variables coding groups. For example, for a three group multicategorical X represented with indicator codes and group 3 as the reference, $c_1 = \overline{Y}_1 - \overline{Y}_3$ and $c_2 = \overline{Y}_2 - \overline{Y}_3$.

For a model such as in Figure 6.1, the relative total effects of X can be quantified by first estimating the relative direct and indirect effects using equations 6.1 and 6.2 and then adding them up or, instead, by regressing Y on the $g-1$ variables coding groups, leaving M out of the model:

$$Y = i_Y + c_1 D_1 + c_2 D_2 + \cdots + c_{g-1} D_{g-1} + e_Y \tag{6.3}$$

Inference about the relative total effects is available in the regression output when estimating equation 6.3, either as confidence intervals for each of the regression coefficients for the $g-1$ variables coding group or, alternatively, p-values for the test of the null that the regression coefficient equals zero. And equation 6.3 will generate the mean of each group when each group's pattern of values on the $g-1$ D variables is substituted into the equation.

Omnibus Tests of the Effect of X

Tests of relative effects provide specific information about various comparisons and contrasts between groups. Typically, studies are designed with specific hypotheses in mind, and when a group coding system is strategically chosen so as to produce quantifications of the relative direct, indirect, and total effects that are informative about those specific hypotheses, then no other inferential tests are needed beyond those discussed above. But you may on occasion have an interest in an *omnibus inference*. For instance, you might ask whether X affects Y, irrespective of whether that effect is direct or indirect. Such a question does not require focusing on specific comparisons between groups that relative effects quantify. Or one could ask whether X directly affects Y, again, without focusing on specific comparisons between groups. The answer to these questions can be determined by an omnibus test.

Omnibus tests usually provide only vague conclusions, but sometimes a vague conclusion is useful or better than nothing. Furthermore, omnibus tests are not influenced by the coding system used for representing the multicategorical X, like tests of relative effects are. For example, you could find that no relative direct effects are different from zero using your chosen system for representing the g groups, yet there may be a statistically significant direct effect of X when tested with an omnibus test. This would leave you with the conclusion that X does directly affect Y, though you may not be able to say anything more precise than this. But that may be better than nothing.

As with relative direct and total effects, omnibus inference about the direct and total effects of X when X is multicategorical is straightforward. The absence of a direct effect of X on Y implies that all $g - 1$ relative direct effects are equal to zero. So if the null hypothesis of no direct effect of X is true, then a model that fixes all $g - 1$ relative direct effects to zero should fit no worse than a model which allows them to differ from zero. In OLS regression, fixing a coefficient to zero is equivalent to leaving the corresponding variable out of the model entirely. Using OLS regression, an omnibus test of the direct effect is undertaken by comparing the fit of two models. The first model estimates Y from M alone. The second model takes the form of equation 6.2, which estimates Y from M as well as the $g - 1$ D variables coding groups. The increase in the squared multiple correlation is a measure of improvement in fit that results when the $g - 1$ D_j variables are added. A test for the difference in R^2 values for the two models was already described in sections 2.6 and 2.7 and is based on a conversion of the increase in R^2 to an F-ratio. A sufficiently small p-value supports the inference that X directly affects Y. The F-ratio and p-value that result from this test are identical the F-ratio and p-value for X in an analysis of covariance comparing the group means on Y using M as the covariate.

No total effect of X implies all $g - 1$ relative total effects are zero. In regression analysis, a test of this null hypothesis is accomplished by testing the significance of R^2 in the model resulting from estimating the $g - 1$ relative total effects in equation 6.3. This test is addressed in sections 2.6 and 2.7 and is exactly the same as a one-way ANOVA comparing the g group means on Y.

An omnibus inference about the indirect effect would allow for a claim as to whether or not M mediates the effect of X on Y without relying on tests of the $g - 1$ relative indirect effects. This would be like testing the null hypothesis that all $_Ta_{j\,T}b = 0$ for all $j = 1$ to $g - 1$. As discussed at the end of this chapter, no omnibus test of this indirect effect has yet been derived that doesn't rely on unrealistic assumptions.

6.2 An Example: Sex Discrimination in the Workplace

Having outlined the fundamentals in generic form in the prior section, I now illustrate a mediation analysis with a multicategorical antecedent X relying on data from Garcia, Schmitt, Branscombe, and Ellemers (2010). The data file is named PROTEST and can be downloaded from *www.afhayes.com*. In this study, 129 participants, all of whom were female, received a written account of the fate of a female attorney (Catherine) who lost a promotion to a less qualified male as a result of discriminatory actions of the senior partners. After reading this story, which was the same in all conditions, the participants were given a description of how Catherine responded to this sexual discrimination. Those randomly assigned to the *no protest* condition (coded PROTEST=0 in the data file) learned that though very disappointed by the decision, Catherine decided not to take any action against this discrimination and continued working at the firm. Those assigned to the *individual protest* condition (coded PROTEST=1) were told that Catherine approached the partners to protest the decision, while giving various explanations as to why the decision was unfair that revolved around *her*, such as that she was more qualified for the job, and that it would hurt her career. But those randomly assigned to a *collective protest* condition (PROTEST=2) were told Catherine protested the decision and framed her argument around how the firm has treated women in the past, that women are just as qualified as men, and that they should be treated equally.

Following this manipulation of Catherine's response to the discrimination, the participants responded to a set of questions measuring how appropriate they perceived her response was for this situation. Higher scores on this variable (RESPAPPR in the data file) reflect a stronger perception of appropriateness of the response. Finally, the participants were asked to respond to six questions evaluating Catherine (e.g., "Catherine has many positive traits," "Catherine is the type of person I would like to be friends with"). Their responses were aggregated into a measure of liking, such that participants with higher scores liked her relatively more (LIKING in the data file).

The purpose of this study was to assess the extent to which Catherine's action—her decision to protest or not and in what form (individually or collectively)–affected perceptions of her. Was she liked more when she protested than when she didn't? And did the form her protest took matter

TABLE 6.1. Descriptive Statistics for Sex Discrimination Study

		M RESPAPPR	Y LIKING	Y adjusted
No Protest (PROTEST = 0)	Mean	3.884	5.310	5.715
	SD	1.457	0.819	
Individual Protest (PROTEST = 1)	Mean	5.145	5.826	5.711
	SD	1.075	0.819	
Collective Protest (PROTEST = 2)	Mean	5.494	5.753	5.495
	SD	0.936	0.936	
	Mean	4.866	5.637	
	SD	1.348	1.050	

in how much she was liked? And is perceived appropriateness of her response a mediator of the effect of her behavior on how she was perceived? Some preliminary answers to these questions can be found in Table 6.1, which shows the mean perceived response appropriateness and how much Catherine was liked in each of the three conditions. As can be seen, it appears Catherine was perceived as more likable when she protested individually, next most when she protested collectively, and least when she didn't protest at all. Furthermore, her behavior was seen as more appropriate when she protested in some form, with collectively protesting seen as somewhat more appropriate than individually protesting, both of which were perceived as more appropriate than not protesting at all.

To conduct the mediation analysis, two variables are constructed to code experimental condition (X). The first variable, D_1, is set to 1 for participants told she individually protested, and all other participants are set to zero on D_1. The second variable, D_2, is set to 1 for participants told she collectively protested, with everyone else set to zero. Using this indicator coding system, the no protest condition is the reference group, as participants in that condition are assigned values of zero on both D_1 and D_2.

The relative total effects of her behavior on how she was perceived are estimated by regressing how much Catherine was liked (LIKING) on experimental condition (X), represented with D_1 and D_2. In SPSS, the code that constructs the indicator variables and does the regression analysis is

```
compute d1=(protest=1).
compute d2=(protest=2).
regression/dep=liking/method=enter d1 d2.
```

In SAS, use

```
data protest;set protest;d1=(protest=1);d2=(protest=2);run;
proc reg data=protest;model liking=d1 d2;run;
```

The resulting regression model can be found in Table 6.2. The model is

$$\hat{Y} = 5.310 + 0.516D_1 + 0.443D_2 \tag{6.4}$$

with $R^2 = .046, F(2, 126) = 3.055, p = .051$. This is equivalent to a single-factor analysis of variance testing equality of the three means. It is also the omnibus test of the total effect discussed in section 6.1. The results suggest that her response to the discrimination did influence how she was perceived.

Notice that equation 6.4 reproduces the three group means when each group's pattern of D_1 and D_2 is used in the equation:

$$\overline{Y}_{NP} = 5.310 + 0.516(0) + 0.443(0) = 5.310$$
$$\overline{Y}_{IP} = 5.310 + 0.516(1) + 0.443(0) = 5.826$$
$$\overline{Y}_{CP} = 5.310 + 0.516(0) + 0.443(1) = 5.753$$

From this regression analysis, the relative total effects are $c_1 = 0.516$ and $c_2 = 0.443$. Looking at the table of group means (Table 6.1), you can verify that these relative total effects correspond to the mean difference in liking of Catherine between those told she individually protested and those told she did not protest ($c_1 = \overline{Y}_{IP} - \overline{Y}_{NP} = 5.826 - 5.310 = 0.516$) and those told she collectively protested and those told she did not protest ($c_2 = \overline{Y}_{CP} - \overline{Y}_{NP} = 5.753 - 5.310 = 0.443$). Both of these relative total effects are statistically significant. Compared to when she didn't protest, Catherine was liked significantly more when she individually protested as well as when she collectively protested.

These two relative total effects partition into relative direct and relative indirect components. To construct these effects, in one regression analysis we estimate perceived response appropriateness (M) from experimental condition (X, represented with D_1 and D_2) to get a_1 and a_2. In a second regression analysis, we regress liking on both experimental condition and perceived response appropriateness, which yields c_1', c_2', and b. In SPSS,

TABLE 6.2. Regression Coefficients, Standard Errors, and Model Summary Information for the Sex Discrimination Mediation Analysis

			Consequent							
			Y (LIKING)				M (RESPAPPR)			
Antecedent			Coeff.	SE	p		Coeff.	SE	p	
D_1	c_1		0.516	0.226	.024	a_1	1.261	0.255	< .001	
D_2	c_2		0.443	0.233	.049	a_2	1.610	0.253	< .001	
M (RESPAPPR)			—	—	—		—	—	—	
Constant	i_Y		5.310	0.161	< .001	i_M	3.884	0.182	< .001	
			$R^2 = .046$				$R^2 = .261$			
			$F(2, 126) = 3.055, p = .051$				$F(2, 126) = 22.219, p < .001$			

			Y (LIKING)			
Antecedent			Coeff.	SE	p	
D_1	c'_1		−0.004	0.219	.987	
D_2	c'_2		−0.220	0.228	.336	
M (RESPAPPR)	b		0.412	0.070	< .001	
Constant	i_Y		3.710	0.307	< .001	
			$R^2 = .263$			
			$F(3, 125) = 14.123, p < .001$			

```
regression/dep=respappr/method=enter d1 d2.
regression/dep=liking/method=enter d1 d2 respappr.
```

In SAS, try

```
proc reg data=protest;model respappr=d1 d2;run;
proc reg data=protest;model liking=d1 d2 respappr;run;
```

The resulting models can be found in Table 6.2. The model of perceived response appropriateness is

$$\hat{M} = 3.884 + 1.261D_1 + 1.610D_2 \tag{6.5}$$

and $R^2 = .261, F(2, 126) = 22.219, p < .001$. Different responses were perceived differently in appropriateness. And observe that equation 6.5 reproduces the three group means on M when each group's pattern of D_1 and D_2 is used in the equation:

$$\overline{M}_{NP} = 3.884 + 1.261(0) + 1.610(0) = 3.884$$
$$\overline{M}_{IP} = 3.884 + 1.261(1) + 1.610(0) = 5.145$$
$$\overline{M}_{CP} = 3.884 + 1.261(0) + 1.610(1) = 5.494$$

Looking at these computations or the table of group means (Table 6.1), notice that a_1 and a_2 correspond to the mean difference in perceived appropriateness of Catherine's response between those told she individually protested and those told she did not protest ($a_1 = \overline{M}_{IP} - \overline{M}_{NP} = 5.145 - 3.884 = 1.261$) and those told she collectively protested and those told she did not protest ($a_2 = \overline{M}_{CP} - \overline{M}_{NP} = 5.494 - 3.884 = 1.610$). Compared to not protesting, protesting the discrimination was seen as more appropriate, regardless of whether she framed the protest around herself or the collective of women.

From Table 6.2, the model of liking of Catherine that includes both experimental condition and perceived response appropriateness is

$$\hat{Y} = 3.710 - 0.004D_1 - 0.220D_2 + 0.412M \tag{6.6}$$

Plugging each group's pattern of D_1 and D_2 into equation 6.6, setting M to the sample mean ($\overline{M} = 4.866$) produces the adjusted group means in Table 6.1:

$$\overline{Y}^*_{NP} = 3.710 - 0.004(0) - 0.220(0) + 0.412(4.866) = 5.715$$
$$\overline{Y}^*_{IP} = 3.710 - 0.004(1) - 0.220(0) + 0.412(4.866) = 5.711$$
$$\overline{Y}^*_{CP} = 3.710 - 0.004(0) - 0.220(1) + 0.412(4.866) = 5.495$$

The regression coefficients for D_1 and D_2 in equation 6.6 are $c_1' = -0.004$ and $c_2' = -0.220$. These are the relative direct effects of individually protesting and collectively protesting, respectively, compared to not protesting at all, on how much Catherine was liked. Neither of these is statistically significant. Notice that these quantify differences between adjusted means in Table 6.1. The relative direct effect for individually protesting compared to not protesting is $c_1' = \overline{Y}_{IP}^* - \overline{Y}_{NP}^* = 5.711 - 5.715 = -0.004$, and the relative direct effect for collectively protesting relative to not protesting is $c_2' = \overline{Y}_{CP}^* - \overline{Y}_{NP}^* = 5.495 - 5.715 = -0.220$.

An omnibus test of the direct effect compares the three adjusted means to each other. This is equivalent to a single-factor analysis of covariance with perceived response appropriateness as the covariate. Using the method described in section 2.6, first entering perceived response appropriateness and then entering the two indicator codes for experimental condition, this test results in a failure to reject the null hypothesis of equality of the adjusted means, $\Delta R^2 = .009, F(2, 125) = 0.729, p = .485$. The code to conduct this omnibus test of the direct effect in SPSS is

```
regression/statistics defaults change/dep=liking/method=enter respappr
    /method=enter d1 d2.
```

In SAS, use

```
proc reg data=protest;model liking=d1 d2 respappr;test d1=0,d2=0;run;
```

Equation 6.6 also provides an estimate of b, the effect of perceived response appropriateness on liking of Catherine among participants told the same thing about her behavior. The more appropriate Catherine's behavior was perceived as being for the situation, the more she was liked. More specifically, among two people told the same thing about Catherine's response, the person who perceived her behavior as one unit higher in appropriateness liked her 0.412 units more.

A test of mediation in a model such as this comes from an estimate and test of the indirect effect of X on Y through M. Complicating things somewhat is the fact there is no single number we can call the indirect effect of X when X is a multicategorical variable. In this example, we instead have two relative indirect effects, one expressing the effect of individually protesting relative to not protesting at all, and one quantifying the effect of collectively protesting relative to not protesting, each operating on how much Catherine is liked by influencing perceptions of the appropriateness of her behavior. These relative indirect effects are estimated as $a_1 b$ and $a_2 b$. From equations 6.5 and 6.6, $a_1 b = 1.261(0.412) = 0.520$ and $a_2 b = 1.610(0.412) = 0.663$. So relative to not protesting at all, protesting with an individualistic focus enhanced the likeability of Catherine by 0.520 units, because individually protesting was seen as more appropriate than not protesting, and this translated into a more positive evaluation. Likewise, collectively protesting enhanced the likeability of Catherine by 0.663 units relative to not protesting, as collectively protesting was seen as more appropriate than not protesting, and this translated into a more positive evaluation of her.

But what about inference for these relative indirect effects? The relative indirect effects are products of two regression coefficients. As discussed in section 3.4, the sampling distribution of two regression coefficients is not normal, so a bootstrap or Monte Carlo confidence interval for these relative indirect effects would be appropriate. Using PROCESS (see the discussion of implementation next) with 5,000 bootstrap samples, 95% bootstrap confidence intervals for the relative indirect effects of individual protesting and collectively protesting are 0.258 to 0.840, and 0.368 to 1.013, respectively. Both of these are entirely above zero, leading to the inference that both of these relative indirect effects are positive. Given that at least one of the relative indirect effects is different from zero, we can conclude that the effect of Catherine's response to the discrimination on how she was perceived is mediated by perceptions of the appropriateness of her chosen response.

To complete this example, as promised in section 6.1, the relative total effects in this model partition cleanly into relative direct and relative indirect effects. That is, $c_1 = c_1' + a_1 b$ and $c_2 = c_2' + a_2 b$. Observe that indeed this is so: $0.516 = -0.004 + 1.261(0.412) = -0.004 + 0.520 = 0.516$, and $0.443 = -0.220 + 1.610(0.412) = -0.220 + 0.663 = 0.443$.

Implementation in PROCESS

PROCESS can estimate a mediation model when X is multicategorical just as easily as when X is dichotomous or continuous, as in the examples in Chapters 3 and 5. The model is still number 4. However, you must tell PROCESS that the values held in the variable specified for X are codes for groups, otherwise they will be interpreted as numbers with at least interval level measurement properties. To tell PROCESS X is multicategorical, use the **mcx** option (for _multicategorical_ _X_), with an argument following an equals sign telling PROCESS how to code the groups. For indicator coding, use a 1 following **mcx**, as in the command below:

```
process y=liking/x=protest/m=respappr/mcx=1/total=1/model=4/seed=30217.
```

In SAS, the equivalent command is

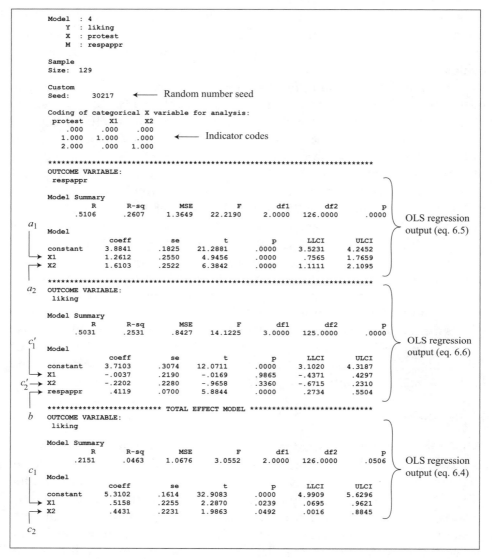

```
Model   : 4
    Y   : liking
    X   : protest
    M   : respappr

Sample
Size:   129

Custom
Seed:       30217    ←——— Random number seed

Coding of categorical X variable for analysis:
    protest     X1        X2
     .000      .000      .000
    1.000     1.000      .000   ←——— Indicator codes
    2.000      .000     1.000

***************************************************************************
OUTCOME VARIABLE:
  respappr

Model Summary
        R        R-sq       MSE        F        df1       df2        p
     .5106      .2607     1.3649    22.2190    2.0000   126.0000    .0000

Model
              coeff       se         t          p        LLCI      ULCI
  constant   3.8841     .1825    21.2881     .0000     3.5231    4.2452
  X1         1.2612     .2550     4.9456     .0000      .7565    1.7659
  X2         1.6103     .2522     6.3842     .0000     1.1111    2.1095

***************************************************************************
OUTCOME VARIABLE:
  liking

Model Summary
        R        R-sq       MSE        F        df1       df2        p
     .5031      .2531      .8427    14.1225    3.0000   125.0000    .0000

Model
              coeff       se         t          p        LLCI      ULCI
  constant   3.7103     .3074    12.0711     .0000     3.1020    4.3187
  X1         -.0037     .2190     -.0169     .9865     -.4371     .4297
  X2         -.2202     .2280     -.9658     .3360     -.6715     .2310
  respappr    .4119     .0700     5.8844     .0000      .2734     .5504

************************** TOTAL EFFECT MODEL **************************
OUTCOME VARIABLE:
  liking

Model Summary
        R        R-sq       MSE        F        df1       df2        p
     .2151      .0463     1.0676     3.0552    2.0000   126.0000    .0506

Model
              coeff       se         t          p        LLCI      ULCI
  constant   5.3102     .1614    32.9083     .0000     4.9909    5.6296
  X1          .5158     .2255     2.2870     .0239      .0695     .9621
  X2          .4431     .2231     1.9863     .0492      .0016     .8845
```

a_1

a_2

c'_1

c'_2

b

c_1

c_2

OLS regression
output (eq. 6.5)

OLS regression
output (eq. 6.6)

OLS regression
output (eq. 6.4)

(continued)

FIGURE 6.2. Output from the PROCESS procedure for SPSS for the sex discrimination mediation analysis.

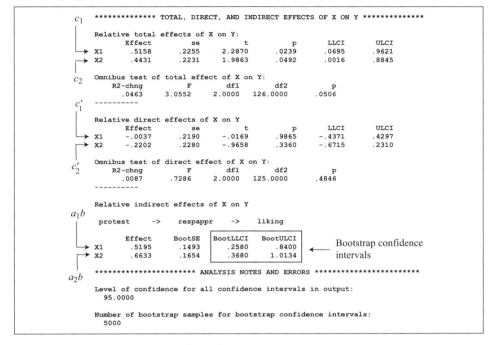

FIGURE 6.2 continued.

```
%process (data=protest,y=liking,x=protest,m=respappr,mcx=1,total=1,
    model=4,seed=30217);
```

The resulting output can be found in Figure 6.2. Toward the top of the output is a table showing that PROCESS has created two indicator variables X1 and X2 representing the three experimental conditions coded in the variable PROTEST. The group coded with PROTEST=0, the no protest group, is specified as the reference group. The indicator variable X1 represents the individual protest group (PROTEST=1) and X2 represents the collective protest group (PROTEST=2). With indicator coding, PROCESS uses the group with the numerically smallest code in the variable specified as X as the reference group. If you would rather have a different group as the reference group, you have to recode X so that the desired reference group is coded with the numerically smallest value.

Following in the output are the models of M and Y, estimated using OLS regression as in the prior section (equations 6.5 and 6.6). The **total=1** option in the PROCESS command tells PROCESS to print the model for the total effect of X (equation 6.4). Everything in this output is consistent with the information provided in the prior section.

The last section of output contains the relative total, relative direct, and relative indirect effects of X, calculated as described in the example. Also provided are tests of the omnibus total and direct effect, described earlier. PROCESS also provides bootstrap confidence intervals for the relative indirect effects, based on 5,000 bootstrap samples. These are found under the headings "BootLLCI" and "BootULCI." The number of bootstrap samples can be changed if desired by using the **boot** option (e.g., **boot=10000** for 10,000 bootstrap samples).

So PROCESS takes much of the work out of a mediation analysis when X is a multicategorical variable. When using the **mcx** option, the variable specified in X can contain up to nine unique numbers coding the groups. That is, X can be multicategorical with up to nine categories. PROCESS has three other systems for coding groups preprogrammed, and you can also construct a custom-defined system using the **xcatcode** option. The next section repeats this analysis using one of the other preprogrammed systems. For a discussion of all of the coding methods PROCESS implements, see the documentation in Appendix A. For a more general discussion of systems for coding a multicategorical predictor variable in regression analysis, see Darlington and Hayes (2017).

6.3   Using a Different Group Coding System

In section 6.2, I applied the procedure discussed in section 6.1 to estimate the relative direct, indirect, and total effects of one form of protesting an act of discrimination relative to not protesting at all on how the protester is perceived, with perceived response appropriateness as the mediator. These effects are specific to the system of coding groups I used, which was indicator coding. In that example, I used the no protest group as the reference group. Had I made a different decision about which of the three experimental conditions would function as the reference group, these relative effects would be different. So the findings you obtain from a mediation analysis when the causal antecedent is multicategorical will depend to some extent on decisions you make about how the groups are represented in the regression math.

Notice that in the analysis just conducted, there is no information about the effects (relative direct, relative indirect, and relative total) of protesting collectively versus protesting individually, yet that might be an effect you would care about. The fact that this effect is missing reflects the choice of reference category and that we can represent only two comparisons in the

TABLE 6.3. Representing the Three Conditions with Two Orthogonal Contrasts

PROTEST	D_1	D_2
0 (no protest)	−2/3	0
1 (individual protest)	1/3	−1/2
2 (collective protest)	1/3	1/2

model when there are three groups. Had we instead used the individual protest group as the reference, then the indicator coding system would yield a relative effect of individually protesting relative to not protesting, and collectively protesting relative to individually protesting.

A simple solution is to just reconduct the analysis, changing the reference group so as to generate these missing relative effects. An alternative is to choose a single coding system in the first place that would yield this comparison as well as another one that may or may not be of interest to you. Recall that we need to use two variables in a regression model to represent membership in three groups. When choosing a coding system, you should think through what effects you most care about, and if possible, choose a single coding system that generates the effects of interest to you. It may not be possible, but often it is.

If you are familiar with analysis of variance, you may have heard about *orthogonal contrasts*. These are comparisons between two groups or two sets of groups that provide nonoverlapping information about how a larger set of g groups differ from one another. In this example, you could imagine that it would be worthwhile to examine the effect of protesting, *whether collectively or individually*, relative to not protesting at all, as well the effect of protesting individually relative to collectively. There is a way of representing the three groups with a coding system that provides precisely this information. That system can be found in Table 6.3. This coding system represents two orthogonal contrasts. It also goes by the name *Helmert coding*, although this term is more often used when the categorical variable represents an ordinal dimension, as it is a useful way of including an ordinal antecedent variable in a regression model.

The SPSS code below constructs D_1 and D_2 using this coding system:

```
if (protest=0) d1=-2/3.
if (protest > 0) d1=1/3.
if (protest=0) d2=0.
```

```
if (protest=1) d2=-1/2.
if (protest=2) d2=1/2.
```

In SAS, use

```
data protest;set protest;
    if (protest=0) then d1=-2/3;if (protest > 0) then d1=1/3;
    if (protest=0) then d2=0;if (protest=1) then d2=-1/2;
    if (protest=2) then d2=1/2;
run;
```

Once D_1 and D_2 are constructed, they can be used as antecedent variables in models of M and Y in a mediation analysis in the same way as described in sections 6.1 and 6.2, using any OLS regression program.

But an ordinary regression program will not generate the relative indirect effects or bootstrap confidence intervals for inference about those relative indirect effects. PROCESS will, and it will even construct the Helmert codes for you. The PROCESS command for this analysis is

```
process y=liking/x=protest/m=respappr/mcx=3/total=1/model=4/seed=30217.
```

In SAS, the equivalent command is

```
%process (data=protest,y=liking,x=protest,m=respappr,mcx=3,total=1,
    model=4,seed=30217);
```

This command is almost identical to the one on page 201. The only difference is the use of **mcx=3** rather than **mcx=1** in the command line. The 3 argument in the **mcx** option tells PROCESS to code the groups using Helmert coding. These are denoted X1 and X2 in the output, and the table at the top of the PROCESS output shows that PROCESS is implementing the coding system in Table 6.3.

The output from this PROCESS command can be found in Figure 6.3. As can be seen, for the model of Y without M in the model (listed as the "Total Effect Model" in the PROCESS output)

$$\hat{Y} = 5.630 + 0.479D_1 - 0.073D_2 \tag{6.7}$$

and so $c_1 = 0.479$ and $c_2 = -0.073$. The F-ratio for the model is statistically significant and identical to the F-ratio for this model when using indicator coding, because this omnibus test of the total effect is not affected by the coding system used. This model generates the group means on Y (in Table 6.1):

$$
\begin{aligned}
\overline{Y}_{NP} &= 5.630 + 0.479(-2/3) - 0.073(0) = 5.310 \\
\overline{Y}_{IP} &= 5.630 + 0.479(1/3) - 0.073(-1/2) = 5.826 \\
\overline{Y}_{CP} &= 5.630 + 0.479(1/3) - 0.073(1/2) = 5.753
\end{aligned}
$$

However, unlike when indicator coding was used, only c_1 is statistically significant; c_2 is not. But what do c_1 and c_2 actually quantify when using this coding system? Whereas with indicator coding, c_1 and c_2 were the relative total effects of one form of protesting relative to not protesting at all, with this coding system, they represent something different. The regression coefficient for D_1, c_1, quantifies the difference between the unweighted average perception of Catherine in the two protest conditions and the mean perception of Catherine for those told she did not protest. That is,

$$
\begin{aligned}
c_1 &= \frac{\overline{Y}_{IP} + \overline{Y}_{CP}}{2} - \overline{Y}_{NP} \\
&= \frac{5.826 + 5.753}{2} - 5.310 \\
&= 5.789 - 5.310 \\
&= 0.479
\end{aligned}
$$

So c_1 is the relative total effect of protesting in either form relative to not protesting at all. This relative total effect is statistically different from zero.

What is c_2? This regression coefficient for D_2 quantifies the effect of protesting collectively relative to protesting individually:

$$
\begin{aligned}
c_2 &= \overline{Y}_{CP} - \overline{Y}_{IP} \\
&= 5.753 - 5.826 \\
&= -0.073
\end{aligned}
$$

but this difference is not statistically significant.

These same computations generate corresponding effects of experimental condition on perceived response appropriateness when M is the dependent variable. Regressing perceived response appropriateness (M) on D_1 and D_2 yields (see the PROCESS output)

$$
\hat{M} = 4.841 + 1.436D_1 + 0.349D_2 \tag{6.8}
$$

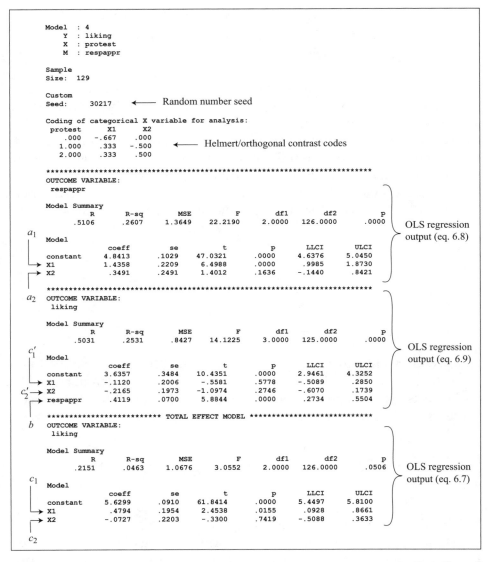

FIGURE 6.3. Output from the PROCESS procedure for SPSS for the sex discrimination mediation analysis.

(continued)

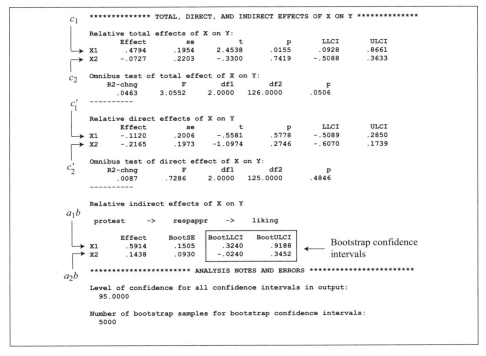

FIGURE 6.3 continued.

and so $a_1 = 1.436$ and $a_2 = 0.349$. As with indicator coding, the model reproduces the group means:

$$\overline{M}_{NP} = 4.841 + 1.436(-2/3) + 0.349(0) = 3.884$$
$$\overline{M}_{IP} = 4.841 + 1.436(1/3) + 0.349(-1/2) = 5.145$$
$$\overline{M}_{CP} = 4.841 + 1.436(1/3) + 0.349(1/2) = 5.494$$

Only a_1 is statistically significant. The meaning of a_1 and a_2 follow from the same mathematics:

$$
\begin{aligned}
a_1 &= \frac{\overline{M}_{IP} + \overline{M}_{CP}}{2} - \overline{M}_{NP} \\
&= \frac{5.145 + 5.494}{2} - 3.884 \\
&= 5.320 - 3.884 \\
&= 1.436
\end{aligned}
$$

which is the difference between the unweighted average perception of the appropriateness of Catherine's response in the two protest conditions and the average perception of appropriateness in the no protest condition. And a_2 is

$$
\begin{aligned}
a_2 &= \overline{M}_{CP} - \overline{M}_{IP} \\
&= 5.494 - 5.145 \\
&= 0.349
\end{aligned}
$$

which is the difference in the perceived appropriateness of collectively protesting compared to individually protesting.

Regressing perceptions of Catherine on experimental condition and perceived response appropriateness results in (from the PROCESS output)

$$
\hat{Y} = 3.636 - 0.112D_1 - 0.217D_2 + 0.412M \tag{6.9}
$$

and so $c_1' = -0.112$, $c_2' = -0.217$, and $b = 0.412$. The F-ratio for the omnibus test of the direct effect is the same as when indicator coding was used. And notice that this model generates the adjusted means of Y when M is set to $\overline{M}$:

$$
\begin{aligned}
\overline{Y}^*_{NP} &= 3.636 - 0.112(-2/3) - 0.217(0) + 0.412(4.866) = 5.715 \\
\overline{Y}^*_{IP} &= 3.636 - 0.112(1/3) - 0.217(-1/2) + 0.412(4.866) = 5.711 \\
\overline{Y}^*_{CP} &= 3.636 - 0.112(1/3) - 0.217(1/2) + 0.412(4.866) = 5.495
\end{aligned}
$$

Only b is statistically significant in this model, reflecting that among those told the same thing about Catherine's behavior, those who perceived her behavior as one unit more appropriate for the situation liked Catherine 0.412 units more. Observe that b is the same as when indicator coding was used. The effect of M on Y when X is held constant will not be affected by the decision of how to represent the three groups with two variables.

The regression coefficients for D_1 and D_2 in equation 6.9 are the relative direct effects. The relative direct effect c_1' is

$$
\begin{aligned}
c_1' &= \frac{\overline{Y}^*_{IP} + \overline{Y}^*_{CP}}{2} - \overline{Y}^*_{NP} \\
&= \frac{5.711 + 5.495}{2} - 5.715 \\
&= 5.603 - 5.715 \\
&= -0.112
\end{aligned}
$$

and quantifies, among people equal in how appropriate they perceived her behavior, the estimated difference between the unweighted mean evaluation of Catherine among those told she protested and the mean evaluation of those told she did not protest. This difference is not statistically significant.

The relative direct effect c_2' is the estimated mean difference in how Catherine was perceived between those told she collectively protested versus individually protested, among those equal in their perceptions of how appropriate her behavior was for the situation:

$$\begin{aligned} c_2' &= \overline{Y}^*_{CP} - \overline{Y}^*_{IP} \\ &= 5.494 - 5.145 \\ &= 0.349 \end{aligned}$$

This relative direct effect is not statistically significant.

The relative indirect effects are constructed by multiplying the paths from X to Y through M in the usual way. The relative indirect effect of protesting *in either form* relative to not is $a_1b = 1.436(0.412) = 0.591$, with a bootstrap confidence interval of 0.324 to 0.919 based on 5,000 bootstrap samples (see the PROCESS output in Figure 6.3). As the bootstrap confidence interval is entirely above zero, we can conclude that this relative indirect effect is significantly positive. The relative indirect effect of collectively protesting relative to individually protesting is $a_2b = 0.349(0.412) = 0.144$, with a bootstrap confidence interval from -0.024 to 0.345. As zero is in the confidence interval, we cannot definitively conclude that this relative indirect effect is different from zero.

Notice that changing the system for representing the three groups with D_1 and D_2 has not changed the fact that relative total effects partition into relative direct and indirect effects. That is, $c_1 = c_1' + a_1b = -0.112 + 0.591 = 0.479$ and $c_2 = c_2' + a_2b = -0.217 + 0.144 = -0.073$.

We can conclude from this analysis that perceived response appropriateness mediates the effect of Catherine's response on how positively she was perceived. When Catherine protested the decision (ignoring the form of the protest), this was perceived as more appropriate than not protesting at all, and this translated into a more positive perception of Catherine. This is the relative indirect effect of protesting versus not protesting. Whether she protested individually or collectively neither directly nor indirectly influenced how positively she was perceived.

It may be apparent to you how this coding system can be useful when X represents an ordinal dimension. It can be used to assess the effects of being in a group ordinally higher compared to one ordinally lower on the dimension X represents. For example, Kalyanaraman and Sundar (2006) manipulated the degree of personal customization of an internet web browser portal to users prior to assessing their attitudes about using the portal after browsing with it. Their manipulation of degree of customization was ordinal, with one group receiving no customization, a second receiving a little customization, and a third receiving lots of customization. The Helmert coding system described in this section would produce a regression coefficient quantifying the effect of customization on attitudes for those who received no customization versus some customization (whether a little or a lot), and another quantifying the effect of lots of customization compared to a little customization. Another coding system useful for an ordinal X is *sequential coding*. See Appendix A for a discussion of the implementation of sequential coding in PROCESS, or Darlington and Hayes (2017) for a more general discussion of this system for representing groups.

6.4 Some Miscellaneous Issues

So the estimation of a mediation model with a multicategorical X is not much different than when X is dichotomous or continuous. Some additional complexity results when X is multicategorical due to having to represent X's effects with a set of variables coding the multicategorical variable. This increases the number of regression coefficients and the number of direct, indirect, and total effects, which are now *relative* effects. In this section, I discuss a few miscellaneous additional topics, including extensions to multiple mediators, the influence of coding choice on whether M can be deemed a mediator, and some cautions about using too few variables to represent the groups.

More Than One Mediator

In this chapter, I discussed and illustrated *simple* mediation analysis with an antecedent X that is a multicategorical variable representing g groups, where $g \geq 3$. A simple mediation analysis has only one mediator. The mathematics and logic of this method generalize to models with more than one mediator operating in parallel or serial. The result is $g - 1$ relative total and direct effects, $g - 1$ *relative total indirect effects*, but possibly more than $g - 1$ *relative specific indirect effects*, depending on the number of pathways from X to Y. For example, in a model with $g = 4$ groups and two mediators operating in parallel, the regression equations representing the model would be

$$
\begin{aligned}
M_1 &= i_{M_1} + a_{11}D_1 + a_{21}D_2 + a_{31}D_3 + e_{M_1} \\
M_2 &= i_{M_2} + a_{12}D_1 + a_{22}D_2 + a_{32}D_3 + e_{M_2} \\
Y &= i_Y + c'_1 D_1 + c'_2 D_2 + c'_3 D_3 + b_1 M_1 + b_2 M_2 + e_Y
\end{aligned}
$$

The three relative direct effects are c'_1, c'_2, c'_3. There are two relative specific indirect effects for each of the three D variables representing X. For instance, the specific indirect effect through mediator 1 for the part of X represented with D_1 is $a_{11}b_1$, and through mediator 2, the relative specific indirect effect is $a_{12}b_2$. Their sum across the two mediators is its relative total indirect effect: $a_{11}b_1 + a_{12}b_2$. The relative total effect for D_1 is the sum of its relative direct and indirect effects: $c'_1 + a_{11}b_1 + a_{12}b_2$. For some examples of the use of this approach with multiple mediators, see Bohns et al. (2016), Brach et al. (2017), and Chew et al. (2017).

The **mcx** option can be used in *all* models that PROCESS can estimate, including model 4 (for the parallel multiple mediator model), model 6 (for the serial multiple mediator model), and models 80, 81, and 82 (which blend parallel and serial mediation processes). So PROCESS can easily handle more complex mediation models with a multicategorical X. And if your model is not represented by a preprogrammed model number, you can build your own model in PROCESS using the procedure documented in Appendix B.

The Importance of Coding Choice

When X is a multicategorical antecedent variable representing g groups, it can be said that X's effect on Y is mediated by mediator M if at least one of the relative indirect effects through M for the $g-1$ variables coding groups is different from zero by an inferential standard, such as a confidence interval that does not include zero. But remember from the two analyses that served as examples in this chapter that the size and sign of relative indirect effects will depend on the system used to code the g groups. It is possible that this criterion to claim mediation is met when one coding system is used but not another. For example, when indicator coding is used, one might find at least one nonzero relative indirect effect when one group is used as the reference group, but no relative indirect effects different from zero when a different group is used as the reference group.

This means that a failure to find at least one relative indirect effect different from zero does not necessarily mean M is not a mediator of the effect of a multicategorical X on Y. It may be that the use of a different system for coding groups would yield a substantively different conclusion from a mediation analysis. This is primarily a problem when one uses a coding system that is not sensitive to the specific hypotheses being tested, or when no argument or theoretical rationale underlies the choice for the coding system used. Absent a principled rationale for the choice, one could pursue a null finding by making a different coding choice and see what happens to the results. In that case, I recommend thinking about the multiple test problem, as such "fishing expeditions" for nonzero effects can produce false positives at a rate that many scientists would find too high to tolerate.

As discussed already, there are omnibus tests of the total effect and direct effect of X in a mediation analysis with a multicategorical X. These tests are not sensitive to the coding system used. There is no such test, at least not one that has been studied or disseminated widely, of the omnibus indirect effect.[1] Such a test, if it existed, would provide an answer to the question as to whether M mediates the effect of X on Y regardless of how the investigator chooses to represent the g groups with $g - 1$ variables in the model. Research in this area would be a worthwhile undertaking. Such a test *could* be done in a structural equation modeling environment by comparing the fit of a model that constrains all of the relative indirect effects to zero to one that does not impose such a constraint. But a formal test of fit would require the assumption of multivariate normality of the distribution of the relative indirect effects. As the sampling distribution of the product of regression coefficients is not normal, the joint distribution of the $g - 1$ relative indirect effects would not be multivariate normal.

A Caution about Using Contrast Coefficients from ANOVA

If you are familiar with analysis of variance, you probably have been exposed to the idea of a *contrast* of means. A contrast of means is a linear combination of means constructed to test a specific hypothesis. For example, in a study with four experimental groups, you may be interested in a test that compares the mean of group 1 to the mean of the means of groups 3 and 4. This contrast is formed as a linear sum of the means, with each mean receiving a weight based on a set of *contrast coefficients* constructed for the test. In this example, the contrast coefficients used to construct the contrast would be −2, 0, 1, and 1 for groups 1 through 4, respectively. Coefficients that result when dividing or multiplying each weight by a constant could also be used, such as −1, 0, 0.5, and 0.5. Or if the experiment contained only three groups, one might choose to use −1, 0, and 1 as the contrast coefficients for a contrast comparing the means of the first and third groups. Once this linear combination of means is constructed, an estimate of its standard error can be used to derive a p-value for null hypothesis testing or to construct a confidence interval.

It is tempting to represent the groups in a mediation analysis when X is a multicategorical variable by a single variable containing contrast coefficients such as these as a substitute for X (for an example of this single-

---

[1]Some of my as of yet unpublished research on this topic can be downloaded from *www.afhayes.com*.

variable practice, see Xu, Bègue, & Bushman, 2014). Resist this temptation, for doing so will usually produce an improper mediation analysis. When X codes g groups, a single variable containing these contrast coefficients cannot be used as a substitute for $g - 1$ variables needed as discussed in this chapter. In a mediation analysis, the goal is to understand how the means of Y differ between the groups as a result of a mediation process in which X influences M which in turn influences Y. Using the method described in this chapter, the regression equations will always reproduce the groups means on the mediator M and the final consequent Y, and the relative direct, indirect, and total effects quantify the separation between the g means resulting from some kind of mechanism (the relative indirect effects) or something not a part of the model (the relative direct effects). The use of a single variable containing ANOVA contrast coefficients as a substitute for X will usually result in a model that does not regenerate the means or quantify their separation resulting from direct and indirect processes.

Furthermore, when these contrast coefficients are used to construct a linear combination of means in the ANOVA tradition, groups with a contrast coefficient of zero are ignored in the construction of the contrast. The size of the mean for groups with a zero coefficient has no influence on the linear sum of means. However, when using contrast coefficients as a substitute for the $g - 1$ codes representing groups in a regression-based mediation analysis, groups with a coefficient of zero are not ignored, because the regression algebra will treat the codes as if they represent an interval-level measurement scale. The resulting direct, indirect, and total effects will be determined in part by the means of M and Y for all of the groups, including those receiving a coefficient of zero. They are not ignored, as you might think they would be if you overgeneralize the use of contrast coefficients from the ANOVA tradition to a mediation analysis with a multicategorical X.

6.5   Chapter Summary

In this chapter, I extended the path analysis algebra and inferential methods in mediation analysis with a dichotomous or continuous antecedent to mediation analysis with a multicategorical antecedent. A multicategorical X representing g groups can be represented with $g - 1$ variables, and these $g - 1$ variables are treated as the causal antecedent variable in a mediation model. The result is $g - 1$ relative direct, relative indirect, and relative total effects of X, one for each of the $g - 1$ variables coding X. Inference for relative total and direct effects can be undertaken using standard inferential approaches available in regression output. The methods of inference for indirect effects when X is dichotomous or continuous can be used for each of the relative indirect effects, including bootstrap confidence intervals. The PROCESS macro makes implementation easy, automates the construction of the $g - 1$ variables representing groups, and it can be used for models involving a single mediator or multiple mediators operating in parallel or serial.

An important limitation of the method discussed here is that the relative effects and their interpretation are dependent on how the g groups are represented with the $g - 1$ variables used in the analysis, and different coding decisions can result in different claims about mediation, including whether X's effect on Y is transmitted indirectly through M. For this reason, care must be exercised when deciding on a system for representing the multi-categorical variable, with the choice ideally determined by and sensitive to the specific hypotheses being tested or theory or theories motivating the study in the first place.

A solid understanding of the concepts and methods described thus far is a strong foundation upon which to build as we move toward more complex models that integrate mediation with moderation analysis in the latter chapters of this book. But before doing so, we must continue to build on this foundation by shifting our attention to moderation analysis, the focus of the next four chapters.

Part III

MODERATION ANALYSIS

7

Fundamentals of Moderation Analysis

Most effects that scientists study are contingent on one thing or another. An effect may be large for women and small for men, or positive among certain types of people and negative among other types, or zero for one category of stimuli but not zero for another category. When an investigator seeks to determine whether a certain variable influences or is related to the size of one variable's effect on another, a moderation analysis is the proper analytical strategy. This chapter introduces the fundamentals of estimation and inference about moderation (also known as *interaction*) using linear regression analysis. In addition to basic principles, this chapter covers some of the subtle details about interpretation of model coefficients, how to visualize moderated effects, and how to probe an interaction in a regression model through the estimation of conditional effects.

Although I consider myself primarily a statistical methodologist, now and then I dabble in substantive research in a variety of different areas, such as public opinion, political communication, and various applied domains such as health psychology. Some years ago, the second U.S. invasion of Iraq prompted me to conduct a number of studies related to war, the media, and public opinion (Hayes & Reineke, 2007; Hayes & Myers, 2009; Myers & Hayes, 2010). One of these studies was conducted in an attempt to replicate a classic finding from 1970s experimental social psychology on reactions to censorship (Worchel & Arnold, 1973). During the first and again in the second invasion of Iraq, the two George Bush administrations (George H. W. and George W.) instituted a policy restricting the access of journalists to locations where they could photograph images of the caskets of U.S. soldiers who had died returning to the United States for repatriation at Dover Air Force base in Delaware. Though not a literal censorship policy as the term is generally understood and used, this policy clearly had the effect of reducing public exposure to images of the human costs of warfare in terms of U.S. lives lost. We wondered whether people who knew about this policy would, in accordance with reactance theory (Wicklund, 1974), express greater interest in viewing such images than people who didn't know about it. We conducted an experiment to answer this question. In a telephone survey administered prior to the 2004 federal election, we told half of the respondents about this policy, and the other half (randomly determined) we did not. We then asked them how interested they would be in seeing such images or video if a local newspaper or television station published them.

Reactance theory predicts that participants told about this policy would perceive it as a threat to their freedom (in this case, their freedom to access information of their choosing) and, as a result, would express greater interest in recovering the lost freedom by seeking out the information they were being prohibited from accessing. But this is not at all what we found. On average, there was no statistically significant difference in interest in viewing the images between those told and not told about the policy. But a closer examination of the data revealed that this lack of effect was contingent on party identification. Republican participants told about the policy actually expressed *less* interest in viewing the images on average than Republicans not told about it, whereas among Democrats, there was no difference in interest caused by exposure to the policy information.

The result of this study illustrates the concept of *moderation*, the topic of this and the next three chapters. The effect of X on some variable Y is moderated by W if its size, sign, or strength depends on or can be predicted by W. In that case, W is said to be a *moderator* of X's effect on Y, or that W and X *interact* in their influence on Y. Identifying a moderator of an effect helps to establish the boundary conditions of that effect or the circumstances, stimuli, or type of people for which the effect is large versus small, present versus absent, positive versus negative, and so forth. In this study, party identification was a moderator of the effect of knowledge of the policy on interest in viewing the images. That is, giving participants information about the Bush administration policy had different effects on interest in viewing the images for people of different political leanings.

Moderation is depicted in the form of a conceptual diagram in Figure 7.1. This diagram represents a process in which the effect of some variable of interest X (called the *focal antecedent*) on Y is influenced by or dependent on W, as reflected by the arrow pointing from W to the line from X to Y. Readers familiar with structural equation modeling programs such as AMOS or EQS that allow the analyst to draw the model to tell the program what to do should not attempt to estimate a moderation model by constructing such a diagram in their program, for this will not work. Nor should you assume that because there is no arrow pointing from W to

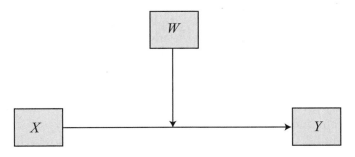

FIGURE 7.1. A simple moderation model depicted as a conceptual diagram.

Y that W is not an antecedent variable in a moderation model. Unlike for mediation, the conceptual diagram of a moderation model is very different in form from its corresponding statistical diagram, which represents how such a model is set up in the form of an equation. As will be described in section 7.1, the statistical diagram corresponding to this moderation model will require not two but three antecedent variables, and W will be one of those antecedents.

Moderation plays an important role in many social science theories. Consider *The Elaboration Likelihood Model of Persuasion* (Petty & Cacioppo, 1986), which attempts to explain the conditions under which messages designed with the intent to persuade are likely to result in short-term, long-term, or no attitude change. Research supporting the elaboration likelihood model almost exclusively is based on evidence of moderation. For instance, in conditions in which participants are motivated to deeply process message content because the message pertains to some issue or policy that will directly affect them, strong arguments result in greater attitude change than do weak ones relative to when participants are less inclined to engage in such message elaboration, such as when the topic or issue has no direct impact on their lives. And high motivation to elaborate on message content reduces the impact of peripheral cues, such as the number of arguments, relative to when motivation is lower. Thus, personal involvement in the topic (W) moderates the effect of argument strength (X) or number of arguments (X) on attitude change (Y).

Cultivation theory (see, e.g., Shanahan & Morgan, 1999) is another explanatory model in which moderation is pivotal. Our understanding about the world outside of our immediate experience comes primarily through television and other media forms. Although the advent of cable and the Internet has changed the media landscape considerably, television remains an important window through which the world is perceived. According to cultivation theory, frequent exposure to the televised world cultivates a perception of the world consistent with that depiction. For example, some argue that the world as portrayed by televised news and popular dramas is a hostile, mean, and dangerous place. Thus, according to cultivation theory, the more exposure to the televised world as depicted as hostile, mean, and dangerous, the more a person will see the world that way. Such cultivation is so theoretically powerful that frequent television viewers will in time become more homogeneous than less frequent viewers in their attitudes and beliefs. In other words, variables such as sex, education, and ethnicity that predict attitudes and beliefs among less frequent viewers are less predictive of such beliefs among frequent television viewers. This homogenization of the frequently viewing public is referred to in cultivation theory as *mainstreaming*, and it is a moderation phenomenon. Television viewing frequency (W) moderates the effect of certain individual differences (X) such as sex and ethnicity on various attitudes and beliefs (Y), such as how violent and dangerous the world is perceived as being.

As a third example, it has been well established by research in public health, communication, and political science that people who differ in education frequently differ in their knowledge of numerous public affairs topics (e.g., various community issues and controversies, the positions held by politicians, etc.), science and health-related information (e.g., cancer prevention) and a variety of other topics (Gaziano, 1983; Hwang & Jeong, 2009). Many have speculated about and there is much research on the potential causes of these *knowledge gaps* and how they can be reduced or eliminated (see, e.g., Tichenor, Donohue, & Olien, 1970). The most obvious means of reducing such gaps in knowledge, it would seem, is some kind of an information campaign targeting the public in the hope that the less educated will become more knowledgeable following exposure to the relevant information. However, it turns out that this does not always work and can even backfire. People who are more educated are more likely to have the cognitive skills and resources to benefit from exposure to information. As a result, information campaigns can sometimes increase rather than narrow knowledge gaps, as the more educated who are exposed to the information (relative to those not exposed) are more likely to acquire the relevant knowledge than those who are less educated. In other words, research has established that sometimes education (W) moderates the effect of exposure to information (X) on knowledge in such a manner that knowledge gaps are increased rather than decreased.

Although mediation analysis is popular throughout the social and behavioral sciences, it is less commonly covered in statistics classes than is moderation. Moderation is very widely covered, although not always in the way I present here. Most burgeoning researchers are exposed to moderation analysis when they take a course that covers analysis of variance, which is a form of regression analysis restricted to categorical antecedent variables. In a *factorial* research design, a researcher has two (or more) categorical variables that are crossed, yielding a cross-classification of some kind, such as in a 2 (experimental condition: control versus treatment) × 2 (sex: male versus female) design. Factorial analysis of variance is used to ascertain whether the effect of one variable on a dependent variable of interest differs across levels of the second variable. If so, then it is said that the two variables *interact* in their influence on the dependent variable. *Statistical interaction* is just another term for moderation, and I use the terms interchangeably in this chapter. So if you know something about testing interactions in analysis of variance, you already know something about moderation.

Mathematically, factorial analysis of variance is identical to the regression-based procedure I emphasize here for moderation analysis, but the regression procedure is more general and flexible. Factorial analysis of variance assumes categorical antecedents (although continuous variables are sometimes used as covariates in analysis of *covariance*). The regression-based procedure I describe beginning in the next section makes no such restriction on the nature of the variables being analyzed. It can be used for categorical antecedent variables, continuous antecedent variables, or any combination thereof.

7.1 Conditional and Unconditional Effects

Consider a multiple regression model of the form $Y = i_Y + b_1 X + b_2 W + e_Y$, which estimates Y from two antecedents X and W. More specifically, suppose $i_Y = 4$, $b_1 = 1$, and $b_2 = 2$ and therefore

$$\hat{Y} = 4 + 1X + 2W$$

Table 7.1 provides values of $\hat{Y}$ from this model for various combinations of X and W, and the model is depicted in visual form in Figure 7.2, panel A.

Try choosing *any* value of W in Table 7.1 and observe that as X increases by one unit (e.g., from −1 to 0, 0 to 1, and so forth) but W is held constant at that value chosen, $\hat{Y}$ changes by 1.00 unit. For example, suppose you choose $W = 1$. When $X = 0$ and $W = 1$, $\hat{Y} = 6$, but when $X = 1$ and $W = 1$, $\hat{Y} = 7$. If you were to choose a different value, say $W = 2$, the same would be true. For example, when $X = -1$ and $W = 2$, $\hat{Y} = 7$, and when $X = 0$ and $W = 2$, $\hat{Y} = 8$. It is no coincidence that this difference in $\hat{Y}$ as X changes by

TABLE 7.1. Fitted Values of Y Generated from Two Models Using X and W as Antecedent Variables

X	W	$\hat{Y} = 4 + 1X + 2W$	$\hat{Y} = 4 + 1X + 2W + 1.5XW$
−1	0	3	3.0
−1	1	5	3.5
−1	2	7	4.0
0	0	4	4.0
0	1	6	6.0
0	2	8	8.0
1	0	5	5.0
1	1	7	8.5
1	2	9	12.0
2	0	6	6.0
2	1	8	11.0
2	2	10	16.0

one unit with W held fixed is b_1. Most generally, for any value $W = w$ and $X = x$,

$$b_1 = [\hat{Y} \mid (X = x, W = w)] - [\hat{Y} \mid (X = x - 1, W = w)]$$

In other words, the effect of a one unit increase in X on $\hat{Y}$ is not dependent on W. Regardless of the value of W, a change of one unit in X translates into a change of b_1 units in $\hat{Y}$. The effect of a one unit change in X on $\hat{Y}$ is *unconditional* on W, in the sense that it does not depend on W.

The same can be said for b_2. Choose any value of X, and when W increases by one unit, $\hat{Y}$ increases by $b_2 = 2$ units. For instance, when $X = 1$ and $W = 0$, $\hat{Y} = 5$, and when $X = 1$ and $W = 1$, $\hat{Y} = 7$. Most generally, for any value $W = w$ and $X = x$,

$$b_2 = [\hat{Y} \mid (W = w, X = x)] - [\hat{Y} \mid (W = w - 1, X = x)]$$

So the effect of a one unit change in W on $\hat{Y}$ is unconditional on X, in that it is not dependent on X.

A regression model in this form is not well-suited to testing questions about moderation. In fact, such a model is the very opposite of what the concept of moderation embodies. If X's effect on Y is moderated by another variable in the model, that means X's effect depends on that other variable. But this model constrains X's effect to be unconditional on W, meaning that it is invariant across all values of W.

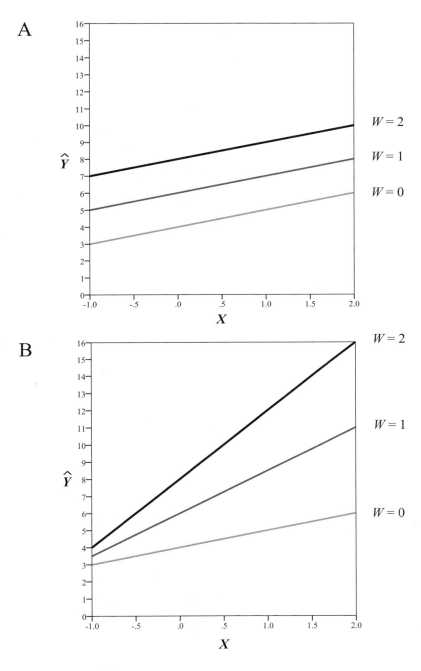

FIGURE 7.2. A graphical representation of the two models in Table 7.1.

Eliminating the Constraint of Unconditionality

We want to get around this constraint in the model such that X's effect can be dependent on W, meaning that for different values of W, X's effect on Y is different. In generic terms, such a model can be written as

$$Y = i_Y + f(W)X + b_2W + e_Y \tag{7.1}$$

where $f(W)$ is a function of W. Consider a simple function of the form $f(W) = b_1 + b_3W$. This function of W looks like a simple linear regression model where b_1 is the constant and b_3 is the regression coefficient for W, except that rather than estimating some consequent variable from W, it is a model of the effect of X on Y. Substituting $b_1 + b_3W$ for $f(W)$ in equation 7.1 yields

$$Y = i_Y + (b_1 + b_3W)X + b_2W + e_Y$$

which can be expanded by distributing X across the two terms defining the function of W, resulting in

$$Y = i_Y + b_1X + b_2W + b_3XW + e_Y \tag{7.2}$$

or, in terms of estimated values of Y,

$$\hat{Y} = i_Y + b_1X + b_2W + b_3XW$$

where XW is a variable constructed as the product of X and W. The resulting equation is the *simple linear moderation model*, depicted conceptually in Figure 7.1 and in the form of a statistical diagram in Figure 7.3. This approach, widely attributed to Saunders (1956), provides a simple means of modeling data in which X's effect on Y is dependent on W or *conditional*, as well as an approach to testing hypotheses about moderation.

To see what effects adding the product of X and W as an antecedent has, consider a specific example where $i_Y = 4$, $b_1 = 1$, $b_2 = 2$, and $b_3 = 1.5$; thus,

$$\hat{Y} = 4 + 1X + 2W + 1.5XW$$

This model is identical to the prior example, except it now includes the term $1.5XW$. Values of $\hat{Y}$ this model generates for different combinations of X and W can be found in Table 7.1, and the model is depicted visually in Figure 7.2, panel B.

Observe what has happened as a result of the addition of b_3XW to the model that constrained X's effect on Y to be unconditional on W. Now a one-unit change in X results in a change in $\hat{Y}$ that depends on W. For instance, when $W = 0$, changing X by one unit changes $\hat{Y}$ by one unit, but

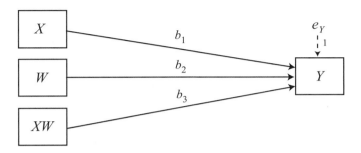

FIGURE 7.3. A simple moderation model depicted as a statistical diagram.

when $W = 1$, changing X by one unit changes $\hat{Y}$ by 2.5 units, and when $W = 2$, changing X by one unit changes $\hat{Y}$ by four units.

More generally, in a model of the form in equation 7.2, the effect of a one-unit change in X on $\hat{Y}$ is expressed by the function

$$\theta_{X \to Y} = b_1 + b_3 W \qquad (7.3)$$

where $\theta_{X \to Y}$ is the *conditional effect of X on Y*, defined as the amount by which two cases that differ by one unit on X are estimated to differ on Y. It should not come as a surprise that this is exactly the same function plugged into equation 7.1 to generate the simple linear moderation model expressed as equation 7.2. In this example, $\theta_{X \to Y} = 1 + 1.5W$. Plugging values of W into this equation yields an estimate of how much a one-unit change in X changes Y given that value of W. Various values of $\theta_{X \to Y}$ for different values of W can be found in Table 7.2. As can be seen, as W increases by one unit, the difference in $\hat{Y}$ between two cases that differ by one unit on X changes by b_3 units.

Figure 7.2 most dramatically illustrates the difference between the model that constrains X's effect to be unconditional and the one that allows X's effect on Y to depend on W. In panel A, X's effect on $\hat{Y}$ is constrained to be independent of W. As a result, the slopes of each line linking X to $\hat{Y}$ are identical and the lines are therefore parallel. However, in panel B, X's effect on $\hat{Y}$ depends on W. Visually, this manifests itself in slopes for each line linking X to Y that differ for different values of W. As a result, the lines are not parallel. The degree of nonparallelism that will exist in a visual representation of moderation will depend on b_3, where b_3 in graphical terms is the change in the slope of the line linking X to $\hat{Y}$ as W increases by one unit. The larger b_3 in absolute value, the more divergent from parallel are the slopes.

TABLE 7.2. The Conditional Effect of X for Values of W and the Conditional Effect of W for Values of X for the Model $\hat{Y} = 4 + 1X + 2W + 1.5XW$

	$\theta_{X \to Y} = b_1 + b_3 W$			$\theta_{W \to Y} = b_2 + b_3 X$	
W	$b_1 + b_3 W$	$\theta_{X \to Y} \mid W$	X	$b_2 + b_3 X$	$\theta_{W \to Y} \mid X$
0	b_1	1.000	-1	$b_2 - b_3$	0.500
1	$b_1 + b_3$	2.500	0	b_2	2.000
2	$b_1 + 2b_3$	4.000	1	$b_2 + b_3$	3.500
3	$b_1 + 3b_3$	5.500	2	$b_2 + 2b_3$	5.000

Symmetry in Moderation

Earlier, I illustrated that the simple moderation model described by equation 7.2 can be expressed as

$$Y = i_Y + (b_1 + b_3 W)X + b_2 W + e_Y \tag{7.4}$$

or, alternatively, as

$$Y = i_Y + \theta_{X \to Y} X + b_2 W + e_Y \tag{7.5}$$

where $\theta_{X \to Y} = b_1 + b_3 W$. Equations 7.4 and 7.5 make it most clear how X's effect on Y is dependent on W. But the simple moderation model can also be written in another mathematically equivalent form that expresses W's effect on Y as moderated by X:

$$Y = i_Y + b_1 X + (b_2 + b_3 X)W + e_Y \tag{7.6}$$

or, alternatively,

$$Y = i_Y + b_1 X + \theta_{W \to Y} W + e_Y \tag{7.7}$$

where $\theta_{W \to Y}$ is the conditional effect of W on $Y = b_2 + b_3 X$. Expressed in this form, it is apparent that in the simple moderation model, W's effect on Y is dependent on X, with that dependency expressed as $b_2 + b_3 X$. Indeed, observe in Table 7.1 that the amount by which two cases that differ by one unit on W differ on $\hat{Y}$ depends on X. For instance, when $X = 0$, two cases differing by one unit on W differ by two units on $\hat{Y}$, but when $X = 1$, two cases differing by one unit on W differ by 3.5 units on $\hat{Y}$. Various values of the conditional effect of W on Y for different values of X can be found in Table 7.2. Observe that as X increases by one unit, the conditional effect of W on Y changes by b_3 units.

Thus, b_3 has two interpretations, depending on whether X or W is construed as the moderator. When W is conceptualized as the moderator of X's effect on Y, then b_3 estimates how much the difference in Y between two cases that differ by a unit on X changes as W changes by one unit. But if X is conceptualized as the moderator of W's effect on Y, then b_3 estimates how much the difference in Y between two cases that differ by a unit on W changes as X changes by one unit. Of course, the mathematics underlying the simple moderation model don't know or care which variable you are conceptualizing as the moderator in your analysis. Both interpretations are correct.

Interpretation of the Regression Coefficients

Above, I described the interpretation of b_3 in the simple moderation model. Most generally, for any value $X = x$ and $W = w$,

$$b_3 = \frac{\left([\hat{Y} \mid (X = x, W = w)] - [\hat{Y} \mid (X = x - 1, W = w)]\right) -}{\left([\hat{Y} \mid (X = x, W = w - 1)] - [\hat{Y} \mid (X = x - 1, W = w - 1)]\right)} \qquad (7.8)$$

But how are b_1 and b_2 interpreted? The interpretation of b_1 is made clear by an examination of equation 7.3. Observe that if W is set to 0, then equation 7.3 reduces to $\theta_{X \to Y} = b_1$. So b_1 is the conditional effect of X on Y when $W = 0$. That is, b_1 quantifies how much two cases that differ by one unit on X but with $W = 0$ are estimated to differ on Y. For any value $X = x$,

$$b_1 = [\hat{Y} \mid (X = x, W = 0)] - [\hat{Y} \mid (X = x - 1, W = 0)] \qquad (7.9)$$

Thus, it is neither appropriate to interpret b_1 as relationship between X and Y controlling for W "on average" or "controlling for W and XW," nor is it the "main effect of X" (to use a term from analysis of variance lingo). Rather, it represents the association between X and Y conditioned on $W = 0$. As depicted in Figure 7.4, b_1 is the slope of the line linking X to Y when $W = 0$. In analysis of variance terms, b_1 is akin to a *simple effect*—the simple effect of X when $W = 0$.

Similarly, examining equations 7.6 and 7.7, notice that when X is set to 0, $\theta_{W \to Y} = b_2$. Thus, b_2 is the conditional effect of W on Y when $X = 0$. For any value $W = w$,

$$b_2 = [\hat{Y} \mid (W = w, X = 0)] - [\hat{Y} \mid (W = w - 1, X = 0)] \qquad (7.10)$$

So like b_1, b_2 is a conditional effect, in that it quantifies how much two cases that differ by one unit on W are estimated to differ on Y conditioned on $X = 0$. It should not be interpreted as W's effect controlling for X and XW or as W's average effect on Y or W's main effect. It describes the association

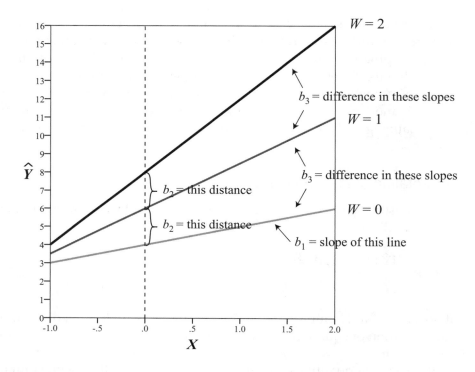

FIGURE 7.4. A visual representation of b_1, b_2, and b_3 in a model of the form $\hat{Y} = i_Y + b_1X + b_2W + b_3XW$. In this figure, $b_1 = 1$, $b_2 = 2$, and $b_3 = 1.5$.

between W and Y when $X = 0$. See Figure 7.4 for a visual representation of b_2.

Notice that these interpretations of b_1 and b_2 are very different from their interpretation when XW is not included as an antecedent variable. When XW is an antecedent along with X and W in the model of Y, b_1 and b_2 are conditional effects. But for a model of the form $\hat{Y} = i_Y + b_1X + b_2W$, without XW as an antecedent, b_1 and b_2 are *partial effects* and *unconditional*. In the unconditional model, b_1 quantifies how much two cases that differ by one unit on X are estimated to differ on Y *holding W constant*, and b_2 quantifies how much two cases that differ by one unit on W are estimated to differ on Y *holding X constant*. These are completely different in meaning, and their substantive interpretation typically is dramatically different as well. Do not confuse these interpretations as many have (see, e.g., Hayes, Glynn, & Huge, 2012). When XW is in a model with X and W, the coefficients for X and W are conditional effects—conditioned on the other variable being zero. When XW is not in the model, these are partial effects.

The Importance of b_3 When Asking about Moderation

The simple moderation model allows X's effect on Y to be a linear function of W. Of course, allowing that effect to depend on W doesn't mean that it actually does in reality. In most any sample of data, b_3 will be different from zero even when X's effect on Y is independent of W. Of interest when testing a moderation hypothesis is not just allowing X's effect to be contingent on W, but also determining whether b_3 deviates too far from zero than would be expected given that b_3, like any statistic, is subject to sampling variance. In other words, an inferential test about $_T b_3$ ultimately determines whether X's effect really depends on W or whether the obtained b_3 is within the realm of what would be expected to occur just by chance given the assumption that W does not linearly moderate X's effect.

Most scientists would agree that evidence that $_T b_3$ is different from zero (as determined by a hypothesis test or a confidence interval) is needed in order to claim that W functions as a linear moderator of X's effect. If the evidence is not consistent with such a claim, a more parsimonious model would fix X's effect on Y to be unconditional on W. In other words, given that b_1 and b_2 are conditional effects when XW is in the model, absent evidence that X's effect is moderated by W, it is best to estimate a model without the product of X and W, which thereby renders b_1 and b_2 as estimates of partial rather than conditional effects.

Such a model cleansing strategy does not apply to b_1 and b_2 whenever XW is in the model. If you choose to retain XW in the model, X and W should be included as well, even if b_1 and b_2 are not statistically significant. Excluding X or W will bias the estimate of the moderation of X's effect by W. There are few circumstances in which you would want to estimate a model including XW as a antecedent without also including X and W. Once of these circumstances is described in Chapter 10. But as a general rule, when XW is in the model, keep X and W in the model as well, *regardless of the outcome of an inferential test of b_1 and/or b_2.*

7.2   An Example: Climate Change Disasters and Humanitarianism

To illustrate how to test for and interpret linear moderation using this procedure, I rely on data from Chapman and Lickel (2016) published in *Social Psychological and Personality Science*. The data file is named DISASTER and can be downloaded from this book's web page at *www.afhayes.com*. In this study, 211 participants read a news story about a famine in Africa that was reportedly caused by severe droughts affecting the region. For half of the participants, the story attributed the droughts to the effects of climate change, whereas for the other half, the story provided no information suggesting that climate change was responsible for the droughts. I refer to these as the "climate change" and "natural causes" conditions, respectively. They are coded in a variable named FRAME in the data, which is set to 0 for those in the natural causes condition and 1 for those in the climate change condition.

After reading this story, the participants were asked a set of questions assessing how much they agreed or disagreed with various justifications for *not* providing aid to the victims, such as that they did not deserve help, that the victims had themselves to blame for their situation, the donations would not be helpful or effective, and so forth. Responses to these questions were aggregated and are held in a variable named JUSTIFY that quantifies the strength of a participant's justifications for withholding aid. So higher scores on JUSTIFY reflect a stronger sense that helping out the victims was not justified. The participants also responded to a set of questions about their beliefs about whether climate change is a real phenomenon. This measure of *climate change skepticism* is named SKEPTIC in the data, and the higher a participant's score, the more skeptical he or she is about the reality of climate change.

The purpose of the analysis I report here is to examine whether framing the disaster as caused by climate change rather than leaving the cause unspecified influences people's justifications for not helping, and also whether this effect of framing is dependent on a person's skepticism about climate change. The group means can be found in Table 7.3, which suggest that participants who read a story attributing the droughts to climate change reported stronger justifications for withholding aid ($\overline{Y} = 2.936$) than those given no such attribution ($\overline{Y} = 2.802$). But an independent groups t-test shows that this difference is not statistically significant, $t(209) = -1.049, p = .295$. Chance is a plausible explanation for the observed difference in justifications for not helping the victims.

A mathematically equivalent procedure that is more consistent with the modeling approach used in this book is to regress justifications for withholding aid (Y) on experimental condition (X):

$$Y = i_Y + b_1 X + e_Y$$

As can be seen in Table 7.4 (model 1), $i_Y = 2.802$ and $b_1 = 0.134$. This simple linear model produces two estimates for Y, depending on whether $X = 0$ or 1. When $X = 0$, meaning those assigned to the natural causes condition,

$$\hat{Y} = 2.802 + 0.134(0) = 2.802$$

TABLE 7.3. Descriptive Statistics for the Climate Change Victims Study

		Y JUSTIFY	W SKEPTIC
Natural causes condition	Mean	2.802	3.339
($X = 0$)	SD	0.849	2.042
Climate change condition	Mean	2.936	3.421
($X = 1$)	SD	1.010	2.032
	Mean	2.867	3.378
	SD	0.930	2.033

and when $X = 1$ (i.e., those assigned to the climate change condition),

$$\hat{Y} = 2.802 + 0.134(1) = 2.936$$

These two values of $\hat{Y}$ correspond to the group means (see Table 7.3).

The regression coefficient for experimental condition (b_1) is positive. Because the two groups are coded such that they differ by a single unit (1 versus 0) on X, b_1 can be interpreted as the difference between the group means. Two cases that differ by one unit on X are estimated to differ by 0.134 units on Y. That is,

$$b_1 = [\hat{Y} \mid (X = 1)] - [\hat{Y} \mid (X = 0)] = 2.936 - 2.802 = 0.134$$

The positive coefficient tells us that those with a higher value on X are estimated as higher on Y. In other words, participants told the disaster was caused by climate change reported stronger justifications for withholding aid, by 0.134 units on the scale, than those in the natural causes condition. However, this not statistically different from zero, with the same t statistic and p-value as the independent group t-test produces. And observe that the regression constant, $i_Y = 2.802$, is the estimated value of Y when $X = 0$. It estimates the mean strength of justifications for withholding aid among those told the disaster was brought about by natural causes (i.e., $X = 0$), consistent with the value reported in Table 7.3.

This analysis only determines that, on average, those told the disaster resulted from natural causes did not differ on average in their justifications for withholding assistance than those told it was brought about by climate change. But this finding says nothing about whether the attribution of cause differentially affected people with different beliefs about whether climate

TABLE 7.4. Various Regression Models Estimating Justifications for Withholding Aid

		Coeff.	SE	t	p
Model 1 $R^2 = 0.005, MSE = 0.864$					
Constant	i_Y	2.802	0.089	31.623	< .001
Frame Condition (X)	b_1	0.134	0.128	1.049	.295
Model 2 $R^2 = 0.198, MSE = 0.700$					
Constant	i_Y	2.132	0.124	17.204	< .001
Frame Condition (X)	b_1	0.118	0.115	1.022	.308
Skepticism (W)	b_2	0.201	0.028	7.071	< .001
Model 3 $R^2 = 0.246, MSE = 0.661$					
Constant	i_Y	2.452	0.149	16.449	< .001
Frame Condition (X)	b_1	−0.562	0.218	−2.581	.011
Skepticism (W)	b_2	0.105	0.038	2.756	.006
$X \times W$	b_3	0.201	0.055	3.640	< .001
Model 4 (mean-centered W) $R^2 = 0.246, MSE = 0.661$					
Constant	i_Y	2.807	0.078	36.201	< .001
Frame Condition (X)	b_1	0.117	0.112	1.045	.297
Skepticism (W')	b_2	0.105	0.038	2.756	.006
$X \times W'$	b_3	0.201	0.055	3.640	< .001
Model 5 (mean-centered W, X coded −0.5 and 0.5) $R^2 = 0.246, MSE = 0.661$					
Constant	i_Y	2.865	0.056	51.136	< .001
Frame Condition (X)	b_1	0.117	0.112	1.045	.297
Skepticism (W')	b_2	0.206	0.028	7.443	< .001
$X \times W'$	b_3	0.201	0.055	3.640	< .001

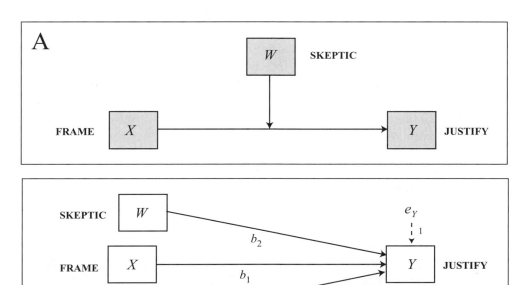

FIGURE 7.5. Moderation of the effect of framing of the cause of the drought on strength of justifications for withholding aid by climate change skepticism, depicted as a conceptual diagram (panel A) and a statistical diagram (panel B).

change is real. *Regardless* of whether the groups differ on average on Y, in order to determine whether the effect depends on another variable, a formal test of moderation should be conducted. Evidence of an association between X and Y is not required in order for X's effect to be moderated, just as the existence of such an association says nothing about whether that association is dependent on something else.

So our interest is in whether the framing of the cause of the drought (X) on strength of justifications for withholding aid (Y) depends on climate change skepticism (W). Such a moderation model is depicted in conceptual form in Figure 7.5, panel A. To test the moderation of X's effect on Y by W, a term is included in the regression model of Y from X and W that allows X's effect to be a function of W. In this case, we estimate the coefficients of a regression model in which the effect of the attribution for the cause of the drought on justifications for withholding aid is allowed to vary linearly with climate change skepticism by including the product of X and W as an antecedent in the model of consequent Y along with X and W:

$$Y = i_Y + b_1 X + b_2 W + b_3 XW + e_Y$$

A statistical diagram of this model can be found in Figure 7.5, panel B. Of interest is the estimate of b_3 along with an inferential test. If b_3 is not statistically different from zero (via a hypothesis test or a confidence interval for $_Tb_3$ that straddles zero), this means that the effect of the framing of the cause of the drought on justifications for withholding aid is not dependent (at least not linearly) on climate change skepticism. But if b_3 is statistically different from zero, we can conclude that whether or not the drought was attributed to climate change has a different effect on people's justifications depending on their beliefs about the reality of climate change.[1]

No special modeling software is needed to estimate the model. Simply construct the product of X and W and include it as an antecedent of Y along with X and W using any OLS regression program. In SPSS, the commands that do the job are

```
compute framskep=frame*skeptic.
regression/dep=justify/method=enter frame skeptic framskep.
```

In SAS, try

```
data disaster;set disaster;framskep=frame*skeptic;run;
proc reg data=disaster;model justify=frame skeptic framskep;run;
```

Table 7.4 (model 3) contains the OLS regression coefficients along with their standard errors, t- and p-values, and 95% confidence intervals. As can be seen, the best fitting OLS regression model is

$$\hat{Y} = 2.452 - 0.562X + 0.105W + 0.201XW \qquad (7.11)$$

In this model, $i_Y = 2.452$, $b_1 = -0.562$, $b_2 = 0.105$, $b_3 = 0.201$. Importantly, observe b_3 is statistically different from zero, $t(207) = 3.640, p < .001$ (though not generated by the commands above, a 95% confidence interval for $_Tb_3$ is 0.092 to 0.310). So we can conclude that the effect of framing of the cause of the disaster on strength of justifications for withholding aid is moderated by participants' climate change skepticism. That is, whether the drought was framed as caused by climate change or not had different effects on different people, depending on their beliefs about whether climate change is real.

Had there been no evidence of moderation (i.e., b_3 was not statistically different from zero), the most sensible approach would be to reestimate the

[1]In practice, an investigator may want to include one or more covariates in the model in order to control for their effects in the estimation of X's effect on Y. Covariates can be included in a moderation model such as this, and the discussion that follows generalizes without modification. A concrete example of a moderation model with covariates is provided in Chapter 8.

model excluding the product, thereby allowing X's effect to be invariant across W. This could take the form of model 1 or model 2 in Table 7.4, depending on whether or not one desires to control for W when assessing X's effect on Y.

In this case, the effect of the attributed cause of the drought is clearly moderated. This moderation component of the model explains about 4.8% of the variance in strength of justifications for withholding aid, as calculated from the difference in R^2 for the model that includes the product (model 3, $R^2 = 0.246$) compared to the model that excludes it (model 2, $R^2 = 0.198$). That is, $R^2_{model\,3} - R^2_{model\,2} = 0.048$. This could be thought of as a measure of the "size" of the moderation effect, though as Darlington and Hayes (2017) discuss, there are many ways of defining the size of an effect in a regression analysis, and reducing effect size to a single number oversimplifies the complexity and subjectivity of this problem.

By expressing the regression model in an equivalent form

$$\hat{Y} = 2.452 + \theta_{X \to Y}X + 0.105W$$

where

$$\theta_{X \to Y} = b_1 + b_3W = -0.562 + 0.201W \tag{7.12}$$

and then plugging various values of W into equation 7.12, one gains insight into how the differences in justifications for withholding aid between the two groups is a function of climate change skepticism. In the data, climate change skepticism ranges between 1 and 9, with most participants between 1.5 and 5.2 or so. Arbitrarily choosing 2, 3.5, and 5 as values of W, when $W = 2$, $\theta_{X \to Y} = -0.562 + 0.201(2) = -0.160$; when $W = 3.5$, $\theta_{X \to Y} = -0.562 - 0.201(3.5) = 0.142$; and when $W = 5$, $\theta_{X \to Y} = -0.562 + 0.201(5) = 0.443$. From these calculations, it appears that participants lower in climate change skepticism reported weaker justifications for withholding aid when told the drought was caused by climate change compared to when not so told. However, among those at the higher end of the continuum of climate change skepticism, the opposite is observed. Participants high in skepticism about climate change who read the story attributing the drought to climate change reported stronger justifications for withholding aid than those who read the story that did not attribute the drought to climate change. If this is not obvious (and it very well may not be until you become fluent in interpreting models of this sort), a picture will help. How to visualize a model such as this is described in section 7.3.

Estimation Using PROCESS

PROCESS can estimate a moderation model such as this, and it also provides a number of valuable output options for visualizing and probing an interaction described later. In SPSS, the PROCESS command for this analysis is

```
process y=justify/x=frame/w=skeptic/model=1/jn=1/plot=1.
```

In SAS, use

```
%process (data=disaster,y=justify,x=frame,w=skeptic,model=1,jn=1,
    plot=1);
```

Output from the SPSS version of PROCESS can be found in Figure 7.6. In PROCESS, a simple moderation model with W moderating the effect of X on Y is estimated by requesting **model=1**. PROCESS saves you the trouble of having to calculate the product of X and W, for it does so automatically and generates a new variable for its own use corresponding to this product labeled "int_1" in the output.

PROCESS also produces the proportion of the variance in Y uniquely attributable to the moderation of X's effect by W in the section of output labeled "R-square increase due to interaction," calculated as described earlier. The p-value for this increase is the same as the p-value for b_3, as these procedures test the same null hypothesis, albeit framed in different ways. For a discussion of the test for the increase in R^2 when a variable is added to a model, see section 2.6. The **jn** and **plot** options in the PROCESS command are described below and in section 7.3.

Interpreting the Regression Coefficients

As discussed on page 229, in a regression model of the form $Y = i_Y + b_1 X + b_2 W + b_3 XW$, b_1 and b_2 are conditional effects. These regression coefficients estimate the effect of X when $W = 0$ and the effect of W when $X = 0$, respectively (see equations 7.9 and 7.10). As will be seen, these coefficients don't always have a sensible substantive interpretation.

Applied to this analysis, the regression coefficient for X is $b_1 = -0.562$. This is the estimated difference in strength of justifications for withholding aid between those told climate change was responsible for the drought and those not so told *among those scoring zero on climate change skepticism* (i.e., $W = 0$). The coefficient is negative, meaning that among those scoring zero in climate change skepticism, those told climate change was responsible for the drought ($X = 1$) had weaker justifications for withholding aid than those not told anything about climate change as the cause ($X = 0$). Although this interpretation is mathematically correct, substantively it is nonsense. The measure of climate change skepticism in this study is mathematically bound between 1 and 9. An estimate of the effect of the manipulation conditioned

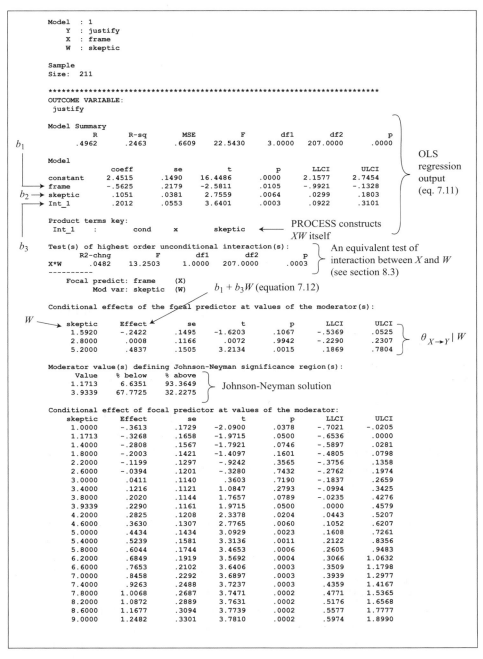

```
Model   : 1
    Y   : justify
    X   : frame
    W   : skeptic

Sample
Size:   211

***************************************************************************
OUTCOME VARIABLE:
 justify

Model Summary
        R        R-sq       MSE         F         df1        df2         p
     .4962      .2463     .6609    22.5430     3.0000   207.0000      .0000

Model
                coeff        se         t          p         LLCI       ULCI
constant       2.4515      .1490   16.4486      .0000      2.1577     2.7454
frame          -.5625      .2179   -2.5811      .0105      -.9921     -.1328
skeptic         .1051      .0381    2.7559      .0064       .0299      .1803
Int_1           .2012      .0553    3.6401      .0003       .0922      .3101

Product terms key:
 Int_1    :        cond     x        skeptic

Test(s) of highest order unconditional interaction(s):
        R2-chng         F         df1        df2         p
X*W      .0482     13.2503     1.0000   207.0000      .0003
----------
     Focal predict: frame    (X)
     Mod var: skeptic  (W)

Conditional effects of the focal predictor at values of the moderator(s):

  skeptic     Effect        se         t          p         LLCI       ULCI
   1.5920     -.2422      .1495   -1.6203      .1067      -.5369      .0525
   2.8000      .0008      .1166     .0072      .9942      -.2290      .2307
   5.2000      .4837      .1505    3.2134      .0015       .1869      .7804

Moderator value(s) defining Johnson-Neyman significance region(s):
      Value     % below    % above
     1.1713     6.6351    93.3649
     3.9339    67.7725    32.2275

Conditional effect of focal predictor at values of the moderator:
  skeptic     Effect        se         t          p         LLCI       ULCI
   1.0000     -.3613      .1729   -2.0900      .0378      -.7021     -.0205
   1.1713     -.3268      .1658   -1.9715      .0500      -.6536      .0000
   1.4000     -.2808      .1567   -1.7921      .0746      -.5897      .0281
   1.8000     -.2003      .1421   -1.4097      .1601      -.4805      .0798
   2.2000     -.1199      .1297    -.9242      .3565      -.3756      .1358
   2.6000     -.0394      .1201    -.3280      .7432      -.2762      .1974
   3.0000      .0411      .1140     .3603      .7190      -.1837      .2659
   3.4000      .1216      .1121    1.0847      .2793      -.0994      .3425
   3.8000      .2020      .1144    1.7657      .0789      -.0235      .4276
   3.9339      .2290      .1161    1.9715      .0500       .0000      .4579
   4.2000      .2825      .1208    2.3378      .0204       .0443      .5207
   4.6000      .3630      .1307    2.7765      .0060       .1052      .6207
   5.0000      .4434      .1434    3.0929      .0023       .1608      .7261
   5.4000      .5239      .1581    3.3136      .0011       .2122      .8356
   5.8000      .6044      .1744    3.4653      .0006       .2605      .9483
   6.2000      .6849      .1919    3.5692      .0004       .3066     1.0632
   6.6000      .7653      .2102    3.6406      .0003       .3509     1.1798
   7.0000      .8458      .2292    3.6897      .0003       .3939     1.2977
   7.4000      .9263      .2488    3.7237      .0003       .4359     1.4167
   7.8000     1.0068      .2687    3.7471      .0002       .4771     1.5365
   8.2000     1.0872      .2889    3.7631      .0002       .5176     1.6568
   8.6000     1.1677      .3094    3.7739      .0002       .5577     1.7777
   9.0000     1.2482      .3301    3.7810      .0002       .5974     1.8990
```

b_1

b_2

b_3

OLS
regression
output
(eq. 7.11)

PROCESS constructs
XW itself

An equivalent test of
interaction between X and W
(see section 8.3)

$b_1 + b_3W$ (equation 7.12)

W

$\theta_{X \to Y} | W$

Johnson–Neyman solution

(continued)

FIGURE 7.6. Output from the PROCESS procedure for SPSS for a simple moderation analysis of the disaster framing study.

```
Data for visualizing the conditional effect of the focal predictor:
Paste text below into a SPSS syntax window and execute to produce plot.

DATA LIST FREE/
      frame    skeptic    justify    .
BEGIN DATA.
      .0000     1.5920     2.6188
     1.0000     1.5920     2.3766
      .0000     2.8000     2.7458
     1.0000     2.8000     2.7466
      .0000     5.2000     2.9980
     1.0000     5.2000     3.4816
END DATA.
GRAPH/SCATTERPLOT=
  skeptic WITH      justify  BY       frame    .

*********************** ANALYSIS NOTES AND ERRORS ************************

Level of confidence for all confidence intervals in output:
  95.0000

W values in conditional tables are the 16th, 50th, and 84th percentiles.
```

Output from the **plot** option

FIGURE 7.6 continued.

on a score of zero on climate change skepticism has no meaning because no such people could even exist. Disregard this estimate and its test of significance, for they are meaningless. Even if it was possible to score so low on the scale, in the data the lowest score is 1, so at best this would represent an interpolation of the results of the model beyond the range of the available data. Such interpolation is generally a bad idea.

The same cannot be said about b_2. The regression coefficient for climate change skepticism is $b_2 = 0.105$ and statistically different from zero ($p = .006$). This is the estimated difference in strength of justifications for withholding aid between two people who differ by one unit in their climate change skepticism *among those who read a story that did not attribute the cause of the drought to climate change* ($X = 0$). Thus, this is the conditional effect of climate change skepticism on strength of justifications for not assisting among those assigned to the natural causes condition. The sign is positive, meaning that among these participants, those who were more skeptical about climate change had stronger justifications for withholding aid to the victims. Unlike b_1, this is substantively meaningful.

The regression coefficient for the product of X and W is $b_3 = 0.201$. This coefficient quantifies how the effect of X on Y changes as W changes by one unit. Here, b_3 is statistically different from zero, meaning that the effect of the framing of the cause of the drought on strength of justifications for withholding aid depends on climate change skepticism. More specifically, as climate change skepticism increases by one unit, the difference in strength of justifications between those told climate change was the cause and those not so told "increases" by 0.201 units, meaning that this effect moves *right* on the number line toward larger values. So b_3 quantifies a difference between differences (see equation 7.8).

Variable Scaling and the Interpretation of b_1 and b_2

As discussed already, b_1 and b_2 must be interpreted with care and considering the scaling of X and W, for depending on the scaling, these coefficients and their tests of significance may have no substantive interpretation. However, typically it is possible to rescale X and/or W prior to analysis in such a fashion that b_1 and b_2 are rendered interpretable.

One handy transformation is variable *centering*, which is accomplished by subtracting a constant from every value of a variable in the data. When X or W (or both) are centered prior to the construction of their product, b_1 and b_2 still represent conditional effects, but they are now conditioned on a value that renders the coefficient interpretable if it wasn't already.

For instance, suppose we *mean-center* climate change skepticism. To do so, the mean of W is subtracted from each value of W in the data to produce a new variable W', as such:

$$W' = W - \overline{W}$$

In this case, we calculate $W' = W - 3.378$, as the sample mean on the climate change skepticism scale is 3.378. This mean-centered version of W has a mean of zero and a standard deviation equal to the standard deviation of W. With this transformation accomplished, the simple moderation model is then estimated in the usual way but substituting W' for W:

$$\hat{Y} = i_Y + b_1 X + b_2 W' + b_3 X W'$$

This model is mathematically equivalent to

$$\hat{Y} = i_Y + b_1 X + b_2 (W - \overline{W}) + b_3 X (W - \overline{W}).$$

In SPSS, this regression analysis is accomplished using the code

```
compute skepticp=skeptic-3.378.
compute framskpp=frame*skepticp.
regression/dep=justify/method=enter frame skepticp framskpp.
```

In SAS, use

```
data disaster;set disaster;skepticp=skeptic-3.378;
    framskpp=frame*skepticp;run;
proc reg data=disaster;model justify=frame skepticp framskpp;run;
```

The resulting model can be found in Table 7.4 as model 4. The model is

$$\hat{Y} = 2.807 + 0.117X + 0.105W' + 0.201XW'$$

Observe that relative to model 3 in Table 7.4, b_2 and b_3 are not changed by this transformation of W, and their interpretations are the same. Their standard errors are identical, as are confidence intervals and p-values. Furthermore, the fit of the model is the same as the model using W in its original form. Indeed, model 4 will produce exactly the same estimates of Y as will model 3, because mathematically they are identical models; one is just a reparameterization of the other.

But the reparameterization caused by centering W has affected b_1. Remember that b_1 is a conditional effect when XW' is in the model. It estimates the effect of X on Y when $W' = 0$. So two cases that differ by one unit on X are estimated to differ by 0.117 units on Y when $W' = 0$. But notice that $W' = 0$ when $W = \overline{W} = 3.378$, so b_1 now estimates the difference in strength of justifications for withholding aid between those told climate change caused the drought and those not so told among those *average* in their climate change skepticism. Among such people with average skepticism about climate change, those told climate change was the cause of the drought were 0.117 units higher, on average, in the strength of their justifications for withholding aid to the victims than those not told climate change was responsible. But this difference between the conditions is not statistically significant ($p = .297$). This is substantively meaningful, unlike when the model was estimated with W in its original metric.

In models 3 and 4 summarized in Table 7.4, b_2 estimates the effect of W on Y when $X = 0$. In this example, b_2 is substantively meaningful as the difference in strength of justifications for withholding aid among two people who differ by one unit in their climate change skepticism but who are not told that the disaster was caused by climate change. While meaningful, b_2 is determined by the arbitrary decision to code experimental conditions using $X = 0$ and $X = 1$. A different decision about how to code groups would most likely change b_2 and it could change b_1 and b_3 as well, depending on the choice made.

To illustrate, suppose we used $X = 0.5$ for the climate change condition and $X = -0.5$ for the natural causes condition, but W was mean-centered as in model 4. The coefficients for the resulting model after this recoding of X can be found in Table 7.4, model 5. This model is mathematically identical to models 3 and 4, fits exactly the same, and generates the same estimates of Y, but the rescaling of X has reparameterized the model. The coefficient for the interaction ($b_3 = 0.201$) is identical to models 3 and 4, as is its standard error and p-value. Rescaling X has not changed b_1 relative to model 4 because the two experimental conditions still differ by a single unit on X. But b_2 has changed. This regression coefficient quantifies the difference in strength of justifications for withholding aid between two people who differ by one unit in their climate change skepticism when $X = 0$. Although $X = 0$ seems senseless given that X is an arbitrary code for two groups, b_2 still has a meaningful interpretation. It is now the unweighted average effect of climate change skepticism on strength of justifications for withholding aid in the two conditions.

As should now be apparent, caution must be exercised when interpreting b_1 and b_2 in a model of the form $Y = i_Y + b_1 X + b_2 W + b_3 XW + e_Y$. Although their mathematical interpretations are the same regardless of how X and W are scaled, their substantive interpretations can be dramatically affected by decisions about scaling, centering, and coding. Different transformations of X and W will change b_1 and b_2 and how they are interpreted. However, as we have changed only the mean of X or W, b_3 and inferences about $_T b_3$ are unaffected.

There is a widespread belief that a transformation such as mean-centering of X and W is mathematically necessary in order to properly estimate a model that includes the product of X and W as an antecedent variable and therefore in order to test a moderation hypothesis correctly. Although there is some value to mean-centering, it is *not* necessary. I will debunk the myth about the need to mean-center in models of this sort in Chapter 9. In the meantime, should you choose to mean-center X and W, PROCESS makes this easy. Simply add **center=1** to the PROCESS command, and all variables involved in the construction of a product will be mean-centered and all output will be based on the mean-centered metrics of X and W.[2]

7.3 Visualizing Moderation

A regression model with the product of two antecedent variables is an abstract mathematical representation of one's data that can be harder to interpret than a model without such a product. As described earlier, the coefficients for X and W are conditional effects that may not have any substantive interpretation, and the coefficient for XW is interpreted as a

[2]There is an exception. The **center** option will not mean-center multicategorical focal antecedents or moderators. See Appendix A.

difference between differences that can be hard to make sense of without more information. Although the sign of b_3 carries unambiguous mathematical meaning, even if the sign is in the direction you anticipated, this does not mean that the results are consistent with your predictions. A picture of the model can be an important interpretive aid when trying to understand a regression model with a product of antecedent variables. To produce such a visual representation of the model, I recommend generating a set of estimates of Y from various combinations of X and W using the regression model and then plotting $\hat{Y}$ as a function of X and W. This can be done using any graphics program that you find handy.

In the climate change study, the model of Y is $\hat{Y} = 2.452 - 0.562X + 0.105W + 0.201XW$ (using W rather than mean-centered W). To generate various values of $\hat{Y}$, select values of X and W that are within the range of the data, and then plug those values into the model to get estimates of Y. The choice of these values may be arbitrary, but it is important that they be within the range of the data and that they cover the distribution. If W is quantitative, one might use the mean and plus and minus one standard deviation from the mean, or various percentiles in the distribution. Many use the mean and a standard deviation below and above. But the problem with that strategy is that if W is highly skewed, a standard deviation below or above the mean may be outside of the range of measurement or may be smaller than the minimum value or larger than the maximum value observed in the data. This will result in a plot that depicts the model in a region of the variables' distributions where you have no data. I think a better strategy is to use the 16th, 50th, and 84th percentiles. If W is exactly normally distributed, these would be equivalent to a standard deviation below the mean, the mean, and a standard deviation above the mean, without the danger that one of them is outside of the range of measurement. Of course, if W is dichotomous, there isn't a choice to make. Simply use the two values of W in the data.

In this example, W is a continuum, so I use the 16th, 50th, and 84th percentiles of the distribution of W. These are 1.592, 2.8, and 5.2, respectively. For X, I use 0 and 1, which are the codes for the natural causes and climate change conditions, respectively. When these values are plugged into the regression model, the values of $\hat{Y}$ in Table 7.5 result. These data can then be plugged into your favorite program for generating graphs and edited in a variety of ways to your taste to produce a nice picture of the model, such as in Figure 7.7.

If your model contains covariates, you can't ignore these when generating $\hat{Y}$ for the various combinations of X and W. In the regression model, each of the covariates will have a regression coefficient. These

TABLE 7.5. Values of $\hat{Y}$ Generated from $\hat{Y} = 2.452 - 0.562X + 0.105W + 0.201XW$

X (FRAME)	W (SKEPTIC)	$\hat{Y}$
0	1.592	2.619
1	1.592	2.377
0	2.800	2.746
1	2.800	2.747
0	5.200	2.998
1	5.200	3.482

regression coefficients should be used along with the mean of the corresponding covariate when producing $\hat{Y}$ for plotting. For example, suppose our climate change analysis included two covariates C_1 and C_2, and their regression coefficients were $b_4 = 0.5$ and $b_5 = -1.8$, respectively. In that case, $\hat{Y}$ would be generated for the six combinations of X and W using $\hat{Y} = 2.452 - 0.562X + 0.105W + 0.201XW + 0.5\overline{C}_1 - 1.8\overline{C}_2$. The resulting estimates of Y as a function of X and W would be estimates among people average on C_1 and C_2. Although it might seem strange, it is appropriate to use the mean of a covariate even if it is dichotomous and coded with two arbitrary numbers. Just use the mean of the arbitrary numbers. This works even when a covariate is multicategorical with g categories. Just use the mean of each of the $g - 1$ codes representing the groups in the model.

If you ask it to, the PROCESS macro for SPSS does you the favor of writing an SPSS program that can be cut out of the output and pasted into a syntax window and executed. You ask PROCESS for the code to produce the plot by specifying **plot=1** in the PROCESS command, as on page 238. Doing so generates the section toward the end of the output in Figure 7.6, repeated below:

```
data list free/
     frame     skeptic     justify .
begin data.
     .0000     1.5920     2.6188
    1.0000     1.5920     2.3766
     .0000     2.8000     2.7458
    1.0000     2.8000     2.7466
     .0000     5.2000     2.9980
    1.0000     5.2000     3.4816
end data.
```

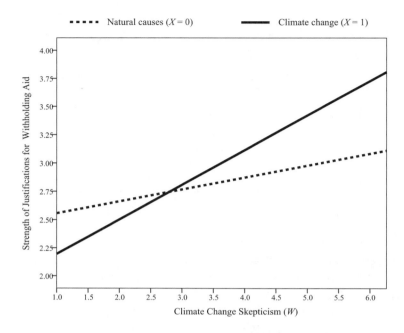

FIGURE 7.7. A visual representation of the moderation of the effect of the disaster cause framing (*X*) on strength of justifications for withholding aid (*Y*) by climate change skepticism (*W*).

```
graph/scatterplot=
    skeptic with  justify by  frame.
```

When you execute this SPSS code, the result is a scatterplot containing six points ($\hat{Y}$ for each combination of *X* and *W*), with different colors for the two conditions.[3] You can edit this within SPSS to produce something like Figure 7.7, which was produced largely in SPSS, but then exported to a more dedicated graphics editing program for fine tuning.

The SAS version of PROCESS has a similar feature, but it will not write the entire program to produce a plot. Instead, it only generates the data in Table 7.5 for you, and you could then write a program around it. An example of such a program is below:

```
data;input frame skeptic justify;
if (frame = 1) then Condition = 'Climate change (X=1)';
if (frame = 0) then Condition = 'Natural causes (X=0)';
datalines;
```

[3]If your model contains covariates, the values of $\hat{Y}$ are produced by PROCESS when setting the covariates to their means.

```
0 1.592 2.619
1 1.592 2.377
0 2.800 2.746
1 2.800 2.747
0 5.200 2.998
1 5.200 3.482
run;
proc sgplot;reg x=skeptic y=justify/group=Condition
nomarkers lineattrs=(color=black);
xaxis label='Climate change skepticism (W)';
yaxis label='Strength of justifications (Y)';run;
```

R is a statistical computing platform that has become popular over the years in part for its excellent graphics capabilities. R can be download at no charge from *www.r-project.org*. The R program below generates a plot depicting the interaction between framing condition and climate change skepticism using the data generated from the procedure just described. With a little background in R, this program can be modified to change colors, styles of the lines, and so forth. Consult a knowledgable R user for assistance if needed.

```
x<-c(0,1,0,1,0,1)
w<-c(1.592,1.592,2.80,2.80,5.20,5.20)
y<-c(2.619,2.377,2.746,2.747,2.998,3.482)
plot(y=y,x=w,pch=15,col="black",xlab="Climate Change Skepticism (W)",
ylab="Negative Justifications (Y)")
legend.txt<-c("Natural causes (X=0)","Climate change (X=1)")
legend("topleft",legend=legend.txt,lty=c(3,1),lwd=c(3,2))
lines(w[x==0],y[x==0],lwd=3,lty=3,col="black")
lines(w[x==1],y[x==1],lwd=2,lty=1,col="black")
```

Regardless of which program you use, a picture of this model, as in Figure 7.7, certainly makes it clearer what is happening in the data than the abstract numerical representation in the form of regression coefficients. The effect of the cause framing manipulation (X) on strength of justifications for withholding aid is reflected in the gap between the two lines. Notice that the gap varies with climate change skepticism. Among those lower in the distribution of climate change skepticism, the model estimates weaker justification for withholding aid among those in the climate change condition than among those in the natural causes condition. But among those more skeptical of the existence of climate change, the opposite is found. Strength of justifications for not providing assistance are higher among climate change skeptics told that climate change is the culprit for the drought relative to those not so told.

Looking at the plot of the interaction in this way may seem counterintuitive to you. Most likely, the first thing that you noticed when looking at Figure 7.7 was two lines with different slopes. Each of these lines reflects the conditional effect of climate change skepticism on strength of justifications for withholding aid. It looks like those conditional effects are different. Indeed, we will see in Chapter 8 that they are statistically different from each other. But thinking of the interaction in that way reverses the roles of focal antecedent and moderator relative to how the question was framed going into the analysis. As the question was asked on page 232, of interest is the extent to which the framing of the drought as caused by climate change or something else would differentially influence a person's justifications for not helping, depending on the person's climate change skepticism. Phrased in this way, experimental condition (framing of the cause) is the focal antecedent and climate change skepticism is the moderator, not the other way around. The gap between the lines represents the effect of the focal antecedent variable in this plot. It varies with the moderator, as can be seen in Figure 7.7.

7.4   Probing an Interaction

They say that a picture is worth a thousand words, but it takes more than a thousand words to convince some. The holistic interpretation of the pattern of results in the climate change study I gave in the prior section is not sufficient for the tastes of many. With evidence of moderation of X's effect on Y by W, this does not establish that, for instance, X has an effect on Y for people high on W but not for people low on W. A test of significance for b_3 (or a confidence interval) establishes that the effect of X on Y depends on W. (Though as discussed in section 7.5, it says a little more than just this.) Framed in terms of this example, neither the interaction itself as manifested by the estimate of b_3 nor the visual picture of that interaction depicted in Figure 7.7 establishes that people who are skeptical of the existence of climate change are inclined to find excuses for not helping victims of a climate change-caused disaster compared to one caused by something else, or that people who believe in climate change are more open to assisting people who are victims of climate change. Descriptively, the results are consistent with that pattern to be sure. But the magnitude of the discrepancy in strength of justifications for withholding aid between the two conditions is subject to sampling error at each and every value of climate change skepticism. That is, there is a certain "chance" component to the estimate of X's effect on Y at any value of W one might choose.

To deal with the uncertainty, it is common to follow up a test of interaction with a set of additional inferential tests to establish where in the distribution of the moderator X has an effect on Y that is different from zero and where it does not. This exercise is commonly known as "probing" an interaction, like you might squeeze an avocado or a mango in the produce section of the grocery store to assess its ripeness. The goal is to ascertain where in the distribution of the moderator X is related to Y and where it is not in an attempt to better discern the substantive interpretation of the interaction. In this section I describe two approaches to probing an interaction, one that is very commonly used, the other less so but that is growing in popularity as computers have made implementation easier.

The Pick-a-Point Approach

The pick-a-point approach (Rogosa, 1980; Bauer & Curran, 2005), sometimes called an *analysis of simple slopes* or a *spotlight analysis*, is perhaps the most popular approach to probing an interaction and is described in most discussions of multiple regression with interactions (e.g., Aiken & West, 1991; Cohen et al., 2003; Darlington & Hayes, 2017; Hayes, 2005; Jaccard & Turrisi, 2003; Spiller, Fitzsimons, Lynch, & McClelland, 2013). This procedure involves selecting a value or values of the moderator W, calculating the conditional effect of X on Y ($\theta_{X \to Y}$) at that value or values, and then conducting an inferential test or generating a confidence interval. To do so, an estimate of the standard error of the conditional effect of X is required for values of W selected (see, e.g., Aiken & West, 1991; Cohen et al., 2003; Bauer & Curran, 2005):

$$se_{\theta_{X \to Y}} = \sqrt{se_{b_1}^2 + (2W)COV_{b_1 b_3} + W^2 se_{b_3}^2} \tag{7.13}$$

where $se_{b_1}^2$ and $se_{b_3}^2$ are the squared standard errors of b_1 and b_3, W is any chosen value of the moderator, and $COV_{b_1 b_3}$ is the covariance of b_1 and b_3 across repeated sampling. All but the covariance between b_1 and b_3 is available as standard output in all OLS regression programs, and $COV_{b_1 b_3}$ is available as optional output.[4] The ratio of $\theta_{X \to Y}$ at a specific value of W to its standard error is distributed as $t(df_{residual})$ under the null hypothesis that $_T\theta_{X \to Y} = 0$ at that value of W. A p-value for the ratio can be obtained

---

[4]In SPSS, the covariance between regression coefficients can be obtained by adding bcov as an argument in a statistics subcommand following the regression command. In SAS, specify covb as an option following the model command in proc reg.

from any t table, or a confidence interval generated using equation 2.16 substituting for $\theta_{X \to Y}$ for b and $se_{\theta_{X \to Y}}$ for se_b.

I do not recommend doing these computations by hand because the potential for error is very high unless you do them to many decimal places and are really comfortable with and confident in what you are doing. In addition, this approach can be implemented fairly easily to a high degree of accuracy by a computer using the regression-centering method described next. Furthermore, PROCESS implements the pick-a-point approach, making even the regression-centering approach unnecessary if you have PRO-CESS handy. Example manual computations for the pick-a-point approach can be found in Aiken and West (1991) and Cohen et al. (2003).

The Pick-a-Point Approach Implemented by Regression Centering. An easy way to implement the pick-a-point approach is by centering W around the value or values at which you would like an estimate of the conditional effect X on Y and its standard error. Recall that in a model of the form $\hat{Y} = i_Y + b_1 X + b_2 W + b_3 XW$, b_1 estimates the effect of X on Y when $W = 0$. On page 241, I described the effects of scaling on the estimate and interpretation of b_1. By centering W around the mean prior to the computation of XW and estimation of the model, the regression analysis generated the effect of X on Y when W equals $\overline{W}$. In more general terms, defining $W' = W - w$, where w is any chosen value of the moderator, b_1 in

$$Y = i_Y + b_1 X + b_2 W' + b_3 XW' + e_Y$$

quantifies $\theta_{X \to Y}|(W = w)$, the conditional effect of X on Y when $W = w$. The standard error of b_1 will be equivalent to the standard error generated by equation 7.13, and the t- and p-value can be used to test the null hypothesis that $_T\theta_{X \to Y}|(W = w) = 0$.

When W is a quantitative variable, as in the climate change study, a common strategy when probing an interaction is to estimate the conditional effect of X on Y when W is equal to the mean, a standard deviation below the mean, and a standard deviation above the mean (see, e.g., Aiken & West, 1991). This allows you to ascertain whether X is related to Y among those "relatively low" ($\overline{W} - SD_W$), "moderate" ($\overline{W}$), and "relatively high" ($\overline{W} + SD_W$) on the moderator. But I recommend that if you are going to use the pick-a-point approach and don't have any other way of selecting values of W, instead use the 16th, 50th, and 84th percentiles of the distribution as operationalizations of relatively low, moderate, and relatively high. As discussed in section 7.3, if W is highly skewed, one standard deviation below or above the mean could be below or above the minimum or maximum observed value in the data, or perhaps even beyond the scale of measurement. You wouldn't want to probe an interaction using values of the moderator that are outside of the bounds of measurement or observation. But the 16th and 84th percentiles of the distribution of W will always be within the range of the observed data, regardless of the shape of the distribution. And the median (the 50th percentile) of the distribution of W is always a sensible description of the center. The mean may not be if W is skewed. Although these might seem like strange percentiles to use (why not nice round numbers like the 25th, 50th, and 75th percentiles, for instance?), the 16th, 50th, and 84th percentiles correspond to a standard deviation below the mean, the mean, and a standard deviation above the mean if W is exactly normally distributed.

The SPSS and SAS code below implements this regression-centering approach to probing the interaction. It does so by estimating the model three times, once after centering W around 1.592 (the 16th percentile), once after centering around 2.8 (the median or 50th percentile), and a last time centering around 5.2 (the 84th percentile). The regression coefficients for b_1 in the three outputs estimate the effect of framing of the cause of the drought among those relatively low in climate change skepticism, moderate or average in skepticism, and relatively high in skepticism, respectively.

```
compute skepticp=skeptic-1.592.
compute framskpp=frame*skepticp.
regression/dep=justify/method=enter frame skepticp framskpp.
compute skepticp=skeptic-2.8.
compute framskpp=frame*skepticp.
regression/dep=justify/method=enter frame skepticp framskpp.
compute skepticp=skeptic-5.2.
compute framskpp=frame*skepticp.
regression/dep=justify/method=enter frame skepticp framskpp.
```

In SAS, use

```
data disaster;set disaster;skepticp=skeptic-1.592;
    framskpp=frame*skepticp;run;
proc reg data=disaster;model justify=frame skepticp framskpp;run;
data disaster;set disaster;skepticp=skeptic-2.8;
    framskpp=frame*skepticp;run;
proc reg data=disaster;model justify=frame skepticp framskpp;run;
data disaster;set disaster;skepticp=skeptic-5.2;
    framskpp=frame*skepticp;run;
proc reg data=disaster;model justify=frame skepticp framskpp;run;
```

This analysis results in $\theta_{X \to Y}|(W = 1.592) = -0.242$, $t(207) = -1.620, p = .107$; $\theta_{X \to Y}|(W = 2.8) = 0.001$, $t(207) = 0.007, p = .994$; $\theta_{X \to Y}|(W = 5.2) =$

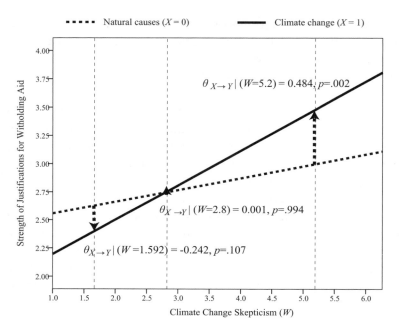

FIGURE 7.8. A visual representation of the conditional effects of disaster cause framing (*X*) on strength of justifications for withholding aid (*Y*) among those relatively low (*W* = 1.592), moderate (*W* = 2.8), and relatively high (*W* = 5.2) in their climate change skepticism.

0.484, $t(207) = 3.213, p = .002$; These conditional effects of *X* correspond to the distance between the lines in Figure 7.7 at the corresponding values of *W* (see Figure 7.8). The framing of the cause of the disaster seems to have had a statistically significant effect on strength of justifications for withholding aid among those relatively high in climate change skepticism. Among such climate change skeptics, justifications for withholding aid are stronger when the drought is framed as caused by climate change rather than by natural causes. But among people low to moderate in climate change skepticism, the framing of the disaster had no statistically significant effect on strength of justifications for withholding assistance.

Keep in mind that the use of percentiles of the distribution of *W* to operationalize low, moderate, and high on the moderator is arbitrary. Furthermore, these are sample specific operationalizations. What you are calling "low" on the moderator someone else might call "high" if his or her sample tends to be lower on *W* on average. Of course, this is true if you use a standard deviation below the mean, the mean, and a standard deviation above the mean as many researchers do. If your moderator is a variable that is widely used in research in your area and there are existing norms and agreed upon definitions of low, moderate, and high, it would probably be more sensible and defensible to use those values instead of values defined by the distribution of the moderator in a specific sample.

Implementation in PROCESS. PROCESS automatically produces output from the pick-a-point approach to probing interactions whenever a moderation model is specified with X's effect on Y moderated by another variable. By default, when W is dichotomous, PROCESS generates $\theta_{X \to Y}$ for the two groups defined by values of W, along with standard errors, p-values for a two-tailed test of the null hypothesis that $_T\theta_{X \to Y} = 0$, and confidence intervals for $_T\theta_{X \to Y}$. When W is a continuous variable, as it is in this example, PROCESS estimates $\theta_{X \to Y}$ for values of W equal to the 16th, 50th, and 84th percentiles of the distribution of W. This information can be found in the PROCESS output in Figure 7.6. Notice that the conditional effects and all the information for inference in that section of the PROCESS output are the same as described earlier when the regression-centering strategy was introduced.

For a continuous moderator W, you are not stuck using the 16th, 50th, and 84th percentiles when probing the interaction with PROCESS. If you prefer a standard deviation below the mean, the mean, and a standard deviation above the mean, add **moments=1** to the PROCESS command line. (In statistics, the mean is known as the first moment of a distribution, and the standard deviation is the second moment; hence, the name "moments" for this option.) When one standard deviation below or above the mean is beyond the range of the observed data, PROCESS will substitute the minimum or maximum value of the moderator for a standard deviation below or above the mean, respectively. That way you won't accidently interpret an estimate of a conditional effect at value of the moderator in a region of the measurement scale where you have no data.

Alternatively, you can provide to PROCESS one or more specific values of W at which to condition the test of the conditional effect of X. This is done with the **wmodval** option (short for W *moderator value*). For example, if you wanted $\theta_{X \to Y}|W = 2.5$ along with its standard error, t- and p-values, and a confidence interval, add **wmodval=2.5** to the PROCESS command. Or if you used **wmodval=2.5,3,5.5**, PROCESS would estimate the conditional effect of X on Y at values of W equal to 2.5, 3, and 5.5. In the SAS version, separate the values of the moderator by a space rather than a comma.

The Johnson–Neyman Technique

The pick-a-point approach suffers from one significant problem. This approach requires the selection of values of W at which to estimate the conditional effect of X on Y. Different choices can lead to different claims, and the choice is often made arbitrarily. Using conventions such as the mean, as well as plus and minus one standard deviation from the mean, or perhaps various percentiles of the distribution of W to represent "low," "moderate," and "high" on the moderator is entirely arbitrary. Although this practice of choosing values of W relying on conventions is widely discussed and recommended in books and journal articles that discuss probing interactions (e.g., Aiken & West, 1991; Cohen et al., 2003), that does not make such values any less arbitrary. And as discussed earlier, such designations are sample specific. What is low in one sample may be moderate or high in another sample, and this can produce false inconsistencies in the literature on a common topic.

You can wash your hands of the arbitrariness of the choice of values of W by using the Johnson–Neyman (JN) technique, dubbed a *floodlight analysis* by Spiller et al. (2013). Originally conceived for dealing with tests of mean differences between two groups in analysis of covariance when the homogeneity of regression assumption is violated (Johnson & Neyman, 1936; Johnson & Fey, 1950; Rogosa, 1980), it was later extended by Bauer and Curran (2005) to regression models more generally. It is growing in popularity. Some examples of the application of the JN technique for probing interactions can be found in Beach et al. (2012), Coronel and Federmeier (2016), Keng, Seah, Wong, and Smoski (2016), Prinzie et al. (2012), Simons et al. (2012), and Walder et al. (2014).

The JN technique, which can be applied only when W is a continuum, is essentially the pick-a-point approach conducted in reverse. Using the pick-a-point approach, one calculates the ratio of the conditional effect of X on Y given W to its standard error. Using the t distribution, a p-value for the obtained ratio is derived and an inference made based on the p-value. Rather than finding p for a given value of t, the JN technique derives the values of W such that the ratio of the conditional effect to its standard error is exactly equal to t_{crit}, the critical t-value associated with $p = \alpha$, where α is the level of significance chosen for the inference. Given the following equation

$$t_{crit} = \frac{\theta_{X \to Y} \mid W}{se_{\theta_{X \to Y} \mid W}}$$

or, in the case of a model of the form $\hat{Y} = i_Y + b_1 X + b_2 W + b_3 XW$,

$$t_{crit} = \frac{b_1 + b_3 W}{\sqrt{se_{b_1}^2 + (2W)COV_{b_1 b_3} + W^2 se_{b_3}^2}}$$

the JN technique derives the roots of the quadratic equation that results when W is isolated. The roots of this equation will be the values of W for which the ratio of the conditional effect to its standard error is exactly t_{crit}, meaning $p = \alpha$. For computational details, see Bauer and Curran (2005) or Hayes and Matthes (2009).

A quadratic equation contains two roots, meaning that the JN technique will produce two solutions for W, which I refer to in my discussion below as JN_{W_1} and JN_{W_2} where $JN_{W_1} < JN_{W_2}$. These values of W demarcate the points along the continuum of W where the conditional effect of X on Y transitions between statistically significant and not significant at the α level of significance. As such, they identify the "region of significance" of the effect of X on Y. In practice, often one or both of these values may be outside of the range of the measurement scale of W or will be in the domain of imaginary numbers. Such values of JN_{W_1} or JN_{W_2} should be ignored as if they didn't exist. Given this caveat, there are three outcomes that are possible when the JN technique is used.

The first possible outcome is that the JN technique generates a single solution within the range of the measurement of the moderator. Call this value JN_{W_1}. When the JN technique produces a single value, this means that the conditional effect of X on Y is statistically significant at the α level when $W \geq JN_{W_1}$ or when $W \leq JN_{W_1}$ but *not* both. This defines either $W \geq JN_{W_1}$ or $W \leq JN_{W_1}$ as the region of significance of X's effect on Y.

The second possibility is that the JN technique generates two solutions within the range of the data. When this occurs, the region of significance of X's effect on Y is either $JN_{W_1} \leq W \leq JN_{W_2}$ or, alternatively, $W \leq JN_{W_1}$ *and* $W \geq JN_{W_2}$. The former means that the conditional effect of X on Y is statistically significant when W is between JN_{W_1} and JN_{W_2} but not beyond those two values. The latter means that the conditional effect of X on Y is statistically significant when W is less than or equal to JN_{W_1} and when W is greater than or equal to JN_{W_2} but not in between these two values.

A final possibility is no solutions within the range of the moderator. This can mean one of two things. One interpretation is that the conditional effect of X on Y is statistically significant across the entire range of the moderator, meaning that there are no points along the continuum of W where the conditional effect transitions between statistically significant and not. The second interpretation is that the conditional effect of X on Y is not statistically significant *anywhere* in the observed distribution of the moderator, again meaning no points of transition. In the former case, the region of significance of the effect X on Y is the entire range of W, whereas in the latter case, there is no region of significance.

Implementation in PROCESS. Derivation of regions of significance by hand computation would be vary tedious. Fortunately, the JN technique is implemented in PROCESS. In a model with an interaction that involves a continuous moderator, the addition of **jn=1** to the PROCESS command, as on page 238 for the disaster framing study, produces the relevant output.[5]

The results of the JN technique can be found in Figure 7.6. As can be seen, PROCESS identifies two values of climate change skepticism as points which demarcate the regions of significance of the effect of causal attribution for the drought on strength of justifications for withholding aid: $W = 1.171$ and $W = 3.934$. But without more information, this is hard to interpret. To ease the interpretation, PROCESS slices the distribution of W into 21 arbitrary values, calculates $\theta_{X \to Y}$ at those values, along with their standard errors, p-values, and confidence interval endpoints, and then displays the results in a table. It also inserts the corresponding conditional effects when W equals the points identified by the JN technique. As can be seen, when $W \geq 3.934$, the framing manipulation had a statistically significant effect, with those told the drought was caused by climate change reporting stronger justifications for withholding assistance than those not so told (because the conditional effect of X is positive and statistically different from zero when $W \geq 3.934$). When $W \leq 1.171$, the framing manipulation had the opposite effect, with those told the drought was caused by climate change reporting weaker justifications for withholding aid. Thus, the region of significance for the effect of the framing of the drought on justifications for withholding aid is $W \leq 1.171$ and $W \geq 3.934$.[6]

A handy means of visualizing the region of significance derived from the JN technique is a plot of $\theta_{X \to Y}$ as a function of W along with confidence bands (see Bauer & Curran, 2005; Preacher, Curran, & Bauer, 2006; Rogosa, 1980). The region of significance is depicted as the values of W corresponding to points where a conditional effect of 0 is outside of the confidence band for $_T\theta_{X \to Y}$. Figure 7.9 displays the region of significance in this example. As can be seen, when $W \leq 1.171$ and $W \geq 3.934$, the confidence bands are entirely above or entirely below zero.

Figure 7.9 was produced using the SPSS code below, then doing considerable editing within SPSS and adding some final touches using a dedicated illustration program. The data between the **begin data** and **end**

---

[5]An earlier SPSS and SAS implementation of the JN technique was published by Karpmann (1986) and Hayes and Matthes (2009).

[6]As described here, the JN technique affords a *nonsimultaneous* inference, meaning that one can claim that for any chosen value of W in the region of significance, the probability of incorrectly concluding the conditional effect of X on Y is different from zero, when it is not, is no greater than α. One cannot make a *simultaneous* inference and say that the conditional effects at all values of W in the region of significance are different from zero while keeping the Type I error rate for this simultaneous claim at α. The probability of a Type I error for this claim is higher than α. Potthoff (1964) describes a version of the JN technique that allows for simultaneous inference of this sort. The Potthoff correction is not implemented in PROCESS, but it is available in MODPROBE (Hayes & Matthes, 2009).

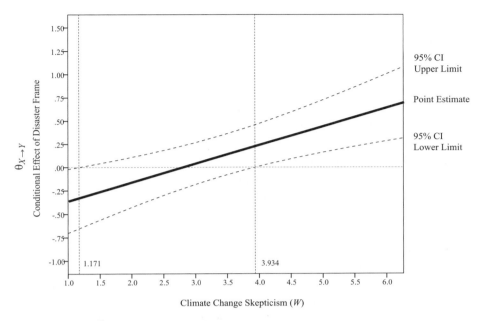

FIGURE 7.9. The conditional effect of the disaster frame manipulation ($\theta_{X \to Y}$) on strength of justifications for withholding aid as a function of climate change skepticism.

data commands in the code were generated by PROCESS, and the output from PROCESS was simply cut and pasted into the code prior to editing.

```
data list free/skeptic effect llci ulci.
begin data.
1.0000    -0.3613    -0.7021    -0.0205
1.1713    -0.3268    -0.6536     0.0000
1.4000    -0.2808    -0.5897     0.0281
   .          .           .         .
   .       (from PROCESS JN table) .
   .          .           .         .
8.2000     1.0872     0.5176     1.6568
8.6000     1.1677     0.5577     1.7777
9.0000     1.2482     0.5974     1.8990
end data.
graph/scatter(overlay)=skeptic skeptic skeptic with llci ulci effect
(pair).
```

The SAS code below produces a similar figure that requires no editing whatsoever.

```
data;input skeptic effect llci ulci;
datalines;
1.0000    -0.3613    -0.7021    -0.0205
1.1713    -0.3268    -0.6536     0.0000
1.4000    -0.2808    -0.5897     0.0281

   .         .          .          .

   .     (from PROCESS JN table) .

   .         .          .          .
8.2000     1.0872     0.5176     1.6568
8.6000     1.1677     0.5577     1.7777
9.0000     1.2482     0.5974     1.8990
run;
proc sgplot;
series x=skeptic y=ulci/curvelabel = '95% upper limit' lineattrs=
    (color=red pattern=ShortDash);
series x=skeptic y=effect/curvelabel = 'point estimate' lineattrs=
    (color=black pattern=Solid);
series x=skeptic y=llci/curvelabel = '95% lower limit' lineattrs=
    (color=red pattern=ShortDash);
xaxis label = 'Climate change skepticism (W)';
yaxis label = 'Conditional effect of disaster framing';
refline 0/axis=y transparency=0.5;refline 3.5 4.98/axis=x
    transparency=0.5; run;
```

An R program that produces a comparable depiction of JN regions of significance is below. The numbers at the top of the code are from the section of PROCESS output in Figure 7.6 showing the Johnson–Neyman results.

```
skeptic<-c(1,1.171,1.4,1.8,2.2,2.6,3,3.4,3.8,3.934,4.2,
        4.6,5,5.4,5.8,6.2,6.6,7,7.4,7.8,8.2,8.6,9)
effect<-c(-.361,-.327,-.281,-.200,-.120,-.039,.041,.122,.202,.229,.282,
        .363,.443,.524,.604,.685,.765,.846,.926,1.007,1.087,1.168,1.248)
llci<-c(-.702,-.654,-.589,-.481,-.376,-.276,-.184,-.099,-.024,0,.044,.105,
        .161,.212,.261,.307,.351,.394,.436,.477,.518,.558,.597)
ulci<-c(-.021,0,.028,.080,.136,.197,.266,.343,.428,.458,.521,.621,.726,.836,
        .948,1.063,1.180,1.298,1.417,1.537,1.657,1.778,1.899)
plot(x=skeptic,y=effect,type="l",pch=19,ylim=c(-1,1.5),xlim=c(1,6),lwd=3,
ylab="Conditional effect of disaster frame",
xlab="Climate Change Skepticism (W)")
points(skeptic,llci,lwd=2,lty=2,type="l")
```

```
points(skeptic,ulci,lwd=2,lty=2,type="l")
abline(h=0, untf=FALSE,lty=3,lwd=1)
abline(v=1.171,untf=FALSE,lty=3,lwd=1)
abline(v=3.934,untf=FALSE,lty=3,lwd=1)
text(1.171,-1,"1.171",cex=0.8)
text(3.934,-1,"3.934",cex=0.8)
```

Although the JN technique eliminates the need to select arbitrary values of W when probing an interaction, it does not eliminate your need to keep your brain tuned into the task and thinking critically about the answer this method gives you. In this example, one interpretation caution is in order. The JN technique reveals that when $W \leq 1.171$, $\theta_{X \to Y}$ is negative and statistically different from zero, meaning weaker justifications for not assisting among such nonskeptics when the drought is framed as caused by climate change than when it is not attributed to climate change. But PROCESS tells us that only 6.635 percent of the cases in the data are in that region of the distribution of the moderator. In a sample of 211, that is 14 people. Ask yourself whether it makes sense to interpret a region of significance such as this when one has only 14 people in the data this low on the moderator. There are no hard and fast rules for deciding this. I would probably be somewhat reluctant to make much out of this section of the region of significance. There simply are not enough data in this end of the distribution for my taste. I don't feel at all concerned, however, about interpreting the region of significance above 3.934. PROCESS tells us 32.228% of the data are in this region of the moderator. That is 68 people, which seems sufficient for a claim about the effect of the message framing among skeptics of this sort. But you may disagree.

7.5   The Difference between Testing for Moderation and Probing It

We test for evidence of moderation when we want to know whether the relationship between X and Y varies systematically as a function of a proposed moderator W. We've seen in this chapter that in a model of the form $\hat{Y} = i_Y + b_1 X + b_2 W + b_3 XW$, X's effect on Y is a linear function of W: $b_1 + b_3 W$. If b_3 is statistically different from zero, then W linearly moderates the effect of X on Y, meaning X and W interact.

When we probe moderation, we are not testing for moderation. Presumably, one would not probe a moderation effect unless one has evidence that such moderation exists. Rather, probing moderation involves ascertaining whether the conditional effect of X on Y is different from zero at certain specified values of W (if using the pick-a-point approach) or exploring where in the distribution of W the conditional effect of X on Y transitions between statistically significant and not significant (if using the Johnson–Neyman technique).

Figure 7.10 illustrates the distinction between testing and probing moderation using the climate change experiment that has been the focus of this chapter. In this figure, the solid line depicts the conditional effect of X on Y, which is defined by the function $\theta_{X \to Y} = b_1 + b_3 W$. In this example, $\theta_{X \to Y} = -0.562 + 0.201W$. The slope of this line is $b_3 = 0.201$, which is also the weight for the product of X and W in the regression equation. A test of moderation is a test of whether the slope of this line deviates significantly from flat, meaning a slope of zero. An affirmative test means that X's effect on Y depends on W. In this example, because b_3 was statistically significant, we can claim that the framing of the disaster as caused by climate change as opposed to natural causes differentially influenced strength of justifications for withholding aid, depending on a person's skepticism about climate change.

Being able to claim that X's effect on Y is dependent on W is inherently meaningful, albeit a somewhat vague claim. But with evidence of interaction, you can be a bit more specific than this. If X's effect depends on W, then X's effect must be different from zero for at least *some* people, or in *some* situation, or whatever W codes or operationalizes. This is because X's effect can't both vary with W but also be zero at all values of W. So when you find evidence of interaction, you can also say that X must have an effect of some kind, somewhere in the distribution of W. Without further analysis, you can't say more specifically where X's effect is different from zero and where it is not.

That's where probing an interaction comes in. When we choose two or more values of W and then test whether X's effect on Y differs from zero at one or more of those values, we are trying to make a more focused claim or set of claims about X's effect on Y than the test of interaction provides. In Figure 7.10 are two dashed arrows pointing from the conditional effect of X on Y given W toward zero. When we probe an interaction, we are testing whether the length of that arrow is significantly different from zero, because the length of that arrow is the distance between $\theta_{X \to Y}|W$ and zero, meaning no effect of X. In this example, we can claim that among people "relatively low" in climate change skepticism, operationalized as $W = 1.592$ on the scale, the framing of the cause of the disaster does not affect their strength of justifications for withholding aid. But among people "relatively high," operationalized as $W = 5.2$, the climate change frame resulted in

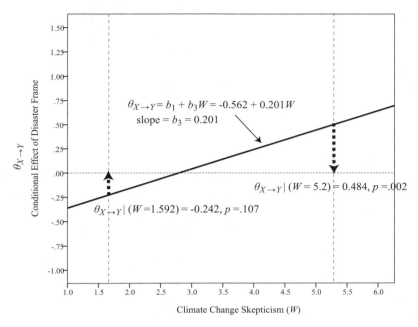

FIGURE 7.10. The difference between testing for moderation (the slope of the line) and probing moderation (the size of the dashed arrows).

stronger justifications for not helping. This is a more definitive claim than merely saying that the climate change frame affected people differently depending on their climate change skepticism. The JN method provides a bit more information than the pick-a-point approach, but the basic goal of the analysis is the same. Where in the distribution of W does X exert an effect on Y and where does it not?

You might think it would be worthwhile to ask whether these conditional effects differ from each other. Is a formal test of the difference between the effect of X on Y on W when $W = w_1$ and the effect of X on Y when $W = w_2$ needed to be able to say whether these two effects differ? For example, is the effect of the framing of the cause of the effect of the disaster different between people low versus high in climate change skepticism?

Such a test is *very* important, but that test has already been done! As Aiken and West (1991) discuss, it turns out that a test of linear moderation of the effect of X on Y by W is equivalent to a test of the difference between any two conditional effects of X on Y that one could construct from this model, regardless of the values of w_1 and w_2 chosen. The difference between the two conditional indirect effects of X at values w_1 and w_2 is

$$(b_1 + b_3 w_2) - (b_1 + b_3 w_2) = b_3(w_2 - w_1)$$

with an estimated standard error of

$$se_{b_3}(w_2 - w_1)$$

The ratio of the difference to its standard error is

$$\frac{b_3(w_2 - w_1)}{se_{b_3}(w_2 - w_1)}$$

which simplifies to b_3/se_{b_3}. But this is the t-value for the regression coefficient for the XW in the regression model, and the degrees of freedom is the same, and so the p-value for testing the null hypothesis of no difference between the two conditional effects of X is the same as the p-value for testing the null hypothesis of no linear moderation. There is no need for a test of the difference between two conditional effects of X. Interaction between X and W implies that any two conditional effects derived from the model are statistically different from each other.

A failure to appreciate the difference between testing and probing an interaction can get you into all kinds of interpretation difficulties. For example, you might find that the conditional effect of X on Y is different from zero for some values of W but not others, and yet b_3 may not be statistically significant. How can it both be true that X's effect differs from zero for some values of W but not others, yet X and W don't interact? It can't. The problem is that one cannot say anything about moderation by qualitatively integrating a pattern of results of hypothesis tests for conditional effects. What matters when testing interaction is not whether X's effect on Y exists for some values of W but not others, but whether those conditional effects of X differ from each other. Difference in significance does not imply significantly different (Gelman & Stern, 2006). If you want to say that X's effect differs as a function of W, you need to test that. The test of interaction between X and W is the proper test.

By the same token, you might find that b_3 is significantly different from zero, and thus X and W interact, yet you may find when probing the interaction that X's effect on Y is not different from zero at any value in the distribution of W. How is this possible? But again, the pattern of p-values in a set of tests of conditional effects of X does not say anything about moderation. Just as difference in significance doesn't imply significantly different, mutual nonsignificance does not imply statistical equivalence. Remember that if X's effect on Y is linearly moderated by W, then X must affect Y somewhere in the distribution of W. Two things in a set can't vary from each other yet both be zero.

A null hypothesis can never be proven true, and any test carries with it a risk of a decision error. One of my cardinal principles of inference is that you should do as few statistical tests as required to support a claim, given that procedures for statistical inference are fallible by nature. A single test of interaction between X and W tests whether or not X's effect on Y varies with W and also whether any two conditional effects of X are different. When you are repeatedly estimating conditional effects and conducting hypotheses tests about their values, you are doing at least two and perhaps more tests and then piecing together the inference from the pattern of results. Given that any hypothesis test can lead to a decision error, would you trust more a claim based on a single test sensitive to the question of interest (does X's effect vary with W?), or several tests, none of which directly answers the question you care about?

7.6 Artificial Categorization and Subgroups Analysis

Those without an understanding of how to test a moderation hypothesis involving a continuous moderator, such as in the example in this chapter, frequently attempt to simplify their analytical problem so that they can analyze their data using procedures with which they are familiar. Most commonly, a mean or median split is used, where cases in the data below the mean or median of a continuous moderator are placed in a "low" group and everyone else is placed in a "high" group. The analysis then proceeds by examining whether X is related to Y differently in one group than another, now defined by a dichotomous W, by conducting a 2×2 factorial ANOVA or, worse, two independent groups t-tests.

Returning to the climate change and humanitarianism example, recall the question asked in section 7.2, which was whether framing the cause of the drought as due to climate change rather than leaving the cause unspecified affected strength of justifications for withholding aid differently for people who differ in their climate change skepticism. An investigator unfamiliar with the principles introduced in this chapter might use a mean split to classify participants as either "low" or "high" in climate change skepticism based on whether they score above or below the sample mean (3.378 in these data). Once participants are categorized in this fashion, two independent groups t-tests might then be conducted in the low and high climate skepticism groups comparing mean strength of justifications for withholding age in the two framing conditions. In SPSS, the commands would be

```
temporary.
select if (skeptic < 3.378).
```

```
ttest groups=frame(0,1)/variables=justify.
temporary.
select if (skeptic >= 3.378).
ttest groups=frame(0,1)/variables=justify.
```

or in SAS, try

```
proc ttest data=disaster;where skeptic < 3.378;
   class frame;var justify;run;
proc ttest data=disaster;where skeptic >= 3.378;
   class frame;var justify;run;
```

This analysis shows that among those relatively low in climate change skepticism, those told the drought was caused by climate change (Mean = 2.519, SD = 0.775) did not differ on average in their justifications for withholding aid compared to those given no information about the cause of the drought (Mean = 2.622, SD = 0.808), $t(124) = 0.733, p = .465$. However, among those high in climate change skepticism, those told the drought was caused by climate change reported stronger justifications for withholding aid (Mean = 3.549, SD = 1.008) than those not told anything about the cause (Mean = 3.073, SD = 0.845), $t(83) = -2.365, p = .020$.

There is a large literature admonishing researchers not to do this. Such artificial categorization of a continuum prior to analysis is almost always difficult to defend, for the split point usually is determined arbitrarily and thus produces groups that are not psychometrically meaningful (e.g., why the mean or the median as opposed to some other number?), it throws out information by treating people who are nearly indistinguishable (i.e., those close to the mean or median) as if they are maximally distinct on the dimension measured, it reduces statistical power of tests, and it can increase Type I error rate in some circumstances. Don't do this. For the many arguments against this practice, see Bissonnette, Ickes, Bernstein, and Knowles (1990), Cohen (1983), Hayes (2005), Humphreys and Fleishman (1974), Hunter and Schmidt (1990), Hutchinson (2003), Irwin and McClelland (2002), MacCallum, Zhang, Preacher, and Rucker (2002), Maxwell and Delaney (1993), Newsom, Prigerson, Schultz, and Reynolds (2003), Preacher, Rucker, MacCallum, and Nicewander (2005), Royston, Altman, and Sauerbrei (2006), Rucker, McShane, and Preacher (2015), Sedney (1981), Streiner (2002), and Vargha, Rudas, and Maxwell (2011).

Even if the resulting groups constructed arbitrarily in this fashion were psychometrically meaningful, or the groups did exist naturally and thus are inherently meaningful (e.g., men versus women), such a subgroup analysis does not actually test whether the effect of X on Y differs as a function of W. Suppose it is sensible to categorize people into either high or low in climate change skepticism, thereby allowing us to quantify $\theta_{X \to Y} \mid W =$ "high" and $\theta_{X \to Y} \mid W =$ "low." In terms of patterns of significance and not, there are four possible outcomes of the two t-tests ($\theta_{X \to Y} \mid W =$ "high" statistically significant and $\theta_{X \to Y} \mid W =$ "low" not significant, $\theta_{X \to Y} \mid W =$ "high" and $\theta_{X \to Y} \mid W =$ "low" also significant, and so forth). Not one of these patterns actually provides evidence as to whether $_T\theta_{X \to Y} \mid (W =$ "high") $=$ $_T\theta_{X \to Y} \mid (W =$ "low"). Statistical significance in one group but not in the other does not imply a difference between the two groups in the effect of X. Furthermore, statistical significance in both groups does not imply no difference between them (cf. Gelman & Stern, 2006). If your question asks about moderation, you need to conduct a formal test of the difference between differences. Subgroups analysis does not accomplish this.

Of course, the differences between the conditional effects of X among those low and high could be tested with a factorial ANOVA if W is dichotomous. A statistically significant interaction means that the simple effect of X given $W =$ "high" is different from the simple effect of X given $W =$ "low." Applied to this example, after dichotomizing participants at the mean of climate change skepticism, the interaction between climate change skepticism (low versus high) and framing of the cause of the drought is statistically significant, $F(1, 207) = 4.257, p = .016$. Although this solves the problem with subgroup analyses—that difference in significance does not imply significance of difference—it does not get around all the problems associated with artificial categorization. Testing for differences between conditional effects of X using a factorial ANOVA would be entirely appropriate if the levels of W were naturally existing categories (e.g., men and women) or experimentally created (e.g., conditions in an experiment). When they are not, respect the continuous nature of W and the differences between cases it quantifies and proceed as described in this chapter.

7.7 Chapter Summary

When the question motivating a study asks *when* or *under what circumstances* X exerts an effect on Y, moderation analysis is an appropriate analytical strategy. This chapter introduced the principles of moderation analysis using OLS regression. If W is related to the magnitude of the effect of X on Y, we say that W moderates X's effect, or that X and W interact in their influence on Y. A hypothesis about moderation can be tested in several ways. The most common approach, widely used by researchers in many disciplines, is to include the product of X and W in the model of Y along with X and W. This allows X's effect on Y to depend linearly on W. If such a dependency is established, it is no longer sensible to talk about X's effect on Y without conditioning that discussion on W.

A regression model that includes a product of two antecedent variables can be difficult to interpret when left in its mathematical form. A picture of a moderation model can go a long way toward better understanding the contingent nature of the association between X and Y. So too can a formal probing of the interaction by estimating the conditional effect of X on Y for various values of W. The pick-a-point approach is the most commonly implemented strategy for probing interactions, but the Johnson–Neyman technique is slowly gaining users and followers, and probably will in time be as popular or even more so than the pick-a-point approach.

The next chapter extends the method introduced in this chapter by applying it to models in which W is dichotomous, as well as when both X and W are quantitative. As you will see, all the principles introduced in this chapter generalize to such models, and once these principles are well understood, you will be in a strong position to tackle the integration of moderation and mediation analysis later in the book.

8

Extending the Fundamental Principles of Moderation Analysis

In Chapter 7 I introduced the principles of moderation analysis and applied them to a study in which the focal predictor was a dichotomous experimental manipulation and the moderator was continuous. In this chapter I illustrate that these principles generalize and can be applied without modification to problems in which the moderator is dichotomous as well as when both focal predictor and moderator are continuous. Following this, I show the equivalence between moderation analysis using multiple regression and the 2 × 2 factorial analysis of variance, with the important caveat that this equivalence depends heavily on how the two dichotomous predictors or "factors" are coded. A failure to appreciate this important condition can lead to a misinterpretation of the results of a regression analysis when used as a substitute for factorial analysis of variance.

In Chapter 7, I introduced the principles of moderation analysis. In a model of the form $Y = i_Y + b_1X + b_2W + e_Y$, b_1 and b_2 quantify unconditional effects, in that X's effect on Y does not depend on W, and W's effect on Y does not depend on X. Adding the product of X and W to the model, thereby producing a model of the form $Y = i_Y + b_1X + b_2W + b_3XW + e_Y$, relaxes this constraint and allows X's effect to depend linearly on W and W's effect to depend linearly on X. Thus, X's and W's effects on Y are conditional in such a model.

If I have done my job well writing Chapter 7, some of this chapter should feel a bit like a review to you, because everything discussed in that chapter applies without modification to the examples of moderation analysis presented here. In this chapter, I show how these principles of moderation analysis are applied when the moderator is dichotomous (rather than a continuum, as in the previous chapter) as well as when both focal antecedent and moderator are continuous. I also illustrate that one of the more common analytical techniques, the 2×2 factorial analysis of variance, is equivalent to multiple regression in which one dichotomous antecedent variable's effect on an consequent is moderated by a second dichotomous variable. However, as will be seen, this equivalence is dependent on how the two dichotomous antecedent variables are coded. Happily, for all the examples presented in this chapter, PROCESS makes the estimation simple and it greatly eases the effort of probing and interpreting interactions regardless of whether the focal antecedent and moderator are dichotomous, continuous, or any combination thereof.

8.1   Moderation with a Dichotomous Moderator

I illustrated the method of moderation analysis introduced in Chapter 7 using data from a study examining whether attributing the cause of a disaster to climate change as opposed to leaving the cause unspecified would affect people's justifications for withholding aid to the victims differentially depending on their beliefs in the reality of climate change. In that example, the focal antecedent variable was a dichotomous variable coding the framing of the cause of the drought, and the moderator was a measured individual difference that located each person on a continuum of skepticism about the reality of climate climate. As described in that analysis, those more skeptical of climate change reported stronger justifications for withholding aid when the disaster was attributed to climate change than when the cause was not specified. No such effect was observed among people relatively lower in climate change skepticism.

But what if our substantive focus was not on the effect of how the cause of the disaster was framed but instead on how climate change skepticism influences willingness to provide aid to disaster victims? This question is easily answered with a simple regression analysis. The best fitting OLS regression model estimating justifications for withholding aid (Y) from climate change skepticism (X) is $\hat{Y} = 2.186 + 0.201X$. Thus, two people who differ by one unit in their skepticism about climate change are estimated to differ by 0.201 units in the strength of their justifications for withholding aid to victims of the famine. This relationship is statistically significant.

But this analysis completely ignores that half of the participants in this study were told that the drought and resulting famine was caused by climate change, whereas others were given no information about the cause. According to the authors of this study, an event labeled as caused by climate change might cause climate change skeptics to be especially doubtful of the value of aiding the victims compared to people who are less skeptical of the reality of climate change. That is, the attribution to

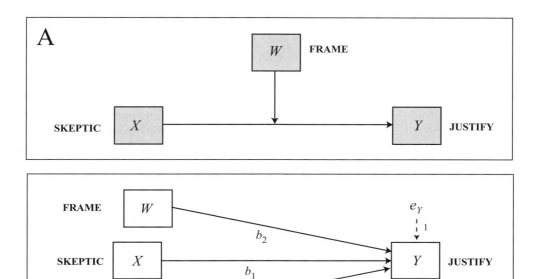

FIGURE 8.1. Moderation of the effect of climate change skepticism on justifications for withholding aid by causal attribution for the disaster, depicted as a conceptual diagram (panel A) and a statistical diagram (panel B).

climate change could prompt a motivated defensiveness, where attitudes about the reality of climate change would better predict attitudes about helping compared to when no such attribution is present. In other words, the attribution could prime people to respond to the needs of victims in a manner more consistent with their attitudes compared to when no cause is provided.

Such reasoning predicts that the relationship between climate change skepticism and justifications for withholding aid should be different among those told that climate change was the cause of the drought compared to those given no information about the cause. Calling climate change skepticism X and the disaster frame W (set to 1 for the climate change condition and 0 for the natural causes condition) we can estimate a simple moderation model just as in Chapter 7 that allows the effect of X on Y to depend on W. Such a process is diagrammed in conceptual form in Figure 8.1, panel A, and translates into a statistical model with X, W, and XW as antecedent variables, as in the statistical diagram in Figure 8.1, panel B. In the form of an equation, the model is

$$Y = i_Y + b_1X + b_2W + b_3XW + e_Y \tag{8.1}$$

TABLE 8.1. Results from a Regression Analysis Examining the Moderation of the Effect of Climate Change Skepticism on Justifications for Withholding Aid by Framing of the Cause of the Disaster

		Coeff.	SE	t	p
Constant	i_Y	2.452	0.149	16.449	< .001
Skepticism (X)	b_1	0.105	0.038	2.756	.006
Frame Condition (W)	b_2	−0.562	0.218	−2.581	.011
Skepticism × Frame (XW)	b_3	0.201	0.055	3.640	< .001

$$R^2 = 0.246, MSE = 0.661$$
$$F(3, 207) = 22.543, p < .001$$

where the focal antecedent is a continuous individual difference variable (X) and the moderator is a dichotomous variable in the form of an experimental manipulation (W). The SPSS and SAS code described on page 236 could be used to estimate the coefficients of the model in equation 8.1. I repeat it here for your convenience. In SPSS, the commands are

```
compute framskep=frame*skeptic.
regression/dep=justify/method=enter skeptic frame framskep.
```

and in SAS,

```
data disaster;set disaster;framskep=frame*skeptic;run;
proc reg data=disaster;model justify=skeptic frame framskep;run;
```

Even easier would be to use PROCESS. The PROCESS command is largely the same as on page 238, except that the roles of experimental condition (FRAME) and climate change skepticism (SKEPTIC) are reversed merely by assigning SKEPTIC to X and FRAME to W. In SPSS, the PROCESS command is

```
process y=justify/x=skeptic/w=frame/model=1/plot=1.
```

In SAS, use

```
%process (data=disaster,y=justify,x=skeptic,w=frame,model=1,plot=1);
```

The PROCESS output can be found in Figure 8.2, and a summary of the model can found in Table 8.1. The best fitting OLS regression model is

$$\hat{Y} = 2.452 + 0.105X - 0.562W + 0.201XW \tag{8.2}$$

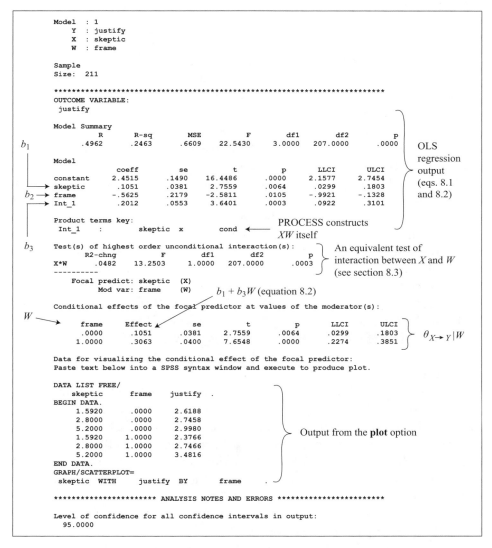

FIGURE 8.2. Output from the PROCESS procedure for SPSS for a simple moderation analysis of the disaster framing study.

The regression coefficient for XW is $b_3 = 0.201$ and is statistically different from zero, $t(207) = 3.640, p < .001$. Thus, the effect of climate change skepticism on strength of justifications for withholding aid depends on whether the drought was attributed to climate change or the cause was not specified. Also provided by this analysis is the conditional effect of climate change skepticism on justifications for withholding aid among those not given information about the cause of the drought. This is b_1 and it is statistically different from zero. The analysis also yields the conditional effect of the attribution of cause for the drought among those scoring zero on climate change skepticism measure. This is b_2, but it along with its test of significance is substantively meaningless because zero is outside of the range of measurement of X. Scores on the climate change skepticism scale, as constructed in this study, cannot be less than one because that is the lower bound of the measurement scale.

This model should look familiar to you because it is exactly the same model estimated in the analysis presented in Chapter 7 (see Table 7.4, model 3). The only differences between these two analyses are how the corresponding question is framed, meaning which variable is deemed the focal antecedent and which is the moderator, and how these variables are symbolically labeled as X and W. In the analysis in Chapter 7, the focal antecedent variable was a dichotomous variable coding the framing of the cause of the disaster (labeled X then, but W now), whereas in this analysis, the focal antecedent is a continuous variable placing each person on a continuum of climate change skepticism (labeled W then, but X now), with the moderator being a dichotomous variable coding experimental condition.

So this example illustrates the symmetry property of interactions introduced in section 7.1. In a regression model of the form in equation 8.1, b_3 estimates both the moderation of X effect on Y by W and W's effect on Y by X. Rejection of the null hypothesis that $_Tb_3 = 0$ allows for either claim, with how the claim is made and the interaction substantively interpreted depending on which variable is construed as the focal antecedent and which is the moderator.

Visualizing and Probing the Interaction

Because this is exactly the same model estimated in Chapter 7, the procedure described in section 7.3 can be used to generate a visual depiction of the model. Naturally, because the model is the same, so too is its visual representation (see Figure 8.3).

Recall in Chapter 7 that interpretation of this model was based on the difference between points on the solid and dashed lines at various values of

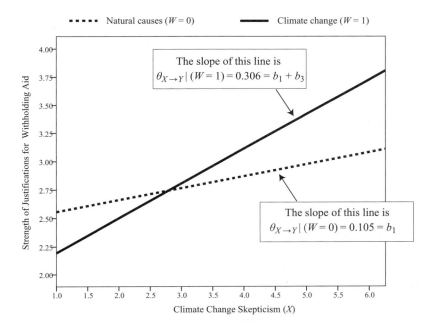

FIGURE 8.3. A visual representation of the moderation of the effect of the climate change skepticism (*X*) on strength of justifications for withholding aid (*Y*) by framing of the cause of the drought (*W*).

climate change skepticism. However, now that experimental condition is the moderator rather than it being the focal antecedent, our interpretation of the model focuses on the slopes of the two lines. As can be seen, the slope linking climate change skepticism to justifications for withholding aid is positive in both groups, meaning that regardless of the attribution of the cause, those who are more skeptical of climate change seem to feel stronger justifications for withholding aid to the disaster victims. However, the slope appears steeper among those told that the drought was caused by climate change compared to those not so told.

The slopes of these lines can be quantified by formally probing the interaction. When the moderator is dichotomous, there is only one option. Using the pick-a-point approach, we can estimate the conditional effect of the focal antecedent *X* on consequent *Y* for the two values of moderator *W*. Using the same mathematics introduced in section 7.1, equation 8.1 can be rewritten as

$$Y = i_Y + \theta_{X \to Y} X + b_2 W + e_Y$$

where

$$\theta_{X \to Y} = b_1 + b_3 W \tag{8.3}$$

Plugging the two values of W representing each experimental condition into equation 8.3 yields the two conditional effects of X. That is, among who received no attribution for the cause of the drought ($W = 0$),

$$\theta_{X \to Y} \mid (W = 0) = b_1 + b_3(0) = b_1 = 0.105$$

and among those told the drought was caused by climate change ($W = 1$),

$$\theta_{X \to Y} \mid (W = 1) = b_1 + b_3(1) = b_1 + b_3 = 0.105 + 0.201 = 0.306$$

So between two people told nothing about the cause of the drought but who differ by one unit in their climate change skepticism, the person higher in skepticism is estimated to be 0.105 units higher in the strength of his or her justifications for withholding aid. But among those told climate change was the cause of the drought, the person one unit higher in climate change skepticism is estimated to be 0.306 units higher in justifications for withholding aid. These two conditional effects correspond to the slopes of the lines in Figure 8.3.

Probing an interaction involves more than just quantifying the conditional effect of X as a function of W. In addition to estimating these conditional effects, an inferential test should be conducted to determine whether the conditional effect of X for a given value of W is statistically different from zero. Equation 7.13 could be used to estimate the standard error of these two conditional effects, and then a p-value derived based on the $t(df_{residual})$ distribution. However, this is a lot of work and subject to error in hand computation.

A much easier approach is to recognize that the regression model already gives us an estimate of the conditional effect of X on Y when $W = 0$ as well as a test of the null hypothesis that $_Tb_1 = 0$. Notice in the PROCESS output in Figure 8.2 that $b_1 = 0.105 = \theta_{X \to Y} \mid W = 0, t(207) = 2.756, p = .006$, with a 95% confidence interval between 0.030 and 0.180. Because $W = 0$ corresponds to the group of participants not told anything about the cause of the drought, we can conclude that when no attribution of the cause is provided, the relationship between climate change skepticism and strength of justifications for withholding aid is positive and statistically different from zero.

So by coding one of the groups $W = 0$ when the moderator is dichotomous, the regression coefficient for X estimates the conditional effect of X on Y in the group coded 0, and a test of significance is available right in the regression output. But the regression model does not provide a test of significance of the conditional effect of X when $W = 1$, which is needed to complete the probing process in this analysis. We do know from these mathematics that this conditional effect is $b_1 + b_3 = 0.306$. But we don't have a test of significance or an interval estimate for this conditional effect. Fortunately, this is easy to generate by exploiting your understanding of the interpretation of the regression coefficients in a moderation model. In equation 8.1, b_1 estimates the effect of X on Y when $W = 0$, which corresponds to the conditional effect of climate change skepticism on strength of justifications for withholding aid among those given no information about the cause of the drought. But the decision to code the climate change group $W = 1$ and the natural causes group $W = 0$ was totally arbitrary. By re-coding the groups such that the climate change group is coded 0 and the natural causes condition is coded 1, b_1 in equation 8.1 will then estimate the conditional effect of climate change skepticism among those told that climate change was responsible for the drought. The SPSS code below accomplishes this.

```
compute framep = 1-frame.
compute frampskp=framep*skeptic.
regression/dep=justify/method=enter skeptic framep frampskp.
```

The equivalent code in SAS is

```
data disaster;set disaster;framep=1-frame;frampskp=framep*skeptic;run;
proc reg data=disaster;model justify=skeptic framep frampskp;run;
```

The first thing this program does is reverse the coding of experimental condition, such that 0 becomes 1 and 1 becomes 0, held in a new variable named FRAMEP and denoted W' below. After this reverse coding, this new variable holding reverse-coded W is multiplied by X to produce the necessary product. Finally,

$$Y = i_Y + b_1 X + b_2 W' + b_3 X W' + e_Y$$

is estimated, which is equivalent to equation 8.1 but substituting W' for W, where $W' = 1 - W$. The resulting model is

$$\hat{Y} = 1.889 + 0.306X + 0.562W' - 0.201XW'$$

In this model, b_1 is the effect of X on Y when $W' = 0$, but this corresponds to the effect of X on Y when $W = 1$, because $W' = 0$ when $W = 1$. Notice that $b_1 = 0.306$, which is the conditional effect of X on Y when $W = 1$, just as calculated by hand earlier. That is, in this model, $b_1 = \theta_{X \to Y} \mid (W' = 0) = \theta_{X \to Y} \mid (W = 1)$. A test of significance is also provided in the regression output; $t(207) = 7.655, p < .001$. A confidence interval can be calculated in the usual way (see equation 2.16), or by requesting it in the SPSS Regression or SAS PROC REG command. Doing so yields a 95%

confidence interval between 0.227 and 0.385. So we can claim that among those told the drought was caused by climate change, those more skeptical of climate change reported stronger justifications for withholding aid than those less skeptical of climate change. This effect is statistically significant.

Albeit reasonably easy to do, not even this simple procedure is necessary when you use PROCESS, as PROCESS automatically implements the pick-a-point procedure. It recognizes that W is a dichotomous moderator without having to be told, because when it scans the data, it finds only two values for the variable specified as W. Thus, it estimates the conditional effect of X for each of the two values of the moderator. This implementation of the pick-a-point procedure can be found at the bottom of Figure 8.2 in the section of output labeled "Conditional effects of the focal predictor at values of the moderator(s)." By default, it provides the conditional effects of X when (in this case) $W = 0$ and $W = 1$, as well as standard errors, t-ratios, p-values, and confidence intervals.

In section 7.5, I addressed how testing for moderation is different than probing it. We have now seen that by probing the statistically significant interaction between the framing of the cause of the drought and climate change skepticism that the relationship between skepticism and strength of justifications for withholding aid is positive and statistically significant in both experimental conditions. In the climate change condition, $\theta_{X \to Y} = 0.105$, and in the natural causes condition, $\theta_{X \to Y} = 0.306$. But are these statistically different from each other? Yes they are. No further test is needed. Remember that a test of moderation of X's effect on Y by W is equivalent to a test of the difference between any two conditional effects of X on Y for any two values of W. So we can say these two conditional effects differ from each other because X and W interact.

To more clearly understand why, recall b_3's interpretation. It quantifies how the effect of X on Y changes as W changes by one unit. In this example, the two framing conditions differ by one unit on W. When $W = 0$, $\theta_{X \to Y} = 0.105$. When W is increased by one unit, $\theta_{X \to Y} = 0.306$. So the effect of X on Y increases by 0.201 units as W increases by one unit. But this is b_3, the weight for XW in the regression model. We know this is statistically different from zero, which means these two conditional effects of X are statistically different from each other.

8.2 Interaction between Two Quantitative Variables

Both examples of moderation analysis thus far illustrate how to test a moderation hypothesis involving a dichotomous variable in the model. In the first example in section 7.2, the dichotomous variable was the focal antecedent (whether the drought was framed as caused by climate change or left unspecified) and the moderator was a quantitative dimension (climate change skepticism). The roles of these two variables were reversed in section 8.1, with framing of the cause of the drought as moderator and climate change skepticism as the focal antecedent. The second example illustrated the generality of the mathematics of moderation analysis introduced at the beginning of Chapter 7. In this section I further demonstrate the generality of this procedure by showing how it is applied to testing moderation involving two quantitative variables. As you will see, no modifications to the procedure are required.

Sticking with climate change as the topic area, recall the global climate change data (file name GLBWARM) used in the review of multiple regression in Chapter 2. In that study, participants were asked about their support for various policies and actions the federal government could implement to help mitigate the causes of climate change. The analysis described in Chapter 2 demonstrated that people who reported feeling more negative emotions about climate change were more supportive of government action, even after accounting for individual differences in positive emotions, political ideology, age, and sex. Though not discussed in these terms then, this model imposed the constraint that any effect of negative emotions was independent of all other variables in the model. Such a constraint may not be realistic. At a minimum, it is an assumption that can be tested. In this example of moderation analysis, we determine whether the effect of negative emotions on support for government action differs among people of different ages. Age is a quantitative variable ranging between 17 and 87 years in the data, and we will ask whether there is any linear association between age and the effect of negative emotions on support for government action. The answer to this question will be derived while controlling for political ideology, sex, and positive emotions.

A conceptual representation of the model can be found in Figure 8.4, panel A, which illustrates that negative emotions is the focal antecedent X and age is the moderator W. In the form of a linear regression equation, the model is

$$Y = i_Y + b_1 X + b_2 W + b_3 XW + b_4 C_1 + b_5 C_2 + b_6 C_3 + e_Y \tag{8.4}$$

where X is negative emotions about global climate change, W is age, and C_1, C_2, and C_3 are positive emotions, ideology, and sex, respectively. If b_3 is statistically different from zero, this provides evidence that the effect of negative emotions on support for government action is moderated by age.

In this model, b_3 will properly estimate the moderation of X's effect by W, and the test of significance for b_3 will be a legitimate test of interaction.

But this model will also generate two regression coefficients that have no meaningful interpretation. As parameterized here, recall that b_1 estimates the effect of X on Y when $W = 0$. In this example, W is age, meaning that b_1 quantifies how much two cases that differ by one unit in their negative emotions about global climate change but who are *0 years old* are estimated to differ in support for government action. This would be nonsensical, of course. Although one could have an age of zero, no newborns participated in this study. The youngest person in the sample is 17 years old. By the same reasoning, b_2 quantifies how much two cases that differ by 1 year in age but measure zero in their negative emotions about climate change are estimated to differ in their support for government action. Zero is outside of the bounds of measurement of negative emotions, so b_2 and its test of significance will also be meaningless. But that is not a problem if you know these aren't meaningful and interpretable. Just don't attempt to interpret them. All the computations described in what follow will still be correct.

The SPSS code below estimates the model.

```
compute negage=negemot*age.
regression/dep=govact/method=enter negemot age negage posemot
    ideology sex.
```

Comparable code for SAS is

```
data glbwarm;set glbwarm;negage=negemot*age;run;
proc reg data=glbwarm;model govact=negemot age negage posemot
    ideology sex;run;
```

The best fitting regression model along with standard errors and p-values for all coefficients can be found in Table 8.2. The model is

$$\hat{Y} = 5.174 + 0.120X - 0.024W + 0.006XW - 0.021C_1 - 0.212C_2 - 0.011C_3$$

Our interest resides in the regression coefficient for the product of age and negative emotions, which is positive and statistically significant, $b_3 = 0.006, t(808) = 4.104, p < .001$, and accounts for about 1.25% of the variance in support for government action (from the PROCESS output, discussed below).

PROCESS provides a lot more information than SPSS or SAS's regression procedure. In addition to estimating the model and providing the coefficients, standard errors, and so forth, it also automatically estimates the conditional effects of negative emotions at various values of age, can generate data to help visualize the interaction, will implement the Johnson–Neyman technique for further probing the interaction, and calculates the proportion of variance in the consequent variable attributable to the interaction. The PROCESS command for this analysis is

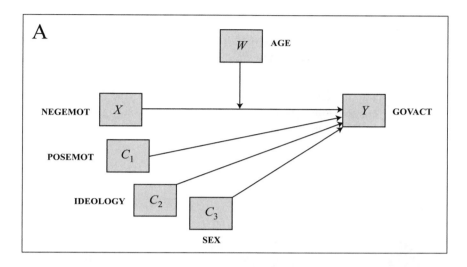

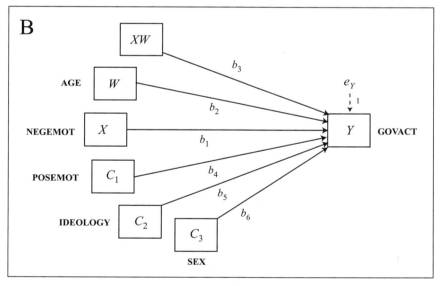

FIGURE 8.4. The moderation of negative emotions about climate change on support for government action by age with various covariates, depicted as a conceptual diagram (panel A) and a statistical diagram (panel B).

TABLE 8.2. Results from a Regression Analysis Examining the Moderation of the Effect of Negative Emotional Responses to Global Climate Change on Support for Government Action by Age, Controlling for Positive Emotions, Political Ideology, and Sex

		Coeff.	SE	t	p
Constant	i_Y	5.174	0.338	15.287	< .001
Negative Emotions (X)	b_1	0.120	0.083	1.449	.148
Age (W)	b_2	−0.024	0.006	−3.993	< .001
Negative Emotions × Age (XW)	b_3	0.006	0.002	4.104	< .001
Positive Emotions (C_1)	b_4	−0.021	0.028	−0.768	.443
Political Ideology (C_2)	b_5	−0.212	0.027	−7.883	< .001
Sex (C_3)	b_6	−0.011	0.076	−0.147	.883

$$R^2 = 0.401, MSE = 1.117$$
$$F(6, 808) = 90.080, p < .001$$

```
process y=govact/x=negemot/w=age/cov=posemot ideology sex/model=1
    /jn=1/plot=1.
```

or in SAS,

```
%process (data=glbwarm,y=govact,x=negemot,w=age,cov=posemot ideology
    sex,model=1,jn=1,plot=1);
```

However, I recommend adding an additional option. By default, PROCESS will produce conditional effects of negative emotions on support for government action among people at the 16th, 50th, and 84th percentiles of the distribution of age. In these data, those ages are 30, 51, and 67. These will also be ages used by PROCESS to produce data useful for visualizing the interaction. But these seem like strange ages to focus on. If we used the **moments=1** option, PROCESS would choose values of age equal to a standard deviation below the sample mean, the mean, and a standard deviation above the mean. In these data, these ages are 33.205, 49.536, and 65.867, respectively. These also seem like odd choices. So let's instead tell PROCESS to use ages of 30, 50, and 70. These are nice round numbers, and it will be easier to talk about conditional effects later using these round numbers. This is accomplished using the **wmodval** option, as below:

```
process y=govact/x=negemot/w=age/cov=posemot ideology sex/model=1/
    jn=1/plot=1/wmodval=30,50,70.
```

```
%process (data=glbwarm,y=govact,x=negemot,w=age,cov=posemot ideology
    sex,model=1,jn=1,plot=1,wmodval=30 50 70);
```

Output from the SPSS version can be found in Figure 8.5. The estimates of the regression coefficients and other statistics at the top of the PRO-CESS output reproduce the information in Table 8.2. Other sections of the PROCESS output are discussed below.

Visualizing and Probing the Interaction

A visual representation of the interaction can be generated using the same procedure described in section 7.3, but because this model involves covariates, an additional step is required. First, select combinations of X and W to be included in the interaction plot. It doesn't matter too much which values you select so long as they are within the range of your data. You could choose various percentiles of the distribution, the minimum and maximum value, plus and minus one standard deviation from the sample mean, or whatever you want. If you plan on using the pick-a-point approach for probing the interaction, it makes most sense to choose values of W corresponding to those values at which you intend to formally estimate the conditional effect of X.

Next, using the best fitting regression model, generate $\hat{Y}$ for the combinations of X and W that you have chosen. However, because the model contains three covariates, these need to be set to a value as well. Although you could choose any values you want to plug into the model along with X and W, convention is to use the means of the covariates. In this example, the means for C_1, C_2, and C_3 are 3.132, 4.083, and 0.488, respectively. Thus, the equation for generating $\hat{Y}$ for values of X and W when the covariates are set to their sample means is

$$\hat{Y} = 5.174 + 0.120X - 0.024W + 0.006XW - 0.021(3.132)$$
$$- 0.212(4.083) - 0.011(0.488)$$

which simplifies to

$$\hat{Y} = 4.237 + 0.120X - 0.024W + 0.006XW$$

The values plugged into the model for the covariates end up merely adding or subtracting from the regression constant, depending on the signs of the regression coefficients for the covariates. This will have the effect of moving the plot up or down the vertical axis. Although it seems coun-terintuitive, you *can* use the sample mean for dichotomous covariates. If a dichotomous variable is coded zero and one, then the sample mean is

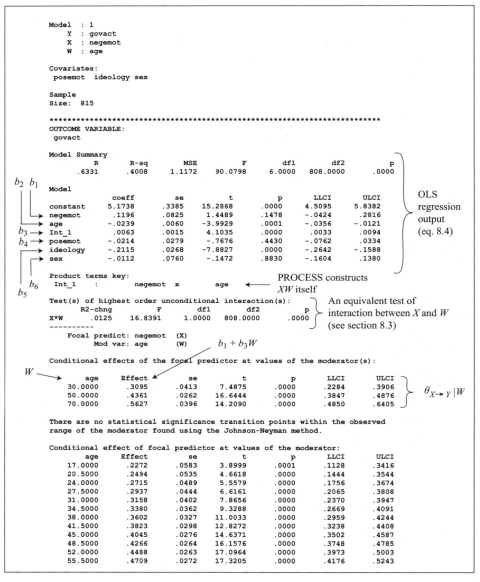

FIGURE 8.5. Output from the PROCESS procedure for SPSS for a simple moderation analysis of the global climate change data.

(continued)

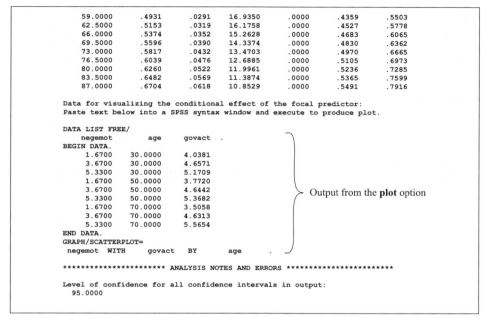

```
      59.0000      .4931      .0291    16.9350    .0000    .4359    .5503
      62.5000      .5153      .0319    16.1758    .0000    .4527    .5778
      66.0000      .5374      .0352    15.2628    .0000    .4683    .6065
      69.5000      .5596      .0390    14.3374    .0000    .4830    .6362
      73.0000      .5817      .0432    13.4703    .0000    .4970    .6665
      76.5000      .6039      .0476    12.6885    .0000    .5105    .6973
      80.0000      .6260      .0522    11.9961    .0000    .5236    .7285
      83.5000      .6482      .0569    11.3874    .0000    .5365    .7599
      87.0000      .6704      .0618    10.8529    .0000    .5491    .7916

Data for visualizing the conditional effect of the focal predictor:
Paste text below into a SPSS syntax window and execute to produce plot.

DATA LIST FREE/
     negemot        age      govact  .
BEGIN DATA.
      1.6700     30.0000     4.0381
      3.6700     30.0000     4.6571
      5.3300     30.0000     5.1709
      1.6700     50.0000     3.7720
      3.6700     50.0000     4.6442
      5.3300     50.0000     5.3682
      1.6700     70.0000     3.5058
      3.6700     70.0000     4.6313
      5.3300     70.0000     5.5654
END DATA.
GRAPH/SCATTERPLOT=
     negemot  WITH     govact   BY       age      .

*********************** ANALYSIS NOTES AND ERRORS ***********************

Level of confidence for all confidence intervals in output:
   95.0000
```

Output from the **plot** option

FIGURE 8.5 continued.

the proportion of the cases in the group coded one. But using the mean works regardless of how the groups are coded, even if the mean is itself meaningless. Regardless, once you have values of $\hat{Y}$ generated for various values of X and W, then you will have a small dataset containing X, W, and $\hat{Y}$, which could be given to whatever graphing program you prefer in order to generate the interaction plot.

PROCESS takes much of the burden out of this procedure. When the **plot** option is used, PROCESS generates a table of estimates of Y for various combinations of the focal antecedent variable and moderator while setting all covariates to their sample means. This table could then be used as input into any program you prefer to generate graphs. The SPSS version of PROCESS will even write the necessary code, which you can then cut and paste out of the PROCESS output and into a syntax window and then execute to produce a plot. This code can be found toward the bottom of the PROCESS output (see the bottom of Figure 8.5 under the heading "Data for visualizing the conditional effect of the focal predictor"). A copy of that section of output is below:

```
DATA LIST FREE/
    negemot      age      govact .
BEGIN DATA.
```

```
    1.6700    30.0000    4.0381
    3.6700    30.0000    4.6571
    5.3300    30.0000    5.1709
    1.6700    50.0000    3.7720
    3.6700    50.0000    4.6442
    5.3300    50.0000    5.3682
    1.6700    70.0000    3.5058
    3.6700    70.0000    4.6313
    5.3300    70.0000    5.5654
END DATA.
GRAPH/SCATTERPLOT=
    negemot WITH  govact BY  age.
```

The values of negative emotions used by PROCESS when it generates this code correspond to the 16th, 50th, and 84th percentiles of the distribution. Had we used the **moments** option, it would have used a standard deviation below the mean, the mean, and a standard deviation above the mean for negative emotions. For age, the values of 30, 50, and 70 correspond to the ages put into the **wmodval** option.

The corresponding commands in SAS to produce a plot are

```
data;input negemot age govact;
datalines;
1.6700 30.0000 4.0381
3.6700 30.0000 4.6571
5.3300 30.0000 5.1709
1.6700 50.0000 3.7720
3.6700 50.0000 4.6442
5.3300 50.0000 5.3682
1.6700 70.0000 3.5058
3.6700 70.0000 4.6313
5.3300 70.0000 5.5654
run;
proc sgplot;reg x=negemot y=govact/group=age
    nomarkers lineattrs=(color=black);
xaxis label='Negative Emotions About Global Climate Change (X)';
yaxis label='Support for Government Action (Y)';run;
```

If you prefer to use R to produce a visual depiction of the model, try this code:

```
x<-c(1.67,3.67,5.33,1.67,3.67,5.33,1.67,3.67,5.33)
w<-c(30,30,30,50,50,50,70,70,70)
y<-c(4.038,4.657,5.171,3.772,4.644,5.362,3.506,4.631,5.565)
wmarker<-c(15,15,15,16,16,16,17,17,17)
```

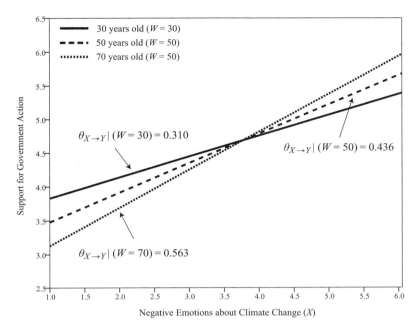

FIGURE 8.6. A visual representation of the moderation of the effect of negative emotions about global climate change (X) on support for government action (Y) by age (W).

```
plot(y=y,x=x,cex=1.2,pch=wmarker,xlab="Negative Emotions (W)",
ylab="Support for Government Action (Y)")
legend.txt<-c("30 years old","50 years old", "70 years old")
legend("topleft", legend = legend.txt,cex=1,lty=c(1,3,6),lwd=c(2,3,2),
pch=c(15,16,17))
lines(x[w==30],y[w==30],lwd=2,col="black")
lines(x[w==50],y[w==50],lwd=3,lty=3,col="black")
lines(x[w==70],y[w==70],lwd=2,lty=6,col="black")
```

A plot produced by the SPSS code after considerable editing can be found in Figure 8.6. As can be seen, the effect of negative emotions about global climate change on support for government action to mitigate climate change appears to be consistently positive, regardless of age. But the slope linking negative emotions to support for government action is more steep among those older. That is, the effect of negative emotions appears to be larger among the relatively older (in this plot, 70-year-olds) than among the relatively younger (here, 30-year-olds).

The slopes of the lines in Figure 8.6 are $\theta_{X \to Y}$ for arbitrarily chosen values of W. These conditional effects of X, sometimes called "simple slopes," can be formally quantified and an inferential test conducted using the pick-a-point approach. As described in Chapter 7, the regression model

$$Y = i_Y + b_1X + b_2W + b_3XW + b_4C_1 + b_5C_2 + b_6C_3 + e_Y$$

can be written in equivalent form as

$$Y = i_Y + (b_1 + b_3W)X + b_2W + b_4C_1 + b_5C_2 + b_6C_3 + e_Y$$

or

$$Y = i_Y + \theta_{X \to Y}X + b_2W + b_4C_1 + b_5C_2 + b_6C_3 + e_Y$$

where $\theta_{X \to Y} = b_1 + b_3W$. In terms of the regression coefficients from the model, $\theta_{X \to Y} = 0.120 + 0.006W$. Plugging in various values of W produces the conditional effect of X at those values of W. You can use any values of W you choose, such as the mean and plus and minus one standard deviation from the mean, various percentiles in the distribution, or anything else. Regardless of the choice, once $\theta_{X \to Y}$ is generated for those values, a standard error can be derived using equation 7.13 and a p-value calculated based on the $t(df_{residual})$ distribution.

PROCESS does all these tedious computations for you, the results of which are found in the first section of output you find labeled "Conditional effects of the focal predictor at values of the moderator(s):" Because the **wmodval** option was used, PROCESS implements the pick-a-point approach using values of 30, 50, and 70 for age. As can be seen in Figure 8.5. PROCESS calculates the conditional effects of negative emotions on support for government action at these values of age for you. They are 0.301, 0.436, and 0.563, respectively, and as can be seen, all are statistically significant from zero with p-values less than .0001. These correspond to the slopes of the lines in Figure 8.6.

The Johnson–Neyman technique described in section 7.4 can be used here because the moderator variable is a quantitative dimension. Doing so eliminates the need to arbitrarily select values of the moderator at which to probe the interaction. But in these data, and according to PROCESS's implementation of the JN technique (requested with the **jn** option), there are no points in the distribution of age where the conditional effect of negative emotions on support for government action transitions between statistically significant and not significant at the $\alpha = 0.05$ level of significance. This is because, as the pick-a-point section of the PROCESS output suggests, the effect of negative emotions is significantly positive for *any* value of age in the data. You can see this by looking at the table in the PROCESS output below the section where it tells you that there are no statistical significance transition points.

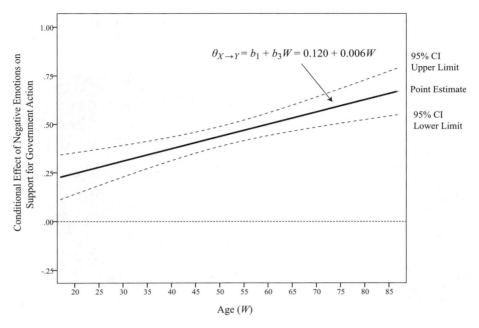

FIGURE 8.7. The conditional effect of the negative emotions about global climate change (X) on support for government action ($\theta_{X \to Y}$) as a function of age (W).

If that isn't apparent to you, Figure 8.7 will make it clearer. In this figure, the solid black line is $\theta_{X \to Y}$, the conditional effect of X, defined by the function $b_1 + b_3 W$, or $0.120 + 0.006W$ based on this analysis. The dotted lines are the upper and lower bounds of a 95% confidence interval for $_T\theta_{(X \to Y)|W}$ (approximately plus and minus two standard errors from $\theta_{X \to Y}$, using the standard error estimator in equation 7.13). Unlike in Figure 7.9, where the confidence interval straddled zero for some values of the moderator but not others, in these data the confidence interval is always above zero. In other words, at any value of age you can choose, negative emotion's effect is significantly positive because the confidence interval is entirely above zero for all values of age. Thus, the region of significance for X is the entire distribution of W.

The visual depiction of the moderation as presented in Figure 8.7 can be a handy alternative relative to the more traditional plot in Figure 8.6. Figure 8.7 provides not only a point estimate of $\theta_{X \to Y}$ for any value of the moderator you can choose, but it also provides an inferential test at any chosen value in the form of a confidence interval and thus conveys much more information than does Figure 8.6.

Figure 8.7 was generated in SPSS using the code below, and then edited using SPSS's graphics editing features. This code could easily be tailored to your own data and model.

```
DATA LIST FREE/age effect llci ulci.
BEGIN DATA.
17.0000    0.2272    0.1128    0.3416
20.5000    0.2494    0.1444    0.3544
24.0000    0.2715    0.1756    0.3674

   .            .         .         .
   .       (from PROCESS JN table) .
   .            .         .         .
80.0000    0.6260    0.5236    0.7285
83.5000    0.6482    0.5365    0.7599
87.0000    0.6704    0.5491    0.7961
END DATA.
GRAPH/SCATTER(OVERLAY)=age age age WITH llci ulci effect (PAIR).
```

In SAS, the code below will produce a similar figure but will require much less editing.

```
data;input age effect llci ulci;
datalines;
17.0000    0.2272    0.1128    0.3416
20.5000    0.2494    0.1444    0.3544
24.0000    0.2715    0.1756    0.3674

   .            .         .         .
   .       (from PROCESS JN table) .
   .            .         .         .
80.0000    0.6260    0.5236    0.7285
83.5000    0.6482    0.5365    0.7599
87.0000    0.6704    0.5491    0.7961
run;
proc sgplot;
series x=age y=ulci/curvelabel='95% upper limit' lineattrs=(color=red
    pattern=ShortDash);
series x=age y=effect/curvelabel='point estimate' lineattrs=(color=
    black pattern=Solid);
series x=age y=llci/curvelabel='95% lower limit' lineattrs=(color=red
    pattern=ShortDash);
xaxis label = 'Age (W)';
yaxis label = 'Conditional effect of negative emotions';
```

```
refline 0/axis=y transparency=0.5;refline 3.5 4.98/axis=x
transparency=0.5;
run;
```

In R, try

```
age<-c(17,20.5,24,27.5,31,34.5,38,41.5,45,48.5,52,55.5,59,62.5,66,69.5,
     73,76.5,80,83.5,87)
effect<-c(.227,.249,.272,.294,.316,.338,.360,.382,.405,.427,.449,.471,
         .493,.515,.537,.560,.582,.604,.626,.648,.670)
llci<-c(.113,.144,.176,.207,.237,.267,.296,.324,.350,.375,.397,.418,
        .436,.453,.468,.483,.497,.511,.524,.537,.549)
ulci<-c(.342,.354,.367,.381,.395,.409,.424,.441,.459,.479,.500,.524,
        .551,.578,.607,.636,.667,.697,.729,.760,.792)
plot(age,effect,type="l",pch=19,ylim=c(-.5,1),xlim=c(15,90),lwd=3,
ylab="Conditional effect of negative emotions",
xlab="Age (W)")
points(age,llci,lwd=2,lty=2,type="l")
points(age,ulci,lwd=2,lty=2,type="l")
abline(h=0,untf=FALSE,lty=3,lwd=1)
```

8.3 Hierarchical versus Simultaneous Entry

Many investigators test a moderation hypothesis in regression analysis using a method that on the surface seems different than the procedure described thus far. This alternative approach is to build a regression model by adding the product of X and W to a model already containing X and W. This procedure is sometimes called *hierarchical regression* or *hierarchical variable entry* (and easily confused by name with *hierarchical linear modeling*, which is an entirely different thing). The goal using this method is to determine whether allowing X's effect to be contingent on W produces a better fitting model than one in which the effect of X is constrained to be unconditional on W. According to the logic of hierarchical entry, if the contingent model accounts for more of the variation in Y than the model that forces X's effect to be independent of W, then the better model is one in which W is allowed to moderate X's effect. Although this approach works, it is a widely believed myth that it is *necessary* to use this approach in order to test a moderation hypothesis.

To test whether W moderates the effect of X on Y using hierarchical regression, the model for Y is built in steps. In the first step, Y is estimated from X and W and any additional variables other than XW of interest, such as various covariates and so forth. Call the resulting model "model 1" and its squared multiple correlation R_1^2. In the second stage, XW is added to model 1 to generate "model 2" and its squared multiple correlation, R_2^2. Under the null hypothesis that W does not linearly moderate the effect of X on Y, model 2 should not fit better than model 1. That is, if the null hypothesis is true, adding the product term will not produce a model that provides any new information about individual differences in Y not already provided by model 1. The difference in the squared multiple correlations, $\Delta R^2 = R_2^2 - R_1^2$, is a descriptive measure of how much better model 2 fits relative to model 1. This is sometimes called the incremental increase in R^2, or simply "change in R^2."

Because R^2 cannot go down when a variable is added to a model, $\Delta R^2 \geq 0$. Even if the null hypothesis is true, expect model 2 to fit better than model 1 from a purely descriptive standpoint, even if only slightly so. In science, we must rule out chance as a plausible explanation for a research finding before advancing other explanations, so the question is not whether model 2 fits better—it will—but whether it fits better than one would expect by chance if the null hypothesis is true. To answer this question, a p-value is needed. The mechanics of the test as to whether model 2 fits better than model 1 more than can be explained by chance has already been spelled out in section 2.6, where inference about a set of variables in a regression model was introduced. The difference in R^2 is converted to an F-ratio using equation 2.17, where $R_2^2 - R_1^2 = \Delta R^2$ and $m = 1$, and a p-value derived from the F distribution with 1 and $df_{residual}$ degrees of freedom.

I illustrate this procedure using the disaster framing experiment. In section 8.1, we asked if attributing the cause of the drought to climate change as opposed to leaving the cause unspecified (W) moderates the effect of climate change skepticism (X) on justifications for withholding aid (Y). The answer was yes, but this answer was derived using a different approach in which X, W, and XW were simultaneously included in the regression model. Using the hierarchical entry method, the fit of a model estimating Y from X and W is first calculated. Doing so yields $R_1^2 = 0.198$. When XW is added to this model, $R_2^2 = 0.246$, which means $\Delta R^2 = 0.246 - 0.198 = 0.048$. The residual degrees of freedom for model 2 is 207. Using either equation 2.17 or calculated more precisely using the SPSS or SAS code on page 63, $F(1, 207) = 13.250, p < .001$. The null hypothesis can be rejected. The effect of climate change skepticism on strength of justifications for withholding aid depends on whether or not the drought was attributed to climate change.

Although this hierarchical entry procedure works, it is not necessary, as it will produce the same decision as the test that $_T b_3 = 0$ when estimating a model of the form $\hat{Y} = i_Y + b_1 X + b_2 W + b_3 XW$. The F-ratio for ΔR^2 is equal to the square of b_3/se_{b_3} (that is, $F = t^2_{b_3}$) and the F- and t-values will have the same p-value. Indeed, observe from Figure 8.2, the t statistic for b_3 is 3.640, which when squared yields $F = 13.250$. Thus, there is no need to conduct or report both tests, as they are mathematically identical and will always give the same answer.

The hierarchical entry method does give ΔR^2—the proportion of variance in Y that is uniquely accounted for by the moderation of X's effect by W. You could argue that this gives the hierarchical entry method some advantage if you want to report the incremental improvement in fit. However, ΔR^2 can be obtained from most regression outputs if you ask for it without using hierarchical entry, because ΔR^2 is equal to the squared semipartial correlation for XW. Most regression programs have the ability to print the semipartial correlations for each variable in the model. If your preferred program does not, it can be calculated from information provided from the regression model with X, W, and XW as antecedent variables:

$$\Delta R^2 = \frac{t^2_{b_3}(1 - R^2)}{df_{residual}}$$

Of course, no one wants to do these computations by hand, and most programs don't automatically produce the semipartial correlation (which then has to be squared, introducing human-generated rounding error into the estimate of ΔR^2). Understanding this, PROCESS was programmed to automatically produce ΔR^2 for the interaction for the simple moderation model in a section of the output labeled "Test of highest order unconditional interaction(s)" but without you having to actually build the model hierarchically. As can be seen in Figure 8.2, $\Delta R^2 = 0.048$, just as computed by calculating the two R^2 for each model and manually calculating their difference. PROCESS also gives the F-ratio and p-value for this change in R^2, but as just described, this provides no information not already contained in the t- and p-values for b_3.

All this said, there are two circumstances in which one might choose to use hierarchical entry. First, sometimes it is convenient from the perspective of describing research results to first talk about the effect of X in unconditional terms as estimated and tested before, if necessary, qualifying that claim after the results of model estimation in the second step are described. Putting X, W, and XW in the model simultaneously yields an estimate of X's effect that is necessarily conditional on W. Second, if more than one regression coefficient is needed to quantify moderation of X's effect on Y, such as when W or X is multicategorical with k levels, hierarchical entry is an easy way to test the simultaneous null hypothesis that the regression coefficients for all $k - 1$ product terms are equal to zero. An example of this procedure is described in Chapter 10. There are other ways, however, as in SAS with the use of the "test" option in PROC REG (see page 63 for example code).

8.4   The Equivalence between Moderated Regression Analysis and a 2 × 2 Factorial Analysis of Variance

Some believe that the method of analysis one uses plays an important role in whether one can infer cause–effect. For this reason, the logic goes, the method of choice for experimentalists is analysis of variance (ANOVA), because multiple regression is used only for correlational studies in which cause–effect cannot be established. I think it has already been shown this belief is misguided. Multiple regression is a legitimate statistical tool for the analysis of experimental data. Even more than just legitimate, analysis of variance is just a special case of multiple regression, so the belief that ANOVA should be the method of choice when cause–effect inferences are desired and sought out through experimentation is misplaced. Remember that inferences are products of mind, not mathematics. Statistical methods do not produce causal inferences. Our inferences stem from the interpretation of the results a statistical model generates and the manner in which the data are collected.

In this section, I show the equivalence between regression analysis with the product of X and W in the model along with X and W and a 2 × 2 factorial ANOVA, which is one of the more common forms of ANOVA used when analyzing data from experimental research. But I also warn by way of example that this equivalence is dependent on how X and W are coded. A failure to appreciate this important caveat can result in a misinterpretation of the coefficients in a regression analysis and a misreporting and misrepresentation of your findings.

We return to the study by Hayes and Reineke (2007) that began Chapter 7. In this study, 541 residents of the state of Ohio in the United States responded to a telephone survey conducted just after the 2004 federal election. This survey included a couple of questions gauging respondents' interest (on a 1 to 5 scale, with higher values representing greater interest) in viewing images of caskets containing the bodies of U.S. servicemen and women killed in action in Iraq returning to the United States for burial. Prior to this question, half of the respondents (randomly assigned) were told about the Bush administration's policy, which restricted journalist access to locations where such images can be recorded, whereas the other half were given no such information. The participants were also classified based on questions they were asked about who they voted for in the 2004 presidential election as either supporters of George W. Bush or supporters of his opponent, Senator John Kerry of Massachusetts.

The data file corresponding to this study is CASKETS, and it can be found at *www.afhayes.com*. The dependent variable is INTEREST. The other two variables pertinent to this analysis are codes holding which of the two policy information conditions a respondent was assigned to (POLICY, with 0 = no information given and 1 = policy information given) as well as whether or not the respondent was a Kerry supporter (KERRY=1) or a Bush supporter (KERRY=0). Using these data, we will determine whether there is evidence that the effect of providing information about the Bush administration policy differentially affected Bush and Kerry supporters' interest in viewing the casket images. Thus, policy information is the focal antecedent variable X, and the candidate the respondent supported in the election is the moderator W. So both X and W are dichotomous.

The typical approach to answering this question is covered in almost every introductory statistics course. When both X and W are dichotomous variables and interest is in the interaction between X and W, factorial ANOVA is most commonly used. Using a factorial ANOVA, it is possible to estimate the *main* and *interactive* effects of X and W on Y. This is a 2 × 2 *between-participants* factorial ANOVA because there are two levels of each variable or *factor*, and participants provide data to one and only one cell of the design, with a *cell* defined as the combination of the two factors.

I assume that you are familiar with the mechanics of factorial ANOVA and thus do not discuss its theory or computation here. For details or to review, see most any introductory statistics book or a good book on the design and analysis of experiments (e.g., Keppel & Wickens, 2004). A 2 × 2 factorial ANOVA can be conducted in most any statistics program, including SPSS and SAS. For instance, in SPSS, the commands below produce Table 8.3 and the ANOVA summary table found in Table 8.4:

```
unianova interest BY policy kerry/emmeans=tables(policy)/emmeans=tables
    (kerry)/emmeans=tables(policy*kerry).
```

In SAS, try

```
proc glm data=caskets;class policy kerry;
    model interest = policy kerry policy*kerry;
    lsmeans policy kerry policy*kerry;run;
```

As can be seen in Table 8.4, the main effect of policy information (X) is statistically significant, $F(1, 537) = 5.394, p = .021$. The estimate of the

TABLE 8.3. Interest in Viewing Casket Images from the Hayes & Reineke (2007) Study

| Candidate Supported (W) | Information about Policy (X) | | Marginal Means |
	No	Yes	
Bush	$\overline{Y}_1 = 1.784$	$\overline{Y}_2 = 1.397$	$\overline{Y}_{12} = 1.590$
Kerry	$\overline{Y}_3 = 2.384$	$\overline{Y}_4 = 2.357$	$\overline{Y}_{34} = 2.370$
Marginal Means	$\overline{Y}_{13} = 2.084$	$\overline{Y}_{24} = 1.877$	

TABLE 8.4. Summary Table for a 2 × 2 Between-Participant Factorial ANOVA of the Caskets Data

Source	SS	df	MS	F	p
Policy Information (X)	5.759	1	5.759	5.394	.021
Candidate Supported (W)	82.110	1	82.110	76.906	< .001
Interaction (X × W)	4.372	1	4.372	4.095	.044
Error	573.338	537	1.068		

main effect of X can be calculated from Table 8.3 in one of two ways. First, it is the unweighted average simple effect of X. A *simple effect* is a mean difference conditioned on a row or column in the table. So the simple effect of policy information among Kerry supporters is $\overline{Y}_4 - \overline{Y}_3 = 2.357 - 2.384 = -0.027$, and the simple effect of policy information among Bush supporters is $\overline{Y}_2 - \overline{Y}_1 = 1.397 - 1.784 = -0.387$. Thus,

$$\text{Main effect of } X = \frac{(\overline{Y}_4 - \overline{Y}_3) + (\overline{Y}_2 - \overline{Y}_1)}{2} = \frac{-0.027 - 0.387}{2} = -0.207$$

Simple algebra shows that this main effect can also be written as the difference in the marginal means for X, where a *marginal mean* is the unweighted mean of cell means in a given row or column in the 2 × 2 table. For instance, from Table 8.3 the marginal mean for the policy information condition is $\overline{Y}_{24} = (\overline{Y}_2 + \overline{Y}_4)/2 = (1.397 + 2.357)/2 = 1.877$, and the marginal mean for the no policy information condition is $\overline{Y}_{13} = (\overline{Y}_1 + \overline{Y}_3)/2 = (1.784 + 2.384)/2 = 2.084$. The difference between these means is

$$\text{Main effect of } X = \overline{Y}_{24} - \overline{Y}_{13} = 1.877 - 2.084 = -0.207$$

This statistically significant main effect of -0.207 is interpreted to mean that participants given information about the policy expressed 0.207 units less interest in viewing the images than participants not given this information.

The main effect of candidate supported is also statistically significant, $F(1, 537) = 76.906, p < .001$. This main effect corresponds to the unweighted average simple effect of candidate supported on interest in the images, or the difference between the marginal means of candidate supported. The simple effect of candidate supported among those given information about the policy is $\overline{Y}_4 - \overline{Y}_2 = 2.357 - 1.397 = 0.960$ and the simple effect of candidate supported among participants not given information about the policy is $\overline{Y}_3 - \overline{Y}_1 = 2.384 - 1.784 = 0.600$. Thus,

$$\text{Main effect of } W = \frac{(\overline{Y}_4 - \overline{Y}_2) + (\overline{Y}_3 - \overline{Y}_1)}{2} = \frac{0.960 + 0.600}{2} = 0.780$$

This is equivalent to the difference between the marginal means for who the candidate supported:

$$\text{Main effect of } W = \overline{Y}_{34} - \overline{Y}_{12} = 2.370 - 1.590 = 0.780$$

In words, Kerry supporters expressed 0.780 more interest, on average, in viewing the casket images than did Bush supporters.

The interaction between policy information and candidate supported is also statistically significant, $F(1, 537) = 4.095, p = .044$, which addresses the central question of interest. The effect of providing information about the policy on interest in the images is indeed moderated by who the participant supported in the 2004 election. According to the symmetry property of interactions, this can also be interpreted as evidence that the difference in interest in viewing the casket images between Kerry and Bush supporters depends on whether information about the policy was provided or not.

In a 2×2 factorial ANOVA, interaction or moderation is quantified as a difference in the simple effect of one variable between levels of the second. When candidate supported is construed as the moderator, this means that the simple effect of policy information among Kerry supporters is different than the simple effect of policy information among Bush supporters. The former simple effect is $\overline{Y}_4 - \overline{Y}_3 = 2.357 - 2.384 = -0.027$ and the latter simple effect is $\overline{Y}_2 - \overline{Y}_1 = 1.397 - 1.784 = -0.387$. Thus,

$$X \times W \text{ interaction} = (\overline{Y}_4 - \overline{Y}_3) - (\overline{Y}_2 - \overline{Y}_1) = -0.027 - (-0.387) = 0.360$$

This interaction can also be conceptualized with policy information as the moderator of differences between Kerry and Bush supporters in interest in viewing the casket images. In that case, the interaction means that the simple effect of candidate supported among those given information about the policy $(\overline{Y}_4 - \overline{Y}_2) = 2.357 - 1.397 = 0.960$ is different than the simple effect of candidate supported among those not given information about the policy $(\overline{Y}_3 - \overline{Y}_1) = 2.384 - 1.784 = 0.600$. That is,

$$X \times W \text{ interaction} = (\overline{Y}_4 - \overline{Y}_2) - (\overline{Y}_3 - \overline{Y}_1) = 0.960 - 0.600 = 0.360$$

Simple Effects Parameterization

A 2×2 factorial analysis of variance is just a special case of multiple regression with dichotomous antecedent variables. As such, the main and interactive effects of X and W can be expressed as a regression model of the form $Y = i_Y + b_1 X + b_2 W + b_3 XW + e_Y$. However, care must be exercised, because whether b_1 and b_2 can be interpreted as equivalent to the main effects from a factorial ANOVA will be highly dependent on the way that X and W are coded.

In the data, whether or not information about the policy was provided (POLICY) and who the respondent supported in the 2004 election (KERRY) are dummy-coded variables, meaning they are coded 0 and 1. If you were to regress Y on X, W, and XW using these dummy codes, the resulting regression coefficients, standard errors, and t- and p-values can be found in Table 8.5 as model 1. In this model, b_1 and b_2 are *not* equivalent to the main effects of X and W in a 2×2 factorial ANOVA and should not be interpreted as such. Rather, when X and W are dummy codes and their product is included as an antecedent variable in a regression model, the resulting model is a *simple effects parameterization* of the 2×2 design. In this model, b_1 estimates the simple effect of X for the level of W coded zero, and b_2 estimates the simple effect of W for the level of X coded zero. These are equivalent to what we've been calling *conditional effects* thus far. That is, b_1 estimates the effect of X (policy information) when $W = 0$ (Bush supporters), and b_2 estimates the effect of W (candidate supported) when $X = 0$ (no policy information given). Indeed, observe that b_1 and b_2 correspond to these simple effects in Table 8.3:

$$b_1 = \overline{Y}_2 - \overline{Y}_1 = 1.397 - 1.784 = -0.387$$

$$b_2 = \overline{Y}_3 - \overline{Y}_1 = 2.384 - 1.784 = 0.600$$

The t statistics and p-values for b_1 and b_2 can be used to test the null hypothesis that the population simple effects are equal to zero. So it is inappropriate to interpret b_1 and b_2 as tests of main effects when dummy coding of the two factors is used. These are simple effects or conditional effects and *not* main effects. However, b_3 in the simple effects parameterization does estimate

TABLE 8.5. Regression Analysis of the Caskets Study Using Simple Effect and Main Effect Parameterizations of the 2 × 2 Design

		Coeff.	SE	t	p
Model 1: Simple Effect Parameterization $R^2 = 0.138, MSE = 1.068$					
Constant	i_Y	1.784	0.089	19.952	< .001
Policy Information (X)	b_1	−0.387	0.127	−3.045	.002
Candidate Supported (W)	b_2	0.600	0.128	4.709	< .001
Information × Candidate Supported	b_3	0.360	0.178	2.024	.044
Model 2: Main Effect Parameterization $(R^2 = 0.138, MSE = 1.068$					
Constant	i_Y	1.980	0.045	44.521	< .001
Policy Information (X)	b_1	−0.207	0.089	−2.322	.021
Candidate Supported (W)	b_2	0.780	0.089	8.770	.001
Information × Candidate Supported	b_3	0.360	0.178	2.024	.044

the interaction between X and W in the ANOVA, defined as the difference between the simple effects of X at levels of W:

$$b_3 = (\overline{Y}_4 - \overline{Y}_3) - (\overline{Y}_2 - \overline{Y}_1) = (2.357 - 2.384) - (1.397 - 1.784) = 0.360$$

or the difference between the simple effects of W at levels of X:

$$b_3 = (\overline{Y}_4 - \overline{Y}_2) - (\overline{Y}_3 - \overline{Y}_1) = (2.357 - 1.397) - (2.384 - 1.784) = 0.360$$

The t statistic for b_3 in this model is the square root of the F-ratio for the interaction from the ANOVA, and they have the same p-value. These are mathematically identical tests.

Main Effects Parameterization

The main effects in a 2 × 2 ANOVA can be reproduced in a linear regression analysis through the use of a *main effects parameterization*. This is done by coding the two levels of both X and W with codes of −0.5 and 0.5 rather than dummy coding them 0 and 1. The resulting regression model estimating Y from X, W, and XW can be found in Table 8.5 as model 2. In this parameterization of the model, b_1 and b_2 now estimate the main effects of X and W, respectively. To verify, observe that indeed,

$$b_1 = \frac{(\overline{Y}_4 - \overline{Y}_3) + (\overline{Y}_2 - \overline{Y}_1)}{2} = \frac{(2.357 - 2.384) + (1.397 - 1.784)}{2} = -0.207$$

$$b_2 = \frac{(\overline{Y}_4 - \overline{Y}_2) + (\overline{Y}_3 - \overline{Y}_1)}{2} = \frac{(2.357 - 1.397) + (2.384 - 1.784)}{2} = 0.780$$

which are the same as the main effects of X and W, respectively, from the ANOVA. Furthermore, the t statistics for each of the regression coefficients are equal to the square root of the corresponding F-ratios for each effect in the 2×2 ANOVA, and the p-values for the regression coefficients are the same as the p-values from these effects in the ANOVA. Mathematically, these are identical analyses and they will produce exactly the same results.

Although coding X and W with -0.5 and 0.5 has dramatically changed b_1 and b_2 relative to when dummy codes are used, notice that b_3 is not at all affected by this change in the coding. b_3 still properly estimates the interaction between X and W, as can be seen in Table 8.5. Notice that b_3 as well as the t- and p-value are the same as in the simple effects parameterization and in the 2×2 ANOVA.

In sum, there is nothing about ANOVA that makes it especially well-suited to the analysis of the 2×2 factorial design relative to multiple regression. Factorial ANOVA is just a special case of regression analysis with categorical antecedent variables. However, care must be taken to parameterize the model correctly so that the coefficients for the variables that define the interaction can be interpreted as main effects rather than simple effects or something else.

Conducting a 2 × 2 Between-Participants Factorial ANOVA Using PROCESS

PROCESS can conduct a 2×2 factorial ANOVA while also simultaneously (and without special instruction) conducting follow-up analyses that probe the interaction through estimation and tests of the simple effects. As POLICY and KERRY are dummy coded in the data, these dummy codes first have to be converted to -0.5 and 0.5 by subtracting 0.5 from each code prior to execution of PROCESS. In SPSS, the commands which conduct the analysis are

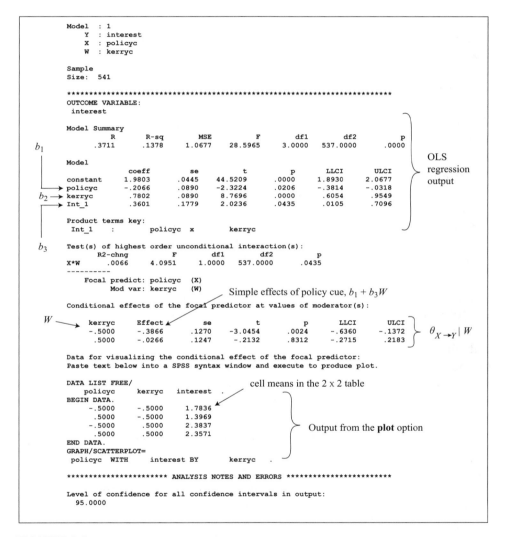

FIGURE 8.8. Output from PROCESS for a 2 × 2 ANOVA examining the main and interactive effects of candidate supported and policy information provided on interest in viewing images containing the caskets of U.S. servicemen and women killed in action.

```
compute kerryc=kerry-0.5.
compute policyc=policy-0.5.
process y=interest/x=policyc/w=kerryc/plot=1/model=1.
```

In SAS, use

```
data caskets;set caskets;kerryc=kerry-0.5;policyc=policy-0.5;run;
%process (data=caskets,y=interest,x=policyc,w=kerryc,plot=1,model=1);
```

The resulting PROCESS output from the SPSS version of this code can be found in Figure 8.8. Because the two factors are coded −0.5 and 0.5, PROCESS generates a model equivalent to the main effects parameterization in Table 8.5. Had POLICY and KERRY been kept in their 0/1 form, PROCESS would produce output equivalent to the simple effects parameterization.

In addition to the main and interaction effects, PROCESS estimates the simple effects of X at each level of W using the pick-a-point approach, which is typically the next step when a significant interaction is found in a 2×2 ANOVA. The use of the **plot** option also generates the cell means. In the section of the PROCESS output labeled "Conditional effect of X on Y at values of the moderator(s)," the simple effect of policy information is statistically significant among Bush supporters, $\theta_{X \to Y} \mid (W = -0.5) = -0.387, t(537) = -3.045, p = .002$. Bush supporters told about the policy expressed less interest in viewing the images (Mean = 1.397) than those not told about the policy (Mean = 1.784). But among Kerry supporters, those told about the policy were no different in their interest in viewing the images (Mean = 2.357), on average, than Kerry supporters not told about the policy (Mean = 2.384), $\theta_{X \to Y} \mid (W = 0.5) = -0.027, t(537) = -0.213, p = .831$. This simple effects analysis does not require splitting the file into groups and conducting separate t-tests among Bush and Kerry supporters, a strategy I discourage in part because it is lower in power than the approach implemented here. Rather, the regression-based procedure exploits information about mean differences contained in the entire model derived from estimates based on the complete sample rather than subgroups of the data.

The alternative simple effects analysis, with candidate supported as X and policy information condition as W, can also be conducted in PROCESS by reversing the roles of X and W in the PROCESS command. Covariates could also be added to the PROCESS command using the **cov** option to produce a 2×2 factorial analysis of *co*variance (ANCOVA).

8.5   Chapter Summary

In a model of the form $Y = i_Y + b_1X + b_2W + b_3XW$, whether or not additional predictors are included in the model, b_3 estimates the extent to which X's relationship with Y depends on W, or W's relationship with Y depends on X. Evidence of such dependency supports a claim of moderation or interaction—that one variable's effect is contingent on another. It makes no difference whether X or W is dichotomous or continuous, both are dichotomous, or both are continuous, as the principles of moderation analysis described in Chapter 7 generalize without modification.

Many investigators who were introduced to ANOVA before multiple regression go away from their first exposure to the principles described in the last two chapters with the mistaken belief that the concept of a "main effect" in ANOVA generalizes to the interpretation of b_1 and b_2 in any regression model that includes an interaction. As demonstrated, b_1 and b_2 are conditional effects and not main effects. These are completely different concepts, and treating a conditional effect and a main effect as synonyms in meaning and interpretation will lead to misinterpretation and misreporting of your findings or worse. The exception is when X and W are dichotomous and coded such that the resulting model does in fact yield main effects as they are defined in ANOVA.

The belief that b_1 and b_2 are main effects is only one of several commonly held misconceptions about the proper estimation and interpretation of models of the sort described in the last two chapters. In the next chapter I debunk some of those additional myths before illustrating the application of the principles of moderation analysis to models with more than one moderator.

9

Some Myths and Additional Extensions of Moderation Analysis

With a solid background in the fundamentals of moderation analysis, we can now address some of the pervasive misunderstandings about its implementation, including the role of variable scaling in model interpretation and how this has given rise to various myths, such as the need to mean-center or standardize antecedent variables prior to testing a moderation hypothesis. I debunk these myths in this chapter. I then discuss models with more than one moderator, including additive multiple moderator and moderated moderation models. I close the chapter with a discussion of how to compare conditional effects in models with two moderators.

When I teach moderation analysis in my university courses and public workshops,[1] at this point in a course I can tell that students are getting really excited but also a bit anxious. On the one hand, those following closely have begun to appreciate just how versatile multiple regression can be. On the other hand, they also begin to seriously question the legitimacy of some of the things they have done in the past, as well as the things they have read in books, journal articles, or even been told by their advisors and collaborators. Most notably, I believe their anxiety reflects their newfound appreciation that b_1 and b_2 in a regression model of the form $Y = i_1 + b_1 X + b_2 W + b_3 XW$ are not "main effects" and may estimate something totally meaningless and uninterpretable. I am certain that many students go back to old data and papers they have written to see whether they have fallen victim to their prior misunderstandings and perhaps have inappropriately interpreted an analysis they have reported. Perhaps the thought has crossed your mind too.

Some of the material I cover in this chapter is perhaps the most exciting to teach, and I hope you find it illuminating. The first section could be

---

[1]See *www.processmacro.org* for a schedule of workshops I teach on the topic of this book.

called the "mythbusting" part of the book, because it emphasizes various myths and misunderstandings about procedures that putatively one must or should follow when testing a moderation hypothesis. These myths include that one must mean-center or standardize X and W prior to estimating an interaction between them in a regression model, or that standardized regression coefficients generated automatically by OLS regression programs are meaningful and should be reported in a moderation analysis. In the second half of the chapter, I discuss models with multiple and higher-order interactions, including "moderated moderation." Better known as three-way interaction, interpreting such a model can be quite complicated, but it doesn't take too much effort to extend the principles of simple moderation to more complex models, and PROCESS makes the estimation of models with multiple interactions as well as probing such interactions quite easy.

9.1   Truths and Myths about Mean-Centering

There is much ado in the literature about the need to mean-center X and W in a model that includes their product as an antecedent variable. That is, rather than estimating a model of the form $Y = i_Y + b_1 X + b_2 W + b_3 XW + e_Y$, many believe one should instead estimate

$$Y = i_Y + b_1(X - \overline{X}) + b_2(W - \overline{W}) + b_3(X - \overline{X})(W - \overline{W}) + e_Y \qquad (9.1)$$

A simpler representation of equation 9.1 is

$$Y = i_Y + b_1 X' + b_2 W' + b_3 X' W' + e_Y \qquad (9.2)$$

where $X' = X - \overline{X}$ and $W' = W - \overline{W}$. This makes it clearer that a regression model with mean-centered focal antecedent and moderator can be thought of as an ordinary moderation model but after subtracting the sample means of X and W from X and W prior to the computation of the product of X and W.

Mean-centering has been recommended in a few highly regarded books on regression analysis (e.g., Aiken & West, 1991; Cohen et al., 2003), and several explanations have been offered for why mean-centering should be undertaken prior to computation of the product and model estimation. The explanation that seems to have resulted in the most misunderstanding is that X and W are likely to be highly correlated with XW and this will produce estimation problems caused by collinearity and result in poor or "strange" estimates of regression coefficients, large standard errors, and reduced power of the statistical test of the interaction. But this is, in large part, simply a myth. As I describe later, there are some reasons that mean-centering the focal antecedent or moderator variables can be a beneficial thing to do, which is why it has been *recommended* by some. However, it is incorrect to claim that it is *necessary*, that a failure to do so will lead one to incorrect inferences about moderation, or that the resulting regression coefficients are somehow strange or inherently uninterpretable.

One means of debunking this myth is to estimate a moderation model with and without mean-centering of X and W and compare the results. Using the emotions and climate change policies example described in Chapters 2 and 8, Table 9.1 provides the regression coefficients, standard errors, and t- and p-values for a model estimating the moderating effect of age (W) on the relationship between negative emotional responses to global climate change (X) and support for government action (Y) to mitigate global climate change. Model 1 is based on the original data, without mean-centering X and W, and model 2 comes from the same model but after first mean-centering X and W and then calculating their product. The SPSS code to estimate model 2 is

```
compute negemotc=negemot-3.558.
compute agec=age-49.536.
compute negage=negemotc*agec.
regression/dep=govact/method=enter negemotc agec negage.
```

and in SAS, the code below accomplishes the analysis:

```
data glbwarm;set glbwarm;negemotc=negemot-3.558;
    agec=age-49.536;negage=negemotc*agec;run;
proc reg data=glbwarm;model govact=negemotc agec negage;run;
```

Observe that there are some differences and some similarities between models 1 and 2 in Table 9.1. They have the same R^2 and $MS_{residual}$. Thus, they fit the data equally well. In fact, they generate exactly the same estimates of Y because these are mathematically equivalent models. Observe as well that although b_1, b_2, and their standard errors, t- and p-values are different, this is not true for b_3. In both models 1 and 2, the regression coefficients for XW are identical, as are their standard errors, t-, and p-values. Clearly, mean-centering has done nothing to the test of the interaction. If your focus is on testing whether W moderates X's effect, you'll get the same results regardless of whether or not you mean-center. The need to mean-center antecedent variables in order to test an interaction between those variables in a regression model is a myth.

TABLE 9.1. The Effects of Mean-Centering and Two Variations of Standardization on the Regression Coefficients in a Model with an Interaction

		Coeff.	SE	t	p
Model 1: Original Data $R^2 = 0.354, MSE = 1.200$					
Constant i_Y		4.335	0.330	13.154	$< .001$
Negative Emotions (X) b_1		0.147	0.085	1.729	.084
Age (W) b_2		−0.031	0.006	−5.009	$< .001$
Negative Emotions × Age (XW) b_3		0.007	0.002	4.476	$< .001$
Model 2: X and W Mean-Centered $R^2 = 0.354, MSE = 1.200$					
Constant i_Y		4.597	0.038	119.596	$< .001$
Negative Emotions (X') b_1		0.501	0.025	19.810	$< .001$
Age (W') b_2		−0.005	0.002	−2.237	.026
Negative Emotions × Age ($X'W'$) b_3		0.007	0.002	4.476	$< .001$
Model 3: Standardized Variant 1 $R^2 = 0.354, MSE = 0.648$					
Constant i_{Z_Y}		0.007	0.028	0.263	.792
Negative Emotions (Z_X) b_1		0.562	0.028	19.810	$< .001$
Age (Z_W) b_2		−0.063	0.028	−2.237	.026
Negative Emotions × Age ($Z_X Z_W$) b_3		0.131	0.029	4.476	$< .001$
Model 4: Standardized Variant 2 $R^2 = 0.354, MSE = 0.648$					
Constant i_{Z_Y}		0.000	0.028	0.000	1.000
Negative Emotions (Z_X) b_1		0.165	0.096	1.927	.084
Age (Z_W) b_2		−0.368	0.073	−5.009	$< .001$
Negative Emotions × Age (Z_{XW}) b_3		0.511	0.114	4.476	$< .001$

The Effect of Mean-Centering on Multicollinearity and the Standard Error of b_3

This misplaced concern about the potential damage to estimation and inference caused by the strong intercorrelation between X, W, and XW is entirely understandable given what we know about the determinants of the standard error of a regression coefficient. In a multiple regression model estimating a consequent variable Y, the standard error for antecedent variable j in that model is

$$se_{b_j} = \sqrt{\frac{1}{1 - R_j^2}} \sqrt{\frac{MS_{residual}}{df_{residual}(s_j^2)}} \tag{9.3}$$

where R_j^2 is the squared multiple correlation when estimating antecedent variable j from the other antecedent variables in the model, s_j^2 is the variance of antecedent j, and $MS_{residual}$ and $df_{residual}$ are the mean squared residual and residual degrees of freedom for the model of Y, respectively (see, e.g., Darlington & Hayes, 2017, p. 107).

In equation 9.3, R_j^2 quantifies the proportion of the variance in antecedent variable j that is explained by the other antecedent variables in the model. Thus, $1 - R_j^2$ is the proportion of the variance in antecedent j unexplained by the other antecedent variables in the regression model. This proportion is known as variable j's *tolerance*. The inverse of a variable's tolerance, $1/(1 - R_j^2)$, is its *variance inflation factor*, or *VIF*. It quantifies how much antecedent variable j's standard error is influenced by its correlation with the other antecedent variables in the model. How a variable's tolerance, and therefore its *VIF*, enters into the standard error is more easily seen by reexpressing equation 9.3 in an equivalent form:

$$se_{b_j} = \sqrt{\frac{MS_{residual} VIF_j}{df_{residual}(s_j^2)}} \tag{9.4}$$

An important insight to take away from equations 9.3 and 9.4 is that the more strongly correlated antecedent variable j is with the other antecedent variables (i.e., the smaller its tolerance, and the larger its *VIF*), the larger is its standard error. That is, the more of the variance in variable j that is explained by the other antecedent variables in the model, the less stable b_j is over repeated sampling. All other things being equal, the larger a statistic's standard error, the lower the power of the hypothesis test of its corresponding parameter, and the wider an interval estimate for the parameter will be. Therefore, anything that can be done to reduce the correlation between variable j and the other antecedent variables in the model would seem to be a good thing.

TABLE 9.2. Correlations, Tolerances (Tol.), and Variance Inflation Factors (*VIF*) before and after Mean-Centering or Standardization in the Climate Change Moderation Analysis

Original Data	X	W	XW	Variance	*Tol.*	*VIF*
Negative Emotions (X)	1.000			2.336	0.087	11.473
Age (W)	−.057	1.000		266.694	0.148	6.776
Neg. Emot. × Age (XW)	.766	.549	1.000	9489.221	0.061	16.357

After Mean-Centering	X'	W'	$X'W'$	Variance	*Tol.*	*VIF*
Negative Emotions (X')	1.000			2.336	0.988	1.012
Age (W')	−.057	1.000		266.694	0.997	1.003
Neg. Emot. × Age ($X'W'$)	.092	−.015	1.000	585.166	0.991	1.009

After Standardization	Z_X	Z_W	$Z_X Z_W$	Variance	*Tol.*	*VIF*
Negative Emotions (Z_X)	1.000			1.000	0.988	1.012
Age (Z_W)	−.057	1.000		1.000	0.997	1.003
Neg. Emot. × Age ($Z_X Z_W$)	.092	−.015	1.000	0.969	0.991	1.009

As can be seen in Table 9.2, this concern about collinearity on the surface seems justified. The correlation between negative emotional responses (X) and age (W) is near zero, but observe the rather large correlation ($r = 0.766$) between the product of negative emotional responses and age (XW) and negative emotions (X). Furthermore, most of the variance in the product is accounted for by X and W, as its tolerance is very small (0.061) and its variance inflation factor is massive (16.357). According to equations 9.3 and 9.4, if this correlation between XW and X could be reduced in some way (which would thereby increase the tolerance of XW and decrease its variance inflation factor), then the standard error of b_3 should decrease, right?

It is not a myth that mean-centering X and W prior to computing their product will reduce this correlation. Table 9.2 displays the correlations, tolerances, and variance inflation factors after mean-centering X and W. Observe that this seems to have made the problem go away entirely. The correlation between XW and X has shrunk considerably ($r = 0.092$), and the tolerance and variance inflation factors are now near 1. Certainly, this must be good.

It turns out, however, that this does not matter one bit, for something else has changed as a result of mean-centering that completely counteracts the effect of reduced collinearity. Observe that the variance for XW has also changed. The variance of an antecedent variable figures into its standard error, and because the variance is in the denominator of the standard error formula, when it goes down, the standard error of its regression coefficient goes up. This counteracting effect of reduced variance relative to collinearity can be best seen by reexpressing equations 9.3 and 9.4 as

$$se_{b_j} = \sqrt{\frac{VIF_j}{s_j^2}} \sqrt{\frac{MS_{residual}}{df_{residual}}}$$

Because mean-centering does not change $MS_{residual}$ or $df_{residual}$ but it does change s_j^2 and VIF_j, any change in the standard error of a regression coefficient resulting from mean-centering is determined by its effect on variances and tolerances (Sheih, 2011). By mean-centering, the variance inflation factor for XW has been reduced by a factor of $16.357/1.009 = 16.21$. But the variance of XW has also been reduced by this same factor: $9489.221/585.166 = 16.21$. As a result, the standard error of XW is completely unaffected by mean-centering X and W prior to computation of the product and estimation of the model. It is a myth that one must mean-center X and W because of the problems produced by collinearity. This collinearity does not cause a problem in the test for the interaction, so there is no problem to solve by mean-centering.

I stated earlier that the need to mean-center is "for the most part" a myth. My condition on this claim stems from the fact that there can be some circumstances in which collinearity could appear to produce estimation problems or might actually do so. For example, if a model includes many antecedent variables that are highly correlated and also includes a product involving several of those antecedents (i.e., includes at least a couple of interactions), this can produce a tolerance that exceeds the minimum tolerance allowed by certain regression programs. For instance, SPSS is programmed to remove variables from a model automatically if the tolerance for any variable is smaller than some default preset (e.g., 0.000001). This default can easily be overriden simply by changing it in the regression command line. Whether doing so then results in problems with estimation will be specific to the data one is analyzing. If a model won't estimate, mean-centering might make it estimable by your regression program. But in my experience, this situation is fairly rare. In most models you are likely to estimate involving one or two interactions, you will not find collinearity produces any concerns and you should trust whatever results your regression program gives you regardless of whether or not you mean-center.

The Effect of Mean-Centering on b_1, b_2, and Their Standard Errors

A second explanation given for why mean-centering is preferred is that it makes b_1 and b_2, the regression coefficients for X and W, more meaningful. This is generally true and thus not a myth, although it is not necessarily true in all circumstances. Recall that in a model of the form $Y = i_Y + b_1X + b_2W + b_3XW$, b_1 estimates the difference in Y between two cases that differ by one unit on X when $W = 0$, and b_2 estimates the difference in Y between two cases that differ by one unit on W when $X = 0$. We saw in section 7.2 that b_1 and b_2 will be dependent on how X and W are scaled. If $W = 0$ is not meaningful in the measurement system for W, then b_1 and its test of significance are meaningless and have no substantive interpretation. But if $W = 0$ is meaningful, then so too is b_1 and its test of significance. The same is true for b_2.

Mean-centering X and W prior to computation of the product and estimation of the model will produce b_1 and b_2 that are always meaningful, rather than meaningful only when X and/or W are meaningful when equal to zero. When X and W are mean-centered and the coefficients in equations 9.1 or 9.2 estimated, b_1 estimates the difference in Y between two cases that differ by one unit on X among cases that are *average* on W. Similarly, b_2 estimates the difference in Y between two cases that differ by one unit on W among cases that are *average* on X. These will always estimate conditional effects of X on Y within the range of the data, and they can always be interpreted.

The difference between b_1 and b_2 and their standard errors in models 1 (original data) and 2 (mean-centered) has nothing whatsoever to do with the reduction in collinearity that results when X and W are mean-centered. Rather, they differ because they estimate different effects—the effects of X and W among people who are average on the other variable rather than who are at zero on the other variable. Naturally, because these estimate different effects, their standard errors, t-, and p-values are different.

Indeed, one need not mean-center to estimate these conditional effects. One could use the coefficients from the model based on uncentered data to estimate the conditional effect of X when $W = \overline{W}$. Simply use b_1 and b_3 from the uncentered model and use $\overline{W}$ for W in equation 7.3. That is,

$$\theta_{X \to Y} \mid (W = \overline{W}) = b_1 + b_3\overline{W} = 0.147 + 0.007(49.536) = 0.501$$

which is exactly equal to b_1 from model 2 based on mean-centered X and W. Even the standard error for b_1 in the centered solution could be derived from the uncentered solution. Using equation 7.13, the estimated standard error for $\theta_{X \to Y} \mid (W = \overline{W})$ in terms of regression coefficients and standard errors from the uncentered solution is

$$
\begin{aligned}
se_{\theta_{X \to Y} \mid (W = \overline{W})} \ &= \ \sqrt{se_{b_1}^2 + (2\overline{W})COV_{b_1 b_3} + \overline{W}^2 se_{b_3}^2} \\
&= \ \sqrt{0.085^2 + (2)(49.536)(0.000003) + (49.536)^2 0.002^2} \\
&= \ 0.025
\end{aligned}
$$

where 0.085 is the standard error for b_1, 0.002 is the standard error for b_3, 0.000003 is the covariance between b_1 and b_3, and $\overline{W} = 49.536$ is used for W. Thus, the standard errors that result after mean-centering are no more or less accurate than those produced when estimating the model using the original, uncentered forms of X and W. The changes in b_1, b_2, and their standard errors have nothing to do with reduction in collinearity that results when mean-centering is employed.[2]

Another reason you might choose to mean-center X and W prior to estimating a model including their product is to protect your reader from misinterpreting something that is not interpretable. Suppose you report the results of a regression analysis in a table in a research article you have published, and you didn't mean-center X or W prior to computing XW and doing the analysis. If you have been following along, you would know that b_1 or b_2 may not be meaningful, and you would know not to interpret one or the other or both if not. But your reader may not have the same understanding as you. He or she may interpret your meaningless and uninterpretable b_1 or b_2 as if they quantify something meaningful and interpretable, perhaps thinking of them as "main effects," the average effect of X or W, or something else they are not. If you reported b_1 and b_2 following mean-centering, then you know you would be reporting something that others could interpret as meaningful. Of course, this doesn't guarantee your readers will interpret it *correctly*. Some of them may have other misunderstandings about how to properly interpret regression coefficients in a model that includes a product of variables. You can't protect a reader from his or her own ignorance. But you can at least make it easier on your reader by not reporting something that is meaningless.

In this section, I have debunked the myth that mean-centering of X and W is necessary prior to the estimation of a model with an interaction

---

[2]Because the mean of age is large and the regression coefficients and standard errors for b_1 and b_3 are small, substantial rounding error is produced in hand computations here unless they are done to a great degree of precision. Though not apparent from what is printed here, I did all these hand computations to many decimal places of resolution. You will get slightly different values if you attempt to verify these computations carrying them out to only three decimal places of accuracy.

between X and W. I cannot take credit for this, however, as this myth and its corollaries have been repeatedly debunked in the methodology literature yet doggedly persist in spite of these debunkings (see, e.g., Cronbach, 1987; Echambadi & Hess, 2007; Edwards, 2009; Friedrich, 1982; Hayes et al., 2012; Irwin & McClelland, 2001; Kam & Franzese, 2007; Kromrey & Foster-Johnson, 1998; Sheih, 2011; Whisman & McClelland, 2005). To be sure, there are interpretational advantages associated with mean-centering, but the differences in model coefficients and standard errors have nothing to do with reduced collinearity that results from mean-centering.

The bottom line is this: If you are going to mean-center, go ahead and do so. The choice is up to you. But don't say that you are doing so "to reduce the problems produced by collinearity" (I am paraphrasing what is often said in one form or another by those who justify this practice.) If you say this, you are just perpetuating a myth. Although mean-centering does reduce collinearity, this has no consequence on the estimation accuracy, hypothesis tests, or standard errors of regression coefficients in most circumstances you are likely to encounter. Instead, say that you are centering to render b_1 and b_2 interpretable and their hypothesis tests meaningful. But only say this if they otherwise would not be meaningful. And if you aren't reporting b_1 and b_2 to the reader, then you aren't even benefiting from this reason to mean-center. In that case, there really isn't much point to centering at all.

The Centering Option in PROCESS

If you choose to center the focal antecedent and moderator, you can do so manually using the syntax available in your chosen software, as on page 305. Alternatively, you can have PROCESS do the centering for you. Adding **center=1** to the command line tells PROCESS to center any variable in a model that is used to construct a product of variables for estimation of a moderated effect. When this option is used, the output should be interpreted as if those variables used to form a product had been centered. PROCESS will provide information at the bottom which variables in the analysis were centered prior to model estimation. When using this option in conjunction with **wmodval**, the values of the moderator provided should be based on the mean-centered metric rather than the original metric of measurement. For instance, if the mean of your moderator W is 10, you use the centering option in PROCESS, and you seek the conditional effect of X on Y when W is 8 and 14, then you should use **modval=-2, 4**, because 8 and 14 are two points below and four points above the mean of 10, respectively.

9.2   The Estimation and Interpretation of Standardized Regression Coefficients in a Moderation Analysis

Mean-centering does nothing to change the scaling of regression coefficients. Whether or not mean-centering is used when estimating a model of the form $\hat{Y} = i_Y + b_1 X + b_2 W + b_3 XW$, b_1, b_2, and b_3 are interpreted with respect to the measured metrics of X, W, and Y (i.e., in *unstandardized* form). Although I generally prefer to report and interpret regression analyses based on unstandardized coefficients, it is possible to generate regression coefficients that are analogous to standardized regression coefficients in regression models without a product term as a predictor. However, one must be careful when doing so. There are two variants of standardization one can use yielding b_1, b_2, and b_3 that can be interpreted as standardized regression coefficients. But one of these should *never* be used or interpreted. In this section, I discuss these two variants.

Throughout this section, I also debunk a version of the mean-centering myth with respect to the need to standardize X and W prior to calculating their product when testing a moderation hypothesis. That is, some researchers mistakenly believe that such standardization is required for the same reasons X and W should be mean-centered; that doing so reduces collinearity, produces more accurate estimates of the variables' effects, and yields a hypothesis test for the interaction that is higher in power. I have also heard people claim that they standardize prior to estimation of the model because it facilitates the interpretation or probing of the interaction. Like with mean-centering, the need to standardize X and W is a myth, and doing so does nothing to facilitate the probing or interpretation of an interaction.

Variant 1

In the first variant of standardization, X and W are standardized to produce Z_X and Z_W. These standardized versions of X and W are then multiplied to produce $Z_X Z_W$. Then standardized Y, Z_Y, is estimated in a multiple regression model from Z_X, Z_W, and $Z_X Z_W$ (and any covariates if desired, which may be but need not be standardized):

$$Z_Y = i_{Z_Y} + b_1 Z_X + b_2 Z_W + b_3 Z_X Z_W + e_{Z_Y} \tag{9.5}$$

Using the emotions and climate change policies as an example, the SPSS code to estimate the moderating effect of age (W) on the relationship between negative emotional reactions to climate change (X) and support for government action to mitigate its effects (Y) is

```
descriptives variables = negemot age govact/save.
compute znegzage = znegemot*zage.
regression/dep=zgovact/method=enter znegemot zage znegzage.
```

In this code, the **save** option in the **descriptives** command generates three new variables in the dataset that are the standardized versions of X, W, and Y. The original variable names are retained by SPSS but with "Z" tacked onto the beginning. In SAS, the corresponding code is

```
proc stdize data=glbwarm out=glbwarmz;var negemot age govact;run;
data glbwarmz;set glbwarmz;znegzage=negemot*age;run;
proc reg data=glbwarmz;model govact = negemot age znegzage;run;
```

When looking at a regression output, i_Y, b_1, b_2, and b_3 will be the coefficients listed wherever *unstandardized* regression coefficients are ordinarily provided (e.g., in SPSS, in the column labeled "Unstandardized Coefficients," or in the column labeled "Parameter Estimate" in SAS). Do not look for these coefficients in any section of the output labeled "Standardized regression coefficients" or something of the sort. That is not where to find them. As we will see soon, the coefficients in the column labeled as standardized should not be interpreted.

The model summary, standardized regression coefficients, and standard errors can be found in Table 9.1, model 3. b_1 is interpreted as the estimated difference in *standard deviations* of Y between two cases that differ by *one standard deviation* on X but are average on W. The "but are average on W" part of the interpretation is due to the fact that b_1 estimates the effect of X on Y when $Z_W = 0$. But $Z_W = 0$ when $W = \overline{W}$. b_2 is similarly interpreted as the estimated difference in *standard deviations* of Y between two cases that differ by *one standard deviation* on W but are average on X, because $Z_X = 0$ when $Z = \overline{Z}$. Finally, b_3 quantifies how much the estimated difference in *standard deviations* of Y between two cases that differ by *one standard deviation* on X changes as W changes by *one standard deviation*.

Observe that b_1 and b_2 are different relative to when X and W are mean-centered (Table 9.1, model 2) or kept in their original metric (Table 9.1, model 1). This is because standardization has changed the metrics of X, W, and Y. b_1 and b_2 in model 2 estimate the effect of X and W on Y when the other variable is set to the sample mean. However, after standardization, the metric of difference on X and W has changed from one unit to one *standard deviation*. So two cases that differ by one standard deviation in negative emotional responses to climate change but that are average in age (as defined by the sample mean in these data) are estimated to differ by $b_1 = 0.562$ standard deviations in support for government action. And two cases that differ by one standard deviation in age but are average in the negative emotions are estimated to differ by $b_2 = -0.063$ standard deviations in support for government action (with the negative sign meaning the older person expresses less support for government action). Because they test the same hypothesis, the t- and p-values for b_1 and b_2 are the same in standardization variant 1 as they are in the version of the model using mean-centered W and X. In both models they test the null hypothesis that X's effect on Y is zero when $W = \overline{W}$ and W's effect on Y is zero when $X = \overline{X}$.

Importantly, notice from Table 9.1 that although the regression coefficient for b_3 is different compared to when the original data or mean-centered data are used in the model, the t statistic and p-values for standardized b_3 are the same. So standardization of X and W has no effect on the test of the interaction, contrary to the myth that standardization is necessary to properly test a moderation hypothesis. As with b_1 and b_2, standardization has changed the metric of difference for X and W, which changes the interpretation of b_3 slightly. We can say that the estimated difference in support for government action between two cases that differ by one standard deviation in negative emotions increases by 0.131 standard deviations as age increases by one standard deviation.

To implement variant 1, I recommend the use of PROCESS rather than SPSS's regression routine or SAS PROC REG because of the options it provides for easily probing the interaction. PROCESS has no option for printing standardized regression coefficients in the output. Instead, simply use the standardized versions of X, W, and Y in a properly formatted PROCESS command rather than the unstandardized versions of X, W, and Y. PROCESS will generate $Z_X Z_W$ for you. The interaction can be probed using either the pick-a-point approach or the Johnson–Neyman technique. Conditional effects of X or regions of significance will be generated for various values of Z_W. If using the **wmodval** option in PROCESS, make sure you specify a value of W in the metric of Z_W rather than W.

Variant 2

Variant 2 is like variant 1 except that the order of standardization and multiplication is reversed. Whereas in variant 1, where X and W are both standardized prior to calculating their product $Z_X Z_W$, in variant 2, X and W are first multiplied to produce XW which is then standardized to produce Z_{XW}. This standardized product Z_{XW} is then included as a predictor of Z_Y along with Z_X and Z_W:

$$Z_Y = i_{Z_Y} + b_1 Z_X + b_2 Z_W + b_3 Z_{XW} + e_{Z_Y} \tag{9.6}$$

Although one could implement variant 2 by standardizing Y, X, W, and XW and then estimating the model in the usual way, it turns out that this is not necessary. The regression coefficients for variant 2 are produced by any OLS regression program that provides standardized regression coefficients in the output. In SPSS, for instance, the regression coefficients in equation 9.6 are found in the regression coefficient summary when estimating $Y = i_Y + b_1 X + b_2 W + b_3 XW$ under the column labeled "Standardized Coefficients: Beta" and are printed whether you want them or not any time you conduct a regression analysis. They can be generated by SAS using the **/stb** option after the model command in PROC REG and will be found under the label "Standardized Estimate."

There is a major problem with this variant that makes it impossible to ever recommend. Although this variant will give you a legitimate test of the interaction (notice in Table 9.1 that the t- and p-values for b_3 are the same as they are for all other methods described in this chapter), this approach to standardization should not be used, because b_1, b_2, and b_3 are meaningless. I bring this variation to your attention not so that you will use it, but to make an important point. Because the regression coefficients in equation 9.6 are equivalent to the standardized regression coefficients generated by an OLS regression program automatically when estimating a model of the form $Y = i_Y + b_1 X + b_2 W + b_3 XW$, this means such standardized regression coefficients generated by your OLS regression program *should never be interpreted, they should never be reported, and you should never probe an interaction using these regression coefficients.* The only thing meaningful about these coefficients is their sign. You can substitute any nonsense symbol for the actual value of the regression coefficients (e.g., happy faces, suns and moons, kitty cats, stop signs) and these will convey just as much information to your reader about your model. So never interpret or report the standardized regression coefficients given to you automatically by an OLS regression program such as SPSS or SAS when the model includes a product of focal antecedent X and moderator W. This is true regardless of whether you have analyzed the original data, mean-centered, or standardized the data manually on your own. Rather, always base your interpretation on the coefficients reported in your regression program as unstandardized, which actually will be standardized regression coefficients if you followed the procedure described for variant 1.

The problem with variant 2 can be illustrated by reconsidering the reason for including XW as an antecedent variable in a regression model. In a model of the form $Y = i_Y + b_1 X + b_2 W$, X's effect on Y is constrained to be independent of W, which is the opposite of what is desired when interest is in testing the moderation of X's effect on Y by W. The model that allows X's effect to depend linearly on W was formed by adding XW as a antecedent variable to this model, resulting in $Y = i_Y + b_1X + b_2W + b_3XW$. This model can be rewritten in the mathematically identical form $Y = i_Y + (b_1 + b_3W)X + b_2W$, which clearly illustrates how X's effect is a linear function of W.

When X and W are standardized and then multiplied to produce Z_XZ_W, the model for variant 1 (equation 9.5) can be rewritten as

$$Z_Y = i_{Z_Y} + (b_1 + b_3Z_W)Z_X + b_2Z_W + e_{Z_Y}$$

In this form, it is clear that X's effect is conditional on W. That is,

$$\theta_{Z_X \to Z_Y} = b_1 + b_3Z_W \qquad (9.7)$$

Thus, all the rules for the computation of conditional effects and the methods for probing an interaction described in Chapters 7 and 8 generalize to models with standardized X and W.

However, the model for variant 2 (equation 9.6) *cannot* be rewritten in a form that allows X's effect to be rewritten as a linear function of W because $Z_{XW} \neq Z_XZ_W$. The implication is that b_1, b_2, and b_3 in equation 9.6 have none of the interpretational properties described in Chapters 7 and 8. The conditional effect of X cannot be estimated using equation 9.7, and an interaction cannot be probed or plotted using the regression coefficients from variant 2.

Whether you choose to report regression coefficients from a moderation model in unstandardized or standardized form is your choice to make.[3] Standardization of X and W prior to estimation of their product yields estimates of each variable's effect on Y gauged in terms of differences between cases that differ by one standard deviation on X or W rather than simply "one unit" in the original metric of measurement. Although standardization does reduce collinearity (as demonstrated in Table 9.2), this has no effect on the test of interaction. The *need* to standardize X and W prior to computation of the product is a myth. Finally, never use variant 2, and never interpret or report the regression coefficients given to you automatically by your regression analysis program that are listed as standardized when including a product of predictors in the model. These are meaningless regardless of which variant you use.

Does Standardization Facilitate the Probing of an Interaction?

Two other reasons I have heard given for why standardization is a good idea is that it facilitates the interpretation of an interaction and makes it

---

[3]Though for reasons discussed in section 2.2, I strongly discourage the reporting of standardized regression coefficients for dichotomous antecedent variables.

easier to probe. In my opinion, standardization does nothing to make an interaction easier to interpret. An interaction is just as easy to interpret when X and W are left in their original metric as it is when standardized. This claim is, I believe, misguided.

If implementing the pick-a-point approach by hand, I suppose there is a grain of truth to the latter claim. There is always the potential for rounding error propagating through computations when doing computations by hand. The more noninteger numbers you can remove from the computation, the less of a problem rounding error will be, and the easier it is to do the computations with a calculator. When W is continuous and standardized and you are interested in estimating the conditional effect of X when $W = \overline{W} - 1SD$, $\overline{W}$, and $\overline{W} + 1SD$, as many researchers do, the values of W at which the conditional effect of X is estimated become $Z_W = -1, 0,$ and 1. Thus, the conditional effects of X for values of W corresponding to "low," "moderate," and "high" are (from equations 7.3 or 9.7) $b_1 - b_3$, b_1, and $b_1 + b_3$, respectively. The elimination of nonintenger values of the moderator makes these hand computations more accurate and easier to do.

But the biggest computational gains are produced through the simplification of the standard error for the conditional effect of X, as some of the terms in equation 7.13 disappear and fewer noninteger numbers or squares are required:

$$se_{\theta_{Z_X \to Z_Y | (Z_W = -1)}} = \sqrt{se_{b_1}^2 - 2COV_{b_1 b_3} + se_{b_3}^2}$$

$$se_{\theta_{Z_X \to Z_Y | (Z_W = 0)}} = \sqrt{se_{b_1}^2}$$

$$se_{\theta_{Z_X \to Z_Y | (Z_W = 1)}} = \sqrt{se_{b_1}^2 + 2COV_{b_1 b_3} + se_{b_3}^2}$$

Although these computations are indeed somewhat less tedious and susceptible to error when conducted by hand, this doesn't seem like a real advantage of standardization given that there is no reason to ever do these computations by hand in the first place. The regression centering method (see page 250) can be used to implement the pick-a-point approach by computer, and PROCESS can do all these computations for you without you having to even think much about the mathematics behind them. Thus, don't standardize X and W just because you think doing so makes it easier to probe the interaction. In this age of computers, it does not.

9.3 A Caution on Manual Centering and Standardization

There may be occasions in which you choose to mean-center or standardize one or more variables prior to analysis. As discussed in section 9.1, PROCESS has an option for mean-centering variables used to form products when testing a moderation hypothesis, though it has no options for standardizing or producing standardized regression coefficients. If you choose to mean-center or standardize the data on your own prior to estimating a model, be aware of the dangers of doing so if your program uses listwise deletion of missing data, as most regression programs (including PROCESS) do by default.

To understand the danger, consider a hypothetical example. You plan on estimating a moderation model and have a sample of 20 people measured on consequent Y, focal antecedent variable X, and moderator W. All 20 cases have data on Y, but 2 cases are missing data on X, and another 3 are missing on W, but those three cases do have data on X. Suppose you decide you want to standardize X, W, and Y prior to estimating the model, so you tell your program to construct standardized versions of each of these variables, using the means and standard deviations of the cases not missing on the variable being standardized. After the standardization is complete, you will have 20 values of Z_Y, 18 values of Z_X, and 17 values of Z_W. The means of each of these variables will be zero, and they will each have a standard deviation of one, as standardized variables should.

But suppose you then give these standardized variables to PROCESS using model 1 to estimate a simple moderation model. PROCESS uses listwise deletion, like almost all regression programs do, so the analysis it conducts will be based on only the 15 cases that contain no missing data on any variable in the analysis. That is, the 5 cases missing on either Z_X or Z_W will be kicked out of the analysis. Now you can see the danger. The means and standard deviations of Z_Y, Z_X, and Z_W for the 15 cases in the analysis are not likely to be zero and one like when they were originally standardized. This is because your standardized variables were each constructed using more than the 15 cases that remain after listwise deletion. So the regression coefficients that PROCESS generates will not be standardized regression coefficients, because you are not actually giving PROCESS variables that are in standardized form.

This same danger applies to centering, as standardization is just centering with an additional rescaling of the variable to have a standard deviation of one. This danger is not unique to analyses done with PROCESS. Rather, it is a problem anytime you manually standardize or mean-center and then give the resulting data to any statistical procedure that uses listwise deletion of missing data. So if you are going to manually standardize or mean-center, make sure that you construct the standardized or mean-centered variables using only the cases that will be left after your statistical procedure boots out cases missing on any of the variables in the analysis.

9.4   More Than One Moderator

Every example of moderation analysis thus far has included a single moderator of a single focal antecedent variable's effect—the simple moderation model. Not infrequently, investigators propose or test hypotheses involving more than one moderator of a variable's effect. In this section, I describe a multiple moderation model in which two variables moderate a single focal antecedent's effect. I also touch upon *moderated moderation*, in which the moderation of one variable's effect by another is itself moderated. Also known as *three-way interaction*, moderated moderation hypotheses are advanced and tested quite regularly in the social sciences.

Although the principles of moderation analysis discussed thus far apply regardless of how many moderators are in a model, interpretation and probing of interactions can become complicated quite rapidly. Space precludes a thorough exposition of this topic, as doing so would require several chapters. But PROCESS has the ability to estimate the kinds of models described in this section, and it implements all the necessary computations for probing interactions and generating data needed to visualize more complex models such as these without you having to think much at all about the mathematics behind them.

Additive Multiple Moderation

Consider a multiple linear regression model with three antecedent variables X, W, and Z:

$$Y = i_Y + b_1 X + b_2 W + b_3 Z + e_Y \qquad (9.8)$$

While a very useful model for assessing the partial association between X and Y controlling for W and Z, the limitation that the effect of X is constrained to be unconditional on both W and Z should be acknowledged. That is, X's effect is quantified holding constant W and Z, such that regardless of which values of W and Z you choose, X's effect on Y is b_1. For instance, suppose X is negative emotional responses to climate change, W and Z are sex and age, respectively, and Y is support for government actions to mitigate climate change. In this model, the influence of negative emotions on support for government action is constrained to be the same for men and women and people of all ages. This constraint is simple enough to demonstrate for yourself using the same procedure described in section 7.1. Choose any arbitrary values of i_Y, b_1, b_2, b_3, as well as W an Z, and you will see that *regardless* of which values of W and Z you substitute into equation 9.8, two hypothetical cases that differ by one unit on X are estimated to differ by b_1 units on Y.

Chapters 7 and 8 illustrated how this constraint can be relaxed by letting X's effect be a function of another variable in the model. But X's effect could also be a function of more than one variable simultaneously, such as both W and Z. Such a model is depicted in the form of a conceptual diagram in Figure 9.1, panel A. Recall from those prior chapters that to do so, b_1 was replaced with a linear function of W to produce the simple moderation model. Instead, we could replace it with a function of both W and Z, as in

$$Y = i_Y + f(W, Z)X + b_2W + b_3Z + e_Y \tag{9.9}$$

For example, consider the additive linear function

$$f(W, Z) = b_1 + b_4W + b_5Z$$

which, when substituted into equation 9.9, yields

$$Y = i_Y + (b_1 + b_4W + b_5Z)X + b_2W + b_3Z + e_Y \tag{9.10}$$

Expanding equation 9.10 by distributing X among all terms in the parentheses yields

$$Y = i_Y + b_1X + b_2W + b_3Z + b_4XW + b_5XZ + e_Y \tag{9.11}$$

where XW and XZ are two variables formed as the product of X and W and X and Z, respectively. This model is represented in the form of a statistical diagram in Figure 9.1, panel B. In this model, X's effect on Y is estimated as an additive linear function of W and Z. Thus, X's effect is conditional on both W and Z. Expressed symbolically, equations 9.10 and 9.11 can be written in equivalent form as

$$Y = i_Y + \theta_{X \to Y}X + b_2W + b_3Z + e_Y$$

where $\theta_{X \to Y}$ is the conditional effect of X on Y, defined as

$$\theta_{X \to Y} = b_1 + b_4W + b_5Z \tag{9.12}$$

Equation 9.12 makes it apparent that b_1 in equation 9.11 estimates the conditional effect of X on Y when both W and Z are zero. Thus, b_1 is not a "main effect," in that it estimates X's effect only when both W and Z are

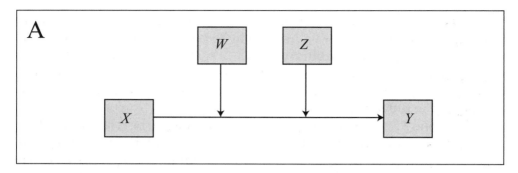

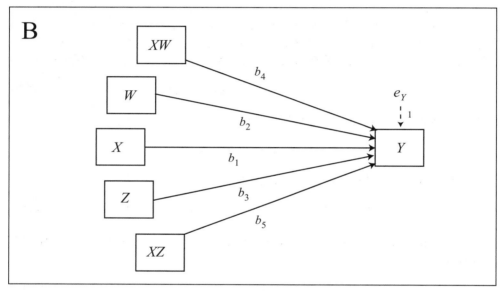

FIGURE 9.1. An additive multiple moderation model depicted as a conceptual (panel A) and a statistical diagram (panel B).

zero rather than X's effect "on average." Regression coefficients b_4 and b_5 determine how much X's effect is contingent on W and Z, respectively. More specifically, b_4 quantifies how much the conditional effect of X on Y changes as W changes by one unit, holding Z constant, and b_5 estimates how much the conditional effect of X on Y changes as Z changes by one unit, holding W constant. Tests of significance or confidence intervals based on b_4 and b_5 answer the question as to whether W moderates X's effect and whether Z moderates X's effect, respectively.

Although not obvious, b_2 and b_3 also estimate conditional effects just as does b_1. b_2 estimates the conditional effect of W on Y when X is zero while holding Z constant, and b_3 estimates the conditional effect of W on

Y when X is zero while holding W constant. These are not equivalent to main effects in ANOVA and should not be interpreted as if they are.

I illustrate the estimation and interpretation of such a model using the climate change data by regressing support for government action (Y) on negative emotions about climate change (X), sex (W), age (Z), the product of negative emotions and sex (XW), and the product of negative emotions and age (XZ). I also include positive emotions (C_1) and political ideology (C_2) as covariates. This is easy enough to do in SPSS or SAS's regression procedures merely by constructing the products prior to estimating. But if there are only two moderators of a single focal antecedent variable's effect, as is the case here, PROCESS does all the necessary computations for you. The SPSS version of the command is

```
process y=govact/x=negemot/w=sex/z=age/cov=posemot ideology/model=2/
    plot=1/zmodval=30,50,70.
```

and in SAS, use

```
%process (data=glbwarm,y=govact,x=negemot,w=sex,z=age,cov=posemot
    ideology,plot=1,model=2,zmodval=30 50 70);
```

The resulting output can be found in Figure 9.2. Specifying **model=2** requests the estimation of a moderation model with X as focal antecedent and W and Z as additive moderators of X's effect on Y (see the model templates in Appendix A). PROCESS constructs the necessary products, estimates the model, and generates conditional effects of X on Y for various values of W and Z. Using the **zmodval** option, this command also asks PROCESS to probe the interaction by estimating the conditional effect of X on Y using ages of 30, 50, and 70. This option works just like the **wmodval** option introduced in section 8.2, but because age is specified as Z in this model, the option used is **zmodval** rather than **wmodval**. If this option were not used, PROCESS would choose the 16th, 50th, and 84th percentiles of the distribution of age. If **moments=1** were used instead, ages corresponding to a standard deviation below the mean, the mean, and a standard deviation above the mean would be used.

From the PROCESS output, the best fitting OLS regression model is

$$\hat{Y} = 5.272 + 0.093X - 0.742W - 0.018Z + 0.205XW + 0.005XZ - 0.024C_1 - 0.207C_2 \tag{9.13}$$

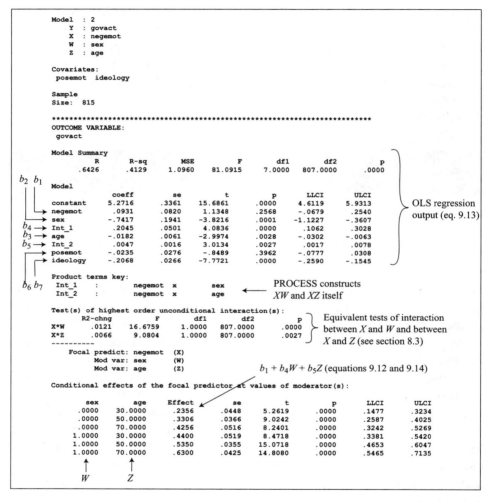

FIGURE 9.2. Output from the PROCESS procedure examining the moderation of the effect of negative emotions about climate change on support for government action by sex and age.

(continued)

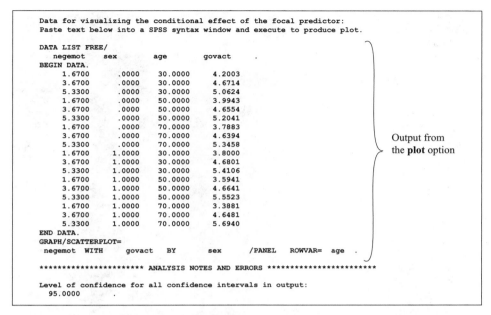

```
Data for visualizing the conditional effect of the focal predictor:
Paste text below into a SPSS syntax window and execute to produce plot.

DATA LIST FREE/
     negemot      sex          age          govact       .
BEGIN DATA.
       1.6700      .0000     30.0000        4.2003
       3.6700      .0000     30.0000        4.6714
       5.3300      .0000     30.0000        5.0624
       1.6700      .0000     50.0000        3.9943
       3.6700      .0000     50.0000        4.6554
       5.3300      .0000     50.0000        5.2041
       1.6700      .0000     70.0000        3.7883
       3.6700      .0000     70.0000        4.6394
       5.3300      .0000     70.0000        5.3458
       1.6700     1.0000     30.0000        3.8000
       3.6700     1.0000     30.0000        4.6801
       5.3300     1.0000     30.0000        5.4106
       1.6700     1.0000     50.0000        3.5941
       3.6700     1.0000     50.0000        4.6641
       5.3300     1.0000     50.0000        5.5523
       1.6700     1.0000     70.0000        3.3881
       3.6700     1.0000     70.0000        4.6481
       5.3300     1.0000     70.0000        5.6940
END DATA.
GRAPH/SCATTERPLOT=
  negemot   WITH       govact   BY        sex      /PANEL   ROWVAR=   age   .

*********************** ANALYSIS NOTES AND ERRORS ************************

Level of confidence for all confidence intervals in output:
   95.0000      .
```

Output from the **plot** option

FIGURE 9.2 continued.

Observe from the PROCESS output that $b_4 = 0.205, t(807) = 4.084, p <$ .001 and $b_5 = 0.005, t(807) = 3.013, p = .003$. Both are statistically different from zero, meaning both sex and age function as moderators of the effect of negative emotions on support for government action. From the section of output titled "Test(s) of highest order unconditional interaction(s)," the moderation of the effect of negative emotions by sex (W) uniquely accounts for 1.21% of the variance [$F(1, 807) = 16.676, p < .001$], whereas the moderation by age (Z) uniquely accounts for 0.66% of the variance, $F(1, 807) = 9.080, p = .003$. These correspond to the change in R^2 when that product is added to the model containing all other antecedents, including the other product, using the method discussed in section 8.3.

A visual depiction of the model can be constructed using the same procedure described in sections 7.3 and 8.2, choosing combinations of W and Z and plugging them into the model (equation 9.13) to generate estimates of Y (setting covariates, if any, to their means). The **plot=1** option in the PROCESS code produces the needed data, and the SPSS version of PROCESS even writes the syntax, found below, to read the data and produce a visual representation of the model, as in Figure 9.3.

```
DATA LIST FREE/
    negemot     sex     age     govact .
```

```
BEGIN DATA.
    1.6700      .0000    30.0000     4.2003
    3.6700      .0000    30.0000     4.6714
    5.3300      .0000    30.0000     5.0624
    1.6700      .0000    50.0000     3.9943
    3.6700      .0000    50.0000     4.6554
    5.3300      .0000    50.0000     5.2041
    1.6700      .0000    70.0000     3.7883
    3.6700      .0000    70.0000     4.6394
    5.3300      .0000    70.0000     5.3458
    1.6700     1.0000    30.0000     3.8000
    3.6700     1.0000    30.0000     4.6801
    5.3300     1.0000    30.0000     5.4106
    1.6700     1.0000    50.0000     3.5941
    3.6700     1.0000    50.0000     4.6641
    5.3300     1.0000    50.0000     5.5523
    1.6700     1.0000    70.0000     3.3881
    3.6700     1.0000    70.0000     4.6481
    5.3300     1.0000    70.0000     5.6940
END DATA.
GRAPH/SCATTERPLOT=
    negemot WITH   govact BY   sex/PANEL   rowvar= age .
```

Corresponding commands in SAS to produce a plot would be

```
data;input negemot sexcode age govact;
if (sexcode=0) then sex='Female';
if (sexcode=1) then sex='Male';
datalines;
1.6700    .0000 30.0000 4.2003
3.6700    .0000 30.0000 4.6714
5.3300    .0000 30.0000 5.0624
1.6700    .0000 50.0000 3.9943
3.6700    .0000 50.0000 4.6554
5.3300    .0000 50.0000 5.2041
1.6700    .0000 70.0000 3.7883
3.6700    .0000 70.0000 4.6394
5.3300    .0000 70.0000 5.3458
1.6700   1.0000 30.0000 3.8000
3.6700   1.0000 30.0000 4.6801
5.3300   1.0000 30.0000 5.4106
1.6700   1.0000 50.0000 3.5941
3.6700   1.0000 50.0000 4.6641
5.3300   1.0000 50.0000 5.5523
1.6700   1.0000 70.0000 3.3881
3.6700   1.0000 70.0000 4.6481
```

```
5.3300 1.0000 70.0000 5.6940
run;
proc sgpanel;
panelby age / columns=1;
series x=negemot y=govact/group=sex lineattrs =(color=black);
colaxis label='Negative Emotions';
rowaxis label='Support for Government Action';run;
```

And here is some R code to produce a similar depiction of the model:

```
par(mfrow=c(3,1))
par(mar=c(3,4,0,0),oma=c(2,2,2,2))
par(mgp=c(5,0.5,0))
x<-c(1.67,3.67,5.33,1.67,3.67,5.33)
w<-c(0,0,0,1,1,1)
yage30<-c(4.2003,4.6714,5.0624,3.800,4.6801,5.4106)
yage50<-c(3.9943,4.6554,5.2041,3.5941,4.6641,5.5523)
yage70<-c(3.7883,4.6394,5.3458,3.3881,4.6481,5.6940)
legend.txt<-c("Female (W=0)","Male (W=1)")
for (i in 1:3){
if (i==1)
    {y<-yage30
    legend2.txt<-c("Age (Z) = 30")}
if (i==2)
    {y<-yage50
    legend2.txt<-c("Age (Z) = 50")}
if (i==3)
    {y<-yage70
    legend2.txt<-c("Age (Z) = 70")}
plot(y=y,x=x,col="white",ylim=c(3,6),cex=1.5,xlim=c(1,6),tcl=-0.5)
lines(x[w==0],y[w==0],lwd=2,lty=2)
lines(x[w==1],y[w==1],lwd=2,lty=1)
legend("topleft",legend=legend.txt,lwd=2,lty=c(2,1))
legend("bottomright",legend=legend2.txt)
box}
mtext("Negative Emotions (X)",side=1,outer=TRUE)
mtext("Support for Government Action",side=2,outer=TRUE)
```

PROCESS also estimates the conditional effect of X for various values of W and Z, defined as

$$\theta_{X \to Y} = b_1 + b_4 W + b_5 Z$$

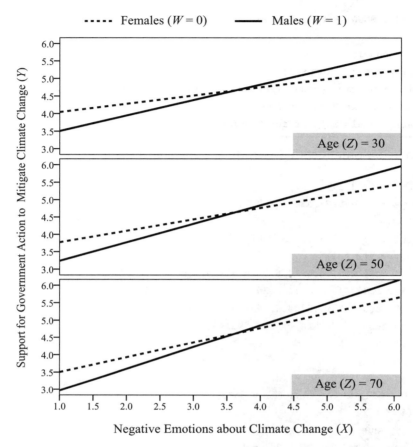

FIGURE 9.3. The conditional effect of negative emotions about climate change on support for government action as a function of sex and age from an additive multiple moderation model.

which, in this example, is

$$\theta_{X \to Y} = 0.093 + 0.205W + 0.005Z \tag{9.14}$$

Six such estimates can be found in the section titled "Conditional effects of the focal predictor at values of moderator(s)." PROCESS sees that W is dichotomous so it uses the two values of W found in the data (0 and 1, for females and males, respectively). And because we used the **zmodval** option, specifying ages of 30, 50, and 70, these are the three ages used for Z. The two values of sex crossed with three values of age produce the six rows in this section of output. PROCESS also calculates the standard errors of these conditional effects, estimated as

$$se_{\theta_{X \to Y|(W,Z)}} = \sqrt{\begin{array}{c} se_{b_1}^2 + W^2 se_{b_4}^2 + Z^2 se_{b_5}^2 + (2W)COV_{b_1 b_4} + \\ (2Z)COV_{b_1 b_5} + (2WZ)COV_{b_4 b_5} \end{array}}$$

where $COV_{b_i b_j}$ is the covariance between b_i and b_j. With this information, a t-ratio and p-value for testing the null hypothesis that $_T\theta_{X \to Y} = 0$ is provided, along with a 95% confidence interval.

As can be seen, the effect of negative emotions on support for government action is consistently positive and statistically significant for both males and females of 30, 50, or 70 years of age. It is apparent both from the estimate of b_4 and the conditional effects produced by PROCESS that the effect of negative emotions on support for government action is larger for men than women. Notice that regardless of which of the three values of age you condition on, the difference in this effect between men and women is $b_4 = 0.205$. For example, the conditional effect for 50-year-old men is 0.330 and for 50-year-old women it is 0.535, a difference of $b_4 = 0.205$. This difference is consistent for all values of age, a constraint inherent in this model. This means that in this model, an interaction between X and W means that the conditional effect of X differs when $W = w_1$ compared to when $W = w_2$, regardless of the value of Z. I elaborate on this point in section 9.5.

In this model, b_5 estimates how much the conditional effect of X on Y changes as Z changes by one unit. Thus, among two hypothetical groups of people who differ by 1 year in age, the conditional effect of negative emotions on support for government action is $b_5 = 0.005$ larger in the older group. For two groups 10 years apart, the difference in the effect is $10b_5 = 0.047$, and so forth.[4] This difference is invariant to where you start on the distribution of age, a constraint built into this model. Furthermore, this difference in the conditional effect due to age is the same in both men and women, also a constraint that is built mathematically into this model. For example, looking at the PROCESS output, notice that among women who differ by 20 years in age, the conditional effect of negative emotions differs by 0.095 (e.g., $0.331 - 0.236$ for 50- versus 30-year-old women, respectively), which is $20b_5$. This is the same as the difference between the conditional effect of negative emotions among among men who differ by 20 years in age (e.g., for 50- versus 30-year-old men, $0.535 - 0.440 = 0.095 = 20b_5$).

Moderated Moderation

Although the additive multiple moderation model is considerably more flexible than a multiple regression model that constrains X's effect to be

---

[4]To more decimal places of precision, $b_5 = 0.0047$, and so $10b_5 = 0.047$.

unconditional (e.g., as does equation 9.8), it still has an important constraint. This constraint is best illustrated by considering the findings from the prior analysis. As discussed, in this model, X's effect is moderated by W and Z, but W's moderation of X's effect is not dependent on Z. That is, b_4 estimates how much X's effect on Y changes as W changes by one unit, but this is constrained to be the same regardless of Z. In other words, as sex increases by one unit (i.e., the difference between women and men), the effect of negative emotions on support for government action increases by b_4 units *regardless* of age. But perhaps the sex differences in the link between negative emotions and support for government action is age dependent. Maybe the sex difference is smaller among younger people than among older people, for instance. The multiple moderation model cannot be used to determine this, because it constrains the interaction between X and W to be independent of Z.

One means of overcoming this constraint is to estimate the model represented not by equation 9.11 but, instead, by equation 9.15:

$$Y = i_Y + b_1X + b_2W + b_3Z + b_4XW + b_5XZ + b_6WZ + b_7XWZ + e_Y \quad (9.15)$$

where XWZ is the product of X, W, and Z. This product allows the moderation of X's effect on Y by W to depend on Z. This model can be rewritten in equivalent form as

$$Y = i_Y + (b_1 + b_4W + b_5Z + b_7WZ)X + b_2W + b_3Z + b_6WZ + e_Y \quad (9.16)$$

which shows that X's effect on Y is a function of W, Z, and their product. So the conditional effect of X in this model is

$$\theta_{X \to Y} = b_1 + b_4W + b_5Z + b_7WZ \quad (9.17)$$

Another means of representing this model is

$$Y = i_Y + (b_1 + b_5Z)X + [(b_4 + b_7Z)W]X + b_2W + b_3Z + b_6WZ + e_Y$$

Expressed in this form, it is apparent that X's effect on Y has two components. One component is determined by Z, expressed in functional form as $b_1 + b_5Z$. The second component is determined by W, expressed in functional form as $b_4 + b_7Z$. So W's influence on X's effect on Y is conditional on Z. Thus, the moderation of X's effect on Y by W is itself moderated by Z, a situation I refer to as *moderated moderation*. A conceptual representation of moderated moderation can be found in Figure 9.4, panel A. Panel B represents moderated moderation in the form of a statistical diagram. Moderated moderation is more widely known as *three-way interaction*, meaning that X, W, and Z interact.

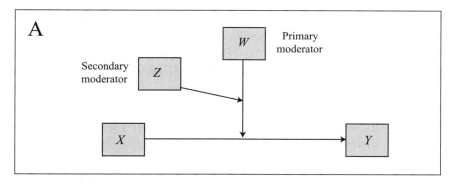

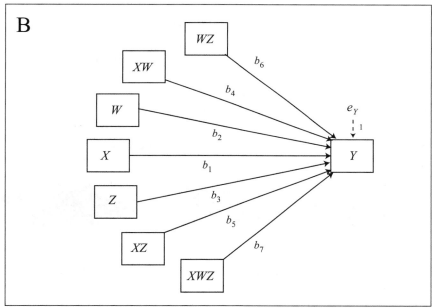

FIGURE 9.4. A moderated moderation model depicted in the form of a conceptual diagram (panel A) and a statistical diagram (panel B).

In equations 9.15 and 9.16, most of the regression coefficients represent conditional effects and should not be interpreted as main effects and interactions as they are in a factorial ANOVA. The exception is b_7, which does estimate the three-way interaction between X, W, and Z. But b_1, b_2, and b_3 are conditional effects or, in the lingo of ANOVA, *simple* effects, and *not* main effects. b_1 estimates the effect of X on Y when both W and Z are zero, b_2 estimates the effect of W on Y when both X and Z are equal to zero, and b_3 estimates the effect of Z on Y when both X and W are equal to zero. By the same token, b_4 estimates the *conditional* interaction between X and W when $Z = 0$, b_5 quantifies the conditional interaction between X and Z when

$W = 0$, and b_6 estimates the conditional interaction between W and Z when $X = 0$. Mean-centering X, W, and Z prior to computation of products and model estimation will make the interpretation of these coefficients closer to their counterparts in ANOVA, but usually not exactly the same. Whether or not mean-centering is used, all six of these terms should be included in a model that includes XWZ, regardless of their statistical significance or lack thereof. A failure to do so will produce an invalid test of the three-way interaction between X, W, and Z.

PROCESS has a model built in that greatly simplifies the estimation of a moderated moderation model such as this. By specifying **model=3** along with consequent variable Y, focal antecedent variable X, the primary and secondary moderators W and Z, and any covariates of interest, PROCESS calculates all the necessary products, estimates the best-fitting OLS regression model, and probes the interaction for you. In the commands below, I also requested implementation of the Johnson–Neyman technique and estimates of Y for generating a plot of the model.

For instance, a PROCESS command that allows the moderation of the effect of negative emotions (X) on support for government action by sex (W) to depend on age (Z) while controlling for positive emotions (C_1) and ideology (C_2) would be

```
process y=govact/x=negemot/w=sex/z=age/cov=posemot ideology/
    model=3/jn=1/plot=1/zmodval=30,50,70.
```

In SAS, use

```
%process (data=glbwarm,y=govact,x=negemot,w=sex,z=age,cov=posemot
    ideology,model=3,jn=1,plot=1,zmodval=30 50 70);
```

The output generated by the SPSS version can be found in Figure 9.5. The best-fitting model is

$$\hat{Y} = 4.560 + 0.273X + 0.529W - 0.003Z - 0.131XW + 0.001XZ$$
$$- 0.025WZ + 0.007XWZ - 0.021C_1 - 0.206C_2$$

Notice that the regression coefficient for XWZ is statistically significant, $b_7 = 0.007, t(805) = 2.096, p = .036$, meaning that there is evidence of a three-way interaction between negative emotions, sex, and age. That is, the magnitude of the moderation by sex of the effect of negative emotions on support for government action depends on age, though this "moderation of moderation" explains only 0.3% of the variance in support for government action (from the PROCESS output under the heading "Tests(s) of highest order unconditional interaction(s)").

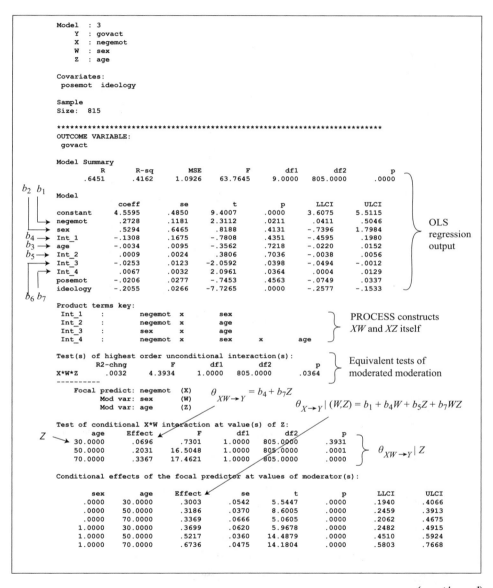

(*continued*)

FIGURE 9.5. Output from the PROCESS procedure for a moderated moderation analysis examining the moderation by age of sex differences in the effect of negative emotions about climate change on support for government action.

```
*Moderator value(s) defining Johnson-Neyman significance region(s):
      Value    % below    % above
     38.1138   28.2209    71.7791    ◄──────────────    Demarcates region of significance
                                                          for the XW interaction
Conditional X*W interaction at values of the moderator Z:
      age      Effect       se         t          p        LLCI     ULCI
    17.0000    -.0172      .1169     -.1475     .8828     -.2467    .2122
    20.5000     .0061      .1069      .0573     .9543     -.2038    .2160
    24.0000     .0295      .0972      .3035     .7616     -.1613    .2203
    27.5000     .0529      .0878      .6019     .5474     -.1196    .2253
    31.0000     .0763      .0789      .9661     .3343     -.0787    .2312
    34.5000     .0996      .0707     1.4100     .1589     -.0391    .2383
    38.0000     .1230      .0633     1.9440     .0522     -.0012    .2472
    38.1138     .1238      .0630     1.9629     .0500      .0000    .2475
    41.5000     .1464      .0571     2.5625     .0106      .0343    .2585
    45.0000     .1697      .0526     3.2246     .0013      .0664    .2731
    48.5000     .1931      .0503     3.8408     .0001      .0944    .2918
    52.0000     .2165      .0503     4.3008     .0000      .1177    .3153
    55.5000     .2399      .0528     4.5425     .0000      .1362    .3435
    59.0000     .2632      .0574     4.5883     .0000      .1506    .3759
    62.5000     .2866      .0636     4.5073     .0000      .1618    .4114
    66.0000     .3100      .0710     4.3647     .0000      .1706    .4494
    69.5000     .3334      .0793     4.2022     .0000      .1776    .4891
    73.0000     .3567      .0883     4.0415     .0001      .1835    .5300
    76.5000     .3801      .0977     3.8920     .0001      .1884    .5718
    80.0000     .4035      .1074     3.7570     .0002      .1927    .6143
    83.5000     .4269      .1174     3.6366     .0003      .1965    .6573
    87.0000     .4502      .1276     3.5297     .0004      .1999    .7006

Data for visualizing the conditional effect of the focal predictor:
Paste text below into a SPSS syntax window and execute to produce plot.

DATA LIST FREE/
    negemot        sex         age        govact .
BEGIN DATA.
    1.6700       .0000     30.0000       4.0561
    3.6700       .0000     30.0000       4.6566
    5.3300       .0000     30.0000       5.1551
    1.6700       .0000     50.0000       4.0190
    3.6700       .0000     50.0000       4.6562
    5.3300       .0000     50.0000       5.1850
    1.6700       .0000     70.0000       3.9820
    3.6700       .0000     70.0000       4.6557
    5.3300       .0000     70.0000       5.2149
    1.6700      1.0000     30.0000       3.9422
    3.6700      1.0000     30.0000       4.6819
    5.3300      1.0000     30.0000       5.2959
    1.6700      1.0000     50.0000       3.6220
    3.6700      1.0000     50.0000       4.6654
    5.3300      1.0000     50.0000       5.5314
    1.6700      1.0000     70.0000       3.3017
    3.6700      1.0000     70.0000       4.6489
    5.3300      1.0000     70.0000       5.7670
END DATA.
GRAPH/SCATTERPLOT=
    negemot  WITH      govact   BY      sex    /PANEL  ROWVAR=  age

*********************** ANALYSIS NOTES AND ERRORS ***********************

Level of confidence for all confidence intervals in output:
  95.0000
```

Output from the **plot** option

FIGURE 9.5 continued.

A visual representation of this model can be found in Figure 9.6, generated with the help of the estimated values of Y for various combinations of X, W, and Z produced with **plot** option in PROCESS and found in the section of output labeled "Data for visualizing the conditional effect of the focal predictor." The SPSS, SAS, and R code below generates a picture of this model. You will find this code is largely identical to the code on pages 325-327. The only difference is the estimated values of Y.

```
DATA LIST FREE/
     negemot     sex      age      govact .
BEGIN DATA.
      1.6700    .0000    30.0000     4.0561
      3.6700    .0000    30.0000     4.6566
      5.3300    .0000    30.0000     5.1551
      1.6700    .0000    50.0000     4.0190
      3.6700    .0000    50.0000     4.6562
      5.3300    .0000    50.0000     5.1850
      1.6700    .0000    70.0000     3.9820
      3.6700    .0000    70.0000     4.6557
      5.3300    .0000    70.0000     5.2149
      1.6700   1.0000    30.0000     3.9422
      3.6700   1.0000    30.0000     4.6819
      5.3300   1.0000    30.0000     5.2959
      1.6700   1.0000    50.0000     3.6220
      3.6700   1.0000    50.0000     4.6654
      5.3300   1.0000    50.0000     5.5314
      1.6700   1.0000    70.0000     3.3017
      3.6700   1.0000    70.0000     4.6489
      5.3300   1.0000    70.0000     5.7670
END DATA.
GRAPH/SCATTERPLOT=
    negemot WITH  govact BY  sex/PANEL  rowvar= age .
```

The corresponding commands in SAS and R to produce a plot would be

```
data;input negemot sexcode age govact;
if (sexcode=0) then sex='Female';
if (sexcode=1) then sex='Male';
datalines;
1.6700   .0000 30.0000 4.0561
3.6700   .0000 30.0000 4.6566
5.3300   .0000 30.0000 5.1551
1.6700   .0000 50.0000 4.0190
3.6700   .0000 50.0000 4.6562
5.3300   .0000 50.0000 5.1850
1.6700   .0000 70.0000 3.9820
3.6700   .0000 70.0000 4.6557
```

```
5.3300   .0000 70.0000 5.2149
1.6700 1.0000 30.0000 3.9422
3.6700 1.0000 30.0000 4.6819
5.3300 1.0000 30.0000 5.2959
1.6700 1.0000 50.0000 3.6220
3.6700 1.0000 50.0000 4.6654
5.3300 1.0000 50.0000 5.5314
1.6700 1.0000 70.0000 3.3017
3.6700 1.0000 70.0000 4.6489
5.3300 1.0000 70.0000 5.7670
run;
proc sgpanel;
panelby age / columns=1;
series x=negemot y=govact/group=sex lineattrs =(color=black);
colaxis label='Negative Emotions';
rowaxis label='Support for Government Action';run;
```

```
par(mfrow = c(3, 1))
par(mar = c(3, 4, 0, 0),oma = c(2,2,2,2))
par(mgp = c(5, 0.5, 0))
x<-c(1.67,3.67,5.33,1.67,3.67,5.33)
w<-c(0,0,0,1,1,1)
yage30<-c(4.0561,4.6566,5.1551,3.9422,4.6819,5.2959)
yage50<-c(4.0190,4.6562,5.1850,3.6220,4.6654,5.5314)
yage70<-c(3.9820,4.6557,5.2149,3.3017,4.6489,5.7670)
legend.txt<-c("Female (W=0)","Male (W=1)")
for (i in 1:3){
if (i==1)
   {y<-yage30
   legend2.txt<-c("Age (Z) = 30")}
if (i==2)
   {y<-yage50
   legend2.txt<-c("Age (Z) = 50")}
if (i==3)
   {y<-yage70
   legend2.txt<-c("Age (Z) = 70")}
plot(y=y,x=x,col="white",ylim=c(3,6),cex=1.5,xlim=c(1,6),tcl=-0.5)
lines(x[w==0],y[w==0],lwd=2,lty=2)
lines(x[w==1],y[w==1],lwd=2,lty=1)
legend("topleft", legend=legend.txt,lwd=2,lty=c(2,1))
```

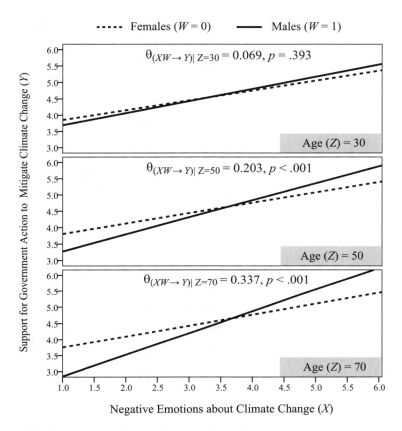

FIGURE 9.6. The conditional effect of negative emotions about climate change on support for government action as a function of sex and age from a moderated moderation model.

```
legend("bottomright",legend=legend2.txt)
box}
mtext("Negative Emotions (X)",side=1,outer=TRUE)
mtext("Support for Government Action",side=2,outer=TRUE)
```

As can be seen, the effect of negative emotions on support for government action is consistently positive, but the difference in its effect between men and women is larger among those who are older. This moderation of the interaction between negative emotions and sex by age is not strong to be sure. Indeed, it accounts for only 0.3% of the variance in support for government action. But when represented visually in this fashion, it is clearly detectable by eye.

There are several options available for probing a three-way interaction in a moderated moderation model. One approach is a variant of the pick-a-point approach in which values of the secondary moderator Z are chosen with the goal of ascertaining whether W moderates X's effect on Y conditioned on these various values of Z. This requires estimation of the conditional effect of the XW interaction given Z and conducting an inferential test for this conditional interaction at that value of Z. The conditional moderation of X by W is estimated as

$$\theta_{XW \to Y} = b_4 + b_7 Z$$

with an estimated standard error of

$$se_{\theta_{XW \to Y}} = \sqrt{se_{b_4}^2 + (2Z)COV_{b_4 b_7} + Z^2 se_{b_7}^2}$$

Under the null hypothesis of no conditional interaction between X and W at a given value of Z, the ratio of $\theta_{XW \to Y}$ to its standard error is distributed as $t(df_{residual})$ or, equivalently, $F(1, df_{residual})$.

PROCESS automatically implements this approach, the results of which can be seen in Figure 9.5 under the heading "Conditional effect of X*W interaction at value(s) of Z." Because we used the **zmodval** option, specifying values of age equal to 30, 50, and 70, PROCESS estimates $\theta_{XW \to Y}$ at values of Z corresponding to ages of 30, 50, and 70. Among 30-year-olds ($Z = 30$), the effect of negative emotions on support for government action is not significantly moderated by sex, $\theta_{XW \to Y}|(Z = 30) = 0.070, F(1, 805) = 0.730, p = .393$. But among 50-year-olds [$\theta_{XW \to Y}|(Z = 50) = 0.203, F(1, 805) = 16.505, p < .001$] and 70-year-olds [$\theta_{XW \to Y}|(Z = 70) = 0.337, F(1, 805) = 17.462, p < .001$], sex significantly moderates the effect of negative emotions on support for government action. As discussed below, these three estimates of the conditional XW interaction are equal to the difference in the conditional effect of negative emotions in men compared to women at those three values of age.

An alternative approach when the secondary moderator is a continuum is to use the Johnson–Neyman technique to ascertain where the conditional interaction between X and W transitions between statistically significant and not along the distribution of Z. The mathematics of the application of the Johnson–Neyman technique is the same as in simple moderation and equally complicated. Leave this to a computer program such as PROCESS. As can be seen in Figure 9.5, the interaction between negative emotions and sex transitions between statistically significant and nonsignificant at age = 38.114. Above this age, there is a significantly positive two-way interaction between negative emotions and sex. That is, there is a statistically significant difference in the effect of negative emotions between men and women among those at least 38.114 years of age. Below this age, sex does not moderate the effect of negative emotions on support for government action.

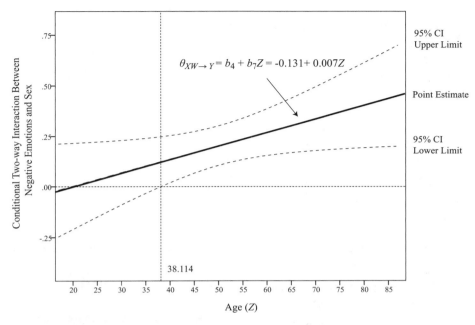

FIGURE 9.7. The conditional two-way interaction between negative emotions and sex $(\theta_{XW \to Y})$ as a function of age (Z).

Figure 9.7 was generated in SPSS using the code below, and then edited using SPSS's graphics editing features. This code could easily be tailored to your own data and model.

```
DATA LIST FREE/age effect llci ulci.
BEGIN DATA.
17.0000    -0.0172    -0.2467    0.2122
20.5000     0.0061    -0.2038    0.2160
24.0000     0.0295    -0.1613    0.2203
   .           .          .         .
   .        (from PROCESS JN table)  .
   .           .          .         .
80.0000     0.4035     0.1927    0.6143
83.5000     0.4269     0.1965    0.6573
87.0000     0.4502     0.1999    0.7006
END DATA.
GRAPH/SCATTER(OVERLAY)=age age age WITH llci ulci effect (PAIR).
```

In SAS, the code below will produce a similar figure but will require much less editing.

```
data;input age effect llci ulci;
datalines;
17.0000    -0.0172    -0.2467    0.2122
20.5000     0.0061    -0.2038    0.2160
24.0000     0.0295    -0.1613    0.2203

    .         .          .          .
    .       (from PROCESS JN table) .
    .         .          .          .
80.0000     0.4035     0.1927    0.6143
83.5000     0.4269     0.1965    0.6573
87.0000     0.4502     0.1999    0.7006
run;
proc sgplot;
series x=age y=ulci/curvelabel = '95% upper limit' lineattrs=(color=red
    pattern=ShortDash);
series x=age y=effect/curvelabel = 'point estimate' lineattrs=(color=
    black pattern=Solid);
series x=age y=llci/curvelabel = '95% lower limit' lineattrs=(color=red
    pattern=ShortDash);
xaxis label = 'Age';
yaxis label = 'Conditional negative emotions by sex interaction';
refline 0/axis=y transparency=0.5;refline 38.114/axis=x
    transparency=0.5;
run;
```

If you prefer R, try

```
age<-c(17,20.5,24,27.5,31,34.5,38,38.11,41.5,45,48.5,52,55.5,59,62.5,66,
    69.5,73,76.5,80,83.5,87)
effect<-c(-.017,.006,.030,.053,.076,.100,.123,.124,.146,.170,.193,.217,
    .240,.263,.287,.310,.333,.357,.380,.404,.427,.450)
llci<-c(-.247,-.204,-.161,-.120,-.078,-.039,-.001,0,.034,.066,.094,.118,
    .136,.151,.162,.171,.178,.184,.188,.193,.197,.200)
ulci<-c(.212,.216,.220,.225,.231,.238,.247,.248,.259,.273,.292,.315,.344,
    .376,.411,.449,.489,.530,.572,.614,.657,.701)
plot(age,effect,type="l",pch=19,ylim=c(-1,1.5),xlim=c(15,90),lwd=3,
ylab="Conditional negative emotions by sex interaction",
xlab="Age")
points(age,llci,lwd=2,lty=2,type="l")
points(age,ulci,lwd=2,lty=2,type="l")
abline(h=0,untf=FALSE,lty=3,lwd=1)
```

```
abline(v=38.114,untf=FALSE,lty=3,lwd=1)
text(38.114,-1,"38.114",cex=0.8)
```

A variant of the pick-a-point approach can be used in which the conditional effect of X is estimated for various values of W and Z, followed by an inferential test for those combinations of W and Z. This is not a formal probing of moderated moderation per se because it is not sensitive to how the conditional effect of X on Y given W is differentially related to Z. However, it can be a handy and informative way of ascertaining how X is differentially related to Y as a function of both W and Z in conjunction. The estimated conditional effect of X on Y given W and Z is

$$\theta_{X \to Y} = b_1 + b_4 W + b_5 Z + b_7 WZ$$

with estimated standard error of

$$se_{\theta_{X \to Y|(W,Z)}} = \sqrt{\begin{array}{c} se_{b_1}^2 + W^2 se_{b_4}^2 + Z^2 se_{b_5}^2 + W^2 Z^2 se_{b_7}^2 + \\ (2W)COV_{b_1 b_4} + (2Z)COV_{b_1 b_5} + \\ (2WZ)COV_{b_1 b_7} + (2WZ)COV_{b_4 b_5} + \\ (2W^2 Z)COV_{b_4 b_7} + (2WZ^2)COV_{b_5 b_7} \end{array}}$$

(see Aiken & West, 1991, p. 54). Under the null hypothesis of no effect of X on Y at the chosen values of W and Z, the ratio of $\theta_{X \to Y}$ to its standard error is distributed as $t(df_{residual})$. Obviously, this you would never want to attempt to do by hand. Leave it up to a computer program such as PROCESS. As can be seen in Figure 9.5, for both men and women, and whether 30, 50, or 70 years of age, the relationship between negative emotions and support for government action is positive and statistically significant.

However, the pattern of differences in the effect of negative emotions between men and women is different here compared to the additive multiple moderator model discussed starting on page 323. Whereas without the XWZ term in the model, the sex difference in the conditional effect of negative emotions on support for government action was constrained to be the same regardless of age, in the moderated moderation model, the sex difference depends on age. Among 30-year-olds, the difference in the effect of negative emotions between men and women is $0.370 - 0.300 = 0.070 = \theta_{XW \to Y} \mid (Z = 30)$, which we know is not statistically different from zero from the implementation of the pick-a-point approach earlier. But among 50-year-olds, the difference in the effect of negative emotions is no longer 0.070 but is, instead, $\theta_{XW \to Y} \mid (Z = 50) = 0.522 - 0.319 = 0.203$ and statistically different from zero ($p < .001$). Finally, among 70-year-olds, the sex difference in the effect of negative emotions is bigger still: $\theta_{XW \to Y} \mid (Z = 70) = 0.674 - 0.337 = 0.337$, $p < .0001$.

9.5   Comparing Conditional Effects

In section 9.4 we saw that the effect of negative emotions (X) on support for government actions to mitigate climate change (Y) varies between people of different sexes (W) and ages (Z). The additive multiple moderation model fixes the extent of the moderation of X's effect by W to be independent of Z, whereas the moderated moderation model releases this constraint, allowing the moderation or X's effect by W to vary with Z. Regression coefficients for products involving X in these models quantify the rate of change of X's effect as one moderator changes when another moderator is held fixed (additive multiple moderation) or as another moderator varies (moderated moderation).

These regression coefficients and corresponding inferential tests are not necessarily sensitive to a different question one might ask: Is X's effect on Y when $W = w_1$ and $Z = z_1$ different than when $W = w_2$ and $Z = z_2$? For instance, is the relationship between negative emotions about climate change and support for government actions among 30-year-old men different than the relationship among 50-year-old women? This is a question about the difference between two conditional effects of X. In this example, $w_1 \neq w_2$ and $z_1 \neq z_2$. But one could imagine variations on this question when W is held fixed but Z varies, or when W varies but Z is fixed. For example, is the relationship between negative emotions and support for government action different between 30-year-old men and 30-year-old women, or between 30-year-old men and 50-year-old men?

In this section, I discuss a test of the difference between two conditional effects in a moderation model. The method I describe is called a "slope difference test" by Dawson (Dawson, 2014; Dawson & Richter, 2006), who offers some guidelines on how to conduct this test for the moderated moderation model. But Dawson's discussion is more complicated than need be, and the method he provides for conducting the test using an Excel spreadsheet is tedious and fraught with potential for data entry error. This test is implemented in PROCESS and it requires no more effort than providing the values of W and Z for the comparison of interest in the PROCESS command. So PROCESS makes this test easy and largely foolproof.

In section 7.5, I described how in a model of the form $\hat{Y} = b_0 + b_1 X + b_2 W + b_3 XW$, the hypothesis test that $_T b_3 = 0$ doubles as a test of the difference between any two conditional effects of X when $W = w_1$ compared to when $W = w_2$ for any two different values of w_1 and w_2. It makes no difference which values of w_1 and w_2 are used. So no special test is needed to compare conditional effects of X in the simple moderation model. All one needs to do is test whether W moderates the effect of X on Y. So this situation is not discussed further.

We want to test whether the difference between two conditional effects of X defined by pairs of values of moderators W and Z are the same or different. In symbolic form, we seek a test of the null hypothesis that

$$\theta_{X \to Y} \mid (w_1, z_1) = \theta_{X \to Y} \mid (w_2, z_2)$$

against the alternative that these conditional effects are different. We can also phrase this test in terms of the difference between the two conditional effects, meaning the null is

$$\theta_{X \to Y} \mid (w_1, z_1) - \theta_{X \to Y} \mid (w_2, z_2) = 0$$

and the alternative is that this difference is not zero. Of course, we could also abandon null hypothesis entirely and phrase the inference in terms of a confidence interval for the difference.

Comparing Conditional Effects in the Additive Multiple Moderation Model

In the additive multiple moderation model of the form $\hat{Y} = b_0 + b_1 X + b_2 W + b_3 Z + b_4 XW + b_5 XZ$, the conditional effect of X when $W = w_1$ and $Z = z_1$ is $b_1 + b_4 w_1 + b_5 z_1$ (from equation 9.12). When $W = w_2$ and $Z = z_2$, the conditional effect of X is $b_1 + b_4 w_2 + b_5 z_2$. So their difference is

$$
\begin{aligned}
\Delta\theta_{X \to Y} &= b_1 + b_4 w_1 + b_5 z_1 - (b_1 + b_4 w_2 + b_5 z_2) & (9.18) \\
&= b_4(w_1 - w_2) + b_5(z_1 - z_2) & (9.19)
\end{aligned}
$$

The standard error of this difference is complicated, but it has some less complicated special cases. This standard error can be estimated as

$$
se_{\Delta\theta_{X \to Y}} = \sqrt{ \begin{array}{c} (w_1 - w_2)^2 se_{b_4}^2 + (z_1 - z_2)^2 se_{b_5}^2 + \\ 2(w_1 - w_2)(z_1 - z_2) COV_{b_4 b_5} \end{array} } \tag{9.20}
$$

The ratio of the estimated difference between the conditional effects to its standard error is distributed as $t(df_{residual})$ under the null hypothesis. Or a 95% confidence interval for the difference can be constructed in the usual way, as approximately the point estimate plus or minus about 2 standard errors.

Clearly, equation 9.20 and the test itself is best left to a computer. But there are two special cases that require no computation at all. In the special case when $z_1 = z_2$, equation 9.19 simplifies to $b_4(w_1 - w_2)$ and equation 9.20

reduces to $se_{b_4}(w_1 - w_2)$. But the ratio of these two quantities is just the t statistic for b_4 in the additive multiple moderation model. So a claim that W moderates X's effect on Y in this model means that any two conditional effects of X at different values of W but the same value of Z can be declared different from each other. Conversely, if W does not moderate the effect of X in this model, then no two conditional effects of X conditioned on the same value of Z but with different values of W can be deemed different from each other. When we estimated this model, we saw that b_4 was statistically significant. So we can say that the conditional effect of negative emotions on support for government actions is different between groups of men and women of the same age. It makes no difference what the ages of those two groups is, so long as their ages are the same.

The second special case is when $w_1 = w_2$. In that case, equation 9.19 simplifies to $b_5(z_1 - z_2)$ and equation 9.20 reduces to $se_{b_5}(z_1 - z_2)$. The ratio of these is the t statistic for b_5 in the additive multiple moderation model. So when you say that Z moderates X's effect on Y in this model, then you can also say any two conditional effects of X at different values of Z but the same value of W are different from each other. But if Z does not moderate the effect of X, then no two conditional effects of X conditioned on the same value of W but with different values of Z are different from each other. From the earlier analysis, we know that b_5 in this model is statistically significant. Therefore, the conditional effect of negative emotions on support for government actions is different among two groups of people of different ages but of the same sex. It makes no difference what the ages of those two groups is. So long as they are of the same sex, we can say the conditional effect of negative emotions is different in those two groups.

Comparing Conditional Effects in the Moderated Moderation Model

In the moderated moderation model, the model of Y is of the form $\hat{Y} = b_0 + b_1X + b_2W + b_3Z + b_4XW + b_5XZ + b_6WZ + b_7XWZ$. The conditional effect of X on Y when $W = w_1$ and $Z = z_1$ is $b_1 + b_4w_1 + b_5z_1 + b_7w_1z_1$ (from equation 9.17), and when $W = w_2$ and $Z = z_2$ the conditional effect of X is $b_1 + b_4w_2 + b_5z_2 + b_7w_2z_2$. The difference between these two conditional effects of X is

$$\begin{aligned}
\Delta\theta_{X\to Y} &= b_1 + b_4w_1 + b_5z_1 + b_7w_1z_1 - (b_1 + b_4w_2 + b_5z_2 + b_7w_2z_2) \\
&= b_4(w_1 - w_2) + b_5(z_1 - z_2) + b_7(w_1z_1 - w_2z_2)
\end{aligned}$$

The standard error of this difference is even more complicated than it is for the additive multiple moderation model:

$$se_{\Delta\theta_{X\to Y}} = \sqrt{\begin{array}{c} (w_1 - w_2)^2 se_{b_4}^2 + (z_1 - z_2)^2 se_{b_5}^2 + \\ (w_1 z_1 - w_2 z_2)^2 se_{b_7}^2 + \\ 2(w_1 - w_2)(z_1 - z_2)COV_{b_4 b_5} + \\ 2(w_1 - w_2)(w_1 z_1 - w_2 z_2)COV_{b_4 b_7} + \\ 2(z_1 - z_2)(w_1 z_1 - w_2 z_2)COV_{b_5 b_7} \end{array}} \qquad (9.21)$$

The ratio of the estimated difference in conditional effects to its standard error is distributed as $t(df_{residual})$ under the null hypothesis of equality of the two conditional effects of X. Although setting $w_1 = w_2$ or $z_1 = z_2$ results in some simplification to these equations, they still contain values of W and Z. Computation is best left to a device such as PROCESS.

Implementation in PROCESS

PROCESS will implement this test of the difference between two conditional effects of X in both the additive multiple moderation and moderated moderation models. This is accomplished by adding the **contrast** statement in the PROCESS line, specifying the (w_1, z_1) and (w_2, z_2) pairs following an equals sign. To illustrate, we shall conduct a test of the difference in the conditional effect of negative emotions about climate change on support for government action between 30-year-old men ($w_1 = 1, z_1 = 30$) and 50-year-old women ($w_2 = 0, z_2 = 50$) from the moderated moderation model reported starting on page 329. In Figure 9.5, which is the PROCESS output from that analysis, you can see that for 30-year-old men, the conditional effect of X is 0.3699, and for 50-year-old women, the conditional effect is 0.3186. So their differerence is $0.3699 - 0.3186 = 0.0513$. Using PROCESS for SPSS, the **contrast** option conducts the test of this difference:

```
process y=govact/x=negemot/w=sex/z=age/cov=posemot ideology/
    model=3/zmodval=30,50,70/contrast=1,30;0,50.
```

In SAS, the command is

```
%process (data=glbwarm,y=govact,x=negemot,w=sex,z=age,cov=posemot
    ideology,model=3,jn=1,plot=1,zmodval=30 50 70,contrast=1 30 0 50);
```

Notice a small difference in the syntax for the **contrast** option between SPSS and SAS. In SPSS, the (w_1, z_1) pair, which comes first, is separated from the (w_2, z_2) pair with a semicolon, and the values of w and z are separated by a comma. In SAS, no commas are used between any of the values of w and z.

In addition to the usual PROCESS output, an additional section is produced when the **contrast** option is used:

```
Contrast between conditional effects of X:

              sex         age      Effect
Effect1:   1.0000     30.0000      .3699
Effect2:    .0000     50.0000      .3186

Test of Effect1 minus Effect2
    Contrast          se          t           p        LLCI        ULCI
      .0513       .0711      .7215       .4708      -.0882       .1908
```

So the null hypothesis of equality of the conditional effects cannot be rejected, $t(805) = 0.722, p = 0.471$. A 95% confidence interval for the difference is -0.088 to 0.191. We don't have sufficient evidence to conclude that the effect of negative emotions on support for government action differs between 30-year-old men and 50-year-old women.

9.6   Chapter Summary

Absent the added flexibility that results when the product of two variables is included in a linear model, multiple regression yields estimates of effects of one variable on another that are unconditional, meaning that they are not dependent on any variable in the model. A simple mathematical trick in which a focal antecedent variable's effect is conceptualized as a linear function of a moderator produces an analytical tool with much greater utility that can be used to determine whether one variable's effect is contingent on another. But this one fairly minor modification to a regression model introduces new complexities in interpretation that can easily trip up those without a good understanding of the principles introduced in this and the prior two chapters. In this chapter, I attempted to illustrate some of these complexities while also debunking some myths circulating about how to test an interaction between two variables in a regression model, such as the need to center or standardize variables prior to constructing products and using them as antecedent variables in a regression model.

Many investigators who were introduced to ANOVA before multiple regression go away from their first exposure to the principles described in the last two chapters with the mistaken belief that the concept of a "main effect" in ANOVA generalizes to the interpretation of regression coefficients in a model that includes a product between two variables. I have discussed how the regression coefficients for X and W in a model that includes XW

represent conditional effects and not main effects. These are completely different concepts, and treating a conditional effect and a main effect as synonyms in meaning and interpretation will lead to misinterpretation and misreporting of your findings or worse. One exception I illustrated in the prior chapter is when X and W are dichotomous and coded such that the resulting model does in fact yield main effects as they are defined in ANOVA.

A moderation model can include more than one moderator. In this chapter, I introduced the additive linear moderation model and the moderated moderation model. The former allows the moderation of X's effect on Y to vary with primary moderator W when secondary moderator Z is held fixed, whereas the latter allows the moderation of X's effect on Y by primary moderator W to vary with secondary moderator Z. Analogues of the pick-a-point and Johnson–Neyman approaches to probing interactions are available in these more complicated multiple moderator models. PROCESS implements these methods, thereby eliminating most of the computational efforts that otherwise would be required.

10

Multicategorical Focal Antecedents and Moderators

My treatment of moderation analysis has focused thus far on those analytical situations where the focal antecedent or moderator is dichotomous or a quantitative continuum. In this chapter, I address the principles and mathematics of moderation analysis when the focal antecedent variable is multicategorical. I show how the fundamentals introduced in the prior chapters apply, allowing the difference between subsets of groups or combinations of groups on a consequent variable to differ linearly as a function of a moderator. I also cover the visualizing and probing of moderation models involving a multicategorical variable. I end by illustrating that the symmetry property of interaction described in Chapters 7 and 8 still applies, and the same model when the focal antecedent variable is a multicategorical variable can be used when the focal antecedent is dichotomous or a continuum and the moderator is multicategorical.

In the last three chapters I demonstrated that a regression model that includes the product of two antecedent variables X and W along with X and W themselves is a flexible one that allows X's effect on Y to vary linearly with a moderator variable W. Chapter 7 introduced the principles of moderation analysis when the focal antecedent variable is dichotomous and the moderator is continuous. In Chapter 8, the principles were generalized to models with a dichotomous moderator variable and a continuous focal antecedent, as well as to models with continuous focal antecedent and moderator. These three scenarios are quite common in the substantive literature.

But what if the focal antecedent variable or moderator is neither continuous nor dichotomous? For example, suppose that X is a multicategorical variable, like when an investigator conducts an experiment with three or more conditions to which participants are randomly assigned. How does one test whether the effect of the manipulation (which takes one of several different forms) on the consequent variable Y depends on a moderator? Or a moderator W might be a categorical variable representing three or more groups, while X is a continuous or dichotomous variable. In that situation, an investigator might want to know whether the relationship between X and Y differs between the three or more groups.

Designs such as these are common. For example, Walsh, Stock, Peterson, and Gerrard (2014) took a photograph of research participants that revealed damage to their skin caused by ultraviolet radiation. Following this, participants were randomly assigned to one of three conditions that varied with respect to instructions they were given about how to respond to the photograph. Some were told they should think logically about their response to the photograph, others were told to focus on their emotional reactions, and those in a control group were given no specific instructions. They found an interaction between participant age and instruction condition on several consequent variables. For instance, age was positively related to perceived vulnerability to skin cancer except among those told to focus on their emotional reactions to their skin damage. And the emotion-focused instructions reduced the number of packets of sunscreen participants took at the end of the experiment, but more so among the relatively older participants. Some other examples in the substantive literature with a multicategorical variable as focal antecedent or moderator in a study designed to test a moderation hypothesis include Ferraro, Krimani, and Matherly (2013), and Nisbet, Hart, Myers, and Ellithorpe (2011).

In this chapter, I extend the principles of moderation analysis described in Chapters 7 and 8 to testing interaction involving a multicategorical focal antecedent variable or moderator. As you will see, the principles discussed in those chapters generalize quite readily, although the model necessarily requires more than one product to capture an interaction between two variables. This makes the formulas a bit more complex, and the visualizing and probing process a bit more involved. But with comfort with the fundamentals described so far, you should not find it difficult to master this extension of multiple regression analysis.

10.1 Moderation of the Effect of a Multicategorical Antecedent Variable

In the review of regression analysis in section 2.7, we saw that a multicategorical variable with g categories can be included as an antecedent variable in a regression model by using a system of coding based on $g - 1$ variables representing the g groups. In that discussion, indicator coding was described as one coding option. Chapter 6 illustrated how to test a mediation hypothesis when the causal agent of interest X is a multicategorical variable. An example was presented there using both indicator coding and a system of two orthogonal contrasts to represent group membership. And then in Chapters 7 and 8, we saw that the effect of a dichotomous or continuous antecedent variable X on a consequent variable Y can be specified as dependent on a moderator W by including the product of X and W in a model of Y along with X and W. When doing so, X's effect on Y becomes a linear function of W. A test of moderation is conducted by estimating the regression weight for XW in this model.

Testing a hypothesis about moderation of the effect of X on Y when the focal antecedent X is a multicategorical variable and moderator W is continuous or dichotomous involves an integration of these lessons about representing g groups in a regression model along with how to allow X's effect to vary linearly with W. If X is a multicategorical variable with g groups, include $g - 1$ variables coding membership in the groups, the moderator variable W, and $g - 1$ products between the $g - 1$ group codes and moderator W in a regression model of Y:

$$Y = i_Y + \sum_{i=1}^{g-1} b_i D_i + b_g W + \sum_{j=g+1}^{2g-1} b_j D_{j-g} W + e_Y \qquad (10.1)$$

Additional variables could be included in equation 10.1 as covariates if desired. The model is represented in the form of a statistical diagram in Figure 10.1.

For example, if X is a multicategorical variable with $g = 4$ groups, the model is

$$Y = i_Y + b_1 D_1 + b_2 D_2 + b_3 D_3 + b_4 W + b_5 D_1 W + b_6 D_2 W + b_7 D_3 W + e_Y \quad (10.2)$$

This model allows X's effect on Y, which is represented by the three variables D_1, D_2, and D_3, to depend linearly on W. Remember that the regression weights for the $g - 1$ variables coding groups quantify differences between pairs of means (such as when using indicator coding) or some combination of subsets of group means (such as when using Helmert coding or some other set of orthogonal contrast codes). Rewriting equation 10.2 in a different form shows that these differences are a linear function of W when the $g - 1$ products involving the D variables and W are included in the model:

$$Y = i_Y + (b_1 + b_5 W)D_1 + (b_2 + b_6 W)D_2 + (b_3 + b_7 W)D_3 + b_4 W + e_Y \quad (10.3)$$

Using the notation introduced in section 7.1, this model can be written in the form of three *relative conditional effects* $\theta_{D_i \to Y}$

$$Y = i_Y + \theta_{D_1 \to Y} D_1 + \theta_{D_2 \to Y} D_2 + \theta_{D_3 \to Y} D_3 + b_4 W + e_Y$$

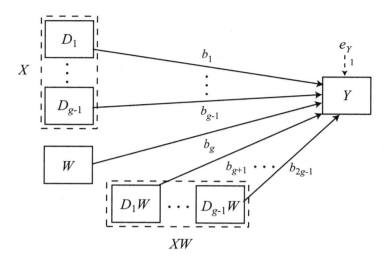

FIGURE 10.1. A statistical diagram of a moderation model with a multicategorical focal antecedent X with g categories.

where $\theta_{D_1 \to Y} = b_1 + b_5 W$, $\theta_{D_2 \to Y} = b_2 + b_6 W$, and $\theta_{D_3 \to Y} = b_3 + b_7 W$. Collectively, these three relative conditional effects represent the conditional effect of X on Y. The conditional effect of X will depend on W, as each of the relative conditional effects are functions of W.

Suppose indicator coding was used to represent the four groups, with group 4 being the reference group, and D_1 is set to 1 for cases in group 1 (0 otherwise), D_2 is set to 1 for cases in group 2 (0 otherwise) and D_3 is set to 1 for cases in group 3 (0 otherwise). Then each of the estimated differences in Y between the group coded with D_i and the reference group is a linear function of W. The extent to which a specific difference depends on W will depend on the weight for W in that linear function. Consider $\theta_{D_1 \to Y} = b_1 + b_5 W$. Using this indicator coding system, D_1 represents the difference in $\hat{Y}$ between group 1 and group 4. If b_5 is equal to 2.0, then the difference in the estimate of Y between group 1 and group 4 changes by 2 units with each one unit increase in W. Suppose the difference in Y between groups 1 and 4 is 3.0 units when $W = 2$. If $b_5 = 2.0$, then when W is increased to 3, the difference in Y between the two groups increases by 2.0 units from 3.0 to 5.0. A negative b_5 would mean that the difference changes in the negative direction. Thus, if $b_5 = -3.0$, then when W increases from 2 to 3, the estimated difference in Y changes from 2.0 to -1.0.

Now consider a special case of equations 10.2 and 10.3 with $b_5 = b_6 = b_7 = 0$. In that situation, none of the differences between each group and the reference group changes with a change in W. That is, none of these differences are a function of W, and therefore X's effect on Y is linearly unrelated to W. If all three of these regression coefficients were exactly zero, then equations 10.2 and 10.3 reduce to a simpler form

$$Y = i_Y + (b_1 + 0W)D_1 + (b_2 + 0W)D_2 + (b_3 + 0W)D_3 + b_4W + e_Y$$
$$Y = i_Y + b_1D_1 + b_2D_2 + b_3D_3 + b_4W + e_Y$$

which is a form of the model with X's effect on Y invariant across values of W.

This logic applies regardless of the coding system representing the four groups that is used in the model. It could be indicator coding, sequential coding, Helmert coding, or any other legitimate coding system representing the multicategorical antecedent X. Regardless of the choice, when b_5, b_6, and b_7 are equal to zero, then X's effect is linearly independent of W, but if any of these regression coefficients for any of the D_iW products is different from zero, this implies that X's effect on Y depends on W.

This logic also applies regardless of the number of groups (g) represented by X. If all of the $g - 1$ regression coefficients for the products between D_i and W are equal to zero, then X's effect is linearly independent of W. But if any of these $g - 1$ regression coefficients is different from zero, then X's effect depends linearly on W. So we can test a hypothesis about moderation of the effect of a multicategorical X on Y by W by comparing the fit of two models estimated using the data available. One model constrains X's effect on Y to be linearly independent of W. That model takes the form

$$Y = i_Y + \sum_{i=1}^{g-1} b_iD_i + b_gW + e_Y \tag{10.4}$$

which is equivalent to equation 10.1 if we assume all regression weights for the $g - 1$ products are zero and so fix them to zero during the estimating by not including the $g - 1$ D_iW products in the equation. The second model, represented by equation 10.1, allows X's effect to depend linearly on W. If the second model fits significantly better than the first (equation 10.4) by a hypothesis test, this is evidence that X interacts with (i.e., X's effect is moderated by) W. But if the second model does not fit any better, meaning that the first, simpler model that fixes X's effect to be linearly independent of W fits no worse, then parsimony would lead us to prefer the simpler model that doesn't allow for linear interaction between X and W.

In section 2.6, I discussed an inferential approach to comparing the fit of two models that differ from each other only by the inclusion of one or more antecedent variables in one model that are not in the other. This involves constructing the difference in R^2 between the two models and converting this difference to a F-ratio, which has a known sampling distribution under the null hypothesis of equality of fit. This null hypothesis of equality of fit is equivalent to the null hypothesis that all of the true regression weights for the antecedent variables in the second model that are not in the first model are equal to zero. In this case, the two models differ by the $g - 1$ products that are in the second model that allow for interaction between X and W that are not in the first model. Under the null hypothesis of no interaction, adding the $g - 1$ products wouldn't improve the fit relative to when the products are absent. But if X and W interact (i.e., W linearly moderates the effect of X), then the model should fit better when the $g - 1$ products are in the model compared to when they are not.

10.2   An Example from the Sex Discrimination in the Workplace Study

In section 6.2, I introduced a study examining how people perceived a person who had been a victim of sexual discrimination as a function of how the victim responded to that discrimination. In this study, women were told about the fate of an attorney (Catherine) who lost a promotion at her law firm to a less qualified male. Participants were randomly assigned to one of three conditions that varied with respect to how Catherine responded. Some were told that she accepted the decision and went about her work at the firm (the no protest condition; PROTEST=0 in the PROTEST data file), some were told that she protested the decision to the senior partners, framing her protest around herself (the individual protest condition; PROTEST=1 in the data), and some were told she protested while framing her arguments around the collective of women (the collective protest condition; PROTEST=2 in the data). Participants then evaluated the attorney on a number of dimensions, with the evaluations aggregated to a single measure of how positively Catherine was perceived or, more simply, how much she was liked (LIKING in the data file).

In this example, X is experimental condition, with three groups distinguished by how Catherine responded, and Y is how much Catherine was liked. The moderator variable is *perceived pervasiveness of sex discrimination in society*, operationalized using the Modern Sexism Scale and available in the data file in the variable labeled SEXISM. Participants who score high on this variable perceive sexism and sex discrimination as rampant and pervasive in society. People who score lower see sexism and sex discrimination as less pervasive than those who score higher. This is a continuous dimension based on a 1 to 7 rating scale for each item in the Modern Sexism Scale, though in the data the measurements range between 2.37 and 7. That is, no participant scored lower than 2.37.

Using these data, I examine whether the effect of the attorney's behavior on how positively she is evaluated depends on the perceiver's beliefs about the pervasiveness of sex discrimination in society. Recall from the example in section 6.2 that Catherine was liked more when she protested in some form relative to when she did not. We now ask whether the effect of her behavior on how much she was liked is related to the perceiver's beliefs about how pervasive sex discrimination and sexism is in society. This is a question about moderation. In this example, the focal predictor X is a multicategorical variable representing three groups and W is a continuous variable proposed as functioning as a moderator of the effect of X.

To test this moderation hypothesis, two models of Y are estimated. The first model includes X and W as antecedent variables. The second model contains the variables in the first model as well as products involving X and W. If X's effect on Y is not linearly moderated by W, then including the products in the second model should not improve the fit of the model relative to the first model, which constrains X's effect on Y to be linearly independent of W.

Slightly complicating this analysis relative to when X is dichotomous or continuous, X must be converted to two variables that represent membership in one of the three groups. Once these variables are constructed, then their products with W can also be constructed and added to the model that includes only the two variables coding group as well as the moderator. For this example, I will use indicator coding, with the no protest group treated as the reference. So the effect for indicator 1 (D_1) will quantify the difference in how Catherine was perceived between those told she individually protested and those told she didn't protest, and the effect for indicator 2 (D_2) will quantify this difference between those told she collectively protested and those told she did not protest the discrimination.

The SPSS code below conducts the analysis, and Table 10.1 contains the regression coefficients and summary statistics for the two models. The first four lines construct the indicator codes and the two products, and the remaining line estimates

$$\hat{Y} = i_Y + b_1 D_1 + b_2 D_2 + b_3 W$$

and then

$$\hat{Y} = i_Y + b_1 D_1 + b_2 D_2 + b_3 W + b_4 D_1 W + b_5 D_2 W$$

and conducts the test of interaction between X and W.

```
compute d1=(protest=1).
compute d2=(protest=2).
compute d1sexism=d1*sexism.
```

TABLE 10.1. Two Regression Models Estimating How Much Catherine Is Liked from Experimental Condition and Perceived Pervasiveness of Sex Discrimination In Society

		Coeff.	SE	t	p
Model 1 $R^2 = 0.053, MSE = 1.069$					
Constant	i_Y	4.762	0.617	7.720	< .001
D_1	b_1	0.497	0.227	2.193	.030
D_2	b_2	0.447	0.223	2.001	< .048
Sexism (W)	b_3	0.108	0.117	0.921	.359
Model 2 $R^2 = 0.135, MSE = 0.992$					
Constant	i_Y	7.706	1.063	7.322	< .001
D_1	b_1	−4.129	1.498	−2.755	.007
D_2	b_2	−3.491	1.408	−2.490	.015
Sexism (W)	b_3	−0.472	0.205	−2.302	.023
$D_1 \times$ Sexism ($D_1 W$)	b_4	0.901	0.288	3.135	.002
$D_2 \times$ Sexism ($D_2 W$)	b_5	0.778	0.275	2.827	.005

```
compute d2sexism=d2*sexism.
regression/statistics defaults change/dep=liking/method=enter d1 d2
   sexism/method=enter d1sexism d2sexism.
```

In SAS, the corresponding set of commands is

```
data protest;set protest;d1=(protest=1);d2=(protest=2);
   d1sexism=d1*sexism;d2sexism=d2*sexism;run;
proc reg data=protest;model liking=d1 d2 sexism d1sexism d2sexism;
   test d1sexism=0,d2sexism=0;run;
```

Unlike the SPSS version, this SAS code will not produce any output for the model that excludes the products (a separate PROC REG command is required to get this model), but it will conduct a simultaneous test that both of the regression coefficients for the two products are zero. This is equivalent to a test of the null hypotheses that the model that includes the two products fits the same as the model that excludes them.

As can be seen in Table 10.1, the model that fixes X's effect to be independent of W is

$$\hat{Y} = 4.762 + 0.497D_1 + 0.447D_2 + 0.108W$$

with $R^2 = 0.053$, whereas the model that allows X's effect to vary linearly with W is

$$\hat{Y} = 7.706 - 4.129D_1 - 3.491D_2 - 0.472W + 0.901D_1W + 0.778D_2W \quad (10.5)$$

with $R^2 = 0.135$. The difference between these two R^2 values is $0.135 - 0.053 = 0.082$, and an increase in the variance in Y explained from 5.3% to 13.5%. This is statistically significant by the test described in section 2.6 and found in the SPSS and SAS output, $F(2, 123) = 5.847, p = .004$. So we conclude that X and W interact, or that W moderates the effect of X. Substantively we conclude that Catherine's decision to protest or not, and the form that protest took, appears to have had different effects on how she was evaluated, depending on the perceiver's beliefs about the pervasiveness of sex discrimination in society.

Implementation in PROCESS

PROCESS takes much of the analytical burden off your shoulders by automatically constructing the necessary products, estimating the model, and conducting the test of interaction. It will even generate the $g - 1$ variables coding groups, produce data to assist in the visualization of the interaction, and it implements various approaches to probing an interaction, discussed later in section 10.4. The model number to use is model 1, just as when X was a dichotomous or continuous dimension, but as discussed in Chapter 6 in the context of mediation analysis, you can tell PROCESS that X is a multicategorical variable by using the **mcx** option.

The PROCESS command that conducts this analysis is

```
process y=liking/x=protest/w=sexism/mcx=1/model=1/plot=1.
```

In SAS, the equivalent command is

```
%process (data=protest,y=liking,x=protest,w=sexism,mcx=1,model=1,
    plot=1);
```

The **mcx=1** specification in the command line tells PROCESS to use indicator coding to represent the three conditions held in the PROTEST variable in the data. Other coding options implemented in PROCESS include Helmert, sequential, and effect coding, or you can feed PROCESS your own coding system if you desire. See Appendix A.

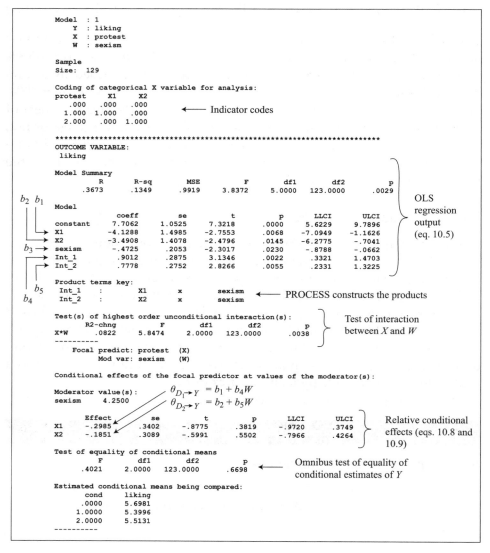

FIGURE 10.2. Output from the PROCESS procedure for SPSS for the sex discrimination moderation analysis.

(continued)

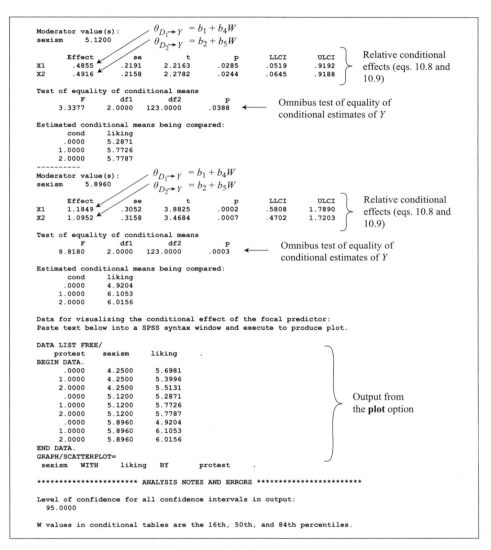

```
Moderator value(s):          θ_{D_1→Y} = b_1 + b_4W
sexism      5.1200           θ_{D_2→Y} = b_2 + b_5W

        Effect      se         t          p       LLCI      ULCI      Relative conditional
X1      .4855     .2191     2.2163     .0285     .0519     .9192      effects (eqs. 10.8 and
X2      .4916     .2158     2.2782     .0244     .0645     .9188      10.9)

Test of equality of conditional means
        F         df1        df2        p               Omnibus test of equality of
     3.3377    2.0000   123.0000     .0388      ←       conditional estimates of Y

Estimated conditional means being compared:
        cond      liking
        .0000     5.2871
       1.0000     5.7726
       2.0000     5.7787
----------
Moderator value(s):          θ_{D_1→Y} = b_1 + b_4W
sexism      5.8960           θ_{D_2→Y} = b_2 + b_5W

        Effect      se         t          p       LLCI      ULCI      Relative conditional
X1     1.1849     .3052     3.8825     .0002     .5808    1.7890      effects (eqs. 10.8 and
X2     1.0952     .3158     3.4684     .0007     .4702    1.7203      10.9)

Test of equality of conditional means
        F         df1        df2        p               Omnibus test of equality of
     8.8180    2.0000   123.0000     .0003      ←       conditional estimates of Y

Estimated conditional means being compared:
        cond      liking
        .0000     4.9204
       1.0000     6.1053
       2.0000     6.0156

Data for visualizing the conditional effect of the focal predictor:
Paste text below into a SPSS syntax window and execute to produce plot.

DATA LIST FREE/
     protest    sexism      liking     .
BEGIN DATA.
       .0000     4.2500     5.6981
      1.0000     4.2500     5.3996
      2.0000     4.2500     5.5131
       .0000     5.1200     5.2871        Output from
      1.0000     5.1200     5.7726        the plot option
      2.0000     5.1200     5.7787
       .0000     5.8960     4.9204
      1.0000     5.8960     6.1053
      2.0000     5.8960     6.0156
END DATA.
GRAPH/SCATTERPLOT=
  sexism    WITH     liking    BY       protest    .

*********************** ANALYSIS NOTES AND ERRORS ************************

Level of confidence for all confidence intervals in output:
  95.0000

W values in conditional tables are the 16th, 50th, and 84th percentiles.
```

FIGURE 10.2 continued.

The resulting output can be found in Figure 10.2. The top of the output shows how the groups are represented with indicator codes (X1 and X2 in the output) and the following section contains the ordinary least squares regression analysis, including all the regression coefficients, standard errors, t- and p-values, confidence intervals, some model summary information, as well as a test of interaction between X and W using the method described in section 2.6 and the end of section 10.1. All the statistics found in this section of the output correspond to statistics described earlier in this example analysis.

Interpretation of the Regression Coefficients

The interpretation of the regression coefficients in a model that includes an interaction between a multicategorical and a continuous antecedent variable can be tricky, but understanding how they are interpreted is important. The regression model estimated earlier is

$$\hat{Y} = i_Y + b_1 D_1 + b_2 D_2 + b_3 W + b_4 D_1 W + b_5 D_2 W \qquad (10.6)$$

From the analysis using the sexual discrimination study data, $i_Y = 7.706$, $b_1 = -4.129$, $b_2 = -3.491$, $b_3 = -0.472$, $b_4 = 0.901$, and $b_5 = 0.778$ (see equation 10.5 and Table 10.1). Equation 10.6 can be written in an equivalent form as

$$\hat{Y} = i_Y + (b_1 + b_4 W)D_1 + (b_2 + b_5 W)D_2 + b_3 W \qquad (10.7)$$

The two terms in parentheses in equation 10.7 are the relative conditional effects of X, expressed in the form of the conditional effects of D_1 and D_2:

$$\theta_{D_1 \to Y} = b_1 + b_4 W = -4.129 + 0.901 W \qquad (10.8)$$

$$\theta_{D_2 \to Y} = b_2 + b_5 W = -3.491 + 0.778 W \qquad (10.9)$$

These are both linear functions of W. $\theta_{D_1 \to Y}$ is the estimated difference in how much Catherine is liked between those told she individually protested and those told she didn't protest. A positive estimate reflects a more positive evaluation of Catherine among those told she individually protested, whereas a negative estimate means that she was liked more when she did not protest compared to when she individually protested. $\theta_{D_2 \to Y}$ has a comparable interpretation, except that it represents the effect of collectively protesting compared to not protesting at all.

From equation 10.8 it is apparent that b_1 quantifies the relative conditional effect of individually protesting compared to not protesting on how positively Catherine was perceived among people who score zero on the Modern Sexism Scale (i.e., $W = 0$). Likewise, from equation 10.9, b_2 estimates the relative conditional effect of collectively protesting compared to not protesting among people who score 0 on the Modern Sexism Scale. But neither of these is substantively meaningful because the Modern Sexism Scale is bound between 1 and 7, and even if zero were on the measurement scale, the smallest value observed in the data is 2.37. So b_1 and b_2 are not substantively interpretable, and their hypothesis tests and confidence intervals are meaningless.

The regression coefficient for $D_1 W$ is $b_4 = 0.901$. This is also the weight for W in equation 10.8 that generates the relative conditional effect of individually protesting relative to not protesting, $\theta_{D_1 \to Y}$. It quantifies how much this relative conditional effect changes as W changes by one unit. In this example, we can say that the effect of individually protesting compared to not protesting differs by 0.901 units between two people who differ by one unit in their perceived pervasiveness of sex discrimination. This difference is statistically significant. Testing whether this regression coefficient is equal to zero is meaningful and useful, because it tells us whether W moderates the effect of individually protesting compared to not protesting at all on how positively Catherine is perceived.

The regression coefficient for $D_2 W$ is $b_5 = 0.778$, which is also the weight for W in equation 10.9. It quantifies how much the relative conditional effect of collectively protesting compared to not protesting at all, $\theta_{D_2 \to Y}$, changes as W changes by one unit. So the effect of collectively protesting compared to not protesting differs by 0.778 units between two people who differ by one unit in their perceived pervasiveness of sex discrimination. This difference is statistically significant, which means that W moderates the effect of collectively protesting relative to not protesting at all on how positively Catherine is perceived.

The interpretation of the remaining regression coefficient, b_3, becomes clear if you set D_1 and D_2 to zero. In that case, equation 10.6 reduces to $\hat{Y} = i_Y + b_3 W$, which looks just like a linear regression model estimating Y from W. But this was simplified by setting D_1 and D_2 to zero, which is the two values of D_1 and D_2 for participants in the no protest condition. So b_3 estimates the relationship between W and Y in this group. We can say that among those told she did not protest, two people who differ by one unit in their perceived pervasiveness of sex discrimination are estimated to differ by -0.472 units in how much they like Catherine. The negative coefficient reflects that the person higher in perceived pervasiveness of sex discrimination likes the nonprotesting Catherine *less* than the person one unit lower in perceived pervasiveness of sex discrimination. This negative relationship is statistically significant.

Note that the interpretation of all these regression coefficients is dependent on how the three groups are represented in the model by the three patterns of D_1 and D_2. A different coding system for the 3 groups will change most if not all of these regression coefficients. However, the test of interaction between X and W will *not* be affected by the coding system used.

10.3   Visualizing the Model

In section 7.3, I described how a regression model that includes the product of antecedent variables is a mathematical abstraction difficult to make sense of without some kind of visual aid. This is even more true when more than one regression coefficient is required to represent an interaction, as when the focal antecedent variable is multicategorical. To gain an understanding of how X's effect on Y varies with W, a procedure largely identical to the one described in section 7.3 can be followed. This involves generating estimates of Y from the regression model by plugging in values of X and W into the regression equation and then plotting the resulting values of $\hat{Y}$ against W and X.

For this example, X represents three groups defined in the analysis by a pattern of values of D_1 and D_2, so these three patterns are used for D_1 and D_2. W is a continuous dimension, so we will choose some values of W to pair up with values of D_1 and D_2. The choice of values of W is frequently arbitrary, and it doesn't really matter so much what values are used so long as they are within the range of the observed data. Using values that are smaller than the minimum value of W or larger than the maximum value of W results in a visual depiction of the model that extrapolates beyond the available data, something I don't recommend doing. To draw a picture of this model, we will use values of W that correspond to the 16th, 50th, and 84th percentiles of the distribution. These values are 4.250, 5.120, and 5.896, respectively. Again, this is somewhat arbitrary, but they correspond to values that PROCESS uses when it generates some output discussed later. We might interpret these values as representing people "relatively low," "relatively moderate," and "relatively high" in their beliefs about the pervasiveness of sex discrimination in society, as defined by the distribution of this variable in the sample. If the model contains covariates, these can be set to their sample mean in the computation of the estimates of Y, as discussed in section 7.3.

With various combinations of X (i.e., a pattern of values of D_1 and D_2) and W, these combinations of values are then plugged into equation 10.5, resulting in various estimates of Y. For example, for a person in the individual protest condition ($D_1 = 1$, $D_2 = 0$) who is "relatively high"

TABLE 10.2. Values of $\hat{Y}$ Generated from the Regression Model (Equation 10.5)

Condition (X)	D_1	D_2	W (SEXISM)	$\hat{Y}$
No Protest	0	0	4.250	5.698
No Protest	0	0	5.120	5.287
No Protest	0	0	5.896	4.920
Individual Protest	1	0	4.250	5.400
Individual Protest	1	0	5.120	5.773
Individual Protest	1	0	5.896	6.105
Collective Protest	0	1	4.250	5.513
Collective Protest	0	1	5.120	5.779
Collective Protest	0	1	5.896	6.016

in perceptions of the pervasiveness of sex discrimination in society ($W = 5.896$), the model generates

$$\hat{Y} = 7.706 - 4.129D_1 - 3.491D_2 - 0.472W + 0.901D_1W + 0.778D_2W$$
$$\hat{Y} = 7.706 - 4.129(1) - 3.491(0) - 0.472(5.896) + 0.901(1)(5.896)$$
$$+ 0.778(0)(5.896)$$
$$\hat{Y} = 6.105$$

as the estimate for how much such a person likes Catherine. These computations for this combination of X and W along with eight other combinations can be found in Table 10.2. These can then be plotted and the dots connected for points corresponding to the same group. The end result of this process can be found in Figure 10.3.

It is now possible to substantively interpret what is happening in the data. Looking at Figure 10.3, your brain probably first noticed three lines with different slopes. These lines represent the relationship between perceived pervasiveness of sex discrimination and how positively Catherine is perceived. It looks like the relationship is positive in two of the conditions but negative in one of them. Although this is true, interpreting Figure 10.3 in this way reverses the focal antecedent variable and moderator relative to the original purpose of the analysis. Our goal was to examine if the effect of her behavior on how she is perceived differs as a function of the perceiver's beliefs about the pervasiveness of sex discrimination in society. Framed in that way, interest with respect to interpretation is not on the different slopes in Figure 10.3, but instead on the *gap between the lines* and how that gap varies as a function of the moderator. It is the gap between the three lines

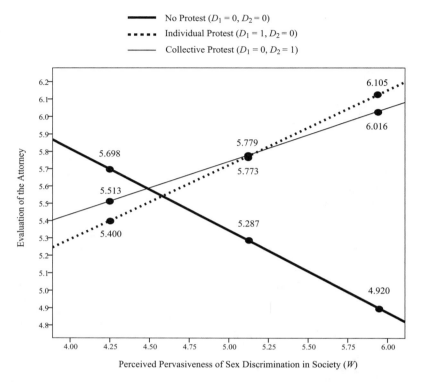

FIGURE 10.3. A visual representation of the moderation of the effect of Catherine's behavior (*X*) on how positively she was perceived (*Y*) by perceived pervasiveness of sex discrimination in society (*W*).

conditioned on a specific value of the moderator that represents differences between the three conditions in how much they liked Catherine, on average, among people who are the same in their beliefs about sex discrimination.

Focusing instead on the gap between the lines, the interpretation is fairly obvious. It appears that among those who are relatively lower in how pervasively they perceive sex discrimination in society, Catherine was liked more when she did not protest compared to when she did. Interpersonally, she appears to have been punished when she framed the argument around herself, but less so when she framed the argument around the collective of women. But when she didn't do anything, she was interpersonally rewarded in the form of a more positive evaluation. However, the pattern is quite different among people who see sex discrimination as more pervasive. Among such people, Catherine was liked more when she protested relative to when she did not. The more pervasive the perception of sex discrimination, the larger the difference in evaluation when Catherine protested relative to when she did not. It appears that such people did not distinguish much between framing the protest collectively or individually. She was liked about the same regardless, but clearly more than when she did not protest, although at the extremes of the distribution of perceived pervasiveness of sex discrimination, she was liked a bit more when she individually rather than collectively protested.

Visualizing the model is an important step in the substantive interpretation process. But you probably aren't going to want to do all the computations described above manually. Fortunately, PROCESS makes the computations needed to generate something like Figure 10.3 quite a bit easier. If you ask for it by using the **plot** option, PROCESS uses the regression model to produce estimates of Y for each group defined by the multicategorical X for cases at various values of W. This information can be found toward the end of the output in Figure 10.2 as well as in the black box below. In this example, the values PROCESS uses correspond to the 16th, 50th, and 84th percentiles of the distribution of SEXISM in the sample, but these can be changed using the **moments** or **wmodval** options. See Appendix A. The SPSS version of PROCESS also writes a little program around the data it generates that can be cut and pasted into SPSS syntax and executed to produce a rough visual representation of the model. This can be edited, or you can use the data in some other graphics production program of your choosing.

```
data list free/
     sexism      protest     liking .
begin data.
     4.2500      .0000      5.6981
     5.1200      .0000      5.2871
     5.8960      .0000      4.9204
     4.2500     1.0000      5.3996
     5.1200     1.0000      5.7726
     5.8960     1.0000      6.1053
     4.2500     2.0000      5.5131
     5.1200     2.0000      5.7787
     5.8960     2.0000      6.0156
end data.
graph/scatterplot=
     sexism with  liking by  protest.
```

The SAS version of PROCESS doesn't write the entire program, but it does generate a table of combinations of X and W as well as $\hat{Y}$ for these. You can then write a program around this table to produce a picture of the model. The SAS code below accomplishes this.

```
data;input sexism protest liking;
if (protest = 0) then Condition = 'No protest condition';
if (protest = 1) then Condition = 'Individual protest condition';
if (protest = 2) then Condition = 'Collective protest condition';
datalines;
4.2500 0.0000 5.6981
5.1200 0.0000 5.2871
5.8960 0.0000 4.9204
4.2500 1.0000 5.3996
5.1200 1.0000 5.7726
5.8960 1.0000 6.1053
4.2500 2.0000 5.5131
5.1200 2.0000 5.7787
5.8960 2.0000 6.0156
run;
proc sgplot;reg x=sexism y=liking/group=Condition
nomarkers lineattrs=(color=black);
xaxis label='Perceived pervasiveness of sex discrimination (W)';
yaxis label='Liking of the attorney (Y)';run;
```

Some people like using R because of its nice graphics production features. An R program that generates a comparable figure is below:

```
x<-c(0,1,2,0,1,2,0,1,2)
w<-c(4.25,4.25,4.25,5.12,5.12,5.12,5.896,5.896,5.896)
y<-c(5.698,5.400,5.513,5.287,5.773,5.779,4.920,6.105,6.016)
plot(y=y,x=w,pch=15,col="white",xlab="Perceived pervasiveness of sex
discrimination (W)",ylab="Liking of the attorney (Y)")
legend.txt<-c("No protest","Individual protest","Collective protest")
legend("topleft",legend=legend.txt,lty=c(1,1,3),lwd=c(4,1,4))
lines(w[x==0],y[x==0],lwd=4,lty=1)
lines(w[x==1],y[x==1],lwd=1,lty=1)
lines(w[x==2],y[x==2],lwd=4,lty=3)
```

10.4 Probing the Interaction

The interpretation I provided for the results of this study using the visual representation of the model in Figure 10.3 is descriptive and holistic. For some people, this would be sufficient. But most investigators would want to go further than this by offering the rigor of statistical inference for particular claims about the effect of X, acknowledging that the picture in Figure 10.3 is sample specific. It is based on the estimated regression coefficients, each of which is estimated with sampling error, which means that so too does the visual depiction of the model contain sampling error. If this study were conducted in exactly the same way but using a different set of 129 participants, the regression coefficients would certainly not be the same as the ones in equation 10.5, which means the picture of the model would also be different. So we can't just look at a picture and start talking about where X affects Y and where it does not. We need to acknowledge sampling variance by formally *probing* the interaction.

The methods for doing so are similar to those discussed in Chapters 7 and 8, but when X is a multicategorical variable, we need to distinguish between an *omnibus test* and a *pairwise test*. This distinction came up in Chapter 6 in the discussion of the omnibus effects and relative effects in a mediation analysis when X is multicategorical. In an analysis of variance, when we claim that g groups differ from each other on average on dependent variable Y because the F-ratio is sufficiently large, we are making an omnibus claim. Analysis of variance provides an omnibus test of equality of a set of g group means. Except in the special case where $g = 2$, an analysis of variance result doesn't say how the groups differ, or which groups differ from which. In contrast, a pairwise test offers a more specific test of the difference between two quantities, such as between the means of groups 1 and 2, or between the average of the means of groups 1 and 2 compared to the mean of group 3. Pairwise tests provide more specific information than does an omnibus test.

With this distinction in mind, probing an interaction involving a multicategorical focal antecedent can yield answers to such questions as whether $\hat{Y}$ differs between the g groups among people high on the moderator, or whether $\hat{Y}$ differs between two groups of people who are average on the moderator. The first is an omnibus claim, while the second is a pairwise claim. My discussion of probing the interaction focuses first on the pick-a-point procedure and its use for making omnibus and pairwise claims. Following this, I address the application of the Johnson–Neyman technique.

Before beginning, it is worth acknowledging a potential question and confusion. Why should we care about differences in $\hat{Y}$ between the groups, since $\hat{Y}$ is just an estimate for a particular person in a particular group based on the model? The answer is that $\hat{Y}$ functions as an estimate of a group mean. When we say the estimate of how much Catherine is liked by someone who scored 5.12 on the Modern Sexism Scale and was told Catherine individually protested is $\hat{Y} = 5.773$, we are making a statement about an estimated mean of a group of such people in that condition who scored 5.12 on this scale. So it is meaningful to determine if $\hat{Y}$ differs between two or more groups, because we are in effect determining whether two or more means are different from each other, conditioned on a value of the moderator. This is possible to do even if no one in the data scored exactly 5.12 or some other value of interest on the Modern Sexism Scale. We are making a model-informed guess what the mean of Y would be for such people based on the relationships between the antecedent variables and their relationships with Y.

The Pick-a-Point Approach

The pick-a-point approach requires you to choose values of the moderator W and then estimate the conditional effect of X on Y at those values and conduct an inferential test. When X is a multicategorical variable, the conditional effect of X when $W = w$ is represented by a set of $g - 1$ relative conditional effects $\theta_{D_i \to Y}|(W = w)$, where $i = 1$ to $g - 1$. An omnibus inferential test answers the question of whether $\hat{Y}$ when $W = w$ is the same for all g groups. A pairwise inference focuses on one of the $g-1$ conditional effects and answers the question of whether $\hat{Y}$ is the same in the two groups or sets of groups corresponding to the comparison that D_i codes, but when $W = w$. Of course, $\hat{Y}$ is not likely to be exactly the same in all the groups when using the estimated regression coefficients. But the estimated model is sample specific. We are interested in whether the $\hat{Y}$ in the three groups differ from each other, on average, more than can be explained by chance.

Omnibus Inference. In equation 10.6, b_1 and b_2 jointly quantify the effect of X on Y when $W = 0$ (also recall equations 10.7, 10.8, and 10.9). A test of the null hypothesis that these two regression weights both equal zero is an omnibus test of the null hypothesis of equality of $\hat{Y}$ in the three groups when $W = 0$. This can be conducted by estimating a model that includes W, $D_1 W$, and $D_2 W$, and then adding D_1 and D_2 to that model. A statistically significant increase in R^2 using the method described in section 2.6 leads to a rejection of the null hypothesis and a corresponding inference that among people who score zero on the Modern Sexism Scale, the attorney's behavior results in a difference in how she is perceived.

But this null hypothesis is not worth testing in this example because a value of zero on the Modern Sexism Scale is below the minimum possible measurement on the scale. The Modern Sexism Scale is bound between 1 and 7. Furthermore, there is no one in the data lower than 2.37, so there is no value in testing whether the attorney's behavior had an effect on how she is perceived at the point $W = 0$. What we want is a test of equality of $\hat{Y}$ in the three groups when W is some value we choose, rather than when $W = 0$. By choosing various values of W and conducting this test for each of those values, we can then say where in the distribution of W there is a statistically significant effect of her behavior on how much she was liked, and where there is no such effect.

Using this logic of building a model in two steps, adding D_1 and D_2 to the model last, we can test the equality of $\hat{Y}$ in the three groups for any value of W we choose using the regression centering strategy described starting on page 250. First, construct a new variable W' defined as $W - w$, where w is some value you choose. Then run a regression analysis estimating Y from W', D_1W', and D_2W':

$$\hat{Y} = i_Y + b_3 W' + b_4 D_1 W' + b_5 D_2 W' \qquad (10.10)$$

With this model estimated, then add D_1 and D_2, resulting in a model of the form:

$$\hat{Y} = i_Y + b_1 D_1 + b_2 D_2 + b_3 W' + b_4 D_1 W' + b_5 D_2 W' \qquad (10.11)$$

Then apply the test of equality of fit of these two models that is discussed in section 2.6. If the second model fits significantly better than the first (i.e., the change in R^2 has a sufficiently small p-value), this means that $\hat{Y}$ is not the same in the three groups conditioned on $W = w$.

The logic of this test becomes clear once you appreciate that equations 10.10 and 10.11 are identical if you assume that the regression coefficients for D_1 and D_2 in equation 10.11 are equal to zero. Remember that b_1 and b_2 quantify the differences between groups in Y when $W' = 0$, but $W' = 0$ when $W = w$. So equation 10.10 assumes that when $W = w$, $\hat{Y}$ is the same in the three groups because the regression coefficients for D_1 and D_2 are fixed at zero. But equation 10.11 allows the regression coefficients for D_1 and D_2 to differ from zero. If doing so produces a better fitting model, then this means that the three groups differ, on average, on $\hat{Y}$, conditioned on $W = w$.

In the sex discrimination study, there were three groups. However, the logic of this test applies to any number of groups. Merely center W around a value of w of your choosing, estimate Y from the centered W and the $g - 1$ products between centered W and each of the D variables coding groups. Then add the $g - 1$ D variables to the model. A significant increase in R^2 when the D variables are added results in a rejection of the null hypothesis of equality of $\hat{Y}$ between the g groups when $W = w$.

I illustrate this procedure by testing whether estimated liking of Catherine is the same in the three groups among people "relatively low" in perceived pervasiveness of sex discrimination. I operationalize "relatively low" as 4.25, which is the 16th percentile of the distribution of W in the sample. From the regression model (see section 10.3 and Table 10.2), we know that for such people, the estimated liking for Catherine is 5.698, 5.400, and 5.513 among those assigned to the no protest, individual protest, and collective protest groups, respectively. These are the three estimates of Y depicted on the left side of the plot of the model in Figure 10.3.

To test whether these differ from each other more than can be explained by chance, a new variable W' is constructed, defined as $W - 4.25$. Two products are then created, one by multiplying W' by D_1, and another by multiplying W' by D_2. With these new variables constructed, the models in equation 10.10 and 10.11 are estimated, along with a test of equality of the fit of the two models. The SPSS code below does the analysis:

```
compute d1=(protest=1).
compute d2=(protest=2).
compute sexismp=sexism-4.250.
compute d1sexp=d1*sexismp.
compute d2sexp=d2*sexismp.
regression/statistics defaults change/dep=liking/method=enter sexismp
    d1sexp d2sexp/method=enter d1 d2.
```

The equivalent code in SAS is

```
data protest;set protest;d1=(protest=1);d2=(protest=2);
    sexismp=sexism-4.25;d1sexp=d1*sexismp;d2sexp=d2*sexismp;run;
proc reg data=protest;model liking=d1 d2 sexismp d1sexp d2sexp;
    test d1=0,d2=0;run;
```

The model without D_1 and D_2 has $R^2 = .129$. When D_1 and D_2 are added, R^2 increases to .135, a change in R^2 of $\Delta R^2 = .135 - .129 = .006$. This is not statistically significant, $F(2, 123) = 0.402, p = .670$. So we can conclude that among people relatively low in their perceived pervasiveness of sex discrimination, Catherine's behavior does not affect how much she is liked.

This procedure would then typically be repeated a few more times for different values of W. I did so for $W = 5.120$ and $W = 5.896$, which are the 50th and 84th percentiles of the distribution of W in the data and represent "relatively moderate" and "relatively high" in perceived pervasiveness of sex discrimination. Among those relatively moderate ($W = 5.120$), the three estimated values of Y are 5.287, 5.773, and 5.779, for the no protest, individual protest, and collective protest groups, respectively (see Table 10.2 and Figure 10.4). These are statistically different from each other, $\Delta R^2 = .047, F(2, 123) = 3.338, p = .039$. And among those relatively high ($W = 5.896$) in perceived pervasiveness of sex discrimination, there is a statistically significant difference in how much Catherine is liked in the three groups, $\Delta R^2 = .124, F(2, 123) = 8.818, p < .001$. The three estimated values of Y being compared in this test are 4.920, 6.105, and 6.016 for the

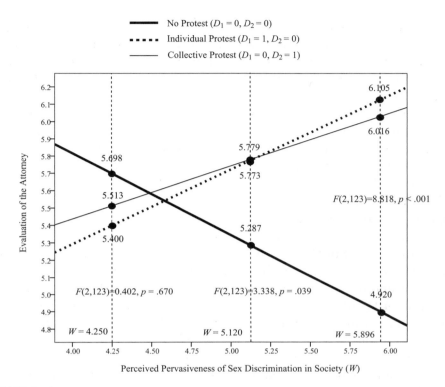

FIGURE 10.4. A visual representation of the moderation of the effect of Catherine's behavior on how positively she was perceived by perceived pervasiveness of sex discrimination in society, along with the results of three omnibus tests of the equality of conditional estimates of Y.

no protest, individual protest, and collective protest groups, respectively (from Table 10.2 and Figure 10.4).

PROCESS takes care of all of this work for you if X is specified as multicategorical using the **mcx** option. When W is a continuum, PROCESS automatically conducts a test of the omnibus null hypothesis that $\hat{Y}$ is the same in the three groups at values of W corresponding to the 16th, 50th, and 84th percentiles of the distribution of W in the data available. You can change the values of W if you want using the **moments** or **wmodval** options. The test is displayed in the section of output in Figure 10.2 titled "Test of equality of conditional means," where you will find the F-ratio and p-value corresponding for this test. Below the test are the estimates of Y that are being compared (and that correspond to those found in Figures 10.3 and 10.4 as well as Table 10.2). Everything you see in this part of the output in Figure 10.2 corresponds to the computations just described. If W is dichotomous, PROCESS will show the results of this test twice, once for each group coded by W.

Pairwise Inference. When probing an interaction involving a multicategorical X, pairwise inferential tests provide more information than omnibus tests. Whereas an omnibus test determines whether g groups differ from each other on $\hat{Y}$ when W is some value w, a pairwise test can be used to determine whether two groups, or two subsets or combinations of groups, differ from each other on $\hat{Y}$ conditioned on W. Whereas omnibus tests are invariant to the choice of the coding system used to represent the g groups, the outcome of pairwise tests will be dependent on the choice. Using a different system for coding groups can produce different results when a pairwise test is used.

When X is multicategorical, X's effect on Y is represented by the effects of the $g - 1$ variables used to code the g groups. From equations 10.3 and 10.7, these $g - 1$ effects are a linear function of moderator W. They are the $g-1$ relative conditional effects $\theta_{D_i \to Y}$. For instance, in the three group case, equations 10.7, 10.8, and 10.9 show that the relative conditional effect of D_1 is $b_1 + b_4 W$ and the relative conditional effect of D_2 is $b_2 + b_5 W$. By plugging any value of W into these functions, you can quantify the difference in $\hat{Y}$ between the groups or subsets of groups that D_1 and D_2 represent. With a standard error derived, you can test whether $\hat{Y}$ differs between the two groups or combinations of groups that D_i represents. The standard error can be estimated with a variant of equation 7.13. For instance, in this example,

$$se_{\theta_{D_1 \to Y}} = \sqrt{se_{b_1}^2 + (2W)COV_{b_1 b_4} + W^2 se_{b_4}^2}$$

and

$$se_{\theta_{D_2 \to Y}} = \sqrt{se_{b_2}^2 + (2W)COV_{b_2 b_5} + W^2 se_{b_5}^2}$$

But there is no need to compute this standard error manually using a formula such as this, as you can get your regression program to do the test for you using the regression-centering approach.

To make this more concrete, consider the effect of Catherine's behavior on how she is perceived among people who are relatively high in their perceptions of the pervasiveness of sex discrimination in society. Defining "relatively high" as $W = 5.896$, or the 84th percentile of the distribution of W in the data, we know from equation 10.5, Table 10.2, and Figures 10.3 and 10.4 that among such people, the estimates of how much Catherine is liked are 4.920, 6.105, and 6.016. Earlier, we saw that these three estimates are not the same according to an omnibus test of equality. But this is a vague claim. A pairwise test provides further information about which of these estimates are different from which.

Earlier, I discussed that b_1 and b_2 in equation 10.6 quantify the effect of D_1 on Y and the effect of D_2 on Y when $W = 0$. We decided that

TABLE 10.3. Three Regression Models Estimating How Much Catherine Is Liked (Y) from Experimental Condition (X) and Perceived Pervasiveness of Sex Discrimination in Society (W) after Centering Perceived Pervasiveness of Sexism around 4.250, 5.120, and 5.896

		Coeff.	SE	t	p
$W' = W - 4.250$					
Constant	i_Y	5.698	0.229	24.846	< .001
D_1	b_1	−0.299	0.340	−0.877	.382
D_2	b_2	−0.185	0.309	−0.599	.550
Sexism (W')	b_3	−0.472	0.205	−2.302	.023
$D_1 \times$ Sexism ($D_1 W'$)	b_4	0.901	0.288	3.135	.002
$D_2 \times$ Sexism ($D_2 W'$)	b_5	0.778	0.275	2.827	.005
$W' = W - 5.120$					
Constant	i_Y	5.287	0.156	33.920	< .001
D_1	b_1	0.486	0.219	2.216	.029
D_2	b_2	0.492	0.216	2.278	.024
Sexism (W')	b_3	−0.472	0.205	−2.302	.023
$D_1 \times$ Sexism ($D_1 W'$)	b_4	0.901	0.288	3.135	.002
$D_2 \times$ Sexism ($D_2 W'$)	b_5	0.778	0.275	2.827	.005
$W' = W - 5.896$					
Constant	i_Y	4.920	0.230	21.398	< .001
D_1	b_1	1.185	0.305	3.883	< .001
D_2	b_2	1.095	0.316	3.468	.001
Sexism (W')	b_3	−0.472	0.205	−2.302	.023
$D_1 \times$ Sexism ($D_1 W'$)	b_4	0.901	0.288	3.135	.002
$D_2 \times$ Sexism ($D_2 W'$)	b_5	0.778	0.275	2.827	.005

these weren't meaningful in the sex discrimination study analysis. But by centering W around a value like $W = 5.986$, then b_1 and b_2 quantify the effect of D_1 and D_2 among people "relatively high" on W. The effect of D_1 is the difference in $\hat{Y}$ between those told Catherine individually protested and those told she didn't protest, $\theta_{D_1 \to Y}$, and the effect of D_2 is the difference in $\hat{Y}$ between those told Catherine collectively protested and those told she didn't protest, $\theta_{D_2 \to Y}$. By centering W around 5.896 prior to construction of products and estimating the model, then our regression program gives us these conditional effects, standard errors, t-values, p-values, and confidence intervals.

Table 10.3 shows b_1 and b_2 when estimating the model after centering W around the values 4.250, 5.120, and 5.896. Notice that b_1 and b_2 differ in these analyses, but b_3, b_4, and b_5 are unaffected by the centering. Also notice in the third model, when W was centered around 5.896, that $b_1 = 1.185$ and $b_2 = 1.095$. The regression coefficient b_1 quantifies the difference in $\hat{Y}$ between those told Catherine individually protested and those told she did not protest: $b_1 = 6.105 - 4.920 = 1.185$. This difference, depicted visually in Figure 10.5 on the top right, is statistically significant. Similarly, the regression coefficient b_2 quantifies the difference in $\hat{Y}$ between those told Catherine collectively protested and those told she did not protest: $b_2 = 6.015 - 4.920 = 1.095$. This difference, depicted in Figure 10.5 on the bottom right, is statistically significant.

So by using the regression centering strategy described earlier in the context of an omnibus test of equality of values of $\hat{Y}$, the regression coefficients b_1 and b_2 provide pairwise inferences consistent with the coding system used to represent the three groups, conditioned on the value that W is centered around. From Table 10.3, you can see that among those "relatively low" in perceived pervasiveness of sex discrimination ($W = 4.250$), Catherine was no more or less liked on average when she individually or collectively protested relative to when she did not [$b_1 = -0.299 = \theta_{D_1 \to Y}|(W = 4.250) = 5.400 - 5.698, p = .382$; $b_2 = -0.185 = \theta_{D_2 \to Y}|(W = 4.250) = 5.513 - 5.698, p = .550$]. These relative conditional effects are depicted in Figure 10.5 on the top and bottom left. But among people "relatively moderate" in perceived pervasiveness of sex discrimination ($W = 5.120$), Catherine was liked more on average when she individually or collectively protested relative to when she did not [$b_1 = 0.486 = \theta_{D_1 \to Y}|(W = 5.120) = 5.773 - 5.287, p = .029$; $b_2 = 0.492 = \theta_{D_2 \to Y}|(W = 5.120) = 5.779 - 5.287, p = .024$; see Figure 10.5 in the middle of the top and bottom panels]. A similar pattern exists among those relatively high in perceived pervasiveness of sex discrimination ($W = 5.986$). She was liked more when she individually

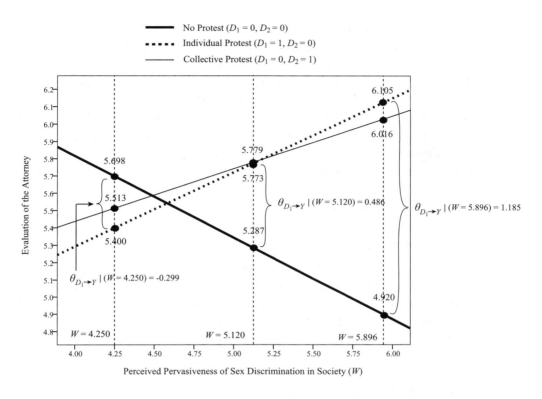

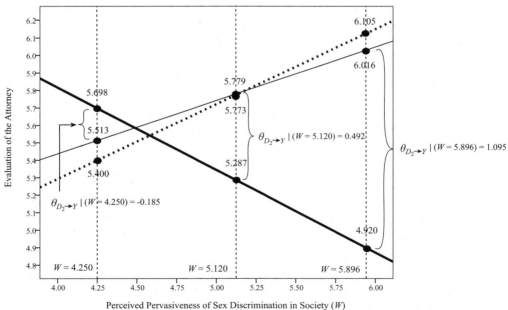

FIGURE 10.5. The relative conditional effects of individually protesting compared to not protesting (top) and collectively protesting compared to not protesting (bottom) conditioned on various values of perceived pervasiveness of sex discrimination.

protested than when she did not protest [$b_1 = 1.185 = \theta_{D_1 \to Y}|(W = 5.986) = 6.105 - 4.920, p < .001$] and when she collectively protested relative to when she did not [$b_2 = 1.095 = \theta_{D_2 \to Y}|(W = 5.896) = 6.016 - 4.920, p < .001$].

Information for pairwise inference when probing an interaction involving a multicategorical X is provided automatically by PROCESS. When X is specified as multicategorical, PROCESS will produce all $g - 1$ estimates of $\theta_{D_i \to Y}$ along with standard errors, t- and p-values and confidence intervals. In Figure 10.2, these are found in the section of output just under the values of W used for conditioning in the rows labeled X1 and X2. A close examination of Figure 10.2 will verify that all the statistics just reported are provided in one PROCESS output.

The Johnson–Neyman Technique

As discussed in section 7.4, a problem with the pick-a-point approach to probing an interaction is having to choose values of the moderator. When the moderator is a continuum, you may not have any basis for choosing some values rather than others, and the choice you make will certainly influence the results of the probing exercise to some extent. Letting a program such as PROCESS make the choice for you through its default use of the 16th, 50th, and 84th percentiles of the distribution of the moderator does not solve this problem. Actively choosing a different system or convention, such as using the sample mean of W, a standard deviation below the mean, and a standard deviation above the mean also does not eliminate the problem. But the Johnson–Neyman (JN) technique avoids this problem entirely. Recall from section 7.4 that the JN technique algebraically derives the value or values of W, if they exist, where the effect of focal antecedent variable X transitions between statistically significant and not at a given α-level. By looking at the p-values for the conditional effect of X above and below the value(s) identified by the JN technique, one can talk about when, or for whom, X is significantly related to Y and when or for whom it is not.

Omnibus Inference. Applied to probing an interaction between a multicategorical X and a continuous W, an omnibus version of the JN technique involves finding the value or values of W where the F-ratio comparing the g estimated values of Y is just statistically significant. Although this is easy to say, Montoya (2016) shows that this is much harder to do. The problem is that the mathematics involves some tedious algebra with complex polynomials. When $g = 3$, W needs to be isolated in a 4th-order polynomial. When $g > 3$, there are some theorems in mathematics suggesting that no solutions can be derived.

To get around this problem, Montoya (2016) provides a computational solution that involves iteratively hunting the moderator space to find the values of W that produce an F-ratio testing the equality of the g values of $\hat{Y}$ with a p-value exactly equal to the α-level used for the inference, with α chosen by you (or convention, such as $\alpha = .05$). So rather than deriving the values of values of W analytically, they can be found through a kind of computational trial and error approach. This requires a computer program. The approach she describes is not implemented in PROCESS, but it is available in a macro for SPSS and SAS named OGRS described in detail in Montoya (2016) and also illustrated in Hayes and Montoya (2017). OGRS can be downloaded at no charge from *www.akmontoya.com*. When I applied the OGRS macro to this analysis, it identified $W = 5.096$ as defining one region of significance, with the effect of the attorney's behavior resulting in a statistically significant difference ($p = .05$) in how much she was liked among people higher than 5.096 on the Modern Sexism Scale. Among people lower than this value, there is no statistically significant difference between the three groups in how much she was liked.

Pairwise Inference. Each of the $g - 1$ variables representing a multicategorical X with g groups represents some kind of comparison between two groups or sets of groups, depending on the coding system used. In the sex discrimination study analysis, D_1 and D_2 are indicator codes with the no protest group used as the reference. D_1 represents the comparison between the individual protest group and the no protest reference group, and D_2 represents the comparison between the collective protest group and the no protest group. The conditional effects of D_1 and D_2 are $\theta_{D_1 \to Y} = b_1 + b_4 W$ and $\theta_{D_2 \to Y} = b_2 + b_5 W$ and so are both linear functions of W. By choosing a value of W, you get an estimate of the difference between the two groups on Y represented by that D variable, as discussed earlier when I described the pick-a-point approach. The ratio of the conditional effect at some value of W relative to its standard error at that W value is a t statistic which has a p-value associated with it, or a confidence interval could be constructed.

A pairwise JN approach to probing the interaction between X and W derives the value or values of W where the conditional effect $\theta_{D_i \to Y}$ transition between statistically significant and not. With g groups, you can get zero, one or two values of W for each conditional effect, and these need not and typically won't be the same. For example, when $g = 3$, the value or values of W identified for $\theta_{D_1 \to Y}$ typically won't be the same as those identified for $\theta_{D_2 \to Y}$.

As discussed in section 7.4, the JN computations are complex and tedious and best left to a computer. The JN technique is implemented in PROCESS, but only when X is dichotomous or continuous. When using the **mcx** option specifying that X is a multicategorical variable, no JN output is provided even when including **jn=1** in the command line. However, it is possible to trick PROCESS into generating JN output for $\theta_{D_i \to Y}$ when X is multicategorical. This requires using D_i as X in model 1 and the remaining $g-2$ D variables as well as the $g-2$ products between the other D variables and W as covariates. This is then repeated for a total of $g-1$ times, once for each of the $g-1$ D_i variables.

For the sex discrimination example, the PROCESS code to identify regions of significance for the conditional effect of individually protesting relative to not protesting (D_1) is

```
compute d1=(protest=1).
compute d2=(protest=2).
compute d2sexism=d2*sexism.
process y=liking/x=d1/w=sexism/cov=d2 d2sexism/jn=1/model=1.
```

Notice that we have to construct the indicator codes manually because we are not using the **mcx** option. In addition, we have to manually construct the product between D_2 and W, because PROCESS won't do this on its own. It will, however, generate D_1W, since PROCESS is programmed to produce the product of X and W, and D_1 is specified as X in the command line. I don't include the **plot** option here like I have in other examples because the output PROCESS generates from this option would be meaningless when using this trick.

After executing this code, PROCESS identifies $W = 5.065$ as the point where the estimated difference in how much Catherine is liked between those told she did not protest and those told she individually protested transitions between statistically significant and not at the $\alpha = .05$ level. Above this value, she was liked more by those told she individually protested. But below this value, there is no statistically significant difference between these two conditions. Actually, there is a second point PROCESS identifies; the value $W = 3.335$, with estimated liking being higher among those told she did not protest. However, there is only one case in the data below this value of W, so I would not be comfortable reporting this region of significance, even though it does make substantive sense.

We then repeat this process for the comparison between the collective protest condition and the no protest condition. With the indicator codes already constructed, the SPSS code below does the analysis:

```
compute d1sexism=d1*sexism.
process y=liking/x=d2/w=sexism/cov=d1 d1sexism/jn=1/model=1.
```

PROCESS shows $W = 5.036$ as a point of transition in the significance of the difference between these two conditions. For people above this value, those told she collectively protested liked Catherine more than those told she did not protest. Below this value, there is no statistically significant difference between these two groups in how much she was liked.

This trick also works in the SAS version of PROCESS. Corresponding SAS code is

```
data protest;set protest;d1=(protest=1);d2=(protest=2);
    d1sexism=d1*sexism;d2sexism=d2*sexism;run;
%process (data=protest,y=liking,x=d1,w=sexism,cov=d2 d2sexism,jn=1,
    model=1);
%process (data=protest,y=liking,x=d2,w=sexism,cov=d1 d1sexism,jn=1,
    model=1);
```

10.5   When the Moderator Is Multicategorical

In section 10.1, we saw that the moderation of the effect of a multicategorical variable X by a dichotomous or continuous moderator W can be estimated using a regression model of the form

$$Y = i_Y + \sum_{i=1}^{g-1} b_i D_i + b_g W + \sum_{j=g+1}^{2g-1} b_j D_{j-g} W + e_Y \qquad (10.12)$$

where the $g - 1$ D variables are constructed using a system for representing membership in one of the g groups, such as indicator coding. But what if instead, X is a continuous or dichotomous focal antecedent variable and W is a multicategorical variable functioning as a moderator of X's effect? In that case, we would think of the $g - 1$ D variables in equation 10.12 as representing the g categories of the *moderator*. But this doesn't change the mathematics of the model, in that X's effect on Y can be estimated as dependent on W by estimating Y from X, the $g - 1$ D variables coding W, and $g - 1$ products involving X and the D variables:

$$Y = i_Y + \sum_{i=1}^{g-1} b_i D_i + b_g X + \sum_{j=g+1}^{2g-1} b_j D_{j-g} X + e_Y \qquad (10.13)$$

This model is presented in statistical diagram form in Figure 10.6. Mathematically, equations 10.12 and 10.13 are the same. All I have done is switch the labeling of W and X. When applied to the same data, these models will produce exactly the same estimates of Y, the models will fit equally well, and all the regression coefficients will be the same.

Earlier, I showed that a model of the form in equation 10.12 can be rewritten as $g - 1$ linear functions of W, each of which represents "the effect

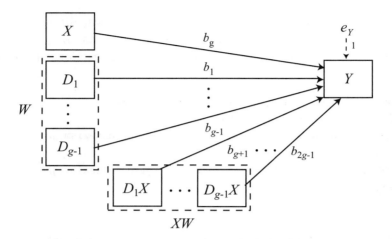

FIGURE 10.6. A statistical diagram of a moderation model with a multicategorical moderator W with g categories.

of D_i," which is a component of the effect of X. For instance, in the sex discrimination study, where X is three groups, the model

$$\hat{Y} = i_Y + b_1 D_1 + b_2 D_2 + b_3 W + b_4 D_1 W + b_5 D_2 W + e_Y \qquad (10.14)$$

can be written in the form

$$\hat{Y} = i_Y + (b_1 + b_4 W)D_1 + (b_2 + b_5 W)D_2 + b_3 W + e_Y$$

which expresses X's effect on Y in the form of two linear functions of moderator W. These are the relative conditional effects of D_1 and D_2 that represent the effect of X on Y for a given value of W.

But equation 10.14 can be rewritten in another form. Before doing so though, let's reexpress equation 10.14 after reversing the roles of X and W, so that D_1 and D_2 represent categories of W rather than X. The model in that form looks like this

$$Y = i_Y + b_1 D_1 + b_2 D_1 + b_3 X + b_4 D_1 X + b_5 D_2 X + e_Y \qquad (10.15)$$

which can written in an alternative form:

$$Y = i_Y + b_1 D_1 + b_2 D_2 + (b_3 + b_4 D_1 + b_5 D_2)X + e_Y \qquad (10.16)$$

Equation 10.16 shows that the effect of X on Y is a function of the multicategorical W:

$$\theta_{X \to Y} = b_3 + b_4 D_1 + b_5 D_2 \qquad (10.17)$$

In equation 10.17, $\theta_{X \to Y}$ is the conditional effect of X on Y. But notice that because there are only three patterns of D_1 and D_2 representing the three groups, equation 10.17 produces only three values. These represent how differences in X relate to differences in Y in each of the three groups.

Notice that if b_4 and b_5 are both zero in equation 10.17, then X's conditional effect is the same in each of the three groups, meaning no moderation of the effect of X on Y. But if either b_4 or b_5 is different from zero, then this implies that the relationship between X and Y is not the same in the three groups. So a test of moderation of X's effect by the multicategorical W can be conducted by testing whether both of the weights for the two products in equation 10.15 are equal to zero. This is equivalent to testing whether a model that includes the products fits no better than the model that excludes them. The test described in section 2.6 can be used.

An important lesson from this derivation is that testing whether a multicategorical X's effect is moderated by a continuous or dichotomous W is mathematically the same as testing whether a multicategorical W moderates the effect of a dichotomous or continuous X. Either way the moderation question is framed, the test of moderation boils down to whether the regression coefficients for the $g - 1$ product terms in the model are all equal to zero. So when we claim from a statistical test of moderation that X's effect is moderated by W, then it is also true that W's effect is moderated by X. This is the symmetry property of interactions first described in section 7.1. But it is convenient for the sake of this discussion to call the focal antecedent X regardless of whether it is the multicategorical variable. Mathematically, the model is the same either way, and so is the test of interaction.

An Example

In the study on sex discrimination in the workplace described earlier, the analysis showed that the attorney's behavior had different effects on how much she was liked, depending on the perceiver's beliefs about the pervasiveness of sex discrimination in society. In that example, experimental condition was a multicategorical focal antecedent and scores on the Modern Sexism Scale served as a continuous moderator. For this illustration, we will switch the roles of the experimental manipulation and scores on the Modern Sexism Scale and ask how the relationship between perceived pervasiveness of sex discrimination (X) and how positively the attorney was perceived (Y) depends on the attorney's choice as to how to respond to the sex discrimination (W). Now the moderator is a multicategorical variable representing three groups, and the focal antecedent variable is a continuous individual difference. We will use the same indicator coding system for representing the three conditions as we did earlier.

We already know from the symmetry property of interactions that the relationship between perceived pervasiveness of sex discrimination and how much Catherine was liked must vary across the three conditions, because we know that how Catherine behaved differently affected how much she was liked depending on the perceiver's beliefs about the pervasiveness of sex discrimination in society. And we just discussed that the model is the same regardless of whether the multicategorical variable is the focal antecedent or moderator. Given this, we know from Table 10.1 that the regression model in equation 10.15 after estimation is

$$\hat{Y} = 7.706 - 4.129D_1 - 3.491D_2 - 0.472X + 0.901D_1X + 0.778D_2X \quad (10.18)$$

and so $i_Y = 7.706$, $b_1 = -4.129$, $b_2 = -3.491$, $b_3 = -0.472$, $b_4 = 0.901$, and $b_5 = 0.778$. We also know from that earlier analysis that the inclusion of the two products produces a better-fitting model than when they are excluded, $\Delta R^2 = .082$, $F(2, 123) = 5.847$, $p = .004$.

Because the model is the same as in the earlier analysis, so too is the visual depiction of the model, which can be found in Figure 10.7 with a few minor changes to reflect that we are now thinking of perceived pervasiveness of sex discrimination as the focal antecedent rather than the moderator. But this change in the roles of experimental condition and perceived pervasiveness of sex discrimination influences how we should look at Figure 10.7. Earlier, focus was on the gaps between the lines and how these gaps varied with perceived pervasiveness of sex discrimination. But now interpretation focuses on the slopes of the three lines, as each of these lines represents the relationship between perceived pervasiveness of sex discrimination (the focal antecedent variable) and how much the attorney was liked. It appears that perceiving sex discrimination as more pervasive translates into liking Catherine more, *if she protested in some form*. If she chose not to protest the discrimination, perceiving sex discrimination as more pervasive translates into liking Catherine *less*.

Probing the Interaction and Interpreting the Regression Coefficients

When a moderator is a continuous variable, the pick-a-point or JN approaches can be used to probe an interaction. But if the moderator is a categorical variable, the JN technique is off the table, as it applies only to continuous moderators. When the moderator is categorical, probing the interaction involves quantifying the relationship between the focal antecedent X and the consequent variable Y in each of the groups that constitute the categorical moderator. One may also be interested in comparing two or more of these conditional effects of X to each other.

Recall equation 10.17, which expresses the conditional effect of X as a function of the three group multicategorical moderator variable W as $\theta_{X \to Y} = b_3 + b_4D_1 + b_5D_2$. In this example, plugging the three patterns of D_1

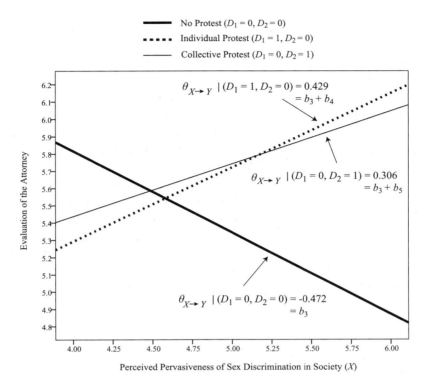

FIGURE 10.7. A visual representation of the moderation of the effect of perceived pervasiveness of sex discrimination in society on how positively the attorney is evaluated as a function of the attorney's response to the sex discrimination.

and D_2 representing how the attorney responded to the sex discrimination into this equation yields three conditional effects of perceived pervasiveness of sex discrimination on how much she was liked:

$$\theta_{X \to Y} | \text{No protest} = -0.472 + 0.901(0) + 0.778(0) = -0.472$$
$$\theta_{X \to Y} | \text{Individual protest} = -0.472 + 0.901(1) + 0.778(0) = 0.429$$
$$\theta_{X \to Y} | \text{Collective protest} = -0.472 + 0.901(0) + 0.778(1) = 0.306$$

These are the slopes of the three lines in Figure 10.7, and each can be interpreted just like a regression coefficient as the estimated difference in Y between two cases that differ by one unit on X. These estimates and their signs reflect the substantive interpretation of Figure 10.7 provided earlier.

It becomes apparent looking at equation 10.17 that b_3 quantifies the relationship between X and Y when D_1 and D_2 both equal zero. So when indicator coding is used, b_3 represents the relationship between X and Y in the reference group. In this example, we know that b_3 is statistically significant (see Table 10.1 and corresponding discussion), so we can say that among those told the attorney did not protest, the relationship between perceived pervasiveness of sex discrimination and how positively she is evaluated is negative and statistically significant.

Reflecting on equation 10.17 results in the recognition that the regression coefficients for D_1X and D_2X, b_4 and b_5, quantify the difference in the relationship between X and Y in the reference group and the group coded with D_1 or D_2. For instance, D_1 in this example captures the comparison between the no protest group and the individual protest group. Thus, b_4 is the difference in the conditional effect of X between these two groups, which corresponds to the difference between the slopes of the lines for these two groups in Figure 10.7. Indeed, notice that this is so: $b_4 = 0.429 - (-0.472) = 0.901$. From Table 10.1 and earlier discussion, we know that b_4 is statistically significant, so we can say that these slopes are significantly different from each other. So the relationship between perceived pervasiveness of sex discrimination and how much Catherine is liked differs between those told she individually protested and those told she did not protest.

The indicator variable D_2 captures the comparison between the no protest group and the collective protest group. So b_5 is the difference in the conditional effect of perceived pervasiveness of sexism on how much Catherine is liked between these two groups: $b_5 = 0.306 - (-0.472) = 0.778$. This is the difference between the slopes of the corresponding lines in Figure 10.7. As this difference is statistically significant, we can conclude that the relationship between perceived pervasiveness of sex discrimination and evaluation of Catherine differs between these two groups.

But we are missing some other inferential tests that might be worth undertaking. For example, notice that b_3, b_4, and b_5 provide no information about the statistical significance of the relationship between X and Y in the other two groups. We do get an inference for the conditional effect of X in the reference group. That is b_3 and its test of significance. But we get this information only because the no protest group was chosen as the reference group. We can undo that choice, making one of the other groups the reference group and rerunning the analysis after modifying the construction of D_1 and D_2 accordingly. When that is done, b_3 and its test of significance correspond to the conditional effect of X on Y in the group made the new reference group.

Doing so reveals that among those told Catherine protested individually, the conditional effect of perceived pervasiveness of sex discrimination, $\theta_{X \to Y} = 0.429$, is statistically significant, $p = .035$. But $\theta_{X \to Y} = 0.306$, the conditional effect of perceived pervasiveness of sex discrimination among those told she collectively protested, is not statistically significant ($p = .098$). Changing the reference group also provides a test of the difference between the conditional effects of perceived pervasiveness of sex discrimination among those told she individually protested and those told she collectively protested. This difference is $0.429 - 0.306 = 0.123$, but it is not statistically significant, $p = .615$.

Have we yet discussed the meaning of b_1 and b_2 in this example? We have, since equation 10.18 is the same as equation 10.5 from when experimental condition was the focal predictor. We saw earlier that b_1 represents the estimated difference in how much Catherine is liked among those told she did not protest and those told she individually protested *among those who score zero on the Modern Sexism Scale*. Similarly, b_2 represents the estimated difference in how much Catherine is liked among those told she did not protest and those told she collectively protested *among those who score zero on the Modern Sexism Scale*. These are not substantively meaningful because zero is outside of the range of possible values of the Modern Sexism Scale. But they could be made meaningful by centering perceived pervasiveness of sex discrimination around some value within the range of measurement prior to model estimation, as discussed in section 10.4.

Implementation in PROCESS

I demonstrated earlier that PROCESS takes care of much of the work required to estimate a model that includes an interaction between a multicategorical focal predictor and a dichotomous or continuous moderator. But you can specify the moderator as multicategorical instead, and PROCESS will take care of all the required computations. To do so, use the **mcw** option, as in

```
process y=liking/x=sexism/w=protest/mcw=1/model=1.
```

In SAS, the equivalent command is

```
%process (data=protest,y=liking,x=sexism,w=protest,mcw=1,model=1);
```

As with the **mcx** option, an equals sign and a number should follow the **mcw** option to tell PROCESS how to represent the multicategorical moderator in the form of a set of $g-1$ variables. Using option 1, as in the command above, specifies indicator coding of W (see the documentation in Appendix A for other coding strategies implemented in PROCESS).[1] The resulting output is in Figure 10.8. The output looks very similar to the first part of the output in Figure 10.2, though the indicator codes are now labeled W1

---

[1] The **mcx** and **mcw** can be used together if both focal predictor and moderator are multicategorical.

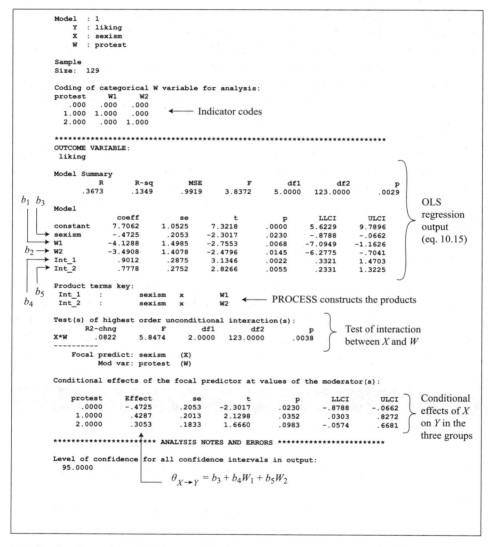

FIGURE 10.8. Output from the PROCESS macro for SPSS for the sexual discrimination study, with experimental condition as the moderator and perceived pervasiveness of sex discrimination as the focal antecedent variable.

and W2 rather than X1 and X2, reflecting the fact that W rather than X is specified as multicategorical. The output provides the regression model and summary and information pertinent to inference such as the test of interaction and p-values and confidence intervals for the regression coefficients. And at the end of the output, PROCESS implements equation 10.17 to generate the conditional effects of X on Y in each of the g groups, along with corresponding information for inference. As can be seen, perceptions of the pervasiveness of sex discrimination are significantly and positively related to how much Catherine is liked among those told she individually protested ($W = 1$), but significantly and negatively related to how much she is liked among those told she did not protest ($W = 0$). Among those told she collectively protested ($W = 2$), the relationship between evaluations of Catherine and perceived pervasiveness of sex discrimination is positive but not quite statistically significant.

10.6   Using a Different Coding System

When either the focal antecedent variable or moderator is a multicategorical variable, it requires $g - 1$ variables in the model to represent membership in one of the g groups. There are many systems you can use for representing group membership. In this chapter, I have focused on indicator coding as an easy and commonly used system. Other systems may be more useful in your analysis.

It may have occurred to you, now that you have seen the results of the two analyses presented in this chapter, that indicator coding may not be the best choice here. From the results of these analyses, it seems that the participants in this study made little distinction between protesting individually and protesting collectively. The relative conditional effects of these forms of protesting relative to not protesting at all are largely identical regardless of the value of perceived pervasiveness of sexism that these effects are conditioned on. And when experimental condition (how the attorney responded to the sex discrimination) was used as the moderator, Figure 10.7 shows that the relationship between perceived pervasiveness of sex discrimination and how the attorney was evaluated is largely the same in the two protest conditions, but very different than in the no protest condition.

Indeed, even before you saw the results, you might have thought from the discussion in Chapter 6 on mediation analysis (see section 6.3) that using D_1 and D_2 to define two orthogonal contrasts representing the three groups would have provided more useful information about differences between them. This set would include one contrast comparing the no protest condition to a combined protest condition (D_1), and another comparing the two protest conditions to each other (D_2). The codes to represent such contrasts would be $D_1 = -2/3$, $D_2 = 0$ for the no protest group, $D_1 = 1/3$, $D_2 = -1/2$ for the individual protest group, and $D_1 = 1/3$, $D_2 = 1/2$ for the collective protest group. See Table 6.3 and the surrounding discussion in section 6.3 for a review of how this coding system works.

If we had used this coding system to represents the groups rather than indicator coding, it would not have changed the answer to the question of whether experimental condition and perceived pervasiveness of sexism interact in their influence on how positively Catherine is evaluated. It also would not have changed omnibus approaches to probing the interaction if experimental condition were the focal antecedent variable. However, it would change various pairwise inferences, because these are determined by how the $g - 1$ variables represent differences between groups or pairs of groups.

I end this chapter without showing the results of a comparable analysis using this alternative coding system, though you might consider it worthwhile to try this as an exercise. In Chapter 13, when I integrate the mediation analysis described in Chapter 6 with the moderation analysis in this chapter, I will use this set of orthogonal contrast codes to represent the groups instead of indicator coding.

10.7   Chapter Summary

This third section of the book on moderation analysis has been dedicated to the use of regression analysis to answer questions about how the effect of an antecedent variable on a consequent varies as a function of a third variable. The inclusion of the product of focal antecedent variable X and moderator W along with X and W allows the effect of X to vary linearly with W. This chapter illustrates that this principle generalizes when the focal antecedent is a multicategorical variable representing membership in three or more groups. When X is multicategorical with g groups, including $g-1$ products constructed from the $g-1$ variables representing the g groups and moderator W allows the differences between the groups on Y to differ linearly with W. A comparison of the fit of a regression model with and without these $g - 1$ products serves as a formal test of moderation of the effect of X on Y by W.

Once such a model is estimated, it can be visualized and probed using a variation on the techniques discussed in prior chapters. The pick-a-point approach to probing an interaction between a multicategorical X and a dichotomous or continuous W involves choosing values of W and then conducting an omnibus test of the difference between groups on Y at those values, or doing two or more specific comparisons between groups conditioned on those values of W. The Johnson–Neyman technique can also be used to identify regions of the distribution of a continuous moderator W where the g groups differ from each other on Y to a statistically significant degree.

The symmetry property of interaction guarantees that if W moderates the effect of X on Y, then X also moderates the effect of W on Y. The models are mathematically identical. The same procedure used for specifying interaction between a multicategorical antecedent variable X and a continuous or dichotomous moderator W can be used when the moderator is multicategorical and the focal predictor is dichotomous or continuous. I Illustrated how so in this chapter.

The computations described here are not difficult to undertake using any program capable of doing linear regression analysis, although they can be somewhat tedious. The PROCESS macro takes away much of the computational burden by estimating the model, conducting a test of interaction, probing the interaction, and producing estimates of Y for various combinations of focal antecedent and moderator useful for visualizing the model.

With the fundamental principles and procedures of mediation and moderation analysis discussed in the last 8 chapters now well in your grasp, you are prepared to tackle the integration of mediation and moderation analysis into a single integrated analytical model. Conditional process analysis—the name I have given to this analytical integration—allows you to examine the extent to which a mechanism or set of mechanisms is contingent on a moderator or moderators. As you will see, lessons learned in the previous chapters cannot just be forgotten as you turn to the next page, for most every concept introduced thus far reappears in this next section of the book dedicated to conditional process analysis.

Part IV

CONDITIONAL PROCESS ANALYSIS

11

Fundamentals of Conditional Process Analysis

Conditional process analysis is used when the analytical goal is to describe and understand the conditional nature of the mechanism or mechanisms by which a variable transmits its effect on another. In this chapter, I describe a number of published examples that illustrate some of the many ways that moderation and mediation can be pieced together into a single integrated analytical model—a conditional process model. Following this, I outline the fundamental principles, concepts, and procedures of conditional process analysis, including the conditional direct and conditional indirect effect. I illustrate the application of these fundamentals by conducting a simple conditional process analysis using data from a study of team performance that illustrates how an indirect effect can be moderated and how to interpret such a phenomenon. Throughout the chapter, I show how PROCESS simplifies the work required to conduct a conditional process analysis.

Let's return to the example that started Chapter 3 on simple mediation analysis. Suppose we have established through a carefully designed experiment that gain frame messages are more effective than loss frame messages at influencing people to abandon their smoking habit. Furthermore, perhaps a mediation analysis reveals that this effect operates through counterarguing, in that loss frame messages invoke more counterarguing in the minds of the recipient, and this counterarguing reduces the persuasiveness of the message. However, even after accounting for individual differences in counterarguing, there is still evidence of a difference in smoking cessation between those exposed to the gain versus the loss frame.

The indirect effect of X (frame) on Y (smoking cessation intentions) through M (counterarguing) contains two components that, when multiplied together, yield an estimate of how much two cases that differ by one unit on X are estimated to differ on Y through the effect of X on M, which in turn affects Y. The first component is the effect of X on M, and the second is the effect of M on Y when holding X constant. In the notation of Chapter 3, these are paths a and b, respectively. Their product functions as a quantification of the mechanism by which gain frame messages influence behavior relative to loss frame messages.

In a mediation analysis, as in any analysis, we are losing some information when we reduce complex responses that no doubt differ from person to person or situation to situation down to a single number or estimate. For instance, when we say from the results of an experiment that people exposed to a loss frame message engage in more counterarguing on average than those exposed to the gain frame message, we are ignoring the very real possibility that for some types of people, or for some types of messages, or in some contexts or circumstances, or for some types of health-related issues, this may be less true or perhaps even false. Perhaps a loss frame message does not produce more counterarguing if the message includes a highly graphic visual image relative to when it does not. Or perhaps people who are less likely to engage in systematic processing of the message are less likely to counterargue regardless of how the message is framed. No doubt there are moderators of the effect of framing on counterarguing. Just because we haven't explicitly modeled an effect as moderated doesn't mean that it isn't. In fact, it almost certainly is.

This same reasoning applies to the effect of M on Y. It certainly makes sense that engaging in counterarguing while processing a message could reduce its persuasive effectiveness. But maybe this is more true for open-minded people whose beliefs and behaviors are amenable to influence through reasoning than for people whose beliefs and behaviors are determined by ideology, religion, or who have deeply ingrained habits. A single estimate of the effect of counterarguing on intentions to quit smoking collapses across all individual differences and ignores the possibility that this effect may be and probably is moderated by *something*.

Finally, the direct effect in a mediation analysis is an effect too. Like all other causal paths in a mediation model, assuming that the direct effect is unmoderated by ignoring potential moderators and reducing the effect down to a single estimate may result in a description of a phenomenon that is incomplete, if not also wrong, if that effect is moderated.

It is safe to say that all effects are moderated by something. This is not to say that any analysis that fails to include moderation or that does not attempt to test for interaction between variables is bad, misguided, or should be avoided. Models are not intended to be complete mathematical representations of a process. Human behavior is too complicated to be reduced to a mathematical model, and no model we could ever imagine, much less estimate or test, would be complete and accurate (MacCallum,

2003). But an analysis that ignores the potential contingencies and boundary conditions of an effect is going to result in a greater oversimplification of complex processes relative to an analysis that acknowledges that complexity by formally modeling it, at least in part. With comfort in the principles of moderation analysis outlined in Chapters 7 to 10 you are now able to rigorously test a moderation hypothesis and examine or explore the potential contingencies that characterize most all phenomena that scientists study.

Thus far in this book, mediation and moderation have been treated as distinct, separate, and independent concepts with different analytical procedures and interpretations. Yet processes modeled with mediation analysis likely are contingent and hence moderated, in that they operate differently for different people or in different contexts or circumstances. A more complete analysis, therefore, should attempt to model the mechanisms at work linking X to Y while simultaneously allowing those effects to be contingent on context, circumstance, or individual differences. This chapter begins the formal integration of mediation and moderation analysis by introducing an analytical method I have termed *conditional process analysis*. Conditional process analysis, or conditional process *modeling*, can be used when your research goal is to understand and describe the conditional nature of the mechanism or mechanisms by which a variable transmits its effect on another and testing hypotheses about such contingent effects.

The notion of combining moderation and mediation is not new. Authors of some of the seminal articles on mediation analysis discussed reasons investigators might want to entertain hypotheses that involve both moderation and mediation simultaneously. For instance, Judd and Kenny (1981) discuss the possibility that a causal antecedent variable X could moderate its own indirect effect on Y through M if the effect of M on Y depends on X. Some have gone so far as to say that *any* mediation analysis should include a component that allows M's effect on Y to be moderated by X (Kraemer et al., 2002; Kraemer, Kiernan, Essex, & Kupfer, 2008; Valeri & VanderWeele, 2013). Similarly, James and Brett (1984) describe how the indirect effect of X on Y through M could be contingent on a fourth variable if that fourth variable W moderates one or more of the relationships in a three-variable causal system. Both of these are examples of what has come to be known as *moderated mediation*. Baron and Kenny (1986) also discuss moderated mediation when they make the point that an indirect effect could be contingent on a moderator variable, while also describing the possibility that an interaction between a moderator W and causal agent X on outcome Y could operate through a mediator M, a phenomenon that has been dubbed *mediated moderation*.

Not long after the turn of the 21st century, there was an explosion of articles in the methodology literature that more formally addressed moderated mediation and mediated moderation, and how moderation and mediation analysis can be analytically integrated. Muller et al. (2005) started the boom with their aptly titled article, "When Moderation Is Mediated and Mediation Is Moderated," in which they describe causal-steps-like criteria to establish mediation of moderation or moderation of mediation while also discussing how moderated indirect and direct effects can be quantified. However, their discussion focused entirely on only one specific form of moderated mediation in which a single variable moderated all three paths in a simple mediation model, and their method suffers from the some of the same flaws as the causal steps approach discussed in section 4.1. Not long after, Morgan-Lopez and MacKinnon (2006) described a formal test of mediated moderation that researchers could use to establish that an interaction effect on some outcome is carried through a mediator.

Almost simultaneously, Edwards and Lambert (2007) and Preacher et al. (2007) published on the topic of moderated mediation but went far beyond the single model delineated by Muller et al. (2005). Edwards and Lambert (2007) described eight different models that could be constructed by allowing a single variable to moderate one or more of the causal paths in a mediation process and how the various direct and indirect effects can be estimated. While more limited in the number of models they discussed compared to Edwards and Lambert (2007), Preacher et al. (2007) introduced *conditional indirect effect* into the lexicon of statistical mediation analysis and showed how conditional indirect effects are calculated and hypotheses are tested through the construction of standard errors and bootstrap confidence intervals. They also illustrated how moderated mediation could be conceptualized in a model with two different moderators of different paths in the causal system. Various other papers have popped up since then in both the methodological and substantive literature addressing means of conceptualizing and quantifying the contingencies of a causal sequence of effects (e.g., Fairchild & MacKinnon, 2009; Hayes, 2015, 2018; Wang & Preacher, 2015).

Although all of these articles in some way contributed to the adoption of the methods and techniques discussed in this collective literature, Preacher et al. (2007) made it very easy for researchers to do so using software with which they were already familiar and using. The release of PROCESS with the first edition of this book probably contributed to the continued growth in the publication of substantive research articles in many different fields that have included an analysis based on the principles of conditional process analysis I illustrate and discuss in this and the next few chapters. In the next section I provide a small sampling of the numerous ways that moderation and mediation can be combined in a single conceptual model. The section following formally defines the conditional indirect and conditional direct effect, concepts that are key in this kind of data analysis exercise. I then apply these ideas by stepping through a single and fairly simple exemplar of a conditional process analysis, showing how PROCESS can be brought into service to simplify the estimation and inference of direct and indirect effects, both conditional and unconditional, and to test whether an indirect effect is moderated.

11.1   Examples of Conditional Process Models in the Literature

The mechanism linking X to Y can be said to be conditional if the indirect effect of X on Y through M is contingent on a moderator. There are many ways this could happen. For instance, the effect of X on M could be moderated by some variable W. The conceptual diagram in Figure 11.1, panel A, represents such a model. Alternatively, the effect of M on Y could be moderated by W, as in Figure 11.1, panel B.

An example of the former is found in Rees and Freeman (2009), who proposed and estimated such a process in a study of 197 male amateur golfers in the United Kingdom. They proposed that athletes with more task-related and emotional social resources available to them (*social support*, X) would perform better next time they played golf (*task performance*, Y) in part because of the boost in confidence such social support provides (*self-efficacy*, M), which in turn helps performance. However, they proposed that this social support $\rightarrow$ self-efficacy $\rightarrow$ task performance effect would be stronger among men experiencing more stress at home (*stressors*, W). Their reasoning was that social support would not be an important or salient source of confidence among people who were content and relaxed at home and so such support would do little to help task performance. But when that support occurred in the presence of a troubled, stressful home life, it would be a particularly effective confidence booster, and this would facilitate better play. Indeed, they found that more social support translated into greater self-efficacy and, in turn, a better golf score only among those experiencing relatively more stress at home. Among those experiencing relatively less stress, there was no indirect effect of social support on performance through self-efficacy. Additional examples of conditional processes in this form being proposed and modeled include Hoyt, Burnette, and Auster-Gussman (2014), Goodboy et al. (2016), Gvirsman (2014), Johnson et al. (2016), Karnal et al. (2016), Penarroja, Orengo, Zornoza,

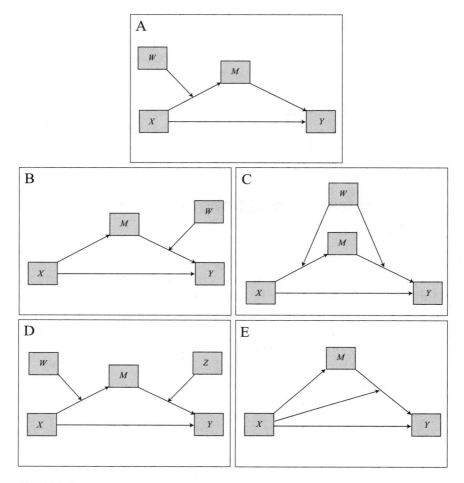

FIGURE 11.1. Some variants of a conditional process model found in published research.

Sanchez, and Ripoll (2015), Pittarello, Leib, Gordon-Hecker, and Shalvi (2016), Quratulain and Khan (2015), Smith et al. (2016), Thomas and Bowker (2015), Torres and Taknint (2015), van Dijke and De Cremer (2010), Wang, Stroebe, and Dovidio (2012), and Zhou, Hirst, and Shipton (2012).

Popan, Kenworthy, Frame, Lyons, and Snuggs (2010) offer an exemplar of a conditional process model with moderation of the effect of M on Y (panel B of Figure 11.1). Their study was designed to examine how the attributions made about the behavior of a member of an outgroup functions as a mechanism by which outgroup contact can influence attitudes held about the outgroup as a whole. Participants in this experiment were randomly assigned to recall up to 10 either positive or negative interactions with an outgroup member—someone with a different political orientation than their own—and provide detail about one of those interactions. They also reflected on the extent to which this person's behavior during the interaction seemed grounded in rational thought. Following this, their attitudes about the outgroup as a whole were assessed. Popan et al. found that participants who were asked to describe a positive interaction rather than negative interaction with a member of the outgroup (*valence of outgroup prime, X*) reported feeling more positive about the outgroup as a whole afterwards (*outgroup attitude, Y*) in part because the outgroup person's behavior was seen as relatively more rational (*rationality attribution, M*), which in turn was associated with a more positive attitude. However, this indirect effect was contingent upon how representative of the outgroup as a whole the outgroup member was perceived as being (*typicality of outgroup member, W*). The indirect effect of contact valence on outgroup attitudes through perceived rationality existed only among people who perceived the outgroup member as typical of the outgroup. Among those who thought the person was atypical, there was no indirect effect of contact valence on attitudes through perceived rationality. Many other examples of conditional process models involving moderation of the $M \rightarrow Y$ effect can be found, including Antheunis, Valkenburg, and Peter (2010), Boren and Veksler (2015), Canfield and Saudino (2016), Cornelissen, Bashshur, Rode, and LeMenestrel (2013), Felipe et al. (2016), Green and Auer (2013), Kung et al. (2016), Luszczynska et al. (2010), and Warner, Schwarzer, Schüz, Wurm, and Tesch-Romer (2012).

A conditional process model can include moderation of more than one path in the causal sequence. For example, the effect of X on M and the effect of M on Y could be moderated by a common variable, as diagrammed in Figure 11.1, panel C. Though less commonly proposed and tested in the empirical literature than models with moderation of only a single path, many examples do exist (e.g., Belogolovsky, Bamberger, & Bacharach, 2012; Chae, 2014; Donegan & Dugas, 2012; Huang, Zhang, & Broniarczyk, 2012; Kim & Labroo, 2011; Li et al., 2013; Malouf, Stuewig, & Tangney, 2012; Parade, Leerkes, & Blankson, 2010; Richter & Schmid, 2010; Silton et al., 2011; Thai et al., 2016; van Leeuwen, Rogers, Gibbs, & Chabrol, 2014; Wu et al., 2015). For instance, Parade et al. (2010) studied 172 females entering university with the goal of examining how feelings that one's parents are responsive the student's needs and are available for discussion and support (*parental attachment security, X*) influence satisfaction with relationships acquired in the first semester of college (*satisfaction with friends, Y*). They proposed that a more secure parental attachment style would result in less discomfort in social situations (*social anxiety, M*) during the transition to college life and this would translate into more positive experiences developing and relating to peers and friends in the university setting. However, this indirect effect was postulated to be moderated by race (*white* versus *minority*, W). They found that the relationship between secure attachment and social anxiety was stronger (i.e., more negative) among minority students than white students (i.e., moderation of $X \rightarrow M$ effect by W), as was the (negative) relationship between social anxiety and satisfaction with friends (i.e., moderation of the $M \rightarrow Y$ effect by W). Their conditional process analysis supported their claim of mediation of the effect of parental attachment security on friendship satisfaction by social anxiety only among minority students. In the white students, no such process appeared to be at work.

A variant of such a model involves the moderation of the effect of X on M by one variable W but moderation of the effect of M on Y by a different moderator Z, as in Figure 11.1, panel D. For instance, Laran, Dalton, and Andrade (2011) examined the mechanism by which slogans, when present in an advertisement, can in some circumstances prompt behavior opposite of the intent of the ad. According to these investigators, slogans are generally seen as attempts at persuasion more so than are brand logos, and the more they are perceived as such by the consumer, the more likely the consumer will unconsciously react against the persuasion attempt by engaging in behavior contrary to the slogan. They exposed participants in the study to brand logos or brand logos combined with slogans (*advertising tactic, X*) that either did or did not emphasize saving money (*behavioral prime, Z*). They also asked how much they felt that the logos and (for some participants) slogans they saw were designed to persuade (*persuasive intent, M*). Before answering the question about persuasive intent, some participants were asked to imagine they had run across the logo or slogan in a magazine filled with advertisements, whereas others were given no such instruction (*persuasion focus, W*). Participants were later presented with a hypothetical scenario in which they were to imagine a shopping trip where they could spend anywhere between \$0 and \$500, and they were asked how much they would spend (*willingness to spend, Y*). They found that logos combined with slogans were perceived as higher in persuasive intent than logos only, but only when participants were not primed to think in terms of the persuasive intent of advertising. This difference in perceived persuasive intent between logos and slogans resulted in an increased willingness to spend money, but only for slogans focused on *saving* money. Thus, they found an indirect effect of advertising tactic on willingness to spend through perceived persuasive intent only when participants were not primed to think in terms of the persuasive intent of advertisements and for slogans that focused on saving money. For another example of such a model, see Li, Shaffer, and Bagger (2015).

An intriguing form of conditional process model is one in which X functions as a moderator of its own indirect effect on Y through M. It may be safe to call this the *original* conditional process model, as this kind of scenario was addressed by Judd and Kenny (1981) in their seminal *Evaluation Review* article published in 1981 on *process analysis*, what later became known as mediation analysis. A causal antecedent X can moderate its own indirect effect on Y through M if it moderates the effect of M on Y, as depicted in Figure 11.1, panel E. MacNeil et al. (2010) offer a good example of such a process in their study of 417 caregivers of elderly persons who suffer from some kind of mental or physical ailment (e.g., Alzheimer's or Parkinson's disease). According to their model, caregivers experiencing certain psychological maladies such as anxiety, depression, or resentment (*caregiver mental health*, X) are more likely to mistreat the person they are caring for (*potentially harmful behavior*, Y), because their own mental states enhance experiences of anger toward the recipient of their care (M), which in turn enhance the likelihood of harmful behavior. Their results were consistent with such a mediation process, but the association between anger and potentially harmful behavior was stronger among those feeling more depressed or resentful. Among the less resentful and depressed caregivers, anger was less likely to prompt maltreatment of the recipient of their care. Thus, the indirect effect of resentment and depression on mistreatment through anger was larger among those feeling more resentful or more depressed. For additional studies examining whether X moderates its own indirect effect, see D'Lima, Pearson, and Kelley (2012), Godin, Belanger-Gravel, and Nolin (2008), Moneta (2011), Oei et al. (2010), Pérez-Edgar et al. (2010), or Wiedemann, Schüz, Sniehotta, Scholz, and Schwarzer (2009).

As these five examples illustrate, moderation can be combined with mediation in a number of different ways. But these examples only scratch the surface of what is possible. Think about the number of possibilities when you increase the number of mediators, distinguish between moderation of paths in a parallel versus serial multiple mediator model, or allow for multiple moderators of different paths or the same path, and so forth. The possibilities are nearly endless. But regardless of the configuration of moderated paths or complexity of the model, conditional process analysis involves the estimation and interpretation of direct and indirect effects, just as in a simple mediation analysis. However, when causal effects in a mediation model are moderated, they will be conditional on those moderators. Thus, an understanding of the concepts of the *conditional direct effect* and the *conditional indirect effect* is required before one should attempt to undertake a conditional process analysis. The next section defines these terms and provides examples of their computation for a few models of increasing complexity.

11.2   Conditional Direct and Indirect Effects

Chapters 3 through 5 described the principles of statistical mediation analysis. In a mediation analysis, interest and effort focus on the estimation and interpretation of the direct and indirect effects of presumed causal agent X on putative outcome Y. The indirect effect in a mediation analysis is the product of a sequence of effects estimated using the available data that are assumed to be causal. For instance, in the simple mediation model, X's indirect effect on Y through M is quantified as the effect of X on M multiplied by the effect of M on Y controlling for X. In the notation of Chapter 3, the indirect effect is product of effects a and b estimated using equations 3.1 and 3.2.

But we've also seen in Chapters 7 through 10 that if a variable's effect is moderated, this means that the variable's effect cannot be quantified with a single number. For instance, suppose that the effect of X on M is moderated by W. In that case, there is no longer a single quantity that can be used to describe X's effect on M. Instead, X's effect on M is a function of W. Or perhaps M's effect on Y controlling for X is moderated by W. Then M's effect on Y cannot be distilled down to a single number. Rather, M's effect on Y is a function of W. Indeed, it could be that both moderation processes are at work simultaneously, where X's effect on M and M's effect on Y are both moderated by W. Or perhaps X's effect on M is moderated by W and M's effect on Y is moderated by a different variable Z.

The moderation of a path in a mediation model does not change the fact that the indirect effect of X on Y through M is still a product of paths of influence. But rather than being a product of two numbers, the indirect effect in such a circumstance becomes a product involving at least one function (depending on which path or paths are moderated), which makes the indirect effect a function of the moderator or moderators that influence the size of the effects in the causal system. That is, the $X \rightarrow M \rightarrow Y$ mechanism differs in size or strength as a function of a moderator variable or set of variables.

A direct effect can also be moderated. In a mediation model, the direct effect of X on Y quantifies the effect of X on Y independent of X's influence on Y through M. In a simple mediation model, it is estimated as c' in equation 3.2. But the direct effect of X on Y could be contingent on a moderator. For instance, if W moderates the effect of X on Y controlling for M, then the direct effect is no longer a single number such as c' but is instead a function of W. It is conditional on a variable in the model rather than unconditional.

When a direct or indirect effect is conditional, analysis and interpretation of the results of the modeling process should be based on a formal estimate of and inference about conditional direct and/or conditional indirect effects. In this section, I illustrate the computation of conditional direct and indirect effects for example models that combine moderation and mediation.

Example 1: Moderation of Only the Direct Effect

The simplest and arguably least interesting conditional process model is a model that combines simple mediation with moderation of the direct effect of X, as depicted in the conceptual diagram in Figure 11.2, panel A, on the left (or in statistical form, on the right). In this model, there is a single indirect effect of X on Y through M, as well as a direct effect that is a function of a fourth variable W. The statistical diagram represents two equations, one for consequent M and one for consequent Y. Assuming linear moderation of the direct effect of X by W, the two equations are

$$M = i_M + aX + e_M \tag{11.1}$$
$$Y = i_Y + c_1'X + c_2'W + c_3'XW + bM + e_Y \tag{11.2}$$

The indirect effect in this model is defined as the product of a and b, just as in any simple mediation model. Because neither the $X \to M$ nor the $M \to Y$ paths are moderated, this indirect effect is unconditional. However, the direct effect of X on Y is conditional, as it is a function of W. As in Chapter 7, this can be seen by rewriting equation 11.2 after grouping terms involving X and factoring out X:

$$Y = i_Y + (c_1' + c_3'W)X + c_2'W + bM + e_Y$$

or, equivalently,

$$Y = i_Y + \theta_{X \to Y}X + c_2'W + bM + e_Y$$

where $\theta_{X \to Y}$ is the *conditional direct effect* of X on Y, defined as

$$\theta_{X \to Y} = c_1' + c_3'W$$

So in this model, X exerts its effect on Y indirectly through M, independent of any other variable, but also directly, with the magnitude of the direct effect being dependent on W.

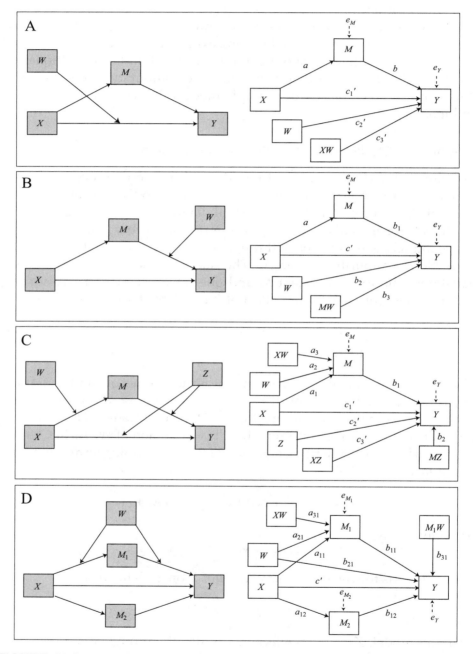

FIGURE 11.2. Some variants of a conditional process model in conceptual (left) and statistical (right) form.

Example 2: Moderation of Only the Indirect Effect

A more interesting conditional process model can be found in Figure 11.2, panel B. This conditional process model is nothing more than a simple mediation model with moderation of the indirect effect of X on Y through M. As depicted here, the indirect effect of X is conditional on W through moderation of the $M \rightarrow Y$ effect by W. When translated into a statistical model, the resulting equations representing such a process are

$$M = i_M + aX + e_M \qquad (11.3)$$
$$Y = i_Y + c'X + b_1M + b_2W + b_3MW + e_Y \qquad (11.4)$$

As in any mediation model, X exerts its effect on Y through both direct and indirect pathways. The direct effect links X to Y independent of M and the indirect effect of X on Y through M is, as always, the product of paths linking X to Y through M. The first of these components of the indirect effect is the path from X to M, estimated as a in equation 11.3, and the second component is the path from M to Y. However, as discussed in Chapter 7, the effect of M on Y (controlling for X) is *not* b_1 in equation 11.4. Rather, the effect of M on Y is a function of W in this model, as revealed by rewriting equation 11.4 in an equivalent form:

$$Y = i_Y + c'X + (b_1 + b_3W)M + b_2W + e_Y$$

Thus, the effect of M on Y is $\theta_{M \rightarrow Y} = b_1 + b_3W$. It is a conditional effect that is a function of W. As a result, the indirect effect of X on Y through M is also a function of W, with the function formed as the product of effects linking X to Y through M. The result is the *conditional indirect effect* of X on Y through M:

$$a\theta_{M \rightarrow Y} = a(b_1 + b_3W) = ab_1 + ab_3W$$

This conditional indirect effect quantifies how differences in X map onto differences in Y indirectly through M depending on the value of W. If the indirect effect of X differs systematically as a function of W, we can say that the mediation of X's effect on Y by M is moderated by W—*moderated mediation*.

The direct effect in this model is not moderated. Because the path from X to Y independent of M is not specified as moderated, it is estimated with c' in equation 11.4.

Example 3: Moderation of the Direct and Indirect Effects

Figure 11.2, panel C, represents a model with both the direct and indirect effects of X moderated, in this case by two moderators. As depicted, W

moderates the indirect effect through its moderation of the effect of X on M, and Z moderates the indirect effect through moderation of the effect of M on Y. At the same time, Z moderates the direct effect of X. The equations corresponding to the model are

$$M = i_M + a_1X + a_2W + a_3XW + e_M \tag{11.5}$$
$$Y = i_Y + c'_1X + c'_2Z + c'_3XZ + b_1M + b_2MZ + e_Y \tag{11.6}$$

From equation 11.5, grouping terms involving X and factoring out X, the effect of X on M is not a_1 but, rather, $\theta_{X \to M} = a_1 + a_3W$. Using the same procedure on equation 11.6, the effect of M on Y is $\theta_{M \to Y} = b_1 + b_2Z$. The indirect effect of X on Y through M is the product of these two conditional effects, meaning it is conditional—the conditional indirect effect—and defined as

$$\theta_{X \to M}\theta_{M \to Y} = (a_1 + a_3W)(b_1 + b_2Z) = a_1b_1 + a_1b_2Z + a_3b_1W + a_3b_2WZ$$

So the indirect effect of X is a function of both W and Z. However, because the direct effect of X is moderated only by Z, it is a function of only Z:

$$\theta_{X \to Y} = c'_1 + c'_3Z$$

Example 4: Moderation of a Specific Indirect Effect in a Parallel Multiple Mediator Model

The model in Figure 11.2, panel D, is a more complex parallel multiple mediator model that includes moderation of effects to and from M_1 by a common moderator W, with all other pathways of influence from X to Y unmoderated. This model translates into the following three equations:

$$M_1 = i_{M_1} + a_{11}X + a_{21}W + a_{31}XW + e_{M_1} \tag{11.7}$$
$$M_2 = i_{M_2} + a_{12}X + e_{M_2} \tag{11.8}$$
$$Y = i_Y + c'X + b_{11}M_1 + b_{12}M_2 + b_{21}W + b_{31}M_1W + e_Y \tag{11.9}$$

The effect of X on M_1 is derived from equation 11.7 by grouping terms involving X and factoring out X, which results in $\theta_{X \to M} = a_{11} + a_{31}W$. Using the same procedure on equation 11.9, the effect of M_1 on Y is $\theta_{M \to Y} = b_{11} + b_{31}W$. The product of these conditional effects yields the conditional *specific* indirect effect of X on Y through M_1:

$$\theta_{X \to M_1}\theta_{M_1 \to Y} = (a_{11}+a_{31}W)(b_{11}+b_{31}W) = a_{11}b_{11}+(a_{11}b_{31}+a_{31}b_{11})W+a_{31}b_{31}W^2$$

which is a curvilinear function of W. There is a second specific indirect effect of X in this model through M_2, but it is unconditional, because none of its constituent paths is specified as moderated. From equations 11.8 and 11.9, the specific indirect effect of X on Y through M_2 is $a_{12}b_{12}$. Finally, the direct effect of X on Y is also unmoderated and therefore unconditional. It is c' in equation 11.9.

11.3 Example: Hiding Your Feelings from Your Work Team

Popular music over the years has reinforced our intuitions as well as advice offered by close friends and extolled by talk show psychologists that little good can come from bottling up our feelings and hiding them from the view of others. We are told by the artists of the day that it is better that you *Express Yourself* (Madonna), to beware that living by a *Code of Silence* (Billy Joel) means you'll never live down your past, and the longer your list of *Things I'll Never Say* (Avril Lavigne), the less likely you are to get the things you long for in life. So when others reach out with the request to *Talk to Me* (Anita Baker), it is important to let your guard down and *Communicate* (B-52s) what is on your mind.

Not necessarily so, at least in some work-related situations, according to research on teamwork by Cole et al. (2008). According to these researchers, sometimes it may be better to hide your feelings from others you work with about the things they do or say that bother you, lest those feelings become the focus of attention of the team and thereby distract the team from accomplishing a task in a timely and efficient manner. This study provides the data for this first example illustrating the mechanics of estimation and interpretation of a conditional process model, held in a data file named TEAMS, which can be found at *www.afhayes.com*.

The study involved 60 work teams employed by an automobile parts manufacturing firm and is based on responses to a survey from over 200 people at the company to a series of questions about their work team, as well as various perceptions of the team supervisor. Some of the variables in the study are measured at the level of the group and are derived from an aggregation of things that members of the same team said. Fortunately, there was much similarity in how team members responded to questions about the team, which justified this kind of aggregation. Other variables are based purely on reports from the team supervisor.

Four variables that are pertinent to this analysis were measured. Members of the team were asked a series of questions about the *dysfunctional behavior* of members of the team, such as how often members of the team did things to weaken the work of others or hinder change and innovation (DYSFUNC in the data file, such that higher scores reflect more dysfunctional behavior in the team). The *negative affective tone* of the group was also measured by asking members of the team how often they felt "angry," "disgusted," and so forth, at work (NEGTONE, with higher scores reflecting a more negative affective tone of the work environment). The team supervisor was asked to provide an assessment of *team performance* in general, such as how efficient and timely the team is, whether the team meets its manufacturing objectives, and so forth (PERFORM in the data, scaled with higher values reflecting better performance). In addition, the supervisor responded to a series of questions gauging how easy it is to read the nonverbal signals team members emote about how they are feeling—their *nonverbal negative expressivity* (NEGEXP in the data file, with higher scores meaning the members of the team were more nonverbally expressive about their negative emotional states).

This goal of the study was to examine the mechanism by which the dysfunctional behavior of members of a work team can negatively affect the ability of a work team to perform well. They proposed a mediation model in which dysfunctional behavior (X) leads to a work environment filled with negative emotions (M) that supervisors and other employees confront and attempt to manage, which then distracts from work and interferes with task performance (Y). However, according to their model, when team members are able to regulate their display of negative emotions (W), essentially hiding how they are feeling from others, this allows the team to stay focused on the task at hand rather than having to shift focus toward managing the negative tone of the work environment and the feelings of others. That is, the effect of negative affective tone of the work environment on team performance is hypothesized in their model as contingent on the ability of the team members to hide their feelings from the team, with a stronger negative effect of negative affective tone on performance in teams that express their negativity rather than conceal it.

The conceptual diagram corresponding to this hypothesized process can be found in Figure 11.3, panel A. This is a conditional process model containing a mediation process ($X \to M \to Y$) combined with moderation of the $M \to Y$ effect by W. This conceptual diagram translates into a set of two equations because there are two consequent variables in the model (M and Y). The two equations representing this model, depicted in the form of a statistical diagram in Figure 11.3, panel B, are

$$M = i_M + aX + e_M \tag{11.10}$$
$$Y = i_Y + c'X + b_1M + b_2W + b_3MW + e_Y \tag{11.11}$$

The regression coefficients can be estimated using two OLS regressions. In SPSS, the commands that accomplish the analysis are

```
compute toneexp=negexp*negtone.
regression/dep=negtone/method=enter dysfunc.
regression/dep=perform/method=enter dysfunc negtone negexp toneexp.
```

The corresponding commands in SAS are

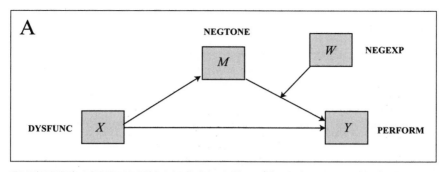

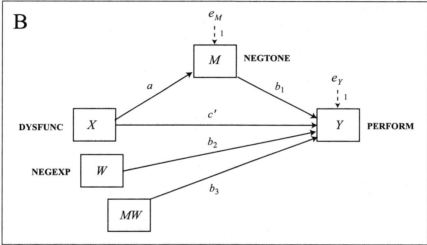

FIGURE 11.3. The conditional process model corresponding to the dysfunctional team behavior study in conceptual (panel A) and statistical (panel B) form.

```
data teams;set teams;toneexp=negtone*negexp;run;
proc reg data=teams;model negtone=dysfunc;run;
proc reg data=teams;model perform=dysfunc negtone negexp toneexp;run;
```

The resulting coefficients and model summary information can be found in Table 11.1. As can be seen, the best fitting OLS regression models are

$$\hat{M} = 0.026 + 0.620X$$
$$\hat{Y} = -0.012 + 0.366X - 0.436M - 0.019W - 0.517MW$$

It appears that the more dysfunctional behavior displayed by team members, the more negative the affective tone of the work environment ($a = 0.620$), just as proposed by Cole et al. (2008). Furthermore, the effect of negative affective tone on work performance is indeed contingent on nonverbal negative expressivity, as evidenced by the statistically significant interaction between M and W in the model of Y ($b_3 = -0.517, p = .036$).

TABLE 11.1. Model Coefficients for the Conditional Process Model in Figure 11.3

		Consequent						
		M (NEGTONE)				Y (PERFORM)		
Antecedent		Coeff.	SE	p		Coeff.	SE	p
X (DYSFUNC)	a	0.620	0.167	< .001	c'	0.366	0.178	.044
M (NEGTONE)		—	—	—	b_1	−0.436	0.131	.002
W (NEGEXP)		—	—	—	b_2	−0.019	0.117	.871
M × W		—	—	—	b_3	−0.517	0.241	.036
Constant	i_M	0.026	0.062	.679	i_Y	−0.012	0.059	.840
		$R^2 = 0.192$				$R^2 = 0.312$		
		$F(1, 58) = 13.800, p < .001$				$F(4, 55) = 6.235, p < .001$		

The regression coefficients for M and W are conditional effects with their product in the model. In this model, b_1 estimates the effect of negative affective tone on team performance in teams measuring zero in negative emotional expressivity but equal in dysfunctional behavior. This effect is negative and statistically different from zero, $b_1 = -0.436, p = 0.002$. This is substantively meaningful because zero is within the bounds of measurement in this study. A score of zero on nonverbal negative expressivity does not mean an absence of expressivity. Rather, zero is just barely above the sample mean ($\overline{W} = -0.008$). So holding constant dysfunctional behavior, among teams just slightly above average in expressivity, those functioning in a relatively more negative emotional climate are perceived by their supervisors as performing relatively less well.

The regression coefficient for nonverbal negative expressivity, b_2, estimates the effect of nonverbal negative expressivity on team performance among teams measuring zero in negative affective tone. Zero is within the bounds of measurement and is just below the sample mean ($\overline{M} = 0.047$). So among teams equal in dysfunctional behavior and slightly below the mean in negative affective tone, those teams whose members are more inclined to express their negative emotions perform less well. However, this effect is not statistically different from zero, $b_2 = -0.019, p = 0.871$.[1]

---

[1]Mean centering or standardization is not required for the same reasons given in Chapter 9. Mean centering M and W prior to the estimation of the model would change the estimates of b_1, b_2, i_M, and i_Y. But doing so would not change a or b_3. Ultimately, it is the direct and indirect effects that matter when it comes to interpretation of the results. Whether or not

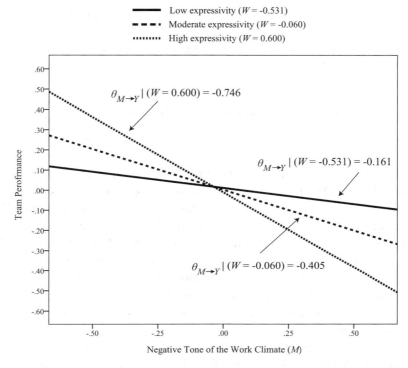

FIGURE 11.4. A visual representation of the moderation of the effect of negative tone of the work climate on team performance by nonverbal negative expressivity.

Evidence of moderation doesn't mean that pattern is as expected or hypothesized. To get a better handle on what the interaction between negative affective tone and nonverbal negative expressivity means, we can visualize the model of Y and also generate the conditional effect of negative affective tone (M) on team performance (Y) for various values of nonverbal negative expressivity (W). A visual depiction of the interaction between negative tone of the work climate and nonverbal negative expressivity can be found in Figure 11.4. This was generated using the same procedure described in section 7.3, with the help of PROCESS.

Notice that the more negative the tone of the work climate, the lower the team's performance, and this pattern is present regardless of the expressivity of the team. However, it appears that the relationship is more negative among the more expressive teams.

you mean center prior to analysis will not change the estimates of the direct and indirect effects in this model, inferential tests about those effects, or their interpretation.

The regression model provides the function defining the slopes of the lines in Figure 11.4. Rewriting equation 11.11 in an equivalent form by grouping terms involving M and then factoring out M yields

$$\hat{Y} = -0.012 + 0.366X + (-0.436 - 0.517W)M - 0.019W$$

Thus, M's effect on Y is conditional on W and takes the form

$$\theta_{M \to Y} = b_1 + b_3W = -0.436 - 0.517W \tag{11.12}$$

Selecting values of W such as the 16th, 50th, and 84th percentiles and plugging these into equation 11.12 yields the effect of negative affective tone on team productivity among teams "low," "moderate," and "high" in emotional expressivity; the slopes of the lines in Figure 11.4. If desired, hypothesis tests could be conducted to determine whether the conditional effect is different from zero at those values, or the Johnson–Neyman technique could be used to identify the region of significance. But ultimately, these hypothesis tests don't matter because we care about the conditional indirect effects in the full conditional process model. But it doesn't hurt to take a look at them.

This could all be done the hard way using the equations and procedures described in Chapters 7 and 8, or PROCESS could be brought into service to take care of most of it. Observe that equation 11.11 can be thought of as a simple moderation model with M as focal antecedent variable, W as moderator, Y as outcome, and X functioning as a covariate. PROCESS model 1 estimates just such a model while also implementing the pick-a-point approach for probing the interaction and generating information necessary to produce a visual picture of the model as in Figure 11.4. In SPSS, the command is

```
process y=perform/x=negtone/w=negexp/cov=dysfunc/model=1/plot=1.
```

In SAS, use

```
%process (data=teams,y=perform,x=negtone,w=negexp,cov=dysfunc,model=1,
    plot=1);
```

This PROCESS command might look peculiar to you, so some explanation is in order. Notice that I have specified X as the negative tone of the work climate in this command, even though it is M in the bigger conditional process model. But this is required because PROCESS model 1 expects the focal antecedent variable in a moderation analysis to be labeled X. So even though negative tone of the work climate is M in the conditional process model, I have to label it X in this PROCESS command because it is serving

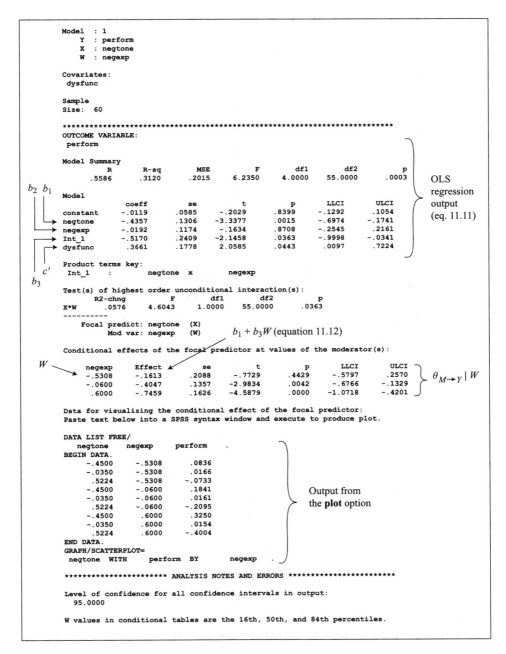

FIGURE 11.5. PROCESS model 1 output for estimating and probing the interaction between negative affective tone and nonverbal negative expressivity.

the role of focal antecedent in the moderation component of the model that I am trying to understand and visualize.

As can be seen in the PROCESS output in Figure 11.5, PROCESS automatically calculates various conditional effects of negative affective tone on performance, along with hypothesis tests for those conditional effects. As mentioned earlier, formal hypotheses tests for these conditional effects of negative affective tone are not required, since ultimately we care about the conditional *indirect* effects to be discussed later and not the conditional effects we are generating here.

The section of output in Figure 11.5 titled "Conditional effects of the focal predictor at values of the moderator(s)" provides estimates of $\theta_{M \to Y}$ using equation 11.12, the conditional effect of negative affective tone (M in the conditional process model, but X in this PROCESS output) on team performance (Y) for various values of nonverbal negative expressivity (W). These values PROCESS used for W are -0.531 (the 16th percentile), -0.060 (the 50th percentile), and 0.600 (the 84th percentile), which we can label as "low," "moderate," and "high" in nonverbal negative expressivity. As can be seen, regardless of the team's nonverbal negative expressivity, teams operating in an environment with a relatively more negative affective tone perform relatively less well, as the conditional effects at these three percentiles of the distribution of nonverbal negative expressivity are all negative. However, this negative association is larger in teams with greater nonverbal negative expressivity, and statistically significant only among teams moderate or high in their expressivity.

Combined, these results are consistent with the process as hypothesized by Cole et al. (2008). Teams whose members engage in relatively more dysfunctional behavior seem to produce a working environment that is relatively more negative in its tone, where team members are feeling irritated, angry, and so forth. And this negative tone is associated with lower team performance, but moreso among teams whose members fail to conceal how they are feeling. Among teams better versed at keeping their feelings to themselves, the negative affective tone produced by dysfunctional behavior does not seem to translate as much into reduced team performance.

11.4 Estimation of a Conditional Process Model Using PROCESS

PROCESS has many models programmed that combine moderation and mediation in some fashion. In addition to doing all the required regression analyses for you, PROCESS will estimate conditional and unconditional direct and indirect effects and provide all that is needed for inference. It knows which effects are conditional and which are not and produces output accordingly. When the direct or indirect effect is moderated, it produces a table containing the conditional effect for various values of the moderator or moderators. For inference, PROCESS generates standard errors, *p*-values, and confidence intervals for direct effects, and bootstrap confidence intervals for conditional indirect effects. Many of the models provide options for the inclusion of multiple moderators of the same path or of different paths, and it can combine moderation with parallel and serial mediation. As in the analyses conducted in prior chapters, all PROCESS needs is a specification of the variables in the model, the model number being estimated (see the model templates beginning on page 584), the role each variable plays in the model (based on the conceptual diagram), and then any additional options you would like implemented.

Many but not all of the options for moderation and mediation analysis are available when estimating models that combine moderation and mediation. For instance, you can tell PROCESS to center variables that are used to form products (using the **center** option), to condition effects that are moderated at the mean and plus and minus one standard deviation from the mean (using the **moments** option), or a specific value or set of values of the moderator (using the **wmodval** or **zmodval** options). For details on the various options available, the models that PROCESS can estimate, and instructions on its use, see Appendix A.

The model estimated in this chapter—a simple mediation model combined with moderation of the path from *M* to *Y* by a single variable *W*—is PROCESS model 14 (see the PROCESS model templates in Appendix A). The SPSS version of the PROCESS command which conducts the analysis is

```
process y=perform/x=dysfunc/m=negtone/w=negexp/model=14/plot=1
   /seed=42517.
```

In SAS, use

```
%process (data=teams,y=perform,x=dysfunc,m=negtone,w=negexp,model=14,
   plot=1,seed=42517);
```

As can be seen by comparing the PROCESS output in Figure 11.6 to the information in Table 11.1, the regression coefficients and their standard errors, the *p*-values, R^2, and so forth provided by PROCESS are the same as those generated by the separate OLS regression analyses conducted using SPSS Regression or SAS PROC REG. However, PROCESS also produces a lot more information needed for interpretation and inference that simply

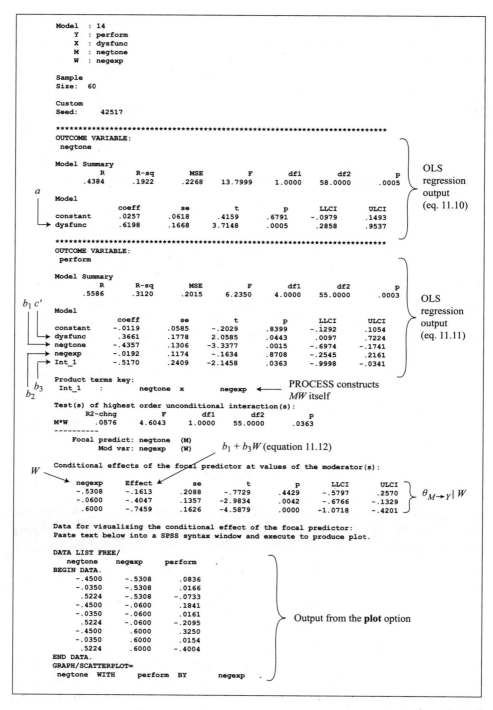

(continued)

FIGURE 11.6. Output from the PROCESS procedure for SPSS for a conditional process model (model 14) of the dysfunctional team behavior study.

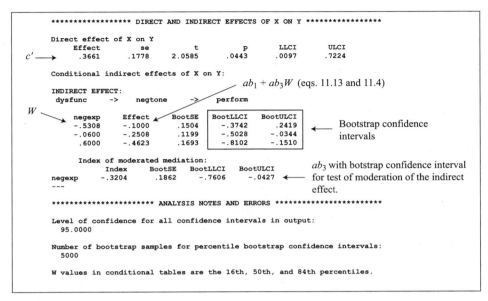

FIGURE 11.6 continued.

isn't available from SPSS or SAS otherwise. Notice, for instance, that PRO-
CESS automatically probes the interaction between M and W in the model
of Y and generates information needed for visualizing the moderation of
the effect of M on Y by W in this part of the model. So it isn't actually
necessary to use model 1, like discussed earlier, to probe and visualize the
interaction between negative tone of the work climate and nonverbal negative expressivity. PROCESS generates the necessary information when
using model 14.

Toward the end of the output, in the section labeled "Direct and Indirect
Effects of X on Y," you will find information about the direct and indirect
effects of dysfunctional team behavior on performance, with the indirect
effect operating through negative tone of the work climate and moderated
by nonverbal negative expressivity. Also in this section of output is a
statistical test of moderated mediation. This part of the PROCESS output
and the underlying concepts are discussed in the next section.

11.5   Quantifying and Visualizing (Conditional) Indirect and Direct Effects

The analysis presented thus far has been piecemeal, in that I have addressed
how to estimate the regression coefficients for each equation in this condi-

tional process model and how to interpret them using standard principles of regression analysis, moderation analysis, and so forth. But a complete analysis goes further by integrating the estimates of each of the effects in the model (i.e., $X \rightarrow M$, $\theta_{M \rightarrow Y}$) to yield the direct and indirect effects of X on Y. That is, the individual effects as quantified with the regression coefficients (conditional or otherwise) in equations 11.10 and 11.11 are not necessarily of immediate interest or relevance. Estimating them is a means to an end. What matters is the estimation of the direct and indirect effects, for they convey information about how X influences Y directly or through a mediator and how those effects are contingent on a moderator. Furthermore, once these effects are estimated, some kind of inferential technique should be applied for the purpose of generalization and ruling out "chance" as an explanation for the effects observed.

The Conditional Indirect Effect of X. As discussed throughout Chapters 3 through 5 as well as section 11.2, indirect effects are calculated as products of estimates of effects assumed to be causal, with those effects quantified with regression coefficients estimated through some kind of modeling method such as OLS regression. The analysis just described has resulted in an estimate of the effect of the proposed causal antecedent variable X (dysfunctional team behavior) on presumed causal consequent M (negative affective tone). The estimate of this $X \rightarrow M$ effect is a in equation 11.10.

The analysis has also generated an estimate of the effect of negative affective tone on team performance, which is the final consequent Y. This $M \rightarrow Y$ effect was proposed by Cole et al. (2008) as moderated by nonverbal negative expressivity (W), and indeed it was. Thus, the effect of M on Y is conditional and estimated with the function $\theta_{M \rightarrow Y} = b_1 + b_3 W$.

The indirect effect of dysfunctional behavior on team performance through negative affective tone is the product of these two effects, one unconditional (a), and one conditional ($\theta_{M \rightarrow Y} = b_1 + b_3 W$). As one of these components of the indirect effect is conditional, then so too is the indirect effect itself (except in the case where the other component is zero), defined as

$$a\theta_{M \rightarrow Y} = a(b_1 + b_3 W) = ab_1 + ab_3 W \qquad (11.13)$$

or, expressed in terms of the estimated regression coefficients (see the PROCESS output in Figure 11.6 or Table 11.1),

$$a\theta_{M \rightarrow Y} = 0.620(-0.436 - 0.517W) = -0.270 - 0.320W \qquad (11.14)$$

So there is no one numerical estimate of the indirect effect that can be used to characterize this process. Rather, in order to talk about the indirect effect of X on Y through M, you must condition that discussion on moderator W.

TABLE 11.2. Constructing the Conditional Indirect Effects of Dysfunctional Team Behavior on Team Performance through Negative Affective Tone for Various Values of Negative Nonverbal Expressivity

Nonverbal Negative Expressivity (W)	a	$\theta_{M \to Y} = b_1 + b_3 W$	$a\theta_{M \to Y} = a(b_1 + b_3 W)$
−0.531	0.620	−0.161	−0.100
−0.060	0.620	−0.405	−0.251
0.600	0.620	−0.746	−0.462

This discussion is facilitated by calculating the conditional indirect effect for various values of W. To do so, choose values of W where you desire an estimate of the conditional indirect effect and then do the computations.

Earlier, we probed the interaction between M and W by estimating the conditional effect of M at values of W corresponding to the 16th, 50th, and 84th percentiles of the distribution of W, so we'll stick with those values here. These three values, representing low, moderate, and high on W, are found in the first column of Table 11.2. The second and third columns provide the effects of X on M and the conditional effects of M on Y at those values of W, respectively. Notice that because the effect of X on M is not estimated as moderated, it is constant across all values of W. The last column is the product of the second and third columns and contains the conditional indirect effect of X on Y through M, conditioned on the value of W in that row.

All of these numbers can be found in the PROCESS output in Figure 11.6. The regression coefficient a is found near the top of the output in the model for negative tone of the work climate. The three conditional effects of negative tone of the work climate on performance at values of nonverbal negative expressivity ($\theta_{M \to Y}$) corresponding to the 16th, 50th, and 84th percentiles are in the section of output for the model of team performance (under the heading "Conditional effects of the focal predictor at values of the moderator(s)"). And the conditional indirect effects are found toward the end of the output in the section titled "Conditional indirect effects of X on Y."

In generic terms, the conditional indirect effect of X on Y through M conditioned on W quantifies the amount by which two cases with a given value of W that differ by one unit on X are estimated to differ on Y indirectly through X's effect on M, which in turn influences Y. So consider two teams $W = 0.600$ units in nonverbal negative expressivity but that differ by one unit in dysfunctional behavior. According to this analysis (see Table 11.2), the team one unit higher in dysfunctional behavior is estimated to be 0.462 units lower (because the conditional indirect effect is negative) in team performance as a result of the more negative affective tone produced by the more dysfunctional behavior (because a is positive), which lowers team performance (because $\theta_{M \to Y}$ when $W = 0.600$ is negative).

As can be seen in Table 11.2, the indirect effect of dysfunctional behavior on team performance through negative affective tone is consistently negative, but it is more negative among teams relatively higher in their nonverbal negative expressivity. So relatively more dysfunctional behavior seems to create a more negative affective tone in a work group, which translates into reduced team performance, more so among teams with members who let their negative emotions be known to the team.

The Direct Effect. The direct effect of X on Y is neither hypothesized to be moderated nor is it estimated as such. Thus, there is only one direct effect of X in this model, estimated with c' in equation 11.11. This quantifies how much two teams that differ by one unit in their dysfunctional behavior are estimated to differ in performance when holding constant negative affective tone and nonverbal negative expressivity. The direct effect is positive, $c' = 0.366$. So two teams differing by one unit in dysfunctional behavior but equal in their negative affective tone and nonverbal negative expressivity are estimated to differ by 0.366 units in team performance, with the team displaying more dysfunctional behavior estimated to perform *better*.

Visualizing the Direct and Indirect Effects

In this example, the indirect effect of X on Y through M is specified as moderated by W. As a result, there is no single number that characterizes the indirect effect. Rather, the indirect effect is a function that generates different values—conditional indirect effects—depending on the value of the moderator plugged into the function. A direct effect can also be a function rather than a single number, but in this example, the direct effect is fixed to be constant, as there is nothing in this model that allows the direct effect to be dependent on a moderator.

A visual representation of the function can aid both interpretation and presentation when the indirect and/or direct effect is specified as dependent on another variable in the model. To visualize conditional direct and/or indirect effects, produce a dataset that contains the estimated direct and indirect effects for various values of the moderator using the function or functions constructed from the coefficients in the model. Then graph the resulting data with the effect on the vertical axis, values of the moderator on the horizontal axis, and different lines for the direct and indirect effects.

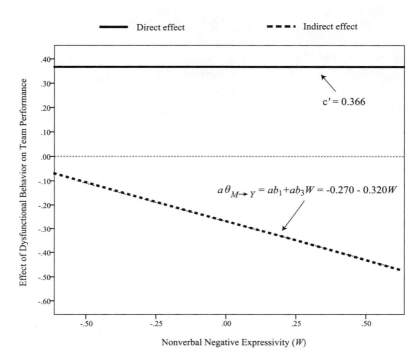

FIGURE 11.7. A visual representation of the conditional indirect and the direct effect of dysfunctional team behavior on team performance, with the indirect effect operating through negative tone of the work climate.

An example for the results in the prior analysis can be found in Figure 11.7. Although your impulse might be to interpret the vertical axis as team performance, that is not the correct interpretation. The vertical axis corresponds to the estimated difference in team performance between two teams that differ by one unit in dysfunctional team behavior—the effect of dysfunctional team behavior on performance. So a positive value means that the team that engages in more dysfunctional team behavior performs better, whereas a negative value means that more dysfunctional team behavior translates into worse performance. Zero on the vertical axis corresponds to no effect of dysfunctional behavior. The slopes of the lines represent how much the effect of the dysfunctional team behavior on team performance is influenced by the difference between teams in their nonverbal negative expressivity.

Figure 11.7 was generated in SPSS with the code below, with some additional editing in a dedicated graphics program:

```
data list free/negexp.
begin data.
-0.531 -0.060 0.600
end data.
compute indirect=-0.270-0.320*negexp.
compute direct=0.366.
graph/scatter(overlay)=negexp negexp WITH direct indirect (pair).
```

In this code, the three values toward the top of the program are values of negative expressivity (W) corresponding to the 16th, 50th, and 84th percentiles of the distribution in the data. The two **compute** commands produce the direct and indirect effects, with the indirect effect generated from equation 11.14 based on the coefficients in the conditional process model. The direct effect is a constant in this model, so the direct effect is set to $c' = 0.366$ regardless of the value of W.

The slope of the line for the indirect effect in Figure 11.7 is $ab_3 = 0.620(-0.517) = -0.320$ and corresponds to how much the indirect effect of dysfunctional behavior on team performance through negative tone of the work climate changes as nonverbal negative expressivity changes by one unit:

$$
\begin{aligned}
a[b_1 + b_3(W + 1)] - a[b_1 + b_3 W] &= ab_1 + ab_3 W + ab_3 - ab_1 - ab_3 W \\
&= (ab_1 - ab_1) + (ab_3 W - ab_3 W) + ab_3 \\
&= ab_3
\end{aligned}
$$

As such, ab_3 quantifies the rate of change of the indirect effect of X on Y through M as W changes. This product also provides a test statistic for a formal test of moderated mediation, discussed in section 11.6.

A comparable figure can be generated in SAS or R with the following code:

```
data;input negexp @@;
indirect = -0.270-0.320*negexp;
direct = 0.366;
datalines;
-0.531 -0.060 0.600
run;
proc sgplot;
series x=negexp y=direct/curvelabel='Direct effect' lineattrs=(color=
    black pattern=Solid);
```

```
series x=negexp y=indirect/curvelabel = 'Indirect effect'
    lineattrs=(color=red pattern=ShortDash);
xaxis label='Nonverbal negative expressivity';
yaxis label='Effect of dysfunctional team behavior on performance';
refline 0/axis=y transparency=0.5;
run;
```

```
x<-c(0,1,0,1,0,1)
w<-c(-0.531,-0.531,-0.060,-0.060,0.600,0.600)
y<-c(0.366,-0.161,0.366,-0.405,0.366,-0.746)
plot(y=y,x=w,pch=15,col="white",
xlab="Nonverbal negative expressivity",
ylab="Effect of dysfunctional team behavior")
legend.txt<-c("Direct effect","Indirect effect")
legend("bottomleft",legend=legend.txt,lty=c(1,3),lwd=c(4,3))
lines(w[x==0],y[x==0],lwd=4,lty=1)
lines(w[x==1],y[x==1],lwd=4,lty=3)
abline(0,0,lwd=0.5,lty=2)
```

11.6 Statistical Inference

My treatment of conditional process analysis thus far has been largely descriptive in nature. Description is important, but usually it is followed up with some kind of inferential technique in order to more rigorously substantiate the descriptive claims one is making. In this section, I discuss inference about the direct and conditional indirect effects quantified in the previous section. I also describe a formal test of moderation of the indirect effect.

Inference about the Direct Effect

In this model, the direct effect of dysfunctional behavior on team performance is $c' = 0.366$. As this effect is not moderated, inference proceeds just as in ordinary mediation analysis by testing the null hypothesis that $_Tc' = 0$ or constructing a confidence interval. This information is available from any OLS regression routine. As shown in the regression summary in Table 11.1 or the PROCESS output in Figure 11.6, the null hypothesis of no direct effect can be rejected, as the p-value for the obtained estimate of 0.366 is less than 0.05. Naturally, therefore, a 95% confidence interval for $_Tc'$ (using equation 2.16) is entirely above zero (0.010 to 0.732). The obtained estimate of 0.366 deviates too far from zero for "chance" to be a plausible alternative explanation. It seems that when holding constant the nonverbal negative expressivity of the team as well as the negative affective tone of the work environment, teams that manifest relatively more dysfunctional behavior perform relatively *better*, at least according to team supervisors.

Although this positive direct effect might seem counterintuitive, there are sensible explanations for this finding. For example, the greater dysfunctional behavior of some teams might reflect a difference in the abilities, ambition, or competitiveness of the members of such teams relative to teams that engage in less dysfunctional behavior. Although they engage in behavior that disrupts others on the team, perhaps these teams are populated by people who are just very good at their job and so, as a collective, perform better in spite of the dysfunctional behavior they exhibit.

Inference about the Indirect Effect

In simple mediation analysis, evidence supporting the existence of a specific mechanism linking X to Y through M is not established by the outcome of a set of hypothesis tests on the constituent paths that define the indirect effect (recall the discussion of this topic in section 4.1). Instead, inferences should be based on an estimate of the quantification of the mechanism— the indirect effect—defined as a product of the paths in the causal system. Complicating matters, however, is the fact that there is no single indirect effect one can quantify when the indirect effect is a function of a moderator. Instead, one must settle for conditioning the inference on a specific value of the moderator and then conducting an inference on the conditional indirect effect at that value. However, before doing so, one should first test whether the indirect effect varies systematically as a function of the moderator. If it does not, then this implies that the indirect effect is better thought of as a constant rather than dependent on a moderator. But if the evidence from such a test supports moderation of the indirect effect, then this moderation can be probed, just as in ordinary moderation analysis.

Historically, the question as to whether an indirect effect is moderated— "moderated mediation"—has been answered using a logic similar to the causal steps approach. An indirect effect is the product of at least two effects (e.g., the effect of X on M and the effect of M on Y controlling for X). In an analysis of moderated mediation, evidence of moderation of the indirect effect, by historical approaches, exists if (a) one of the paths defining the indirect effect is moderated by a formal statistical test, and (b) the other effect is statistically significant (or also moderated by an inferential test, if both paths are proposed as moderated). By this logic, if one of the paths is dependent on a moderator, then so too must be the indirect effect, since the indirect effect is a product of two paths at least one of which is moderated.

Using this approach, we could claim that the indirect effect of dysfunctional behavior on team performance through negative tone of the work climate is moderated, and hence the mediation is moderated, because the effect of dysfunctional team behavior on negative tone of the work climate is statistically significant, and the effect of the negative tone of the work climate on performance is significantly moderated by the expressivity of the team.

But more recent thinking focuses not on the individual pieces of the model, as this approach does, but rather on the model as a whole by examining whether the weight for the moderator in the function defining the size of the indirect effect is different from zero. From equation 11.13, the indirect effect in this model is a function of the form $ab_1 + ab_3 W$. The weight for moderator W in this function is ab_3. In Hayes (2015), I call this weight the *index of moderated mediation* for this model. The index of moderated mediation is the slope of the dashed line in Figure 11.7. If this slope is flat (i.e., if $ab_3 = 0$), then this means that the indirect effect is not related to moderator. But if this slope is not flat (i.e., if $ab_3 \neq 0$), then the indirect effect depends on the moderator, and hence the mediation is moderated. So a test of moderated mediation can be conducted by testing whether the index of moderated mediation is different from zero by an inferential test of some kind.

The index of moderated mediation is a product of two regression coefficients, and we know from our discussion of indirect effects in Chapters 3 through 6 that the sampling distribution of a product of two regression coefficients is irregular in shape. For this reason, as in mediation analysis without a moderation component, a bootstrap confidence interval is preferred for inference. PROCESS automatically constructs the index of moderated mediation for this model and provides a bootstrap confidence interval. This can be found in the section of output in Figure 11.6 titled "Index of moderated mediation." As can be seen, the index $ab_3 = -0.320$, with a bootstrap confidence interval from -0.761 to -0.043. Zero is not within the interval, which leads to the conclusion that the indirect effect is negatively related to the moderator. That is, the mediation of the effect of dysfunctional team behavior on performance through negative affective tone of the work climate is moderated by the expressivity of the team. The mediation is moderated. Had the confidence interval included zero, we could not definitively claim that the indirect effect was related to the moderator.

When using this approach to testing whether an indirect effect is moderated, it doesn't matter whether an interaction involving one of the paths defining the indirect effect is statistically significant by a formal test. What matters is whether the index of moderated mediation is different from zero. As discussed in detail in Hayes (2015), this test of moderated mediation is philosophically and practically appealing because it requires only a single inferential test (rather than two using the piecemeal approach), it is based on a statistic that directly quantifies the relationship between the moderator and the indirect effect (rather than on two statistics, a and b_3, neither of which quantify the relationship between the indirect effect and the moderator), and uncertainty about the relationship between the indirect effect and the moderator can be expressed formally in the form of a confidence interval. A confidence interval cannot be constructed for the inference using the piecemeal approach.

In sections 3.1 and 4.1, I said that the size or statistical significance of the total effect of X on Y has no bearing on whether X indirectly affects Y, so you should not require evidence of an association between X on Y as a precursor to mediation analysis. And in section 7.2, I said a significant relationship between X and Y is not a requirement of moderation of X's effect on Y. Similarly, the existence or lack of evidence of an unconditional indirect effect of X on Y through M has no bearing on whether the indirect effect of X is moderated. So it is appropriate to conduct this test of moderation of mediation without worrying about whether X is indirectly related to Y through M in a simpler model without a moderation component, as this tells you nothing about whether X's indirect effect on Y is moderated.

Probing Moderation of Mediation

In ordinary moderation analysis, evidence of moderation is usually followed up by probing the moderation to ascertain where the effect of the focal antecedent variable is different from zero and where it is not. In conditional process analysis, evidence of moderation of an indirect effect as revealed by a confidence interval for the index of moderated mediation that does not include zero would prompt a similar probing exercise. An analogue of the pick-a-point procedure first introduced in section 7.4 can be applied to probing moderation of mediation. This involves selecting values of the moderator and estimating the conditional indirect effect of X on Y through M at the values chosen.

One of the contributions of Preacher et al. (2007) to the literature on moderated mediation analysis was their discussion of inference for conditional indirect effects. They suggested two approaches, one a normal theory-based approach that is an analogue of the Sobel test in unmoderated mediation analysis, and another based on bootstrapping. I discuss the normal theory approach first but do not recommend its use. Instead, I advocate the use of bootstrap confidence intervals when one wishes to make a statistical inference about an indirect effect conditioned on a value of a moderator.

Normal Theory Approach. The normal theory approach to inference about conditional indirect effects is based on the same philosophy as the normal theory-based Sobel test in unmoderated mediation models. For a conditional process model of this form, the conditional indirect effect of X on Y through M is $a(b_1 + b_3 W)$ (from equation 11.13). An estimate of the standard error of conditional indirect effect is used in the denominator of the ratio of the conditional indirect effect to its standard error. A two-tailed p-value for this ratio is derived from the standard normal distribution in the usual way to test a null hypothesis that the conditional indirect effect of X at the value of W is chosen. Or a confidence interval for the conditional indirect effect can be constructed as the point estimate plus or minus 1.96 standard errors. This is repeated for as many values of W as desired.

Preacher et al. (2007) provide standard error estimators for conditional indirect effects for a variety of different conditional process models. The formulas are complicated and not something you would want to implement by hand. For details on their derivation and the formulas themselves, see their Appendix. But this approach suffers from the same limitation as the Sobel test described in Chapters 3 and 5 for indirect effects in simple and multiple mediator models. The conditional indirect effect is a product of normally distributed regression coefficients and thus its sampling distribution will not be normal. Yet the p-value for the ratio of the conditional effect to its standard error is derived in reference to the standard normal distribution—a reference distribution that is not appropriate. Furthermore, Preacher et al. (2007) show through simulation that this method is lower in power than bootstrap confidence intervals, which is the approach I do recommend. For these reasons, I don't recommend the normal theory approach.

Bootstrap Confidence Intervals. The rationale for using bootstrap confidence intervals for inference about conditional indirect effects is the same as the rationale for preferring this approach when the indirect effect is not estimated as moderated. The sampling distribution of the conditional indirect effect of X is not likely to be normal and may be extremely non-normal. Bootstrap confidence intervals respect this non-normality because they are based on an empirically generated representation of the sampling distribution of the conditional indirect effect rather than a (typically) inaccurate assumption about its shape.

A bootstrap confidence interval for a conditional indirect effect is constructed in exactly the same way as described in Chapter 3. Many, many bootstrap samples of the data are taken and the conditional indirect effect

TABLE 11.3. Bootstrap Confidence Intervals for Three Conditional Indirect Effects

Nonverbal Negative Expressivity (W)	$a(b_1 + b_3 W)$	95% Bootstrap Confidence Interval
−0.531	−0.100	−0.734 to 0.242
−0.060	−0.251	−0.503 to −0.034
0.600	−0.462	−0.810 to −0.151

using equation 11.13 is calculated for a chosen value of W in each of these bootstrap samples. The endpoints of a confidence interval are then calculated using the percentiles of the bootstrap distribution of the conditional indirect effect over this repeated bootstrap sampling and estimation. This process is repeated for various values of W.

Using the function defining the conditional indirect effect in equation 11.13, 95% bootstrap confidence intervals for the conditional indirect effect of dysfunctional behavior on team performance through negative affective tone at low (16th percentile, $W = −0.531$), moderate (50th percentile, $W = −0.060$), and high (84th percentile, $W = 0.600$) values of nonverbal negative expressivity can be found in the last column of Table 11.3. These were generated by PROCESS (see section 11.4) and are shown in the PROCESS output in Figure 11.6. As can be seen, in teams low in nonverbal negative expressivity, the bootstrap confidence interval straddles zero. But in teams moderate and high in negative nonverbal expressivity, the confidence interval is entirely below zero. This supports the claim that the indirect effect when nonverbal negative expressivity is at least moderate is indeed negative. Chance cannot credibly explain the discrepancy between the point estimates and zero.

So the results of this conditional process analysis are consistent with the claim that when team members reveal their negative emotions in response to the negative working climate that dysfunctional behavior produces, team performance suffers. But if they are able to hide how they are bothered by such behavior and thereby avoid having to manage the conflict, team performance is less affected. However, it may not be correct to conclude that dysfunctional behavior results in a net reduction in team performance, as the direct effect of dysfunctional behavior on performance was actually positive after accounting for differences between teams in negative affective tone and nonverbal negative expressivity. Whether dysfunctional behavior results in a net reduction of performance or a net gain will depend on the balance of these direct and indirect influences.

A Johnson–Neyman Approach. The Johnson–Neyman approach to probing an interaction introduced in section 7.4 gets around the problem of having to choose values of the moderator a priori. In principle, a Johnson–Neyman approach could be generalized to probing the moderation of an indirect effect in conditional process analysis. This would involve finding the value or values of the moderator at which point the conditional indirect effect of X transitions between statistically significant and not. However, this can't be done without making an assumption about the shape of the sampling distribution of the conditional indirect effect. Indeed, Preacher et al. (2007) did just this by showing how the regions of significance for a conditional indirect effect can be derived using the same computational logic as in ordinary moderation analysis. However, their computations assumed that the sampling distribution of the conditional indirect effect is normal. Given that the sampling distribution of the conditional indirect effect is not normal, the approach they describe yields, at best, an approximate solution. To my knowledge, no one has ever proposed a bootstrapping-based analogue of the Johnson–Neyman method for probing the moderation of an indirect effect.

Comparing Two Conditional Indirect Effects. If the indirect effect of X on Y through M depends on a moderator, that means that the indirect effect is a function of that moderator. It might seem that a sensible question to ask when an indirect effect is moderated is whether the conditional indirect effect when the moderator equals one value is statistically different from the conditional indirect effect when the moderator equals some different value. For example, we could ask whether the indirect effect of dysfunctional behavior on team performance through negative affective tone of the work climate differs between teams moderate versus high in nonverbal negative expressivity. A bootstrap confidence interval for this difference would be a sensible inferential approach.

However, as I discuss in Hayes (2015), in a model such as the one that is the focus of this chapter, it is not necessary to conduct such a test if you have already determined whether the indirect effect is moderated using the test based on a bootstrap confidence interval for the index of moderated mediation. If this confidence interval does not contain zero, then it follows that any two conditional indirect effects of X are different regardless of the two values of the moderator chosen. But if this bootstrap confidence interval contains zero, then no two conditional indirect effects of X can be deemed different, regardless of the two values of the moderator chosen.

To understand why, consider the function defining the conditional indirect effect of X in equation 11.13: $ab_1 + ab_3W$. So the difference between the conditional indirect effect of X on Y through M when $W = w_1$ versus $W = w_2$ is

$$
\begin{aligned}
(ab_1 + ab_3w_1) - (ab_1 + ab_3w_2) &= ab_3w_1 - ab_3w_2 \\
&= ab_3(w_1 - w_2)
\end{aligned}
$$

which is the index of moderated mediation multiplied by the difference between the two moderator values. But notice that because $w_1 - w_2$ is a constant across bootstrap samples (i.e., it doesn't vary from bootstrap sample to bootstrap sample), the outcome of this test is entirely determined by the bootstrap confidence interval for the index of moderated mediation, ab_3. If a 95% confidence interval for the index of moderated mediation does not contain zero, then a 95% confidence interval for the index multiplied by a constant will also not contain zero. But if a confidence interval for the index of moderated mediation does contain zero, then so too does the confidence interval for the index multiplied by a constant. This is true regardless of the values of w_1 and w_2 chosen (except for the special case when $w_1 = w_2$, but you would never choose two values of the moderator that are the same).

11.7　Chapter Summary

Knowledge of the mechanics, mathematics, and principles of conditional process analysis opens up analytical doors. This chapter has introduced the fundamentals of conditional process analysis using a relatively simple example that combines mediation of the effect of X on Y by M along with simple moderation of one of the paths in the causal sequence. Additional examples of a conditional process model in this form can be found in the literature with ease, but it is only one of the numerous ways that mediation and moderation can be and have been pieced together and combined into an integrated model. When a direct or indirect effect is moderated, it is conditioned on the variable that moderates it, meaning that there is not one single effect that characterizes how X influences Y directly or indirectly. Rather, the indirect or direct effect in such a circumstance is a function rather than a constant. Key to understanding the fundamentals of conditional process analysis is knowing how to estimate, make inferences about, and interpret conditional direct and indirect effects and how to test whether an indirect effect is moderated. The next chapter extends the principles introduced here by applying them to a more complicated model involving moderation of both the direct and the indirect effect of X on Y.

12

Further Examples of Conditional Process Analysis

In this chapter, I provide an additional example of a conditional process analysis in which both the direct and indirect effects of *X* on *Y* are estimated as moderated by a common moderator. I also make the distinction here between moderated mediation and mediated moderation and show how a conditional process model in the form described in this chapter can be interpreted in terms of either moderated mediation or mediated moderation. I argue that mediated moderation rarely has a meaningful substantive interpretation and it is better to reframe a question about mediated moderation in terms of moderated mediation by focusing on the estimation and interpretation of conditional indirect effects rather than the indirect effect of a product of two variables through a mediator.

To someone learning about science, it may seem like scientists intentionally try to make things difficult. Our vocabulary is a case in point. Think about how many ways the word *validity* is used in science. No one wants his or her conclusions to be invalid. If we are worried about capitalizing on chance when exploring data, we are told to set aside half of our data so we can cross-validate our findings. People who conduct experiments are often criticized for producing results or laboratory conditions low in external or ecological validity, even when the internal validity of the design is pristine. We validate measurement instruments by considering criteria such as face validity, content validity, predictive validity, concurrent validity, and criterion-related validity. But even if we meet these tests of validation, our work can be panned if an instrument we have developed is low in discriminant validity. Scientists are great at making fine distinctions between related ideas, but not always so good at coming up with labels for those ideas that clearly distinguish them from each other.

Chapter 11 was dedicated to the fundamentals of conditional process analysis. In this chapter I build on the foundation laid by stepping through an analysis of a more complicated conditional process model that includes moderation of both the indirect and the direct effects in a simple mediation model. I do so by first using a piecemeal approach that focuses on each pathway in the model. With some understanding gained by this examination of the components of the process, I then bring the pieces together into an integrated conditional process analysis. I also describe a means of visualizing the conditional direct and indirect effects by plotting them as a function of a moderator of those effects.

When an indirect effect of X on Y through M is moderated, we call this phenomenon *moderated mediation*. In such a scenario, the mechanism represented by the $X \rightarrow M \rightarrow Y$ chain of events operates to varying degrees (or not at all) for certain people or in certain contexts. A similar-sounding phenomenon is *mediated moderation*, which refers to the scenario in which an interaction between X and some moderator W on Y is carried through a mediator M. I show in this chapter that a mediated moderation analysis is really nothing other than a mediation analysis with the product of two variables serving as the causal agent of focus. However, I argue that rarely can much meaningful come out of a mediated moderation analysis, because conceptualizing a process in terms of mediated moderation misdirects attention toward a variable in the model that actually doesn't measure anything.

So I will admit up front that parts of this chapter perhaps further contribute to the perception that scientists have a problem with their vernacular. But I hope my discussion of the difference between moderated mediation and mediated moderation toward the end clarifies rather than confuses the distinction.

12.1   Revisiting the Disaster Framing Study

In Chapter 7, I introduced a study by Chapman and Lickel (2016) in which participants read a story about a humanitarian crisis caused by a drought in Africa. Half of the participants were told that the drought was caused by climate change (the climate change condition), whereas the other half were not told anything about the specific cause of the drought and thus had no reason to believe it wasn't the result of natural causes (the natural causes condition). The participants were also asked a series of questions to assess the extent to which they felt that it was justified to withhold aid to the victims of the resulting famine (because, for instance, they deserved their fate). Their skepticism about whether climate change is a real phenomenon was also measured.

In this section, I further the analysis presented in Chapter 7 while also expanding the discussion of conditional process analysis I began in Chapter 11 by introducing a new variable that was measured in this study. In addition to the variables already described, the participants' willingness to donate to the victims was assessed using a set of questions. Responses were made on a set of 7-point scales, with higher scores reflecting a greater willingness to donate to the victims. This variable is in the DISASTER data set and is named DONATE.

Was willingness to donate to the victims influenced by whether or not the drought was attributed to climate change? To answer this question, we regress willingness to donate (Y: DONATE) on experimental condition (X: FRAME; 0 = natural causes, 1 = climate change). The resulting model is $\hat{Y} = 4.565 + 0.084X$. The regression coefficient for X is the mean difference between the two conditions in willingness to donate to the victims and reflects that those told the drought and resulting famine were caused by climate change were slightly more willing to donate to the victims than those not so told (by a difference of 0.084 scale points). However, this difference is not statistically significant, $t(213) = 0.461, p = .645$, which leads to the conclusion that the framing of the cause of the disaster did not seem to affect willingness to donate.

We learned in the section of this book on mediation analysis that absence of an association between X and Y does not mean that X isn't causally influencing Y in some manner. Although a causal relationship between X and Y often manifests itself in the form of a correlation between X and Y, this correlation is not a necessary condition of cause. Furthermore, absence of association between X and Y doesn't say anything about whether the relationship between X and Y is dependent on (that is, moderated by) something else. For instance, the relationship between X and Y might be positive for some types of people and negative for other types, but when these two subpopulations are pooled and analyzed, the resulting relationship between X and Y is zero or nearly so. So we should not be discouraged from looking for mediators or moderators of the effect of the framing of the cause of the disaster on willingness to donate just because these two variables are not significantly associated in the data available.

Let's consider first whether the attribution frame manipulation might have had a different effect on people who differ in their climate change skepticism. That is, let's consider climate change skepticism as a possible moderator of the effect of the message frame manipulation on willingness to donate. Using PROCESS, we can estimate

$$Y = b_0 + b_1 X + b_2 W + b_3 XW + e_Y$$

with model 1, which specifies linear interaction between climate change skepticism (W) and the effect of the framing manipulation (X) on willingness to donate (Y). The PROCESS command that accomplishes this analysis is

```
process y=donate/x=frame/w=skeptic/model=1/plot=1.
```

```
%process (data=disaster,y=donate,x=frame,w=skeptic,model=1,plot=1);
```

The resulting output can be found in Figure 12.1. The model is

$$\hat{Y} = 5.030 + 0.679X - 0.140W - 0.171XW \qquad (12.1)$$

and the regression coefficient for XW, $b_3 = -0.171$, is statistically significant. The model is visualized in Figure 12.2, with the help of the **plot** option in PROCESS. As can be seen, it appears that among those low in climate change skepticism, framing the drought as caused by climate change produced a greater willingness to donate compared to when climate change was not described as the cause. However, among climate change skeptics (i.e., those high on the skepticism scale), the opposite pattern is observed, with willingness to donate to the victims lower among those who read the story attributing the cause to climate change.

However, when the interaction is probed using the pick-a-point approach at the 16th, 50th, and 84th percentiles of the distribution of climate change skepticism, none of the conditional effects of message framing are statistically significant (see the PROCESS output). Of course, these are arbitrary values of the moderator. Perhaps different choices would yield at least one conditional effect that is statistically significant. Using the Johnson-Neyman technique eliminates the ambiguity caused by the arbitrary choice. But the JN method (with the **jn** option, not specified in the PROCESS command here) results in no regions of significance. That is, at no value of W within the range of the data is X's effect statistically significant. This can happen, obviously, because it has. But as mentioned in section 7.5, it is not possible for X's effect on Y to be moderated by W while at the same time being zero at all values of W. So we can only conclude that being told the drought was caused by climate change, as opposed to having no cause attributed, had *some* effect on willingness to donate, but

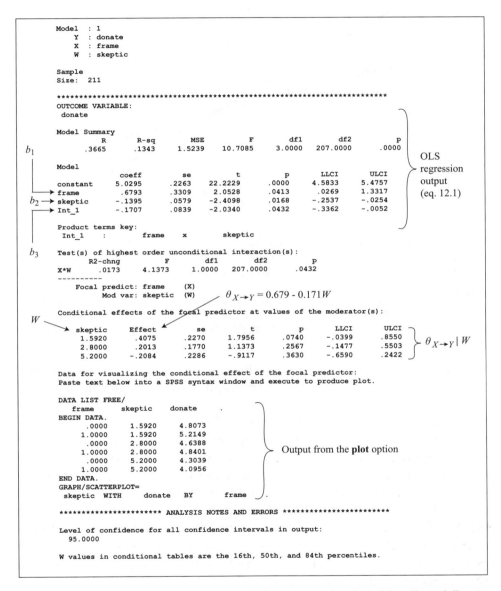

FIGURE 12.1. SPSS PROCESS output examining the moderation of the effect of disaster framing on willingness to donate by climate change skepticism.

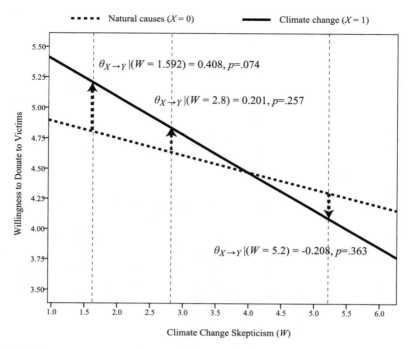

FIGURE 12.2. A visual representation of the conditional effects of disaster cause framing (*X*) on strength of justifications for withholding aid (*Y*) among those relatively low (*W* = 1.592), moderate (*W* = 2.8), and relatively high (*W* = 5.2) in their climate change skepticism.

we can't be more precise than this. The holistic, qualitative interpretation based on Figure 12.2 in the prior paragraph is the best we can do at this point.

We next consider whether the effect of the framing of the disaster on willingness to donate might operate by influencing people's beliefs about whether providing aid to the victims is justified. If a person feels that the victims of a drought caused by climate change don't deserve assistance (because they deserved their fate, or that assisting them wouldn't help), this could reduce such a person's willingness to donate to the victims compared to when the drought is interpreted as produced by natural causes. This is a mediation hypothesis and proposes an indirect effect of the framing of the cause of the drought on willingness to donate through the strength of justifications for not providing aid.

The results of a simple mediation analysis using the procedure described in Chapter 3 is consistent with this proposal. Figure 12.3 contains PROCESS output from a simple mediation analysis using disaster frame as the causal agent *X*, justification for withholding aid as *M*, and willingness to donate as *Y*. As described in Chapter 3, such a model involves two equations, one estimating M from X and the other estimating Y from both X and M. The SPSS PROCESS command that generates this output is

```
process y=donate/x=frame/m=justify/model=4/total=1/seed=280417.
```

whereas in SAS, the command is

```
%process (data=disaster,y=donate,x=frame,m=justify,model=4,total=1,
    seed=280417);
```

The resulting equations (see the PROCESS output) are

$$\hat{M} = 2.802 + 0.134X \tag{12.2}$$
$$\hat{Y} = 7.235 + 0.212X - 0.953M \tag{12.3}$$

As can be seen in Figure 12.3, the indirect effect of the disaster framing manipulation on willingness to donate through strength of justifications for withholding aid is −0.218. This negative indirect effect reflects that participants told the disaster was caused by climate change reported stronger justifications for withholding aid than those not told the drought was attributed to climate change ($a = \overline{M}_{climate\ change} - \overline{M}_{natural\ causes} = 0.134$), and the stronger those justifications for withholding aid, the lower one's willingness to donate ($b = -0.953$). However, the bootstrap confidence interval for this indirect effect straddles zero, so we cannot rule out zero as the size of the indirect effect. We can't even be certain whether the sign is positive or negative. Notice as well as that there is no statistically significant direct effect of disaster framing on willingness to donate. These results do not support an argument that strength of justifications for withholding aid is operating as a mediator of any effect that the disaster frame might be having on willingness to donate.

Yet there is something unsatisfying about this simple mediation analysis. Specifically, it ignores the results from the moderation analysis that started this chapter showing that disaster framing had different effects on willingness to donate among people who differ in their climate change skepticism. Nothing in this mediation analysis allows for systematic individual differences in how the attribution for the drought affected willingness to donate. But even worse, recall from Chapter 7 when this study was first introduced that climate change skepticism moderated the effect of the disaster frame on justifications for withholding aid. The results of that earlier analysis, depicted in Figure 7.8, revealed that among climate change skeptics, strength of justifications for withholding aid from the victims was significantly higher on average among those told the drought was caused by climate change compared to those not so told. The opposite

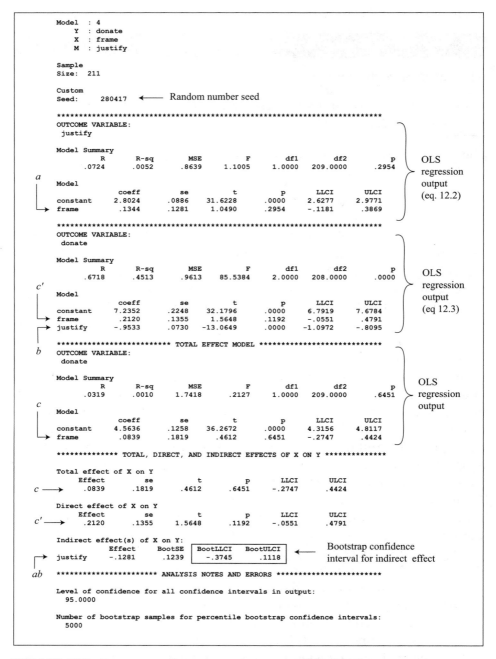

FIGURE 12.3. SPSS PROCESS output from a simple mediation analysis examining the direct and indirect effects of disaster cause framing on willingness to donate to the victims.

effect was observed among believers in climate change, where strength of justifications for withholding aid was lower on average among those told the drought was caused by climate change. The mediation analysis just reported fails to consider this individual difference in the effect of X (disaster frame) on M (justifications for withholding aid).

All these analyses, when qualitatively integrated into a story about how the framing of the disaster influences willingness to donate to the victims, suggest that at least one of the pathways of influence (the indirect effect) if not both (the direct effect too) is contingent on climate change skepticism. Climate change skeptics seem to feel that victims of a climate change-induced disaster (compared to one not attributed to climate change) don't deserve assistance, and this belief may translate into a reduced willingness to personally donate to the victims. This is a negative indirect effect. But among believers in climate change, the opposite effect is observed, with a climate change induced disaster leading believers to see the victims as more worthy of assistance than if the disaster wasn't caused by climate change, and this is related to a greater willingness to donate. This is a positive indirect effect. Ignoring the contingency of the indirect effect by failing to include moderation by climate change skepticism in the mediation model obscures the conditional nature of the mechanism at work.

In the following sections, I reconceptualize the analyses just undertaken by approaching them from two different interpretational perspectives, while simultaneously integrating them into a coherent conditional process model. The first approach formally estimates the conditional direct and indirect effects of the disaster frame on willingness to donate, with the indirect effect operating through strength of justifications for withholding aid—*moderated mediation*. This analysis also includes a formal statistical test of the moderation of the indirect effect. I then show how the identical model can be interpreted from the perspective of *mediated moderation* by estimating and attempting to substantively interpret the indirect effect of a product of variables. As will be seen, doing the latter is a bit of a challenge. To forecast where we are headed, I recommend that any question framed in terms of mediated moderation be reframed in terms of moderated mediation. Doing so will almost always produce results that are substantively more meaningful and interpretable.

12.2 Moderation of the Direct and Indirect Effects in a Conditional Process Model

The two analyses described in section 12.1 combined with the analysis in Chapter 7 involve four variables measured or manipulated by Chapman and Lickel (2016). I label these variables Y, X, M, and W in this section. Participants' willingness to donate (DONATE, Y) served as a consequent variable in two of those analyses and never an antecedent. Second, whether a participant was told the drought was caused by climate change ($X = 1$) or the cause was left unspecified ($X = 0$) (FRAME) was experimentally manipulated and functioned as an antecedent variable in all three of those analyses. The third variable was participants' skepticism about the reality of climate change (SKEPTIC, W). This variable always played the role of moderator in these analyses. Finally, participants were measured with respect to the extent to which they felt that it was justified to withhold aid from the victims (JUSTIFY, M). This variable functioned as either consequent or antecedent, depending on the analysis; in one analysis it was a mediator (and so both antecedent and consequent in the same model).

These three analyses are depicted in the form of conceptual diagrams in Figure 12.4. Panel A depicts the analysis that started this chapter—a simple moderation analysis with the effect of the attribution of the cause of the drought on willingness to donate to the victims moderated by participants' skepticism about the reality of climate change. Panel B reflects the simple mediation analysis assessing the direct and indirect effects of the attribution framing on willingness to donate through strength of justifications for withholding aid to the victims. And in Panel C is a conceptual representation of the moderation analysis conducted in section 7.2. This analysis assessed the moderation of the effect of the framing of the cause of the drought on justifications for withholding aid from the victims by climate change skepticism.

Now imagine you could lift panels A, B, and C off the page and merge them into one diagram, such that the grey boxes labeled X, M, W, and Y in each panel completely overlap each other. The resulting diagram would appear as in Figure 12.4, panel D. This conceptual diagram represents an integration of these three analyses into a single coherent model—a conditional process model. This model depicts mediation of the effect of X on Y by M, with both the direct and indirect effects of X moderated by W. Moderation of the indirect effect is depicted in this model as resulting from moderation of the effect of X on M by W. This moderation renders the indirect effect conditional on W. The direct effect is also proposed as moderated by W, so the direct effect is also conditional on W. So there is no single direct or indirect effect of X on Y. Instead, the indirect and direct effects are functions of W. When these are conceptualized in this fashion as a single integrated model, analysis should focus on whether the direct and indirect effects are moderated and, if so, the estimation and interpretation of the conditional indirect and direct effects.

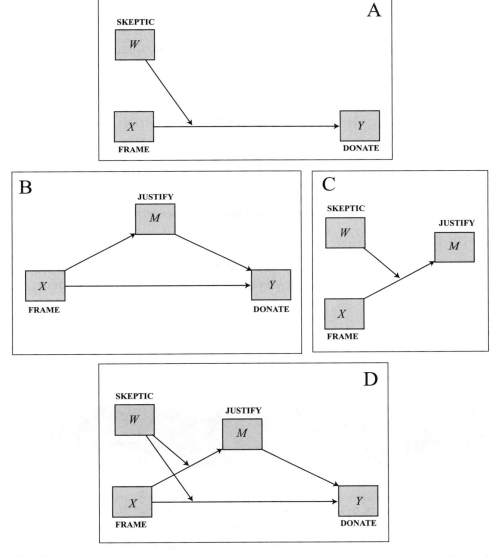

FIGURE 12.4. Conceptual diagrams of the three models estimated in sections 7.2 and 12.1 (panels A, B, and C) and their integration in the form of a conditional process model (panel D).

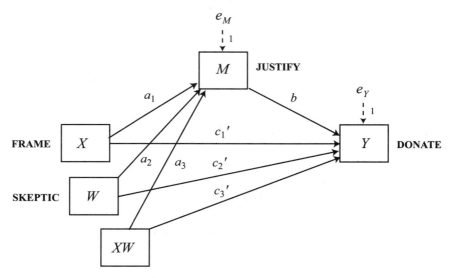

FIGURE 12.5. A statistical diagram of the conditional process model depicted in Figure 12.4, panel D.

Figure 12.4, panel D, translates into the statistical diagram in Figure 12.5. This diagram represents two equations, one for M and one for Y,

$$M = i_M + a_1X + a_2W + a_3XW + e_M \tag{12.4}$$
$$Y = i_Y + c_1'X + c_2'W + c_3'XW + bM + e_Y \tag{12.5}$$

the regression coefficients of which can be estimated using two OLS regression analyses. In SPSS, the commands that accomplish the analysis are

```
compute framskep=frame*skeptic.
regression/dep=justify/method=enter frame skeptic framskep.
regression/dep=donate/method=enter frame skeptic framskep justify.
```

whereas in SAS, the commands below do the job:

```
data disaster;set disaster;framskep=frame*skeptic;run;
proc reg data=disaster;model justify=frame skeptic framskep;run;
proc reg data=disaster;model donate=frame skeptic framskep justify;run;
```

The resulting regression coefficients, standard errors, p-values, and model summary information can be found in Table 12.1. Expressed in the form of the two equations, the models for M and Y are

$$\hat{M} = 2.452 - 0.562X - 0.105W + 0.201XW$$
$$\hat{Y} = 7.291 + 0.160X - 0.043W + 0.015XW - 0.923M$$

TABLE 12.1. Model Coefficients for the Conditional Process Model in Figure 12.5

		Consequent						
		M (JUSTIFY)				Y (DONATE)		
Antecedent		Coeff.	SE	p		Coeff.	SE	p
X (FRAME)	a_1	−0.562	0.218	.011	c_1'	0.160	0.268	.550
M (JUSTIFY)		—	—	—	b	−0.923	0.084	< .001
W (SKEPTIC)	a_2	−0.105	0.038	.006	c_2'	−0.043	0.047	.365
X × W	a_3	0.201	0.055	< .001	c_3'	0.015	0.069	.829
Constant	i_M	2.452	0.149	< .001	i_Y	7.291	0.274	< .001
		$R^2 = 0.246$				$R^2 = 0.454$		
		$F(3, 207) = 22.543, p < .001$				$F(4, 206) = 42.816, p < .001$		

It is important to acknowledge and recognize that a few of the coefficients in Table 12.1 have no substantive interpretation because of the scaling of climate change skepticism (SKEPTIC, W). The regression coefficients for the attribution manipulation (FRAME, X) in both equations (a_1 and c_1') are conditioned on $W = 0$, which is beyond the scale of measurement. Had climate change skepticism been mean-centered prior to analysis, then a_1 and c_1' would estimate the effect of the framing manipulation among those average in climate change skepticism. This would be substantively meaningful and interpretable.

However, this lack of interpretability does not generalize to a_2 and c_2'. Although they too estimate conditional effects (of W when $X = 0$), these are interpretable and substantively meaningful. They estimate the effect of climate change skepticism on justifications for withholding aid and willingness to donate, respectively, among those assigned to the natural causes condition ($X = 0$).

I argue in section 9.1 that it may be a good idea to get into the habit of mean-centering the variables that constitute a product if you are concerned about the possibility of others misinterpreting your results (due to the lack of familiarity of many with the subtleties of how variable scaling affects the interpretation of regression models with products of variables as predictors). I don't mean-center in this analysis to continue to highlight that doing so is not necessary. And in this kind of analysis, where the focus is the estimation and interpretation of the conditional direct and indirect effects, it makes no difference whatsoever, because the conditional direct and indirect effects of X will be the same regardless of whether mean-centering is done prior to model estimation.

Estimation Using PROCESS

Any OLS regression program can be used to estimate the model coefficients. However, some of the statistics we need to compute to make sense of the results, as well as inferential tests based on those statistics, require integration of information across the equations for M and Y. In addition to estimating the required regression equations and providing information helpful for visualizing parts of the model and probing the interactions, PROCESS will compute conditional direct and indirect effects, conduct a test of moderation of the indirect effect of X, and probe the moderation of direct and indirect effects in one fell swoop, packaging it all for you in one tidy output.

The SPSS version of the PROCESS command that conducts the analysis is

```
process y=donate/x=frame/w=skeptic/m=justify/model=8/plot=1/
    seed=280417.
```

whereas in SAS, use

```
%process (data=disaster,y=donate,x=frame,w=skeptic,m=justify,
    model=8,plot=1,seed=280417);
```

By specifying **model=8** in the command line, PROCESS estimates the model depicted in Figure 12.5. It does all the hard work for you. All you have to do is tell PROCESS which variables in the data play the roles of X, M, W, and Y in the model, and request any options you would like PROCESS to carry out and produce in the output.

The output that results from running this PROCESS command can be found in Figure 12.6. PROCESS automatically estimates the coefficients in equations 12.4 and 12.5 using OLS regression. Estimates of a_1, a_2, and a_3 in equation 12.4 are found in the "Outcome Variable: justify" section of the output, along with tests of significance and confidence intervals. These should look familiar, as the model of Y here is exactly the same as the moderation model estimated in section 7.2. PROCESS will automatically probe any interaction in a model if its p-value is 0.10 or less, as it is here. Unless it is told otherwise, PROCESS uses the pick-a-point approach when probing interactions, and because the moderator is continuous, it chooses the 16th, 50th, and 84th percentiles of the distribution of the moderator W

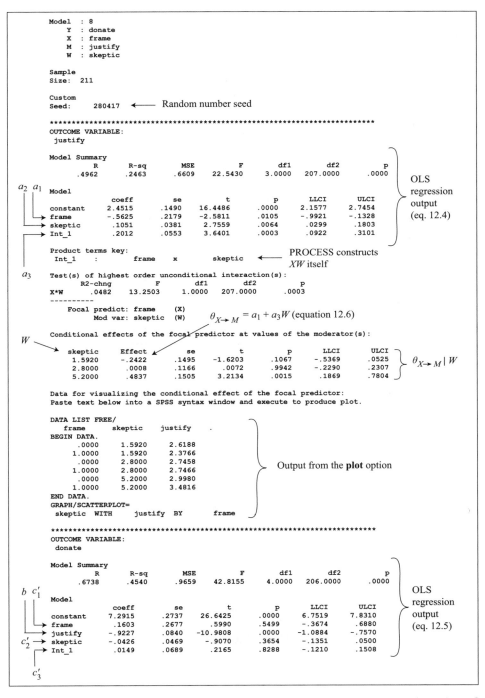

FIGURE 12.6. Output from the PROCESS procedure for SPSS for a conditional process analysis of the disaster framing study.

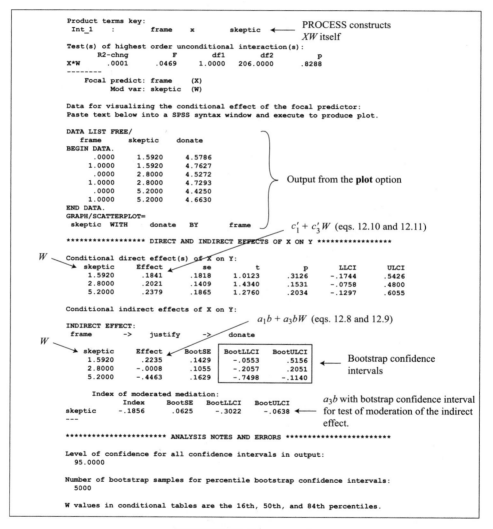

FIGURE 12.6 continued.

when estimating the conditional effect of X. The **plot** option tells PROCESS to generate data that can be used to visualize the interaction. All the information contained in this section of the PROCESS output is discussed further in section 7.2 because this part of the conditional process model (i.e., the equation for M) is just a simple moderation model.

In the section of PROCESS output labeled "Outcome Variable: donate" you will find c_1', c_2', c_3', and b (see equation 12.5). Also in this section of the output, resulting from the **plot** option, is a table of data for plotting the moderation of the direct effect of X. However, as discussed later, the evidence does not support moderation of the direct effect in this model. As the p-value for the regression coefficient for the product of X and W in the equation for Y is larger than 0.10, PROCESS does not produce any information in the output for probing this (non)moderation.[1]

Quantifying Direct and Indirect Effects

In a conditional process model, the direct and indirect effects must be quantified and interpreted. A formal test of moderation of the indirect and direct effect of X should also be conducted before focusing interpretation on the conditional effects. Using the same logic described in Chapter 11, these effects can be derived by piecing together the coefficients from models of M and Y. An indirect effect in a model such as this one is the product of the effect of X on M and the effect of M on Y controlling for X, and the direct effect is the effect of X on Y controlling for M. But in this model, both of these effects are specified as moderated and so become functions of W.

The Conditional Indirect Effect of X. We start first with the derivation of the indirect effect. Observe that the integrated model in statistical form (Figure 12.5 or equations 12.4 and 12.5) contains the product of X and W in the model of M. The model is (see equation 12.4)

$$\hat{M} = 2.452 - 0.562X - 0.105W + 0.201XW$$

and so $a_1 = -0.562$, $a_2 = -0.105$ and $a_3 = 0.201$. This model was visualized and probed in sections 7.3 and 7.4. But the PROCESS output in Figure 12.6 when using model 8 provides the same information that PROCESS did back in Chapter 7 when using model 1 for understanding the conditional nature of the relationship between disaster frame and strength of justifications for withholding aid. That effect is a linear function of climate change skepticism. This function is

$$\theta_{X \to M} = a_1 + a_3 W \tag{12.6}$$

[1]The value of 0.10 is the default in the **intprobe** option. Change this to a larger or smaller number if desired. Including **intprobe=1** in the command line will tell PROCESS to probe any interaction in a model, regardless of its p-value. See Appendix A for details.

As a_3 is statistically different from zero this means that X's effect on M is dependent on W. In this function, a_3 quantifies the linear relationship between W and the effect of X on M. However, whether a_3 is statistically different from zero does not tell us anything specific about the *indirect effect* of X, because a_3 does not quantify the relationship between the indirect effect of X on Y through M. That is, statistically significant moderation of the $X \rightarrow M$ path in this model is not a requirement of moderation of the indirect effect. More on this below.

Equation 12.6 is the first component of the indirect effect of X on Y through M. The second component is the effect of M on Y controlling for X. This effect is not proposed or modeled as moderated here, so this effect can be represented with a single estimate b from equation 12.5. The model of Y in this analysis is

$$\hat{Y} = 7.291 + 0.160X - 0.043W + 0.015XW - 0.923M \qquad (12.7)$$

and so $b = -0.923$. This tells us that the stronger a person's justifications for withholding aid from the victims, the less willing the person is to donate to the victims. This is statistically significant, but the outcome of this hypothesis test is not important, as b does not quantify the indirect effect of X on Y or the relationship between W and the indirect effect.

To get the indirect effect of X on Y through M, we need to multiply the two components defining the indirect effect. The two components are the effect of X on M and the effect of M on Y controlling for X. When these are multiplied, the result is

$$\theta_{X \rightarrow M}b = (a_1 + a_3W)b = a_1b + a_3bW \qquad (12.8)$$

or, expressed in terms of the estimated regression coefficients from the analysis,

$$\theta_{X \rightarrow M}b = (-0.562 + 0.201W)(-0.923) = 0.519 - 0.186W \qquad (12.9)$$

Equation 12.9 quantifies the indirect effect of the disaster frame on willingness to donate through justifications for withholding aid. It is a linear function of climate change skepticism. This means that there is no one number we can say is the indirect effect of X on Y through M. Rather, the indirect effect depends on the value of W plugged into equation 12.9. When you choose a value of W and do the math, the result is a conditional indirect effect of X that quantifies the indirect effect of X on Y through M at that value of W.

You can choose any values of W you want when calculating the conditional indirect effects. Table 12.2 shows the conditional indirect effects

TABLE 12.2. Conditional Direct and Indirect Effects for the Conditional Process Model in Figure 12.5

	Indirect Effect			Direct Effect
W	$a_1 + a_3 W$	b	$(a_1 + a_3 W)b$	$\theta_{X \to Y} = c_1' + c_3' W$
1.592	−0.242	−0.923	0.224	0.184
2.800	0.001	−0.923	−0.001	0.202
5.200	0.484	−0.923	−0.446	0.238

for values of W corresponding to the 16th, 50th, and 84th percentiles of the distribution of W in the data. These conditional indirect effects are also available in the PROCESS output in the section titled "Direct and Indirect Effects of X on Y." These are constructed by calculating the conditional effect of X on M, $\theta_{X \to Y} \mid W$, and multiplying it by the effect of M on Y (b). As can be seen in Table 12.2 and the PROCESS output in Figure 12.6, among those relatively low in climate change skepticism, the indirect effect of the disaster frame is positive (meaning the climate change frame results in a greater willingness to donate) because relative to the natural causes frame, the climate change frame resulted in less strong negative justifications for withholding aid ($\theta_{X \to M} \mid (W = 1.592) = -0.242$), which in turn translates to a greater willingness to donate (because the sign of b is negative). The indirect effect of disaster frame is near zero among those moderate in climate change skepticism, largely because among such people, there is little difference in justifications for withholding aid in the two framing conditions ($\theta_{X \to M} \mid (W = 2.8) = 0.001$), and multiplying this effect near zero by b results in a conditional indirect effect that is essentially zero. Finally, among those relatively high in climate change skepticism, the indirect effect of the disaster frame is *negative*, meaning the climate change frame results in less willingness to donate to the victims. Relative to the natural causes frame, the climate change frame resulted in stronger justifications for withholding aid to the victims ($\theta_{X \to M} \mid (W = 5.2) = 0.484$), which in turn is associated with less willingness to donate.

The Conditional Direct Effect of X. The direct effect of X on Y estimates how differences in X relate to differences in Y holding constant the proposed mediator (or mediators in more complex models). In this example, observe that the direct effect is proposed as moderated by W and is estimated as such by inclusion of the product of X and W in equation 12.5. As a result, the indirect effect of X becomes a function of W, which can be seen by grouping terms in equation 12.5 involving X and then factoring out X. The resulting expression is

$$\theta_{X \to Y} = c_1' + c_3'W \tag{12.10}$$

or, in terms of the estimated regression coefficients from equation 12.7,

$$\theta_{X \to Y} = 0.160 + 0.015W \tag{12.11}$$

which is a linear function of climate change skepticism. Using equation 12.11, conditional direct effects of X at values of W can be constructed by choosing values of W and doing the math. Using the 16th, 50th, and 84th percentiles of the distribution, these three conditional direct effects are found in Table 12.2 and also in the PROCESS output in Figure 12.6. As can be seen, the direct effect is positive at these three values of climate change skepticism. These positive conditional direct effects of X reflect a greater willingness to donate among those exposed to the climate change frame compared to those in the natural causes condition. But these are direct effects, and require the inclusion of the condition "among those equal in the strength of their justifications for withholding aid."

Visualizing the Direct and Indirect Effects

Direct and indirect effects that are specified as moderated become functions of the moderator. Because there is no single number that characterizes the effect in such a case, and given that the function itself is just an abstract mathematical representation of the relationship between the moderator and the effect, a visual representation can aid both presentation and interpretation. To visualize conditional direct and/or indirect effects, produce a dataset that contains the estimated direct and indirect effects for various values of the moderator using the functions constructed from the coefficients in the model. Then graph the resulting data with the effect on the vertical axis, values of the moderator on the horizontal axis, and different lines for the direct and indirect effects.

An example for the results in the prior analysis can be found in Figure 12.7. Although your impulse might be to interpret the vertical axis as willingness to donate, that is not the correct interpretation. The vertical axis corresponds to the estimated difference in willingness to donate between those told the drought was caused by climate change compared to those in the natural causes condition. So a positive value means those who read the story attributing the drought to climate change were more willing to donate, whereas a negative value means those in the climate change condition were less willing to donate. Zero on the vertical axis corresponds to no difference between the two framing conditions. The slopes of the lines represent how

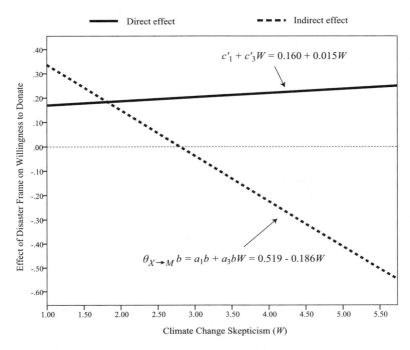

FIGURE 12.7. A visual representation of the conditional indirect and direct effects of the disaster frame on willingness to donate to the victims.

much the effect of the framing manipulation on donation attitude varies with individual differences in climate change skepticism.

Figure 12.7 was generated in SPSS with the code below, with some additional editing in a dedicated graphics program:

```
data list free/skeptic.
begin data.
1.592 2.800 5.200
end data.
compute indirect=0.519-0.186*skeptic.
compute direct=0.160+0.015*skeptic.
graph/scatter(overlay)=skeptic skeptic WITH direct indirect (pair).
```

In this code, the input to the functions are values of climate change skepticism corresponding to the 16th, 50th, and 84th percentiles in the sample distribution. The two **compute** commands produce the direct and indirect effects using the functions in equations 12.9 and 12.11 based on the coefficients in the conditional process model.

Comparable figures can be generated in SAS and R with the following code. The resulting figures require much less editing than the SPSS version.

```
data;input skeptic @@;
indirect=0.519-0.186*skeptic;
direct=0.160+0.015*skeptic;
datalines;
1.592 2.800 5.200
run;
proc sgplot;
series x=skeptic y=direct/curvelabel = 'Direct effect'
    lineattrs=(color=black pattern=Solid);
series x=skeptic y=indirect/curvelabel = 'Indirect effect'
    lineattrs=(color=red pattern=ShortDash);
xaxis label='Climate change skepticism';
yaxis label='Effect of frame on willingness to donate';
refline 0/axis=y transparency=0.5;
run;
```

```
x<-c(0,1,0,1,0,1)
w<-c(1.592,1.592,2.800,2.800,5.200,5.200)
y<-c(0.184,0.224,0.202,-0.001,0.238,-0.446)
plot(y=y,x=w,pch=15,col="white",
xlab="Climate change skepticism",
ylab="Effect of frame on willingness to donate")
legend.txt<-c("Direct effect","Indirect effect")
legend("bottomleft",legend=legend.txt,lty=c(1,3),lwd=c(4,3))
lines(w[x==0],y[x==0],lwd=4,lty=1)
lines(w[x==1],y[x==1],lwd=4,lty=3)
abline(0,0,lwd=0.5,lty=2)
```

The values in Table 12.2 are points on these lines. The slopes of the lines can be derived from equations 12.9 and 12.11. The slope of a line corresponds to how much the output of the function changes as the input to the function changes by one unit. From equation 12.10, the slope of the line for the direct effect is c_3', meaning that $\theta_{X \to Y}$ increases by c_3' units as W increases by one unit. The slope of the line for the conditional indirect effect is not as obvious. From equation 12.8, the conditional indirect effect of X on Y through M is $(a_1 + a_3 W)b$. If W increases by one unit, then the conditional indirect effect of X on Y through M would be $[a_1 + a_3(W + 1)]b$. The slope of the line for the conditional indirect effect is the difference between these two values:

$$[a_1 + a_3(W + 1)]b - (a_1 + a_3W)b = a_1b + a_3bW + a_3b - a_1b - a_3bW$$
$$= (a_1b - a_1b) + (a_3bW - a_3bW) + a_3b$$
$$= a_3b$$

This result of this derivation has an important interpretation. Consider two groups of people that differ by one unit in their climate change skepticism. According to this derivation, the indirect effect of the framing manipulation on willingness to donate through strength of justifications for withholding aid is a_3b units larger in the group that is more skeptical of climate change. That is, a_3b is the difference between the conditional indirect effects in these two groups. This will be relevant to my discussion and critique of mediated moderation in section 12.4. This product also provides a test statistic for a formal test of moderated mediation in this model, described in the next section.

12.3 Statistical Inference

My discussion thus far has largely remained squarely in the realm of statistical description. We see from the prior section that in this model, the direct and indirect effects are both functions of W. With these functions, you can quantify the direct and indirect effects of X on Y for any value or values of W you choose. But before doing so and substantively interpreting the results, some inferential rigor is needed. In this section, I discuss inference about moderation of the direct and indirect effects in this model as well as the process of probing any such moderation found.

Inference about the Direct Effect

In this model, the direct effect is specified as a linear function of W:

$$\theta_{X \to Y} = c_1' + c_3'W$$

In this function, c_1' estimates the conditional direct effect of X when $W = 0$, and c_3' estimates how much the conditional direct effect of X changes as W changes by one unit. As discussed earlier, c_3' is the slope of the line in Figure 12.7. If the direct effect is moderated by W, then the slope of this line—the weight for W in the function defining the conditional direct effect—should be different from zero. It is here, of course; $c_3' = 0.015$. But $c_3' = 0.015$ is just an estimate that contains some sampling error. If we want to test whether

TABLE 12.3. Inference for the Conditional Direct and Indirect Effects in the Disaster Framing Study

	Indirect Effect		Direct Effect		
W	$(a_1 + a_3 W)b$	95% Bootstrap CI	$c_1' + c_3' W$	SE	p
1.592	0.224	−0.055 to 0.516	0.184	0.182	.313
2.800	−0.001	−0.206 to 0.205	0.202	0.141	.153
5.200	−0.446	−0.750 to −0.114	0.238	0.187	.203

the direct effect is moderated, we can conduct an inferential test for c_3' using a hypothesis testing procedure or constructing a confidence interval. This can be done using the output from any regression analysis program, and PROCESS also produces this information. As can be seen in Table 12.1 and the PROCESS output in Figure 12.6, this regression coefficient is not statistically significant, $t(206) = 0.217, p = 0.829$, 95% CI = −0.121 to 0.151. So we conclude that the direct effect of the disaster frame on willingness to donate is not significantly related to climate change skepticism.

Had the direct effect been significantly moderated by W, the next step would be to probe it. This could be done with the pick-a-point approach or the Johnson-Neyman technique. The former requires estimating the conditional direct effect of X on Y at values of W, deriving its standard error, and then computing a p-value for testing the null that this conditional direct effect equals zero, or constructing a confidence interval. The results of this exercise, the details of which are discussed in section 7.4 because the procedure is identical for this model, can be found in Table 12.3. PROCESS does the computations for you automatically in the section of output in Figure 12.6 titled "Direct and Indirect Effects of X on Y," regardless of whether the evidence is consistent with moderation of the direct effect. It is up to you to know whether or not it is worth looking at this section of the output. As can be seen, not only is the direct effect of the disaster frame not significantly moderated by climate change skepticism, but the conditional direct effects are not statistically different from zero at the three values of the moderator defining "relatively low," "relatively moderate," and "relatively high" in climate change skepticism.

It not necessary to test whether any of the conditional direct effects of X in Table 12.3 are significantly different from each other. As discussed in section 7.5, the absence of moderation of the direct effect of X by W in this model means that no two conditional direct effects can be deemed statistically different from each other, regardless of the relative sizes of their p-values.

Inference about the Indirect Effect

Inference about an indirect effect in a conditional process model focuses first on testing whether the indirect effect is moderated. With affirmative evidence of moderation of the indirect effect, conditional indirect effects are then derived and inference about these conditional indirect effects conducted.

A Statistical Test of Moderated Mediation. You might be tempted to think that you can claim that the indirect effect is moderated in this example because there is a statistically significant interaction between X and W in the model of M and the effect of M on Y is statistically significant in the model of Y. Until recently, this piecemeal approach to testing whether the indirect effect is moderated was the dominant one. However, as discussed in section 11.6 and Hayes (2015), a more sensible approach is to determine whether the weight for the moderator in the function defining the indirect effect of X is different from zero. This is the most direct test of moderated mediation, in that it relies on a quantification of the relationship between the moderator and the size of the indirect effect, it requires only a single inferential test rather than two tests for different components of the model, and it is possible to construct a confidence interval for this weight, thereby communicating the uncertainty in the size of the relationship between the moderator and the indirect effect.

Recall that in this model, the indirect effect of X on Y through M is, from equation 12.8, $(a_1 + a_3W)b = a_1b + a_3bW$. This is a function of W. Using the estimated regression coefficients from the model in this analysis, this function is

$$(-0.562 + 0.201W)(-0.923) = 0.519 - 0.186W$$

.

and is visualized in Figure 12.7. The slope of the line representing this function is $a_3b = -0.186$ and it quantifies the change in the indirect effect of X on Y through M as W changes by one unit. I call a_3b the *index of moderated mediation* for this model. If this index is zero, that would mean that there is no linear relationship between the indirect effect of X and proposed moderator W. If this index is exactly zero, then the slope of the line for the indirect effect in Figure 12.7 would be flat. Of course, in the data, the index is not zero, and the slope of the line is not flat. But because a_3 and b are both sample specific, so too is a_3b. We want to know whether the index of moderated mediation deviates further from zero in the data than would be expected by chance if in fact $_Ta_{3T}b = 0$, meaning there is no linear relationship between the moderator and the size of the indirect effect. If it does by an inferential test, then we can say that W moderates the indirect effect of X—moderated mediation. But if it does not, then the indirect effect of X does not vary linearly with W. This means that W does not moderate any mediation of the effect of X on Y through M.

As a_3b is a product of regression coefficients, its sampling distribution will be irregular in form. A bootstrap confidence interval would be a good tool for the inference, for the same reasons we have been using bootstrap confidence intervals when making an inference about a product of regression coefficients. PROCESS takes care of this automatically in any model it can estimate in which the indirect effect can be expressed as a linear function of the moderator.[2] This confidence interval can be found in the PROCESS output in Figure 12.6 near the end. As can be seen PROCESS gives $a_3b = -0.186$ for the index of moderated mediation, with a 95% bootstrap confidence interval between -0.302 and -0.064. As this confidence interval does not straddle zero, this is evidence that the indirect effect of the framing of the disaster on willingness to donate through justifications for withholding aid is moderated by climate change skepticism. In other words, climate change skepticism moderates the mediation. If the confidence interval straddled zero, then we could not claim definitively that the indirect effect varies linearly as a function of climate change skepticism.

Probing Moderation of Mediation. With evidence of moderation of the indirect effect, probing this moderation is the next step. As discussed in section 11.6, a Johnson–Neyman approach cannot be used without making the unwarranted assumption of normality of the sampling distribution of the indirect effect. So the pick-a-point approach is the only viable method for probing this moderation of mediation. This requires selecting values of the moderator, estimating the conditional indirect effect of X at those values, and conducting an inference. We will stick with the use of the 16th, 50th, and 84th percentiles of the distribution of W, or 1.592, 2.8, and 5.2, respectively. Plugging these numbers into equation 12.9 generates the conditional indirect effects among people relatively low, moderate, and high in climate change skepticism. These conditional indirect effects are found in Table 12.2 and again in Table 12.3. As these are products of regression coefficients, a bootstrap confidence interval can be used for inference. PROCESS does this automatically for you, as can be seen toward

[2]The indirect effect is a *linear* function of a moderator W if W is specified as a moderator of only one of the paths that define the indirect effect. Otherwise, the indirect effect will be a nonlinear function of W. In that case, PROCESS will not produce an index of moderated mediation.

the bottom of the output in Figure 12.6. Also see Table 12.3. If the confidence interval straddles zero, you cannot say definitively that the conditional indirect of X at that value of W is different from zero. But if the confidence interval does not straddle zero, this is evidence that the conditional indirect effect is different from zero.

As can be seen in the PROCESS output and in Table 12.3, among people relatively low in climate change skepticism ($W = 1.592$), the conditional indirect effect is estimated as 0.224, but a 95% bootstrap confidence interval includes zero (-0.055 to 0.516). Among those moderate in climate change skepticism ($W = 2.8$), the conditional indirect effect is 0.202 with a 95% bootstrap confidence interval between -0.206 and 0.205. This straddles zero as well. But among those relatively high in climate change skepticism, we can conclude definitively that the indirect effect is negative. The point estimate is -0.447, and the 95% bootstrap confidence interval is entirely below zero (-0.750 to -0.114). Combined, these results support the claim that among climate change skeptics, justifications for withholding aid functions as a mediator of the effect of the framing of the cause of the drought on willingness to donate to the victims. The negative indirect effect means that framing the drought as caused by climate change, as opposed to leaving it unspecified, reduced willingness to donate to the victims by increasing the strength of their justifications for withholding aid, which in turn reduces willingness to donate. However, such justifications do not significantly mediate the effect of framing on willingness to donate among those less skeptical of climate change, as the two conditional indirect effects among those moderate and low in climate change skepticism are not significantly different from zero.

When probing the moderation of an indirect effect in a model of this form, it is not necessary to formally compare two conditional indirect effects at different values of W to determine if they differ from each other. The test of moderated mediation based on the index of moderated mediation doubles as a test of the difference between any two conditional indirect effects one can construct for two different values of W. The logic and mathematics of this claim is identical to that provided in section 11.6 for a different model. The conditional indirect effect in this model is estimated as $(a_1 + a_3 W)b$, and so the difference between two conditional indirect effects when $W = w_1$ compared to when $W = w_2$ is

$$
\begin{aligned}
(a_1 + a_3 w_1)b - (a_1 + a_3 w_2)b &= a_1 b + a_3 w_1 b - a_1 b - a_3 w_2 b \\
&= a_3 w_1 b - a_3 w_2 b \\
&= a_3 b(w_1 - w_2)
\end{aligned}
$$

which is the index of moderated mediation multiplied by the difference between the two values of W. A bootstrap confidence interval could be used as a test of significance of the difference between these two conditional indirect effects. But as $w_1 - w_2$ is a constant across all bootstrap samples, if a confidence interval for $_Ta_{3T}b$ does not contain zero, then a confidence interval for $_Ta_{3T}b(w_1 - w_2)$ also will not contain zero *regardless* of the choice of values of w_1 and w_2. Similarly, if the confidence interval for the index of moderated mediation staddles zero, then so too will a confidence interval for the index multiplied by a constant.

Pruning the Model

In this analysis, we found that although the indirect effect of the disaster frame manipulation on willingness to donate was significantly moderated by climate change skepticism, the direct effect was not. Given this, you might choose to simplify the model by forcing the direct effect to be linearly independent of climate change skepticism. This is more easily done than said when using PROCESS. Just change the model number in the PROCESS command on page 444 from 8 to 7 (compare the template for models 7 and 8 in Appendix A), and it is done. If you did this, you would find that substantively, the results are not any different. The indirect effect is still significantly moderated by climate change skepticism according to a bootstrap confidence interval for the index of moderated mediation, and bootstrap confidence intervals for conditional indirect effects reveal that among those relatively high but not moderate or relatively low in climate change skepticism, the effect of the framing of the cause of the drought on willingness to donate is mediated (negatively) by strength of justifications for withholding aid to the victims. And the direct effect of framing is not statistically significant.

However, if you use model 7 rather than model 8, climate change skepticism is not included in the equation for the model of willingness to donate. If you wanted to keep climate change skepticism in the model of willingness to donate while still fixing the direct effect of the disaster frame to be un-moderated by climate change skepticism, a modification to the PROCESS command accomplishes this. The command is

```
compute skeptcpy=skeptic.
process y=donate/x=frame/w=skeptic/m=justify/model=7/plot=1/
   cov=skeptcpy/cmatrix=0,1/seed=280417.
```

whereas in SAS, use

```
data disaster;set disaster;skeptcpy=skeptic;run;
%process (data=disaster,y=donate,x=frame,w=skeptic,m=justify,model=7,
    plot=1,cov=skeptcpy,cmatrix=0 1,seed=280417);
```

See Appendix B for a discussion of this trick for telling PROCESS how to make a moderator in one part of a conditional process model a covariate in another part.

12.4 Mediated Moderation

Mediation is moderated if the indirect effect of X on Y through one or more mediators is contingent on a moderator. With evidence of moderated mediation, one can claim that the $X \to M \to Y$ chain of events functions differently or to varying degrees for different people, in different contexts or conditions, or whatever the moderator variable represents. Although similar in name and pronunciation to moderated mediation, the term *mediated moderation* refers to the phenomenon in which an interaction between X and a moderator W in a model of Y is carried through a mediator.

Mediation moderation hypotheses are regularly articulated and tested by scientists. For example, Clark, Wegener, Briñol, and Petty (2011) showed participants the cognitive test performance of a child who did either very well or very poorly and then asked them to list their thoughts about the child's performance. Following this, the participants were given information about the socioeconomic status of the child and his family that was either stereotypically consistent or inconsistent with the child's performance, after which they were asked to indicate how confident they were about the validity of their prior thoughts. They were also asked to make a recommendation as to whether the child should be placed in a program for gifted children or for children in need of remedial instruction.

Clark et al. (2011) found an interaction between performance and socioeconomic status in a model predicting placement recommendations, such that participants' recommendations were consistent with the child's performance only when the child's performance was consistent with the performance implied by the socioeconomic stereotype. According to their analysis, this interaction was mediated by thought confidence, in that participants were more confident about the thoughts they listed prior to being told about the child's socioeconomic status when those thoughts were consistent with performance implied by the stereotype, and accounting for thought confidence statistically reduced the size of the interaction in the model estimating placement recommendation. Additional examples of mediated moderation in the empirical literature include Ashton-James and

Tracy (2012), Cohen, Sullivan, Solomon, Greenberg, and Ogilvie (2011), Ein-Gar, Shiv, and Tormala (2012), Gao et al. (2014), Grant, Gino, and Hofmann (2011), Hentshel, Shemla, Wegge, and Kearney (2013), Jiang, Bazarova, and Hancock (2011), Morrison (2011), Rabinovich and Morton (2012), Riglin et al. (2016), Rueggeberg, Wrosch, Miller, and McDade (2012), Wan, Xu, and Ding (2014).

Although there is an abundance of published examples of mediated moderation analysis, their frequency of occurrence in the literature should not be confused with meaningfulness of the procedure itself. I will argue toward the end of this section that rarely is the phenomenon of mediated moderation interesting when interpreted as such. It is almost always substantively more meaningful to conceptualize a mediated moderation process in terms of moderated mediation. But before doing this, I will describe how a mediated moderation analysis is undertaken.

Mediated Moderation as the Indirect Effect of a Product

Consider the simple moderation model, where X's effect on Y is moderated by a single variable, W:

$$Y = i_Y + c_1 X + c_2 W + c_3 XW + e_Y \qquad (12.12)$$

This equation is represented in the form of a statistical diagram in Figure 12.8, panel A. If c_3 is statistically different from zero, then one can claim that the effect of X on Y depends on W.

An investigator interested in testing a hypothesis about mediated moderation would attempt to ascertain whether the interaction between X and W in the model of Y operates through a mediator, M. Baron and Kenny (1986) describe the application of the causal steps approach for establishing mediated moderation. After first demonstrating that c_3 is statistically different from zero, one then tests whether W moderates X's effect in a model of the proposed mediator by estimating the coefficients in

$$M = i_M + a_1 X + a_2 W + a_3 XW + e_M \qquad (12.13)$$

If a_3 is statistically different from zero, then one proceeds to the next stage of the analysis by testing whether M is related to Y in

$$Y = i_Y + c_1' X + c_2' W + c_3' XW + bM + e_Y \qquad (12.14)$$

If b is statistically different from zero and c_3' is closer to zero than c_3, this establishes that the interaction between X and W in determining Y is mediated by M. If c_3' is statistically significant, then it is said that M partially

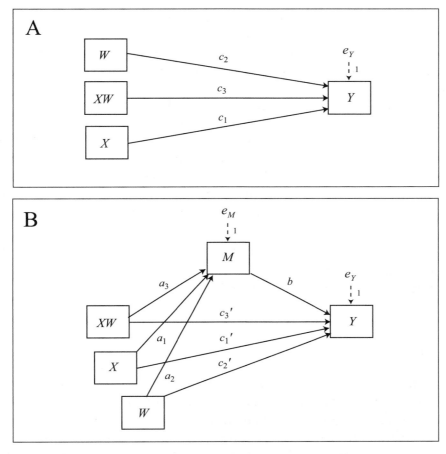

FIGURE 12.8. A statistical diagram representing mediated moderation, with the model of the total effect of *XW* (panel A) as well as the mediation of *XW*'s effect by *M* (panel B).

mediates the interaction, whereas if c_3' is not statistically significant, M is branded a complete mediator of the interaction.

Although the underlying mathematics of the modeling process just described are sound, this causal steps approach to mediated moderation analysis suffers from the same limitations in this application as it does in any mediation analysis (see section 4.1 for a discussion), and so I cannot recommend testing mediated moderation in this fashion. The preferred procedure to test whether moderation is mediated is to estimate the indirect effect of XW on Y through proposed mediator M and then conduct an inferential test for this indirect effect (see, e.g., Fairchild & MacKinnon, 2009; Morgan-Lopez & MacKinnon, 2006).

A mediated moderation model is represented in the form of a statistical diagram in Figure 12.8, panel B, which translates into equations 12.13 and

12.14. The indirect effect of the product is, like any indirect effect, quantified as the product of paths linking the causal agent to the presumed outcome through the proposed mediator. In Figure 12.8, panel B and equations 12.13 and 12.14, the indirect effect of XW is therefore estimated as the product of a_3 and b.

A close examination of Figure 12.8, panel B, reveals that this statistical diagram could be construed as a representation of a simple mediation model with XW as the causal agent and X and W as covariates. Indeed, the same path analysis rules described in Chapter 3 and section 4.2 apply here. c'_3 is the direct effect of XW, and the indirect effect of XW through M is a_3b, as just derived. Together, these sum to yield the total effect of XW, estimated with c_3 in equation 12.12 and represented in Figure 12.8, panel A. That is,

$$c_3 = c'_3 + a_3b$$

Isolating the indirect effect reveals that the indirect effect of XW on Y through M is the difference between the total and direct effects of XW:

$$a_3b = c_3 - c'_3$$

The outcome of an inferential test demonstrating that $_Ta_{3T}b \neq 0$ establishes that XW influences Y indirectly through M. It would also establish that the direct effect of XW on Y is statistically different than the total effect of XW (i.e., $_Tc_3 - _Tc'_3 \neq 0$). Any of the inferential methods discussed in Chapter 3 could be used. I recommend a bootstrap confidence interval.

To illustrate this procedure, I conduct a mediated moderation analysis using the data from the disaster framing study by examining whether the moderation of the effect of the disaster frame on donation attitude by climate change skepticism operates through justifications for withholding aid. That is, is justifications for withholding aid to the disaster victims (M) the mechanism carrying this interaction between the framing of the disaster as caused by climate change rather than natural causes (X) and climate change skepticism (W) in determining willingness to donate (Y)?

The regression coefficients in equations 12.12, 12.13, and 12.14 could be estimated with any program capable of OLS regression, but you wouldn't get a proper inferential test of the indirect effect with most programs. PROCESS provides all that is needed. The statistical diagram of the model in Figure 12.8 can be construed as a simple mediation model with XW as the causal agent sending its effects on Y through M, with X and W as covariates. So PROCESS model 4 would be appropriate. The product of X and W first has to be created and this product is then used as X in the PROCESS command. In SPSS, the commands that conduct the analysis are

```
compute framskep=frame*skeptic.
process y=donate/x=framskep/m=justify/cov=frame skeptic/model=4/total=1
  /seed=280417.
```

In SAS, use

```
data disaster;set disaster;framskep=frame*skeptic;run;
%process (data=disaster,y=donate,x=framskep,m=justify,cov=frame
  skeptic,model=4,total=1,seed=280417);
```

The resulting output can be found in Figure 12.9. The total, direct, and indirect effects of the product of frame condition and climate change skepticism can be found in the section of output labeled "Total, Direct, and Indirect Effects of X on Y."

The total effect of the product of frame condition and climate change skepticism (XW, but listed as X in the PROCESS output) is $c_3 = -0.171, t(207) = -2.034, p = .043$. This total effect of the product of X and W partitions into indirect and direct components. The indirect effect of XW is -0.186, calculated as the product of the effect of XW in the model of justifications for withholding aid (M, $a_3 = 0.201$) and the effect of justifications for withholding aid on willingness to donate (Y, $b = -0.923$). This indirect effect is statistically different from zero according to a 95% bootstrap confidence interval (-0.302 to -0.064). The direct effect of XW is not statistically significant, $c_3' = 0.015, t(207) = 0.217, p = .829$. After accounting for negative justifications for withholding aid, climate change skepticism does not moderate the effect of frame on willingness to donate.

Notice that as promised, and just as in the mediation analyses presented in Chapters 3 through 5, the total effect of XW is the sum of the direct and indirect effects of XW. That is,

$$c_3 = c_3' + a_3b = -0.171 = 0.015 - 0.186$$

Therefore, the indirect effect of XW on Y through M is the difference between the total effect of XW on Y and the direct effect of XW on Y:

$$a_3b = c_3 - c_3' = -0.186 = -0.171 - 0.015$$

The results of this analysis are consistent with the claim that the moderation of the effect of the framing of the cause of the drought on willingness to donate to the victims by people's climate change skepticism is mediated by the strength of their justifications for withholding aid. The coefficient for the product of frame and climate change skepticism in the simple moderation model estimating willingness to donate is significantly reduced after controlling for justifications for withholding aid. This difference between

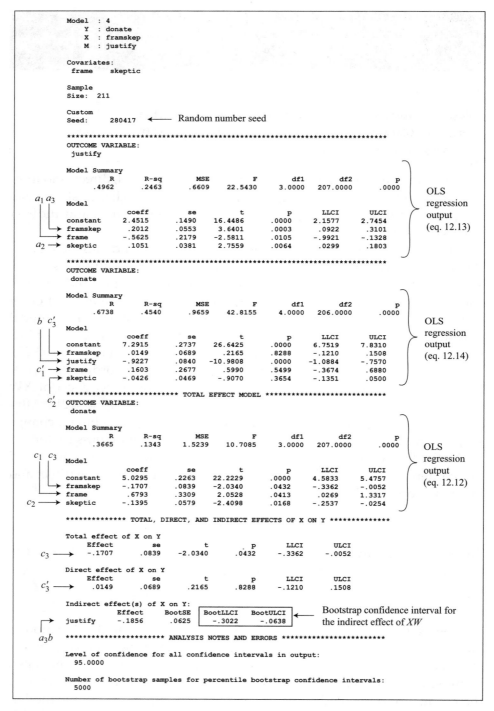

FIGURE 12.9. PROCESS output from a mediated moderation analysis of the data from the climate change and humanitarianism study.

the total and direct effect of the product is the indirect effect of the product through strength of justifications for withholding aid, and it is statistically different from zero according to a bootstrap confidence interval.

Why Mediated Moderation Is Neither Interesting Nor Meaningful

If at this point you feel like you are experiencing déjà vu or wonder if you have been reading the same page repeatedly, then you are paying attention. Many of the numbers in the last couple of paragraphs should look familiar because you've seen them before. Compare the two statistical diagrams in Figures 12.5 and 12.8, panel B. Observe that they are the same. This is because the mediated moderation model just estimated is mathematically identical to the conditional process model estimated in section 12.2 when the analysis was framed in terms of moderated mediation. Indeed, notice the similarities in the PROCESS outputs corresponding to these two analyses (compare Figures 12.6 and 12.9), save differences in formatting and output options. The models are the same, the equations of M and Y used to estimate the coefficients in the model are the same, and when they are each estimated on the same data, they will yield identical results. The only difference between them is how they are interpreted, and on what part of the model your attention is focused.

Moderated mediation focuses on the conditional nature of an indirect effect—how an indirect effect is moderated. If you think of the terms "mediation" and "indirect effect" as essentially synonymous conceptually, then moderated mediation means a moderated indirect effect. Interpretive focus in a moderated mediation analysis is directed at estimating the indirect effect and how that effect varies as a function of a moderator. Mediated moderation, by contrast, asks about the mechanism through which an interaction between X and a moderator W operates, where the product of X and W is construed as the causal agent sending its effect to Y through M. Focus in mediated moderation is the estimation of the indirect effect of the product of X and W.

The problem I have with mediated moderation as a concept is that the product of X and W is meaningless. It is not a measure of anything. Remember that the product of X and W in equations 12.12 and 12.13 originates from conceiving X's effect on Y as a linear function of the moderator W. When that linear function is conceived as X's effect rather than a single number represented by a single regression coefficient, the product pops out of the algebra as an additional variable included in the model estimating Y along with X and W (to refresh your memory, see the derivation beginning on page 226). So the product serves no function in the model other than to allow X's effect on Y to be contingent on W. Its presence in the model builds in flexibility, in that X's effect is not constrained to be invariant across values of W so long as XW is included as an additional antecedent variable. Unlike X and W, both of which carry information about some construct measured or some variable manipulated, XW has no substantive grounding in the measurement or manipulation process. The product doesn't quantify anything. And if XW has no meaning and no substantive interpretation, then what does the indirect effect of a product mean? The answer, in my opinion, is that it means nothing. Therefore, so too is mediated moderation largely meaningless and substantively uninteresting. For a related discussion, see Edwards (2009, pp. 156–157).

It turns out that the indirect effect of the product of XW, a_3b, does have an interpretation, but it is an interpretation that makes sense only if you conceptualize the process being modeled in terms of moderated mediation rather than mediated moderation. Recall the derivation of the slope of the line for the conditional indirect effect of X on Y through M in the conditional process analysis described in section 12.2 (see page 453 and Figure 12.7). The slope of that line is a_3b and can be interpreted as how much the conditional indirect effect of X on Y through M changes as W changes by one unit. We called this the index of moderated mediation in the conditional process analysis described earlier. So an inference that the indirect effect of XW on Y through M is different from zero is really an inference about how much the indirect effect of X on Y through M changes as W is changing. Of course, this means nothing if one is not thinking about the process in terms of the conditional nature of the mechanism linking X to Y through M. In order for a_3b to be substantively interpretable, one must reconceptualize the process being studied in moderated mediation terms rather than mediated moderation terms.[3]

I believe the elusiveness of the substantive interpretation of the indirect effect in mediated moderation is in part due to misdirecting one's analytical focus away from where it belongs, which is on X rather than XW. If you phrase your research question not as "Does XW carry its effect on Y through M?" but as "Does the indirect effect of X on Y through M depend on W?" then a_3b becomes meaningful as a measure of how the size of the indirect effect linking X to Y through M differs as a function of W. Furthermore, one ends up with a better understanding of the conditional nature of the process being investigated when one quantifies conditional indirect effects that are by their nature meaningful and substantively interpretable. So I

[3]Notice that the PROCESS output in Figure 12.6 shows that the index of moderated mediation and its confidence interval is identical to the indirect effect of XW in the PROCESS output in Figure 12.9. So it is not necessary to test mediated moderation in PROCESS using model 4. Model 8 accomplishes the job just as well, but it also generates the conditional direct and indirect effects of X, which model 4 does not provide.

recommend avoiding the articulation of hypotheses or research questions in terms of the mediation of the effect of a product, abandoning the term *mediated moderation* entirely, and instead reframing such hypotheses and research questions in terms of the contingencies of an indirect effect—moderated mediation.

12.5 Chapter Summary

The indirect effect of X on Y through M represents the mechanism by which X affects Y. An indirect effect of X, meaning the mechanism by which X affects Y, can vary as a function of a moderator. A conditional indirect effect quantifies the indirect effect of some proposed causal agent X on a presumed outcome Y through a putative mediator M conditioned on the value of a moderator. By contrast, a conditional direct effect quantifies the effect of X on Y independent of the mediator but conditioned on a value of a moderator variable. Any path in a mediation model can be moderated, and which path is moderated determines the function that mathematically defines the conditional indirect effect. In Chapter 11, I illustrated conditional process analysis by estimating a simple mediation model that included moderation of the effect of M on Y. This chapter extended the principles introduced in Chapter 11 to a model which included moderation of the effect of X on M along with moderation of the direct effect of X. By quantifying conditional indirect and direct effects in an integrated conditional process model, one is in a position to better numerically describe how the $X \rightarrow M \rightarrow Y$ mechanism is contingent compared to a piecemeal approach that focuses only on specific paths or steps in the process the model represents rather than the process as a whole.

If the indirect effect of X on Y through M is moderated by W, this means that mediation of the effect of X on Y is moderated, a phenomenon called *moderated mediation*. This is different from *mediated moderation*, which refers to the phenomenon in which the product of X and a moderator of X's effect (W) on Y carries its effect on Y through M. Although mediated moderation hypotheses are tested in abundance in the literature, the indirect effect of a product is substantively meaningless because XW is not a measure of anything. However, in a conditional process model in the form estimated in this chapter, the indirect effect of the product can be interpreted as an estimated difference between conditional indirect effects in a moderated mediation process. Thus, I recommend that questions about mediated moderation be recast in terms of a moderated mediation process. This takes the focus off the meaningless XW as the causal agent and shifts it back where it belongs on X.

With the principles of conditional process modeling introduced in this book more or less mastered, you are in a good position to branch out beyond the examples presented in this and the prior chapter and try alternative models, potentially more complex than these. An example of a more complex model is the topic of Chapter 13.

13

Conditional Process Analysis with a Multicategorical Antecedent

---

In this chapter, I build on the principles of conditional process analysis introduced in Chapters 11 and 12 by estimating and interpreting a conditional process model with a multicategorical causal antecedent variable X. This requires an integration of the fundamentals of conditional process analysis with the lessons learned in Chapters 6 and 10 on mediation and moderation involving a multicategorical variable. I introduce and define the terms *relative conditional indirect effect* and *relative conditional direct effect* and show how the index of moderated mediation can be used to test whether the indirect effect of a multicategorical X on Y through M is moderated by W.

At the end of any great fireworks show is the grand finale, where the pyrotechnicians throw everything remaining in their arsenal at you at once, leaving you amazed, dazed, and perhaps temporarily a little hard of hearing. Although this is not the final chapter of this book, I am now going to throw everything at you at once with an example of the most complicated conditional process model I will cover in this book. Although things can certainly get more complicated than this (e.g., Hayes, 2018), and PROCESS can make the analysis of more complicated models quite a bit simpler than it otherwise would be, nothing in the rest of this book will require your close attention quite so much as what follows.

The second section of this book (Chapters 3 through 6) was dedicated to mediation analysis, where we covered the estimation of *indirect* and *direct effects* of X and discussed how to determine whether X's effect on Y is mediated by at least one intervening variable M. That section of the book closed with a treatment of mediation analysis when X is a multicategorical variable and how to quantify *relative* indirect and direct effects of X.

In the third section of the book (Chapters 7 through 10), I described how to specify a regression model that allows focal antecedent variable X's effect on Y to be linearly dependent on a moderator W. We saw how to set up a moderation model in regression analysis, visualize the resulting model, and probe it by estimating the *conditional effect of X*, so as to make claims about how X's effect on Y differs depending on the value of one or more moderators. I closed that section of the book with a discussion of moderated regression analysis when X is a multicategorical variable, at which point I defined the *relative conditional effect of X*.

The fourth section of the book, beginning with Chapter 11 and ending with the one you are reading now, is about the integration of moderation and mediation in the form of a conditional process model. The theme of this section of the book has been how to test hypotheses about whether a mechanism—an indirect effect of X on Y through mediator M—is moderated. We have seen two examples thus far, one with a continuous X and one with a dichotomous X, and during the discussion of these two examples I defined the *conditional indirect* and *conditional direct effect of X*.

Given the pattern of the prior two sections, it seems fitting to end this section of the book with an example of a conditional process analysis with a multicategorical X. As you know from earlier chapters, when X is a multicategorical variable representing g groups, X's effect can be expressed in the form of $g - 1$ relative effects of X. But when a multicategorical X is part of a mediation model that allows for the indirect or direct effect to be moderated, it is necessary to introduce yet additional statistics with names that combine all of the adjectives we have used to describe effects to this point: the *relative conditional indirect* and *relative conditional direct effect of X*. I start the discussion by reminding you of some of the analyses we conducted using a study examining the interpersonal effects of responding to an act of discrimination.

13.1 Revisiting Sexual Discrimination in the Workplace

In Chapter 6, I introduced a study by Garcia et al. (2010) in which participants evaluated an attorney (Catherine) subjected to sexual discrimination at the law firm at which she worked. Recall that some of the participants in this study were told that following news that she lost a promotion to a less qualified male attorney at the firm, Catherine protested the decision by approaching the senior partners and making a case as to why it was unfair and that she should have been promoted. Some of the participants were told that she protested the decision by framing her argument around why she deserved the promotion (the individual protest condition), whereas others were told she framed her argument around the collective of women (the collective protest condition). But some participants were told that she chose *not* to protest and, instead, accepted the decision, kept quiet, and went about her job at the firm. So in this study, there were three conditions representing the manipulation of Catherine's behavior, and participants were randomly assigned to one of the three conditions. The purpose of this study was to see how Catherine would be perceived as a function of her decision to protest the discrimination rather than remaining silent.

In the analysis presented in Chapter 6, we saw that Catherine was evaluated more positively on average—she was liked more—when she protested the decision of the partners to promote the man rather than when she did nothing and just accepted their decision. The pattern of means suggested that little distinction was made in the minds of the perceivers between protesting individually and collectively. She was liked about the same amount on average regardless, but clearly more than when she did not protest the decision. In that same analysis, perceived appropriateness of her response was assessed as a mediator of this effect. The analysis supported the claim that her behavior resulted in a difference in how positively she was perceived because different behaviors were seen as more or less appropriate for the circumstance, depending on what that behavior was. Protesting was seen as more appropriate than not protesting, and the more appropriate her behavior was perceived as being, the more she was liked. In that analysis, both of the relative indirect effects (one for individually protesting relative to not protesting, and one for collectively protesting relative to not protesting) were significantly different from zero. As at least one of these relative indirect effects was different from zero, this supported a claim of mediation of the effect of her behavior on how much she was liked by perceived appropriateness of the response.

Later, in Chapter 10, the relevance of perceived appropriateness of the response as a mediator was ignored and focus shifted to perceived pervasiveness of sex discrimination as a moderator of the effect of Catherine's behavior on how she was perceived. Recall from that analysis that how much Catherine was liked as a function of her decision to protest or not and how was dependent on the perceiver's beliefs about the pervasiveness of sex discrimination in society. Among those who perceived sexism and sex discrimination as rampant in society, Catherine was liked more when she protested than when she did not. But the opposite pattern was observed among those who saw sex discrimination as less pervasive. Among such people, she was liked more when she did not protest.

Interesting though these findings may be, Garcia et al.'s (2010) reasoning about the process linking the protesting of an act of discrimination to evaluation of the protester was a bit more sophisticated than as reflected in

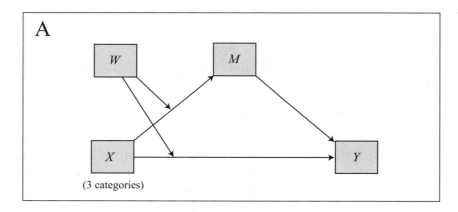

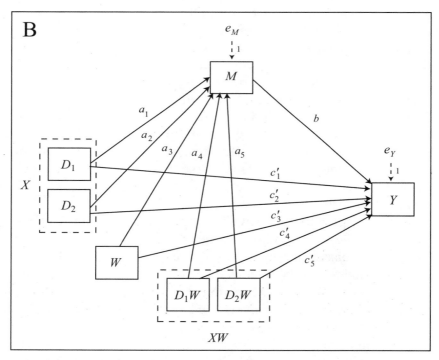

FIGURE 13.1. A conceptual (panel A) and statistical diagram (panel B) of a conditional process model with a multicategorical antecedent X with 3 categories and a continuous moderator of the $X \to M$ and $X \to Y$ paths.

these two analyses. Garcia et al. (2010) proposed that Catherine's decision to protest would be perceived as entirely justified and even necessary in a world unfair to women. Among those who see the world in this fashion, her decision to protest would be considered reasonable, even noble, and this would translate into a more positive evaluation because she acted appropriately and how she *should* have acted. But if she chose to remain silent and not defend herself against such unfairness when sticking up for herself was the more appropriate course of action, she'd be evaluated less positively. So the more a participant perceived sex discrimination to be rampant in society, the more protesting would be seen as appropriate relative to not protesting, and the more positively Catherine would be perceived as a result of acting approopriately.

This process is depicted conceptually in Figure 13.1, panel A. This is similar to the model used in Chapter 12, in that it allows both the direct and indirect effects of X on Y to vary with moderator W, with the moderation of the indirect effect resulting from the moderation of the effect of X on M. However, unlike in that example, here X is a multicategorical variable coding the three experimental conditions in this study. This requires integrating the lessons learned in Chapters 6 and 10, which focused on moderation and mediation when X, the antecedent variable of focus, is multicategorical. As X consists of three categories, it must be represented in the regression equations with two variables, D_1 and D_2, coding membership in one of the three groups. W is a continuous dimension, so it can be included in the model as is. Two products between the two variables coding X and the moderator W in the equations for mediator M and consequent Y allow X's effect on both M and Y to vary linearly with W, with Y also being affected by M.

When this is all combined, the result is the statistical diagram in Figure 13.1, panel B. This diagram represents two regression equations:

$$M = i_M + a_1 D_1 + a_2 D_2 + a_3 W + a_4 D_1 W + a_5 D_2 W + e_M \quad (13.1)$$
$$Y = i_Y + c_1' D_1 + c_2' D_2 + c_3' W + c_4' D_1 W + c_5' D_2 W + b M + e_Y \quad (13.2)$$

Equation 13.1 allows for the effect of Catherine's behavior on how appropriate it is perceived as being for the situation to depend linearly on the perceiver's beliefs about the pervasiveness of sex discrimination in society. Equation 13.2 is similar, except that the consequent variable is how positively Catherine is perceived, and it includes the effect of perceived appropriateness of her response on how she is perceived as an additional antecedent. Collectively, these two equations allow for moderation of both the indirect and direct effects of this multicategorical X on Y through M to vary linearly with moderator W.

Given that the other analyses of this study conducted in earlier chapters suggests that participants didn't appear to make much distinction between individually and collectively protesting in terms of how they perceived Catherine, in this analysis the three conditions will be represented with the orthogonal contrast codes used in section 6.3 and provided in Table 6.3. This coding system results in one variable D_1 that captures the effect of protesting versus not protesting, regardless of the form that protest took, and the second, D_2, captures the effect of collectively versus individually protesting. The SPSS code below constructs the contrast codes in Table 6.3, multiplies D_1 and D_2 by W to capture any moderation of the effect of X by W, and then estimates equations 13.1 and 13.2 using SPSS's OLS regression routine:

```
if (protest=0) d1=-2/3.
if (protest > 0) d1=1/3.
if (protest=0) d2=0.
if (protest=1) d2=-1/2.
if (protest=2) d2=1/2.
compute d1sexism=d1*sexism.
compute d2sexism=d2*sexism.
regression/dep=respappr/method=enter d1 d2 sexism d1sexism d2sexism.
regression/dep=liking/method=enter d1 d2 sexism d1sexism d2sexism
    respappr.
```

The corresponding commands in SAS are

```
data protest;set protest;
    if (protest=0) then d1=-2/3;if (protest > 0) then d1=1/3;
    if (protest=0) then d2=0;if (protest=1) then d2=-1/2;
    if (protest=2) then d2=1/2;
    d1sexism=d1*sexism;d2sexism=d2*sexism;
run;
proc reg data=protest;
    model respappr=d1 d2 sexism d1sexism d2sexism;
    model liking=d1 d2 sexism d1sexism d2sexism respappr;
run;
```

TABLE 13.1. Model Coefficients for the Conditional Process Model in Figure 13.1

		Consequent						
		M (RESPAPPR)				Y (LIKING)		
Antecedent		Coeff.	SE	p		Coeff.	SE	p
D_1	a_1	−2.940	1.450	.045	c_1'	−2.732	1.176	.022
D_2	a_2	1.671	1.620	.305	c_2'	0.025	1.299	.985
SEXISM (W)	a_3	0.042	0.130	.749	c_3'	0.072	0.104	.489
$D_1 \times$ SEXISM	a_4	0.856	0.281	.003	c_4'	0.526	0.233	.026
$D_2 \times$ SEXISM	a_5	−0.244	0.311	.434	c_5'	−0.034	0.249	.892
RESPAPPR		—	—	—	b	0.367	0.072	< .001
Constant	i_M	4.607	0.673	< .001	i_Y	3.477	0.631	< .001
		$R^2 = 0.316$				$R^2 = 0.287$		
		$F(5, 123) = 11.342, p < .001$				$F(6, 122) = 8.177, p < .001$		

The regression coefficients, standard errors, and miscellaneous additional information for the models of M and Y can be found in Table 13.1. As can be seen, the regression equations are

$$\hat{M} = 4.607 - 2.940D_1 + 1.671D_2 + 0.042W + 0.856D_1W \quad (13.3)$$
$$- 0.244D_2W$$

$$\hat{Y} = 3.477 - 2.732D_1 + 0.025D_2 + 0.072W + 0.526D_1W \quad (13.4)$$
$$- 0.034D_2W + 0.367M$$

But as is probably now clear to you at this point in the book, the use of the regression routines built into SPSS and SAS can only get you so far for this kind of analysis. We will eventually need to compute some statistics based on regression coefficients in both equations and also construct bootstrap confidence intervals for those statistics. PROCESS takes care of all of this and much more. We will use PROCESS model 8, as it allows for moderation of the $X \rightarrow M$ and $X \rightarrow Y$ effects by a common moderator W while fixing the effect of M on Y to be constant. The SPSS PROCESS command to estimate this model is

```
process y=liking/x=protest/m=respappr/w=sexism/plot=1/mcx=3/
    model=8/seed=290417.
```

whereas in SAS, the command is

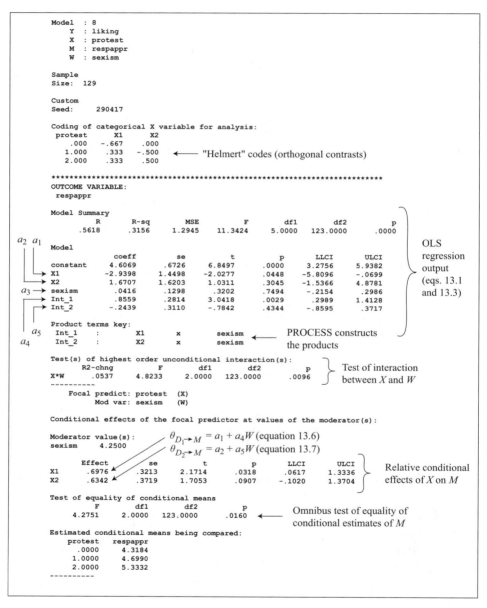

FIGURE 13.2. Output from the PROCESS procedure for SPSS for the sex discrimination conditional process analysis.

(continued)

Moderator value(s): $\theta_{D_1 \to M} = a_1 + a_4 W$ (equation 13.6)
sexism   5.1200 $\theta_{D_2 \to M} = a_2 + a_5 W$ (equation 13.7)

	Effect	se	t	p	LLCI	ULCI
X1	1.4422	.2161	6.6736	.0000	1.0145	1.8700
X2	.4221	.2449	1.7232	.0874	-.0628	.9069

Relative conditional effects of X on M

Test of equality of conditional means

F	df1	df2	p
23.9623	2.0000	123.0000	.0000

Omnibus test of equality of conditional estimates of M

Estimated conditional means being compared:

protest	respappr
.0000	3.8582
1.0000	5.0894
2.0000	5.5115

Moderator value(s): $\theta_{D_1 \to M} = a_1 + a_4 W$ (equation 13.6)
sexism   5.8960 $\theta_{D_2 \to M} = a_2 + a_5 W$ (equation 13.7)

	Effect	se	t	p	LLCI	ULCI
X1	2.1064	.3121	6.7487	.0000	1.4886	2.7242
X2	.2328	.3371	.6906	.4911	-.4345	.9001

Relative conditional effects of X on M

Test of equality of conditional means

F	df1	df2	p
22.8591	2.0000	123.0000	.0000

Omnibus test of equality of conditional estimates of M

Estimated conditional means being compared:

protest	respappr
.0000	3.4477
1.0000	5.4377
2.0000	5.6705

Data for visualizing the conditional effect of the focal predictor:
Paste text below into a SPSS syntax window and execute to produce plot.

```
DATA LIST FREE/
    protest     sexism    respappr   .
BEGIN DATA.
      .0000      4.2500    4.3184
     1.0000      4.2500    4.6990
     2.0000      4.2500    5.3332
      .0000      5.1200    3.8582
     1.0000      5.1200    5.0894
     2.0000      5.1200    5.5115
      .0000      5.8960    3.4477
     1.0000      5.8960    5.4377
     2.0000      5.8960    5.6705
END DATA.
GRAPH/SCATTERPLOT=
   sexism    WITH     respappr BY      protest
```

Output from the **plot** option

```
************************************************************************
```

OUTCOME VARIABLE:
 liking

Model Summary

R	R-sq	MSE	F	df1	df2	p
.5355	.2868	.8245	8.1767	6.0000	122.0000	.0000

c_2' c_1'

Model

	coeff	se	t	p	LLCI	ULCI
constant	3.4767	.6309	5.5108	.0000	2.2278	4.7256
X1	-2.7315	1.1763	-2.3222	.0219	-5.0601	-.4030
X2	.0252	1.2987	.0194	.9846	-2.5458	2.5962
respappr	.3668	.0720	5.0969	.0000	.2243	.5092
sexism	.0719	.1037	.6940	.4890	-.1333	.2771
Int_1	.5256	.2328	2.2573	.0258	.0647	.9866
Int_2	-.0340	.2488	-.1365	.8917	-.5265	.4586

OLS regression output (eqs. 13.2 and 13.4)

$b \to$ respappr
$c_3' \to$ sexism

Product terms key:

| Int_1 | : | X1 | x | sexism |
| Int_2 | : | X2 | x | sexism |

c_4' c_5'

PROCESS constructs the products

Test(s) of highest order unconditional interaction(s):

	R2-chng	F	df1	df2	p
X*W	.0298	2.5479	2.0000	122.0000	.0824

Test of moderation of the direct effect of X

(continued)

FIGURE 13.2 continued.

```
        Focal predict: protest   (X)
           Mod var: sexism      (W)

Conditional effects of the focal predictor at values of the moderator(s):
(These are also the relative conditional direct effects of X on Y)
```

Moderator value(s):

```
sexism      4.2500
```

$$\theta_{D_1 \to Y} = c'_1 + c'_4 W \text{ (equation 13.16)}$$
$$\theta_{D_2 \to Y} = c'_2 + c'_5 W \text{ (equation 13.17)}$$

```
      Effect      se         t         p       LLCI      ULCI
X1    -.4977     .2613    -1.9048    .0592    -1.0149    .0195
X2    -.1192     .3003     -.3968    .6922     -.7137    .4754
```

Relative conditional direct effects

```
Test of equality of conditional means
      F        df1        df2        p
   1.9642    2.0000    122.0000    .1447
```

Omnibus test of equality of conditional estimates of Y

```
Estimated conditional means being compared:
   protest     liking
    .0000      5.8991
   1.0000      5.4610
   2.0000      5.3418
----------
```

Moderator value(s):

```
sexism      5.1200
```

$$\theta_{D_1 \to Y} = c'_1 + c'_4 W \text{ (equation 13.16)}$$
$$\theta_{D_2 \to Y} = c'_2 + c'_5 W \text{ (equation 13.17)}$$

```
      Effect      se         t         p       LLCI      ULCI
X1    -.0404     .2013     -.2007    .8413     -.4389    .3581
X2    -.1487     .1978     -.7517    .4537     -.5403    .2429
```

Relative conditional direct effects

```
Test of equality of conditional means
      F        df1        df2        p
    .2942    2.0000    122.0000    .7457
```

Omnibus test of equality of conditional estimates of Y

```
Estimated conditional means being compared:
   protest     liking
    .0000      5.6568
   1.0000      5.6908
   2.0000      5.5421
----------
```

Moderator value(s):

```
sexism      5.8960
```

$$\theta_{D_1 \to Y} = c'_1 + c'_4 W \text{ (equation 13.16)}$$
$$\theta_{D_2 \to Y} = c'_2 + c'_5 W \text{ (equation 13.17)}$$

```
      Effect      se         t         p       LLCI      ULCI
X1     .3675     .2916     1.2603    .2100     -.2097    .9447
X2    -.1751     .2696     -.6494    .5173     -.7087    .3586
```

Relative conditional direct effects

```
Test of equality of conditional means
      F        df1        df2        p
   1.0646    2.0000    122.0000    .3480
```

Omnibus test of equality of conditional estimates of Y

```
Estimated conditional means being compared:
   protest     liking
    .0000      5.4407
   1.0000      5.8957
   2.0000      5.7207
```

```
Data for visualizing the conditional effect of the focal predictor:
Paste text below into a SPSS syntax window and execute to produce plot.

DATA LIST FREE/
   protest    sexism      liking    .
BEGIN DATA.
    .0000      4.2500      5.8991
   1.0000      4.2500      5.4610
   2.0000      4.2500      5.3418
    .0000      5.1200      5.6568
   1.0000      5.1200      5.6908
   2.0000      5.1200      5.5421
    .0000      5.8960      5.4407
   1.0000      5.8960      5.8957
   2.0000      5.8960      5.7207
END DATA.
GRAPH/SCATTERPLOT=
  sexism    WITH      liking   BY       protest  .
---------
```

Output from the **plot** option

(continued)

FIGURE 13.2 continued.

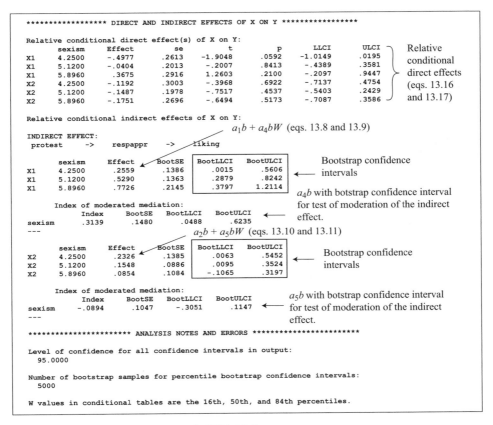

FIGURE 13.2 continued.

```
%process (data=protest,y=liking,x=protest,m=respappr,w=sexism,
    plot=1,mcx=3,model=8,seed=290417);
```

The output, which is quite lengthy, can be found in Figure 13.2. This PRO-CESS command is very similar to the one from Chapter 12, which uses model 8 as well. However, unlike in that example, here X is specified as a multicategorical variable using **mcx=3**, with the 3 telling PROCESS to use Helmert coding to represent the three groups. This coding system produces relative effects that correspond to two orthogonal contrasts. PRO-CESS constructs the codes for X on its own as well as all necessary products to represent the moderation for model 8, it estimates the models of M and Y, probes any interactions, produces data for visualizing those interactions (requested with the **plot** option), constructs conditional direct and indirect effects of X and two indices of moderated mediation, and provides bootstrap confidence intervals when required for inference. In the rest of this chapter, we will work through this output, looking at the pieces of the model and then bringing those pieces together when needed.

13.2   Looking at the Components of the Indirect Effect of *X*

A mediation process contains at least two "stages." The first stage is the effect of the presumed causal antecedent variable X on the proposed mediator M, and the second stage is the effect of the mediator M on the final consequent variable Y. More complex models, such as the serial mediation model, will contain more stages. In a model such as the one that is the focus of this chapter with only a single mediator, the indirect effect of X on Y through M is quantified as the product of the effects in these two stages. When one or both of the stages of a mediation process is moderated, making sense of the indirect effect requires getting intimate with each of the stages, so that when they are integrated or multiplied together, you can better understand how differences or changes in X map on to differences in Y through a mediator differently depending on the value of a moderator.

Examining the First Stage of the Mediation Process

In this example, the first stage of the mediation process is specified as moderated. This first stage is the effect of Catherine's behavior (X) on how appropriately her behavior is perceived for the situation (M). But X is a multicategorical variable with three groups, meaning that it requires two variables to represent its effect on M. And with W as a continuous moderator of the effect of X on M, two products constructed from W and the two variables representing X are required to allow X's effect on M to be moderated linearly by W. The result is a moderation model like the one described in Chapter 10. So to understand the first stage of the mediation process, we need to visualize and interpret the model of M. We have already estimated this model, and the PROCESS output corresponding to this part of the full conditional process model can be found in Figure 13.2 in the section titled "Outcome Variable: respappr." The model is

$$\hat{M} = 4.607 - 2.940D_1 + 1.671D_2 + 0.042W + 0.856D_1W - 0.244D_2W \quad (13.5)$$

and so $a_1 = -2.940$, $a_2 = 1.671$, $a_3 = 0.042$, $a_4 = 0.856$, and $a_5 = -0.244$. This model is depicted visually in Figure 13.3. The skeleton of this figure was constructed using the procedure described in section 10.3, made simpler with the use of **plot** option in PROCESS.

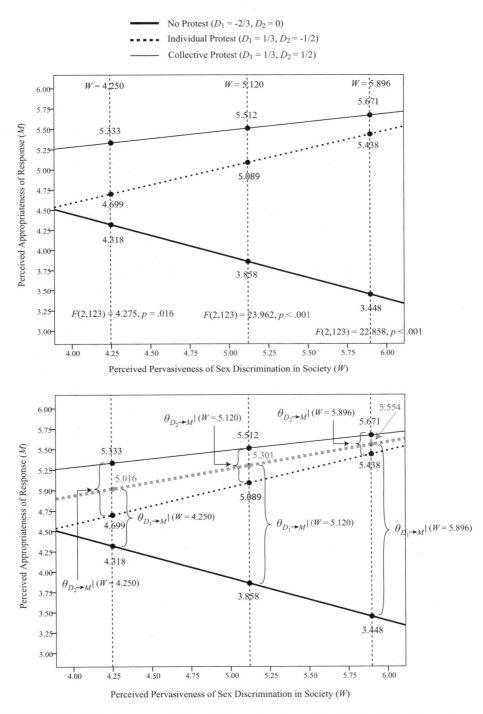

FIGURE 13.3. A visual representation of the moderation of the effect of the attorney's behavior on appropriateness of her response by perceived pervasiveness of sex discrimination. Omnibus tests of the conditional effects are in top panel, and the relative conditional effects are depicted in the bottom panel.

As Catherine's behavior is the focal antecedent variable here, our interpretation should focus on the gap between the three lines and how this gap varies as a function of perceived pervasiveness of sex discrimination in society. The consequent variable in this part of the full conditional process model is perceived appropriateness of the response. As you can see, among those who see sex discrimination as highly pervasive ($W = 5.896$; the 84th percentile of the distribution), protesting was seen as more appropriate than not protesting, with little distinction made between collectively and individually protesting. This pattern largely holds up among those moderate ($W = 5.120$; the 50th percentile of the distribution) in their perceptions of the pervasiveness of sex discrimination in society. But among those relatively low ($W = 4.250$; the 16th percentile), it appears a distinction is being made between collectively and individually protesting. Among such people, collectively protesting seems to be perceived as quite a bit more appropriate than either individually protesting or not protesting at all, with little distinction in appropriateness between not protesting at all and individually protesting.

But perhaps this interpretation is a bit premature, since we haven't yet even formally tested for interaction between Catherine's behavior and perceived pervasiveness of sex discrimination in the model of perceived appropriateness of the response. In Chapter 10, we saw how to test whether X's effect on some consequent variable (M in this case) is moderated when X is multicategorical with g categories and W is continuous or dichotomous. This involves comparing the fit of two models. The first model includes the $g - 1$ variables coding the categories of the multicategorical variable as well as W. The second adds the $g - 1$ products between the variables coding X and the moderator W. A significant increase in R^2 leads to the inference that X's effect on M is moderated by W. This test is formally discussed in sections 2.6 and 10.4. PROCESS implements it automatically; it can be found in Figure 13.2 in the section for the model of perceived response appropriateness titled "Test(s) of highest order unconditional interaction(s)." As can be seen, $\Delta R^2 = 0.054, F(2, 123) = 4.823, p = .010$. So we can say that $_T a_4$ and $_T a_5$ aren't both equal to zero. At least one of them is different from zero. This is equivalent to saying that X and W interact, or X's effect on M is moderated by W.

We can probe this interaction by looking at the conditional effects of Catherine's behavior at values of perceived pervasiveness of sex discrimination corresponding to the 16th, 50th, and 84th percentiles of the distribution, or what we have been calling relatively low, relatively moderate, and relatively high, respectively. An omnibus approach to probing the interaction, using the procedure described in section 10.4 and conducted automatically by PROCESS, leads to the inference that there are statistically significant differences in the perceived appropriateness of Catherine's behavior at each of these three values of perceived pervasiveness of sex discrimination in society. Among those relatively low ($W = 4.250$), $F(2, 123) = 4.275, p = .016$; among those relatively moderate ($W = 5.120$), $F(2, 123) = 23.962, p < .001$; among those relatively high ($W = 5.896$), $F(2, 123) = 22.858, p < .001$. See the top of Figure 13.3 and the PROCESS output in Figure 13.2.

These omnibus tests provide only vague information about differences between groups. Furthermore, they provide no information needed later for calculating what I will call the *relative conditional indirect effects* of X. Instead, we will use a pairwise approach to probing the interaction by looking at the relative conditional effects of X on M, as these relative conditional effects will be useful later. Recall from Chapter 10 that there are $g - 1$ relative effects of X when X is a multicategorical variable representing g groups. In this example, one of the relative effects of X on M quantifies the difference in how appropriate Catherine's behavior is perceived between those told she protested and those told she did not. The second relative effect quantifies the difference in how appropriate her behavior is perceived as being between those told she collectively protested and those told she individually protested. These are $\theta_{D_1 \to M}$ and $\theta_{D_2 \to M}$, respectively and are derived from equations 13.1 and 13.3 as

$$\theta_{D_1 \to M} = a_1 + a_4 W = -2.940 + 0.856W \tag{13.6}$$

$$\theta_{D_2 \to M} = a_2 + a_5 W = 1.671 - 0.244W \tag{13.7}$$

both of which are functions of W. By plugging values of W into equations 13.6 and 13.7, the result is the difference between two groups or combinations of groups in how appropriately they perceived Catherine's behavior, conditioned on the value of perceived pervasiveness of sex discrimination used in the computation. The conditional effect will be dependent on the coding system used to represent the groups. In this example, we used the two sets of orthogonal contrasts in Table 6.3 to represent the groups. So D_1 represents the difference in perceived appropriateness of response between those told Catherine protested versus those in the no protest condition. Among those "relatively low" in perceived pervasiveness of sex discrimination ($W = 4.250$), this relative conditional effect is

$$\theta_{D_1 \to M} = -2.940 + 0.856(4.250) = 0.698$$

meaning those who were told Catherine protested felt her behavior was 0.698 units more appropriate than those told she did not protest.

Using this group coding system, D_2 represents the difference in the perceived appropriateness of her response between those told Catherine collectively protested and those told she individually protested. Among those "relatively low" in perceived pervasiveness of sex discrimination ($W = 4.250$), this relative conditional effect is

$$\theta_{D_2 \to M} = 1.671 - 0.244(4.250) = 0.634$$

meaning those who were told Catherine collectively protested felt her behavior was 0.634 units more appropriate than those told she individually protested.

These relative conditional effects are perhaps better understood by thinking of them as differences between estimates of M from the model. Using equation 13.3, you can generate an estimate of M for each of the three groups conditioned on any value of W by plugging in a group's values on D_1 and D_2 and a chosen value of W and then doing the math. For example, for those "relatively low" in perceived pervasiveness of sex discrimination, equation 13.3 generates estimates of $\hat{M}_{NP} = 4.318$, $\hat{M}_{IP} = 4.699$, and $\hat{M}_{CP} = 5.333$ for the no protest, individual protest, and collective protest conditions, respectively. These can also be found in the PROCESS output in the section corresponding to the model of M under the heading "Estimated conditional means being compared." The black dots in Figure 13.3 correspond to the estimates of M for the three groups conditioned on W being 4.250, 5.120, and 5.896.

With these estimates of M in the three groups derived, the relative conditional effects when $W = 4.250$ are

$$
\begin{aligned}
\theta_{D_1 \to M} \mid (W = 4.250) &= \frac{\hat{M}_{IP} + \hat{M}_{CP}}{2} - \hat{M}_{NP} \\
&= \frac{5.333 + 4.699}{2} - 4.318 \\
&= 5.016 - 4.318 \\
&= 0.698
\end{aligned}
$$

$$
\begin{aligned}
\theta_{D_2 \to M} \mid (W = 4.250) &= \hat{M}_{CP} - \hat{M}_{IP} \\
&= 5.333 - 4.699 \\
&= 0.634
\end{aligned}
$$

The bottom half of Figure 13.3 visually depicts these differences. $\theta_{D_1 \to M} \mid (W = 4.250) = 0.698$ is the gap between the dot on the grey line (representing the unweighted average of the estimates of M in the two protest conditions) and the black dot on the line for the no protest group over the value

$W = 4.250$ (representing the estimate of M in this group when $W = 4.250$). And $\theta_{D_2 \to M} \mid (W = 4.250) = 0.634$ is the gap between the black dot on the collective protest line and the black dot on the individual protest line over the value $W = 4.250$.

PROCESS does all these computations for you and also provides standard errors, t- and p-values for testing the null hypothesis that the relative conditional effect is zero, as well as 95% confidence intervals for the relative conditional effects. These can be found in Figure 13.2 under the heading "Conditional effects of the focal predictor at values of the moderator(s)" in the model of M. $\theta_{D_1 \to M} \mid (W = 4.250)$ is in the X1 row, and $\theta_{D_2 \to M} \mid (W = 4.250)$ is in the X2 row. As can be seen, among those relatively low in perceived pervasiveness of sex discrimination, those told she protested saw her behavior as significantly more appropriate than those told she did not protest, $\theta_{D_1 \to M} \mid (W = 4.250) = 0.698, t(123) = 2.171, p = .031$, 95% CI = 0.062 to 1.334. But the difference in perceived appropriateness between those told she collectively protested and those told she individually protested is not quite statistically significant, $\theta_{D_2 \to M} \mid (W = 4.250) = 0.634, t(123) = 1.705, p = .091$, 95% CI = -0.102 to 1.370.

These computations can be repeated for as many values of W as desired. When $W = 5.120$ ("relatively moderate"),

$$\theta_{D_1 \to M} = -2.940 + 0.856(5.120) = 1.442$$

and

$$\theta_{D_2 \to M} = 1.671 - 0.244(5.120) = 0.422$$

which correspond to

$$
\begin{aligned}
\theta_{D_1 \to M} \mid (W = 5.120) &= \frac{\hat{M}_{IP} + \hat{M}_{CP}}{2} - \hat{M}_{NP} \\
&= \frac{5.512 + 5.089}{2} - 3.858 \\
&= 5.301 - 3.858 \\
&= 1.442
\end{aligned}
$$

$$
\begin{aligned}
\theta_{D_2 \to M} \mid (W = 5.120) &= \hat{M}_{CP} - \hat{M}_{IP} \\
&= 5.512 - 5.089 \\
&= 0.422
\end{aligned}
$$

(see Figure 13.3). From the PROCESS output, only $\theta_{D_1 \to M}$ is statistically significant. Those told Catherine protested felt her behavior was more appropriate than those told she did not protest, $\theta_{D_1 \to M} \mid (W = 5.125) = 1.442, t(123) = 6.674, p < .001$, 95% CI = 1.015 to 1.870. But the difference in perceived appropriateness of collectively protesting compared to individually protesting is not quite statistically significant, $\theta_{D_2 \to M} \mid (W = 5.120) = 0.422, t(123) = 1.723, p = .087$, 95% CI = −0.063 to 0.907.

One last time. When $W = 5.896$ ("relatively high"),

$$\theta_{D_1 \to M} = -2.940 + 0.856(5.896) = 2.106$$

and

$$\theta_{D_2 \to M} = 1.671 - 0.244(5.896) = 0.233$$

which correspond to

$$
\begin{aligned}
\theta_{D_1 \to M} \mid (W = 5.896) &= \frac{\hat{M}_{IP} + \hat{M}_{CP}}{2} - \hat{M}_{NP} \\
&= \frac{5.671 + 5.438}{2} - 3.448 \\
&= 5.554 - 3.448 \\
&= 2.106
\end{aligned}
$$

$$
\begin{aligned}
\theta_{D_2 \to M} \mid (W = 5.896) &= \hat{M}_{CP} - \hat{M}_{IP} \\
&= 5.671 - 5.438 \\
&= 0.233
\end{aligned}
$$

(see Figure 13.3). Those told Catherine protested felt her behavior was more appropriate than those told she did not protest, $\theta_{D_1 \to M} \mid (W = 5.896) = 2.106, t(123) = 6.749, p < .001$, 95% CI = 1.489 to 2.724. But there was no significant difference in perceived appropriateness of collectively protesting compared to individually protesting, $\theta_{D_2 \to M} \mid (W = 5.896) = 0.233, t(123) = 0.691, p = .491$, 95% CI = −0.435 to 0.900.

There is another pairwise approach to probing the interaction between experimental condition and perceived pervasiveness of sex discrimination in this study. Equations 13.6 and 13.7 that define the conditional effect of X on M are both functions of W, with a_4 and a_5 the weights for W. Observe that the gap between the no protest line and the gray line representing the average of the protest conditions in Figure 13.3 grows with increases in perceived pervasiveness of sex discrimination. The rate of change of this gap is a_4, which is also the regression coefficient for $D_1 W$ in equations 13.1 and 13.3. Inference about $_T a_4$ is an inference about whether this gap varies with W. In this case, $a_4 = 0.856, p = 0.003$ (see Table 13.1 or Figure 13.2). So we can say that the difference in the perceived appropriateness of Catherine's behavior between those told she protested and those told she did not is significantly related to (i.e., is moderated by) perceived pervasiveness of sex discrimination.

Using the same logic, a_5, the regression coefficient for D_2W in equations 13.1 and 13.3, quantifies rate of change in the gap between the lines for the individual and collective protest groups as perceived pervasiveness of sex discrimination increases. As can be seen in Table 13.1 and Figure 13.2, this rate of change is not statistically significant ($a_5 = -0.244, p = 0.434$). So we cannot say that perceived pervasiveness of sex discrimination moderates the effect of collectively protesting relative to individually protesting on perceived appropriateness of Catherine's behavior.

Examining the Second Stage of the Mediation Process

The second stage of a mediation model with only one mediator is the effect of M on Y when X is held constant. In this model, our discussion of this second stage component of the model is much simplified by the fact that it is fixed to be independent of W and any other variable in the model. That is, it is not a function but is, rather, a constant. The effect of perceived appropriateness of Catherine's response on how positively she is perceived is estimated with b in equation 13.2. As can be seen in the PROCESS output in Figure 13.2 as well as in Table 13.1, $b = 0.367$ and is statistically significant. Those who perceived Catherine's response as more appropriate for the situation liked Catherine more than did those who saw her behavior as less appropriate for the situation.

13.3 Relative Conditional Indirect Effects

An indirect effect in a model with a single mediator is the product of two effects: the effect of X on M and the effect of M on Y when X is held constant. To construct the indirect effect of Catherine's behavior (X) on how much she is liked (Y) through perceived appropriateness of her response M), we multiply the effect of X on M by the effect of M on Y. But when X is a multicategorical variable representing $g = 3$ groups, there are two indirect effects, which we called *relative* indirect effects in Chapter 10. But these relative indirect effects are still products of effects. In this example, because one of these effects is a function, then the relative indirect effects become a function as well.

In section 13.2 we saw that X's effect on M breaks into two relative effects, each of which is a function of moderator W. The effect of protesting relative to not protesting on how appropriate the response is perceived as being is

$$\theta_{D_1 \to M} = a_1 + a_4 W$$

and the effect of collectively protesting relative to individually protesting is

$$\theta_{D_2 \to M} = a_2 + a_5 W$$

both of which are functions of W. To get the two relative indirect effects of X, each of these relative conditional effects of X on M is multiplied by the effect of M on Y, which is b from equation 13.2. The result is the relative indirect effects of X on Y through M. So the relative indirect effect of protesting relative to not protesting is the product of the conditional effect of protesting versus not on perceived appropriateness of the response ($\theta_{D_1 \to M}$) multiplied by the effect of perceived appropriateness of the response on how much Catherine is liked (b):

$$\theta_{D_1 \to M} b = (a_1 + a_4 W)b = a_1 b + a_4 bW \tag{13.8}$$

Substituting the estimated regression coefficients (equations 13.3 and 13.4; see Table 13.1) into equation 13.8 yields

$$
\begin{aligned}
\theta_{D_1 \to M} b &= (-2.940 + 0.856W)(0.367) \tag{13.9} \\
&= -2.940(0.367) + 0.856(0.367)W \\
&= -1.079 + 0.314W
\end{aligned}
$$

which is a function of perceived pervasiveness of sex discrimination in society (W). Using the same logic, the relative indirect effect of collectively protesting compared to individually protesting is the product of the conditional effect of collectively versus individually protesting on the perceived appropriateness of the response ($\theta_{D_2 \to M}$) multiplied by the effect of perceived appropriateness of the response on how much Catherine is liked (b):

$$\theta_{D_2 \to M} b = (a_2 + a_5 W)b = a_2 b + a_5 bW \tag{13.10}$$

After substituting the estimated regression coefficients into equation 13.10, the result is

$$
\begin{aligned}
\theta_{D_2 \to M} b &= (1.671 - 0.244W)(0.367) \tag{13.11} \\
&= 1.671(0.367) - 0.244(0.367) \\
&= 0.613 - 0.089W
\end{aligned}
$$

which is also a function of W.

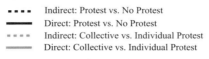

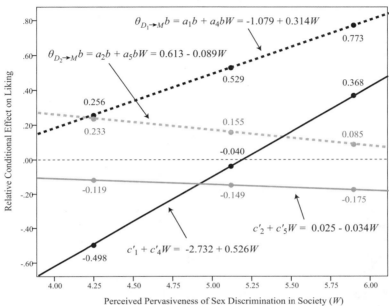

FIGURE 13.4. A visual representation of the relative conditional direct and indirect effects of the attorney's behavior on how positively she is perceived.

You probably recognize that equations 13.9 and 13.11 are mathematical formulas for lines, with intercepts a_1b and a_2b and slopes a_4b and a_5b. These equations can be visually represented in the form of lines by plugging in various values of W into the equations and doing the math. Repeated many times for many values of W and then plotting the results produces the two dashed lines in Figure 13.4.

These lines, or the equations that they represent, generate relative *conditional* indirect effects of X when a specific value of W is used in the computations. For example, for people "relatively low" in perceived pervasiveness of sex discrimination ($W = 4.250$; the 16th percentile of the distribution), equation 13.9 produces

$$\theta_{D_1 \to M} b \mid (W = 4.25) = -1.079 + 0.314(4.250) = 0.256$$

as the relative conditional indirect effect of protesting versus not protesting on how much Catherine is liked. Likewise, equation 13.11 produces

$$\theta_{D_2 \to M} b \mid (W = 4.250) = 0.613 - 0.089(4.250) = 0.232$$

TABLE 13.2. The Relative Conditional Indirect Effects of the Attorney's Behavior on How Positively She Is Perceived

				Indirect Effect	
W	$\theta_{D_1 \to M}$	$\theta_{D_2 \to M}$	b	$\theta_{D_1 \to M} b$	$\theta_{D_2 \to M} b$
4.250	0.698	0.634	0.367	0.256	0.232
5.125	1.442	0.422	0.367	0.529	0.155
5.896	2.106	0.233	0.367	0.773	0.085

as the relative conditional indirect effect of collectively versus individually protesting on how much Catherine is liked among people relatively low in perceived pervasiveness of sex discrimination. The result of these computations can be found in Table 13.2, along with relative conditional indirect effects when $W = 5.120$ (relatively moderate in perceive pervasiveness of sex discrimination) and $W = 5.896$ (relatively high).

As is true for any indirect effect, the substantive interpretation of these conditional relative indirect effects requires knowing the signs of their components. In this example, they are the product of the conditional effect of X on M given W and the unconditional effect of M on Y. As can be seen in Table 13.2, all of the conditional effects of X on M conditioned on these three values of W are positive, meaning that protesting is seen as more appropriate for the circumstance than not protesting (i.e., $\theta_{D_1 \to M} > 0$ for all three values of W), and collectively protesting is perceived as more appropriate than individually protesting (i.e., $\theta_{D_2 \to M} > 0$ for all three values of W). When these positive effects are multiplied by the positive effect of M on Y, the result is positive relative conditional indirect effects. So Catherine is liked more when she protests relative to when she does not because protesting is perceived as more appropriate than not protesting, and she is liked more when she does the more appropriate thing. Similarly, collectively protesting is seen as more appropriate than individually protesting, and she is liked more when she engages in a more appropriate behavior.

These relative conditional indirect effects are all measured on the same scale. They are, essentially, differences between groups in how much Catherine is liked resulting from the joint effect of her behavior on the perceived appropriateness of her response to the situation which in turn influences how positively she is perceived. So we can legitimately say that the largest of these indirect effects is the indirect effect of protesting (relative to not protesting) among those who see sex discrimination as highly pervasive. And we can also say that conditioned on these three values of W, the indirect effects of protesting compared to not are larger than the indirect effects of collectively protesting relative to individually protesting.

13.4   Testing and Probing Moderation of Mediation

This prior discussion of relative conditional indirect effects is holistic and descriptive in nature. There is nothing stopping us from calculating how a relative indirect effect varies as a function of moderator and talking about how the relative indirect effect seems to differ across values of a moderator. But at this point we have not formally determined through statistical inference whether the indirect effect varies more from moderator value to moderator value in a way greater than would be expected to occur just by chance. After all, the relative conditional indirect effects are calculated using regression coefficients that are estimated with uncertainty. This uncertainty translates to sampling variance in the estimation of relative conditional indirect effects. In this section, we deal with sampling variance by talking about inference, first focused on whether an indirect effect varies with a moderator, and then by probing any evidence of moderation of an indirect effect.

A Test of Moderation of the Relative Indirect Effect

In the examples in Chapters 11 and 12, a test of moderation of the indirect effect was based on the index of moderated mediation. Recall that the index of moderated mediation is the weight for the moderator in a linear function relating the size of the indirect effect of X on Y to the moderator. If this index is different from zero, as assessed with a bootstrap confidence interval for the index, then this means the indirect effect is linearly related to the moderator and supports a claim of moderated mediation. But if the confidence interval does not include zero, this implies that the indirect effect is not (linearly) related to the moderator and, hence, no moderation of mediation.

   The same logic can be applied to this model, but it is made slightly more complex by the fact that in this model we have two relative indirect effects rather than a single indirect effect, and each of these relative indirect effects is a function of moderator W. In section 13.3 (see equations 13.8 and 13.9), we saw that the relative indirect effect of protesting compared to not is

$$\theta_{D_1 \to M}b = (a_1 + a_4 W)b = a_1 b + a_4 bW = -1.079 + 0.314W$$

which is a linear function of perceived pervasiveness of sex discrimination in society (W). In this function, $a_4 b$ is the index of moderated mediation of the indirect effect of protesting (relative to not) on perceptions of Catherine through perceived appropriateness of her response. It is the slope of the black dashed line in Figure 13.4, which is $a_4b = 0.314$. A bootstrap confidence interval for the index of moderated mediation provides an inference for whether the slope of this line—the weight for W in the function linking the moderator to the size of the relative indirect effect—is different from zero. PROCESS provides this automatically in the output. As can be seen in Figure 13.2 toward the very bottom of the output, the confidence interval for the index is entirely above zero (0.049 to 0.624). This is evidence of moderation of the indirect effect of protesting relative to not on how Catherine is perceived through perceived response appropriateness by perceived pervasiveness of sex discrimination in society. The mediation of X's indirect effect on Y through M is moderated.

There is a second index of moderated mediation we can construct, this one quantifying the relationship between perceived pervasiveness of sex discrimination in society and the size of the indirect effect of collectively protesting relative to individually protesting. Recalling equations 13.10 and 13.11 from section 13.3:

$$\theta_{D_2 \to M}b = (a_2 + a_5W)b = a_2b + a_5bW = 0.613 - 0.089W$$

In this function, $a_5b = -0.089$ is the index of moderated mediation of the indirect effect of protesting collectively relative to individually on perceptions of Catherine through perceived appropriateness of her response. It is the slope of the gray dashed line in Figure 13.4. A bootstrap confidence interval yields an inference for whether the slope of this line is different from zero. As can be seen in Figure 13.2 the confidence interval for the index includes zero (−0.305 to 0.115).

In Chapter 6 (see section 6.4), I said that when X is a g-category multicategorical variable in a mediation model, evidence of mediation of X's effect on Y through M exists if at least one of the $g - 1$ relative indirect effects is different from zero based on a bootstrap confidence interval. The same argument applies here, but to moderation of the indirect effect of X. If X represents g categories and the indirect effect of X is estimated as moderated by W, then it can be said that the mediation of X's effect on Y through M is moderated if at least one of the $g - 1$ relative indirect effects is moderated by W. That means that we can say that X's indirect effect is moderated if at least one of the bootstrap confidence intervals for the $g - 1$ indices of moderated mediation does not contain zero. This analysis meets this requirement, as the index of moderated mediation for the relative indirect effect of protesting relative to not protesting is different from zero, reflected in the bootstrap confidence interval that is entirely above zero.

However, I also said in section 6.4 that the outcome of a test of mediation based on confidence intervals for the relative indirect effects when X is a multicategorical variable may be dependent on the coding system used. This is true for moderation of mediation with a multicategorial X as well. It could be that had we used a different coding system for representing the 3 groups, the confidence interval for both of the indices of moderated mediation would have contained zero, resulting in a lack of evidence of moderation of the indirect effect. This is a shortcoming of this approach. The recommendation I offer in section 6.4 for dealing with the lack of invariance of test outcome across coding systems applies here too.

Probing Moderation of Mediation

Evidence of moderation of an effect is usually followed by some kind of analytical probing procedure to better understand where in the distribution of the moderator the effect is different from zero and where it is not. A pick-a-point procedure is easy to implement once it is determined that a relative indirect effect varies systematically as a function of a moderator. This involves choosing values of the moderator, quantifying relative conditional indirect effects at those values, and then conducting an inference about those relative conditional indirect effects.

I already provided the derivation of the relative conditional indirect effects in this example (see section 13.2). The relative conditional indirect effects of protesting versus not protesting at values of perceived pervasiveness of sex discrimination that operationalize "relatively low" ($W = 4.250$, the 16th percentile), "moderate" ($W = 5.120$, the 50th percentile) and "relatively high" ($W = 5.986$, the 84th percentile) can be found in Table 13.2. Probing requires the additional step of inference. As relative conditional indirect effects are products of regression coefficients, a bootstrap confidence interval for each relative conditional indirect effect is a sensible inferential strategy. If a 95% bootstrap confidence interval includes zero, then the evidence does not definitively support a claim that the effect of protesting (relative to not) indirectly influences how positively Catherine is perceived through beliefs about the appropriateness of her behavior among a group of people who measure at the chosen value of W. But if the confidence interval does not include zero, this is evidence of mediation at that value of W.

PROCESS automatically constructs bootstrap confidence intervals for relative conditional indirect effects. These can be found in Figure 13.2 toward the very end of the PROCESS output under the heading "Relative conditional indirect effects of X on Y." The relative conditional indirect effects for protesting versus not are found in the X1 rows. As can be seen, at all three of these values of W, the bootstrap confidence intervals are all above zero (0.002 to 0.561 when $W = 4.250$; 0.288 to 0.824 when $W = 5.120$; 0.380 to 1.211 when $W = 5.896$). So we can say not only that this relative indirect effect is moderated and seems to increase with increasing (perceived) prevalence of sexism in society, but it is significantly larger than zero at these values. And as I say at the end of this discussion, we can also say that the three relative conditional indirect effects are significantly different from each other.

PROCESS also produces another set of relative conditional indirect effects—those for collectively protesting relative to individually protesting. These are found in the same section of output, in the rows labeled X2. Recall that according to the confidence interval for the index of moderated mediation for this relative indirect effect, we cannot say that the indirect effect of collectively versus individually protesting is moderated by perceived pervasiveness of sex discrimination. This might seem inconsistent with the bootstrap confidence intervals for the three relative conditional indirect effects found in this section of the output. Notice that the relative indirect effect of collectively relative to individually protesting is significantly positive among those low to moderate in perceived pervasiveness of sex discrimination, but not significant among those relatively high.

This conflict was addressed in section 7.5. A test of moderation of an effect is not the same as a set of tests that two or more conditional effects are equal to zero. There is nothing in the mathematics that requires internal consistency in the results of tests of different hypotheses. Your impulse might be to talk about the relative indirect effect of collectively protesting compared to individually protesting as different among those lower compared to high in perceived pervasiveness of sex discrimination. But you can't technically say this, a point made below. This puts you in a rhetorical box, for talking about these relative effects as different implies moderation, something that you can't say given that the confidence interval for the index of moderated mediation for this relative indirect effect includes zero.

Comparing Relative Conditional Indirect Effects

With evidence of moderation of a relative indirect effect using the index of moderated mediation, it is not necessary to conduct any further tests comparing conditional indirect effects to each other. The rationale given in sections 11.6 and 12.3 for conditional indirect effects applies to relative conditional indirect effects as well. The difference between two relative conditional indirect effects (e.g., when $W = w_1$ compared to when $W = w_2$) is equal to the index of moderated mediation for the relative indirect effect multiplied by the difference between the two moderator values, $w_2 - w_1$. As $w_2 - w_1$ is a constant, it does not determine sampling variance of the difference between relative conditional indirect effects, nor does it influence whether a confidence interval for the difference includes zero. So if a relative indirect effect is moderated according to the index of moderated mediation test, then *any* two relative conditional indirect effects conditioned on different values of the moderator can be deemed different from each other. But if the evidence does not support moderation of the relative indirect effect, then no two relative conditional indirect effects can be deemed different from each other.

13.5   Relative Conditional Direct Effects

The direct effect of X represents the part of X's effect on Y that does not operate through the mediator(s) in the model. In this example, the direct effect of X is specified as moderated by W. As the effect of X is represented with two contrast codes D_1 and D_2, there are two relative direct effects. But because, as shown below, these are functions of W, the direct effects become dependent on W.

The model for Y is

$$Y = i_Y + c'_1 D_1 + c'_2 D_2 + c'_3 W + c'_4 D_1 W + c'_5 D_2 W + bM + e_Y \qquad (13.12)$$

which can be expressed in the form

$$Y = i_Y + (c'_1 + c'_4 W)D_1 + (c'_2 + c'_5 W)D_2 + c'_3 W + bM + e_Y \qquad (13.13)$$

which shows that the direct effect of X on Y can be expressed in the form of two relative direct effects,

$$\theta_{D_1 \to Y} = c'_1 + c'_4 W \qquad (13.14)$$

$$\theta_{D_2 \to Y} = c'_2 + c'_5 W \qquad (13.15)$$

both of which are linear functions of W.

A test of moderation of the direct effect can be undertaken by testing the null hypothesis that both of the regression coefficients for $D_1 W$ and $D_2 W$ in equation 13.12 (which are also the modifiers of the relative direct effects of D_1 and D_2 by W in equations 13.13, 13.14, and 13.15) are equal to zero. Using the mathematics of the test described in sections 2.6 and 10.4, PROCESS implements this test in the model of Y and shows the result under the heading "Test(s) of highest order unconditional interactions(s)." The output in Figure 13.2 shows that the addition of the two products

D_1W and D_2W results in a change in R^2 of 0.030, $F(2, 122) = 2.548, p = .082$. Although this is not quite statistically significant, for the sake of illustration, we will plot the model and probe this near-interaction. The p-value is close to statistically significant. Furthermore, c'_4 and c'_5 quantify the relationship between the relative direct effect and W, and as can be seen in Table 13.1 and the PROCESS output, c'_4 is statistically significant, suggesting that the direct effect of protesting relative to not protesting is dependent on perceived pervasiveness of sex discrimination. Whether or not we interpret these results as consistent with moderation of the direct effect, it is worth going through the exercise of probing this possible moderation so that you will understand how to do it to your own analyses.

With the use of the **plot** option, PROCESS provides the code necessary to visualize the moderation of the relative direct effect of X on Y by W in the model of Y, using the procedure described in section 7.3. Executing that code and doing some editing of the resulting graph produces something like the top panel in Figure 13.5. The relative direct effects are reflected in the gaps between the lines, and the estimated means of Y for the three groups for three different values of W are depicted with the black circles. Although it looks like the gaps between the lines change quite a bit as a function of W, observe the scaling on the vertical axis. The movement in the size of the gaps you are seeing between the lines as a function of W reflects very small differences in Y, generally less than one scale point on the liking scale. But if we were to interpret this graph at face value, it would appear that when controlling for perceived appropriateness of Catherine's response, Catherine is liked more when she didn't protest compared to when she did among those who see sex discrimination as relatively less pervasive. Among those who see sex discrimination as highly pervasive, it appears she is liked more when she protested than when she did not. Among those moderate in perceived pervasiveness of sex discrimination, there appears to be little if any difference between the three groups in how much they liked Catherine.

Recall from Chapter 10 that the moderation of the effect of a multicate-gorical focal antecedent X by a continuous moderator W can be probed by focusing on omnibus tests of differences between groups or pairwise com-parisons between pairs of means. In the former case, using the pick-a-point approach, a test of equality of the estimates of the consequent variable in the groups conditioned on a value of the moderator is conducted. The top section of Figure 13.5 provides omnibus tests of the equality of estimates of how much Catherine is liked in the three experimental conditions among people relatively low ($W = 4.250$; the 16th percentile of the distribution), moderate ($W = 5.120$; the 50th percentile) and relatively high ($W = 5.896$;

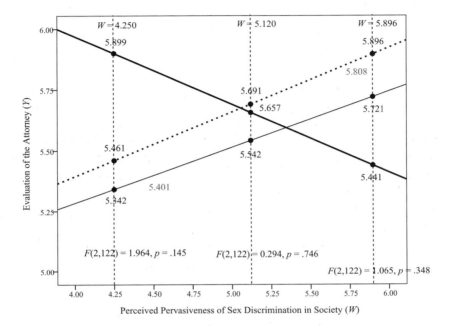

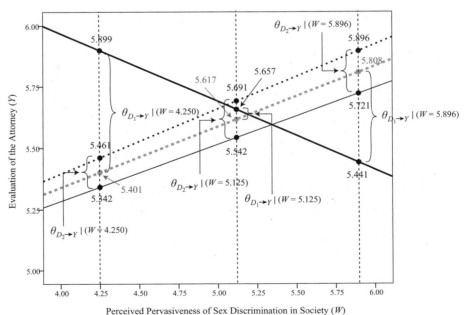

FIGURE 13.5. A visual representation of the moderation of the direct effect of the attorney's behavior on how positively she was evaluated by perceived pervasiveness of sex discrimination. Omnibus tests of the conditional direct effects are in top panel, and relative conditional direct effects are depicted in the bottom panel.

the 84th percentile) in perceived pervasiveness of sex discrimination, based on the procedure described in section 10.4. These tests are also available in the PROCESS output for the model of Y. As can be seen, none of these tests results in a rejection of the null hypothesis of equality of the conditional estimates of how much Catherine is liked. All the F-ratios are small, and the p-values are all large.

An omnibus test provides only vague information about differences between groups, regardless of the outcome of the test. Pairwise tests provide more specific information. In the regression model, X is coded with a set of two orthogonal contrast codes. In this coding system D_1 represents a comparison between the unweighted average estimate of the consequent in the two protest conditions and the no protest condition, and D_2 represents a comparison between the individual protest and the collective protest conditions. The effects of D_1 and D_2, which collectively represent the effect of X, are functions of perceived pervasiveness of sex discrimination (W) in this model.

Substituting the estimated regression coefficients into equations 13.14 and 13.15 defining the relative direct effects, we have

$$\theta_{D_1 \to Y} = c'_1 + c'_4 W = -2.732 + 0.526W \tag{13.16}$$
$$\theta_{D_2 \to Y} = c'_2 + c'_5 W = 0.025 - 0.034W \tag{13.17}$$

which are the equations for the solid lines in Figure 13.4 representing the relationship perceived pervasiveness of sex discrimination and the two relative direct effects of Catherine's behavior on how positively she is evaluated. Values of W can be plugged into equations 13.16 and 13.17 to produce the relative direct effects conditioned on W, and then an inferential test conducted. For instance, when W is set to "relatively low" ($W = 4.25$), the relative *conditional* direct effects are

$$\theta_{D_1 \to Y} = -2.732 + 0.526(4.250) = -0.498$$
$$\theta_{D_2 \to Y} = 0.025 - 0.034(4.250) = -0.119$$

These can be interpreted as the differences between estimates of Y for the three groups, plugging values of D_1 and D_2 and W for each group into equation 13.4 while setting M to $\overline{M} = 4.866$. Nine of these estimates can be found in Figure 13.5 for the three groups for three values of W; they are the black dots in the figure. So the relative conditional direct effects $\theta_{D_1 \rightarrow Y}$ and $\theta_{D_2 \rightarrow Y}$ when $W = 4.250$ correspond to

$$
\begin{aligned}
\theta_{D_1 \rightarrow Y} \mid (W = 4.250) &= \frac{\hat{Y}_{IP} + \hat{Y}_{CP}}{2} - \hat{Y}_{NP} \\
&= \frac{5.461 + 5.342}{2} - 5.899 \\
&= 5.401 - 5.899 \\
&= -0.498
\end{aligned}
$$

$$
\begin{aligned}
\theta_{D_2 \rightarrow Y} \mid (W = 4.250) &= \hat{Y}_{CP} - \hat{Y}_{IP} \\
&= 5.342 - 5.461 \\
&= -0.119
\end{aligned}
$$

These can be found in two places in the PROCESS output in Figure 13.2, once in the section for the model of Y and under the heading "Relative conditional direct effect(s) of X on Y," and once in the section toward the end under the heading "Direct and Indirect Effects of X on Y." In both these sections of output, effects for D_1 are found in the X1 row, and effects for D_2 are in the X2 row. These relative conditional direct effects are visualized in the bottom panel of Figure 13.5. As can be seen in the PROCESS output, neither of these relative conditional direct effects is statistically significant.

This procedure can be repeated for different values of perceived pervasiveness of sex discrimination. When $W = 5.120$, or "moderate" in perceived pervasiveness of sex discrimination,

$$
\begin{aligned}
\theta_{D_1 \rightarrow Y} &= -2.732 + 0.526(5.120) = -0.040 \\
\theta_{D_2 \rightarrow Y} &= 0.025 - 0.034(5.120) = -0.149
\end{aligned}
$$

which correspond to

$$
\begin{aligned}
\theta_{D_1 \rightarrow Y} \mid (W = 5.120) &= \frac{\hat{Y}_{IP} + \hat{Y}_{CP}}{2} - \hat{Y}_{NP} \\
&= \frac{5.691 + 5.542}{2} - 5.657 \\
&= 5.617 - 5.657 \\
&= -0.040
\end{aligned}
$$

$$
\begin{aligned}
\theta_{D_2 \rightarrow Y} \mid (W = 5.120) &= \hat{Y}_{CP} - \hat{Y}_{IP} \\
&= 5.542 - 5.691 \\
&= -0.149
\end{aligned}
$$

and are visualized in Figure 13.5. As can be seen in the PROCESS output in Figure 13.2, neither of these is statistically significant.

Finally, among those "relatively high" ($W = 5.896$),

$$\theta_{D_1 \to Y} = -2.732 + 0.526(5.896) = 0.368$$
$$\theta_{D_2 \to Y} = 0.025 - 0.034(5.896) = -0.175$$

which correspond to

$$
\begin{aligned}
\theta_{D_1 \to Y} \mid (W = 5.896) &= \frac{\hat{Y}_{IP} + \hat{Y}_{CP}}{2} - \hat{Y}_{NP} \\
&= \frac{5.896 + 5.721}{2} - 5.441 \\
&= 5.808 - 5.441 \\
&= 0.368
\end{aligned}
$$

$$
\begin{aligned}
\theta_{D_2 \to Y} \mid (W = 5.896) &= \hat{Y}_{CP} - \hat{Y}_{IP} \\
&= 5.721 - 5.896 \\
&= -0.175
\end{aligned}
$$

(see Figure 13.5). In the PROCESS output in Figure 13.2, you can see that neither of these is statistically significant.

All of these findings are consistent with the nonsignificant omnibus test of interaction presented earlier. There is no compelling evidence that the direct effect of Catherine's behavior on how much she is liked depends on the perceiver's beliefs about the pervasiveness of sex discrimination in society. Given this, it would be sensible to simplify the model by fixing the direct effect to be unmoderated. This can be done in PROCESS merely by changing the model number. Whereas model 8 allows W to moderate the direct effect of X, model 7 fixes the direct effect to be independent of W. If you reconduct this analysis using model 7 rather than model 8, you will find that substantively the results are unaffected by fixing the direct effect to be independent of W. If you want to include W in the model of Y (as model 7 would remove W from the equation for Y), you can employ the trick described in section 12.3 and in Appendix B.

13.6 Putting It All Together

A complex conditional process analysis such as this requires keeping track of many statistics, as well as various tests of hypotheses such as moderated mediation and whether a relative conditional indirect or direct effect is different from zero. Don't forget that ultimately, we conduct analyses not to talk about those analyses but to make substantive claims about psychological, cognitive, or biological processes at work relating antecedent X to consequent Y. I punctuate this chapter by trying to substantively interpret the collection of analyses I just conducted.

From this analysis, it appears that compared to not protesting, when Catherine protested the decision of the senior partners, she was liked more because protesting was perceived as more appropriate, especially among those who see sex discrimination as highly pervasive throughout society, and when Catherine behaved appropriately she was liked more. This indirect effect of protesting on how positively she was perceived was significantly larger among those who see sex discrimination as more pervasive. Collectively protesting also seemed to positively enhance Catherine's image because doing so was perceived as more appropriate for the circumstance, though the strength of this mechanism was not dependent on the perceiver's beliefs about the pervasiveness of sex discrimination in society.

Independent of this process, the evidence did not definitively support a direct effect of Catherine's behavior on how she was perceived. Although the direct effect of protesting relative to not protesting was related to perceived pervasiveness of sex discrimination in society (indicating a nonzero direct effect *somewhere* in the distribution of perceived pervasiveness of sex discrimination), no relative direct effects (for protesting versus not, or collectively protesting versus individually) were statistically significant conditioned on being relatively low, relatively moderate, or relatively high in perceived pervasiveness of sex discrimination.

13.7 Further Extensions and Complexities

In this example, X was a multicategorical variable, the moderation of the indirect effect was modeled as occurring in the first stage of the mediation process (i.e., the $X \rightarrow M$ effect), and the model contained only a single mediator. Many variations and extensions of this model exist. One could imagine a minor variation on this model where, for example, the moderator W is multicategorical and X is a dichotomous or continuous dimension. If the moderator represented g groups, there would be g indirect effects of X on Y through M, one for each group, as well as g direct effects if X's effect was also specified as moderated by the multicategorical W. PROCESS can estimate such a model and produce the output necessary for visualization and interpretation, including some tests of the equality of pairs of indirect effects.

Or instead, suppose that the moderation was in the second stage of the mediation process (i.e., the $M \rightarrow Y$ effect). The derivation of the conditional relative direct and indirect effects would be different. They would be different functions, as would the indices of moderated mediation, but they would be constructed using the same general principles as discussed in this chapter and relying on the fundamentals described throughout this book. Or maybe your model is like this example but instead contains two or more mediators operating in parallel, or in serial, but still with a multicategorical X. In that case, you'd have to estimate and interpret a set of conditional relative *specific* indirect effects. Adding additional complexity, perhaps one day you will want to estimate a model like this but containing a second moderator Z modify one or more of the paths of influence from X to Y. Depending on where Z resides in the model relative to W, you may have a case of *partial moderated mediation, conditional moderated mediation*, or *moderated moderated mediation*, concepts I introduce in Hayes (2018).

The specifics of estimation and interpretation of models such as these is beyond the scope of this book. Indeed, another lengthy book could be written (and perhaps will be one day) just about variations on the kinds of models I have described in these pages. PROCESS can estimate such models and many others of even greater complexity while taking much of the computational burden off your shoulders. Feel free to experiment with PROCESS, and also take a close look at Appendices A and B, where you will learn just what PROCESS can (and cannot) do.

13.8   Chapter Summary

The complexity of the analysis of the contingencies of a mechanism—conditional process analysis—is directly related to the complexity of the components of the model that define an indirect effect. When the presumed causal antecedent X is multicategorical, the analysis can be quite complex indeed. But with organization and an understanding of the principles, the complexity can be reduced, and a tool such as PROCESS further turns down the heat on the difficulty of the analysis.

This chapter tackled conditional process analysis with a multicategorical X. We did only one example, and only for one type of model that allows the indirect and direct effects to be moderated by the same variable, with the moderation of the indirect effect operating in the "first stage" of the mediation process. Building on the concepts of relative indirect and direct effects from Chapter 6 and conditional direct and indirect effects from Chapters 11 and 12, I introduced the relative conditional indirect effect and relative conditional direct effect in this chapter. Relative conditional direct and indirect effects are contingent on the coding system used for representing a multicategorical variable. But with this caveat in mind, the principles of conditional process analysis applied to simpler models in earlier chapters generalize to this more complex model. Relative indirect effects can be moderated, and the index of moderated mediation can be constructed to quantify how a relative indirect effect is related to a moderator. With evidence of moderation of a relative indirect effect, that moderation can be probed using the pick-a-point approach, estimating relative conditional indirect effects at values of the moderator, and conducting an inference about those relative conditional indirect effects.

Given my reference to fireworks that started this chapter, you may feel my grande finale has been a bit anticlimactic and disappointing. But if you feel comfortable with the ideas presented in this chapter, you are now in a good position to be able to generalize your understanding to at least some conditional process models that I have not explicitly discussed in this book. And you will find that PROCESS is able to help you along the way. Of course, many questions no doubt remain unanswered. In the final, closing chapter of this book that comes next, I hope to address some of those questions.

Part V
MISCELLANEA

14

Miscellaneous Topics and Some Frequently Asked Questions

In this closing chapter, I touch on a variety of interesting controversies and address some frequently asked questions. I begin by offering a strategy for approaching a conditional process analysis that acknowledges the need to balance hypothesis testing with data exploration. Following this is a treatment of writing, both in general but also about moderation, mediation and conditional process analysis. I address whether it is possible for a variable to simultaneously moderate and mediate one variable's effect on another, and also the assumption that X and M do not interact in a mediation process. I criticize a subgroups analysis approach to answering questions about moderated mediation and discuss a conditional process model that allows all paths to vary systematically as a function of a common moderator. I close with a brief treatment, with references to consult, on repeated measures data and modeling discrete, ordinal, count, or survival outcomes.

The vast majority of scientists would probably argue that when push comes to shove, the theoretical horse should pull the statistical cart. Statistical methods are mathematical tools, some of them quite amazing in what they do, which can help us to discern order amid the apparent chaos in a batch of data. But ultimately, the stories that statistical methods help us tell are told by our brains, not by the mathematics, and our brains are good at making sense of things—of coming up with stories to explain what we perceive. The problem is that the same pattern of results can be interpreted in many different ways, especially if the pattern is found after an extensive round of exploratory data analysis. Without a theoretical orientation to guide our attempts at making sense of our data or, better still, to guide our research design and data collection efforts, our awesome storytelling ability can lead us astray by invoking explanations for findings that may sound good but that are mere conjecture even if we can find a theoretical hook on which to hang them post hoc.

I won't argue against this perspective, as I believe it is for the most part right on the money. But I also believe that statistical methods can play an important role in theory development as well—that the statistical cart need not always, should not always, and often does not follow the theoretical horse. When we learn something new analytically, this can change the way we think of things theoretically and how we then go about testing the ideas that our newfound awareness of an analytical method inspired (cf. Slater, Hayes, & Snyder, 2008, p. 2). Indeed, as Greenwald (2012) observed, many of the advancements in science over the last few decades or more resulted as much from innovations in method as from innovations in theory.

Although I may be a victim of selective exposure and memory, I believe things have changed since the publications of Edwards and Lambert (2007), Muller et al. (2005), and Preacher et al. (2007). I don't recall seeing investigators combining moderation and mediation analysis nearly as frequently prior to 2007 as I see it now. If I am right, it is likely that this is in part the result of the occasional reversal of the horse and cart that these three articles may have prompted in some. Knowing how to quantify and test the contingencies of mechanisms may have helped to stimulate investigators to think more about how their favored mechanisms might be contingent and why. Asking these questions is in part what theory refinement is, and this may be an example of what Greenwald (2012, p. 99) was talking about when he said that there is "nothing so theoretical as a good method." My hope is that Chapters 11 through 13 on conditional process analysis have stimulated you to think about your own research questions and theories in a different way.

In this final chapter, I touch upon a number of interesting questions, controversies, and procedures related to the principles and practice of mediation, moderation, and conditional process analysis. I first address some basic issues in modeling, such as how to organize one's analysis and strike a balance between exploration and justification. I then talk about writing before entertaining the question as to whether structural equation modeling is better than the regression-based approach I describe in this book. I make the case for why splitting one's data into subgroups and conducting a mediation analysis in each group should be avoided as a means of testing hypotheses about the contingent nature of mechanisms. I then ponder whether it is conceivable that a variable could simultaneously play the role of both moderator and mediator of one variable's effect on another. This brings up the topic of interaction between X and M in mediation analysis. I provide some guidance on mediation analysis with repeated measures designs before closing the chapter and the book by providing some references to consult if your mediators or final outcome variable are not continuous, interval-level measurements and therefore better analyzed with methods other than ordinary least squares regression.

14.1   A Strategy for Approaching a Conditional Process Analysis

People who write about methodology have an advantage over those who don't. I can pick and choose any study I want to illustrate certain principles and procedures. I don't even have to conduct the study myself or collect any data, as I can always call in a favor or get on my knees and ask for donations of data to my methodological causes. If I can't find a real study that works for this purpose, I can just make data up from a hypothetical study (and, of course, describe it as such). Naturally, when using real data I choose examples where the results are clean, all effects of interest are statistically significant, and the interpretation is obvious and elegant.

But everyone else has to cope with the realities of the messiness of science when they analyze their data. Things don't always turn out as we expected and articulated in hypotheses 1, 2, and 3. And sometimes after looking at the data, our thinking about the process at work changes and new hypotheses come to mind that are worth testing. Scientists routinely switch back and forth between the context of justification and the context of discovery, testing hypotheses conceived before the data were analyzed while also exploring one's data to see what else can be learned from patterns observed but not anticipated.

I say this in anticipation of criticism that could be lodged at some of the suggestions I offer below for how you can approach a conditional process analysis. I realize there is much room for differences in opinion here, and in no way am I saying the outline I provide below is how you *should* organize your analysis or that doing it differently than I outline here is ill advised. People have their own philosophies about how science should best proceed, and what I offer below may clash with your philosophy.

Step 1: Construct Your Conceptual Diagram of the Process

Throughout this book, I have used the conceptual diagram as a visual representation of a process. Decide what your single "focal antecedent" is for the analysis you are currently doing, for this is the variable whose effect you are most interested in estimating in the analysis. This will be X in your conceptual diagram. Then draw out the paths of influence from X to your consequent of interest Y, through whatever mediator variables you think X influences and that in turn are thought to influence Y. Always include the direct effect in your conceptual (and statistical) model, for you should be open to the possibility that X influences Y through mechanisms other than those that you are explicitly modeling. When completed, you will have a diagram of the mediation component of the process.

Once you have the mediation component of your conditional process model depicted, then depict moderation of whatever paths you believe are contingent, and by what moderators. Moderation is denoted by connecting a variable to a path with an arrow, as in the examples throughout this book.

Keep things simple at this point. Don't worry about every conceivable path of influence from any variable to any other variable. Focus on X and its direct and indirect effects, moderated or not, for X is your primary interest—your focal antecedent. Once you complete the second step, some of the things that seem missing in the conceptual diagram may end up in the statistical model anyway, such as paths linking moderators to consequent variables. Conditional process modeling as described in this book is not about finding the best fitting model of the data given the variables available, in the way that structural equation modeling is sometimes practiced. It is about estimating effects and interpreting them. Your focus should be on the various coefficients in the statistical model, and how they combine to quantify contingencies in the effect of X on Y through one or more mediators. Determining whether your model is the best fitting model you can justify is not the point. In fact, some models described in this book are "saturated," meaning fit would be perfect when assessed quantitatively with various measures of fit used in structural equation modeling.

Step 2: Translate the Conceptual Model into a Statistical Model

We don't estimate the conceptual model. A conceptual model must be translated into a statistical model in the form of at least two equations, depending on the number of proposed mediators in the model. With an understanding of the principles of moderation and mediation analysis described in this book, you should be able to do this without too much difficulty. As a general rule, if variable A points an arrow at variable B in your conceptual diagram, then variable A should be an antecedent variable in the equation for consequent B. And if variable A's effect on variable B is proposed as moderated by variable C, then the equation for B will also include C and the product of A and C as antecedent variables (assuming you are interested in *linear* moderation). Don't violate these rules, because a failure to follow them can result in a statistical model that does not correspond to the conceptual model you have diagrammed for the process of interest to you.

In complex models, this translation procedure can be tricky. Hayes and Preacher (2013) describe the steps required to accurately translate a complex conceptual model into a statistical model for a conditional process model involving moderated moderation and serial multiple mediation. These principles generalize to simple models. Fortunately, PROCESS is programmed to automatically translate the conceptual model you specify into a set of equations. Using the procedure described in Appendix B, you can deviate from the preprogrammed models built into PROCESS and construct your own model from scratch, and PROCESS will know how to set up the equations for your model. However, it may be still be the case on occasion that PROCESS cannot estimate precisely the model you want. So at some time, you may have learn to translate the principles described in this book into code understood by a structural equation modeling program such as Mplus or LISREL. See Hayes and Preacher (2013) for some guidance if you want to deviate from what PROCESS does for you.

Step 3: Estimate the Statistical Model

Once the equations corresponding to the mediator(s) and outcome are specified, then you estimate the coefficients of the statistical model. Throughout this book I have been assuming you believe OLS regression is appropriate for your data, so the coefficients could be estimated using any OLS regression program. PROCESS does all this for you once you specify the model desired and tell it which variables play which roles.

Step 4: Determine Whether Expected Moderation Exists

Here is where things get controversial. Suppose you have proposed, for instance, that X's effect on M is moderated by W, and that M's effect on Y is moderated by Z (something like model 21 in Appendix A). After estimating the coefficients in the statistical model, perhaps you find that the interaction between X and W in the model of M is statistically significant, but the interaction between M and Z in the model of Y is not. Should you modify your model at this point based on this evidence, or should you forge ahead since your interest is on the conditional (or unconditional) direct and indirect effects of X and not on the individual components of the model? Your decision determines whether you move to step 4a or step 5. Of course, it may be that all paths you proposed as moderated actually are. In that case, proceed to step 5.

I can't tell you what to do, but I can offer you some thoughts about how you might think about proceeding. Your model proposes moderation of a path in the process that it turns out is not moderated as expected, at least according to the results of a hypothesis test. If you leave the interaction in the model, this will influence the estimate of the indirect effect of X on Y through M (which is necessarily conditional with this interaction in the model) along with all inferential tests thereof. But if you have little evidence that the path is actually moderated as you expected, wouldn't it be more sensible to constrain it to be unconditional rather than conditional on that moderator? If you believe so, you should remove it and start fresh, reconceptualizing your thinking in light of this evidence you now have based on the data. But remember that a null hypothesis can never be proven true. Just because an interaction is not significant, that doesn't mean your proposed moderator does not moderate the path you proposed it moderates. Parsimony might dictate that your model should be cleansed of this interaction, but null hypotheses tests are fallible, and sometimes real effects are so weak that we don't have the power to detect them given the limitations of our resources or other things out of our control.

It is important to point out that it is possible (even if perhaps somewhat uncommon) for an indirect effect to depend on a moderator absent evidence that a particular path is moderated by a formal test of significance. I make this point through argument and illustration in Hayes (2015), where I introduce the index of moderated mediation. Furthermore, as Fairchild and MacKinnon (2009) discuss, it is possible for an indirect effect to be constant across all values of a moderator or moderators even when one has evidence that one or more of the constituent paths are moderated. Thus, use step 4 as a guide rather than a hard and fast rule for deciding whether you want to change your model.

Step 4A: If you have decided to prune your model of nonsignificant interactions, then go back to step 1 and start fresh by redrawing your conceptual diagram in light of the evidence you now have and proceed through these steps again. A certain moral or ethical logic might dictate that you not pretend when describing your analysis that this is where you started in the first place. Yet Bem (1987) makes the argument that spending lots of time talking about ideas that turned out to be "wrongheaded" isn't going to produce a particularly interesting paper. You'll have to sort out for yourself where you stand on this continuum of scientific ethics.

Step 5: Probe and Interpret Interactions Involving Components of the Indirect Effect

At this stage, probe any interactions involving components of the indirect effect of X so that you will have some understanding of the contingencies of the various effects that are the components of the larger conditional process model you are estimating. This exercise will help inform and clarify your interpretation of the conditional indirect effect(s) of X later on. This will require you to shift your thinking about the analysis toward pure moderation for the time being rather than condition process modeling. PROCESS will simplify this task considerably, as it has procedures built in to help you visualize and probe any interaction in your model regardless of where it occurs.

Step 6: Quantify and Test Conditional Indirect Effects (If Relevant)

Once you get to this step, you will have a model you either have accepted as is regardless of whether the data are consistent with every part of it, or one that has been cleansed of any moderation components that weren't consistent with the data. It could be that you have cleansed so thoroughly that you no longer have any moderation components left in your model, because none of them was statistically significant, and all that is left is a mediation model. In that case, you can stop what you are doing and consider my advice in section 14.2.

Assuming you have evidence of moderation of an indirect effect, you will now want to quantify the indirect effects as a function of the moderator(s) and conduct various inferential tests for those conditional indirect effects. Chapters 11 through 13 describe how this is done for a few models, but the principles apply to more complex models. Although it is not difficult to do these computations by hand, a computer program that does it for you is handy, and such a program will be necessary if you want to use bootstrap confidence intervals for inference as I recommend throughout this book. PROCESS both quantifies the indirect effects and generates bootstrap confidence intervals for you, without requiring any effort on your part. If you are doing your analysis with a structural equation modeling program with the ability to estimate functions of parameters, you'll need to hard-program the computation of those functions yourself. This requires a bit more effort than does the use of PROCESS, and it is easy to slip up during the programming. I provide example code for Mplus for a complex model in Hayes and Preacher (2013).

Step 7: Quantify and Test Conditional Direct Effects (If Relevant)

If your model includes moderation of the direct effect of X, you will want to probe this interaction by estimating the conditional direct effects. This is just moderation analysis, discussed in Chapters 7 to 10. PROCESS will also take the labor out of this, because it will automatically quantify the conditional direct effects for you and provide inferential tests at various values of the moderator, depending on the options for probing the interaction that you request.

Step 8: Tell Your Story

Once you have compiled the results from these various stages of the analysis, you are in a position to frame the story you now want to tell given what you know from the analysis just completed. I provide some writing advice in section 14.2.

I realize that these steps may run contrary to the way that the business of science is typically described in research methods and statistics texts. We are taught to formulate hypotheses, design a study that will allow us to test those hypotheses, test those hypotheses with the data available, and then tell the world whether our hypotheses are supported or not. Yet my outline sounds a bit like data mining in places, as if the analyses are dictating the hypotheses rather than the other way around.

But real science does not proceed in the manner described in research methods and statistics textbooks. Rather, we routinely straddle the fence between the hypothetico-deductive approach and a more discovery-oriented or inquisitive mindset that is open to any story the data may inform. Sometimes the story we originally conceived prior to data analysis is simply wrong and we know it after analyzing the data. No one wants to read (as Daryl Bem once put it rather bluntly) "a personal history about your stillborn thoughts" (Bem, 1987, p. 173). Sometimes our data speak to us in ways that change the story we thought we were going to tell into something much more interesting, and hopefully more accurate.

Of course, there is always the danger of capitalizing on chance when you let your explorations of the data influence the story you tell. We are great at explaining patterns we see. Our brains are wired to do it. So replication is important, and it may be the only way of establishing the generality of our findings and claims in the end. If replication is not likely to happen by you in your lifetime but you have the luxury of lots of data (i.e., if you have "power to burn," as some say), randomly set aside half of your data before analyzing the other half. Explore all you want in one half, but don't report anything you find as real that doesn't replicate in the other half you have set aside.

14.2   How Do I Write about This?

Over my years as an academic, one of my administrative duties has been to serve on my department's graduate studies committee. One of this committee's responsibilities each year is to sort through stacks of applications for graduate school and figure out who is likely to succeed in a rigorous and quantitatively driven social science Ph.D. program. But to be honest, nobody really knows how to do this, yet everyone has their own beliefs about what it takes to succeed that they are sure are predictive of actual success. For some time, I put much more emphasis on quantitative Graduate Record Examination scores and grades in quantitative courses (such as statistics, mathematics, and economics) than other committee members. As I have taught nothing but data analysis for the last two decades, I have repeatedly seen firsthand the struggles of students who aren't prepared to think abstractly and quantitatively. But after several years of following this strategy, I began to realize that the students who were comfortable with the mathematics weren't necessarily the ones getting the best jobs after graduate school. Although there are many determinants of success no doubt, I have become convinced that the ability to communicate in writing is at least as if not more important than the ability to manipulate numbers and think in abstractions. You don't have to be a good data analyst to be a good scientist, but your future on the front lines of science is limited if you can't write effectively.

I have been asked several times if I would be willing to write a paper on "best practices" in the reporting of mediation, moderation, and conditional process analysis. I have always refused these invitations, because I am reluctant to provide strict advice or spell out explicit rules about how to write about data analysis. I believe writing the results section of a scientific article is not much different than writing about anything else, whether it is a biography, science fiction, or a trashy romance. There are as many ways to write a good scientific article as there are ways to write a good novel. There is no specific formula that will produce good scientific prose, for so much of what makes writing good is what you bring to the task that is unique to you—your style, your background, and writing models who have inspired you. Most important is that you be interesting and engaging, focus on the human dimensions that make your research matter, minimize your use of jargon as much as possible, and deemphasize things that the reader won't care about. If you do that, almost anything else goes. You should have fun when you write, and if you have passion for and interest in your subject matter, it will come across in your writing if you let it. That said, I recognize that writing about data analysis can be a challenge until you get used to it and develop your own style, and it can be difficult to know what is and is not important.

In my experience, respectable writing comes in spurts with long delays between, and what comes out between periods of inspiration often is drivel that ends up getting cut. It took me several weeks to write some of the chapters in this book. Often my time was spent procrastinating because I wasn't sure how I wanted it to start and I had other things I wanted to do. But with time running out to deliver this manuscript to the publisher, I had no choice but to force myself to sit and do it. But once I start typing, things usually come out without lots of effort, and I find myself impressed with how much I accomplished in one sitting when I was dreading the idea going into it.

My point is that you should give yourself plenty of time to write. Your first couple of drafts of a paper are not what you want others to read, and if you don't give yourself the opportunity to think about what you want to say, choose your words carefully, and then reflect on what you have written, you are not going to be communicating as effectively as you probably can and must. From my experience editing a journal and reviewing for many, I know how poor writing is perceived by other scholars. Most reviewers don't have the patience or time to read the work of others that wasn't ready to be submitted. They will simply reject and move on to the next thing in their busy schedules, and they will do so without feeling the least bit guilty about it.

It takes time to develop a writing style that is your own and conveys your research findings in ways that are informative, interesting, and engaging to the reader. Science should be fun to communicate and fun to read, but it doesn't always seem that way given how many scientific articles are framed and written. Don't let your assumptions about science—that it should be cold, objective, and conveyed in third-person perspective—turn something that could and should be lively and fun into something dreadfully dull. Don't be afraid to say "I did" this or "We did" that, so long as you keep the focus on the science rather than the scientist. Take a look at some of the advice offered by Silva (2007) on writing, who is quite critical of the way scientists communicate with each other, but who also offers some tips for how you can break the cycle. Along the way, you will acquire some skills for writing productively as well as better.

It never hurts to have a good model to follow when writing about anything. Although I encourage scientific writers to find their own voice rather than rely on conventions and the expectations of others, sometimes following the lead of a good writer whose work you admire can go a long way toward improving your own scientific communication and developing your own style. For instance, I have always been a big fan of the prose of social psychologist Daniel T. Gilbert. His writing has a degree of levity not found in most journal articles, and I find his playfulness with words and the stories he tells when framing his work keeps me interested in reading more. After all, who begins a scientific article with stories about bubblegum-chewing robots (Gilbert & Osborne, 1989) or aliens descending from space to peek in on the work of psychologists (Gilbert & Krull, 1988), and who dares describe the goal of social psychology as figuring out how Aunt Sofia reasons about the behavior of her nephews (Gilbert & Malone, 1995)? I believe my writing is better in part because of my early exposure to his.

If you are feeling all warm and empowered by my words above, recognize that I haven't actually provided any practical guidance. You still have to face a blank screen and start typing. In the rest of this section I will offer what little guidance I am comfortable giving, considering the perspective on writing I have expressed above. I start first with general advice that applies regardless of the kind of analysis you are reporting before discussing some of the specifics of mediation, moderation, and conditional process analysis. But some of those specifics generalize to other kinds of analysis as well.

First, remember that you are a reader as well as a writer, and you don't want to read boring things. It is easy to bore the reader with excessive discussion of regression coefficients, tests of significance, and statements of hypotheses supported or not. Try to pack as much of the pallid statistical information as you can into a table or figure summarizing the analysis (such as in Figures 3.3 or 5.3 or Tables 3.2 or 5.1). Let the reader scan this information as he or she chooses while you walk the reader through the analytical procedure and the substantive interpretation of the results in the text. Use statistics in the text as support for substantive claims being made, but as punctuation for those claims rather than as the subject and focus of the results. Unless necessary when using them in formulas, try to avoid the use of symbolic representations for variables in the text itself (with variable names in the dataset such as COND, PMI, ESTRESS, etc.).

For instance, consider the following description of a simple mediation analysis:

> A mediation analysis was conducted by estimating perceived media influence (PMI) from article location (COND) as well as reactions to the story (REACTION) from both article location and perceived media influence. Supporting hypothesis 1, COND was positively related to PMI ($a = 0.477, p = .045$). Supporting hypothesis 2, PMI positively predicted REACTION while controlling for COND ($b = 0.506, p < .001$). A bootstrap confidence interval for the indirect effect of COND (ab) using 10,000 bootstrap samples was 0.004 to 0.524, meaning that there was evidence of an indirect effect of COND on REACTION through PMI. Contrary to hypothesis 3, the direct effect of COND on REACTION of $c' = 0.254$ was not statistically significant ($p = .322$).

Now compare this to the one below:

From a simple mediation analysis conducted using ordinary least squares path analysis, article location indirectly influenced intentions to buy sugar through its effect on beliefs about how others would be influenced. As can be seen in Figure 3.3 and Table 3.2, participants told that the article would be published on the front page believed others would be more influenced to buy sugar than those told that the article would appear in an economic supplement ($a = 0.477$), and participants who believed others would be more influenced by the story expressed a stronger intention to go buy sugar themselves ($b = 0.506$). A bootstrap confidence interval for the indirect effect ($ab = 0.241$) based on 5,000 bootstrap samples was entirely above zero (0.007 to 0.526). There was no evidence that article location influenced intention to buy sugar independent of its effect on presumed media influence ($c' = 0.254, p = .322$).

Notice how much more interesting and understandable the second description is. Unlike the first, the second paragraph focuses on the results in terms of the constructs measured rather than symbols, while still providing some of the descriptive and inferential statistics for the reader. However, those statistics are primarily used as punctuation for substantive claims rather than as the focus of the text itself. And by avoiding explicit discussion of hypotheses supported or not, attention is kept off the investigator and his or her clairvoyance or lack thereof. Most readers will not care whether an investigator correctly forecasted his or her results, nor is the reader likely to remember what hypotheses 1, 2, and 3 were at this point in a scientific article.

Second, I will repeat a point made way back in section 2.2 because it is important. Avoid the use of terms such as "beta coefficient" or symbols such as b or β when talking about any regression analysis without first telling your reader what these mean in table notes, footnotes, or the text itself. Many researchers throw such symbols around casually and without definition, believing that they are understood by all as conventions for talking about regression analysis.[1] Although there may be some such conventions in some disciplines, they are not universal, and I generally recommend assuming when you write that you are writing for an interdisciplinary audience. Different people trained in a different field than you or who learned regression analysis from a different book or instructor

---

[1] A colleague of mine once asked a presenter at a talk we both attended whether he was reporting "bees or betas." Although I understood the question, it sounded bizarre and revealed his ignorance of variation within and between fields in how people are trained and talk about regression analysis.

may have learned to use different symbols or conventions. Using symbols undefined makes your writing seem somewhat parochial.

Third, throughout this book, I emphasize estimation and interpretation of effects in their unstandardized metric, and I report unstandardized effects when I report the results in my own research. There is a widespread belief that standardized effects are best reported, because the measurement scales used in most sciences are arbitrary and not inherently meaningful, or that standardized effects are more comparable across studies or investigators using different methods. But standardization simply changes one arbitrary measurement scale into another arbitrary scale, and because standardized effects are scaled in terms of variability in the sample, they are not comparable across studies conducted by different investigators regardless of whether the same measurement scales are used. By keeping the results in an unstandardized metric, the analytical results (equations, regression coefficients, etc.) map directly onto the measurement scales used in the study and as described, and they can be directly compared across studies conducted using the same measurement system. If you provide information about the variability of each variable in the model, a reader interested in standardized effects can generate them for him- or herself. Of course, there is no harm in reporting both if you would rather not take a stand on this, with the exception of the caveat below.

For reasons discussed in sections 2.2, 2.4, and 4.3, I very strongly discourage reporting standardized effects involving a dichotomous X. Standardized regression coefficients (and therefore direct, indirect, and total effects) for a dichotomous X are not meaningful, as they are influenced by the distribution of the cases between the two groups as well as differences between the group means. Furthermore, standardization of X destroys the interpretation of the effects in terms of differences between the means of the two groups on M and Y. If you feel compelled to report some kind of standardized metric for the effects in a mediation analysis involving a dichotomous X, use the partially standardized effect size measure discussed in section 4.3. For good discussions of the pros and cons of the reporting of standardized versus unstandardized effects, see Baguley (2009), Kim and Ferree (1976), and Kim and Mueller (1981).

Ultimately the choice to report standardized or unstandardized effects is yours to make. Report both if you desire. Regardless of your choice, make sure you tell the reader somewhere (in table notes or the text itself) whether the effects are expressed in a standardized or unstandardized metric. Don't assume that symbolic representations or text such as β or "beta coefficient" will be understood by all.

Reporting a Mediation Analysis

Mediation is a causal phenomenon. You will find some people skeptical of the use of mediation analysis in studies based on data that are purely correlational in nature and involve no experimental manipulation or measurement over time. Some people are quite fanatical about this, and if you are unlucky enough to get such an extreme reviewer when trying to publish your work, there may not be much you can to do to convince him or her otherwise. I made my perspective on this clear in sections 1.4 and 4.2. Inferences are products of our minds and not the mathematics we use to analyze our data, and we can use most any mathematical tool we want to help guide the story we tell from the data we have collected. But you can do a lot to preempt unnecessary criticism from those who take extreme positions by presenting a compelling story as to why you believe, even if you cannot empirically justify, that the relationships that define your mediation process constitute a sensible causal process. Theory and logical argument is important. Make your case, and make it strongly, and recognize the limitations of your data. If you don't, you are largely to blame for the criticism you receive.

Although there is no harm in reporting hypothesis tests or confidence intervals for the paths that define the indirect effect (a and b), whether those effects are statistically significant need not be a part of the argument supporting evidence of the existence of an indirect effect. The days of the "criteria to establish mediation" described in Baron and Kenny (1986) are gone and will not be returning. Notice that the description of the mediation analysis I provide on page 517 does not provide p-values for a or b (though p-values are provided in the table), because whether a and b is statistically significant is not pertinent to whether the indirect effect is different from zero. An indirect effect is quantified as the product of paths. Provide your point estimate of the indirect effect, as well as an inferential test supporting your claim that the indirect effect is not zero. Whether or not a and b are statistically different from zero can be useful supplementary information for the reader, but it need not be part of your claim that an indirect effect exists. As discussed in section 3.2, their signs certainly do matter, for the signs of a and b determine the sign of ab and therefore its interpretation in terms of the process at work being modeled. You absolutely should focus on the signs of a and b when talking about the indirect effect. Just don't worry so much about p-values for these, because you care about ab, not a and b.

Be precise in your language when talking about direct and indirect effects. In mediation analysis, X exerts an effect on Y directly and/or indirectly through M. It is not correct to talk about the "indirect effect of M"

unless there is another variable causally between M and Y. Although M affects Y in a mediation process, it does not do so indirectly except in serial multiple mediator models. It is X that affects Y indirectly *through M*. I also find the term "mediated effect," which some use as a synonym for indirect effect, to be an awkward label. To call the indirect effect the mediated effect suggests that *ab* or M is the causal agent of interest, but in fact it is X that is the cause of Y, which exerts its effect indirectly through M, not *ab* or M itself.

You should report both the direct and the indirect effect(s) in a mediation analysis as well as an inferential test for each. I don't recommend using the Sobel test, and most experts in this area agree with me. Instead, I recommend the use of bootstrap confidence intervals when conducting inferential tests of indirect effects, for they respect the irregularity of the sampling distribution of the indirect effect. However, merely stating that bootstrapping was used is not sufficient. Make sure your description includes both the number of bootstrap samples and the method used for constructing confidence intervals (i.e., percentile, bias-corrected). And it wouldn't hurt to report the seed used for the random number generator so that others could exactly reproduce any results you report using your data and model.

Finally, I often see mediation analyses overreported, with a description of multiple methods used that seems to track the evolution of mediation analysis. A report might include a discussion as to whether the causal steps criteria for mediation are met, followed by a Sobel test, and perhaps (if the investigator has been keeping up with the literature in mediation analysis) end with a more appropriate and modern test of the indirect effect using a bootstrap confidence interval or some other method that respects the nonnormality of the sampling distribution of a product of regression coefficients. See Bond (2015) for an example of this multiple-method approach to reporting. My guess is that investigators who do this realize that publishing is partly a political process and by describing multiple approaches and tests, one's bases are covered against any potential critics. I understand this, yet it also seems like analytical overkill to me. There is value to establishing converging evidence through multiple analytical strategies, but pick a method, defend it if need be, and focus your description of the analysis on the one you have chosen. If you feel a need to satisfy potential critics by describing alternative methods and the results they yield, do so in footnotes.

Reporting a Moderation Analysis

Some of the more interesting studies you will find show that what is commonly assumed turns out to be true only sometimes, or that a well-known manipulation only works for some types of people. When writing about moderation, you have the opportunity to tell the scientific world that things aren't as simple as perhaps they have seemed or been assumed to be, and that there are conditions that must be placed on our understanding of the world. It is up to you how to tell your story about the contingencies of the effects you have found in your research. I offer only a few guidelines below for how you might think about articulating your results, how to contemplate the reporting of findings that seem inconsistent or contradictory (as often happens when we analyze real data), and what you should try to always include in a description of an analysis so as to provide the reader what he or she needs to make sense of it.

First, at some point in your research career, you are going to come across one of three scenarios and wonder how to talk about your results under such circumstances. One scenario is a statistically significant interaction between focal antecedent X and moderator W but no evidence of a statistically significant conditional effect of X at any value of W. The second scenario is a nonsignificant interaction but evidence that X is significantly related to Y for some but perhaps not all values of W. A third scenario is evidence of an interaction between X and W with additional evidence that X is related to Y at any value of W. Such results seem contradictory or paradoxical, but really they are not at all if you keep in mind that these are entirely different tests. A test of interaction is a test as to whether X's effect on Y depends linearly on W (or, in the case of a dichotomous W, whether X's effect on Y is different for the two groups defined by W). By contrast, a test of a conditional effect of X is a test as to whether X is significantly related to Y at a specific value of W chosen (or derived using the Johnson–Neyman technique). The outcome of one test implies nothing about the outcome of the other.

In the first scenario, you can claim that X's effect depends on W but you won't be able to say specifically where on the continuum of W or for whom the effect of X on Y is different from zero. It may be that this doesn't bother you at all. Perhaps your primary focus is on whether X's effect depends on W and probing the interaction with the goal of making more specific claims is not important to you. But if the exercise and outcome of probing is important to you, this scenario requires some carefully chosen language, and though it may seem unsatisfying not to be able to provide a more specific claim, such is the nature of science at times. But remember if you are using the pick-a-point approach that whatever values of W you choose are entirely arbitrary. Just because X is not significantly related to Y at a few arbitrarily chosen values of W does not mean that X is unrelated to Y anywhere on the continuum of W. You are not wedded to the use of arbitrary operationalizations of "low," "moderate," and "high." Probe elsewhere if you choose. Alternatively, abandon the pick-a-point approach entirely and use the Johnson–Neyman technique instead, thereby eliminating the need to choose values of W when probing an interaction. If there is evidence that X is related to Y somewhere within the range of the data on W, the Johnson–Neyman technique will usually find where.

The second scenario can get you into trouble if you aren't careful when interpreting and writing, because a hypothesis about interaction is a hypothesis about the relationship between W and X's effect on Y. Establishing that X is significantly related to Y for one value of W but not for another does not establish that X's effect depends on W. Remember from section 7.5 that differences in degrees of significance or lack thereof does not imply significance of a difference. To say, for example, that X is significantly and positively related to Y in males but not in females does not mean that the relationship between X and Y is different between men and women. The claim that a conditional effect is not statistically different from zero does not mean that it actually is zero. Therefore, you can't claim that two things are different from each other just because one is not statistically different from zero when another is. A claim of difference between conditional effects should be based on an actual test as to whether X's effect on Y depends on W—a test of moderation. Most critics of your work will take you to task if you imply interaction in your interpretation and discussion by talking about differences in significance if you can't establish convincingly with statistical evidence of interaction that X's effect on Y is actually related to W.

The third scenario is not nearly as difficult to deal with from a writing perspective as the first or second. Interaction between X and W does not mean that X's effect must be zero for some values of W but not others. It may be that X is significantly related to Y at all values of W in the range of the data, or none of them. Just because you can't find some value of W where the conditional effect of X is not different from zero does not mean that W does not moderate X's effect on Y. W is a moderator of X's effect if X's effect depends on W. It may be that X is related to Y for both men and women, for example. If X is moderated by sex, that means that these conditional effects differ from each other. That does not preclude the possibility that X is related to Y in both groups. In this situation, you can claim both that X is related to Y wherever you look, and that X's effect also depends on W.

Second, as discussed in section 7.2, the interpretation of the regression coefficients for X and W in a model that includes XW are highly dependent on the scaling of X and W. If you have centered a variable, say so. If one or both of these variables is dichotomous, tell the reader what numerical codes were used to represent the two groups. Preferably, choose codes for the two groups that differ by one unit. The more information you give to the reader about how your variables are scaled or coded, the more the reader will be able to look at your results in the text, tables, or figures, discern their meaning, and interpret them correctly.

Third, as discussed in section 9.1, the decision to mean center or not has no effect on the estimate of the interaction between X and W. Whether to center or not is your choice to make. Personally, I think mean centering X or W, if not both, is a good idea in many circumstances, but my reasons have nothing to do with collinearity between X, W, and XW. As illustrated in section 7.2 and further discussed in section 9.1, b_1 and b_2 and their tests of significance in a model of the form $\hat{Y} = i_Y + b_1 X + b_2 M + b_3 XW$ are heavily influenced by the scaling of X and W. b_1 estimates the effect of X on Y when $W = 0$ and b_2 estimates the effect of W on Y when $X = 0$. If X and W are kept in their original metric, one or both of these coefficients will be meaningless if zero is outside of the bounds of the metric of measurement. If you get in the habit of mean centering X and W, you know that b_1 and b_2 and their tests of significance will always be interpretable and meaningful because they estimate conditional effects of X and W when the other variable is at the sample mean. If W is dichotomous and mean-centered, b_1 estimates the weighted average effect of X between the two groups coded by W. If X is dichotomous and mean-centered, b_2 estimates the weighted average effect of W between the two groups coded by X.

With knowledge of the effects of scaling of X and W on the interpretation of the coefficients in a regression model with an interaction, you are less likely to fall victim to incorrect interpretation. However, don't assume that your reader will be equally informed, and so even if you know not to interpret a coefficient or hypothesis test that is meaningless, by mean centering you reduce the likelihood that your reader will do so. When X's effect is moderated by W, readers of your work unfamiliar with the interpretational principles described in this book are likely to misinterpret b_1 and b_2 as "main effects" when they are not. Mean centering X and W does not make these main effects either, but they are closer to main effects than when X and W are uncentered. A "main effect" is a term from analysis of variance that does not generalize to all regression models. Although you can't stop people from misinterpreting a model, you can reduce the severity of their mistakes through mean centering. So if this is something that concerns you, go ahead and mean center.

Fourth, as with mean centering, the decision to standardize X and W or to report standardized or unstandardized regression coefficients is your choice to make. But if you choose to do so, don't say you are doing so to reduce the effects of collinearity. Personally, I prefer to talk about regression results in unstandardized form. If you choose to report standardized regression coefficients, use variant 1 described in section 9.2. When doing so, make sure that you are reporting and interpreting the coefficients corresponding to the *unstandardized* model in the output of your program and not the standardized model. Indeed, as a general rule, *never* report or interpret the coefficients listed in a standardized section of the output when your model includes the product of two variables along with the components of that product, and don't use these coefficients to probe an interaction. And don't standardize dichotomous variables or report standardized coefficients for a dichotomous antecedent. Keep standardized variables in their original metric or, better still, use a 0/1 or −0.5/0.5 coding system (or any two values that differ by one unit) so that the regression coefficient for this antecedent variable can be interpreted in a mean difference metric.

Fifth, the choice is up to you how much to focus your discussion of a model with an interaction between X and W on the regression coefficients for X and W. If you have evidence that W moderates X's effect, it typically is not particularly useful to spend too much time talking about the regression coefficients for X and W, because they will reflect a variable's association with Y conditioned on a single value of the other variable. Usually, the story to be told concerns the relationship between the moderator and the focal antecedent's effect whenever you have evidence that X and W interact.

This would apply even if you choose to enter the XW product in a later step using hierarchical entry as described in section 8.3. It is common when using hierarchical regression to first enter X and W, substantively interpret the regression coefficients in that first stage with respect to one or more of the goals of the original study, and then enter the product to see if that earlier discussion needs to be qualified in light of evidence as to whether X's effect is contingent on W. Personally, I often don't see the value in spending lots of time telling your reader about relationships in step 1 of a hierarchical modeling procedure that ultimately must be qualified because those effects are contingent. In my opinion, often it makes more sense to go right step 2, describe the conditional nature of X's effect on Y, and probe the interaction. In other words, if you know X's effect is moderated by W, why hassle with hierarchical regression in the first place, describing a bunch of results from preliminary stages of the model-building process that ultimately aren't the complete story? Of course, it is your story to tell how you want, and if you feel that the results from preliminary stages of the model-building process are valuable, interesting, and/or of theoretical relevance, go ahead and include those results in your narrative.

Reporting a Conditional Process Analysis

One of the challenges you are likely to face when writing about a conditional process analysis is staying within the page allowance that most journal editors provide. A well-written analysis will usually contain multiple tables, perhaps a figure or two to depict the conceptual model and perhaps an interaction or two, and enough text to describe what was found in substantive terms while also providing sufficient detail about the analysis for the reader to understand what was done. Many reviewers, editors, and readers will not be familiar with this approach and may need to be educated within the text, further lengthening the manuscript. Yet I am also amazed how much I am able to cut from my own writing with sufficient editing, so don't be wedded to every word you write, and don't be afraid to delete that sentence or two you spent much time pondering, crafting, and fine-tuning but that upon third or fourth reading really isn't necessary to convey what needs to be conveyed.

That said, I would err on the side of presenting more information rather than less whenever space allows it. Conditional direct and indirect effects are functions of regression coefficients. I recommend providing these functions for the reader in the text itself, or in a text box in figures if you are graphically depicting your results, in order to better help your readers understand how the conditional effects you present and interpret map on to the regression coefficients you might be presenting in a table or elsewhere. Cole, Bedeian, and Bruch (2011) provides a good example of this (also see Berndt et al., 2013). Tables can also be an effective way of presenting how a conditional effect (direct or indirect) varies systematically as a function of a moderator or moderators. With a bit of creativity, you pack a lot of information pertinent to the moderation of mediation into a table, including bootstrap confidence intervals or p-values for conditional effects, as in Table 12.2.

The first section of Chapter 12 contained three analyses which I described as a "piecemeal" approach to conditional process modeling. I commented that this approach fails to integrate the three analyses into a coherent conditional process analysis, and then I proceeded to do so in section 12.2. This might suggest that this piecemeal approach is to be avoided because it is somehow wrong or misguided. Not so. Although this piecemeal approach is incomplete, there is nothing inherently wrong about describing and analyzing the components of a larger model first in order to better understand what your data are telling you. In fact, starting with a piecemeal approach and then following through with an integrated conditional process analysis can be an effective way of conveying your logic and argument. An alternative is to reverse the order of these two sets of analyses, first starting with the integrated model and presenting the findings, and then breaking it into its components and doing a more fine-grained analysis of different parts of the model to better understand what the integrated model is telling you. Neither of these two ways of telling the story is any better or worse than the other. How you tell your story is up to you.

Other than this advice, all of the recommendations and guidelines I offer for describing mediation and moderation analysis apply to conditional process analysis as well, since a conditional process model is an integration of a mediation and a moderation model. Don't leave certain details unstated, such as whether you centered variables used to construct products, whether your regression coefficients are unstandardized or standardized, and how dichotomous or multicategorical variables are coded. When using indicator coding, make sure you make it clear what the reference group is. Try not to use symbols without defining them for your reader. Avoid reporting standardized coefficients for dichotomous variables. Never report regression coefficients listed as "standardized" in a model that includes a product of antecedent variables. Specify how many bootstrap samples were generated when bootstrapping is used for inference, and provide the random number seed used.

14.3   Should I Use Structural Equation Modeling Instead of Regression Analysis?

The use of OLS regression when estimating a simple mediation model is commonplace. But as more boxes and arrows are added to a model, there is the widespread belief that a move to a maximum likelihood-based structural equation modeling (SEM) program such as LISREL, AMOS, or Mplus is required for model estimation or that doing so is in some sense better. Although there are some advantages to the use of SEM, doing so is not necessarily better or more appropriate. It depends on the context. For observed variable models as discussed in this book, it makes little difference, and your results will be unaffected by the choice. For a more detailed discussion of this topic than I provide here, including how the regression-based method implemented in PROCESS differs from SEM, see Hayes, Montoya, and Rockwood (2017).

To illustrate the similarity in results between the two approaches to model estimation, I estimated the serial mediation model for the presumed media influence analysis described beginning on page 172, but using Mplus and LISREL, two popular SEM programs. Using the PMI data, the corresponding Mplus MODEL command is

```
MODEL:
reaction ON import pmi cond;
import ON cond;
pmi ON import cond;
```

In LISREL, the code below[2] estimates the same model:

```
TI pmi example
DA NO=123 NI=4 MA=CM ME=ML
CM
0.25123284
0.15747035 3.01572704
0.11971878 0.64720778 1.74573504
0.12453352 1.25128282 0.91457584 2.40342196
LA
cond import pmi reaction
MO NY=4 NE=4 BE=FU,FI LY=ID PS=DI,FR TE=ZE
LE
xcond ximport xpmi xreaction
FR BE 2 1 BE 3 1 BE 3 2 BE 4 1 BE 4 2 BE 4 3
PD
OU SC ND=3
```

Excerpts of the resulting Mplus and LISREL output containing the coefficients for each of the paths as well as their standard errors can be found in Figure 14.1. Compare these to the OLS regression coefficients and standard errors from the PROCESS output in Figure 5.7 and you will find them to be extremely similar. In fact, notice that the OLS regression coefficients are the same as the maximum likelihood (ML) estimates from Mplus and LISREL to three decimal places. There are tiny differences between the standard errors, as would be expected given differences between OLS and ML in how these are calculated. Indeed, observe that the standard errors from Mplus and LISREL are even different from each other. These results are not specific to this example and apply to more complex models too (see Hayes et al., 2017).

The claim that some have made (e.g., Iacobucci, Saldanha, & Deng, 2007; Pek & Hoyle, 2016) that SEM is better or more appropriate than a set of OLS regressions for estimating an observed variable model is, in my

---

[2]I am not and probably never will be a LISREL user. I thank Kristopher Preacher for writing this LISREL code for me.

A

	Estimate	S.E.	Est./S.E.	Two-Tailed P-Value
REACTION ON				
IMPORT	0.324	0.070	4.662	0.000
PMI	0.397	0.091	4.336	0.000
COND	0.103	0.235	0.440	0.660
IMPORT ON				
COND	0.627	0.307	2.040	0.041
PMI ON				
IMPORT	0.196	0.066	2.959	0.003
COND	0.354	0.230	1.540	0.124

B

BETA

	xcond	ximport	xpmi	xreactio
xcond	- -	- -	- -	- -
ximport	0.627	- -	- -	- -
	(0.306)			
	2.048			
xpmi	0.354	0.196	- -	- -
	(0.229)	(0.066)		
	1.546	2.971		
xreactio	0.103	0.324	0.397	- -
	(0.234)	(0.069)	(0.091)	
	0.441	4.681	4.353	

FIGURE 14.1. Mplus (panel A) and LISREL (panel B) output corresponding to the serial multiple mediator model of the presumed media influence data.

opinion, simply not justified. In general, it makes no difference that should be of any concern to you, and you will probably find PROCESS far easier to use than any SEM program. Any difference you observe between OLS regression and SEM will be specific to the SEM program you are using, the algorithms for estimation and iteration used by your favored SEM program, convergence criteria set as defaults, how the covariance matrix is calculated, the number of decimal places of accuracy used when inputting data as a covariance matrix rather than using individual data, and so forth. Indeed, it could even be argued that inferential tests for the path coefficients from an SEM program are more likely to be slightly in error in smaller samples, as p-values from an SEM program are usually derived from the normal distribution rather than the t distribution. In large samples this won't matter, but in small samples, the t distribution used by an OLS regression procedure is more appropriate for the derivation of p-values for regression coefficients.

I am not saying that there are not advantages to the use of a SEM program when conducting a mediation analysis. An SEM program gives the user considerable control over the estimation method and how variables are configured in the model. Although a computational tool like PROCESS is valuable, it is still limited in what it can do, even with features discussed in Appendix B for building your own model. SEM programs also provide some measures of fit for models that are useful when a model is not saturated, thereby allowing for model comparisons. In complex models which involve constraints of some kind, it is possible to measure the fit of a model using various measures built into SEM programs and compare fit of nested models that differ by constraints imposed by the analyst.

But perhaps the biggest advantage to the use of SEM over OLS regression is the ability of an SEM program to estimate latent variable models, or models that combine observed and latent variables. Random measurement error in regression-based observed variable models such as those described in this book can bias estimates in various directions, depending on the reliability of the observed variables and whether variables measured with error are antecedents or consequents (see, e.g., Cole & Preacher, 2014; Darlington & Hayes, 2017; Ledgerwood & Shrout, 2011). Combining a structural model with a properly specified latent variable measurement model using SEM can reduce though will not necessarily eliminate the deleterious effects of random measurement error. I do not cover latent variable models in this book. Discussions of mediation analysis with latent variables can be found in Cheung and Lau (2008), Lau and Cheung (2012), or MacKinnon (2008). An example of a latent variable conditional process model can be found in Hayes and Preacher (2013).

14.4   The Pitfalls of Subgroups Analysis

There are numerous examples in the literature in which investigators attempted to test a moderated mediation hypothesis through the use of a *subgroups analysis*. When the proposed moderator is categorical, this approach involves conducting separate mediation analyses in each of the groups defined by levels of the moderator. Most typically, the moderator is dichotomous, such as two experimental conditions (Martinez, Piff, Mendoza-Denton, & Hinshaw, 2011; Tsai & Thomas, 2011), biological sex (e.g., Carvalho & Hopko, 2011; Dockray, Susman, & Dorn, 2009; Goldstein, Flett, & Wekerle, 2010; Hasan, Begue, & Bushman, 2012; Magee, Caputi, & Iverson, 2011; Molloy, Dixon, Hamer, & Sniehotta, 2010), children versus adolescents (Grøntved et al., 2011), or some other distinction such as school attended (Oldmeadow & Fiske, 2010). In some instances, the causal steps approach has been used in each group and claims of moderated mediation based on whether the criteria for mediation are met in one group but not another. Other researchers have based their claims of differential mediation across groups on formal tests of the indirect effect using more defensible inferential approaches such as bootstrap confidence intervals. However, the mediation analyses are conducted separately in the groups and claims of moderated mediation are based on the pattern of significance or nonsignificance of the indirect effects in the two groups.

For example, in a study of 111 children and adolescents, Dockray et al. (2009) examined whether the direct and indirect effects of depression on body mass, with cortisol reactivity as a possible mediator, differed between boys and girls. Using the causal steps approach along with a Sobel test for the indirect effect in separate analyses of the 56 boys and the 55 girls in the study, they found evidence of mediation only in girls. In girls, the estimated indirect effect of depression on Body Mass Index through cortisol reactivity was four times larger than the indirect effect in boys, but statistically significant only in girls. They also report evidence of a statistically significant association between depression and cortisol reactivity only in girls.

The goal of such an analysis is the same as the goal in conditional process analysis described in the last two chapters. Of interest is establishing whether the direct and/or indirect effects of X on Y vary systematically as a function of a moderator. But there are several problems associated with this subgroups approach to answering questions about the contingencies of mechanisms. These problems are severe enough that I cannot recommend using this approach.

First, the subgroups approach may not accurately reflect the process purportedly at work. For instance, if it is hypothesized that the indirect effect of X on Y through M is moderated due to the moderation of M's effect on Y by W, a subgroups analysis does not respect the implied equality of the other paths in the mediation model. A subgroups analysis, in the lingo of structural equation modeling, *freely* estimates *all* paths in the mediation model, thereby allowing them all to differ across groups. If one's moderated mediation hypothesis is not specific about which path is moderated, this is not a problem, but for more precise hypotheses about how the mechanism linking X to Y through M differs between groups, subgroups analysis is not a good choice.

Second, a direct or indirect effect may be descriptively different in the two groups but may not actually be different when subjected to a formal statistical test of differences. Alternatively, when the causal steps approach is used for assessing mediation in each group separately, the criteria for mediation (now outdated) may be met in one group but not in another, but that doesn't mean there is an indirect effect in one group but not another. A subgroups analysis provides no formal test of moderation of any of the paths in the model, nor does it provide a test of difference between direct or indirect effects across groups.

Third, the subgroups approach conflates statistical significance with sample size. If the groups differ in sample size, power to detect direct or indirect effects in the groups will differ. For instance, it may be that the indirect effect of X on Y through M is actually the same in the groups, but if one group is smaller than another, power to detect the indirect effect in the smaller group will be less than power in the larger group. The probability of a Type II error is inversely related to sample size, so Type II errors are more likely in the analysis of the smaller subgroups in the set. Thus, it can appear that the effects differ between groups when in fact the difference in results is due to differences in statistical power between the separate analyses.

Finally, this approach requires that the proposed moderator be categorical. Although it may be by design or measurement, this approach cannot be used when the moderator is a continuous variable. That in itself is not a problem, but the temptation to artificially categorize a continuous proposed moderator so that the subgroups analysis approach can be used may be too strong for some to resist, thereby resulting in two problems (artificial categorization and subgroups analysis). As discussed in section 7.6, rarely is artificial categorization of a continuum a good idea.

Two alternative approaches mitigate these problems to varying degrees. One is multiple-group structural equation modeling. This approach involves the simultaneous estimation of the paths in separate mediation models, but the fit of models that impose various equality constraints across groups on one or more paths is compared to the fit of models that freely estimate the paths across groups. For examples of this technique in action, see Dittmar, Halliwell, and Stirling (2009) and Lehmann, Burkert, Daig, Glaesmer, and Brähler (2011).

Multiple-group structural equation modeling provides a more formal test of moderation of various paths in the model, but it does not provide a formal test of difference between indirect effects unless additional steps are taken. For instance, if a model that constrains the paths from X to M and from M to Y to be the same across groups does not fit any worse than a model that freely estimates those paths across groups, this suggests that the indirect effect of X on Y through M is the same in the groups. Alternatively,

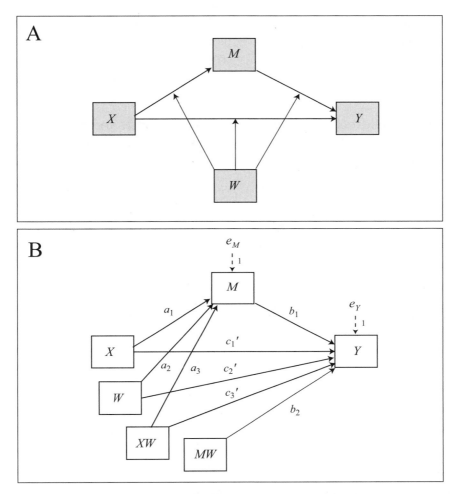

FIGURE 14.2. A conceptual (panel A) and statistical (panel B) diagram representing a simple mediation model with all three paths moderated by a common moderator.

a program such as Mplus could be used to impose an equality constraint on the product of paths across groups to see if such a model fits no worse than one that allows the product to differ across groups.

The second alternative is the kind of regression-based conditional process analysis that has been the focus of the last three chapters. The form of the conceptual and corresponding statistical model will depend on which paths in the causal system are believed to be moderated and which are not. For the sake of illustration, consider a model that allows all three of the paths to be moderated by W. Such a model is represented in conceptual form in Figure 14.2, panel A. This model in the form of a statistical diagram appears as in Figure 14.2, panel B, which represents two equations:

$$M = i_M + a_1 X + a_2 W + a_3 XW + e_M \qquad (14.1)$$
$$Y = i_Y + c_1' X + c_2' W + c_3' XW + b_1 M + b_2 MW + e_Y \qquad (14.2)$$

The indirect effect of X on Y through M is defined as the product of the $X \to M$ and $M \to Y$ effects, each of which is moderated. The effect of X on M is derived from equation 14.1 by grouping terms involving X and then factoring out X, resulting in

$$\theta_{X \to M} = a_1 + a_3 W$$

which is a function of W. Likewise, the effect of M on Y comes from equation 14.2 and is constructed in the same fashion, grouping terms involving M and factoring out M:

$$\theta_{M \to Y} = b_1 + b_2 W$$

So the effect of M on Y is also a function of W. The indirect effect of X on Y through M is the product of these two functions:

$$\theta_{X \to M}\theta_{M \to Y} = (a_1 + a_3 W)(b_1 + b_2 W) \qquad (14.3)$$

which is itself a conditional effect, in that it is a function of W.

The direct effect of X on Y is also conditional. From equation 14.2, grouping terms involving X and then factoring out X yields

$$\theta_{X \to Y} = c_1' + c_3' W \qquad (14.4)$$

So the direct effect is conditional because it is a function of W.

When W is a dichotomous moderator variable, estimation of this model faithfully represents the spirit of a subgroups analysis approach in that it allows all three paths to differ between the two groups, but the paths are estimated using the entire dataset rather than two separate analyses, each based on a subset of the data. A test of moderation for each path in the model is available in the form of the regression coefficients for the products along with their tests of significance. For instance, c_3' estimates the difference in the direct effect between the two groups, and an inferential test that $_Tc_3' = 0$ can be used to rule out "chance" as the explanation for the observed difference. Equation 14.3 can be used to derive estimates of the indirect effect for different values of W, and the direct effect conditioned on a value of the moderator can be derived from equation 14.4.

This model can be estimated by PROCESS using model 59. In addition to the regression coefficients, PROCESS will provide tests of significance and confidence intervals for the conditional direct and indirect effects, the latter based on a bootstrap confidence interval. Important to the point I am making about the deficiencies of subgroups analysis, PROCESS will automatically conduct a test of the difference between the indirect effects in the two groups in the form of a bootstrap confidence interval for the index of moderated mediation, which is equal to the difference between the two conditional indirect effects when W is dichotomous.

Unlike when using multigroup structural equation modeling, the regression based approach implemented by PROCESS does not require the moderator to be categorical. As noted earlier, equation 14.3 is a function that involves W. This is more easily seen by expressing it in an alternative form

$$
\begin{aligned}
\theta_{X \to M} \theta_{M \to Y} &= (a_1 + a_3 W)(b_1 + b_2 W) \\
&= a_1 b_1 + a_1 b_2 W + a_3 b_1 W + a_3 b_2 W^2 \\
&= a_1 b_1 + (a_1 b_2 + a_3 b_1)W + a_3 b_2 W^2
\end{aligned}
\tag{14.5}
$$

By plugging a value of W into equation 14.5, you get the conditional indirect effect of X on Y through M at that value of W. So the indirect effect can be derived for any hypothetical or real set of people with a given value of W. This can be repeated for as many values of W as desired to examine how the indirect effect varies with W.

But how do you formally test the difference between two indirect effects when W is equal to some value w_1 compared to when W equals a different value w_2? In Chapters 11 and 12, I introduced an approach based on the index of moderated mediation and discussed that, in those examples, a bootstrap confidence interval for the index of moderated mediation simultaneously provides both a test of moderation of the indirect effect and a test of the difference between two conditional indirect effects conditioned on two different values of W, *regardless* of the values of W you use.

But this model is different than the two used in those chapters. In those models, W was specified as a moderator of only one of the paths defining the indirect effect. The mathematical consequence of this is that the conditional indirect effect is a linear function of W, and an inference about the weight for W in that function provides a test of the difference between two conditional indirect effects. But when W is specified as a moderator of more than one path that defines an indirect effect, the conditional indirect effect becomes a nonlinear function of W, as in equation 14.5. There are two weights for W in this function that determine the relationship between W and the indirect effect. So a test of moderation of the indirect effect does not reduce to a test on a single weight for W in the function. There is no index of moderated mediation for this model.

To test moderation of mediation in a model that specifies a quantitative W as a moderator of more than one path that defines an indirect effect, choose two values of W and generate a bootstrap confidence interval for the difference between the two conditional indirect effects at those values of W. PROCESS makes this easy with the use of the **contrast** option. When this option is used in estimating a conditional process model, PROCESS generates bootstrap confidence intervals for all possible pairwise comparisons between the conditional indirect effects in the output. For example, if PROCESS generates the conditional effect effect of X when W is equal to the 16th, 50th, and 84th percentiles of the distribution, the inclusion of **contrast=1** in the command line produces all possible comparisons between these three conditional indirect effects. Or if you choose the values of W using the **wmodval** option, PROCESS will produce bootstrap confidence intervals for all the possible differences between the conditional indirect effects at the values of W you choose.

Using this approach, you can say that W moderates the indirect effect of X on Y through M if any bootstrap confidence interval for a difference between any pair of conditional indirect effects does not include zero. However, if all of the bootstrap confidence intervals include zero, this does *not* mean that W is not a moderator of the indirect effect. It could be that you simply haven't correctly identified values of W where the two conditional indirect effects are different. So this approach can confirm moderation of mediation in a model of this sort, but it cannot disconfirm it.

14.5 Can a Variable Simultaneously Mediate and Moderate Another Variable's Effect?

Can a variable both mediate and moderate another variable's effect on a third? In Chapter 1, I described a process in which internalization of the "thin-as-ideal" standard as portrayed in health and beauty magazines could be construed as either a mediator or moderator of the effect of exposure to the standard on various mental and physical health consequences. Frequent childhood exposure to the thin-as-ideal standard could prompt a greater internalization of the norm relative to those with less frequent exposure, with greater internalization leading to consequences such as negative body image and disordered eating at adolescence. More exposure during adolescence could then differentially affect subsequent body image and disordered eating, depending on the extent to which internalization of the standard had occurred in childhood.

So, in principle, it seems that a variable could play the roles of both moderator and mediator. However, it could be argued that exposure and health consequences measured at two different times really aren't the same variables, even if they are given the same name. Furthermore, this example does not by any means establish that it is sensible or even possible to construe a variable as *simultaneously* mediating and moderating one variable's effect on another.

To be sure, there are examples in the literature in which investigators used a variable as a mediator of X's effect on Y in one analysis but that same variable played the role of moderator of the *same* X's effect on the *same* Y in a second analysis. For instance, D'Lima et al. (2012) conducted a study on college students examining the relationship between general self-regulation (e.g., goal planning, tracking progress toward goals) and problems experienced as a result of alcohol use. They found that protective behavioral strategies (e.g., eating before drinking, not playing drinking games) functioned as a mediator of this association, with self-regulators more likely to engage in protective behavioral strategies, which in turn was related to the likelihood of experiencing alcohol-related problems. Yet in a subsequent analysis, they found that the association between self-regulation and alcohol-related problems was more pronounced among students who did not use protective behavioral strategies relative to those who did. This is moderation.

Nir and Druckman (2008) offer another such example in a study of a local election in the Minneapolis area. They examined the extent to which regular voter exposure to balanced, two-sided news coverage of the candidates running for political office increased the length of time it took a voter to decide whom to vote for. They found that more of such exposure was associated with a more delayed time to decision relative to those with less exposure, but only among voters who expressed ambivalence about the candidates running for office. Thus, ambivalence moderated the association between exposure to balanced coverage and decision timing. They also examined whether ambivalence mediated the effect of exposure to balanced coverage on voting timing. That is, perhaps exposure to balanced coverage causes ambivalence, which in turn increases time to decision. But they found no evidence of such a process at work.

These two examples as well as others (e.g., Comello & Farman, 2016; Dakanalis et al., 2014; Kapikiran, 2012; Peltonen, Quota, Sarraj, & Punamäki, 2010; Ning, 2012; Sharma-Patel & Brown, 2016; Sirgy, Yu, Lee, Wei, & Huang, 2012; Somer, Ginzberg, & Kramer, 2012; Versey & Kaplan, 2012) suggest that investigators are comfortable with the idea that the same variable could both mediate and moderate the effect of X on Y. Yet according to the analytical logic of what has come to be known as the MacArthur approach to mediation and moderation analysis (Kraemer et al., 2002, 2008;

Kraemer, 2011), it is not possible for a variable M that is construed as an effect of X to moderate X's effect. According to this school of thought, moderators must precede X and be uncorrelated with X, in which case M could not possibly transmit X's effect on Y.

The position that a moderator of X's effect must be uncorrelated with X is a fringe, unorthodox position. As an ideal, this may be a defensible position to take, but as a *requirement*, I disagree. Furthermore, the very model that Kraemer et al. (2002, 2008) recommend as being the best approach to testing for mediation of the effect of X on Y by M is one in which M simultaneously plays the role of both moderator and mediator, at least mathematically. According to their approach, to establish M as a mediator of X's effect on Y, X must precede M in time and also be related to M, as established by statistical significance of X in a model of M. In addition, in a model of Y that includes X, M, and their product XM, one must find evidence of either a "main effect" of M on Y or an interaction between X and M.

Their model is depicted in conceptual form in panel A of Figure 14.3 and in statistical form in panel B. This model translates into the following equations:

$$M = i_M + aX + e_M \tag{14.6}$$
$$Y = i_Y + c_1'X + bM + c_2'XM + e_Y \tag{14.7}$$

After estimating the coefficients in equations 14.6 and 14.7, the MacArthur approach deems M a mediator if a is statistically different from zero and either b or c_2' is statistically different from zero. Kraemer et al. (2008) recommend centering M around a "central value" such as the median or zero, depending on the scaling of M, so that b estimates a "main effect" of M on Y. Whether b estimates a main effect as the concept is defined in ANOVA will depend on whether and how M is centered. They also recommend coding X with values of -0.5 and 0.5 if X is dichotomous (as it typically is in their treatment of this topic because they focus their discussion primarily on moderation and mediation in randomized clinical trials).

The MacArthur approach is essentially a modification to the causal steps approach described by Baron and Kenny (1986) and thus suffers from the same weakness, in that it uses a statistical significance criterion at each step in the causal model in order to claim M is a mediator. In addition, Kraemer et al. (2002, 2008) don't discuss formally quantifying the indirect effect. In this model, M's effect on Y is not b but, rather, $b + c_2'X$. Thus, the indirect effect of X on Y through M is $a(b + c_2'M)$, meaning it is a function of X (see, e.g., Preacher et al., 2007). I discuss this further in section 14.6

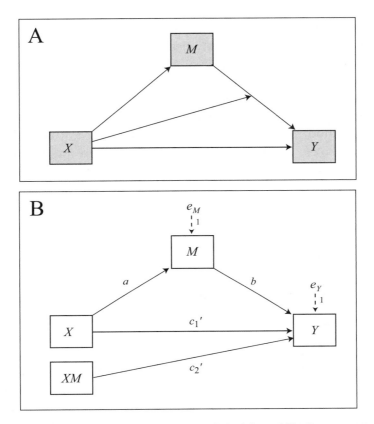

FIGURE 14.3. A conceptual (panel A) and statistical (panel B) diagram representing a conditional process model in which X moderates its own indirect effect.

In the model they recommend using to test for mediation, X is estimated to affect Y indirectly through M, as well as directly independent of M. But the direct effect of X in this model is not c_1' as it might seem. Grouping terms in equation 14.7 involving X and then factoring out X yields the direct effect of X on Y:

$$\theta_{X \rightarrow Y} = c_1' + c_2'M$$

So the direct effect of X is conditioned on M. In other words, if c_2' in equation 14.7 is statistically different from zero, M moderates X's direct effect on Y. The MacArthur camp would reject this as a possibility, as a moderator can't be correlated with X. By their criteria, M *can* be deemed a mediator of X's effect if a and c_2' are both statistically different from zero, but that very circumstance implies that M is *not* uncorrelated with X. At the same time, a statistically significant c_2' means that X's direct effect on Y is moderated by M. Thus, in the model Kraemer et al. (2002, 2008) recommend as the best approach to testing mediation, meeting one subset of their criteria for establishing M as a mediator also means that M could be construed as a moderator of X's effect, at least statistically or mathematically so.

Just because something is mathematically possible doesn't mean that it is sensible theoretically or substantively interpretable when it happens (as it does, as evidenced in some of the example studies cited on page 401). I will not take a firm position on whether construing M as a simultaneous mediator and moderator of a variable's effect could ever make substantive or theoretical sense. I am uncomfortable categorically ruling out the possibility that M could be a moderator just because it is correlated with X. My guess is that there are many real-life processes in which things caused by X also influence the size of the effect of X on Y measured well after X. But M would have to be causally prior to Y in order for this to be possible, implying that M could also be construed as a mediator if M is caused in part by X but also influences Y in some fashion.

14.6 Interaction between *X* and *M* in Mediation Analysis

We saw in Chapters 11 through 13 that an indirect effect can be moderated if one or more of the paths linking X to Y through a mediator M is a function of a moderator W. There are many ways to combine moderation and mediation, depending on the number of mediators and which paths in the mediation process are specified as moderated and by which and how many moderators.

Thus far we have ignored the possibility that X may moderate M's effect on Y. We have, essentially, assumed that the relationship between M and Y does not vary as a function of X. But we could make M's effect on Y a function of X in a mediation model by including the product of X and M in the model of Y. The resulting set of equations for a simple mediation model with X moderating M's effect on Y is

$$M = i_M + aX + e_M \tag{14.8}$$
$$Y = i_Y + c_1'X + bM + c_2'XM + e_Y \tag{14.9}$$

which you probably recognize from the discussion of the MacArthur approach to mediation analysis just described in section 14.5 (that is, equations 14.8 and 14.9 are the same as equations 14.6 and 14.7). If we were to fix c_2' to zero, then this set of equations reduces to the equations for a simple mediation model as described in earlier chapters. In that sense, we are assuming no interaction between X and M when we fail to include XM in the model of Y by fixing c_2' to zero.

Without this assumption, X becomes a moderator of its own indirect effect, as the indirect effect of X on Y is the product of the effect of X on M and the effect of M on Y. The effect of X on M is estimated with a in equation 14.8 and the effect of M on Y is $\theta_{M \to Y} = b + c_2' X$ from equation 14.9. So the indirect effect of X on Y through M is

$$a\theta_{M \to Y} = a(b + c_2' X) = ab + ac_2' X \qquad (14.10)$$

which is a function of X. If X is continuous, this means that the change in Y that results from a change in X through the effect of X on M depends on where you start on X. This wouldn't make sense if X were dichotomous, as there is only one "change" in X that is possible—the transition between the two states of X that code the two groups. And observe that in this model, M can also be construed as a moderator of the direct effect of X, since X's direct effect on Y is $c_1' + c_3' M$. So M mathematically functions as both mediator and moderator of X's effect (as discussed in section 14.5).

There is a camp of methodologists who recommend always allowing X and M to interact in a mediation model, with or without any empirical evidence of such interaction. This complicates things somewhat, and requires the introduction of new terms such as *natural*, *pure*, and *controlled* direct and indirect effects. The mathematics of this approach relies on the counterfactual or potential outcomes approach to causal analysis that is popular in statistics, less widely known in the social science research community, and, to many, a little harder to digest. For discussions of this approach, see Imai, Keele, and Tingley (2010), Muthén and Asparouhov (2015), Valeri and VanderWeele (2013), and VanderWeele (2015).

14.7 Repeated Measures Designs

In all examples throughout this book, cases were measured on mediator(s) M and outcome Y only once. In nonexperimental studies, they were measured once on the causal antecedent X, whereas in experimental studies they were assigned to one of two or three experimental conditions used as X in the model. Although such research designs are common, also common are "repeated measures" designs that involve measuring cases more than once on the variables in a mediation model. There are several forms such designs take, and there are approaches to mediation and conditional process analysis that can be used depending on the form of the design.

For example, suppose participants in an experiment are asked to look at two advertisements for a product, with the advertisements different from each other on some dimension coded in variable X, such as its price, or whether it contains a customer testimonial or a picture. Perhaps following exposure to each advertisement, participants are asked to provide some kind of emotional response to each ad, and also how likely they would be to purchase the product. A variation on this design would involve exposing a person to many different versions of an advertisement (rather than just two) that are manipulated on X, with emotional responses and willingness to purchase measurements following exposure to each of the many advertisements he or she sees. Whether two or many, of interest is whether the effect of X on Y operates indirectly through M. But unlike in the examples in this book, there are at least two measurements of M and two measurements of Y.

For the two-condition version of such a study, Judd, Kenny, and Mc-Clelland (2001) discuss a simple-to-implement approach to mediation and moderation analysis. Their treatment of mediation analysis relies on the causal steps logic described in section 4.1. Montoya and Hayes (2017) offer a mathematically equivalent approach that is based on an estimate of the indirect effect of X on Y through M with inference for the indirect effect using bootstrap or Monte Carlo confidence intervals. PROCESS has no implementation of this method, but Montoya and Hayes (2017) provide and document MEMORE, a macro for SPSS and SAS that does all of the computations. MEMORE can be downloaded from *www.akmontoya.com*.

In the many-versions of X variation on this study, multilevel mediation analysis is the appropriate analytical approach. In a multilevel media-tion analysis, the direct and indirect effect of X on Y can be estimated in each participant in the study, and the average direct and indirect ef-fect derived. Multilevel mediation is flexible in that you can fix paths in the mediation process to be the same across participants or different. Multilevel mediation can also be combined with moderation, resulting in multilevel conditional process analysis. Some journal article-length treat-ments of multilevel mediation analysis include Bauer et al. (2006), Kenny, Korchmaros, and Bolger (2003), Preacher, Zypher, and Zhang (2010), and Zhang (2009). Multilevel mediation analysis is usually done in a structural equation modeling program capable of multilevel analysis, such as Mplus. PROCESS cannot do multilevel analysis, but a macro for SPSS exists called MLMED that can conduct multilevel mediation and some forms of con-ditional process analysis. For the latest version of MLMED, point your browser to *www.njrockwood.com*.

It is common to measure M and Y repeatedly over time, with the goal of understanding how variation in X influences change in Y over time through changes in M over time. In such a design, X may be experimentally manipulated with each participant receiving one version of X, or X could be observed once or also measured over time. An example would be a

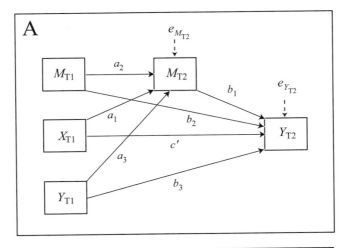

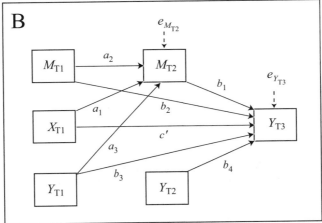

FIGURE 14.4. Statistical diagrams of longitudinal panel mediation models with two (A) and three (B) waves of measurement.

study in which participants in a randomized clinical trial receive one of two forms of therapy (i.e., X is manipulated, with participants randomly assigned to one of the forms), and symptoms of some kind of ailment Y measured at the time therapy starts as well as at one or two (or more) follow up periods. If a proposed mediator M is also measured repeatedly over time, it is possible to examine how the therapy influences Y through its effect on M.

Your impulse in such a design might be to calculate difference scores by subtracting earlier measurements from later measurements and then using these difference scores as M and Y in an ordinary mediation analysis. Although this is common, I discourage the use of difference scores such as this when interest is in change over time. Difference scores tend to be negative correlated with earlier measurements, and artifacts related to regression to the mean or measurement ceilings or floors can make it difficult to interpret the results of such an analysis. Models of difference scores also tend to be suboptimal, in that they force some of the weights in a regression model to one rather than letting the OLS criterion figure out how to best weight the variables (see, e.g., Darlington & Hayes, 2017).

Like Valente and MacKinnon (2017), I recommend modeling later measurements while using earlier measurements (a.k.a. "lags") as covariates. So a mediation model with X measured at time 1 and M and Y measured at both time 1 and time 2 would be set up as in Figure 14.4, panel A. This diagram visually represents the following equations:

$$M_{T2} = i_{M_{T2}} + a_1 X_{T1} + a_2 M_{T1} + a_3 Y_{T1} + e_{M_{T2}}$$
$$Y_{T2} = i_{Y_{T2}} + c' X_{T1} + b_1 M_{T2} + b_2 M_{T1} + b_3 Y_{T1} + e_{Y_{T2}}$$

The direct effect of X on Y is c' and the indirect effect is $a_1 b_1$. Additional covariates could be included in the equations of M_{T2} and Y_{T2} if desired. Any moderators could be included anywhere in the system to allow the indirect or direct effects to be moderated.

Structural equation modeling is often used for analyses of *panel* data such as this. But PROCESS can estimate a mediation or conditional process model of this type by using lags of variables as covariates:

```
process y=y2/x=x1/m=m2/cov=m1 y1/model=4.
```

replacing y2, x1, m2, m1, and y1 in the code above with your variable names would estimate the model in Figure 14.4, panel A. Assuming the data were held in a file named TIME, the equivalent SAS PROCESS command is

```
%process (data=time,y=y2,x=x1,m=m2,cov=m1 y1,model=4);
```

When a third measurement period is available and Y is measured in that third period, the temporal ordering of the measurement of M and Y can be taken advantage of by modeling Y at time 3 from M at time 2 and X at time 1. The equations for such a model, depicted in Figure 14.4, panel B, are

$$M_{T2} = i_{M_{T2}} + a_1 X_{T1} + a_2 M_{T1} + a_3 Y_{T1} + e_{M_{T2}}$$
$$Y_{T3} = i_{Y_{T3}} + c' X_{T1} + b_1 M_{T2} + b_2 M_{T1} + b_3 Y_{T1} + b_4 Y_{T2} + e_{Y_{T3}}$$

The direct and indirect effects of X on Y are still c' and $a_1 b_1$, respectively. In PROCESS, we have to use the **cmatrix** command to tell PROCESS to put Y_{T2} in the model of Y_{T3} but not M_{T2}:

```
process y=y3/x=x1/m=m2/cov=m1 y1 y2/cmatrix=1,1,0,1,1,1/model=4.
```

The equivalent SAS PROCESS command is

```
%process (data=time,y=y3,x=x1,m=m2,cov=m1 y1 y2,cmatrix=1 1 0 1 1 1,
    model=4);
```

More complex models can be set up with more than one mediator, and any path in the system could also be moderated by a variable measured at any point in time. Lags could also be used as moderators, or any other variable you believe may influence the size of the direct or indirect effect. For example, the relationship between M_{T2} and Y_{T3} could be specified as dependent on Y_{T2} or M_{T1}, or some other individual difference measured only once. For a more detailed discussion of mediation in panel designs like this, see Cole and Maxwell (2003), Little, Preacher, Selig, and Card (2007), and Selig and Preacher (2009).

Another analytical option is available when M and Y are measured at least three times, regardless of the number of measurements of X. *Parallel process latent growth modeling* allows for X (either in a single measurement or manipulation, or its change over time) to influence the trajectory in change in the mediator, which in turn can influence the trajectory in the change in Y over time. PROCESS cannot do latent growth modeling, but it can be done in most structural equation modeling programs. See Cheong et al. (2003) and Selig and Preacher (2009) for discussions of the mathematics of mediation analysis in a latent growth context.

14.8   Dichotomous, Ordinal, Count, and Survival Outcomes

This book is focused squarely and exclusively on linear regression analysis using the least squares criterion as the computational backbone of mediation, moderation, and conditional process analysis. In all examples that included a mediation component, all mediator(s) M and final consequent variable Y were always treated as continuous dimensions with at least interval level measurement properties. But no doubt you will find yourself in a situation where M and/or Y is dichotomous, or an ordinal scale with only a few scale points, or perhaps a count variable. Although such variables can be modeled with OLS regression, doing so is controversial because there are better methods that respect the special statistical considerations that come up when such variables are on the left sides of equations.

There are many books on the analysis of outcome variables such as these, some that include discussions of moderation analysis through the inclusion of the product of focal antecedent and moderator. There is also a growing literature on mediation analysis with noncontinuous, ordinal, discrete variables. Construction of direct and indirect effects is not always as simple as multiplying model coefficients, and the path analysis algebra that partitions total effects into direct and indirect components discussed in Chapters 3 through 6 sometimes breaks down.

As of the date of publication of this book, you will find two books on mediation analysis that offer a more general treatment than I offer in this one that includes discussions of dealing with ordinal, count, or dichotomous mediators or outcomes. VanderWeele (2015) focuses primarily on the use STATA and SAS, whereas Muthén, Muthén, and Asparouhov (2016) is dedicated to Mplus, but there are lessons to be learned in these books about the mechanics that generalize across software platforms. Many journal articles exist as well that focus on methods for dealing with specific types of variables in mediation analysis that cannot or should not be modeled with OLS regression. See, for example, Breen, Karlson, and Holm (2013), Imai et al. (2010), MacKinnon and Dwyer (1993), MacKinnon, Lockwood, Brown, Wang, and Hoffman (2007), Valeri and VanderWeele (2013), and VanderWeele and Vansteelandt (2010)

If your analytical problem focuses on modeling of time-to-event data, where censoring is typical because an event doesn't occur for some people during the measurement period, you might find an interest in reading some of the literature on mediation analysis with survival data. See Gelfand, MacKinnon, DeRubeis, and Baraldi (2016), Lange and Hansen (2011), and VanderWeele (2011) for treatments of this topic.

14.9   Chapter Summary

We often approach the study design phase of a study with clear ideas about what we will find when the study is conducted and the kind of paper we will write after the data are in and analyzed. But things can go wrong along the way. Reality sometimes intervenes and shows us something we didn't expect. Sometimes our a priori conceptions about the processes we are trying to study turn out to be incorrect. Good data analysis often requires making decisions about how to proceed when various stages of the analysis reveal things unexpected. What to do isn't always obvious, and the course of action you take will depend on your own philosophy about science and the modeling enterprise as a whole. Of course, your course of action will influence how you tell your story, and I provide some guidance on writing about mediation, moderation, and conditional process analysis in this chapter.

Medation, moderation, and conditional process models can be estimated using either OLS regression-based path analysis, as described in this book, or using SEM software. When all variables are *manifest* or *observed*, it generally doesn't make any difference which approach you use. You will get the same results. Most researchers will find PROCESS much easier to use than the typical SEM program, and PROCESS generates many statistics automatically that would be much harder to generate in the typical SEM program. But SEM programs can be used for latent variable models that combine structural and measurement components and that better deal with random measurement error than does PROCESS.

There are many interesting controversies and debates in the mediation and moderation analysis literature, only a small fraction of which I even attempt to address in this book. One controversy I do address pertains to whether mediation and moderation are mutually exclusive. Can a variable function as both a mediator and a moderator in the same analysis? Can a variable both mediate and moderate another variable's effect? Although I do not take a stand on this controversy, I do illustrate in this chapter that mathematically it is possible, even if it turns out it could never make sense substantively or theoretically. I also show that a model with M both mediating and moderating X's effect requires an interaction between X and M. I also provide some references to methodological approaches to mediation analysis that allow for interaction between X and M rather than assuming it absent.

I take a stand in this chapter on the practice of subgroups analysis when attempting to answer questions about whether mediation is moderated. Conditional process modeling allows you to model the conditional nature of mechanisms without having to slice the data up and conduct separate mediation analyses on subsets of the data. There are various arguments for avoiding this method of analysis, and I recommend you avoid it. With an understanding of the principles described in Chapters 11 through 13, there are few legitimate excuses for employing this procedure.

Mediation, moderation, and conditional process analysis is possible when people are repeatedly measured on one or more variables. I have neglected this topic in this book, but in this final chapter I provided some guidance on statistical approaches available and showed how PROCESS can be used to model the mechanisms and the contingencies of mechanisms for some repeated measures designs. Also neglected in this book is how to test mediation hypotheses when the variables being modeled are not amenable to ordinary least squares regression. I provide some references you can consult when you are in this situation.

I said in the preface to my first book that a book is never finished, you simply run out of time. Twelve years and a couple of additional books later, this remains true to me. I am again out of time and out of space, having only scratched the surface of how the ideas described in this book can be applied and extended. Furthermore, I imagine that there are many new questions you may now have about mediation and moderation analysis, whether epistemological or practical, that perhaps a future edition will better address. I know that if you have been following along, you have certainly developed some skills that will help you to answer some of these questions on your own. I hope that you have found some of the principles and procedures I have described here useful in advancing your own research agenda and that PROCESS makes your analytical life a little bit easier. So enjoy PROCESS, and happy modeling!

APPENDICES

APPENDICES

Appendix A
Using PROCESS

This appendix describes how to install and execute PROCESS, how to set up a PROCESS command, and it documents its many features, some of which are not described elsewhere in this book. As PROCESS is modified and features are added, supplementary documentation will be released at *www.processmacro.org*. Check this web page regularly for updates.

This documentation focuses on the SPSS version of PROCESS. Most features and functions described below are available in the SAS version as well and work as described here, with minor modifications to the syntax. A section of this documentation (starting on page 580) describes some of the differences in syntax structure for the SAS version compared to what is described below.

Overview

PROCESS is a computational tool for observed variable path analysis-based moderation and mediation analysis as well as their integration as conditional process analysis. In addition to estimating model coefficients, standard errors, t- and p-values, and confidence intervals using ordinary least squares regression, PROCESS generates direct and indirect effects in mediation models, conditional effects (i.e., "simple slopes") in moderation models, and conditional indirect effects in conditional process models with a single or multiple mediators. PROCESS offers various methods for probing two- and three-way interactions and can construct percentile bootstrap and Monte Carlo confidence intervals for indirect effects. In mediation models, multiple mediator variables can be specified to operate in parallel, in serial, or combinations of parallel and serial. Preprogrammed models can be modifed or a custom model constructed from scratch. Heteroscedasticity-consistent standard errors are available for inference about model coefficients, in the Sobel test and construction of Monte Carlo confidence intervals for indirect effects, and when testing and probing interactions in moderation analysis. Various measures of effect size for indirect, direct, and total effects are generated in simple as multiple mediator models, along with bootstrap confidence intervals for effect size inference. Paths in conditional process models can be estimated as moderated by one or two variables either additively or multiplicatively. Bootstrap confidence intervals for all model coefficients are also available.

PROCESS operates differently than a structural equation modeling program, although the use of structural equation modeling will frequently generate results that are similar or identical to those produced by PROCESS. For a discussion of the similarities and differences between, and strengths and weaknesses of PROCESS relative to structural equation modeling, see Hayes et al. (2017).

Users familiar with PROCESS version 2 should take note of the changes to the syntax structure in this most current release, beginning on page 578, prior to attempting to use PROCESS.

Preparing for Use

PROCESS can be used as either a syntax-driven macro or installed as a custom dialog menu item for setting up the model using SPSS's point-and-click user interface. When executed as a macro, the process.sps file (an SPSS syntax file available from *www.processmacro.org*) should first be opened as a *syntax* file (not as a *script* file). Once it has been opened, execute the entire file exactly as is. *Do not modify the code at all prior to executing it*. Once the process.sps program has been executed, it can be closed and the PROCESS command is available for use in any SPSS program. Running process.sps activates the macro, and it will remain active so long as SPSS remains open. The PROCESS file must be loaded and reexecuted each time SPSS is opened in order to use the features of the PROCESS command. See the "Examples" section starting on page 554 for how to set up a PROCESS command in a syntax window. Please also read "Model Specification" (page 558) and the "Notes" section (page 582) for important details pertinent to execution, including calling PROCESS with the SPSS INSERT command.

To install PROCESS as a custom dialog into the SPSS menus, install process.spd (a dialog builder file available from *www.processmacro.org*) from the Utilities or Extensions menu (depending on your version of SPSS). Administrative access to the machine on which PROCESS is being installed is required when using a Windows operating system, and you must execute SPSS as an administrator to install a custom dialog file. Once successfully installed, PROCESS will appear as a new menu item in SPSS nested under Analyze → Regression (though this location may change with new releases of SPSS). If you do not have administrative access, contact your local information technology specialist for assistance in setting up administrative access to the machine on which you wish to install PROCESS.

Although the dialog box offers a "Paste" button, it should not be used, as doing so will produce thousands of lines of syntax in your syntax window. Some options available in the macro cannot be accessed through the dialog box (see page 580). Users interested in embedding PROCESS commands in their own syntax should use the syntax-driven macro (process.sps) rather than the custom dialog. Execution of process.sps as described earlier is not necessary when the model is set up using a dialog box. Conversely, installing the dialog menu does not eliminate the need to first execute process.sps if PROCESS is to be operated using the PROCESS command through the execution of syntax rather than using the dialog box.

Syntax Structure

The first line of syntax below is required for all PROCESS commands. The remaining commands in brackets are either optional or model dependent. Brackets, parentheses, and asterisks should not be included in the PROCESS command. "**" denotes the default argument when the option is omitted.

```
process y=yvar/x=xvar
                [/m=mvlist]
                [/w=wvar]
                [/z=zvar]
                [/model=num]
                [/cov=covlist]
                [/wmodval=wval]
                [/zmodval=zval]
                [/boot=z(5000**)]
                [/maxboot=maxz(10000**)]
                [/mc=g(0**)]
                [/conf=ci(95**)]
                [/effsize=(0**)(1)]
                [/normal=(0**)(1)]
                [/jn=(0**)(1)]
                [/hc=(0**)(1)(2)(3)(4)]
                [/covmy=(0**)(1)(2)]
                [/total=(0**)(1)]
                [/center=(0**)(1)]
                [/covcoeff=(0**)(1)]
                [/moments=(0**)(1)]
```

```
[/mcx=(0**)(1)(2)(3)(4)(5)]
[/mcw=(0**)(1)(2)(3)(4)(5)]
[/mcz=(0**)(1)(2)(3)(4)(5)]
[/xcatcode=xcodes]
[/wcatcode=wcodes]
[/zcatcode=zcodes]
[/plot=(0**)(1)(2)]
[/seed=sd]
[/intprobe=alpha(.10**)]
[/modelbt=(0**)(1)]
[/decimals=dec(F10.4**)]
[/save=(0**)(1)(2)]
[/contrast=(0**)(1)(2)(wval1,zval2;wval2,zval2)]
[/bmatrix=bmat]
[/wmatrix=wmat]
[/zmatrix=zmat]
[/wzmatrix=wzmat]
[/cmatrix=cmat].
```

Examples

(1) Simple Moderation

```
process y=newlaws/x=alcohol/w=concerns/cov=use age/model=1/center=1
    /plot=1/jn=1.
```

- Estimates a simple moderation model with the effect of alcohol on newlaws moderated by concerns.

- use and age are included in the model as covariates.

- alcohol and concerns are mean centered prior to analysis.

- Generates the conditional effects of alcohol on newlaws at values of concerns equal to the 16th, 50th, and 84th percentiles of the distribution in the sample.

- Produces a table of estimated values of newlaws for various values of alcohol and concerns.

- Implements the Johnson–Neyman technique to identify the values on the continuum of concerns at which point the effect of alcohol on `newlaws` transitions between statistically significant and nonsignificant at the .05 level.

(2) Moderated Moderation

```
process y=mathprob/x=treat/w=explms/z=gender/model=3/wmodval=4,5.
```

- Estimates a moderated moderation model predicting `mathprob` from `treat` while including a three-way interaction between `treat`, `explms`, and `gender` in the model along with all required two-way interactions.

- Generates the conditional effect of `treat` on `mathprob` for both males and females when `explms` = 4 and when `explms` = 5.

(3) Simple Mediation

```
process y=votes/x=donate/m=winner/model=4/total=1/effsize=1/boot=10000.
```

- Estimates the total and direct effect of `donate` on `votes`, as well as the indirect effect of `donate` on `votes` through `winner`.

- Generates a 95% percentile bootstrap confidence interval for the indirect effect using 10,000 bootstrap samples.

- Produces estimates of various indices of effect size for the direct, indirect, and total effects.

(4) Parallel Multiple Mediation

```
process y=know/x=educ/m=attn elab/cov=sex age/model=4/contrast=1
    /normal=1/conf=90/save=1.
```

- Estimates the direct effect of `educ` on `know`, as well as the total and specific indirect effects of `educ` on `know` through `attn` and `elab`, with `attn` and `elab` functioning as parallel mediators.

- `sex` and `age` are included in the model as covariates.

- Produces the Sobel test for the specific indirect effects.

- Generates 90% bootstrap confidence intervals for the indirect effects using 5,000 bootstrap samples.

- Calculates the difference between the two specific indirect effects and produces a bootstrap confidence interval for the difference.

- Creates a new data window containing 5,000 bootstrap estimates of each of the regression coefficients.

(5) Serial Multiple Mediation

```
process y=happy/x=commit/m=close desire/hc=3/effsize=1/model=6
    /boot=10000.
```

- Estimates the direct effect of `commit` on `happy`, as well as the total and all possible specific indirect effects of `commit` on `happy` through `close` and `desire`.

- `close` and `desire` function as mediators in serial, with `close` affecting `desire`.

- Standard errors for model coefficients are based on the HC3 heteroscedasticity-consistent standard error estimator.

- Generates 95% percentile bootstrap confidence intervals for the indirect effects using 10,000 bootstrap samples.

- Produces various measures of effect size for the total, direct, and indirect effects.

(6) Conditional Process Model Example 1

```
process y=turnout/x=frame/m=risk/w=euskept/z=peffic/model=68
    /moments=1/boot=20000/mcx=1/wmodval=2/center=1.
```

- Estimates the direct effect of `frame` on `turnout`, as well as the conditional indirect effects of `frame` on `turnout` through `risk`. The effect of `frame` on `risk` is modeled as multiplicatively moderated by both `peffic` and `euskept`, and the effect of `risk` on `turnout` is modeled as moderated by `euskept`.

- `euskept`, `peffic`, and `frame` are mean centered prior to analysis.

- `frame` is specified as a multicategorical variable, with PROCESS using indicator coding to represent the groups.

- Calculates the conditional indirect effects of `frame` on `turnout` through `risk` among cases 2 units above the sample mean on `euskept` and with values of `peffic` at the sample means, as well as with `peffic` one standard deviation above and below the sample mean.

- Generates 95% percentile bootstrap confidence intervals for the conditional indirect effects using 20,000 bootstrap samples.

(7) Conditional Process Model Example 2

```
process y=jobsat/m=carcomm workmean/x=calling/w=livecall/model=7
    /boot=1000/seed=34421.
```

- Estimates the direct effect of `calling` on `jobsat`, as well as the conditional indirect effects of `calling` on `jobsat` through both `carcomm` and `workmean` operating in parallel. The effects of calling on both `carcomm` and `workmean` are modeled as moderated by `livecall`.

- Produces the conditional indirect effects of `calling` when `livecall` is equal to the 16th, 50th, and 84th percentiles of the sample distribution.

- Generates 95% bootstrap confidence intervals for the conditional indirect effects using 1,000 bootstrap samples.

- Seeds the random number generator for bootstrapping with the value 34421.

(8) Conditional Process Model Example 3

```
process y=liking/x=protest/m=respappr anger/w=sexism/cov=sex age
    /mcx=3/model=8/moments=1/wmatrix=1,0,0,1,0,0/save=1.
```

- Estimates the effect of `protest` on `liking` directly as well as indirectly through `respappr` and `anger`, with the direct and indirect effects moderated by `sexism`. The effect of `protest` on `respappr` is modeled as moderated by `sexism`.

- `protest` is specified as a multicategorical variable, with PROCESS using Helmert coding to represent the groups.

- `age` and `sex` are included in the model as covariates.

- Generates 95% percentile bootstrap confidence intervals based on 5,000 bootstrap samples for the conditional indirect effect of `protest` at the sample mean, a standard deviation below the mean, and a standard deviation above the mean of `sexism`.

- Eliminates the interaction between `protest` and `sexism` in the model of `anger` that model 8 otherwise specifies.

- Saves the bootstrap estimates of all regression coefficients to a new data file.

(9) Conditional Process Model Example 4

```
process vars=behavior/x=friends/m=attract similar/w=weight
   /z=bmi/mcz=2/cov=cancer/bmatrix=1,1,1,0,1,1/wmatrix=1,1,1,0,0,0
   /zmatrix=1,0,0,0,0,0.
```

- Constructs a custom serial moderated mediation model. The direct effect of `friends` on `behavior` is fixed to zero.

- The effects of `friends` on `attract`, `friends` on `similar`, and `attract` on `similar` are estimated as moderated by `weight`.

- The effect of `friends` on `attract` is estimated as moderated by `bmi`.

- `cancer` is included in the model as a covariate.

- Generates 95% percentile bootstrap confidence intervals based on 5,000 bootstrap samples for the conditional indirect effects of `friends` on `behavior` at the 16th, 50th, and 84th percentiles of `weight` and for the groups defined by `bmi`.

- `bmi` is specified as a multicategorical variable with PROCESS using sequential coding to represent the groups.

Model Specification

PROCESS has various mediation, moderation, and conditional process models that are preprogrammed and specified in a PROCESS command by model number. The preprogrammed models are depicted starting on page 584, along with their corresponding model number as recognized by PROCESS in the **model** statement. You can also edit a numbered model or produce a custom model. For instructions on editing or customizing a model, see Appendix B.

Each model has certain minimum requirements as to which variables must be designated and provided in the PROCESS command. All models require

- A single consequent variable *yvar* listed in the **y=** statement (i.e., **y**=*yvar*), where *yvar* is the name of the variable in your data functioning as Y in the model.

- A single antecedent variable *xvar* listed in the **x=** statement (i.e., **x**=*xvar*), where *xvar* is the name of the variable in your data functioning as X in the model.

- Either a single moderator variable listed in the **w=** statement (i.e., **w**=*wvar*), or at least one mediator listed in *mvlist* in the **m=** statement (i.e, **m**=*mvlist*).

- When a preprogrammed model is being used, a model number corresponding to one of the model templates must be specified following **model=**.

- When a custom model is built, a sequence of zeros and ones separated by commas and following the **bmatrix=** option. See Appendix B.

Other than these requirements, remaining required inputs to PROCESS are model dependent. In general, any variable that is a part of the conceptual model in a numbered model template must be provided as an input to PROCESS, and any variable that is not a part of the conceptual model must be left out. For instance, observe in the model templates section (see page 584) that model 21 has, in addition to X, M, and Y, two moderators W and Z. Thus, PROCESS must be told which two variables in the dataset correspond to W and Z in the diagram. This would be done with the use of the **w=** and **z=** statements (e.g., **w**=*wvar* and **z**=*zvar*), where *wvar* and *zvar* are the names of the variables in the data file corresponding to W and Z.

The **y=**, **x=**, **w=**, and **z=** specifications each allow only one variable, and a variable can be listed in one and only one of the *yvar*, *xvar*, *mvlist*, *wvar*, and *zvar* arguments. For instance, a variable cannot be listed as both **w** in *wvar* and **m** in *mvlist*. The one exception is model 74, which requires that *xvar* by listed following both **x=** and **w=**.

As PROCESS uses ordinary least squares regression for model estimation, it will assume *yvar* and *mvlist* have at least interval level measurement properties. Unless specified otherwise, *xvar*, *wvar*, and *zvar* should be either dichotomous or numerical with interval level properties. Multicategorical variables (i.e., categorical with three or more categories) are acceptable as *xvar*, *wvar*, or *zvar* only if specified as such with the **mcx**, **mcw**, and/or **mcz** options and PROCESS is told what coding system to employ to represent the categories. See the section titled "Multicategorical Variables for X, W, and/or Z" starting on page 562. Covariates listed as *covlist* using the **cov** option are assumed to be either dichotomous or numerical with interval level properties. Multicategorical covariates must be represented with a proper coding system with the codes constructed outside of PROCESS and given to PROCESS in *covlist*.

PROCESS recognizes variable names longer than eight characters but represents variable names internally with no more than eight characters. If two variables in the data file have the same first eight characters in their variable names, PROCESS may confuse them and produce inaccurate output if one or more of them is used in a PROCESS command. For this reason, it is recommended that variable names be restricted to eight characters in length. Variables formatted as string are not acceptable to PROCESS. All variables must be in numeric format. The SPSS version of PROCESS ignores the "Measure" designation for variables available in the SPSS Variable View window.

Although PROCESS has a number of error-trapping routines built in, it will not catch all errors produced by improper formatting of a PROCESS command, improper listing of variables and variable names, and so forth. Any errors it has trapped will be displayed in an errors section of the PROCESS output. Errors it has not successfully trapped will appear as a long list of SPSS execution errors that will be largely unintelligible.

Covariates

Covariates can be included in a model by listing one or more variable names in *covlist* following the **cov=** option in a PROCESS command line (e.g., **cov=sex age attitude**). Covariates must be either dichotomous or quantitative. Multicategorical covariates should be represented with an appropriate categorical coding system (e.g., indicator coding) with codes constructed outside of PROCESS if they are to be used as covariates. A variable listed as a covariate cannot be also specified as X, M, Y, W, or Z (but see Appendix B for a way of a specifying a moderator in one part of the model as a covariate in another part).

By default, covariates are included as antecedent variables in the models of all mediators (i.e., all models of the variables in *mvlist*) as well as in the model of *yvar*. This can be changed through the use of the **covmy** or **cmatrix** options. The **covmy** option allows the specification for the covariates to be included only in the model of *yvar* or only in the models of the variables in *mvlist*. Setting the **covmy** argument to 1 (i.e., **covmy=1**) includes the covariates in the model of all mediators in *mvlist* but not the model of the *yvar*. Using an argument of 2 (i.e., **covmy=2**) specifies estimation of a model that includes all covariates in the model of *yvar* but not the mediator variables in *mvlist*.

The **cmatrix** option provides a more flexible means of assigning co-variates to models of the variables in *mvlist* and *yvar* using a pattern of zeros and ones separated by commas. Consider a C matrix with consequent variables as rows and covariates as columns. The order of the rows in this matrix are in the order med1 med2 ... medk dv, where med1, med2 ... medk are the names of mediators M_1, M_2, and so forth in the data file and in the order listed in *mvlist*, and dv is the variable specified as *yvar*. Similarly, the columns are in the order the covariates are specified in *covlist*. A cell in the C matrix is set to 1 if the covariate in the column is to be included in the equation of the consequent variable in the row, and 0 if that covariate is to be left out of that equation.

For example, suppose you were estimating model 4 and the model includes two mediators med1 and med2 in *mvlist* in that order, Y variable dv, and three covariates cov1, cov2, and cov3 listed in *covlist* in that order. Further, suppose you wanted cov1 and cov2 but not cov3 in the model of med1, only cov3 in the model of med2, and cov1, cov2, and cov3 in the model of dv. The corresponding C matrix is

	cov1	cov2	cov3
med1	1	1	0
med2	0	0	1
dv	1	1	1

To set up this assignment of covariates to equations in a PROCESS command, list a corresponding sequence of zeros and ones separated by commas following **cmatrix=** in the PROCESS command. The sequence of zeros and ones should correspond to the cells of this matrix reading from left to right, top to bottom. So in this example, the **cmatrix** option would be **cmatrix=1,1,0,0,0,1,1,1,1**. The complete PROCESS command (ignoring other possible options) would be

```
process y=dv/m=med1 med2/x=xvar/cov=cov1 cov2 cov3/model=4/
    cmatrix=1,1,0,0,0,1,1,1,1.
```

Working from **cmatrix** to C matrix rather than the reverse, assuming four covariates, three mediators, and one Y the specification **cmatrix=1,0,1,0,1,1,0,1,1,0,0,0,1,0,1,1** corresponds to the C matrix on the next page and represents cov1 and cov3 in the model of med1; cov1, cov2, and cov4 in the model of med2; cov1 in the model of med3; and cov1, cov3, and cov4 in the model of dv. Assuming model 4, the PROCESS command would be

	cov1	cov2	cov3	cov4
med1	1	0	1	0
med2	1	1	0	1
med3	1	0	0	0
dv	1	0	1	1

```
process y=dv/m=med1 med2 med3/x=xvar/cov=cov1 cov2 cov3 cov4/
   model=4/cmatrix=1,0,1,0,1,1,0,1,1,0,0,0,1,0,1,1.
```

If you want to exclude a covariate from all model equations, the proper approach is to exclude that variable from *covlist*, as each column in the covariate matrix must include at least one 1. If unsure whether your *cmatrix* specification correctly corresponds to the model you want to estimate, check the individual models in the PROCESS output, or tell PROCESS to display all model matrices by adding **matrices=1** to the PROCESS command line.

Multicategorical Variables for *X*, *W*, and/or *Z*

The variables listed in a PROCESS command as X, W, and/or Z can be specified as multicategorical (i.e., categorical with three or more categories) using the **mcx**, **mcw**, and **mcz** options. PROCESS automatically implements four coding systems for groups, with the system to be used designated using the arguments 1, 2, 3, or 4. For example, **mcx=2** tells PROCESS that *xvar* is a multicategorical variable and to use sequential coding for groups, and **mcw=1** specifies the moderator *wvar* as multicategorical variable and to use simple indicator (a.k.a "dummy variable") coding to represent groups. A variable specified as multicategorical cannot contain more than 9 categories. PROCESS discerns the number of categories using the number of unique numerical codes in the variable specified as multicategorical. Each group must contain at least two cases.

For a multicategorical variable with g groups, PROCESS automatically constructs $g - 1$ variables and includes them as antecedent variables in the model equations where appropriate. If the multicategorical variables is a moderator or its effect is specified as moderated, PROCESS also constructs the necessary products to specify the interaction. In addition, an omnibus test of interaction involving the multicategorical variable is provided in the form of an F-ratio and p-value.

These $g - 1$ variables are constructed using one of four coding systems preprogrammed into PROCESS, depending on the argument. Acceptable arguments are 1 for dummy coding, 2 for sequential coding, 3 for Helmert coding, and 4 for effect coding. The variables representing the codes are in the output as X, W, or Z following by numbers (e.g., X1, X2, and so forth), and a table mapping categories to codes is provided at the top of the output. The examples below assume that the variable called cond represents four groups coded in the data with the numbers 1, 3, 4, and 6.

When the argument is set to 1, simple indicator coding is used with the group coded with the smallest numerical code treated as the reference category. The indicator codes will correspond to groups as coded in *xvar, wvar,* or *zvar* in ascending sequential order. For example, **mcx=1** implements the coding system below:

cond	X1	X2	X3
1	0	0	0
3	1	0	0
4	0	1	0
6	0	0	1

There is no option in PROCESS for changing which group is treated as the reference. If you want to designate a different group as the reference group, recode *xvar, wvar,* or *zvar* prior to using PROCESS so that the reference group you desire is coded with the numerically smallest code.

When the argument is set to 2, sequential coding is used. Sequential coding allows for the comparison of group *j* to the group one ordinal position higher on the categorical variable. PROCESS will assume that the ascending ordinality of the multicategorical variable corresponds to the ascending sequence of arbitrary numerical codes in *xvar, wvar,* or *zvar.* For example, **mcw=2** implements the coding system below:

cond	W1	W2	W3
1	0	0	0
3	1	0	0
4	1	1	0
6	1	1	1

When the argument is set to 3, Helmert coding is used. Helmert coding allows for the comparison of group *j* to all groups ordinally higher on the categorical variable. PROCESS will assume that the ascending ordinality of the multicategorical variable corresponds to the ascending sequence of arbitrary numerical codes in *xvar, wvar*, or *zvar*. Helmert coding is also useful for setting up certain orthogonal contrasts for a nominal multicategorical variable. For example, **mcz=3** implements the coding system below:

cond	Z1	Z2	Z3
1	−3/4	0	0
3	1/4	−2/3	0
4	1/4	1/3	−1/2
6	1/4	1/3	1/2

When the argument is set to 4, effect coding is used, with the group coded with the smallest number left out of the coding scheme. The dummy variables correspond to groups in ascending sequential order in the coding of the multicategorical variable. For example, **mcx=4** implements the coding system below:

cond	X1	X2	X3
1	−1	−1	−1
3	1	0	0
4	0	1	0
6	0	0	1

Specifying a Set of Custom Group Codes

PROCESS also allows for the specification of a set of user-provided codes for a multicategorical variable by setting the argument for the **mcx, mcw**, and/or **mcz** option to 5. A string of numbers separated by commas corresponding to the coding system in a g (number of groups) $\times$ $g-1$ matrix of codes should also be provided using the **xcatcode, wcatcode**, or **zcatcode** options.

For example, suppose cond is a multicategorical variable representing $g = 4$ groups (with the groups coded 1, 3, 4, and 6 as in the examples above), and the coding system in the table on the next page is desired, with cond as W in model 1. If the X and Y variables are named extra and intent, respectively, the PROCESS command would be

cond	W1	W2	W3
1	−0.5	−0.5	0
3	−0.5	0.5	0
4	0.5	0	−0.5
6	0.5	0	0.5

```
process y=intent/x=extra/w=cond/model=1/mcw=5/
   wcatcode=-0.5,-0.5,0,-0.5,0.5,0,0.5,0,-0.5,0.5,0,0.5.
```

The entries in the string of numbers are assigned to the cells in the $g \times (g-1)$ matrix of codes in order from right to left, top to bottom. Note that the matrix of codes must be of the order $g \times (g-1)$ in order to properly represent the groups, and so the set of codes following the **xcatcode=**, **wcatcode=**, or **zcatcode=** options must contain $g^g - g$ numbers or an error will result. The matrix of codes cannot be singular, or a model estimation error will occur and PROCESS will terminate.

Models with More Than One Mediator

Most numbered models with a mediation component can have up to 10 mediators. Exceptions are certain serial mediation models (models 6 and 83–92) or custom models, which can contain between 2 and 6 mediators. Mediators operating in parallel are all modeled as affected by *xvar* and, in turn, affect *yvar*, but they are not modeled to transmit their effects to any other mediators in the model (see section 5.1). Mediators operating in serial are linked in a causal chain, with the first mediator affecting the second, the second the third, and so forth (see section 5.4). The order of the mediators in *mvlist* is not consequential to the estimation of a parallel multiple mediator model. But for serial multiple mediator models (models 6 and 83–92 and any custom serial model), the first variable in *mvlist* is assumed to be causally prior to the second variable in *mvlist*, which is causally prior to the third, and so forth.

Models 7 and higher include the moderation of an effect either to or from a mediator. The model templates starting on page 584 illustrate which path is moderated for a specific model number. In numbered models and when more than one mediator is listed in **mvlist**, by default the moderation applies to all corresponding paths for each mediator. For example, if model 7 is specified with two mediators med1 and med2, then both the effect from *xvar* to med1 and the effect from *xvar* to med2 will be estimated as linearly moderated by *wvar*. To eliminate one or more moderated paths in a numbered model, the model must be editing using the **wmatrix** or **zmatrix** options. Alternatively, a custom model can be specified. See Appendix B for a discussion of how to edit a numbered model or build a new model from scratch.

Inference for Indirect Effects

PROCESS offers percentile bootstrap confidence intervals for inference about indirect effects in models with a mediation component, as well as the Sobel test and Monte Carlo confidence intervals in some mediation models without a moderation component.

Bootstrap confidence intervals are the default for inference about indirect effects because of the unrealistic assumption the Sobel tests makes about the shape of the sampling distribution of the indirect effect. By default PROCESS generates 95% percentile bootstrap confidence intervals for all indirect effects in any model that involves a mediation component (models 4 and higher). The number of bootstrap samples can be set with the z argument in the **boot** option (e.g., **boot=10000** for $10,000$ bootstrap samples; the default number of bootstrap samples is 5,000). Set z to 0 to turn off bootstrapping. The level of confidence for confidence intervals can be changed by setting ci to the desired number anywhere between 50 and 99.9999 (90, 99, etc.) in the **conf** option (e.g., **conf=99** for 99% confidence intervals). If the number of bootstrap samples requested is too small given the requested level of confidence desired, PROCESS will automatically increase the number of bootstrap samples as required. A note will be produced at the bottom of the output to this effect when it occurs.

Though not recommended, the Sobel test can be generated by PROCESS by setting the argument in the **normal** option to 1 (i.e., **normal=1**), PROCESS generates this test in simple and parallel multiple mediator models (models 4 and 5) only. The second-order standard error estimator is used, and the p-value is derived using the standard normal distribution. This test is not available for the total indirect effect or conditional indirect effects in mediation models with moderated paths, nor is it available in models that include a serial indirect effect (such as models 6 and models 83–92).

Monte Carlo confidence intervals can be requested instead of bootstrap confidence intervals for simple and parallel multiple mediator models (models 4 and 5) through the use of the **mc** option, setting the argument to the number of samples desired. For example, **mc=5000** requests Monte Carlo confidence intervals for the indirect effect based on 5,000 samples. The Monte Carlo option takes precedence over the bootstrapping option, so if **mc** is used in conjunction with **boot**, Monte Carlo confidence intervals will result. The **mc** option is ignored for serial mediation models and any model that involves a moderation component. In that case, bootstrap confidence intervals are generated.

In addition to the point estimate of the indirect effect and the endpoints of a confidence interval, PROCESS will also generate a bootstrap or Monte Carlo estimate of the standard error of the indirect effect. The standard error of the indirect effect is defined as the standard deviation of the bootstrap or Monte Carlo estimates. The bootstrap standard error will be printed in the PROCESS output under the column heading "BootSE."

On occasion, the model cannot be estimated on a bootstrap sample. This occurs when the data matrix in a bootstrap sample contains a singularity or a variable is a constant. When this occurs, the bootstrap sample will be replaced. A note in the output will indicate how many times this occurred during the bootstrapping routine. It is more likely to occur when the model contains a variable that is discrete or multicategorical with a small number of cases in a group. Dichotomous variables that heavily favor one category are especially likely to produce this problem. PROCESS will continue replacing such bootstrap samples during the bootstrap sampling process until it completes the number of bootstrap samples requested or it exceeds the number of attempts set in the **maxboot** option. If the maximum number of bootstrap attempts is not specified, the replacement of bootstrap samples will occur until it has attempted twice as many bootstrap samples as specified in the **boot** option.

Because bootstrapping and Monte Carlo methods are based on random sampling from the data (for bootstrapping) or from theoretical distributions (for Monte Carlo confidence intervals), confidence intervals and standard errors will differ slightly each time PROCESS is run as a result of the random sampling process. The more bootstrap or Monte Carlo samples that are requested, the less this variation between runs. It is possible to replicate a set of random samples by seeding the random number generator, setting sd in the **seed** option to any integer between 1 and 2,000,000,000 prior to running PROCESS (e.g., **seed=23543**). By default, the random number generator is seeded with a random number. When a seed is specified, it will be printed at the top of the output. If no seed is specified, it is not possible to recover the seed used by SPSS's random number generator.

Comparing Indirect Effects

Pairwise comparisons between specific indirect effects can be conducted for any multiple mediator model. This is accomplished by setting the argument in the **contrast** option to either 1 or 2 (i.e., **contrast=1**). Option 1 constructs differences between specific indirect effects, and option 2 constructs differences between the absolute values of specific indirect effects. These comparisons will appear in the output in the indirect effects section with labels (C1), (C2), and so forth. A table that maps the label to the specific indirect effects being compared is provided at the bottom of the section of output containing the comparisons. Bootstrap or Monte Carlo confidence intervals are provided for inference for these pairwise comparisons when the contrast option is used in conjunction with bootstrapping or the Monte Carlo option. See section 5.3 for a discussion of contrasts between indirect effects.

In conditional process models, PROCESS generates a table of specific indirect effects at various values of the moderator or moderator(s). In such models, the **contrast** option generates bootstrap confidence intervals for all pairwise comparisons between conditional indirect effects through a specific mediator. If the model includes more than one mediator, the comparisons are made within mediator. Comparisons for specific indirect effects between different mediators are not produced.

In models with more than one mediator but without a moderation component, the **contrast** option accepts a vector of weights for constructing a bootstrap confidence interval for a linear combination of specific indirect effects. When using this option, as many weights should be included as there are specific indirect effects, the weights must be separated by a comma, and the weights for each specific indirect effect must appear in the order the specific indirect effects appear in the output. For example, the command

```
process y=donate/x=educ/m=neuro extra agree conscien open/model=4
    /contrast=1,1,0,0,0.
```

estimates a parallel multiple mediator model and constructs a bootstrap confidence interval for the sum of the indirect effects of educ on donate through neuro and extro. Negative weights can also be included, as in

```
process y=donate/x=educ/m=neuro extra agree conscien open/model=4
    /contrast=1,1,-1,-1,0.
```

which constructs a bootstrap confidence interval for the difference between the sum of the indirect effects through neuro and extra and the sum of the indirect effects through agree and conscien.

Effect Size Indices for Indirect, Direct, and Total Effects

When estimating a mediation model without a moderation component, adding **effsize=1** to the PROCESS command generates the partially and the completely standardized direct, indirect, and total effects of *xvar* on *yvar* discussed in Chapter 4. When this option is used in conjunction with the bootstrapping option, bootstrap confidence intervals for these effect sizes are produced for the indirect effects. The **effsize** option has no effect if the model includes moderation of any path in the mediation process. Completely standardized effects are not generated when *xvar* is dichotomous or specified as multicategorical.

The Total Effect in Unmoderated Mediation Models

In some mediation models with no moderated effects (e.g, models 4 and 6), the total effect of *xvar* on *yvar* can be quantified with the regression coefficient for *xvar* in the model of *yvar* without the proposed mediators in the model. The model generating the total effect is produced in the output by including the option **total=1** in the PROCESS command.

For custom models, the total effect will not be produced for any mediation models that fix any pathway between *xvar* and *yvar*, between *xvar* and a mediator, or between a mediator and *yvar* to zero. The total effect will also not be provided if some of the covariates listed in **covlist** are excluded from the models of either **yvar** or one of the mediators in **mvlist**.

Visualizing Interactions

To help visualize and interpret the nature of the moderation of an effect in any regression equation in a model, the **plot** option generates a table of predicted values of a consequent variable from the model using various values of the focal antecedent and moderator or moderators. This table is generated by setting the argument in the **plot** option to 1 (i.e., **plot=1**). Any covariates in the equation are set to their sample mean when deriving the predicted values in the table generated. In addition to this table, PROCESS will write a program around this table that can be cut and pasted into a syntax window and executed to produce a visual depiction of the interaction. This can be edited for style and attractiveness using SPSS's editing features.

The **plot=1** option will only produce the estimates of the outcome variable resulting from the regression model. If you desire correspond-

ing standard errors and confidence intervals for the estimated values, use
plot=2.

Probing Interactions

When an effect in a model is specified as moderated, that moderation is automatically specified as linear through the inclusion of the product of focal
antecedent and moderator in the relevant model equation. Such interaction between variables can be better understood and described through the
probing process first introduced in Chapter 7. By default, PROCESS will
produce output for probing an interaction only if it is statistically significant
at or below the $\alpha = 0.10$ level. To use a different α-level, use the **intprobe**
option, with the desired α-level following an equals sign. For example,
intprobe=.05 will tell PROCESS to probe only those interactions in the
model with a p-value no larger than .05. Specifying **intprobe=1** results in
all interactions being probed regardless of the interaction's p-value.

In any model that involves a moderation component for any effect and
when the p-value for the interaction is no larger than the argument used in
the **intprobe** option described above, PROCESS will produce estimates of
the conditional effect of the focal antecedent variable at various values of
the moderator or moderators, along with statistics for inference. It will do
this only for the highest-order interaction involving the focal antecedent
that is not conditioned on another moderator.

By default, when a moderator is dichotomous, conditional effects of the
focal antecedent at the two values of the moderator are generated. If the
moderator is multicategorical and specified as such using the **mcw** or **mcz**
options, PROCESS generates the conditional effect of the focal antecedent
in each of the groups defined by the multicategorical moderator variable.
When a moderator is quantitative, conditional effects are estimated by default at the 16th, 50th, and 84th percentiles of the distribution of the moderator. For a discrete quantitative moderator (i.e., a quantitative moderator
with relatively few observed values), some of the percentile values of the
moderator may be identical. For example, the 16th and 50th percentile of
the moderator may be the same value. This will produce some redundancy
in the output.

Three alternatives for probing interactions are available in PROCESS.
For quantitative moderators, adding **moments=1** to the PROCESS command
generates conditional effects at the sample mean of the moderator as well
as plus and minus one standard deviation from the moderator mean. The
second alternative is to request the conditional effect of the focal antecedent
at a specific value of the moderator or moderators. This is accomplished

through the use of the **wmodval** and/or **zmodval** options for moderators W and Z, respectively, setting the corresponding *wval* or *zval* arguments to the value or values of the moderator at which you'd like the estimate of the conditional effect. For example, model 3 includes two moderators, W and Z. To generate an estimate of the conditional effect of *xvar* on *yvar* when $W = 1$ and $Z = 2$, add **wmodval=1** and **zmodval=2** to the PROCESS command. Or **wmodval=1,3** would condition the effect of X on Y when $W = 1$ and when $W = 3$. When the **wmodval** or **zmodval** options are used in conjunction with the **center** option (discussed on page 572), values of the moderator provided should be based on the mean-centered metric rather than the original metric of measurement. The **wmodval** and **zmodval** options are not available for multicategorical moderators.

The third alternative is the Johnson–Neyman technique, requested by adding **jn=1** to the command line. This approach identifies the value(s) on the moderator variable continuum at which point (or points) the effect of the focal antecedent variable on the consequent variable transitions between statistically significant and not, using the α-level of significance as the criterion. By default, $\alpha = 0.05$. This can be changed using the **conf** option, setting the desired confidence to $100(1 - \alpha)$. For example, for $\alpha = 0.01$, specify **conf=99**. In addition to identifying points of transition, PROCESS produces a table to aid in the identification of the regions of significance as well as information about the percentage of cases in the data above ("% Above") and below ("% Below") the points of transition in significance on the moderator this procedure identifies. See section 7.4 for a discussion of the Johnson–Neyman technique.

If the moderation component of the model involves a three-way interaction with *wvar* and *zvar* as moderators and *zvar* is a continuous variable, PROCESS identifies values of *zvar* at which point the two-way interaction between the focal antecedent and *wvar* transitions between statistically significant and not significant.

When a model includes more than one moderator, a table of conditional effects is generated for all combinations of the moderators based on the options or defaults used and described earlier. For example, in model 21, if **wmodval=1** is specified but the **zmodval** option is not used and Z is a quantitative moderator, PROCESS will generate a table of conditional indirect effects when $W = 1$ and Z is equal to 16th, 50th, and 84th percentiles of the distribution of *zvar*.

Comparing Conditional Effects in Moderation Analysis

In models with only a moderation component (models 1, 2, and 3), two conditional effects of X on Y can be formally compared with a statistical test. In model 1, evidence of moderation of *xvar*'s effect on *yvar* by *wvar* leads to the corresponding claim that any two conditional effects of X on Y for different values of W are different from each other, so no test of the difference between conditional effects is required. But in models 2 and 3, you can choose values of the two moderators and ask whether the conditional effect of X on Y differs between two groups defined by those values of the moderators. For a discussion of this test, see section 9.5. To conduct this test in models 2 or 3, add **contrast=*wval1,zval1;wval2,zval2*** to the PROCESS command line. This tests the difference between the conditional effect of X on Y when W=*wval1* and Z=*zval1* compared to when W=*wval2* and Z=*zval2*. For example,

```
process y=mathprob/x=treat/w=explms/z=gender/model=3/contrast=3,0;4,1.
```

tests the difference between the conditional effect of `treat` on `mathprob` when `explms=3` and `gender=0` compared to when `explms=4` and `gender=1`.

If W or Z is specified as multicategorical, the values for *wval1, zval1, wval2,* and/or *zval2*, should be one or more of the numerical codes in *wvar* or *wvar* representing the groups.

Mean-Centering in Models with a Moderation Component

In models that include regression coefficients for estimating interaction effects, moderation is assumed to be linear, with products of variables serving to represent the moderation. You can ask PROCESS to mean-center all variables used in the construction of products of antecedent variables prior to model estimation by setting the argument in the **center** option to 1 (i.e., **center=1**). All output for conditional effects will be based on moderator values using the mean-centered metric (e.g., the conditional effect of *xvar* on *yvar* at values of *wvar* will be based on values of *wvar* after mean-centering).

When mean centering is requested, arguments of options used for estimating conditional effects at specific values of the moderator(s) should be values based on a mean-centered metric. For example,

```
PROCESS y=smoking/x=surgery/m=anxiety/w=addict/model=7/wmodval=1.5.
```

will produce the conditional indirect effect of surgery on smoking through anxiety and the conditional effect of surgery on anxiety when addict = 1.5, whereas

```
PROCESS y=smoking/x=surgery/m=anxiety/w=addict/model=7/center=1/
   wmodval=1.5.
```

produces the conditional indirect effect of surgery on smoking through anxiety and the conditional effect of surgery on anxiety when addict is 1.5 measurement units above the sample mean of addict.

When an interaction in a model involves a multicategorical variable, the multicategorical variable is not mean-centered, as such centering has no meaning for a multicategorical variable.

Bootstrap Confidence Intervals for Regression Coefficients

PROCESS generates ordinary least squares confidence intervals for all regression coefficients. To request bootstrap confidence intervals for the regression coefficients in each regression equation defining the model, add the option **modelbt=1** to the PROCESS command line. These bootstrap confidence intervals will be provided near the end of the PROCESS output under the columns "BootLLCI" and "BootULCI." The mean and standard deviation of the bootstrap estimates are displayed under the columns headed "BootMean" and "BootSE." The original regression coefficients are found under the column labeled "Coeff."

Note that use of the **modelbt** option does not eliminate the printing of the ordinary least squares confidence intervals for the regression coefficients found in each of the tables of regression coefficients for the regression equations defining the complete model. Furthermore, because the default number of bootstrap samples for models 1, 2, and 3 is zero, the **modelbt** option will have no effect for these models unless the number of bootstrap samples is explicitly stated by using the **boot** option.

Saving Point and Bootstrap Estimates of Model Coefficients

The bootstrap estimates of all regression coefficients can be saved for examination or additional analysis by setting the argument in the **save** option

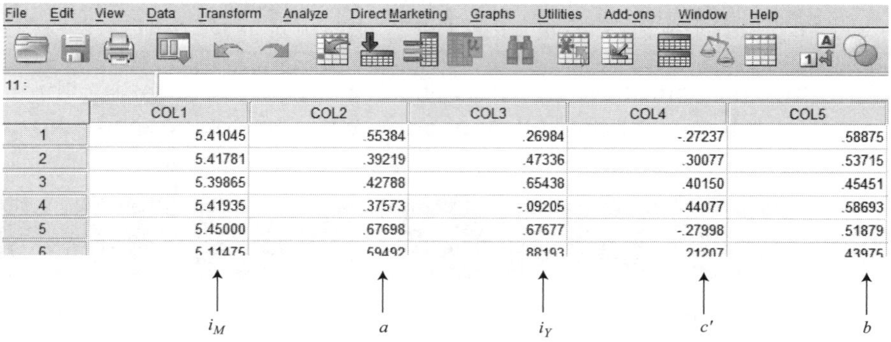

FIGURE A.1. A file of bootstrap estimates of regression coefficients and regression constants from a simple mediation analysis.

to 1 (i.e., **save=1**). This will produce a new data file in the SPSS session with as many rows as bootstrap samples requested, and as many columns as regression coefficients in the model being estimated. The columns of the data file containing the bootstrap samples will be in the order from left to right that the regression coefficients appear in the PROCESS output from top to bottom, and the PROCESS output will contain a table mapping column names in this file to regression coefficients. Parameter estimates for the total effect of X will not be included in this file when the **save** option is used in conjunction with the **total** option. The resulting data file must be saved in order to store it permanently, as subsequent runs of the PROCESS command with the **save=1** option will overwrite the prior file if it is not first saved permanently.

The resulting file containing the bootstrap estimates of the regression constant(s) and regression coefficients can be used in a variety of ways. For instance, the bootstrap sampling distribution for an indirect effect can be visualized by creating a new variable in this data file containing the product of entries in the columns that contain the bootstrap estimates for the $X \rightarrow M$ and $M \rightarrow Y$ effects and then generating a histogram of the resulting product. Or two statistics formed as functions of regression coefficients can be computed using the bootstrap estimates and then a confidence interval for the difference generated to test a hypothesis about the equality of the two parameters the statistics estimate.

To illustrate, using the data from the presumed media influence study described in Chapter 3, the commands below generate a bootstrap confidence interval for the difference between the direct effect of article location on reaction to the news story (c') and the indirect effect of article location on reactions to the story through presumed media influence (ab).

	conseqnt	antecdnt	coeff	se	t	p	LLCI	ULCI	df
1	pmi	constant	5.37692	.16185	33.22223	.00000	5.05650	5.69734	121.00000
2	pmi	cond	.47653	.23569	2.02182	.04540	.00991	.94314	121.00000
3	reaction	constant	.52687	.54968	.95849	.33974	-.56147	1.61520	120.00000
4	reaction	cond	.25435	.25582	.99426	.32210	-.25216	.76087	120.00000
5	reaction	pmi	.50645	.09705	5.21852	.00000	.31430	.69860	120.00000

FIGURE A.2. A file of regression coefficients, standard errors, t- and p-values, and confidence intervals.

```
process y=reaction/x=cond/m=pmi/model=4/seed=31216/save=1.
compute diff=col4-col2*col5.
frequencies variables = diff/percentiles 2.5 97.5.
graph/histogram=diff.
```

The PROCESS command does the mediation analysis in section 3.3 and creates a data file containing the 5,000 bootstrap estimates of i_M, a, i_Y, c', and b in equations 3.1 and 3.2. In this data file (see Figure A.1), the direct effect c' is in column 4 (variable name COL4), the a path is in column 2 (variable name COL2), and the b path is in column 5 (variable name COL5).

With this file active in SPSS prior to executing the rest of the code, the **compute** command produces a variable named DIFF defined as $c' - ab$, and the **frequencies** command prints the 2.5th and 97.5th percentile of the distribution of DIFF. These are the endpoints for a 95% percentile bootstrap confidence interval for the difference between the direct and indirect effects. The confidence interval for the difference is −0.603 to 0.587, so we cannot conclude that the direct and indirect effects differ. The **graph** command produces a histogram of the bootstrap distribution of the difference between c' and ab.

A second **save** option is available. Adding **save=2** to the PROCESS command will produce a new SPSS data file containing the point estimates, standard errors, t- and p-values, confidence intervals, and degrees of freedom for all of the regression coefficients and regression constants that define the full model, as in Figure A.2.

The resulting data file should be permanently saved, if desired, prior to repeated uses of the **save** option, as subsequent runs of PROCESS using this option will overwrite the file produced by a prior run.

Heteroscedasticity-Consistent Standard Errors

By default, PROCESS uses an estimator for the standard errors of the regression coefficients that assumes homoscedasticity of the errors in estimation of the outcome variable. PROCESS can also generate standard errors using heteroscedasticity-consistent covariance matrix estimators HC0, HC1, HC2, HC3, and HC4, described in Long and Ervin (2000) and Hayes and Cai (2007). One of these heteroscedasticity-consistent methods is requested by setting the argument in the **hc** option to a number 0 through 4 (e.g., for the HC3 estimator, specific **hc=3**). Any computation that uses the standard error of a regression coefficient will automatically employ the HC estimator when this option is requested, including the Sobel test, Monte Carlo confidence intervals for indirect effects, the Johnson–Neyman method, tests of conditional effects in moderation analysis, and the test of the significance of R^2 for models of *yvar*, as well as for tests of interactions based on the difference in R^2 when the interaction is included versus excluded from the model.

Confidence Level for Confidence Intervals

By default, 95% confidence intervals are provided for regression coefficients and various other effects generated by PROCESS. The level of confidence can be changed to any value between 50 and 99.9999% using the **conf** option. For example, adding **conf=99** to the PROCESS command generates 99% confidence intervals. The **conf** option also controls the α-level for deriving regions of significance from the Johnson-Neyman technique. For example, **conf=90** and **conf=99** correspond to $\alpha = 0.10$ and $\alpha = .01$, respectively.

Covariance Matrix of Regression Coefficients

PROCESS will display the variance–covariance matrices for the regression coefficients in each part of the model by specifying **covcoeff=1** in the PROCESS command line. By default, the variance–covariance is not produced in the output.

Displaying the Model in its Matrix Representation

All models PROCESS can estimate are represented with a set of zeros and ones in five matrices: the B matrix, the W matrix, the Z matrix, the WZ matrix, and the C matrix. The C matrix is discussed on page 560, and the remaining matrices are discussed in Appendix B. By adding **matrices=1** to the PROCESS command line, PROCESS will print the matrices corresponding to the model estimated at the end of the output. Only matrices that contain at least one 1 will be printed. Matrices that are not produced in the output contain all zeros.

Long Variable Names

Although PROCESS will recognize variable names longer than eight characters, they are represented internally in PROCESS by name with no more than eight characters. Variables in the data file with names longer than eight characters but that share the same first eight characters can be confused for each other by PROCESS. Make sure that all variable names in the data file are unique in the first eight characters before using PROCESS. A warning will be printed at the bottom of the output when variables with names longer than eight characters in length are included in a PROCESS command.

Missing Data

PROCESS assumes complete data and will exclude cases from the analysis that are missing on any of the variables in the model. Any missing data substitution or imputation desired should be conducted prior to the execution of PROCESS. PROCESS does not integrate with the multiple imputation routine in SPSS. Attempting to analyze a data file with stacked multiple-imputed data sets will produce an error.

Decimal Place Precision in Output

PROCESS generates numerical output to four decimals places of resolution. This can be changed with the *dec* argument when using the **decimals** option. This argument is set to F10.4 by default, meaning numbers in the output will contain up to ten characters, with four of these to the right of the decimal. In this argument, **Fa.b** sets the number of characters allocated to numbers to *a* and the number of decimal places to display to the right of the decimal point to *b*. For example, **decimals=F12.6** specifies twelve characters with six to the right of the decimal place. In the *dec* argument, **a** should be larger than **b**.

Mapping PROCESS Models onto MODMED and Edwards and Lambert (2007) Models

PROCESS can estimate conditional indirect effects for all models described in Preacher et al. (2007) and implemented in MODMED for SPSS. However, the model numbers are different. Edwards and Lambert (2007) describe various models that combine moderation and mediation using names rather than numbers, all of which can also be estimated by PROCESS. The table below maps model numbers in MODMED to corresponding model numbers in PROCESS and the model names used by Edwards and Lambert (2007).

MODMED	Edwards and Lambert (2007)	PROCESS
1	—	74
2	Direct effect and first-stage moderation	8
3	Second-stage moderation	14
4	—	22
5	Total effect moderation	59
—	First-stage moderation	7
—	First- and second-stage moderation	58
—	Direct effect moderation	5
—	Direct effect and second-stage moderation	15

Important Changes Compared to PROCESS Version 2

Users familiar with PROCESS version 2 (originally released with the first edition of this book) will find a number of important differences involving syntax structure, model specification, options available, and defaults in this latest release. These include

- Variables in the model no longer should be listed following **vars=**. Variables can now be directly assigned to their roles as X, Y, M, W, and so forth.

- Covariates are now listed following a new **cov=** option.

- In models 1, 2, and 3, moderators are now W and Z rather than M and W.

- *V* and *Q* have been eliminated as moderators from all models and model templates.

- Unlike in earlier releases of PROCESS, *Y* cannot be dichotomous in the current release.

- The number of preprogrammed numbered models has been reduced, with all models containing more than 2 moderators eliminated from the current release (models 23–27 and 30–57 from version 2).

- Thirteen new numbered models have been added that combine moderation with serial mediation or parallel and serial mediation (examples include models 80 and 84).

- The **quantile** option has been eliminated. When conditional effects are generated involving continuous moderators, by default the conditioning is the 16th, 50th, and 84th percentiles of the distribution of the moderator. Use the **moments** option to override this default.

- All interactions are automatically probed if $p \leq .10$ wherever they appear in the model and regardless of model (in earlier releases, interactions were probed only for models 1, 2, and 3). Use the **intprobe** option to change the default (e.g., **intprobe=0.05** for $p \leq .05$; **intprobe=1** to probe interactions regardless of *p*-value).

- Bootstrap confidence intervals are constructed using the percentile method. Bias-corrected bootstrap confidence intervals are not available in this release.

- *X* as well as moderators *W* and *Z* can be specified as multicategorical with up to nine categories each.

- The **wmodval** and **zmodval** options now allow for more than one value for conditioning effects.

- Covariates can now be assigned to different equations in whatever configuration desired rather than being forced to be in the models of *M*s, *Y*, or both.

- The **plot** option for generating data to visualize interactions now works in all models that include an interaction, wherever that interaction appears in the model (in version 2, **plot** worked only in models 1, 2, and 3).

- Bootstrap confidence intervals can be generated for all the regression coefficients in all the equations rather than for just indirect effects.

- Models can be constructed from scratch, bypassing entirely the model number system, through the use of the **bmatrix**, **wmatrix**, **zmatrix**, **wzmatrix** statements. And preprogrammed models can now be edited to remove unwanted moderation or to specify desired moderation of paths preprogrammed to be unmoderated. See Appendix B.

- The **cluster**, **ws**, **varorder**, and **percent** options have been eliminated.

Options Not Available in the PROCESS Dialog Box

Installation of the custom dialog file produces a PROCESS menu item in SPSS that can be used to set up a model. Although this may be more convenient for users more comfortable working with SPSS's graphical user interface, some features available in the PROCESS syntax are not implemented in the PROCESS dialog box. These include **bmatrix**, **wmatrix**, **zmatrix**, **wzmatrix**, **cmatrix**, **wmodval**, **zmodval**, **xcatcode**, **wcatcode**, **zcatcode**, **seed**, **maxboot**, and the **contrast** option for construction of a linear combination of indirect effects in mediation analysis or comparing two conditional effects in moderation analysis. The dialog box also limits the confidence level for confidence intervals with the **conf** option to one of three choices (90%, 95%, and 99%), the level of significance for probing interactions with the **intprobe** option is limited to four values (1, .20, .10, .05), and the number of bootstrap samples for construction of confidence intervals is limited to 6 choices (1,000, 2,000, 5,000, 10,000, and 20,000, and 50,000). And the Monte Carlo approach to construction of confidence intervals is not available as an option in the dialog box.

Installation, Execution, and Syntax Modifications for SAS Users

The SAS version of PROCESS functions similarly to the SPSS version, and most of the instructions described in this appendix apply to the SAS version, with only the minor modifications described below. Like the SPSS version, the SAS version is a program file (process.sas), which when executed creates a new command that SAS understands called **%process**. Once process.sas is executed (without changing the file whatsoever), then the **%process** command is available for use and the program can be closed. Once you close SAS, you have to define the **%process** command by executing process.sas again. **PROCESS for SAS requires the PROC IML**

module. To determine whether you have the PROC IML module installed, run the following commands in SAS:

```
proc iml;
print "PROC IML is installed";
quit;
```

When this code is executed, check the log for any errors, as well as your output window for the text "PROC IML is installed." Any errors in the log or a failure to see this text suggests that PROC IML is not installed on your version of SAS. If not, contact your local SAS representative to obtain the PROC IML product.

The syntax structure for PROCESS for SAS is almost identical to the SPSS version, with some important exceptions:

- The command name is **%process** rather than **process**.

- All parts of the command between **%process** and the ending semi-colon (**;**) must be in parentheses.

- The data file being analyzed must be specified in the command as **data=**file where file is the name of a SAS data file.

- Options and specifications must be delimited with a comma (**,**) rather than a forward slash (**/**). For example, suppose the data corresponding to example 7 on page 557 were stored in a SAS work file named "jobs." The SAS version of the PROCESS command corresponding to example 7 would be

```
%process (data=jobs,y=jobsat,m=carcomm workmean,x=calling,w=livecall,
    model=7,boot=1000,seed=34421);
```

- The **save** option requires an additional file name for the result-ing file. This should be listed following **file=**. For example, **save=1,file=mod14bt** tells SAS to save the bootstrap estimates of the regression coefficients to a temporary work file named "mod14bt." If a file name is not provided, the resulting file will be named "savefile." When using **save=2**, SAS will also create an additional file named "vars" containing information mapping regression coefficients to rows of the data file that the save option produces.

- Moderator values or contrast weights when using the **wmodval**, **zmodval** and **contrast** options should separated by a space rather than a comma (e.g., **wmodval=2 3 4**).

- When using the **contrast** option to compare conditional effects of X on Y in models 2 and 3 (see page 572), moderator values should be separated by a space rather than a comma, and should be provided in the order $w_1\ z_1\ w_2\ z_2$ with no semicolon separating the (W,Z) pairs. For example, to compare the conditional effect of X on Y when $w = 1$ and $z = 3$ compared to when $w = 2$ and $z = 5$, use **contrast=1 3 2 5**.

- When specifying the number of decimal places in output using the **decimals** option, the "F" should be left off the *dec* argument. For example, to set 12 characters for numbers with six after the decimal, use **decimals=12.6**.

- The **plot** option in PROCESS for SAS produces a table of data for visualizing an interaction but does not write the corresponding SAS code to read the data and produce a plot of the model.

Notes

- The SPSS version of PROCESS ignores the properties of the data specified in the "Measure" column of the Variable View section of the data file.

- A case will be deleted from the analysis if user- or system-missing on any of the variables in the model.

- Do not use STRING formatted variables in any of your models. Doing so will produce errors. All variables should be NUMERIC format.

- Dichotomous and multicategorical variables are not allowed as mediators in *mvlist* or as Y in *yvar*.

- PROCESS for SPSS does not honor split files as set up with the SPLIT command.

- Regression coefficients for all model equations are estimated using OLS regression. PROCESS has no options for maximum-likelihood based estimation of discrete, ordinal, or count outcomes.

- The *yvar, xvar, wvar*, and *zvar* arguments are limited to one variable each. Up to 10 variables can be listed in *mvlist*, except when estimating model 6 or building a custom model, in which case *mvlist* is limited to between two and six variables, depending on the model. Each variable should be specified in only one of these arguments, except in model 74.

- All regression coefficients in the output are unstandardized. PROCESS does not have an option for generating standardized regression coefficients. Users interested in standardized coefficients should standardize the variables in the model prior to execution of PROCESS. In mediation models based on standardized variables as input, a bootstrap confidence interval for an indirect effect produced by PROCESS should not be interpreted as a confidence interval for the standardized indirect effect. To get a confidence interval for a standardized indirect effect, use the **effsize** option. As discussed in Chapter 2, standardized regression coefficients for dichotomous antecedent variables generally are not meaningful and their interpretation or use should be avoided.

- In PROCESS, the bootstrapping routine is used only for the construction of bootstrap confidence intervals and bootstrap standard errors of indirect effects (conditional or unconditional) in models with a mediation component. Neither model regression coefficients, their standard errors, nor any other inferential tests are based on bootstrap methods. Bootstrap inference is available for regression coefficients only when the **modelbt** option is used.

- Bootstrapping takes time. The larger the sample, and the more complex the model, the longer the computations take. If you see the message "Running matrix" in the bottom right-hand corner of one of the SPSS windows, this means PROCESS is working on your data. Be patient.

- Some user-generated errors will result in the message "Running CONTINUE..." at the bottom of one of the SPSS windows. In this case, the SPSS processor must be stopped manually by choosing "Stop Processor" under the "File" menu before the use of PROCESS or any other SPSS functions can proceed.

- The PROCESS procedure code cannot be imbedded in a syntax file with an INCLUDE command in SPSS, but it can be called with an INSERT command. This eliminates the need to manually load and run PROCESS.sps prior to execution of a set of commands which call the PROCESS macro. See the *Command Syntax Reference* available through the Help menu in SPSS for details on the use of the INSERT command.

Model 1

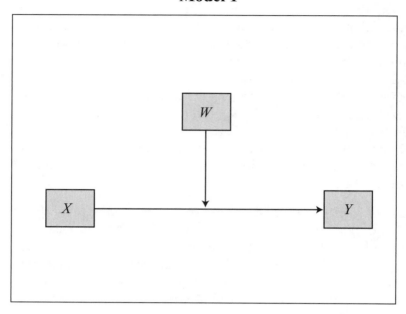

Model 2

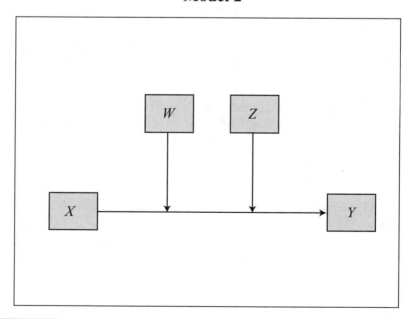

Model 3

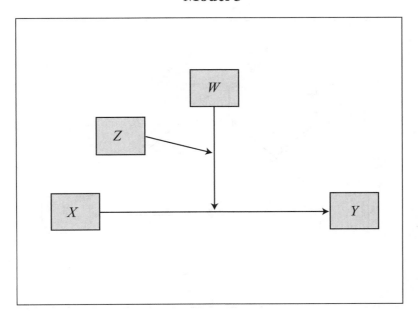

Model 4

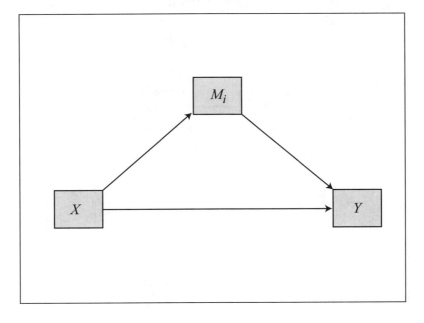

Model 5

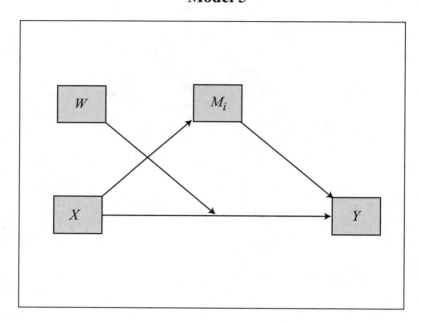

Model 6
(2 mediators)

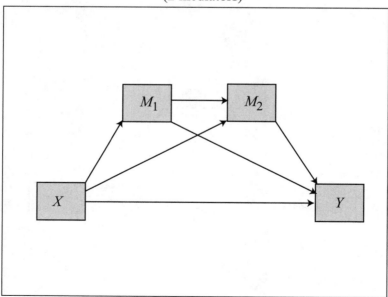

Model 6
(3 mediators)

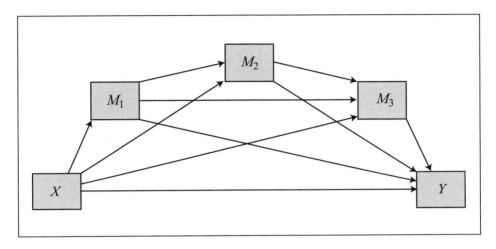

Model 6
(4 mediators)

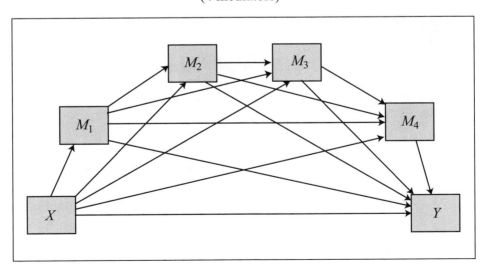

Model 7

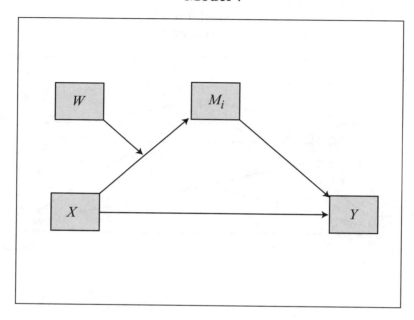

Model 8

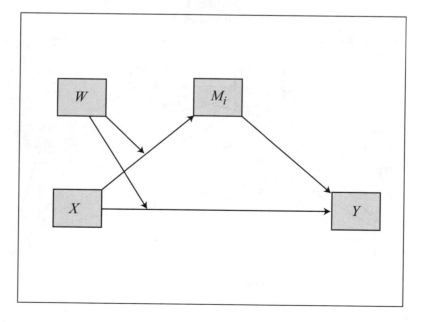

Model 9

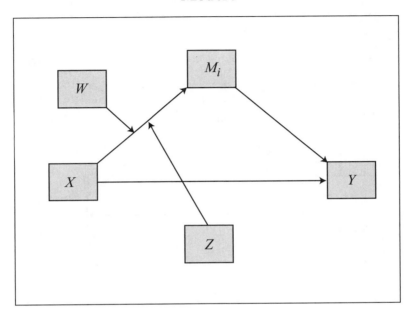

Model 10

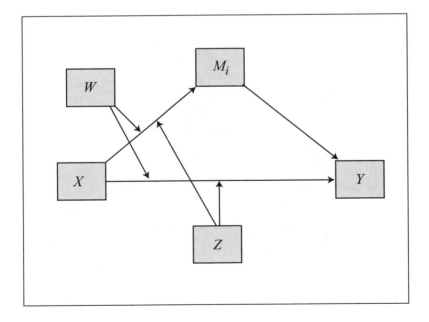

Model 11

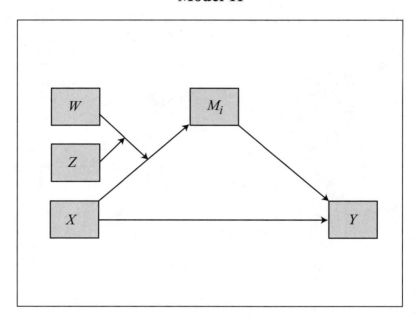

Model 12

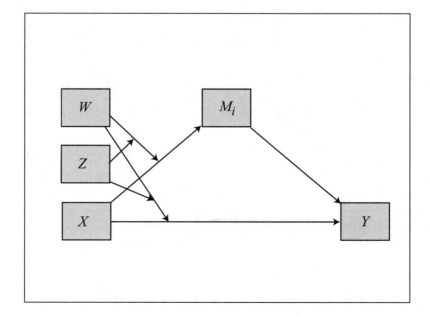

Model 13

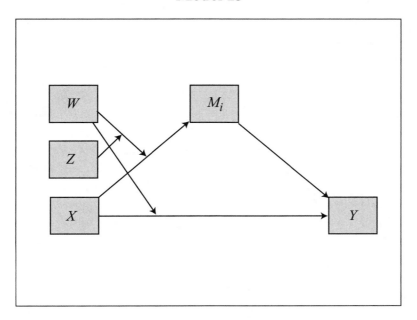

Model 14

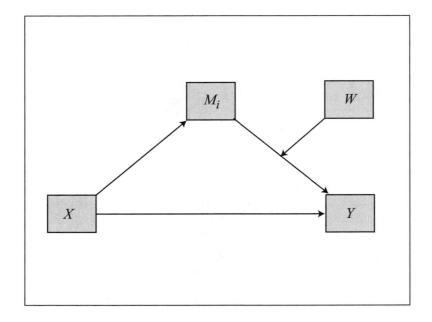

Model 15

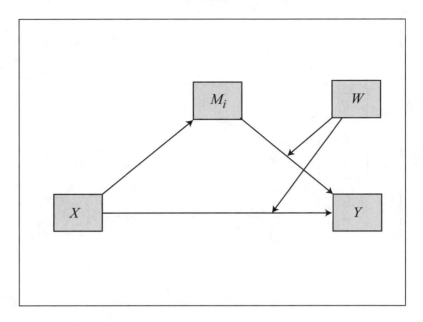

Model 16

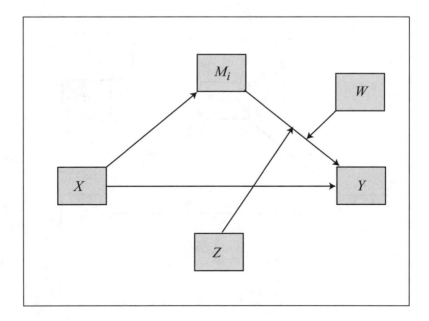

Model 17

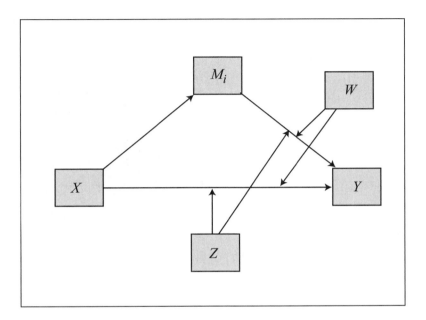

Model 18

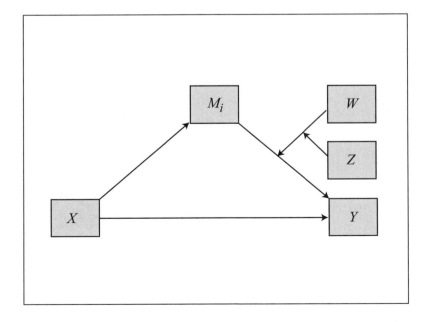

Model 19

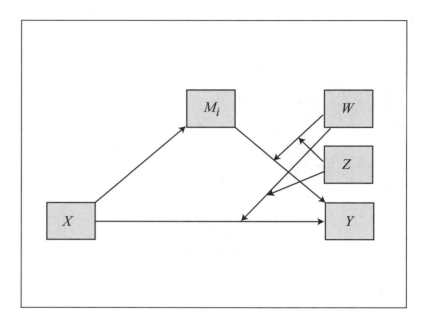

Model 20

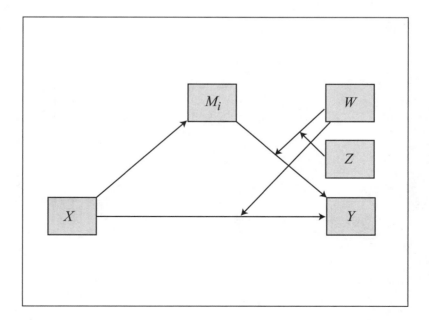

Model 21

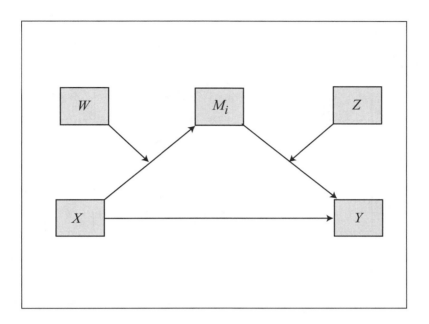

Model 22

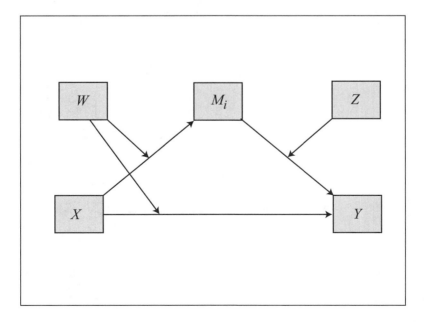

Model 28

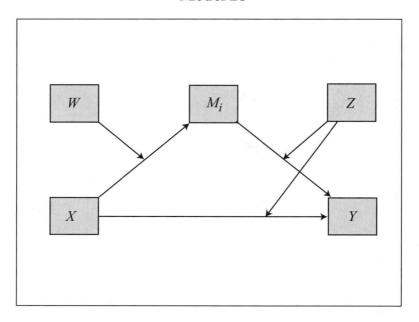

Model 29

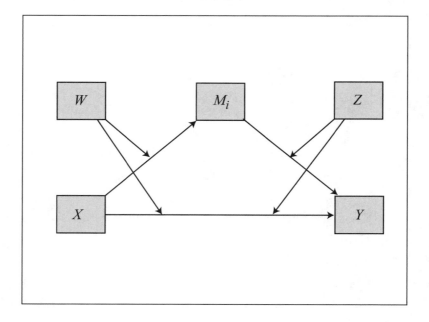

Model 58

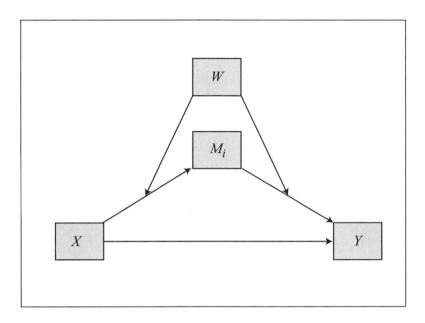

Model 59

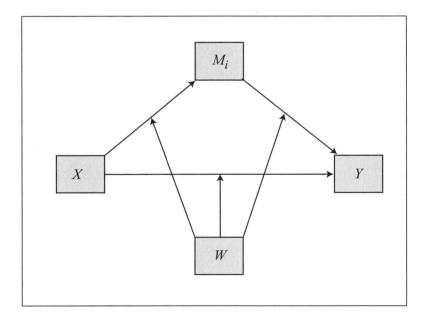

Model 60

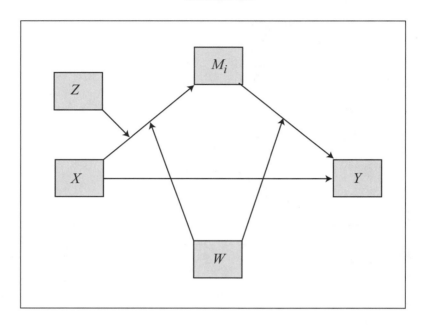

Model 61

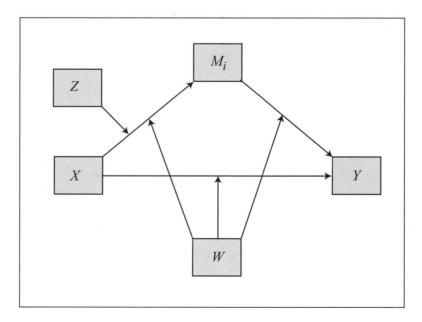

Model 62

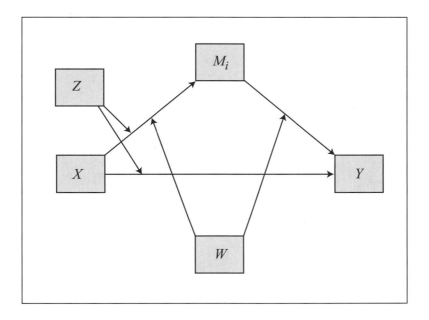

Model 63

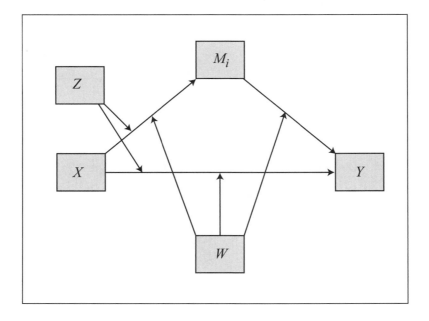

Model 64

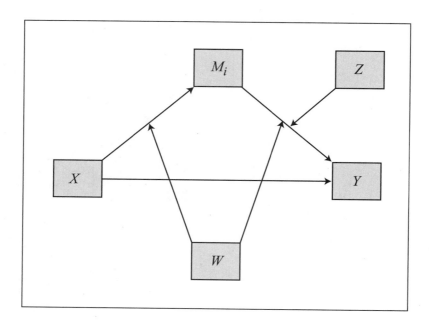

Model 65

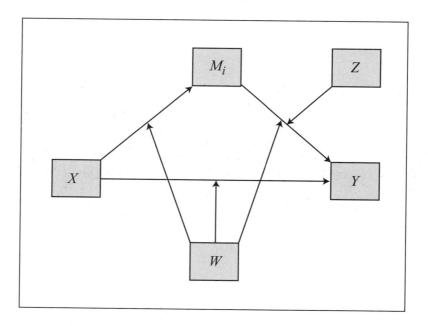

Model 66

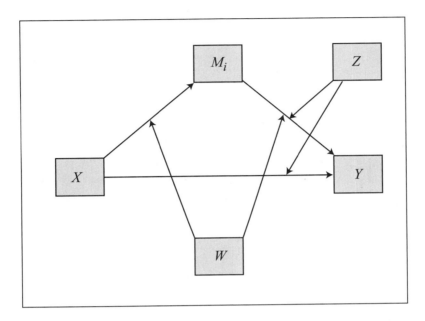

Model 67

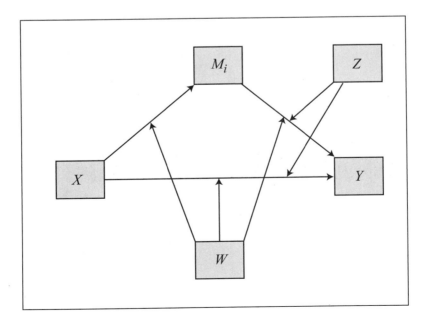

Model 68

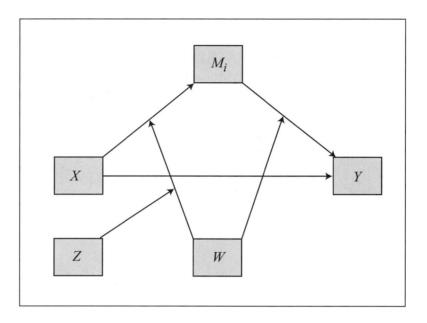

Model 69

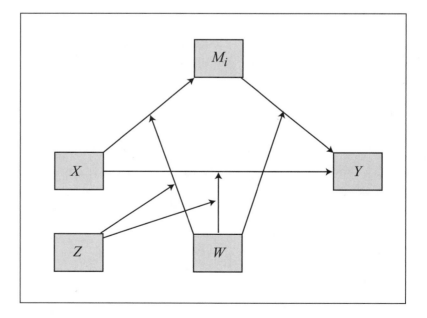

Model 70

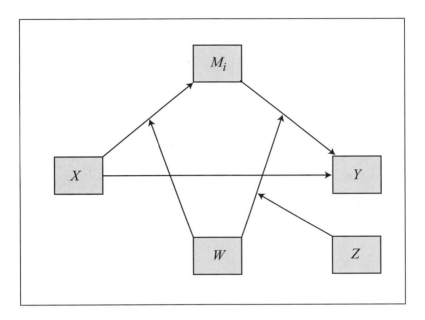

Model 71

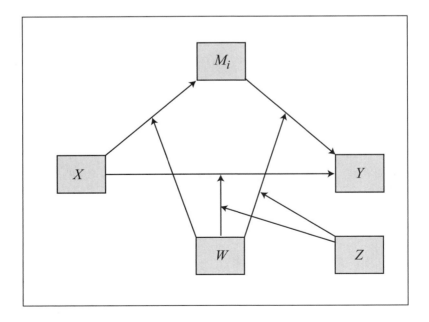

Model 72

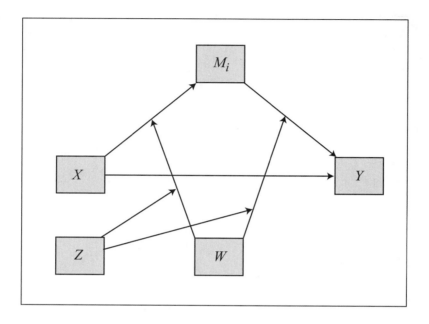

Model 73

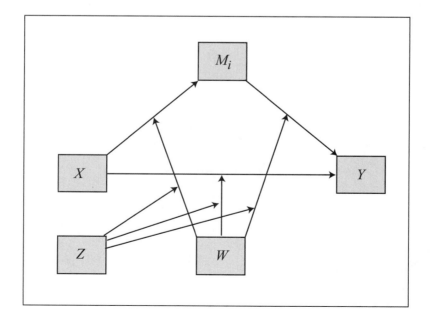

Model 74

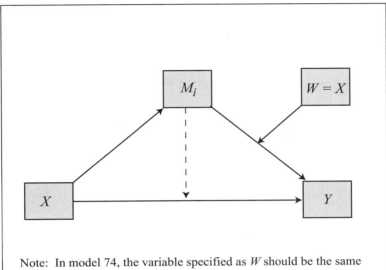

Note: In model 74, the variable specified as W should be the same variable as specified for X.

Model 75

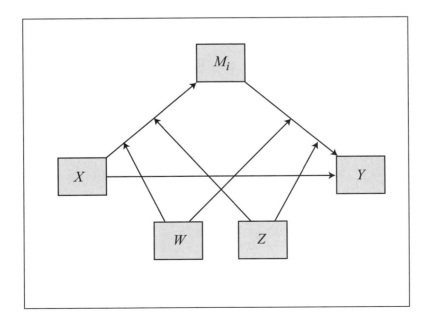

Model 76

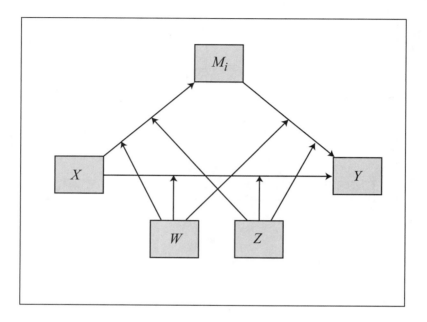

Model 80

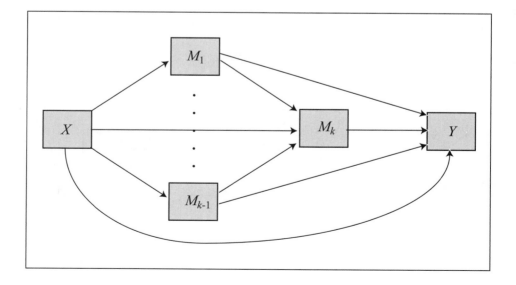

Model 81

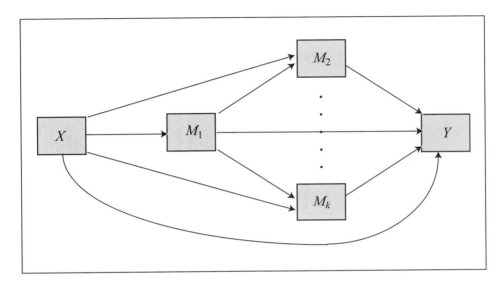

Model 82

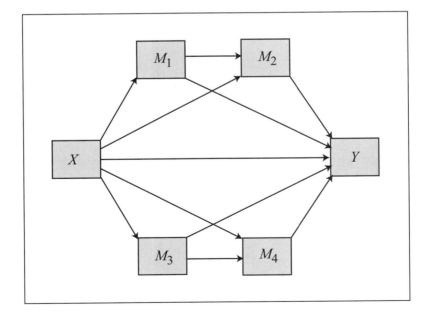

Model 83

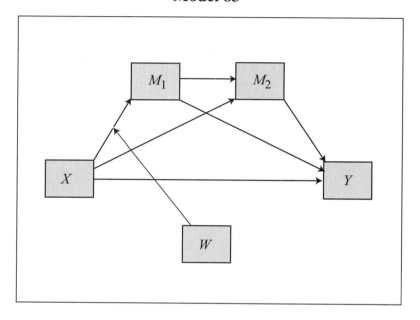

Model 84

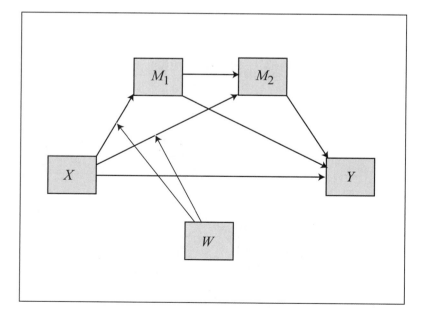

Model 85

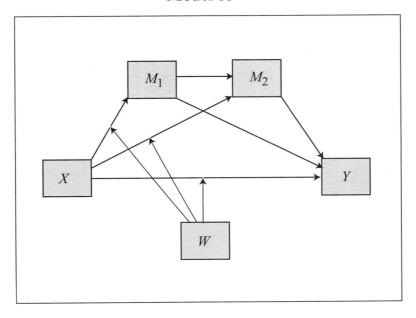

Model 86

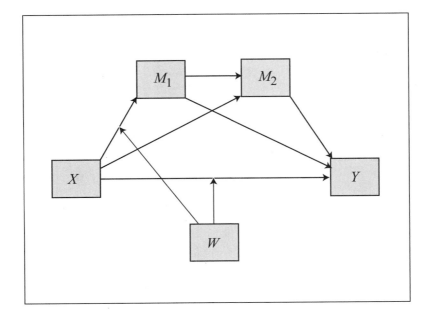

Model 87

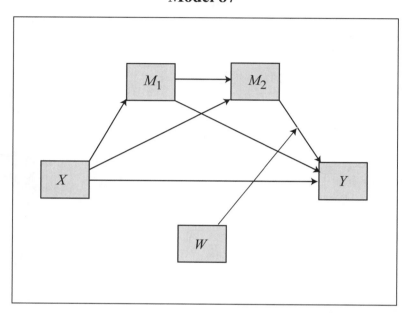

Model 88

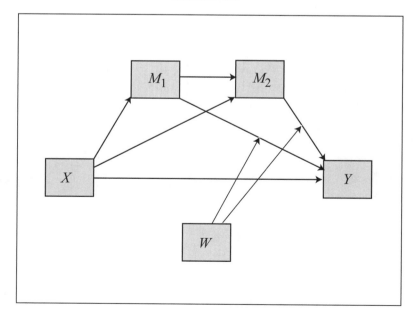

Model 89

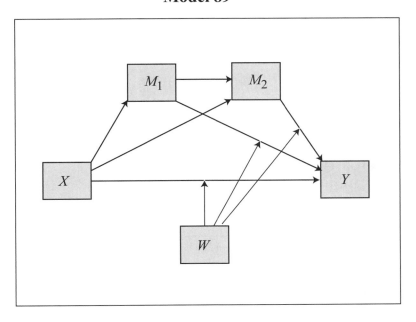

Model 90

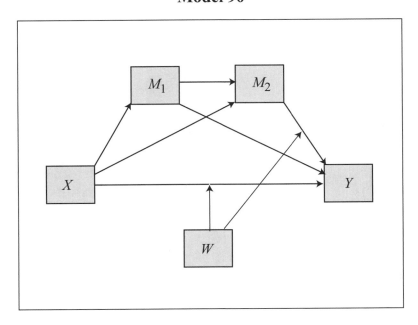

Model 91

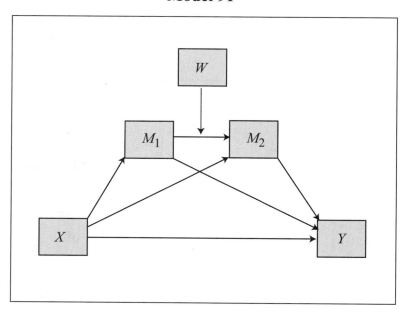

Model 92

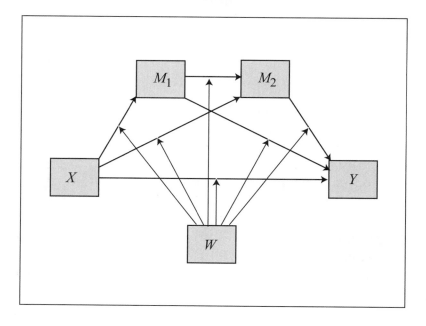

Appendix B
Constructing and Customizing Models in PROCESS

PROCESS uses a model number system for specifying how a mediation, moderation, or conditional process model is defined and translated into a set of regression equations. These preprogrammed models represent many of the popular models that researchers find useful in their work. However, there likely will be occasions when the model you want to estimate is not among the numbered, preprogrammed models. It may be that one of the models is close to the model you would like to estimate, but differs in a small way, perhaps by the presence of an undesired interaction, the absence of one you would like to estimate, or a path freely estimated you would rather have fixed to zero. It is possible to modify a numbered model, customizing it so that it conforms to the model you want to estimate. It is also possible to construct a model from scratch, completely bypassing the model numbering system. This appendix describes how to construct custom models, either by editing a numbered model or building one entirely from scratch.

Before beginning, it is worth pointing out some constraints that are built into PROCESS you cannot override even by editing or customizing a model. First, in a mediation, moderation, or conditional process analysis, you estimate the effect of a causal antecedent variable X on a consequent variable Y, perhaps moderated by W, Z, or both, or mediated through one or more mediators. PROCESS produces the direct and indirect effects of X on Y. But PROCESS allows only one X and one Y in a model. So any model you attempt to construct and estimate must focus on one X and one Y. Second, the model must be recursive, meaning no feedback loops or bidirectional causal influences. Third, only two moderators can be specified in a model. These moderators are always denoted W or Z. Finally, if you are building a model entirely from scratch, without referring to a model number, the maximum number of mediators allowed is six.

With these constraints always in mind, in order understand how to produce a custom model in PROCESS, you need to first understand how PROCESS represents a model in its inner workings. Inside PROCESS, a numbered model is represented as a set of four matrices, denoted here as the B, W, Z, and WZ matrices. These matrices specify which antecedent variables send effects to which consequent variables, and which effects are estimated as moderated and by what moderators. We start first with the B matrix, which represents the core of a mediation and conditional process model.

A Matrix Representation of a Mediation Process

For a recursive model with k mediators, consider a matrix denoted as B, with $k + 1$ rows and columns, as in Figure B.1. The columns of the B matrix correspond to antecedent variables in the model that send an effect to a consequent variable, with X in the first column and the k mediators in the remaining columns in the same order as listed following **m=** in the PROCESS command. The rows correspond to variables that receive effects (the consequent variables in the model), with the k mediators in the first k rows and Y in the last row.

In this matrix, the cell in row i, column j, is set to 1 if the antecedent variable in column j is proposed as affecting the consequent variable in row i, meaning that this effect is to be estimated rather than fixed to zero. But if that effect is fixed to zero, then that cell is set to zero in the B matrix. Because the model is recursive (with no bidirectional paths of influence), all (i, j) cells $j > i$ are always set to zero. These are represented with the black squares in Figure B.1.

With this notation, any mediation model with X as the causal antecedent or "independent variable," Y as the final effect or consequent "dependent

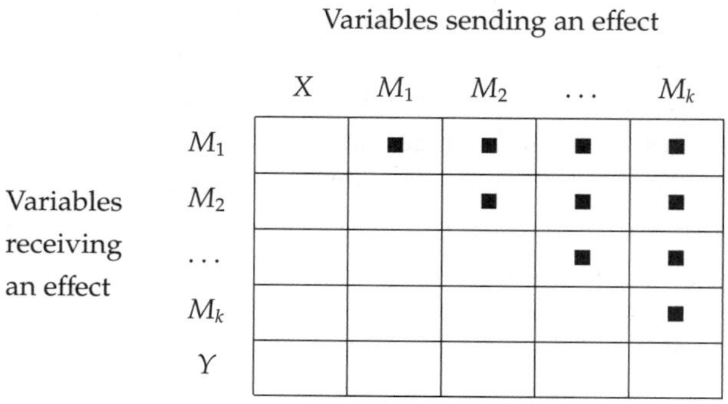

FIGURE B.1. The B matrix.

variable," and M as mediator(s) can be represented by a pattern of 0s and 1s. For example, a simple mediation model (i.e., one mediator) as depicted in Figure B.2, panel A, is represented by a 2×2 matrix containing all ones. All the entries are one because in this model, X sends an effect to M (the 1 in the X column and M row), M sends an effect to Y (the 1 in the M column and Y row), and X sends an effect to Y (the 1 in the X column, Y row).

The matrix representation of a parallel multiple mediator model with three mediators, as in Figure B.2, panel B, is a bit more complex because it has three mediators and involves some paths that are fixed to 0. These are represented with a 0 in the cells in the matrix corresponding to M_j sending an effect to M_i. All other cell entries are 1, meaning that X sends an effect to all mediators, and all mediators send an effect to Y. These effects are not fixed to zero but, rather, are freely estimated.

The zeros in the B matrix for the parallel multiple mediator represent constraints that no mediator affects any other mediator. If this constraint is relaxed, the result will be a model with at least one serial pathway from X to Y. Figure B.2, panel C, represents a serial multiple mediator model with two mediators. As X sends a path to all mediators, all mediators send an effect to the Y, and M_1 is allowed to effect M_2, the result is a matrix that contains all 1s.

Using this system of representing a mediation model always results in a matrix that is square with $k + 1$ rows and columns, where k is the number of mediators. Not counting the black squares (which are implied zeros), the matrix will contain $0.5(k + 1)(k + 2)$ cells containing either 0 or 1.

The BMATRIX Statement

When the user specifies a model number, PROCESS creates a matrix such as just described to represent the model. For example, model 4 with three mediators is represented internally by PROCESS with the matrix in Figure B.2, panel B. Similarly, model 6 with two mediators is presented by the matrix in Figure B.2, panel C. Rather than relying on a model number, you can program your own B matrix representing the effects that are freely estimated and those that are fixed to zero. This is accomplished by using the **bmatrix** statement, followed by a string of zeros and ones separated by commas (in SAS, no commas should separate the 0s and 1s). To understand how this works, imagine reading the cells in one of the matrices in Figure B.2, left to right, top to bottom, and listing out the 0s and 1s as they are encountered, skipping the cells with black squares. For instance, the simple mediation model in Figure B.2, panel A, is a sequence of three 1s. Knowing that your model contains only one mediator (meaning only one variable

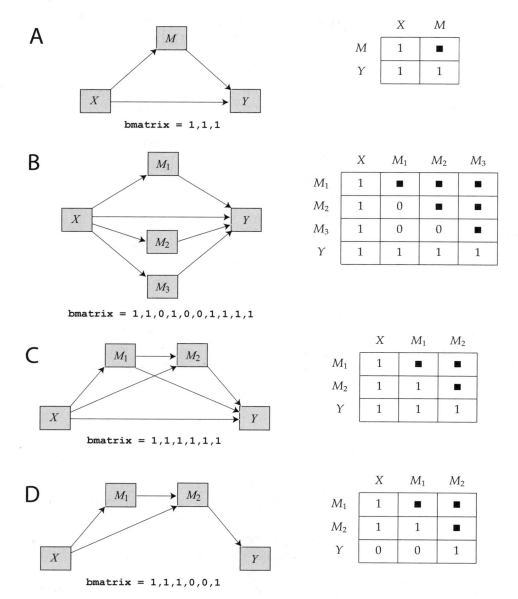

FIGURE B.2. Some mediation models and their representations as a *B* matrix.

is listed following **m=** in the PROCESS command), you can program this matrix with the statement

```
bmatrix=1,1,1
```

Likewise, the parallel multiple mediator model with three mediators in Figure B.2, panel B, would be programmed as

```
bmatrix=1,1,0,1,0,0,1,1,1,1
```

And the serial model with two mediators (Figure B.2, panel C) is

```
bmatrix=1,1,1,1,1,1
```

But if the direct effect of X on Y and the effect of M_1 on Y in this model were fixed to 0, as in Figure B.2, panel D, then use

```
bmatrix=1,1,1,0,0,1
```

Using this system, you can program any mediation model you desire into PROCESS, with the constraint that it must be a recursive model. Furthermore, as discussed earlier, the limit to the number of mediators when programming a custom model is six. A couple of other important limitations are discussed later.

PROCESS figures out the B matrix from your input in the **bmatrix** statement. When using the **bmatrix** statement, PROCESS reads the string of 0s and 1s and fills the matrix from left to right, top to bottom, with the order of the mediators in the resulting rows and columns being the same as the order the mediators are listed following **m=** in the PROCESS line. For example, the command

```
process y=tile/m=wine tent sand/x=baby/bmatrix=1,0,1,1,0,1,1,1,0,1.
```

```
%process (data=four,y=tile,m=wine tent sand,x=baby,
    bmatrix=1 0 1 1 0 1 1 1 0 1);
```

corresponds to

		baby	wine	tent	sand
	wine	1	■	■	■
$B =$	tent	0	1	■	■
	sand	1	0	1	■
	tile	1	1	0	1

Of course, you would probably do your programming of the model in PROCESS by first drawing your model on a piece of paper, then determining what the matrix should look like in order to figure out the required sequence of 0s and 1s in a **bmatrix** statement.

There are three other important constraints to keep in mind when programming a model using the **bmatrix** statement. First, every variable must send at least one effect. That means that each column of the B matrix must contain at least one 1. Second, every variable must receive at least one effect. This means that each row must contain at least one 1. Third, any variable specified as a mediator in the PROCESS command, meaning in the variable list following **m=**, must send and receive an effect. By definition, a mediator is causally between two variables, so if a variable does not send and receive an effect, it could not possibly be a mediator. If you violate this rule, PROCESS will generate a "dangling mediator" error.

All of the requirements for programming a model using the **bmatrix** statement are listed below:

- The model must be recursive, meaning no feedback loops or bidirectional cause.

- The model cannot have more than six mediators.

- All variables must send at least one effect.

- All variables must receive at least one effect.

- All variables specified as a mediator in the PROCESS command must both send and receive at least one effect.

- The **bmatrix** option must contain only zeros and ones following an equal sign and separated by commas (in SPSS; in SAS they should be separated by a space).

- With k mediators, the **bmatrix** option must contain a sequence of $0.5(k + 1)(k + 2)$ 0s and 1s.

Specifying Moderation of One of More Paths in the Mediation Model

In a conditional process model, one or more of the paths in the mediation component of the model is specified as moderated. PROCESS allows for up to two moderators in any model, and the moderator(s) can be specified as moderating any one or more of those paths. It also allows for moderated moderation, meaning that the moderation of a path by W can itself be moderated by Z. This section describes how to specify which paths, if any, in a mediation model are moderated.

The WMATRIX and ZMATRIX Statements

As discussed earlier, the B matrix, defined by the **bmatrix** statement, specifies which paths in the mediation process are estimated and which are fixed to zero. Now consider a matrix W identical in form to Figure B.1, but rather than specifying which paths are freely estimated versus fixed in the mediation model, the 0s and 1s in this matrix specify whether that path in the mediation model represented in the B matrix is linearly moderated by variable W. For example, for a model with two mediators, a W matrix of the form

		X	M_1	M_2
	M_1	1	■	■
$W =$	M_2	0	0	■
	Y	0	0	1

specifies linear moderation of the paths from X to M_1 and M_2 to Y by W. This is represented by the 1s in the X column and M_1 row, and in the M_2 column and Y row. All other entries in this matrix are 0, meaning that these paths are fixed to be invariant across values of W (i.e., not moderated by W). Such a matrix is programmed into PROCESS with the **wmatrix** statement, using a sequence of 0s and 1s and following the same rules as for the **bmatrix** statement. So this W matrix is specified in a PROCESS command using the statement

wmatrix=1,0,0,0,0,1

with the sequence of 1s and 0s in the series generated by reading the matrix from upper left to lower right. Working instead from the **wmatrix** statement to the W matrix,

wmatrix=1,1,0,1,1,0,0,0,0,1

corresponds to the matrix at the top of the next page for a three mediator model with moderation by W of the paths from X to M_1, M_2 and M_3, from M_1 to M_3, and from M_3 to Y.

PROCESS allows up to two moderators in a model, and up to two moderators per path. A second moderator Z and the paths in the mediation model it moderates is represented with a Z matrix and programmed with

		X	M_1	M_2	M_3
	M_1	1	■	■	■
$W =$	M_2	1	0	■	■
	M_3	1	1	0	■
	Y	0	0	0	1

a corresponding **zmatrix** statement, using the same procedure described for the W matrix and **wmatrix** statement.

Through the use of the **bmatrix**, **wmatrix**, and **zmatrix** statements, complex conditional process models can be programmed. Consider, for example, the model diagrammed in Figure B.3. The B, W, and Z matrices corresponding to this model can be found in Figure B.3 along with the **bmatrix**, **wmatrix**, and **zmatrix** statements corresponding to these matrices. The PROCESS command that estimates this model is

```
process y=tile/m=wine tent sand/x=baby/w=milk/z=hair/
   bmatrix=1,1,0,0,1,1,1,1,0,1/wmatrix=1,0,0,0,1,0,1,0,0,0/
   zmatrix=1,1,0,0,0,0,0,0,0,0.
```

```
%process (data=four,y=tile,m=wine tent sand,x=baby,w=milk,z=hair,
   bmatrix=1 1 0 0 1 1 1 1 0 1,wmatrix=1 0 0 0 1 0 1 0 0 0,
   zmatrix=1 1 0 0 0 0 0 0 0 0);
```

The WZMATRIX Statement

In a conditional process model with two moderators, moderators W and Z can moderate the same paths or different paths. Moderator Z can also moderate the moderation of a path by W, a circumstance known as *moderated moderation* or *three-way interaction* (see Chapter 9). In moderated moderation as defined by PROCESS, W is the *primary* moderator and Z is the *secondary* moderator. The secondary moderator moderates the moderation by the primary moderator of an effect in the mediation model. So, for example, if W is a moderator of the effect of X on M_1, then moderated moderation means that Z moderates the moderation by W of the effect of X on M_1.

Moderated moderation of a path in a conditional process model is specified using the WZ matrix, which is identical in form to the B, W, and Z matrices. A 1 in the WZ matrix specifies that the corresponding path in the B matrix is moderated by W, with that moderation itself moderated by Z. A 0 entry means no moderated moderation of that path. The WZ

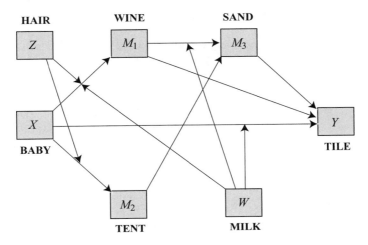

```
bmatrix = 1,1,0,0,1,1,1,1,0,1
wmatrix = 1,0,0,0,1,0,1,0,0,0
zmatrix = 1,1,0,0,0,0,0,0,0,0
```

B Matrix

	baby	wine	tent	sand
wine	1	■	■	■
tent	1	0	■	■
sand	0	1	1	■
tile	1	1	0	1

W Matrix

	baby	wine	tent	sand
wine	1	■	■	■
tent	0	0	■	■
sand	0	1	0	■
tile	1	0	0	0

Z Matrix

	baby	wine	tent	sand
wine	1	■	■	■
tent	1	0	■	■
sand	0	0	0	■
tile	0	0	0	0

FIGURE B.3. A conditional process model and its representation as three matrices.

matrix is programmed with the **wzmatrix** statement, using the same 0 and 1 sequence format as used in the **bmatrix**, **wmatrix**, and **zmatrix** statements.
 Consider the WZ matrix

$$WZ = \begin{array}{c} \\ wine \\ tent \\ sand \\ tile \end{array} \begin{array}{cccc} baby & wine & tent & sand \\ \hline 1 & \blacksquare & \blacksquare & \blacksquare \\ 0 & 0 & \blacksquare & \blacksquare \\ 0 & 0 & 0 & \blacksquare \\ 1 & 0 & 0 & 0 \end{array}$$

which is programmed with

wzmatrix=1,0,0,0,0,0,1,0,0,0

and specifies the moderation by Z of the moderation of the paths from "baby" to "wine" (X to M_1) and "baby" to "tile" (X to Y) by W. When combined with a **bmatrix** such as

$$B = \begin{array}{c} \\ wine \\ tent \\ sand \\ tile \end{array} \begin{array}{cccc} baby & wine & tent & sand \\ \hline 1 & \blacksquare & \blacksquare & \blacksquare \\ 1 & 0 & \blacksquare & \blacksquare \\ 1 & 0 & 0 & \blacksquare \\ 1 & 1 & 1 & 1 \end{array}$$

the resulting model, depicted in Figure B.4, is different than any model that is preprogrammed into PROCESS. This model is estimated in PROCESS using

```
process y=tile/m=wine tent sand/x=baby/w=milk/z=hair/
   bmatrix=1,1,0,1,0,0,1,1,1,1/wzmatrix=1,0,0,0,0,0,1,0,0,0.
```

```
%process (data=four,y=tile,m=wine tent sand,x=baby,w=milk,z=hair,
   bmatrix=1 1 0 1 0 0 1 1 1 1,wzmatrix=1 0 0 0 0 0 1 0 0 0);
```

When the **wzmatrix** statement is used, any corresponding cell in the W and Z matrices will be set to 1 by PROCESS, because a model with a three-way interaction should always include all possible two-way interactions. There is no way of overriding this rule. So the commands above would be equivalent to

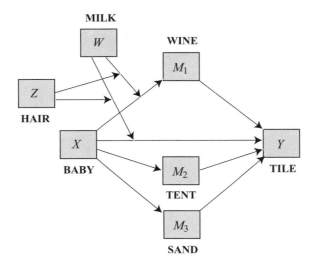

FIGURE B.4. A customized conditional process model resulting from the use of the **wzmatrix** statement.

```
process y=tile/m=wine tent sand/x=baby/w=milk/z=hair/
    bmatrix=1,1,0,1,0,0,1,1,1,1/wmatrix=1,0,0,0,0,0,1,0,0,0/
    zmatrix=1,0,0,0,0,0,1,0,0,0/wzmatrix=1,0,0,0,0,0,1,0,0,0.
```

```
%process (data=four,y=tile,m=wine tent sand,x=baby,w=milk,z=hair,
    bmatrix=1 1 0 1 0 0 1 1 1 1,wmatrix=1 0 0 0 0 0 1 0 0 0,
    zmatrix=1 0 0 0 0 0 1 0 0 0,wzmatrix=1 0 0 0 0 0 1 0 0 0);
```

Even if you use **wmatrix** and **zmatrix** statements and attempt to set such a cell to 0, PROCESS will override your code and set that cell to 1. But otherwise, the entries in the W and Z matrices are independent of the corresponding entries in the WZ matrix. So the PROCESS command

```
process y=tile/m=wine tent sand/x=baby/w=milk/z=hair/
    bmatrix=1,1,0,1,0,0,1,1,1,1/wmatrix=1,0,0,1,0,0,1,0,0,0/
    zmatrix=1,0,0,0,0,0,1,0,0,1/wzmatrix=1,0,0,0,0,0,1,0,0,0.
```

```
%process (data=four,y=tile,m=wine tent sand,x=baby,w=milk,z=hair,
    bmatrix=1 1 0 1 0 0 1 1 1 1,wmatrix=1 0 0 1 0 0 1 0 0 0,
    zmatrix=1 0 0 0 0 0 1 0 0 1,wzmatrix=1 0 0 0 0 0 1 0 0 0);
```

programs the model in Figure B.5.

The rules for the specification of moderated paths in a PROCESS model are summarized below:

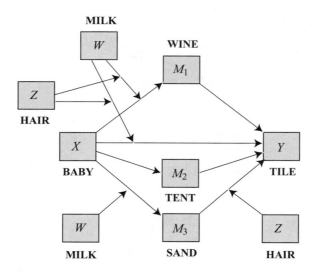

FIGURE B.5. A customized conditional process model resulting from the use of the **wmatrix**, **zmatrix**, and **wzmatrix** statements.

- Up to two moderators, W and Z, can be specified in any model. They can be assigned to any path in the mediation model, but no more than two moderators can be used.

- A path fixed to zero cannot be moderated. So if a cell in the B matrix for the model is 0, then all corresponding cells in the W, Z, and WZ matrices must be zero. A failure to follow this rule will result in an error message stating that a path fixed to zero cannot be moderated.

- If your model contains only a single moderator, that moderator must be W. In other words, if the W matrix contains all zeros, then so too must the Z matrix contain all zeros.

- When building a model from scratch (i.e., no model number is specified in the PROCESS command), all the cells in the W, Z, and WZ matrices are set to zero by default. They are changed through the use of the **wmatrix**, **zmatrix**, and **wzmatrix** statements. So if all of the entries in a W, Z, or WZ matrix for your model are zero, then the **wmatrix**, **zmatrix**, or **wzmatrix** need not be included in the PROCESS command.

- Any cell in the WZ matrix set to 1 will result in the corresponding cells in W and Z matrices set to 1, regardless of whether they are set to 1 by the user with the **wmatrix** and **zmatrix** statements. So any zero provided in a **wmatrix** or **zmatrix** statement that is inconsistent with a 1 in a **wzmatrix** statement will be set to 1 by PROCESS when the command is read. This cannot be overridden

Editing a Numbered Model

PROCESS represents a model with a set of four matrices that define which paths in a mediation model are estimated versus fixed at zero, and which of these paths are moderated and by which moderator or moderators and how. When you specify a model number in a PROCESS command, this is essentially a shortcut to setting up a model from scratch like discussed in the prior section. A call to PROCESS with a specific model number tells PROCESS how to set up the matrices that define the model, eliminating the need to use **bmatrix**, **wmatrix**, **zmatrix**, and **wzmatrix** statements. The cost of this shortcut is that a numbered model may not correspond exactly to the model you prefer to estimate, perhaps because it misses something you want in your model, or your model includes something that is not a part of the closest, preprogrammed model number.

Midway between using a preprogrammed model number and building a model entirely from scratch is editing a numbered model. This feature of PROCESS allows you to work with the convenient model number system while allowing for the tailoring of the model to your specific needs and wants for the analysis at hand. To illustrate, consider the model in Figure B.6, which is a parallel multiple mediator model with three mediators. All three paths from X to a mediator are moderated by W. And the path from M_1 to Y is specified as moderated by Z. Looking through the diagrams of numbered models, there is no such model preprogrammed into PROCESS.

You could just program this model from scratch using the procedures already described. Alternatively, the task could be made slightly simpler by recognizing that although none of the preprogrammed numbered models correspond exactly to this model, a few are close. For example, model 7 is nearly identical, except that model 7 does not include the moderation of any of the paths from mediators to Y. Model 21 does include moderation of the paths from X to each M by W and from each M to Y by Z, but this is not quite right, because the desired model does not include moderation of the M_2 and M_3 paths to Y. I illustrate here how each of these preprogrammed numbered models can be edited to conform to this desired model. The first approach adds the missing moderated path in model 7. The second approach involves deleting the undesired moderation from model 21.

Editing a model involves reprogramming the matrices that define it so that the resulting model is different than the original. All but the B matrix can be reprogrammed when editing a model, and all models num-

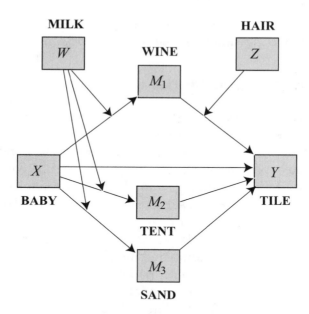

FIGURE B.6. A conditional process model similar to but not the same as models 7 and 21.

bered 4 and higher, with the exception of model 74, can be edited. So the editable components of a numbered model include only the moderation components as defined in the W, Z, and WZ matrices. If you want to fundamentally change the model by modifying the mediation component as defined in the B matrix, you must instead program the model from scratch using the procedure described earlier.

Knowing the rules for how to create a custom model, you could probably figure out what the B, W, Z, and WZ matrices look like for models 7 and 21 just by looking at the preprogrammed model diagrams. But sometimes it is easier to have PROCESS just show you what those matrices look like. This can be done using the **matrices** statement. The command below estimates model 7, which is not the model we want to estimate. But I have added the statement **matrices=1** to the PROCESS command. The section of output that results from the inclusion of this statement follows the PROCESS command.

```
process y=tile/m=wine tent sand/x=baby/w=milk/model=7/matrices=1.
```

```
%process (data=four,y=tile,m=wine tent sand,x=baby,w=milk,
    model=7,matrices=1);
```

```
*********************** MODEL DEFINITION MATRICES *************************

FROM variables are columns, TO variables are rows.

BMATRIX: Paths freely estimated (1) and fixed to zero (0):
     baby wine tent sand
wine  1
tent  1    0
sand  1    0    0
tile  1    1    1    1

WMATRIX: Paths moderated (1) and not moderated (0) by W:
     baby wine tent sand
wine  1
tent  1    0
sand  1    0    0
tile  0    0    0    0
```

When the **matrices** statement is used, all model matrices containing at least one 1 will be printed toward the bottom of the PROCESS output. In model 7, there is no Z in the model at all, and so no moderation by Z. Furthermore, model 7 does not contain a moderated moderation component. So the Z and WZ matrices contain all zeros, and hence their printing is suppressed. Only the B and W matrices in model 7 contain at least one 1, so they are produced in the output. Using the logic described in the prior section, you should be able to discern why the B and W matrices above define model 7.

The desired model includes all the components of model 7, plus moderation of the path from M_1 to Y by Z. If that model did exist and we used the **matrices** statement, an additional matrix would be found in the output that looked like this:

```
ZMATRIX: Paths moderated (1) and not moderated (0) by Z:
     baby wine tent sand
wine  0
tent  0    0
sand  0    0    0
tile  0    1    0    0
```

This matrix is all zeros, except for the cell in the "wine" column and "tile" row, reflecting the moderation of the effect of wine (M_1) on tile (Y) by Z. Of course, this model does not exist. But we can program such a model by adding Z as a variable in the PROCESS command for model 7, and adding a **zmatrix** statement corresponding to this matrix. The **zmatrix** that would program this matrix would be, following the rules described in the prior section,

zmatrix=0,0,0,0,0,0,0,1,0,0

and so the PROCESS command becomes

```
process y=tile/m=wine tent sand/x=baby/w=milk/z=hair/model=7/
    zmatrix=0,0,0,0,0,0,0,1,0,0.
```

```
%process (data=four,y=tile,m=wine tent sand,x=baby,w=milk,z=hair,
    model=7,zmatrix=0 0 0 0 0 0 0 1 0 0);
```

After executing the PROCESS command, check the output to make sure you have correctly programmed this model, in this case by looking at the equation for Y to make sure it now includes Z and M_1Z as predictors. Adding a **matrices=1** statement to verify PROCESS understood your **zmatrix** statement would also be helpful as verification.

The prior example illustrated how to edit a model by adding something missing from a preprogrammed numbered model. A model can also be modified by removing something unwanted. To illustrate this, consider that the desired model is similar to model 21, which includes moderation of all the paths from X to mediators by W and moderation of all paths from mediators to Y by Z. This is not quite the desired model, as it contains two additional moderated paths, one from M_2 to Y, and one from M_3 to Y. So the offending part of model 21 is in the Z matrix, as it contains too many 1s. This can be seen by estimating model 21 and telling PROCESS to show the matrices that define it:

```
process y=tile/m=wine tent sand/x=baby/w=milk/z=hair/model=21/matrices=1.
```

```
%process (data=four,y=tile,m=wine tent sand,x=baby,w=milk,z=hair,
    model=21,matrices=1);
```

```
************************* MODEL DEFINITION MATRICES *************************

FROM variables are columns, TO variables are rows.

BMATRIX: Paths freely estimated (1) and fixed to zero (0):
     baby wine tent sand
wine   1
tent   1    0
sand   1    0    0
tile   1    1    1    1
```

```
WMATRIX: Paths moderated (1) and not moderated (0) by W:
        baby wine tent sand
wine  1
tent  1    0
sand  1    0    0
tile  0    0    0    0

ZMATRIX: Paths moderated (1) and not moderated (0) by Z:
        baby wine tent sand
wine  0
tent  0    0
sand  0    0    0
tile  0    1    1    1
```

As discussed in the prior example, we want the Z matrix to contain a 1 only in the "wine" (M_1) column and "tile" (Y) row because that is the only path in the model that should be moderated by "hair" (Z). The other two 1s (in the "tent" and "sand" columns, "tile" row) produce interactions we do not want in the model. So to remove them, reprogram the Z matrix:

```
process y=tile/m=wine tent sand/x=baby/w=milk/z=hair/model=21/
    zmatrix=0,0,0,0,0,0,0,1,0,0.
```

```
%process (data=four,y=tile,m=wine tent sand,x=baby,w=milk,z=hair,
    model=21,zmatrix=0,0,0,0,0,0,0,1,0,0);
```

Notice that this PROCESS command is largely identical to the version using model 7. The only difference is what is happening in the inner workings of PROCESS. With model 7, we are adding to a Z matrix that is otherwise set to all zeros by model 7, whereas with model 21, we were taking away 1s from the Z matrix that would otherwise be there.

Post Hoc Pruning of a Model

Editing a model by removing unwanted effects can be useful when you want to "prune" from a model an effect that was hypothesized but does not appear worth having in the model after analysis. For example, suppose you had estimated the model in Figure B.6 using either of the approaches just described, and you found no compelling evidence supporting moderation of the effect of X on M_2 by W. In that case, you might want to fix the effect of X on M_2 to be independent of W, meaning not moderated by W. This would be accomplished by editing the W matrix, removing the 1 in the cell that specifies that effect to be moderated by W. In the W matrix, this is the 1 in the "baby" column, "tent" row. So we want to turn

```
WMATRIX: Paths moderated (1) and not moderated (0) by W:
     baby wine tent sand
wine  1
tent  1    0
sand  1    0    0
tile  0    0    0    0
```

into the matrix below:

```
WMATRIX: Paths moderated (1) and not moderated (0) by W:
     baby wine tent sand
wine  1
tent  0    0
sand  1    0    0
tile  0    0    0    0
```

Either of the PROCESS commands below accomplishes this, while retaining everything else that is a part of the original model:

```
process y=tile/m=wine tent sand/x=baby/w=milk/z=hair/model=7/
    zmatrix=0,0,0,0,0,0,0,1,0,0/wmatrix=1,0,0,1,0,0,0,0,0,0.
```

```
%process (data=four,y=tile,m=wine tent sand,x=baby,w=milk,
    model=7,zmatrix=0 0 0 0 0 0 0 1 0 0,wmatrix=1 0 0 1 0 0 0 0 0 0);
```

or, alternatively,

```
process y=tile/m=wine tent sand/x=baby/w=milk/z=hair/model=21/
    zmatrix=0,0,0,0,0,0,0,1,0,0/wmatrix=1,0,0,1,0,0,0,0,0,0.
```

```
%process (data=four,y=tile,m=wine tent sand,x=baby,w=milk,
    model=21,zmatrix=0 0 0 0 0 0 1 0 0,wmatrix=1 0 0 1 0 0 0 0 0 0);
```

Because editing a model is very much like starting from scratch, all the rules and constraints discussed earlier about the W, Z, and WZ matrices and corresponding statements apply to editing a model.

Making a Moderator a Covariate in the Same Model

A variable can play only a single role in a PROCESS command. This means that a variable specified as a moderator cannot also serve as a covariate in the same model. So, for example, you cannot specify a variable as W by listing it following **w=** while also including it as a covariate following **cov=**. When a variable is specified as a moderator in a model of a consequent,

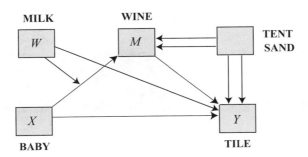

FIGURE B.7. A conditional process model with W serving as moderator in the equation for one consequent and covariate in the equation for a different consequent.

that variable automatically ends up in the regression equation for that consequent.

But there may be occasions when you want a variable serving as a moderator of one or more paths in the model to also be in the equation of a consequent variable that does not include an effect specified as moderated by that variable. As an example, consider model 7, which specifies W as a moderator of the effect of X on M but not of the effect of M or X on Y in a mediation model. This means that W cannot be included in the model of Y because it is already serving the role of moderator in the equation for M. But what if you want to estimate the effect of M or the effect of X on Y while controlling for W?

It would seem that this constraint that a variable can't serve as both covariate and moderator would preclude including W in the equation for Y in model 7. But there is a trick that works that allows you to make a moderator in one part of the model a covariate in another part. It requires making a copy of W but with a different name so that PROCESS will not detect that you are assigning the same variable to two different roles. But to avoid a singularity in the data matrix (which will result in an error), you have to keep that copy of W out of the equation for the consequent variable in which it plays the role of moderator. This can be done using the **cmatrix** command. This is required because W will automatically be included in the equation for a consequent in which it serves the role of moderator of an effect of a variable in that equation. If you fail to exclude the copy of W from the equation for the consequent in which W serves as a moderator, you'll end up with W in the model of that consequent twice.

To illustrate, consider the model in Figure B.7. The model has two covariates "sand" and "tent" in the equations of M and Y, but W ("milk"), the moderator of the X to M path, is also serving as a covariate in the equation for Y. In PROCESS, this model can be estimated using the code below:

```
compute milkcopy=milk.
process y=tile/m=wine/x=baby/w=milk/model=7/cov=sand tent milkcopy/
    cmatrix=1,1,0,1,1,1.
```

```
data four;set four;milkcopy=milk;run;
%process (data=four,y=tile,m=wine,x=baby,w=milk,model=7,cov=sand
    tent milkcopy,cmatrix=1 1 0 1 1 1);
```

The **cmatrix** option is explained in Appendix A. The C matrix is, in this example, a 2×3 matrix with consequents as rows and covariates as columns. The **cmatrix** option in this PROCESS command sets all cells in this matrix to 1 except for the cell in the "wine" row, "milkcopy" column, which is set to 0. The 0 in this cell tells PROCESS that "milkcopy" should not be included in the model of "wine," because "milk" is already in this equation as it is serving as a moderator of the effect of "baby" on "wine." The 1s elsewhere in the matrix tell PROCESS to include the covariate in the column in the equation of the consequent in the row.

Appendix C
Monte Carlo Confidence Intervals in SPSS and SAS

The code in this appendix defines a macro for the generation of a Monte Carlo confidence interval for the indirect effect of X on Y through M in a mediation analysis. The code can be typed into SPSS or SAS or downloaded from *www.afhayes.com*, saved for later use if desired, and then executed. Running this code defines a new command called MCMED. The main arguments for the macro are the a and b coefficients (**a=** and **b=**) corresponding to the $X \rightarrow M$ and $M \rightarrow Y$ paths, respectively, and their standard errors (**sea=** and **seb=**, both default to 1 if omitted). In addition, the number of Monte Carlo samples can be set (**samples=**, defaults to 10,000 if omitted), as can the covariance of a and b (**covab=**, defaults to zero if omitted) and the desired confidence (**conf=**, defaults to 95 if omitted).

The SPSS version of MCMED will construct a new data file containing the Monte Carlo samples of a, b, and ab. This file can be used to produce a visual representation of the sampling distribution of ab. The SAS version constructs a temporary work data file named MCVALS and automatically produces a histogram of the estimates of ab.

Lines in the code below with a "print" command must be entered as one continuous line. Do not break print commands up into multiple lines of code, as this will produce errors.

SPSS version:

```
define mcmed (a=!charend ('/') !default(0)/b=!charend ('/') !default(0)
   /sea=!charend('/') !default(1)/seb=!charend('/') !default(1)
   /samples=!charend ('/') !default(10000)/covab=!charend ('/')
   !default(0)/conf=!charend ('/') !default(95)).
preserve.
set printback=off.
```

```
matrix.
compute r={(!sea)*(!sea),!covab;!covab,(!seb)*(!seb)}.
compute errchk=0.
do if (det(r) <= 0).
compute errchk=2.
end if.
do if (!seb <= 0 or !sea <=0).
compute errchk=1.
end if.
compute cilow=((100-!conf)/200).
compute cihigh=1-cilow.
compute cilow=trunc(!samples*cilow).
compute cihigh=trunc((!samples*cihigh)+.999)+1.
do if (cilow < 1 or cihigh > !samples).
compute errchk=3.
end if.
compute pars={!a;!sea;!b;!seb;!covab;!samples;!conf}.
print pars/title="*** Input Data ***"/rlabels="a:", "SE(a):", "b:",
   "SE(b):", "COV(ab):", "Samples:", "Conf:"/format = F8.4.
do if (errchk=0).
compute mns=make(!samples,1,!a),make(!samples, 1, !b).
compute x1=sqrt(-2*ln(uniform(!samples,2)))&*cos((2*3.14159265358979)*
   uniform(!samples,2)).
compute x1=(x1*chol(r))+mns.
compute ab=x1(:,1)&*x1(:,2).
compute x1={x1,ab}.
compute abtmp=ab.
compute abtmp(GRADE(ab))=ab.
compute ab=abtmp.
save x1/outfile=*/variables=a b ab.
compute mc={(!a*!b), ab(cilow,1), ab(cihigh,1)}.
print mc/title="**** Monte Carlo Confidence Interval ****"/clabels=
   "ab", "LLCI", "ULCI"/format = F8.4.
end if.
do if (errchk=1).
print/title="ERROR: Standard errors must be positive".
else if (errchk=2).
print/title="ERROR: Entered covariance is not compatible with the
   standard errors of a and b".
else if (errchk=3).
print/title="ERROR: Number of samples is too small for this level of
```

```
        confidence".
end if.
end matrix.
restore.
!enddefine.
```

SAS version:

```
%macro mcmed (a=0,sea=1,b=0,seb=1,samples=1000,conf=95,covab=0);
proc iml;
r=((&sea*&sea)||(&covab))//((&covab)||(&seb*&seb));
errchk=0;
if (det(r)<=0) then;do;errchk=2;end;
tmp=det(r);
if ((&sea<=0) | (&seb<=0)) then;do;errchk=1;end;
cilow=((100-&conf)/200);cihigh=1-cilow;
cilow=floor(&samples*cilow);cihigh=floor((&samples*cihigh)+0.999)+1;
if ((cilow < 1) | (cihigh > &samples)) then;do;errchk=3;end;
pars=&a//&sea//&b//&seb//&covab//&samples//&conf;
rwnm="a:"//"SE(a):"//"b:"//"SE(b):"//"COV(ab):"//"Samples:"//"Conf:";
print pars [label="*** Input Data ***" rowname=rwnm];
create mcvals from pars;append from pars;close mcvals;
if (errchk=0) then;do;
mns=j(&samples,1,&a)||j(&samples,1,&b);
x1=rannor(j(&samples,2,0));x1=(x1*root(r))+mns;
ab=x1[,1]#x1[,2];x1=x1||ab;
create mcvals from x1[colname='a' 'b' 'ab'];append from x1;
abtmp=ab;abtmp[rank(abtmp)]=ab;ab=abtmp;
mc=(&a*&b)||ab[cilow,1]||ab[cihigh,1];
clnm="ab"||"LLCI"||"ULCI";
print mc [label="*** Monte Carlo Confidence Interval ***" colname=clnm
    format=12.4];
end;
if (errchk=1) then;do;print "ERROR: Standard errors must be
    positive";end;
if (errchk=2) then;do;print "ERROR: Entered covariance is not
    compatible with the standard errors of a and b";end;
if (errchk=3) then;do;print "ERROR: Number of samples is too small for
    this level of confidence";end;
quit;
```

```
proc univariate data=mcvals noprint;var ab;histogram;run;
%mend;
```

Once the macro is defined by running the code, a properly formatted MCMED command can be executed. For example, the SPSS code below produces a 95% Monte Carlo confidence interval for the indirect effect in the analysis reported in section 3.5, based on 10,000 Monte Carlo samples:

```
mcmed a=0.173/b=0.769/sea=0.030/seb=0.103.
```

In SAS, the corresponding command is

```
%mcmed (a=0.173,b=0.769,sea=0.030,seb=0.103);
```

In some applications of mediation analysis, the covariance between a and b is not zero. When an estimate of this covariance is available, it can be included in the MCMED command. The confidence width can also be modified, or the number of Monte Carlo samples set at some value larger than 10,000. For example, the SPSS code below generates a 99% Monte Carlo confidence interval for the indirect effect based on 100,000 samples, given estimates of a, b, their covariance, and their standard errors:

```
mcmed a=0.5/b=1.2/sea=0.35/seb=0.65/covab=0.08/samples=100000/conf=99.
```

In SAS, the corresponding command is

```
%mcmed (a=0.5,b=1.2,sea=0.35,seb=0.65,covab=0.08,samples=100000,conf=99);
```

References

Aiken, L. S., & West, S. G. (1991). *Multiple regression: Testing and interpreting interactions*. Thousand Oaks, CA: Sage Publications.

Alvarez, A. N., & Juang, J. P. (2010). Filipino-Americans and racism: A multiple mediation model of coping. *Journal of Counseling Psychology, 38*, 545–556.

Alwin, D. F., & Hauser, R. M. (1975). The decomposition of effects in path analysis. *American Sociological Review, 40*, 33–47.

Amato, P. R. (2001). Children of divorce in the 1990s: An update of the Amato and Keith (1991) meta-analysis. *Journal of Family Psychology, 15*, 355–370.

Amato, P. R., & Keith, B. (1991). Parental divorce and the well-being of children: A meta-analysis. *Psychological Bulletin, 110*, 26–46.

An, M., Colarelli, S. M., O'Brien, K., & Boyajian, M. E. (2016). Why we need more nature at work: Effects of natural elements and sunlight on employee mental health and work attitudes. *Plos One, 11*, 1–17.

Anagnostopoulos, F., Slater, J., & Fitzsimmons, D. (2010). Intrusive thoughts and psychological adjustment to breast cancer: Exploring the moderating and mediating role of global meaning and emotional expressivity. *Journal of Clinical Psychology in Medical Settings, 17*, 137–149.

Andela, M., & Truchot, D. (2016). Job stressors and burnout in hospitals: The mediating role of emotional dissonance. *International Journal of Stress Management, 23*, 298–317.

Anderson, C. A., & Bushman, B. J. (2001). Effects of violent video games on aggressive behavior, aggressive cognition, aggressive affect, physiological arousal, and prosocial behavior: A review of the scientific literature. *Psychological Science, 12*, 353–359.

Anderson, C. A., Shibuya, A., Ibori, N., Swing, E. L., Bushman, B. J., Sakamoto, A., et al. (2010). Violent video game effects on aggression, empathy, and prosocial behavior in Eastern and Western countries: A meta-analytic review. *Psychological Bulletin, 136*, 151–173.

Andreeva, V. A., Yaroch, A. L., Unger, J. B., Cockburn, M. G., Rueda, R., & Reynolds, K. D. (2010). Moderated mediation regarding the sun-safe behavior of U.S. Latinos: Advancing the theory and evidence for acculturation-focused research and interventions. *Journal of Immigrant Minority Health, 12*, 691–698.

Antheunis, M. L., Valkenburg, P. M., & Peter, J. (2010). Getting acquainted through social network sites: Testing a model of online uncertainty reduction and social attraction. *Computers in Human Behavior, 26*, 100–109.

Aragón, O. R., Clark, M. S., Dyer, R. L., & Bargh, J. A. (2015). Dimorphous expressions of positive emotion: Displays of both care and aggression in response to cute stimuli. *Psychological Science, 26*, 259–273.

Aroian, L. A. (1947). The probability function of the product of two normally distributed variables. *Annals of Mathematical Statistics, 18*, 265–271.

Ashton-James, C. E., & Tracy, J. L. (2012). Pride and prejudice: How feelings about the self influence judgments of others. *Personality and Social Psychology Bulletin, 38*, 466–476.

Augustine, J. M. (2014). Maternal education and the unequal significance of family structure for children's early achievement. *Social Forces, 93*, 687–718.

Baguley. (2009). Standardized or simple effect size: What should be reported? *British Journal of Psychology, 100*, 603–617.

Banks, J. B., Tartar, J. L., & Welhaf, M. S. (2014). Where's the impairment? an examination of factors that impact sustained attention following a stressor. *Cognition and Emotion, 28*, 856–866.

Barnhofer, T., & Chittka, T. (2010). Cognitive reactivity mediates the relationship between neuroticism and depression. *Behaviour Research and Therapy, 48*, 275–281.

Baron, R. M., & Kenny, D. A. (1986). The moderator–mediator variable distinction in social psychological research: Conceptual, strategic, and statistical considerations. *Journal of Personality and Social Psychology, 51*, 1173–1182.

Barz, M., Lange, D., Parschau, L., Lonsdale, C., Knoll, N., & Schwarzer, R. (2016). Self-efficacy, planning, and prepatory behaviours as joint predictors of physical activity: A conditional process analysis. *Psychology and Health, 31*, 65–78.

Bauer, D. J., & Curran, P. J. (2005). Probing interactions in fixed and multilevel regression: Inferential and graphical techniques. *Multivariate Behavioral Research, 40*, 373–400.

Bauer, D. J., Preacher, K. J., & Gil, K. M. (2006). Conceptualizing and testing random indirect effects in moderated mediation in multilevel models: New procedures and recommendations. *Psychological Methods, 29*, 142–163.

Baumgartner, J., & Morris, J. S. (2006). *The Daily Show* effect: Candidate evaluations, efficacy, and American youth. *American Politics Research, 34*, 341–367.

Beach, S. R. H., Lei, M. K., Brody, G. H., Simons, R. L., Cutrona, C., & Philibert, R. A. (2012). Genetic moderation of contextual effects on negative arousal and parenting in African-American parents. *Journal of Family Psychology, 26*, 46–55.

Bear, G. (1995). Computationally intensive methods warrant reconsideration of pedagogy in statistics. *Behavior Research Methods, Instruments, and Computers, 27*, 144–147.

Belogolovsky, E., Bamberger, P. A., & Bacharach, S. B. (2012). Workforce disengagement stressors and retiree alcohol misuse: The mediating effects of sleep problems and the moderating effects of gender. *Human Relations, 65*, 705–728.

Bem, D. (1987). Writing the empirical journal article. In M. P. Zanna & J. M. Darley (Eds.), *The complete academic: A practical guide for the beginning social scientist* (pp. 171–201). Mahwah, NJ: Lawrence Erlbaum Associates.

Berger, V. W. (2000). Pros and cons of permutation tests in clinical trials. *Statistics in Medcine, 19*, 1319–1328.

Bergman, K. N., Cummings, E. M., & Davies, P. T. (2014). Interparental aggression and adolescent adjustment: The role of emotional insecurity and adrenocortical activity. *Journal of Family Violence, 29*, 763–771.

Berndt, N. C., Hayes, A. F., Verboon, P., Lechner, L., Bolman, C., & De Vries, H. (2013). Self-efficacy mediates the impact of craving on smoking abstinence in low to moderately anxious patients: Results of a moderated mediation approach. *Psychology of Addictive Behaviors, 27*, 113–124.

Berry, W. D. (1993). *Understanding regression assumptions*. Thousand Oaks, CA: Sage Publications.

Beullens, K., & Vandenbosch, L. (2016). A conditional process analysis on the relationship between the use of social networking sites, attitudes, peer norms, and adolescents' intentions to consume alcohol. *Media Psychology, 19*, 310–333.

Biesanz, J. C., Falk, C. F., & Savalei, V. (2010). Assessing mediational models: Testing and interval estimation for indirect effects. *Multivariate Behavioral Research, 45*, 661–701.

Bissonnette, V., Ickes, W., Bernstein, I., & Knowles, E. (1990). Personality moderating variables: A warning about statistical artifact and a comparison of analytic techniques. *Journal of Personality, 58*, 567–587.

Bizer, G. Y., Hart, J., & Jekogian, A. M. (2012). Belief in a just world and social dominance orientation: Evidence for a mediational pathway predicting negative attitudes and discrimination against individuals with mental illness. *Peronality and Individual Differences, 52*, 661–701.

Blashill, A. J., & Wal, J. S. V. (2010). The role of body image dissatisfaction and depression on HAART adherence in HIV positive men: Tests of mediation models. *AIDS and Behavior, 14*, 280–288.

Bohns, V. K., Newark, D. A., & Xu, A. Z. (2016). For a dollar, would you? how (we think) money affects compliance with our requests. *Organizational Behavior and Human Decision Processes, 134*, 45–62.

Bollen, K. A. (1989). *Structural equations with latent variables*. New York, NY: John Wiley and Sons.

Bollen, K. A., & Stine, R. (1990). Direct and indirect effects: Classical and bootstrap estimates of variability. *Sociological Methodology, 20*, 115–140.

Bombay, A., Matheson, K., & Anisman, H. (2012). Expectations among aboriginal people in Canada regarding the potential impacts of a government apology. *Political Psychology, 34*, 443–460.

Bond, B. J. (2015). The mediating role of self-discrepancies in the relationship between media exposure and well-being among lesbian, gay, and bisexual adolescents. *Media Psychology, 18*, 51–73.

Boren, J. P. (2014). The relationship between co-rumination, social support, stress, and burnout among working adults. *Management Communication Quarterly, 28*, 3–25.

Boren, J. P., & Veksler, A. E. (2015). Communicatively restricted organizational stress CROS I: Conceptualization and overview. *Management Communication Quarterly, 29*, 28–55.

Brach, S., Walsh, G., & Shaw, D. (2017). Sustainable consumption and third-party certification labels: Consumers' perceptions and reactions. *European Management Journal.*

Brandt, M. J., & Reyna, C. (2010). The role of prejudice and the need for closure in religious fundamentalism. *Personality and Social Psychology Bulletin, 36,* 715–725.

Breen, R., Karlson, K. B., & Holm, A. (2013). Total, direct and indirect effects in logit and probit models. *Sociological Methods and Research, 42,* 164–191.

Breitborde, N. J. K., Srihari, V. H., Pollard, J. M., Addington, D. N., & Woods, S. W. (2010). Mediators and moderators in early intervention research. *Early Intervention in Psychiatry, 4,* 143–152.

Breusch, T. S., & Pagan, A. R. (1979). A simple test for heteroscedasticity and random coefficient variation. *Econometrica, 47,* 1287–1294.

Broeren, S., Muris, P., Bouwmeester, S., van der Heijden, K. B., & Abee, A. (2011). The role of repetitive negative thoughts in the vulnerability for emotional problems in non-clinical children. *Journal of Child and Family Studies, 20,* 135–148.

Brown, J. E., Nicholson, J. M., Broom, D. H., & Bittman, M. (2011). Television viewing by school-age children; associations with physical activity, snack food consumption, and unhealthy weight. *Social Indicators Research, 101,* 221–225.

Brown-Iannuzzi, J. L., Dotsch, R., Cooley, E., & Payne, B. K. (2017). The relationship between mental representations of welfare recipients and attitudes toward welfare. *Psychological Science, 28,* 92–103.

Bryan, A., Schmiege, S. J., & Broaddus, M. R. (2007). Mediational analysis in HIV/AIDS research: Estimating multivariate path analytic models in a structural equation modeling framework. *AIDS and Behavior, 11,* 365–383.

Buckland, S. T. (1984). Monte Carlo confidence intervals. *Biometrics, 40,* 811–817.

Cafri, G., Yamamiya, Y., Brannick, M., & Thompson, J. K. (2005). The influence of sociocultural factors on body image: A meta-analysis. *Clinical Psychology: Science and Practice, 12,* 421–433.

Canfield, C. F., & Saudino, K. J. (2016). The influence of infant characteristics and attention to social cues on early vocabulary. *Journal of Experimental Child Psychology, 150,* 112–129.

Cao-Lei, L., Veru, F., Elgbeili, G., Szyf, M., Laplante, D. P., & King, S. (2016). DNA methylation mediates the effect of exposure to prenatal maternity stress on cytokine production in children at age 13.5 years: Project Ice Storm. *Clinical Epigenetics, 8.*

Carvalho, J. P., & Hopko, D. R. (2011). Behavioral theory of depression: Reinforcement as a mediating variable between avoidance and depression. *Journal of Behavior Therapy and Experimental Psychiatry, 42,* 154–162.

Casciano, R., & Massey, D. S. (2012). Neighborhood disorder and anxiety symptoms: New evidence from a quasi-experimental study. *Health and Place, 18,* 180–190.

Cerin, E., & MacKinnon, D. P. (2009). A commentary on current practice in mediating variable analyses in behavioural nutrition and physical activity. *Public Health Nutrition, 12,* 1182–1188.

Chae, J. (2014). Interest in celebrities' post-baby bodies and korean women's body image disturbance after childhood. *Sex Roles, 71,* 419–435.

Chapman, D. A., & Lickel, B. (2016). Climate change and disasters: How framing affects justifications for giving or withholding aid to disaster victims. *Social Psychological and Personality Science, 7,* 13–20.

Chen, C., Green, P. G., & Crick, A. (1998). Does entrepreneurial self-efficacy distinguish entrepreneurs from managers? *Journal of Business Venturing, 13,* 295–316.

Cheong, J., MacKinnon, D. P., & Khoo, S. T. (2003). Investigation of mediational processes using parallel process latent growth curve modeling. *Structural Equation Modeling, 10,* 238–262.

Cheung, G. W., & Lau, R. S. (2008). Testing mediation and suppression effects of latent variables. *Organizational Research Methods, 11,* 296–325.

Cheung, M. W. (2009). Comparison of methods for constructing confidence intervals for standardized indirect effects. *Behavior Research Methods, 41,* 425–438.

Chew, J., Haase, A. M., & Carpenter, J. (2017). Individual and family factors associated with self-esteem in young people with epilepsy: A multiple mediation analysis. *Epilepsy & Behavior, 66,* 19–26.

Chugani, S. K., Irwin, J. R., & Redden, J. P. (2015). Happily ever after: The effect of identity-consistency on product satiation. *Journal of Consumer Research, 42,* 564–577.

Clark, J. K., Wegener, D. T., Briñol, P., & Petty, R. E. (2011). Discovering the shoe that fits: The self-validating role of stereotypes. *Psychological Science, 20,* 846–852.

Coetzee, M. (2014). Exploring the mediation role of graduate attributes in relation to academic self-directedness in open distance learning. *Higher Education Research and Development, 33,* 1085–1098.

Cohen, F., Sullivan, D., Solomon, S., Greenberg, J., & Ogilvie, D. M. (2011). Finding everland: Flight fantasies and the desire to transcend mortality. *Journal of Experimental Social Psychology, 47,* 88–102.

Cohen, J., Cohen, P., West, S. G., & Aiken, L. S. (2003). *Applied multiple regression and correlation for the behavioral sciences* (3rd ed.). Mahwah, NJ: Lawrence Erlbaum Associates.

Cohen, J. B. (1968). Multiple regression as a general data analytic system. *Psychological Bulletin, 70,* 426–443.

Cohen, J. B. (1983). The cost of dichotomization. *Applied Psychological Measurement, 7,* 240–253.

Cole, D. A., & Maxwell, S. E. (2003). Testing mediational models with longitudinal data: Questions and tips in the use of structural equation modeling. *Journal of Abnormal Psychology, 112,* 558–577.

Cole, D. A., & Preacher, K. J. (2014). Manifest variable path analysis: Potential serious and misleading consequences due to uncorrected measurement error. *Psychological Methods, 19,* 300–315.

Cole, M. S., Bedeian, A. G., & Bruch, H. (2011). Linking leader behavior and leadership consensus to team performance: Integrating direct consensus and dispersion models of group composition. *Leadership Quarterly, 22,* 383–398.

Cole, M. S., Walter, F., & Bruch, H. (2008). Affective mechanisms linking dysfunctional behavior to performance in work teams: A moderated mediation study. *Journal of Applied Psychology, 93,* 945–958.

Comello, M. L. G., & Farman, L. (2016). Identity as a moderator and mediator of communication effects: Evidence and implications for message design. *Journal of Psychology, 150,* 822–836.

Cook, R. D., & Weisberg, S. (1983). Diagnostics for heteroscedasticity in regression. *Biometrika, 70,* 1–10.

Cornelissen, G., Bashshur, M. R., Rode, J., & LeMenestrel, M. (2013). Rules or consequences: The role of ethnical mind-sets in moral dynamics. *Psychological Science, 24,* 492–488.

Coronel, J. C., & Federmeier, K. D. (2016). The effects of gender cues and political sophistication on candidate evaluation: A comparison of self-report and eye movement measures of stereotyping. *Communication Research, 43,* 922–944.

Cortina, J. M., & Dunlap, W. P. (1997). On the logic and purpose of significance testing. *Psychological Methods, 2,* 161–172.

Coyle, T. R., Pillow, D. R., Snyder, A. C., & Kochunov, P. (2011). Processing speed mediates the development of general intelligence (g) in adolescence. *Psychological Science, 22,* 1265–1269.

Craig, C. C. (1936). On the frequency function of xy. *The Annals of Mathematical Statistics, 7,* 1–15.

Cronbach, L. J. (1987). Statistical tests for moderator variables: Flaws in analyses recently proposed. *Psychological Bulletin, 102,* 414–417.

Cuijpers, P., van Straten, A., Warmeredam, L., & Andersson, G. (2009). Psychotherapy versus the combination of psychotherapy and pharmcotherapy in the treatment of depression: A meta-analysis. *Depression and Anxiety, 26,* 279–288.

Cukor, J., Wyka, K., Jayasinghe, N., Weathers, F., Giosan, C., Leck, P., et al. (2011). Prevalence and predictors of posttraumatic stress symptoms in utility workers deployed to the World Trade Center following the attacks of September 11, 2001. *Depression and Anxiety, 28,* 210–217.

Dakanalis, A., Timko, C. A., Zanetti, M. A., Rinaldi, L., Prunas, A., Carra, G., . . . Clerici, M. (2014). Associations between components of rumination and autobiographical memory specificity as measured by a minimal instructions autobiographical memory test. *Psychiatry Research, 215,* 176–184.

Darlington, R. B., & Hayes, A. F. (2017). *Regression analysis and linear models: Concepts, applications, and implementation.* New York, NY: Guilford Press.

Davis, J. A. (1985). *The logic of causal order.* Newbury Park, CA: Sage Publications.

Davis, M. J. (2010). Contrast coding in multiple regression analysis: Strengths, weaknesses, and utility of popular coding structures. *Journal of Data Science, 8,* 61–73.

Davydov, D. M., Shapiro, D., & Goldstein, I. B. (2010). Relationship of resting baroflex activity to 24-hour blood pressure and mood in healthy people. *Journal of Psychophysiology, 24,* 149–160.

Dawson, J. F. (2014). Moderation in management research: What, why, when, and how. *Journal of Business and Psychology, 29,* 1–19.

Dawson, J. F., & Richter, A. W. (2006). Probing three-way interactions in moderated multiple regression: Development and application of a slope difference test. *Journal of Applied Psychology, 91*, 917–926.

de Zavala, A. G., & Cichocka, A. (2011). Collective narcissism and anti-Semitism in Poland. *Group Processes and Intergroup Relations, 15*, 213–229.

Dearing, E., & Hamilton, L. C. (2006). Contemporary advances and classic advice for analyzing mediating and moderating variables. In K. McCartney, M. R. Burchinal, & K. L. Bub (Eds.), *Best practices in quantitative methods for developmentalists* (pp. 88–104). Boston, MA: Blackwell.

de Moore, J. (2015). External efficacy and political participation revisited: The role of perceived output structures for state- and non-state-oriented action forms. *Partliamentary Affairs, 69*, 642–662.

Desorsiers, A., Vine, V., Curtiss, J., & Klemanski, D. H. (2014). Observing nonreactively: A conditional process model linking mindfulness facets, cognitive emotional regulation strategies, and depression anxiety symptoms. *Journal of Affective Disorders, 165*, 31–37.

Dickert, S., Kleber, J., Västfjäll, D., & Slovic, P. (2016). Mental imagery, impact, and affect: A mediation model for charitable giving. *Plos One, 11*, 1–15.

DiGrande, L., Perrin, M. A., Thorpe, L. E., Thalji, L., Murphy, J., Wu, D., et al. (2008). Posttraumatic stress symptoms, PTSD, and risk factors among lower Manhattan residents 2–3 years after the September 11, 2001 terrorist attacks. *Journal of Traumatic Stress, 21*, 264–273.

Dittmar, H., Halliwell, E., & Stirling, E. (2009). Understanding the impact of thin media models on women's body-focused affect: The roles of thin-ideal internalization and weight-related self-discrepancy activation in experimental exposure effects. *Journal of Social and Clinical Psychology, 28*, 43–72.

D'Lima, G. M., Pearson, M. R., & Kelley, M. L. (2012). Protective behavioral strategies as a mediator and moderator of the relationship between self-regulation and alcohol-related consequences in first-year college students. *Psychology of Addictive Behaviors, 26*, 330–337.

Dockray, S., Susman, E., & Dorn, L. D. (2009). Depression, cortisol reactivity, and obesity in childhood and adolescence. *Journal of Adolescent Health, 45*, 344–350.

Donegan, E., & Dugas, M. (2012). Generalized anxiety disorder: A comparison of symptom change in adults receiving cognitive-behavioral therapy or applied relaxation. *Journal of Consulting and Clinical Psychology, 80*, 490–496.

Doue, C. M., & Roussiau, N. (2016). The role of mediators in the indirect effects of religiosity on therapeutic compliance in African migrant HIV-positive patients. *Journal of Religion and Health, 55*, 1850–1863.

Downs, G. W., & Rocke, D. M. (1979). Interpreting heteroscedasticity. *American Journal of Political Science, 23*, 816–828.

Druckman, D., & Albin, C. (2011). Distributive justice and the durability of peace agreements. *Review of International Studies, 37*, 1137–1168.

Dubois-Comtois, K., Moss, E., Cyr, C., & Pascuzzo, K. (2014). Behavior problems in middle childhood: The predictive role of maternal stress, child attachment, and mother-child interactions. *Journal of Abnormal Clinical Psychology, 41*, 1311–1324.

Duncan, G. T., & Layard, M. W. (1973). A Monte-Carlo study of asymptotically robust tests for correlation coefficients. *Biometrika, 60,* 551–558.

Echambadi, R., & Hess, J. D. (2007). Mean-centering does not alleviate collinearity problems in moderated regression models. *Marketing Science, 26,* 438–445.

Edgell, S. E., & Noon, S. M. (1984). Effect of violation of normality on the *t* test of the correlation coefficient. *Psychological Bulletin, 95,* 576–583.

Edgington, E. S. (1964). Randomization tests. *Journal of Psychology, 57,* 445–449.

Edgington, E. S. (1978). Firmly rooted in tradition. *Contemporary Psychology, 23,* 20–22.

Edgington, E. S. (1995). *Randomization tests.* New York, NY: Dekker.

Edwards, J. R. (2009). Seven deadly myths of testing moderation in organizational research. In C. E. Lance & R. J. Vanderberg (Eds.), *Statistical and methodological myths and urban legends* (pp. 143–164). New York, NY: Routledge.

Edwards, J. R., & Lambert, L. S. (2007). Methods for integrating moderation and mediation: A general analytical framework using moderated path analysis. *Psychological Methods, 12,* 1–22.

Efron, B. (1987). Better bootstrap confidence intervals. *Journal of the American Statistical Association, 82,* 171–185.

Efron, B., & Tibshirani, R. J. (1993). *An introduction to the bootstrap.* Boca Raton, FL: Chapman & Hall.

Ein-Gar, D., Shiv, B., & Tormala, Z. L. (2012). When blemishing leads to blossoming: The positive effect of negative information. *Journal of Consumer Research, 38,* 846–859.

Emery, L. F., Romer, D., Sheerin, K. M., Jamieson, K. H., & Peters, E. (2014). Affective and cognitive mediators of the impact of cigarette warning labels. *Nicotine and Tobacco Research, 16,* 263–269.

Eveland, W. P. (1997). Interactions and nonlinearity in mass communication: Connecting theory and methodology. *Journalism and Mass Communication Quarterly, 74,* 400–416.

Fairchild, A. J., & MacKinnon, D. P. (2009). A general model for testing mediation and moderation effects. *Prevention Science, 10,* 87–99.

Fairchild, A. J., MacKinnon, D. P., Toborga, M. P., & Taylor, A. B. (2009). *R*-squared effect-size measures for mediation analysis. *Behavior Research Methods, 41,* 486–498.

Fairchild, A. J., & McQuillin, S. D. (2010). Evaluating mediation and moderation effects in school psychology: A presentation of methods and review of current practice. *Journal of School Psychology, 48,* 53–84.

Falk, C. F., & Biesanz, J. C. (2016). Two cross-platform programs for inferences and interval estimation about indirect effects in mediational models. *SAGE Open, January–March,* 1–13.

Feldman, L. (2011). The effects of journalist opinionation on learning from the news. *Journal of Communication, 61,* 1183–1201.

Felipe, C. M., Rodan, J. L., & Leal-Rodriguez, A. L. (2016). An exploratory and predictive model for organizational agility. *Journal of Business Research, 10,* 4624–4631.

Ferraro, R., Krimani, A., & Matherly, T. (2013). Look at me! Look at me!: Conspicuous brand usage, self-brand connection, and dilution. *Journal of Marketing*

Research, 50, 477–488.

Fillo, J., Alfano, C. A., Paulus, D. J., Smits, J. A. J., Davis, M. L., Rosenfield, D., . . . Zvolensky, M. J. (2016). Emotion dysregulation explains relations between sleep disturbance and smoking quit-related cognition and behavior. *Addictive Behaviors, 57,* 6–12.

Finkel, S. E. (1995). *Causal analysis with panel data.* Thousand Oaks, CA: Sage Publications.

Fox, J. (1991). *Regression diagnostics.* Thousand Oaks, CA: Sage Publications.

Frazier, P. A., Tix, A. P., & Barron, K. E. (2004). Testing moderator and mediator effects in counseling psychology research. *Journal of Counseling Psychology, 51,* 115–134.

Frick, R. W. (1998). Interpreting statistical testing: Process and propensity, not population and random sampling. *Behavior Research Methods, Instruments, and Computers, 30,* 527–535.

Friedrich, R. J. (1982). In defense of multiplicative terms in multiple regression equations. *American Journal of Political Science, 26,* 797–833.

Fries, S. D., Brown, A. A., Carroll, P. J., & Arkin, R. M. (2015). Shame, rage, and unsuccessful motivated reasoning in vulnerable narcissism. *Journal of Social and Clinical Psychology, 34,* 877–895.

Fritz, M. S., & MacKinnon, D. P. (2007). Required sample size to detect the mediated effect. *Psychological Science, 18,* 233–239.

Fritz, M. S., Taylor, A. B., & MacKinnon, D. P. (2012). Explanation of two anomolous results in statistical mediation analysis. *Multivariate Behavioral Research, 47,* 61–87.

Gao, L., Huang, Y., & Simonson, I. (2014). The influence of initial possession level on consumers' adoption of a collection goal: A tipping point effect. *Journal of Marketing, 78,* 143–156.

Garcia, D. M., Schmitt, M. T., Branscombe, N. R., & Ellemers, N. (2010). Women's reactions to ingroup members who protest discriminatory treatment: The importance of beliefs about inequality and response appropriateness. *European Journal of Social Psychology, 40,* 733–745.

Gaunt, R., & Scott, J. (2014). Parents' involvement in childcare: Do parental and work identities matter? *Psychology of Women Quarterly, 38,* 475–489.

Gaziano, C. (1983). The knowledge gap: An analytical review of media effects. *Communication Research, 19,* 447–486.

Gelfand, L. A., MacKinnon, D. P., DeRubeis, R. J., & Baraldi, A. N. (2016). Mediation analysis with survival outcomes: Accelerated failure time vs. proportional hazard models. *Frontiers in Psychology, 7,* 1–10.

Gelman, A., & Stern, H. (2006). The difference between "significant" and "not significant" is not itself statistically significant. *The American Statistician, 60,* 328–331.

Gibbs, J. L., Ellison, N. B., & Lai, C. H. (2011). First comes love, then comes Google: An investigation of uncertainty reduction strategies and self-disclosure in online dating. *Communication Research, 38,* 70–100.

Gilbert, D. T., & Krull, D. S. (1988). Seeing less and knowing more: The benefits of perceptual ignorance. *Journal of Personality and Social Psychology, 54,* 193–202.

Gilbert, D. T., & Malone, P. S. (1995). The correspondence bias. *Psychological Bulletin, 117*, 21–38.

Gilbert, D. T., & Osborne, R. E. (1989). Thinking backward: Some curable and incurable consequences of cognitive business. *Journal of Personality and Social Psychology, 57*, 940–949.

Giner-Sorolla, R., & Chapman, H. A. (2017). Beyond purity: Moral disgust toward bad character. *Psychological Science, 28*, 80–91.

Godin, G., Belanger-Gravel, A., & Nolin, B. (2008). Mechanism by which BMI influences leisure-time physical activity behavior. *Obesity, 16*, 1314–1317.

Gogineni, A., Alsup, R., & Gillespie, D. F. (1995). Mediation and moderation in social work research. *Social Work Research, 19*, 57–63.

Goldfeld, S. M., & Quandt, R. E. (1965). Some tests for homoscedasticity. *Journal of the American Statistical Association, 60*, 539–547.

Goldman, Z. W., & Goodboy, A. K. (2016). Explaining doctoral students' relational maintenance with their advisor: A psychosocial development perspective. *Communication Education, 66*, 70–89.

Goldman, Z. W., Goodboy, A. K., & Weber, K. (2016). College students' psychological needs and intrinsic motivation to learn: An examination of self-determination theory. *Communication Quarterly, 65*, 167–191.

Goldstein, A., Flett, G. I., & Wekerle, C. (2010). Child maltreatment, alcohol use, and drinking consequences among male and female college students: An examination of drinking motives as mediators. *Addictive Behaviors, 35*, 636–639.

Golubickis, M., Tan, L. B. G., Falben, J. K., & Macrae, C. N. (2016). The observing self: Diminishing egocentrism through brief mindfulness meditation. *European Journal of Social Psychology, 46*, 521–527.

Gong, T. Y., Shenkar, O., Luo, Y., & Nyaw, M.-K. (2007). Do multiple partners help or hinder international joint venture performance?: The mediating roles of contract completeness and partner cooperation. *Strategic Management Journal, 28*, 1021–1034.

Gonzales, V. M., Reynolds, B., & Skewes, M. C. (2011). Role of impulsivity in the relationship between depression and alcohol problems among emerging college drinkers. *Experimental and Clinical Psychopharmacology, 19*, 303–313.

Good, P. I. (2001). *Resampling methods: A practical guide to data analysis* (2nd ed.). Boston, MA: Birkhauser.

Goodboy, A. K., Martin, M. M., & Brown, E. (2016). Bullying on the school bus: Deleterious effects on public school bus drivers. *Journal of Applied Communication Research, 44*, 434–452.

Goodin, B. R., McGuire, L. M., Stapleton, L. M., Quinn, N. B., Fabian, L. A., Haythornthwaite, J. A., et al. (2009). Pain catastrophizing mediates the relationship between self-reported strenuous exercise involvement and pain ratings: Moderating role of anxiety sensitivity. *Psychosomatic Medicine, 71*, 1018–1025.

Goodman, L. A. (1960). On the exact variance of products. *Journal of the American Statistical Association, 55*, 708–713.

Grabe, S., Ward, L. M., & Hyde, J. S. (2008). The role of the media in body image concerns among women: A meta-analysis of experimental and correlational studies. *Psychological Bulletin, 134,* 460–476.

Grant, A. M., Gino, F., & Hofmann, D. A. (2011). Reversing the extraverted leadership advantage: The role of employee proactivity. *Academy of Management Journal, 54,* 528–550.

Gratz, K. L., Bardeen, J. R., Levy, R., Dixon-Gordon, K. L., & Tull, M. T. (2015). Mechanisms of change in an emotion regulation group therapy for deliberate self-harm among women with borderline personality disorder. *Behaviour Research and Therapy, 65,* 29–35.

Grawitch, M. J., & Munz, D. C. (2004). Are your data nonindependent?: A practical guide to evaluating nonindependence and within-group agreement. *Understanding Statistics, 3,* 231–257.

Green, E. G. T., & Auer, F. (2013). How social dominance orientation affects union participation: The role of union identification and perceived union instrumentality. *Journal of Communication and Applied Social Psychology, 23,* 143–156.

Greenwald, A. G. (2012). There is nothing so theoretical as a good method. *Psychological Science, 7,* 99–108.

Greitemeyer, T., & McLatchie, N. (2011). Denying humanness to others: A newly discovered mechanism by which violent video games increase aggressive behavior. *Psychological Science, 22,* 659–665.

Griffin, D., & Gonzales, R. (1995). Correlational analysis of dyad-level data in the exchangeable case. *Psychological Bulletin, 118,* 430–439.

Groetz, L. M., Levine, M. P., & Murnen, S. K. (2002). The effect of experimental presentation of thin media images on body satisfaction: A meta-analytic review. *International Journal of Eating Disorders, 31,* 1–16.

Grøntved, A., Steene-Johannessen, J., Kynde, I., Franks, P. W., Helge, J. W., Froberg, K., et al. (2011). Association between plasma leptin and blood pressure in two population-based samples of children and adolescents. *Journal of Hypertension, 29,* 1093–1100.

Grund, A., & Fries, S. (2014). Study and leisure interferences as mediators between students' self-control capacities and their domain-specific functioning and general well-being. *Learning and Instruction, 31,* 23–32.

Guendelman, M. D., Cheryan, S., & Monin, B. (2011). Fitting in but getting fat: Identity threat and dietary choices among U.S. immigrant groups. *Psychological Science, 22,* 959–967.

Gunn, R. L., & Finn, P. R. (2013). Impulsivity partially mediates the association between reduced working memory capacity and alcohol problems. *Alcohol, 47,* 3–8.

Gurmen, M. S., & Rohner, R. P. (2014). Effects of marital distress on Turkish adolescents' psychological adjustment. *Journal of Child and Family Studies, 23,* 1155–1162.

Gvirsman, S. D. (2014). It's not that we don't know, it's that we don't care: Explaining why selective exposure polarizes attitudes. *Mass Communication and Society, 17,* 74–97.

Hahl, O. (2016). Turning back the clock in baseball: The increased prominence of extrinsic rewards and demand for authenticity. *Organizational Science, 27,* 929–953.

Hammond, S. I., Müller, U., Carpendale, J. I. M., Bibok, M. B., & Liebermann-Finestone, D. P. (2012). The effects of parental scaffolding on preschoolers' executive function. *Developmental Psychology, 48*, 271–281.

Han, Z. R., & Shaffer, A. (2014). Maternal expressed emotion in relation to child behavior problems: Differential and mediating effects. *Journal of Child and Family Studies, 23*, 1491–1500.

Hart, P. S. (2011). One or many?: The influence of episodic and thematic climate change frames on policy preferences and individual change behavior. *Science Communication, 33*, 28–51.

Harty, S., Sella, F., & Kadosh, R. C. (2017). Transcranial electrical stimulation and behavioral change: The intermediary influence of the brain. *Frontiers in Human Neuroscience, 11*, 112.

Hasan, Y., Begue, L., & Bushman, B. J. (2012). Viewing the world through blood-red tinted glasses: The hostile expectation bias mediates the link between violent video game exposure and aggression. *Journal of Experimental Social Psychology, 48*, 953–956.

Havlicek, L. L., & Peterson, N. L. (1977). Effect of violation of assumptions upon significance levels of the Pearson *r*. *Psychological Bulletin, 84*, 373–377.

Hayes, A. F. (1996). The permutation test is not distribution-free: Testing $H_0 : \rho = 0$. *Psychological Methods, 1*, 184–198.

Hayes, A. F. (2005). *Statistical methods for communication science.* New York: Routledge.

Hayes, A. F. (2009). Beyond Baron and Kenny: Statistical mediation analysis in the new millennium. *Communication Monographs, 76*, 408–420.

Hayes, A. F. (2015). An index and test of linear moderated mediation. *Multivariate Behavioral Research, 50*, 1–22.

Hayes, A. F. (2018). Partial, conditional, and moderated moderated mediation: Quantification, inference, and interpretation. *Communication Monographs, 85*.

Hayes, A. F., & Cai, L. (2007). Using heteroscedasticity-consistent standard error estimators in OLS regression: An introduction and software implementation. *Behavior Research Methods, 39*, 709–722.

Hayes, A. F., Glynn, C. J., & Huge, M. E. (2012). Cautions regarding the interpretation of regression coefficients and hypothesis tests in linear models with interactions. *Communication Methods and Measures, 6*, 1–11.

Hayes, A. F., & Matthes, J. (2009). Computational procedures for probing interactions in OLS and logistic regression: SPSS and SAS implementations. *Behavior Research Methods, 41*, 924–936.

Hayes, A. F., & Montoya, A. K. (2017). A tutorial on testing, visualizing, and probing an interaction involving a multicategorical variable in linear regression analysis. *Communication Methods and Measures, 11*, 1–30.

Hayes, A. F., Montoya, A. K., & Rockwood, N. J. (2017). The analysis of mechanisms and their contigencies: PROCESS versus structural equation modeling. *Australasian Marketing Journal, 25*, 76–81.

Hayes, A. F., & Myers, T. A. (2009). Testing the proximate casualties hypothesis: Local troop loss, attention to war news, and support for military intervention. *Mass Communication and Society, 12*, 379–402.

Hayes, A. F., & Preacher, K. J. (2013). Conditional process modeling: Using structural equation modeling to examine contingent causal processes. In G. R. Hancock & R. O. Mueller (Eds.), *A second course in structural equation modeling* (2nd ed., pp. 219–266). Greenwich, CT: Information Age Publishing.

Hayes, A. F., & Preacher, K. J. (2014). Statistical mediation analysis with a multi-categorical independent variable. *British Journal of Mathematical & Statistical Psychology, 67*, 451–470.

Hayes, A. F., & Reineke, J. (2007). The effects of government censorship of war-related news coverage on interest in the censored coverage. *Mass Communication and Society, 10*, 423–438.

Hayes, A. F., & Rockwood, N. J. (2017). Regression-based statistical mediation and moderation analysis: Observations, recommendations, and implementation. *Behaviour Research and Therapy*.

Hayes, A. F., & Scharkow, M. (2013). The relative trustworthiness of inferential tests of the indirect effect in statistical mediation analysis: Does method really matter? *Psychological Science, 24*, 1918–1927.

Hentshel, T., Shemla, M., Wegge, J., & Kearney, E. (2013). Perceiving diversity and team functioning: The role of diversity beliefs and affect. *Small Group Research, 44*, 33–61.

Hofmann, S. G., & Smits, J. A. J. (2008). Cognitive-behavioral therapy for adult anxiety disorders: A meta-analysis of randomized placebo-controlled trials. *Journal of Clinical Psychiatry, 69*, 621–632.

Holbert, R. L., & Stephenson, M. T. (2003). The importance of indirect effects in media effects research: Testing for mediation in structural equation modeling. *Journal of Broadcasting and Electronic Media, 47*, 556–572.

Holland, P. W. (1986). Statistics and causal inference. *Journal of the American Statistical Association, 81*, 945–960.

Hoyt, C. L., Burnette, J. L., & Auster-Gussman, L. (2014). "Obesity is a disease": Examining the self-regulatory impact of this public health meassage. *Psychological Science, 25*, 997–1002.

Hsu, L., Woody, S. R., Lee, H. J., Peng, Y., Zhou, X., & Ryder, A. G. (2012). Social anxiety among East Asians in North America: East Asian socialization or the challenge of acculturation? *Cultural Diversity and Ethnic Minority Psychology, 18*, 181–191.

Huang, J. Y., Sedlovskaya, A., Ackerman, J. M., & Bargh, J. A. (2011). Immunizing against prejudice: Effects of disease protection on attitudes toward out-groups. *Psychological Science, 22*, 1550–1556.

Huang, S., Zhang, Y., & Broniarczyk, S. M. (2012). So near and yet so far: The mental presentation of goal progress. *Journal of Personality and Social Psychology, 103*, 225–241.

Huang, V., Peck, K., Mallya, S., Lupien, S. J., & Fiocco, A. J. (2016). Subjective sleep quality as a possible mediator in the relationship between personality traits and depressive symptoms in middle-aged adults. *Plos One, 11*, 1–18.

Huang-Pollock, C. L., Mikami, A. Y., Pfiffner, L., & McBurnette, K. (2009). Can executive functions explain the relationship between attention deficit hyperactivity disorder and social adjustment? *Journal of Abnormal Child Psychology,*

37, 679–691.

Humphreys, L. G., & Fleishman, A. (1974). Pseudo-orthogonal and other analysis of variance designs involving individual-differences variables. *Journal of Educational Psychology, 66*, 464–472.

Hunter, J. E., & Schmidt, F. L. (1990). Dichotomization of continuous variables: The implications for meta-analysis. *Journal of Applied Psychology, 75*, 334–349.

Hutchinson, P. T. (2003). Dichotomization and manipulation of numbers. *Canadian Journal of Psychiatry, 48*, 429–430.

Hwang, Y., & Jeong, S.-H. (2009). Revising the knowledge gap hypothesis: A meta-analysis of thirty five years of research. *Journalism and Mass Communication Quarterly, 86*, 513–532.

Iacobucci, D., Saldanha, N., & Deng, X. (2007). A mediation on mediation: Evidence that structural equations models perform better than regressions. *Journal of Consumer Psychology, 17*, 140–154.

Imai, K., Keele, L., & Tingley, D. (2010). A general approach to causal mediation analysis. *Psychological Methods, 15*, 309–334.

Irwin, J. R., & McClelland, G. H. (2001). Misleading heuristics and moderated multiple regression models. *Journal of Marketing Research, 38*, 100–109.

Irwin, J. R., & McClelland, G. H. (2002). Negative consequences of dichotomizing continuous predictor variables. *Journal of Marketing Research, 40*, 366–371.

Jaccard, J., & Turrisi, R. (2003). *Interaction effects in multiple regression* (2nd ed.). Thousand Oaks, CA: Sage Publications.

James, L. R., & Brett, J. M. (1984). Mediators, moderators, and tests for mediation. *Journal of Applied Psychology, 69*, 307–321.

Jiang, L. C., Bazarova, N. N., & Hancock, J. T. (2011). The disclosure–intimacy link in computer-mediated communication: An attributional extension of the hyperpersonal model. *Human Communication Research, 37*, 58–77.

Johnson, B. K., Slater, M. D., Silver, N. A., & Ewoldsen, D. R. (2016). Entertainment and expanding boundaries of the self: Relief from the constraints of the everyday. *Journal of Communication, 66*, 386–408.

Johnson, P. O., & Fey, L. C. (1950). The Johnson–Neyman technique, its theory and application. *Psychometrika, 15*, 349–367.

Johnson, P. O., & Neyman, J. (1936). Tests of certain linear hypotheses and their application to some educational problems. *Statistical Research Memoirs, 1*, 57–93.

Jones, D. A., Willness, C. R., & Madey, S. (2014). Why are job seekers attracted by corporate social performance? Experimental and field tests of three signal-based mechanisms. *Academy of Management Journal, 57*, 383–404.

Jones, D. J., Lewis, T., Litrownik, A., Thompson, R., Proctor, L. J., Isbell, P., ... Runyan, D. (2013). Linking childhood sexual abuse and early adolescent risk behavior: The intervening role of internalizing and externalizing problems. *Journal of Abnormal Child Psychology, 41*, 139–150.

Jordan, A. B. (2010). Children's television viewing and childhood obesity. *Pediatric Annals, 39*, 569–573.

Joseph, A., Afifi, T. D., & Denes, A. (2016). (Unmet) standards for emotional support and their short- and medium-term consequences. *Communication Monographs, 83*, 163–193.

Judd, C. M., & Kenny, D. A. (1981). Process analysis: Estimating mediation in treatment evaluations. *Evaluation Review, 5,* 602–619.

Judd, C. M., Kenny, D. A., & McClelland, G. H. (2001). Estimating and testing mediation and moderation in within-subject designs. *Psychological Methods, 6,* 115–134.

Judge, T. A., Piccolo, R. F., Podsakoff, N. P., Shaw, J. C., & Rich, B. L. (2010). The relationship between play and job satisfaction: A meta-analysis of the literature. *Journal of Vocational Behavior, 77,* 157–167.

Kalyanaraman, S., & Sundar, S. S. (2006). The psychological appeal of personalized content in web portals: Does customization affect attitudes and behavior? *Journal of Communication, 31,* 254–270.

Kam, C. D., & Franzese, R. J. (2007). *Modeling and interpreting interactive hypotheses in regression analysis.* Ann Arbor, MI: University of Michigan.

Kan, C., Lichtenstein, D. R., Grant, S. J., & Janiszwski, C. (2014). Strengthening the influence of advertised reference prices through information priming. *Journal of Consumer Research, 40,* 1078–1096.

Kapikiran, N. A. (2012). Positive and negative affectivity as mediator and moderator of the relationship between optimism and life satisfaction in Turkish university students. *Social Indicators Research, 106,* 333–345.

Karnal, N., Machiels, C. J. A., Orth, U. R., & Mai, R. (2016). Healthy by design, but only when in focus: Communicating non-verbal health cues through symbolic meaning in packaging. *Food Quality and Preference, 52,* 106–119.

Karpmann, M. B. (1986). Comparing two non-parallel regression lines with the parametric alternative to the analysis of covariance using SPSS-X or SAS: The Johnson–Neyman technique. *Educational and Psychological Measurement, 46,* 639–644.

Keng, S.-L., Seah, S. T. H., Wong, E. M. W., & Smoski, M. (2016). Effects of brief mindful acceptance induction on implicit dysfunctional attitudes and concordance between implicit and explicit dysfunctional attitudes. *Behaviour Research and Therapy, 83,* 1–10.

Kennedy, P. E. (1995). Randomization tests in econometrics. *Journal of Business and Economic Statistics, 13,* 85–94.

Kenny, D. A., & Judd, C. M. (1986). Consequences of violating the independence assumption in analysis of variance. *Psychological Bulletin, 99,* 422–431.

Kenny, D. A., & Judd, C. M. (2014). Power anomalies in testing mediation. *Psychological Science, 25,* 354–339.

Kenny, D. A., Korchmaros, J. D., & Bolger, N. (2003). Lower level mediation in multilevel models. *Psychological Methods, 8,* 115–128.

Kenny, D. A., Mannetti, L., Pierro, A., Livi, S., & Kashy, D. A. (2002). The statistical analysis of data from small groups. *Journal of Personality and Social Psychology, 83,* 126–137.

Keppel, G., & Wickens, T. D. (2004). *Design and analysis: A researcher's handbook* (4th ed.). Upper Saddle River, NJ: Prentice Hall.

Kim, J. O., & Ferree, G. D. (1976). Standardization in causal analysis. *Sociological Methods and Research, 10,* 187–210.

Kim, J. O., & Mueller, C. W. (1981). Standardized and unstandardized coefficients in causal analysis: An expository note. *Sociological Methods and Research, 4,*

428–438.

Kim, S., & Labroo, A. A. (2011). From inherent value to incentive value: When and why pointless effort enhances consumer preference. *Journal of Consumer Research, 38*, 712–742.

Kimki, S., Eshel, Y., Zysberg, L., & Hantman, S. (2009). Getting a life: Gender differences in postwar recovery. *Sex Roles, 61*, 554–565.

Kirby, A., Jones, C., & Copello, A. (2014). The impact of massively multiplayer online role playing games MMORPGs on psychological well being and the role of play motivations and problematic use. *International Journal of Mental Health Addiction, 12*, 36–51.

Kley, H., Tuschen-Caffier, B., & Heinrichs, N. (2012). Safety behaviors, self-focused attention and negative thinking in children with social anxiety disorder, socially anxious, and nonanxious children. *Journal of Behavior Theory and Experimental Psychiatry, 43*, 548–555.

Knobloch-Westerwick, S. (2014). The selective exposure self and affect-management (SESAM) model: Applications in the realms of race, politics, and health. *Communication Research, 42*, 959–985.

Knobloch-Westerwick, S., & Hoplamazian, G. J. (2012). Gendering the self: Selective magazine reading and reinforcement of gender conformity. *Communication Research, 39*, 358–384.

Kraemer, H. C. (2011). Discovering, comparing, and combining moderators of treatment on outcome after randomized clinical trials: A parametric approach. *Statistics in Medicine, 32*, 1964–1973.

Kraemer, H. C., Kiernan, M., Essex, M., & Kupfer, D. J. (2008). How and why criteria defining moderators and mediators differ between the Baron and Kenny & MacArthur approaches. *Health Psychology, 27*, S101–S108.

Kraemer, H. C., Wilson, G. T., Fairburn, C. G., & Agras, W. S. (2002). Mediators and moderators of treatment effects in randomized clinical trials. *Archives of General Psychiatry, 59*, 877–883.

Krause, M. R., Serlin, R. C., Ward, S. E., & Rony, Y. Z. (2010). Testing mediation in nursing research: Beyond Baron and Kenny. *Nursing Research, 59*, 288–294.

Krieger, J. L., Katz, M. L., Kam, J. A., & Roberto, A. (2012). Appalachian and non-Appalachian pediatricians' encouragement of the Human Papillomavirus Vaccine: Implications for health disparities. *Women's Health Issues, 22*, e19–e26.

Krieger, J. L., & Sarge, M. A. (2013). A serial mediation model of message framing on intentions to receive the human papillomavirus (HPV) vaccine: Revising the role of threat and efficacy perceptions. *Health Communication, 28*, 5–19.

Kromrey, J. D., & Foster-Johnson, L. (1998). Mean centering in moderated multiple regression: Much ado about nothing. *Educational and Psychological Measurement, 58*, 42–68.

Kung, F. Y. H., Eibach, R. P., & Grossmann, I. (2016). Culture, fixed-world beliefs, relationships, and perceptions of identity change. *Social Psychological and Personality Science, 7*, 631–639.

Kurti, A. N., & Dallery, J. (2014). Effects of exercise on craving and cigarette smoking in the human laboratory. *Addictive Behaviors, 39*, 1131–1137.

Kuwabara, K., Yu, S., Lee, A. J., & Galinsky, A. D. (2016). Status decreases dominance in the west but increases dominance in the east. *Psychological Science, 27,* 127–137.

Lachman, M. E., & Agrigoroaei, S. (2012). Low perceived control as a risk factor for episodic memory: The mediational role of anxiety and task interference. *Memory and Cognition, 40,* 287–296.

Landreville, K. D., Holbert, R. L., & LaMarre, H. L. (2010). The influence of late-night TV comedy viewing on political talk: A moderated-mediation model. *International Journal of Press-Politics, 15,* 482–498.

Lange, T., & Hansen, J. V. (2011). Direct and indirect effects in a survival context. *Epidemiology, 22,* 575–581.

Laran, J., Dalton, A. N., & Andrade, E. B. (2011). The curious case of behavioral backlash: Why brands produce priming effects and slogans produce reverse priming effects. *Journal of Consumer Research, 37,* 999–1014.

Lau, R., & Cheung, G. W. (2012). Estimating and comparing specific mediation effects in complex latent variable models. *Organizational Research Methods, 15,* 3–16.

Lau, R. R., Silegman, L., Heldman, C., & Babbit, P. (1999). The effects of negative political advertisements: A meta-analytic assessment. *The American Political Science Review, 93,* 851–875.

Lavenure, S., Fogel, S., Lungu, O., Albouy, G., Sevigny-Dupont, P., Vien, C., ... Doyon, J. (2016). NREM2 and sleep spindles are instrumental to the consolidation of motor sequence memories. *Plos One, 14,* 1-11.

LeBreton, J. M., Wu, J., & Bing, M. N. (2009). The truth(s) on testing for mediation in the social and organizational sciences. In C. E. Lance & R. J. Vanderberg (Eds.), *Statistical and methodological myths and urban legends* (pp. 107–141). New York: Routledge.

Lecheler, S., Bos, L., & Vliegenthart, R. (2015). The mediating role of emotions: News framing effects on opinions about immigration. *Journalism and Mass Communication Quarterly, 92,* 812–838.

Lecheler, S., de Vreese, C., & Slouthuus, R. (2011). Issue importance as a moderator of framing effects. *Communication Research, 79,* 400–425.

Ledgerwood, A., & Shrout, P. E. (2011). The trade-off between accuracy and precision in latent variable models of mediation processes. *Journal of Personality and Social Psychology, 101,* 1174–1188.

Lee, J.-S., Ahn, Y.-S., Jeong, K.-S., Chae, J.-H., & Choi, K.-S. (2014). Resilience buffers the impact of traumatic events on the development of PTSD symptoms in firefighters. *Journal of Affective Disorders, 162,* 128–133.

Lehmann, A., Burkert, S., Daig, I., Glaesmer, H., & Brähler, E. (2011). Subjective underchallenge at work and its impact on mental health. *International Archives of Occupational and Environmental Health, 84,* 655–664.

Lemmer, G., & Gollwitzer, M. (2017). The "true" indirect effect won't (always) stand up: When and why reverse mediation testing fails. *Journal of Experimental Social Psychology, 69,* 144–149.

Leone, L., & Chirumbolo, A. (2008). Conservatism as motivated avoidance of affect: Need for affect scales predict conservativism measures. *Journal of Research in Personality, 42,* 755–762.

Levine, M. P., & Murnen, S. K. (2009). "Everybody knows that mass media are/are not [pick one] a cause of eating disorders": A criticial review of evidence for a causal link between media, negative body image, and disordered eating in females. *Journal of Social and Clinical Psychology, 28,* 9–42.

Li, A., Shaffer, J., & Bagger, J. (2015). The psychological well-being of disability caregivers: Examining the roles of family strain, family-to-work conflict, and perceived supervisor support. *Journal of Occupational Health Psychology, 20,* 40–49.

Li, A., Shaffer, J., & Bagger, J. (2016). Supporting the professional learning of teachers in China: Does principal leadership make a difference? *Teaching and Teacher Education, 59,* 79–91.

Li, D., Li, X., Wang, Y., Zhao, L., Bao, Z., & Win, F. (2013). School connectedness and problematic internet use in adolescents: A moderated mediation model of deviate peer affiliation and self-control. *Journal of Abnormal Child Psychology, 41,* 1231–1242.

Li, N. P., Patel, L., Balliet, D., Tov, W., & Scollon, C. N. (2011). The incompatibility of materialism and the desire for children: Psychological insights into the fertility discrepancy among modern countries. *Social Indicators Research, 101,* 391–404.

Liao, Y., Ho, S. S., & Yang, X. (2016). Motivators of pro-environmental behavior: Examining the underlying processes in the influence of presumed media influence model. *Science Communication, 38,* 51–73.

Little, K., Olsson, C. A., Youssef, G. J., Whittle, S., Simmons, J. G., Yücel, M., . . . Allen, N. B. (2015). Linking the seratonin transporter gene, family environments, hippocampal volume and depression onset: A prospective imaging gene by environment analysis. *Journal of Abnormal Psychology, 124,* 834–849.

Little, T. D., Preacher, K. J., Selig, J. P., & Card, N. A. (2007). New developments in latent variable panel analyses of longitudinal data. *International Journal of Behavioral Development, 31,* 357–365.

Livingston, N. A., Christianson, N., & Cochran, B. N. (2016). Minority stress, psychological distress, and alcohol misuse among sexual minority young adults: A resiliency-based conditional process analysis. *Addictive Behaviors, 63,* 125–131.

Lockhart, G., MacKinnon, D. P., & Ohlrich, V. (2011). Mediation analysis in psychosomatic medicine research. *Psychosomatic Medicine, 73,* 29–43.

Long, J. S. (1997). *Regression models for categorical and limited dependent variables.* Thousand Oaks, CA: Sage Publications.

Long, J. S., & Ervin, L. H. (2000). Using heteroscedasticity-consistent standard errors in the linear regression model. *The American Statistician, 54,* 217–224.

Lopez-Guimera, G., Levine, M. P., Sanchez-Cerracedo, D., & Fauquet, J. (2010). Influence of mass media on body image and eating disordered attitudes and behaviors in females: A review of effects and processes. *Media Psychology, 13,* 387–416.

Ludbrook, J., & Dudley, H. (1998). Why permutation tests are superior to *t* and *F* tests in biomedical research. *The American Statistician, 52,* 127–132.

Luke, D. A. (2004). *Multilevel modeling.* Thousand Oaks, CA: Sage Publications.

Luksyte, A., & Avery, D. R. (2010). The effects of citizenship dissimilarity and national pride on attitudes toward immigrants: Investigating mediators and moderators of intergroup contact. *International Journal of Intercultural Relations, 34,* 629–641.

Lunneborg, C. E. (2000). *Data analysis by resampling.* Pacific Grove, CA: Duxbury.

Luszczynska, A., Cao, D. S., Mallach, N., Petron, K., Mazurkiewicz, M., & Schwarzer, R. (2010). Intentions, planning, and self-efficacy predict physical activity in Chinese and Polish adolescents: Two moderated mediation analyses. *International Journal of Clinical and Health Psychology, 10,* 265–278.

Ma, Z., & Zeng, W. (2014). A multiple mediator model: Power analysis based on Monte Carlo simulation. *American Journal of Applied Psychology, 3,* 72–79.

MacCallum, R. C. (2003). Working with imperfect models. *Multivariate Behavioral Research, 38,* 113–139.

MacCallum, R. C., Zhang, S., Preacher, K. J., & Rucker, D. D. (2002). On the practice of dichotomization of quantitative variables. *Psychological Methods, 7,* 19–40.

MacKinnon, D. P. (2000). Contrasts in multiple mediator models. In J. Rose, L. Chassin, C. C. Presson, & S. J. Sherman (Eds.), *Multivariate applications in substance use and research: New methods for new questions* (pp. 141–160). Mahwah, NJ: Lawrence Erlbaum Associates.

MacKinnon, D. P. (2008). *An introduction to statistical mediation analysis.* New York: Routledge.

MacKinnon, D. P., & Dwyer, J. H. (1993). Estimating mediated effects in prevention studies. *Evaluation Review, 17,* 144–158.

MacKinnon, D. P., Fairchild, A. J., & Fritz, M. S. (2007). Mediation analysis. *Annual Review of Psychology, 58,* 593–614.

MacKinnon, D. P., Fritz, M. S., Williams, J., & Lockwood, C. M. (2007). Distribution of the product confidence limits for the indirect effect: Program PRODCLIN. *Behavior Research Methods, 39,* 384–389.

MacKinnon, D. P., Lockwood, C. M., Hoffman, J. M., & West, S. G. (2002). A comparison of methods to test the significance of the mediated effect. *Psychological Methods, 7,* 83–104.

MacKinnon, D. P., Lockwood, C. M., & Williams, J. (2004). Confidence limits for the indirect effect: Distribution of the product and resampling methods. *Multivariate Behavioral Research, 39,* 99–128.

MacKinnon, D. P., Lockwood, C. P., Brown, C. H., Wang, W., & Hoffman, J. M. (2007). The intermediate endpoint effect in logistic and probit regression. *Clinical Trials, 4,* 499–513.

MacKinnon, D. P., Warsi, G., & Dwyer, J. H. (1995). A simulation study of mediated effect measures. *Multivariate Behavioral Research, 30,* 41–62.

MacNeil, G., Kosberg, J. I., Durkin, D. W., Dooley, W. K., DeCoster, J., & Williamson, G. M. (2010). Caregiver mental health and potentially caregiving behavior: The central role of caregiver anger. *The Gerontologist, 50,* 76–86.

Magee, C. A., Caputi, P., & Iverson, D. C. (2011). Short sleep mediates the association between long work hours and increased Body Mass Index. *Journal of Behavioral Medicine, 34,* 83–91.

Magill, M. (2011). Moderators and mediators in social work research: Toward a more ecologically valid evidence base for practice. *Journal of Social Work, 11,*

387–401.

Maguen, S., Luxton, D. D., Skopp, N. A., Gahm, G. A., Reger, M. A., Metzler, T. J., & Marmar, C. R. (2011). Killing in combat, mental health symptoms, and suicidal ideation in Iraq war veterans. *Journal of Anxiety Disorders, 25,* 563–567.

Malouf, E., Stuewig, J., & Tangney, J. (2012). Self-control and jail inmates' substance misuse post-release: Mediation by friends' substance use and moderation by age. *Addictive Behaviors, 37,* 1198–1204.

Maric, M., Wiers, R. W., & Prins, P. J. M. (2012). Ten ways to improve the use of statistical mediation analysis in the practice of child and adolescent treatment research. *Clinical Child and Family Psychological Review, 15,* 177–191.

Martinez, A. G., Piff, P. K., Mendoza-Denton, R., & Hinshaw, S. P. (2011). The power of a label: Mental illness diagnoses, ascribed humanity, and social rejection. *Journal of Social and Clinical Psychology, 30,* 1–23.

Mascha, E. J., Dalton, J. E., Kurz, A., & Saager, L. (2013). Understanding the mechanism: Mediation analysis in randomized and nonrandomized studies. *Anesthesia and Analgesia, 117,* 980–994.

Maxwell, S. E., Cole, D. A., & Mitchell, M. A. (2011). Bias in cross-sectional analyses of longitudinal mediation: Partial and complete mediation under an autoregressive model. *Multivariate Behavioral Research, 46,* 816–841.

Maxwell, S. E., & Delaney, H. D. (1993). Bivariate median splits and spurious statistical significance. *Psychological Bulletin, 113,* 181–190.

May, R. B., & Hunter, M. A. (1993). Some advantages of permutation tests. *Canadian Psychology, 34,* 401–407.

May, R. B., Masson, M. E. J., & Hunter, M. A. (1989). Randomization tests: Viable alternatives to normal curve tests. *Behavior Research Methods, Instruments, and Computers, 21,* 482–483.

Meade, C. S., Conn, N. A., Skalski, L. M., & Safren, S. A. (2011). Neurocognitive impairment and medication adherence in HIV patients with and without cocaine dependence. *Journal of Behavioral Medicine, 34,* 128–138.

Merino, H., Senra, C., & Ferreiro, F. (2016). Worry- and rumination-specific pathways linking neuroticism and symptoms of anxiety and depression in patients with generalized anxiety disorder, major depressive disorder, and mixed anxiety-depressive disorder. *Plos One, 11,* 1–14.

Micceri, T. (1989). The unicorn, the normal curve, and other improbable creatures. *Psychological Bulletin, 105,* 156–166.

Mijanovich, T., & Weitzman, B. C. (2010). Disaster in context: The effects of 9/11 on youth distant from the attacks. *Community Mental Health Journal, 46,* 601–611.

Mittal, M., Senn, T. E., & Carey, M. P. (2013). Fear of violent consequences and condom use among women attending an STD clinic. *Women and Health, 53,* 795–807.

Molloy, G. J., Dixon, D., Hamer, M., & Sniehotta, F. F. (2010). Social support and regular physical activity: Does planning mediate this link? *British Journal of Health Psychology, 15,* 859–870.

Moneta, G. B. (2011). Metacognition, emotion, and alcohol dependence in college students: A moderated mediation model. *Addictive Behaviors, 36,* 781–784.

Montoya, A. K. (2016). *Extending the Johnson-Neyman procedure to categorical independent variables: Mathematical derivations and computational tools.* Unpublished master's thesis, The Ohio State University.

Montoya, A. K., & Hayes, A. F. (2017). Two condition within-participant statistical mediation analysis: A path-analytic framework. *Psychological Methods, 22,* 6–27.

Mook, D. G. (1987). In defense of external invalidity. *American Psychologist, 38,* 379–387.

Mooney, C. Z., & Duval, R. D. (1993). *Bootstrapping: A nonparametric approach to statistical inference.* Newbury Park, CA: Sage Publications.

Morano, M., Colella, D., Robazza, C., Bortoli, L., & Capranica, L. (2011). Physical self-perception and motor performance in normal-weight, overweight, and obese children. *Scandanavian Journal of Medicine and Science in Sports, 21,* 465–473.

Morgan, J. I., Jones, F. A., & Harris, P. R. (2013). Direct and indirect effects of mood on risk decision making in safety-critical workers. *Accident Analysis and Prevention, 50,* 472–482.

Morgan, S. L., & Winship, C. (2007). *Counterfactuals and causal inference: Methods and principles for social research.* Cambridge, UK: Cambridge University Press.

Morgan-Lopez, A., & MacKinnon, D. P. (2006). Demonstration and evaluation of a method for assessing mediated moderation. *Behavior Research Methods, 38,* 77–89.

Morrison, K. R. (2011). A license to speak up: Outgroup minorities and opinion expression. *Journal of Experimental Social Psychology, 47,* 756–766.

Moyer-Guse, E., Chung, A. H., & Jain, P. (2011). Identification with characters and discussion of taboo topics after exposure to an entertainment narrative about sexual health. *Journal of Communication, 61,* 387–406.

Muller, D., Judd, C. M., & Yzerbyt, V. Y. (2005). When moderation is mediated and mediation is moderated. *Journal of Personality and Social Psychology, 89,* 852–863.

Muthén, B., & Asparouhov, T. (2015). Causal effects in mediation modeling: An introduction with applications to latent variables. *Structural Equation Modeling, 22,* 12–23.

Muthén, B. O., Muthén, L. K., & Asparouhov, T. (2016). *Regression and mediation analysis using Mplus.* Los Angeles, CA: Muthén & Muthén.

Myers, T. A., & Hayes, A. F. (2010). Reframing the casualties hypothesis: (Mis)perception of troop casualties and public opinion about military intervention. *International Journal of Public Opinion Research, 22,* 256–275.

Namazi, M., & Namazi, N.-R. (2016). Conceptual analysis of moderator and mediator variables in business research. *Procedia Economics and Finance, 56,* 540–554.

Napier, J. L., & Jost, J. T. (2008). Why are conservatives happier than liberals? *Psychological Science, 19,* 565–572.

Nathanson, A. I., & Fries, P. T. (2014). Television exposure, sleep time, and neuropsychological function among preschoolers. *Media Psychology, 17,*

237–261.

Nelson, B. D., Shankman, S. A., & Proudfit, G. H. (2014). Intolerance of uncertainty mediates reduced reward anticipation in major depressive disorder. *Journal of Affective Disorders, 158,* 108–113.

Newheiser, A.-K., & Barreto, M. (2014). Hidden costs of hiding stigma: Ironic interpersonal consequences of concealing a stigmatized identity in social interactions. *Journal of Experimental Social Psychology, 52,* 58–70.

Newsom, J. T., Prigerson, H. G., Schultz, R., & Reynolds, C. F. (2003). Investigating moderator hypotheses in aging research: Statistical, methodological, and conceptual difficulties with comparing separate regressions. *International Journal of Aging and Human Development, 57,* 119–150.

Ning, H. K. (2012). Influence of student learning experience on academic performance: The mediator and moderator effects of self-regulation and motivation. *British Educational Research Journal, 38,* 219–237.

Nir, L., & Druckman, J. N. (2008). Campaign mixed-message flows and timing of vote decision. *International Journal of Public Opinion Research, 20,* 326–346.

Nisbet, E. C., Hart, P. S., Myers, T., & Ellithorpe, M. (2011). Attitude change in competitive framing environments? Open-/closed mindedness, framing effects, and climate change. *Journal of Communication, 22,* 1101–1106.

O'Connor, B. P. (2004). SPSS and SAS programs for addressing interdependence and basic levels-of-analysis issues in psychological data. *Behavior Research Methods, Instruments, and Computers, 36,* 17–28.

Oei, N. Y. L., Tollenaar, M. S., Elzinga, B. M., & Spinhoven, P. (2010). Propranolol reduces emotional distraction in working memory: A partial mediating role of propranolol-induced cortisol increases? *Neurobiology of Learning and Memory, 93,* 388–395.

Oishi, S., & Diener, E. (2014). Residents of poor nations have a greater sense of meaning in life than residents of wealthy nations. *Psychological Science, 25,* 422–430.

Oishi, S., Seol, K. O., Koo, M., & Miao, F. F. (2011). Was he happy?: Cultural difference in conceptions of Jesus. *Journal of Research in Personality, 45,* 84–91.

Oja, H. (1987). On permutation tests in multiple regression and analysis of variance problems. *Australian Journal of Statistics, 29,* 91–100.

O'Keefe, D. J. (2011). The asymmetry of predictive and descriptive capabilities in quantitative communication research: Implications for hypothesis development and testing. *Communication Methods and Measures, 5,* 113–125.

O'Keefe, D. J., & Jensen, J. D. (1997). The relative persuasiveness of gain-framed and loss-framed messages for encouraging disease prevention behaviors: A meta-analysis. *Journal of Health Communication, 12,* 623–644.

Oldmeadow, J. A., & Fiske, S. T. (2010). Social status and the pursuit of positive social identity: Systematic domains of intergroup differentiation and discrimination for high- and low- status groups. *Group Processes and Intergroup Relations, 13,* 425–444.

Orom, H., Penner, L. A., West, B. T., Downs, T. M., Rayfords, W., & Underwood, W. (2009). Personality predicts prostate cancer treatment decision making. *Psycho-Oncology, 18,* 290–299.

Osberg, T. M., Billingsley, K., Eggert, M., & Insana, M. (2012). From animal house to old school: A multiple mediation analysis of the association between college drinking movie exposure and freshman drinking and its consequences. *Addictive Behaviors, 37,* 922–930.

Osborne, D., Huo, Y. J., & Smith, H. J. (2015). Organizational respect dampens the impact of group-based relative deprivation on willingness to protest pay cuts. *British Journal of Social Psychology, 54,* 159–174.

Paige, D. D., Rasinski, T., Magpuri-Lavell, T., & Smith, G. S. (2014). Interpreting the relationship among prosody, automaticity, accuracy, and silent reading comprehension in secondary students. *Journal of Literacy Research, 46,* 123–156.

Palmer, A., Koenig-Lewis, N., & Assad, Y. (2016). Brand identification in higher education: A conditional process analysis. *Journal of Business Research, 69,* 3033–3040.

Panno, A., Lauriola, M., & Pierro, A. (2016). Regulatory mode and risk-taking: The mediating role of anticipated regret. *Plos One, 10,* 1–19.

Papadaki, E., & Giovalolias, T. (2015). The protective role of father acceptance in the relationship between maternal rejection and bullying: A moderated-mediation model. *Journal of Child and Family Studies, 24,* 330–340.

Parade, S. H., Leerkes, E. M., & Blankson, A. N. (2010). Attachment to parents, social anxiety, and close relationships of female students over the transition to college. *Journal of Youth and Adolescence, 39,* 127–137.

Pearl, J. (2009). *Causality: Models, reasoning, and inference* (2nd ed.). Cambridge, UK: Cambridge University Press.

Pek, J., & Hoyle, R. H. (2016). On the (in)validity of tests of simple mediation: Threats and solutions. *Social and Personality Psychology Compass, 10,* 150–163.

Peltonen, K., Quota, S., Sarraj, E. E., & Punamäki, R. (2010). Military trauma and social development: The moderating and mediating role of peer and sibling relations in mental health. *International Journal of Behavioral Development, 34,* 554–563.

Penarroja, V., Orengo, V., Zornoza, A., Sanchez, J., & Ripoll, P. (2015). How team feedback and team trust influence information processing and learning in virtual teams: A moderated mediation model. *Computers in Human Behavior, 48,* 9–16.

Peréz, L. G., Abrams, M. P., López-Martínez, A. E., & Asmundson, G. J. G. (2012). Trauma exposure and health: The role of depressive and hyperarousal symptoms. *Journal of Traumatic Stress, 25,* 641–648.

Pérez-Edgar, K., Bar-Haim, Y., McDermott, J. M., Chronis-Tuscano, A., Pine, D. S., & Fox, N. A. (2010). Attention biases to threat and behavioral inhibition in early childhood shape adolescent social withdrawal. *Emotion, 10,* 349–357.

Petrocelli, J. V., Rubin, A. L., & Stevens, R. L. (2016). The sin of prediction: When mentally simulated alternatives compete with reality. *Personality and Social Psychology Bulletin, 42,* 1635–1652.

Petty, R. E., & Cacioppo, J. T. (1986). The elaboration likelihood model of persuasion. In L. Berkowitz (Ed.), *Advances in experimental social psychology* (Vol. 19, pp. 123–205). San Diego, CA: Academic Press.

Pittarello, A., Leib, M., Gordon-Hecker, T., & Shalvi, S. (2016). Justifications shape ethical blind spots. *Psychological Science, 26,* 794–804.

Pitts, B. L., & Safer, M. A. (2016). Retrospective appraisals mediate the effects of combat experiences on PTS and depression symptoms in U.S. Army medics. *Journal of Traumatic Stress, 29,* 65–71.

Pollack, J. M., VanEpps, E. M., & Hayes, A. F. (2012). The moderating effect of social ties on entrepreneurs' depressed affective and withdrawal intentions in response to economic stress. *Journal of Organizational Behavior, 33,* 789–810.

Popan, J. R., Kenworthy, J. B., Frame, M. C., Lyons, P. A., & Snuggs, S. J. (2010). Political groups in contact: The role of attributions for outgroup attitudes in reducing antipathy. *European Journal of Social Psychology, 40,* 86–104.

Potthoff, R. F. (1964). On the Johnson–Neyman technique and some extensions thereof. *Psychometrika, 29,* 241–256.

Preacher, K. J., Curran, P. J., & Bauer, D. J. (2006). Computational tools for probing interactions in multiple linear regression, multilevel modeling, and latent curve analysis. *Journal of Educational and Behavioral Statistics, 31,* 437–448.

Preacher, K. J., & Hayes, A. F. (2004). SPSS and SAS procedures for estimating indirect effects in simple mediation models. *Behavior Research Methods, Instruments, and Computers, 36,* 717–731.

Preacher, K. J., & Hayes, A. F. (2008a). Asymptotic and resampling strategies for assessing and comparing indirect effects in multiple mediator models. *Behavior Research Methods, 40,* 879–891.

Preacher, K. J., & Hayes, A. F. (2008b). Contemporary approaches to assessing mediation in communication research. In A. F. Hayes, M. D. Slater, & L. B. Snyder (Eds.), *The Sage sourcebook of advanced data analysis methods for communication research* (pp. 13–54). Thousand Oaks, CA: Sage Publications.

Preacher, K. J., & Kelley, K. (2011). Effect size measures for mediation models: Quantitative strategies for communicating indirect effects. *Psychological Methods, 16,* 93–115.

Preacher, K. J., Rucker, D. D., & Hayes, A. F. (2007). Assessing moderated mediation hypotheses: Theory, methods, and prescriptions. *Multivariate Behavioral Research, 42,* 185–227.

Preacher, K. J., Rucker, D. D., MacCallum, R. C., & Nicewander, W. A. (2005). Use of the extreme groups approach: A critical reexamination and new recommendations. *Psychological Methods, 10,* 178–192.

Preacher, K. J., & Selig, J. P. (2012). Advantages of Monte Carlo confidence intervals for indirect effects. *Communication Methods and Measures, 6,* 77–98.

Preacher, K. J., Zypher, M. J., & Zhang, Z. (2010). A general multilevel SEM framework for assessing multilevel mediation. *Psychological Methods, 15,* 209–233.

Prinzie, P., Dekovic, M., van den Akker, A. L., de Haan, A. D., Stoltz, S. E. M. J., & Hendriks, A. A. J. (2012). Fathers' personality and its interaction with children's personality as predictors of perceived parenting six years later. *Personality and Individual Differences, 52,* 183–189.

Quratulain, S., & Khan, A. K. (2015). How does employees' public service motivation get affected? A conditional process anlaysis of the effects of person–job fit and work pressure. *Public Personnel Management, 44,* 266–289.

Rabinovich, A., & Morton, T. A. (2012). Ghosts of the past and dreams of the future: The impact of temporal focus on responses to contextual ingroup devaluation. *Personality and Social Psychology Bulletin, 38,* 397–410.

Raudenbush, S. W., & Bryk, A. S. (2002). *Hierarchical linear models: Applications and data analysis methods* (2nd ed.). Thousand Oaks, CA: Sage Publications.

Rees, T., & Freeman, P. (2009). Social support moderates the relationship between stressors and task performance through self-efficacy. *Journal of Social and Clinical Psychology, 28,* 244–263.

Richard, J. E., & Purnell, F. (2017). Rethinking catalogue and online B2B buyer channel preferences in the education supplies market. *Journal of Interactive Marketing, 37,* 1–15.

Richman, J. A., Shannon, C. A., Rospenda, K. M., Flaherty, J. A., & Fendrich, M. (2009). The relationship between terrorism and distress and drinking: Two years after September 11, 2001. *Substance Use and Abuse, 44,* 1665–1680.

Richter, T., & Schmid, S. (2010). Epistemological beliefs and epistemic strategies in self-regulated learning. *Metacognition and Learning, 5,* 47–65.

Riglin, L., Collishaw, S., Shelton, K. H., McMannus, I. C., Ng-Knight, T., Sellers, R., . . . Rice, F. (2016). Development and psychopathology. *Development and Psychopathology, 28,* 97–109.

Ro, H. (2012). Moderator and mediator effects in hospitality research. *International Journal of Hospitality Management, 31,* 952–961.

Robinson, E., & Sutin, A. R. (2017). Parents' perceptions of their children as overweight and children's weight concerns and weight gain. *Psychological Science, 28,* 320–329.

Rodgers, J. L. (1999). The bootstrap, the jackknife, and the randomization test: A sampling taxonomy. *Multivariate Behavioral Research, 34,* 441–456.

Rodriguez, D. N., & Berry, M. A. (2016). Sensitizing potential jurors to variation in eyewitness evidence quality using counterfactual thinking. *Applied Cognitive Psychology, 30,* 600–612.

Rogosa, D. (1980). Comparing nonparallel regression lines. *Psychological Bulletin, 88,* 307–321.

Royston, P., Altman, D. G., & Sauerbrei, W. (2006). Dichotomizing continuous predictors in multiple regression: A bad idea. *Statistics in Medicine, 25,* 127–141.

Rucker, D. D., McShane, B. B., & Preacher, K. J. (2015). A researcher's guide to regression, discretization, and median splits of continuous variables. *Journal of Consumer Psychology, 25,* 666–678.

Rucker, D. D., Preacher, K. J., Tormala, Z. L., & Petty, R. E. (2011). Mediation analysis in social psychology: Current practice and new recommendations. *Personality and Social Psychology Compass, 5/6,* 359–371.

Rueggeberg, R., Wrosch, C., Miller, G. E., & McDade, T. W. (2012). Associations between health-related self-protection, dirunal cortisol, and C-reactive protein in lonely older adults. *Psychosomatic Medicine, 74,* 937–944.

Saunders, D. R. (1956). Moderator variables in prediction. *Educational and Psychological Measurement, 16,* 209–222.

Schaerer, N., Swaab, R. I., & Galinsky, A. D. (2015). Anchors weigh more than power: Why absolute powerlessness liberates negotiators to achieve better outcomes. *Psychological Science, 26,* 170–181.

Schmidt, S. J., & Scimmelmann, B. G. (2014). Mechanisms of change in psychotherapy for children and adolescents: Current state, clinical implications, and methodology and conceptual recommendations for mediation analysis. *European Child and Adolescent Psychiatry, 24,* 249–253.

Schrift, R. Y., & Moty, A. (2015). Pain and preferences: Observed decisional conflict and the convergence of preferences. *Journal of Consumer Research, 42,* 515–534.

Scogin, F., Morthland, M., DiNapoli, E. A., LaRocca, M., & Chaplin, W. (2015). Pleasant events, hopelessness, and quality of life in rural older adults. *Journal of Rural Health, 32,* 102–109.

Sedney, M. A. (1981). Comments on median split procedures for scoring androgyny measures. *Sex Roles, 7,* 217–222.

Seehuus, M., Clifton, J., & Rellini, A. H. (2015). The role of family environment and multiple forms of childhood abuse in the shaping of sexual function and satisfaction in women. *Archives of Sexual Behavior, 44,* 1595–1608.

Selig, J. P., & Preacher, K. J. (2009). Mediation models for longitudinal data in developmental research. *Research in Human Development, 6,* 144–164.

Shanahan, J. E., & Morgan, M. (1999). *Television and its viewers: Cultivation theory and research.* London, UK: Cambridge University Press.

Sharma-Patel, K., & Brown, E. J. (2016). Emotion regulation and self blame as mediators and moderators of trauma-specific treatment. *Journal of Consumer Research, 6,* 400-409.

Sheih, G. (2011). Clarifying the role of mean centering in multicollinearity of interaction effects. *British Journal of Mathematical and Statistical Psychology, 64,* 462–477.

Shenk, C. E., Noll, J. G., & Cassarly, J. A. (2010). A multiple meditational test of the relationship between childhood maltreatment and non-suicidal self-injury. *Journal of Youth and Adolescence, 39,* 335–342.

Shrout, P. E., & Bolger, N. (2002). Mediation in experimental and nonexperimental studies: New procedures and recommendations. *Psychological Methods, 7,* 422–445.

Shrum, L. J., Lee, J., Burroughs, J. E., & Rindfleisch, A. (2011). An online process model of second-order cultivation effects: How television cultivates materialism and its consequences. *Human Communication Research, 37,* 34–57.

Sibley, C. G., & Perry, R. (2010). An opposing process model of benevolent sexism. *Sex Roles, 62,* 438–452.

Silton, R. L., Heller, W., Engels, A. S., Towers, D. N., Spielberg, J. M., Edgar, C. J., et al. (2011). Depression and anxious apprehension distinguish frontocingulate cortical activity during top-down attentional control. *Journal of Abnormal Psychology, 120,* 272–285.

Silva, P. J. (2007). *How to write a lot.* Washington, DC: American Psychological Association.

Simons, R. L., Lei, M. K., Stewart, E. A., Beach, S. R. H., Brody, G. H., Philibert, R. A., et al. (2012). Social adversity, genetic variation, street code, and aggression: A genetically informed model of violent behavior. *Youth Violence and Juvenile Justice, 10,* 3–24.

Simpson, H. B., Maher, M. J., Wang, Y., Bao, Y., Foa, E. B., & Franklin, M. (2011). Patient adherence predicts outcome from cognitive behavioral therapy in obsessive–compulsive disorder. *Journal of Consulting and Clinical Psychology, 79,* 247–252.

Sirgy, M. J., Yu, G. B., Lee, D. J., Wei, S., & Huang, M. W. (2012). Does marketing activity contribute to a society's well-being?: The role of economic efficiency. *Journal of Business Ethics, 107,* 91–102.

Slater, M. D., Hayes, A. F., & Snyder, L. B. (2008). Overview. In A. F. Hayes, M. D. Slater, & L. B. Snyder (Eds.), *The Sage sourcebook of advanced data analysis methods for communication research* (pp. 1–12). Thousand Oaks, CA: Sage Publications.

Smith, J. (2016). The motivational effects of missing matching: A lab-experimental test of a moderated mediation model. *Public Administration Review, 76,* 626–637.

Smith, N. A., Martinez, L. R., & Sabat, I. E. (2016). Weight and gender in service jobs: The importance of warmth in predicting customer satisfaction. *Cornell Hospitality Quarterly, 57,* 314–328.

Sobel, M. E. (1982). Asymptotic confidence intervals for indirect effects in structural equation models. In S. Leinhart (Ed.), *Sociological methodology* (pp. 290–312). San Francisco, CA: Jossey-Bass.

Somer, E., Ginzberg, K., & Kramer, L. (2012). The role of impulsivity in the association between childhood trauma and dissociative psychopathology: Mediation versus moderation. *Psychiatry Research, 196,* 133–137.

Spencer, S. J., Zanna, M. P., & Fong, G. T. (2005). Establishing a causal chain: Why experiments are often more effective than mediational analyses in examining psychological processes. *Journal of Personality and Social Psychology, 89,* 845–851.

Spiller, S. A., Fitzsimons, G. J., Lynch, J. G., & McClelland, G. H. (2013). Spotlights, floodlights, and the magic number zero: Simple effects tests in moderated regression. *Journal of Marketing Research, 50,* 277–288.

Spinhoven, P., Penninx, B. W., Krempeniou, A., van Hemert, A. M., & Elzinga, B. (2015). Trait rumination predicts onset of post-traumatic stress disorder through trauma-related cognitive appraisals: A 4-year longitudinal study. *Behaviour Research and Therapy, 71,* 101–109.

Still, A. W., & White, A. P. (1981). The approximate randomization test as an alternative to the *F* test in analysis of variance. *British Journal of Mathematical and Statistical Psychology, 34,* 243–252.

Stone, C. A., & Sobel, M. E. (1990). The robustness of total indirect effects in covariance structure models estimated with maximum likelihood. *Psychometrika, 55,* 337–352.

Stone-Romero, E. F., & Raposa, P. J. (2010). Research design options for testing mediation models and their implications for facets of validity. *Journal of Managerial Psychology, 25,* 697–712.

Streiner, D. L. (2002). Breaking up is hard to do: The heartbreak of dichotomizing continuous data. *Canadian Journal of Psychiatry, 47,* 262–266.

Takeuchi, R., Yun, S., & Wong, K. F. E. (2011). Social influence of a coworker: A test of the effect of employee and coworker exchange ideologies on employees' exchange qualities. *Organizational Behavior and Human Decision Processes, 115*, 226–237.

Tal-Or, N., Cohen, J., Tsfati, Y., & Gunther, A. C. (2010). Testing causal direction in the influence of presumed media influence. *Communication Research, 37*, 801–824.

Taylor, A. B., MacKinnon, D. P., & Tein, J.-Y. (2008). Tests of the three-path mediated effect. *Organizational Research Methods, 11*, 241–269.

Teixeira, P. J., Silva, M. N., Coutinho, S. R., Palmeira, A. L., Mata, J., Vieira, P. N., et al. (2010). Mediators of weight loss and weight loss maintenance in middle-aged women. *Obesity, 18*, 725–735.

ter Braak, C. J. F. (1992). Permutation versus bootstrap significance tests in multiple regression and ANOVA. In K. J. Jöckel, G. Rothe, & W. Sendler (Eds.), *Bootstrapping and related techniques* (pp. 79–85). Berlin, Germany: Springer-Verlag.

Thai, N., Taber-Thomas, B. C., & Pérez-Edgar, K. E. (2016). Neural correlates of attention biases, behavioural inhibition, and social anxiety in children: An ERP study. *Developmental Cognitive Neuroscience, 19*, 200–210.

Thoemmes, F. (2015). Reversing arrows in mediation models does not distinguish plausible models. *Basic and Applied Social Psychology, 37*, 226-234.

Thomas, K. K., & Bowker, J. C. (2015). Rejection sensitivity and adjustment during adolescence: Do friendship self-silencing and parent support matter? *Journal of Child and Family Studies, 24*, 608–616.

Tichenor, P. A., Donohue, G. A., & Olien, C. N. (1970). Mass media flow and differential growth in knowledge. *Public Opinion Quarterly, 34*, 159–170.

Tofighi, D., & MacKinnon, D. P. (2011). RMediation: An R package for mediation analysis confidence intervals. *Behavior Research Methods, 43*, 692–700.

Torres, L., & Taknint, J. T. (2015). Ethnic microaggressions, traumatic stress symptoms, and latino depression: A moderated mediation model. *Journal of Counseling, 62*, 393–401.

Trafimow, D. (2015). Introduction to the special issue on mediation analysis: What if planetary scientists used mediation analysis to infer causation? *Basic and Applied Social Psychology, 37*, 197–201.

Traut-Mattausch, E., Wagner, S., Pollatos, O., & Jones, E. (2015). Complaints as starting point for vicious cycles in customer-employee interactions. *Frontiers in Psychology, 6*, 1–17.

Tsai, C. I., & Thomas, M. (2011). When does feeling of fluency matter?: How abstract and concrete thinking influences fluency effects. *Psychological Science, 22*, 348–354.

Tsang, J., Carpenter, T. P., Robers, J. A., Frisch, M. B., & Carlisle, R. D. (2014). Why are materialists less happy? The role of gratitude and need satisfaction in the relationship between materialism and life satisfaction. *Personality and Individual Differences, 64*, 62–66.

Usborne, E., & Taylor, D. M. (2010). The role of cultural identity clarity for self-concept clarity, self-esteem, and subjective well-being. *Personality and Social Psychology Bulletin, 36*, 883–897.

Valdesolo, P., & Graham, J. (2014). Awe, uncertainty, and agency detection. *Psychological Science, 25*, 170–178.

Valente, M. J., & MacKinnon, D. P. (2017). Models of change to estimate the mediated effect in the pretest-posttest control group design. *Structural Equation Modeling, 24*, 428–450.

Valentine, K. A., Li, N. P., Penki, L., & Perrett, D. I. (2014). Judging a man by his face: The role of facial ratios and dominance in mate choice at speed-dating events. *Psychological Science, 25*, 806–811.

Valeri, L., & VanderWeele, T. J. (2013). Mediation analysis allowing for exposure-mediator interactions and causal interpretation: Theoretical assumptions and implementation with SAS and SPSS macros. *Psychological Methods, 18*, 137–150.

van Dijke, M., & De Cremer, D. (2010). Procedural fairness and endorsement of prototypical leaders: Leader benevolence or follower control? *Journal of Experimental Social Psychology, 46*, 85–96.

Van Jaarsveld, D. D., Walker, D. D., & Skarlicki, D. P. (2010). The role of job demands and emotional exhaustion in the relationship between customer and employee incivility. *Journal of Management, 36*, 1486–1504.

van Leeuwen, N., Rogers, R. F., Gibbs, J. C., & Chabrol, H. (2014). Callous emotional traits and antisocial behavior among adolescents: The role of self-serving cognitions. *Journal of Abnormal Child Psychology, 42*, 229–237.

VanderWeele, T. J. (2011). Causal mediation analysis with survival data. *Epidemiology, 22*, 582–585.

VanderWeele, T. J. (2015). *Explanation in causal inference: Methods for mediation and interaction.* New York, NY: Oxford University Press.

VanderWeele, T. J. (2016). Mediation analysis: A practitioner's guide. *Annual Review of Public Health, 37*, 17–32.

VanderWeele, T. J., & Vansteelandt, S. (2010). Odds ratios for mediation analysis for a dichotomous outcome. *American Journal of Epidemiology, 172*, 1339-1348.

Vargha, A., Rudas, T., & Maxwell, S. E. (2011). Dichotomization, partial correlation, and conditional independence. *Journal of Educational and Behavioral Statistics, 58*, 264–282.

Veilleux, J. C., Skinner, K. D., Reese, E. D., & Shaver, J. A. (2014). Negative affect intensity influences drinking to cope through facets of emotion dysregulation. *Personality and Individual Differences, 49*, 96–101.

Versey, H. S., & Kaplan, G. A. (2012). Mediation and moderation of the association between cynical hostility and systolic blood pressure in low-income women. *Health Education and Behavior, 39*, 219–238.

Vigil, J. M. (2010). Political leanings vary with facial expression processing and psychosocial functioning. *Group Processes and Intergroup Relations, 13*, 547–558.

Von Hippel, C., Issa, M., Ma, R., & Stokes, A. (2011). Stereotype threat: Antecedents and consequences for working women. *European Journal of Social Psychology, 41*, 151–161.

Vraga, E. K., Johnson, C. N., Carr, D. J., Bode, L., & Bard, M. T. (2014). Filmed in front of a live studio audience: Laughter and aggression in political entertainment programming. *Journal of Broadcasting and Electronic Media, 58*, 131–150.

Walder, D. J., Laplante, D. P., Sousa-Pires, A., Veru, F., Brunet, A., & King, S.

(2014). Prenatal maternal stress predicts autism traits in six and a half year-old children: Project Ice Storm. *Psychiatry Research, 219,* 353–360.

Waldinger, R. J., & Schultz, M. S. (2016). The long reach of nurturing family environments: Links with midlife emotion-regulatory styles and late-life security in intimate relationships. *Psychological Science, 27,* 1443–1450.

Walker, J. L., Harrison, T. C., Brown, A., Thorpe, R. J., & Szanton, S. L. (2016). Factors associated with disability among middle-aged and older African-American women with osteoarthritis. *Disability and Health Journal, 9,* 510–517.

Walsh, L. A., Stock, M. L., Peterson, L. M., & Gerrard, M. (2014). Women's sun protection cognitions in response to UV photography: The role of age, cognition, and affect. *Journal of Behavioral Medicine, 37,* 553–563.

Wan, E. W., Xu, J., & Ding, Y. (2014). The effect of social exclusion on consumer choice. *Journal of Consumer Research, 40,* 1109–1122.

Wang, K., Stroebe, K., & Dovidio, J. F. (2012). Stigma consciousness and prejudice ambiguity: Can it be adaptive to perceive the world as biased? *Personality and Individual Differences, 53,* 241–245.

Wang, L., & Preacher, K. J. (2015). Moderated mediation using Bayesian methods. *Structural Equation Modeling, 22,* 249–263.

Warner, L. M., Schwarzer, R., Schüz, B., Wurm, S., & Tesch-Romer, C. (2012). Health-specific optimism mediates between objective and perceived physical functioning in older adults. *Journal of Behavioral Medicine, 35,* 400–406.

Weaver, J. M., & Schofield, T. J. (2015). Mediation and moderation of divorce effects on children's behavior problems. *Journal of Family Psychology, 29,* 39–48.

Webb, J. B., Fiery, M. F., & Jafari, N. (2016). "You better not leave me shaming!": Conditional indirect effect analyses of anti-fat attitudes, body shame, and fat talk as a function of self-compassion in college women. *Body Image, 18,* 5–13.

Webster, R. J., & Saucier, D. A. (2011). The effects of death reminders on sex differences in prejudice towards gay men and women. *Journal of Homosexuality, 58,* 402–426.

Weikamp, J. G., & Göritz, A. S. (2016). Organizational citizenship behaviour and job satisfaction: The impact of occupational future time perspective. *Human Relations, 69,* 2091–2115.

Weiss, J. A. (2015). Thriving in youth with autism spectrum disorder in intellectual disability. *Journal of Autism and Developmental Disorders, xx,* xxx–xxx.

Wen, Z., & Fan, X. (2015). Monotonicity of effect sizes: Questioning kappa-squared as a mediation effect size measure. *Psychological Methods, 20,* 193–203.

Whisman, M. A., & McClelland, G. H. (2005). Designing, testing, and interpreting interactions and moderator effects in family research. *Journal of Family Psychology, 19,* 111–120.

White, H. (1980). A heteroskedasticity-consistent covariance matrix estimator and a direct test for heteroskedasticity. *Econometrica, 48,* 817–838.

Wicklund, R. A. (1974). *Freedom and reactance.* Potomac, MD: Lawrence Erlbaum Associates.

Wiedemann, A. U., Schüz, B., Sniehotta, F., Scholz, U., & Schwarzer, R. (2009). Disentangling the relation between intentions, planning, and behaviour: A moderated mediation analysis. *Psychology and Health, 24,* 67–79.

Williams, J., & MacKinnon, D. P. (2008). Resampling and distribution of the product methods for testing indirect effect in complex models. *Structural Equation Modeling, 15,* 23–51.

Windgassen, S., Goldsmith, K., Moss-Morris, R., & Chalder, T. (2016). Establishing how psychological therapies work: The importance of mediation analysis. *Journal of Mental Health, 25,* 93-99.

Windscheid, L., Bowes-Sperry, L., Kidder, D. L., Cheung, H. K., Morner, M., & Lievens, F. (2016). Actions speak louder than words: Outsiders' perceptions of diversity mixed messages. *Journal of Applied Psychology, 101,* 1329–1341.

Wohl, M. J. A., & Branscombe, N. R. (2009). Group threat, collective angst, and ingroup forgiveness for the war in Iraq. *Political Psychology, 30,* 193–217.

Woo, J. S. T., Brotto, L. A., & Gorzalka, B. B. (2011). The role of sex guilt in the relationship between culture and women's sexual desire. *Archives of Sexual Behavior, 40,* 385–394.

Wood, M. (2005). Bootstrapped confidence intervals as an approach to statistical inference. *Organizational Research Methods, 8,* 454–470.

Worchel, S., & Arnold, S. E. (1973). The effects of censorship and attractiveness of the censor on attitude change. *Journal of Experimental Social Psychology, 9,* 365–377.

Wu, J., Balliet, D., & Van Lange, P. A. M. (2015). When does gossip promote generosity? Indirect reciprocity under the shadow of the future. *Social Psychological and Personality Science, 6,* 923–930.

Xenos, M., & Becker, A. (2009). Moments of Zen: Effects of *The Daily Show* on information seeking and political learning. *Political Communication, 26,* 317–332.

Xu, H., Bègue, L., & Bushman, B. J. (2014). Washing the guilt away: Effects of personal versus vicarious cleansing on guilty feelings and prosocial behavior. *Frontiers in Neuroscience, 8,* 1–5.

Yuan, Y., & MacKinnon, D. P. (2009). Bayesian mediation analysis. *Psychological Methods, 14,* 301–322.

Zadeh, Z. Y., Farnia, F., & Ungerleider, C. (2010). How home enrichment mediates the relationship between maternal education and children's achievements in reading and math. *Early Education and Development, 21,* 568–594.

Zhang, Z. (2009). Testing multilevel mediation using hierarchical linear models: Problems and solutions. *Organizational Research Methods, 12,* 695–719.

Zhang, Z. (2014). Monte Carlo based statistical power analysis for mediation models: Methods and software. *Behavior Research Methods, 46,* 1184–1198.

Zhao, X., Lynch, J. G., & Chen, Q. (2010). Reconsidering Baron and Kenny: Myths and truths about mediation analysis. *Journal of Consumer Research, 37,* 197–206.

Zhou, Q., Hirst, G., & Shipton, H. (2012). Promoting creativity at work: The role of problem-solving demand. *Applied Psychology: An International Review, 61,* 56–80.

Author Index

Subject Index

Note. *f* or *t* following a page number indicates a figure or table.

About the Author

Andrew F. Hayes, PhD, is Professor of Quantitative Psychology at The Ohio State University. His research and writing on data analysis has been published widely. Dr. Hayes is the author of *Statistical Methods for Communication Science* as well as coauthor, with Richard B. Darlington, of *Regression Analysis and Linear Models*. He teaches data analysis, primarily at the graduate level, and frequently conducts workshops on statistical analysis throughout the world. His website is *www.afhayes.com*.